CURRENTS OF INQUIRY
Readings for Academic Writing

CURRENTS OF INQUIRY
Readings for Academic Writing

Nancy Morrow
Michigan State University

Marlene Clarke
University of California, Davis

Mayfield Publishing Company
Mountain View, California
London • Toronto

Copyright © 1998 by Mayfield Publishing Company

All rights reserved. No portion of this book may be reproduced in any form or by any means without written permission of the publisher.

Library of Congress Cataloging-in-Publication Data
Morrow, Nancy.
  Currents of inquiry : readings for academic writing / Nancy Morrow, Marlene Clarke.
    p. cm.
  Includes bibliographical references and index.
  ISBN 1-55934-818-6
  1. College readers. 2. English language—Rhetoric—Problems, exercises, etc. 3. Academic writing—Problems, exercises, etc.
  I. Clarke, Marlene. II. Title.
PE1417.M633 1997
808'.0427—dc21   97-36270
                                                                CIP

Manufactured in the United States of America

10 9 8 7 6 5 4 3 2 1

Mayfield Publishing Company
1280 Villa Street
Mountain View, California 94041

Sponsoring editor, Renée Deljon; production editor, Carla White; manuscript editor, Stuart Hoffman; text and cover designer, Linda Robertson; cover art, Don Bishop © 1997 Artville, LLC; art manager, Jeanne Schreiber; manufacturing manager, Randy Hurst. The text was set in 11/12 Bembo by Archetype Book Composition and printed on 45# Glatfelter Restorecote by Malloy Lithographing, Inc.

To the Instructor

Currents of Inquiry is designed for college and university courses in critical reading and expository writing, particularly those courses that aim to teach academic discourse and provide students with a foundation for reading and writing across the curriculum. Although we had the freshman course most clearly in mind as we developed the book, we suspect that at many campuses it may be even more appropriate for sophomore-level courses in research and expository writing. *Currents of Inquiry* may also be suitable for general advanced composition courses, especially those that focus on academic discourse or on the connections between academic and professional writing.

Chapter 1 offers students a more extensive analysis of academic reading than is found in most textbooks. Grounded in theories about the connections between reading and writing and in the phenomenology of reading, this chapter is designed to help students understand how critical reading differs from other kinds of reading. We explain theoretical issues in clear, simple terms, and offer students practical suggestions about how to approach the types of readings they will encounter throughout the text. Such an introductory chapter is especially important in a book such as this that includes challenging readings of the nature that students encounter in other college courses. We believe that many students misread because they misunderstand the nature of the reading process; with more direct advice about that process, students are fully capable of understanding even the most difficult and complex texts.

Our goal in the subsequent chapters is to provide students and instructors with challenging readings, interesting questions to explore through discussion, research, or writing, and flexibility in using these materials. With these goals in mind, we have collected articles from academic journals, recently published books, and intellectual and opinion periodicals and grouped them according to four broad intellectual concerns in contemporary American culture. The chapter topics progress outward, from those related to students' immediate experiences as students to those related to past and future experiences of work and play. From there the text moves on to increasingly abstract questions about the roles of technology and the media in our society and about the legal and ethical values that lie at its foundation.

In addition, the readings within each chapter repeat the m from the personal to the more abstract, moving from those in writers have relied more on personal experience to those in writers have developed their ideas using various types of research. This arrangement reflects our own understanding of how assignments might best be sequenced.

Chapter 2 explores connections between the campus and the community. The readings here invite the class to consider the problems and the challenges that higher education in America faces as the twenty-first century approaches. Given that students have their own attitudes toward and experiences of education, this theme offers an excellent common ground for reading, discussion, and writing. It also lends itself well to interdisciplinary and cross-disciplinary discussion of issues and problems. Some of the readings help define key concepts, while others explore problems and issues related to different aspects of education.

Chapter 3 emphasizes issues surrounding work and play in contemporary society. Readings explore a variety of disciplinary perspectives on such issues as job performance, connections between work and education, the psychology of work and play, and the history of labor. Each reading reveals intersections between play and work as fundamental attitudes in our society. Because many students are concerned about finding personal and economic fulfillment in their future careers, we believe the readings in chapter 3 will invite stimulating discussions about how we perceive the functions of work and play.

Chapter 4 includes readings related to media, technology, and literacy. These readings examine the ways in which new technological advances, as well as the media, have changed the way we perceive—in essence, how we "read"—the world in which we live and how we think about literacy. Some readings ask students to consider ethical questions surrounding the use of such innovations as television, video, and computers, while others examine the cross-fertilization of ideas between scientists and humanists and the relationship between technology and literacy.

In chapter 5, the readings explore questions about the relationship between the individual and the state in contemporary American culture as well as questions about freedom and responsibility in a general sense. While the problems of crime and law enforcement figure significantly in the readings, so, too, do questions about ethics and about making fine distinctions between such terms as "legal," "moral," and "ethical."

Two appendices, designed to help instructors and students enhance and supplement the readings in the book, complete the text. Appendix A contains an annotated bibliography of historical sources for the contemporary selections in the preceding chapters. We have referred to a variety of texts, some of them specifically mentioned in the readings and others offering background or context for one or more readings. Instructors may use this bibliography to design assignments that link nonfiction and literature or that ask students to take a historical perspective on some topic or problem. At the end of Appendix A is a helpful list of questions linking the contemporary and historical sources that address similar issues.

Finally, because many of our suggested topics and questions ask students to do various types of independent research, we have included Appendix B, which outlines a variety of traditional and nontraditional research strategies and information sources. Appendix B will be useful in all courses where students use outside sources of any kind in their writing assignments.

We hope that students who use this book will develop as both readers and writers, that they will ultimately be able to analyze the arguments of other writers and develop arguments of their own. In short, we want students to become active participants in the conversations taking place both inside and outside of the university community.

This project began in the summer of 1994 with an Undergraduate Instructional Improvement Program Grant from the Teaching Resources Center at the University of California, Davis. As director and assistant director of the English Department's Composition Program at the time, we developed thematic materials for use in our freshman expository writing course. From that initial work, the present book evolved. We would therefore like to thank our colleagues at U.C. Davis for reviewing those initial materials and providing useful suggestions for future development. We are especially grateful to all of the talented graduate student instructors who used those materials in their classes and who offered thoughtful comments about our original selections and made suggestions about possible alternative readings. We especially thank Lara Gary, who not only used the materials and commented upon them, but took on the sometimes arduous task of obtaining the necessary permissions for the book.

We would like to thank the editors at Mayfield Publishing Company with whom we worked on this project, including Tom Broadbent, James Bull, and Renée Deljon. We are grateful to the reviewers who offered many important and useful suggestions for revision: Ervene Gulley, Bloomsburg University of Pennsylvania; Michael W. Munley, Ball State University; Robert L. Root, Jr., Central Michigan University; James Seitz, University of Pittsburgh; Robert Thompson, Syracuse University; Irwin Weiser, Purdue University; Donna Winchell, Clemson University.

Finally, we offer our thanks to all those in the Composition Program at U.C. Davis and the Department of American Thought and Language at Michigan State University who have supported our attempts to reenvision and revitalize first-year composition courses and who continue to provide students with an interesting and challenging introduction into the world of the university.

To the Student

We designed this book to help you develop the critical reading and writing skills you will need as a college or university student. It may seem odd to devote so much energy to such seemingly basic tasks. After all, you have been reading and writing for so long now that, even when you feel frustrated by a particular assignment, you may take these skills for granted. Nevertheless, we think it will help you to examine more closely what happens in the reading-writing process, especially as you encounter increasingly difficult academic texts and the rising demands and assumptions of a variety of academic disciplines.

Throughout this book we use the idea of a "conversation" to help you think about the exchange of knowledge in the academic setting. As a student, you will enter into many different conversations as you move from course to course and from classroom to classroom. We refer here not just to the classroom discussions, but also to all the reading and writing for all your classes. Across the academic disciplines, reading and writing provide crucial means for making and exchanging knowledge. They are tools we use to raise important questions and to explore possible answers. Your education will prepare you to participate in the exchange of ideas on a variety of topics—or, as teacher and writer Mike Rose puts it in the first selection of this book, you will feel increasingly confident about entering conversations where everything seems, at first, strange and unfamiliar. By developing your ability to read critically and to write effectively, you will be able to make your own significant contributions to these conversations.

You may find that the readings in this book are more challenging than those you have encountered elsewhere. We have chosen such challenging articles to help you become a more careful, critical reader, able to adapt easily to different situations. Even the most inexperienced readers can make sense out of a simple story or gather useful information from a clearly written book. But as you will learn as your academic career progresses, the meaning in some texts is difficult to construct, requiring considerable effort and carefully developed analytical reading skills. Difficulty in reading may arise for a variety of reasons: because the author has more expertise about the subject than you do as the reader; because the language of the text is highly technical or comes from a different time period or culture than yours; because the argument is complex or developed using ideas from a number of unfamiliar sources; or even because the author communicates more subtly or indirectly than you have come to expect. These readings and the questions that follow them aim to help you develop the skills necessary to overcome such difficulties and to construct meanings from sophisticated texts.

The readings here come from writers representing a variety of different disciplinary perspectives and theoretical backgrounds. Think about how these different texts—and the disciplines they represent—"talk" to one another, and reflect upon *your* response to each. While different academic disciplines concern themselves with distinct issues and problems, scholars are increasingly thinking in terms of conversations that cut across disciplines. In the United States today, interdisciplinary conversations are in many instances revitalizing scholarship and teaching. On campuses around the country, some academic programs draw from different disciplines, allowing both students and teachers to cross boundaries that once kept them pursuing ideas in separate spheres. In fact, to use a metaphor suggested by Arabella Lyon, a professor of English at Temple University, the different disciplines are distinct "territories," separated from each other by clearly delineated boundaries, but "rivers" or "currents" that all converge into a common flow of knowledge.

In fact, it is this idea of currents that has provided us with the central metaphor—and the title—for this book. We want you to think of the readings in this book as "currents of inquiry," ideas coming from a variety of sources and disciplinary perspectives and joining to make possible a rich, interdisciplinary exchange. To that end, we have chosen four themes with great potential for this kind of interdisciplinary exchange. Chapters 2 through 5 explore four of these currents of inquiry that have engaged scholars and writers from various backgrounds and perspectives. To help you see how scholars from different disciplines interact with one another, and how the academic community interacts with those outside it, we have chosen broad topics that concern many aspects of our lives in a variety of settings.

In chapter 2, the readings explore issues of great importance in higher education today. In your role as a student, you certainly think about the nature and function of colleges and universities and may ask yourself what you hope to gain from an education or whether your campus is providing you with an "ideal" education. The readings in chapter 2 invite you to draw upon your own experiences and opinions and join a broader conversation about what it means to be an educated person as we move into the twenty-first century. Are there some things that *every* educated person should know?

Chapter 3 presents readings that examine the connections between work and play. All of us have had to juggle the sometimes conflicting demands of work and play, and balance is often hard to achieve. These readings explore the different ways that people balance—or attempt to balance—the two.

In chapter 4, the readings focus on the intersection of three influences in contemporary culture: media, technology, and literacy. It is difficult today to escape discussions of how computer use affects the ways we think, do business, and learn. But the readings in this chapter ask you to look beyond popular conceptions and misconceptions and to take a more serious look at how technology and the media shape our world and our ways of responding to that world. We once thought of "literacy" simply as a matter of reading and writing words on a page. However, in an increasingly technological society, "literate" people need to know how to manipulate and analyze a wider range of communication techniques and the texts they create.

Finally, chapter 5 examines ethics, law, and justice. Is it possible to find justice in today's world? How do we act as ethical individuals in our work and our play? Indeed, what impact can the individual have in the face of this social force we call the "law?" Together with your own experiences and observations, the readings in chapter 5 will lead you to discover just how much both old and new questions of law and ethics permeate every facet of modern life.

In short, we have chosen four topics that engage teachers and scholars across the college and university community. Equally important, these are topics with which you are certain to have some experience and about which you are sure to have some opinion, even if those experiences are scattered and those opinions not yet fully formed. Because you *do* have some experience and some opinions, you are ready to join the conversation, to send your ideas forth into the river of ideas. In reading the essays in this text, you will begin to see how conversations flow back and forth among academic disciplines and in the wider community as well. But in order to follow the flow of ideas between and among these topics, you will need to read actively and critically.

Chapter 1, therefore, presents some practical ideas for becoming a better reader. We have tried to offer advice you can use. However, this chapter has much more than simply homespun wisdom or rules to obey; it presents carefully developed ideas drawn from research and theory about what happens when we read what writers have put on the page. By thinking more fully about the act of reading and by recognizing that readers need to develop multiple ways of reading, we want you to reenvision your ideas of what it means to be a reader, what it means to be a writer, and what it means for readers and writers to share ideas.

We have also included two appendices in the book. Appendix A identifies some of the historical sources of today's concerns and issues. The bibliography of American cultural texts—some of which may be familiar, while others may not—helps you connect the ideas in chapters 2 through 5 with the past. Appendix B offers you a brief guide to some of the strategies that academic researchers use when they develop new ideas and construct new ways of looking at a topic. This guide should help you move from being an academic reader to an academic writer, developing new ideas of your own.

Brief Contents

To the Instructor *v*
To the Student *viii*
Alternate Contents by Academic Genre *xxi*
Alternate Thematic Contents *xxiii*

CHAPTER 1

Finding Your Place in the Conversation: Becoming an Academic Reader 1

CHAPTER 2

The Campus and the Wider Community 19

    Chapter Introduction *19*
    MIKE ROSE, Entering the Conversation *22*
    CHESTER E. FINN, JR., AND BRUNO V. MANNO, Behind the Curtain *44*
    PHILLIP E. JOHNSON, The Creationist and the Sociobiologist: Two Stories about Illiberal Education *57*
    DAPHNE PATAI and NORETTA KOERTGE, Introduction to the World of Women's Studies *79*
    J. WADE GILLEY, The Distributed University *87*
    GEORGE D. KUH, JOHN H. SCHUH, and ELIZABETH J. WHITT, Some Good News about Campus Life: How "Involving Colleges" Promote Learning outside the University *94*
    DAVID M. HUMMON, College Slang Revisited: Language, Culture, and Undergraduate Life *106*
    Crosscurrents: Questions for Connecting the Readings in Chapter 2 *128*

CHAPTER 3

Work and Play 131

    Chapter Introduction *131*
    REG THERIAULT, Old Blue Collars, Young Blue Collars, and That Little Place You're Going to Get in the Country *133*
    STANTON WHEELER, Double Lives *143*
    JOAN RYAN, Little Girls in Pretty Boxes *152*

LOTTE BAILYN, Two Women at Work: Balancing Work and
   Family *163*
MERLISA LAWRENCE CORBETT, Telecommuting: The New
   Workplace Trend *176*
JULIET B. SCHOR, Time Squeeze: The Extra Month of Work *182*
SUSAN WILLIS, Public Use/Private State *210*
HERBERT APPLEBAUM, Work—Past, Present, and Future *224*
Crosscurrents: Questions for Connecting the Readings
   in Chapter 3 *237*

CHAPTER 4
Media, Technology, and Literacy *239*

Chapter Introduction *239*
NEIL POSTMAN, The Medium Is the Metaphor *242*
CHARLES MCGRATH, The Internet's Arrested Development *252*
DEBORAH BRANDT, Accumulating Literacy: Writing and Learning
   to Write in the Twentieth Century *263*
MICHAEL C. BERTHOLD, *Jeopardy!*, Cultural Literacy, and the
   Discourse of Trivia *274*
DON ADAMS AND ARLENE GOLDBARD, Steal This TV: How Media
   Literacy Can Change the World *286*
SUSAN B. NEUMAN, Television and Reading in the Lives of Young
   Children *292*
LANA F. RAKOW AND VIJA NAVARRO, Remote Mothering and the
   Parallel Shift: Women Meet the Cellular Telephone *316*
PAMELA E. KRAMER AND SHEILA LEHMAN, Mismeasuring
   Women: A Critique of Research on Computer Ability
   and Avoidance *332*
Crosscurrents: Questions for Connecting the Readings
   in Chapter 4 *346*

CHAPTER 5
Ethics, Law, and Justice *348*

Chapter Introduction *348*
BENJAMIN SELLS, What Does the Law Want? *350*
LEON KASS, Am I My Brother's Keeper?: Reflections on
   Compassion and Justice *360*
ALBERT W. ALSCHULER, Our Faltering Jury *376*
CRAIG HOROWITZ, Law and Disorder: How the Juvenile Justice
   System Is Letting Kids Get Away with Murder *386*
MARK HANSEN, Final Justice: Limiting Death Row
   Appeals *403*

LYNN HECHT SCHAFRAN, Is the Law Male? *413*
ELLEN ALDERMAN AND CAROLINE KENNEDY, The Right to Privacy:
   High-Tech Monitoring in the Workplace *425*
HADLEY ARKES, Moral Obtuseness in America *433*
RICHARD WEISBERG, From Jefferson to the Gulf War: How
   Lawyers Have Lost Their Golden Tongue *443*
Crosscurrents: Questions for Connecting the Readings
   in Chapter 5 *454*

APPENDIX A

Voices from Our Past: Conversations from American Cultural History—An Annotated Bibliography of Documents from America's Past *457*

APPENDIX B

Research and Knowledge: A Short Guide to Gathering and Using Outside Sources *473*

CREDITS 490

INDEX 493

Contents

To the Instructor *v*
To the Student *viii*
Alternate Contents by Academic Genre *xxi*
Alternate Thematic Contents *xxiii*

CHAPTER 1

Finding Your Place in the Conversation: Becoming an Academic Reader 1

> The Reading-Writing Relationship 1
> Why Do We Read? 2
> The Reader's Role in the Reading Process 4
> Understanding Rhetorical Context 5
> Reading for the Intended Meaning 7
> Using Genre Conventions to Construct Meaning 10
> Using the Rules of Argument to Interpret Texts 12
> Some Final Thoughts about Academic Reading and Writing 17

CHAPTER 2

The Campus and the Wider Community 19

> Chapter Introduction 19
>
> MIKE ROSE, Entering the Conversation 22
>
> > How does it feel to enter a conversation in which the participants are discussing a subject you know nothing about in a language you haven't yet mastered? That question forms the basis for Mike Rose's very personal exploration of his anxieties as he entered the university and its academic "conversations."
>
> CHESTER E. FINN, JR., AND BRUNO V. MANNO, Behind the Curtain 44
>
> > What kind of education should colleges and universities provide and to what standards should students be held? Today, fewer funds are flowing into colleges and universities and many students view college as a means to a job rather than to an education. Finn and Manno argue that an interest in the "bottom line" may have degraded the purpose of higher education. They offer some provocative solutions.
>
> PHILLIP E. JOHNSON, The Creationist and the Sociobiologist: Two Stories about Illiberal Education 57
>
> > Examining two cases in which university professors made controversial statements that some students (and members of the public) might find offensive, Johnson asks us to think about how we should balance issues of free speech, academic freedom, and

tolerance. *When two (or more) sets of beliefs and values collide, how should the university—its administrators, faculty, and students—respond?*

DAPHNE PATAI AND NORETTA KOERTGE, Introduction to the World of Women's Studies 79

Patai and Koertge introduce their readers to the debates and disagreements that often beset women's studies departments. In showing just how intense these internal debates are, they offer both a corrective to those who see feminism as a single approach and an insight into the ways in which disciplinary values and assumptions are formed.

J. WADE GILLEY, The Distributed University 87

Gilley examines distance learning, a university system in which classes are conducted across computer lines. He sees in the idea of the "distributed university" an exciting opportunity for students and faculty to overcome the geographical and intellectual obstacles that now exist in university classrooms bounded by time and place.

GEORGE D. KUH, JOHN H. SCHUH, AND ELIZABETH J. WHITT, Some Good News about Campus Life: How "Involving Colleges" Promote Learning Outside the Classroom 94

Concentrating on what they call "involving colleges," the authors of this article examine what's going right at some colleges and universities across the country. Encouraged to see themselves as part of a campus community and to exhibit "educationally purposeful behavior," students at these schools receive a different kind of education than their peers on other campuses.

DAVID M. HUMMON, College Slang Revisited: Language, Culture, and Undergraduate Life 106

People of different generations and with different cultural and ethnic backgrounds often use different kinds of slang. Those differences in our use of language sometimes make it difficult for us to communicate easily with one another, but they can also help us establish a sense of community with others like us. How aware are we, though, of the ways in which our use of slang reveals our lifestyles and values? David Hummon analyzes the slang of college students from different campuses to help us understand how it reveals their similarities and their differences.

Crosscurrents: Questions for Connecting the Readings in Chapter 2 128

CHAPTER 3

Work and Play 131

Chapter Introduction 131

REG THERIAULT, Old Blue Collars, Young Blue Collars, and That Little Place You're Going to Get in the Country 133

Most of us need and maybe even want to work. But do we all look at work in the same way? Theriault looks at the dreams and values of older and younger workers from various cultural and ethnic backgrounds.

STANTON WHEELER, Double Lives 143

Have you ever felt that you live your most important moments when you are passionately engaged in a kind of play that is more real to you than the worlds of school and work? Have you ever imagined a future in which you use your job—your vocation—primarily to support your avocation? Wheeler examines just that kind of double life.

JOAN RYAN, Little Girls in Pretty Boxes   152

> Many of us have been charmed by gymnasts who look like pixies and perform like seasoned veterans. Why are we so entranced by these little girls who step out onto the world stage? What price do they pay for their training and our adulation? Ryan, comparing them to the children in factories and mines in the nineteenth century, explores the dark side of athletics.

LOTTE BAILYN, Two Women at Work: Balancing Work and Family   163

> What happens when a worker wants to do a good job and be a good parent? In the days of working fathers and stay-at-home mothers, it was easier to establish an appropriate and comfortable balance between work and family. Today, when many women work outside the home and many men want to share more child-rearing responsibilities, employers and employees frequently have a harder time deciding how family and job should be balanced. Bailyn examines the choices two women and their employers made.

MERLISA LAWRENCE CORBETT, Telecommuting: The New Workplace Trend   176

> Are you intrigued and excited by the idea of doing your work out of your home, sending and receiving information over modem lines and saving yourself the aggravation and expense of long and wearing traffic commutes? How successfully do you think you would telecommute? In this short article, Corbett examines the elements of successful telecommuting.

JULIET B. SCHOR, Time Squeeze: The Extra Month of Work   182

> Americans often live with two contradictory "realities": we pride ourselves in the technology that has brought us time-saving devices and, at the same time, we complain about how little time we have. Schor examines the interesting, and surprising, connections between technology, consumer consumption, and our constant feeling that we don't have enough time.

SUSAN WILLIS, Public Use/Private State   210

> Just the mention of Disneyland or Disney World evokes for many of us images of play and fantasy that remind us of the joys of childhood. Willis asks us to look a little deeper into what drives those images. Are these fantasy lands actually structuring creativity in ways that make spontaneous play impossible? Are they appealing as much— or more—to our consumer instincts than to our sense of play?

HERBERT APPLEBAUM, Work—Past, Present, and Future   224

> What kinds of work do you value? What kinds of workers do you most respect? In his short history of attitudes toward work, Applebaum asks us to consider the extent to which we think of work as not only a way of making money but as a way of establishing our identities and our relationships with other members of our societies.

Crosscurrents: Questions for Connecting the Readings in Chapter 3   237

CHAPTER 4

Media, Technology, and Literacy 239

Chapter Introduction *239*

NEIL POSTMAN, The Medium Is the Metaphor *242*

> How much has our fascination with new technology and entertainment influenced both the way we talk and the way we think? How much has it trivialized thought? Using sources from earlier times as well as our own, Postman examines the relationship among technology, the media, and human thought.

CHARLES MCGRATH, The Internet's Arrested Development *252*

> All around us people are talking about the "information age" and about the need to explore the Internet, the "information superhighway." The Internet is, we are told, a wonderful tool for research, one that allows us to follow new paths of thought and to explore the nooks and crannies of human opinion and experience. But McGrath asks us to step back for a moment and ask ourselves whether those are the paths we should follow and the nooks and crannies we should visit.

DEBORAH BRANDT, Accumulating Literacy: Writing and Learning to Write in the Twentieth Century *263*

> What does it mean to be "literate" in today's society? What did it mean several years, even several generations, ago? Looking at the literacy narratives of three generations of the same family, Brandt traces the ways that ideas of and about literacy have changed.

MICHAEL C. BERTHOLD, *Jeopardy!*, Cultural Literacy, and the Discourse of Trivia *274*

> What does it mean to be "culturally literate"? What kinds of information and knowledge should every American have? Looking at the ways in which television, especially the game show Jeopardy!, disseminates information, ideas, and values, Berthold joins the debate about "cultural literacy."

DON ADAMS AND ARLENE GOLDBARD, Steal This TV: How Media Literacy Can Change the World *286*

> Knowledge is power, and in today's world, knowledge of the electronic media represents a particularly important power. Adams and Goldbard argue that, for those who want to gain control over their own lives and to influence society, it's as crucial now to master the electronic media as it once was to master the written word.

SUSAN B. NEUMAN, Television and Reading in the Lives of Young Children *292*

> We've all heard television vilified as a time waster, a "great wasteland" in which children lose their imaginations and become addicted to mindless pursuits. But how valid are those accusations? Neuman examines the extent to which television watching influences children's reading habits and takes time away from other, more worthwhile, activities.

LANA F. RAKOW AND VIJA NAVARRO, Remote Mothering and the Parallel Shift: Woman Meet the Cellular Telephone *316*

> Do men and women use, and respond to, technology differently? Do those who create and market new technological innovations value and appeal to the needs of male users over those of their female counterparts? Rakow and Navarro look at how new technologies both respond to and shape our environments, our relationships, and our futures.

PAMELA E. KRAMER AND SHEILA LEHMAN, Mismeasuring Women:
A Critique of Research on Computer Ability and Avoidance   *332*

For a long time, many have believed that men are more comfortable with computers and other forms of technology than women are. Kramer and Lehman examine the truth of that commonly held opinion, asking us to examine not only our conclusions about gender and technology but also the methods by which we have arrived at those conclusions.

Crosscurrents: Questions for Connecting the Readings in Chapter 4   *346*

CHAPTER 5

Ethics, Law, and Justice   348

Chapter Introduction   *348*

BENJAMIN SELLS, What Does the Law Want?   *350*

If you were to personify the Law, how would you do so? And how would your personification reveal your ideas about what the Law is and should be? In asking us such questions, Sells challenges us to think about the place, problems, and promise of Law in modern society.

LEON KASS, Am I My Brother's Keeper?: Reflections on Compassion and Justice   *360*

What is the appropriate relationship between compassion and justice? If someone behaves foolishly, are the rest of us responsible for helping that person escape or moderate the consequences of the foolish behavior? To what extent is each of us obligated to sacrifice even a little bit of our own comfort and safety for the good of another? In exploring these questions, Kass asks us to think about whether compassion and justice are as clearly linked as we sometimes think.

ALBERT W. ALSCHULER, Our Faltering Jury   *376*

How effective is our jury system? Examining the strategies attorneys use as they make their jury selections, Alschuler asks us to analyze the extent to which today's jury system can ensure the fair trial to which we are all entitled. In the end, he also proposes a series of reforms that some readers will find controversial and all, we think, will find thought-provoking.

CRAIG HOROWITZ, Law and Disorder: How the Juvenile Justice System Is Letting Kids Get Away with Murder   *386*

What happens when children and teenagers commit murder or other serious crimes? How should the court system balance the compassion due a young offender against the violence done to the victim and the victim's family? Examining one court in New York, Horowitz asks us to face the very real question of how we ensure justice for criminal and victim alike.

MARK HANSEN, Final Justice: Limiting Death Row Appeals   *403*

Many people—both advocates and opponents—have very strong opinions about the death penalty, but even those who agree with each other may find that their opinions are based on very different assumptions. Hansen assesses the reasons for limiting the kinds and numbers of legal appeals made by death-row inmates and their attorneys. In examining the appeals process, he also focuses on the death penalty itself.

LYNN HECHT SCHAFRAN, Is the Law Male?   *413*

> Do men and women have different experiences and expectations of the law? How does the fact that most legislators, attorneys, and judges are male influence the laws that are made and the ways they are enforced? Schafran argues that the legal system must pay greater attention to "the diversity of human experience."

ELLEN ALDERMAN AND CAROLINE KENNEDY, The Right to Privacy: High-Tech Monitoring in the Workplace   *425*

> To how much privacy is an employee entitled while using the employer's equipment? Although many employees think that their e-mail correspondence is confidential, many employers argue that they have the right to read any correspondence written on company time using company equipment. Examining a particular conflict between an employee who argues for privacy rights and an employer who argues that business correspondence is automatically open to the boss's scrutiny, Alderman and Kennedy study the effect that emerging technologies have on our right to privacy—and on the legal system's desire and ability to protect that right.

HADLEY ARKES, Moral Obtuseness in America   *433*

> Where do your moral values and beliefs come from? How much are they the product of a higher moral law? Of cultural or family values? Of professional codes or the expedience of the moment? Arkes asks us to examine the origins of our personal moral codes and to think about how we resolve conflicts between two competing moral systems.

RICHARD WEISBERG, From Jefferson to the Gulf War: How Lawyers Have Lost Their Golden Tongue   *443*

> Do today's lawyers make the same kinds of appeals and use the same kind of rhetoric that lawyers of the past did? Using examples from over 200 years of American legal rhetoric, Weisberg argues that the language of the courtroom has become degraded and, in the process, so has our understanding of the law itself.

Crosscurrents: Questions for Connecting the Readings in Chapter 5   *454*

APPENDIX A

Voices from Our Past: Conversations from American Cultural History—An Annotated Bibliography of Documents from America's Past   *457*

Selected Bibliography of Historical Sources   *458*
   From Revolution to Civil War   *458*
   The Age of Progress and Reform   *461*
   The Post-Industrial Age   *465*
More Connections: Questions for Linking Past and Present   *469*

APPENDIX B

Research and Knowledge: A Short Guide to Gathering and Using Outside Sources   *473*

Identify a Research Question That Will Lead You to a Thesis Question   *474*
Develop Good Notetaking Skills   *475*

Find Out What Sources Your Library Has, and
    Learn How to Locate Them   *476*
Consider Using Nonprint Sources of Information   *477*
Start Your Own Clipping File of Current Magazine
    and Newspaper Articles   *477*
Browse the World Wide Web   *478*
Use Observations and Site Visits to Learn More about your Topic   *480*
Gather Information from Research Interviews   *481*
Conduct Research Surveys   *483*
Evaluate Your Sources   *486*
Integrate Sources and Incorporate Quotations   *487*

CREDITS   490

INDEX   493

Alternate Contents by Academic Genre

Since many instructors use genre as an important concept in writing courses, we have provided this genre index which identifies several different types of academic or professional texts. While there clearly might be other categories we could have used or different ways of placing these texts into categories, we felt that such a list might be useful to instructors in designing their courses or in developing writing assignments. Although many of the readings in *Currents of Inquiry* have been excerpted from longer works, we have classified each piece as if it were an independent text.

Case Studies

LOTTE BAILYN, Two Women at Work: Balancing Work and Family   163

DEBORAH BRANDT, Accumulating Literacy: Writing and Learning to Write in the Twentieth Century   263

SUSAN B. NEUMAN, Television and Reading in the Lives of Young Children   292

ELLEN ALDERMAN and CAROLINE KENNEDY, The Right to Privacy: High-Tech Monitoring in the Workplace   425

Cultural Criticism

DAPHNE PATAI and NORETTA KOERTGE, Introduction to the World of Women's Studies   79

SUSAN WILLIS, Public Use/Private State   210

NEIL POSTMAN, The Medium Is the Metaphor   242

MICHAEL C. BERTHOLD, *Jeopardy!*, Cultural Literacy, and the Discourse of Trivia   274

RICHARD WEISBERG, From Jefferson to the Gulf War: How Lawyers Have Lost Their Golden Tongue   443

Feature Articles

GEORGE D. KUH, JOHN H. SCHUH, and ELIZABETH J. WHITT, Some Good News about Campus Life: How "Involving Colleges" Promote Learning outside the University   94

JOAN RYAN, Little Girls in Pretty Boxes   152

MERLISA LAWRENCE CORBETT, Telecommuting: The New Workplace Trend   176

CHARLES MCGRATH, The Internet's Arrested Development   252

CRAIG HOROWITZ, Law and Disorder: How the Juvenile Justice System Is Letting Kids Get Away with Murder   386
MARK HANSEN, Final Justice: Limiting Death Row Appeals   403

Personal Essays

MIKE ROSE, Entering the Conversation   22
REG THERIAULT, Old Blue Collars, Young Blue Collars, and that Little Place You're Going to Get in the Country   133

Position Papers

CHESTER E. FINN, JR., and BRUNO V. MANNO, Behind the Curtain   44
J. WADE GILLEY, The Distributed University   87
DON ADAMS and ARLENE GOLDBARD Steal This TV: How Media Literacy Can Change the World   286
ALBERT W. ALSCHULER, Our Faltering Jury   376

Research Studies

DAVID M. HUMMON, College Slang Revisited: Language, Culture, and Undergraduate Life   106
HERBERT APPLEBAUM, Work—Past, Present, and Future   224
JULIET B. SCHOR, Time Squeeze: The Extra Month of Work   182
LANA F. RAKOW and VIJA NAVARRO, Remote Mothering and the Parallel Shift   316
PAMELA E. KRAMER and SHEILA LEHMAN, Mismeasuring Women: A Critique of Research on Computer Ability and Avoidance   332

Review Article

PHILLIP E. JOHNSON, The Creationist and the Sociobiologist: Two Stories about Illiberal Education   57

Theory

STANTON WHEELER, Double Lives   143
BENJAMIN SELLS, What Does the Law Want?   350
LEON KASS, Am I My Brother's Keeper? Reflections on Compassion and Justice   360
LYNN HECHT SCHAFRAN, Is the Law Male?   413
HADLEY ARKES, Moral Obtuseness in America   433

Alternate Thematic Contents

Several specific themes and issues run through the readings organized into four broad topical clusters in this book. To help instructors make connections between readings that address similar themes and issues, we have provided this thematic contents. It may be useful in course design or in developing writing assignments.

Amusement

    STANTON WHEELER, Double Lives   143
    SUSAN WILLIS, Public Use/Private State   210
    NEIL POSTMAN, The Medium Is the Metaphor   242
    CHARLES MCGRATH, The Internet's Arrested Development   252

Childhood and Adolescence

    DEBORAH BRANDT, Accumulating Literacy: Writing and Learning to Write in the Twentieth Century   263
    JOAN RYAN, Little Girls in Pretty Boxes   152
    SUSAN B. NEUMAN, Television and Reading in the Lives of Young Children   292
    CHARLES MCGRATH, The Internet's Arrested Development   252
    CRAIG HOROWITZ, Law and Disorder: How the Juvenile Justice System Is Letting Kids Get Away with Murder   386

Computer Technology

    J. WADE GILLEY, The Distributed University   87
    MERLISA LAWRENCE CORBETT, Telecommuting: The New Workplace Trend   176
    PAMELA E. KRAMER and SHEILA LEHMAN, Mismeasuring Women: A Critique of Research on Computer Ability and Avoidance   332
    CHARLES MCGRATH, The Internet's Arrested Development   252
    ELLEN ALDERMAN and CAROLINE KENNEDY, The Right to Privacy: High-Tech Monitoring in the Workplace   425

Education in the United States

    MIKE ROSE, Entering the Conversation   22
    CHESTER E. FINN, JR., and BRUNO V. MANNO, Behind the Curtain   44

PHILLIP E. JOHNSON, The Creationist and the Sociobiologist: Two Stories About Illiberal Education   57

DAPHNE PATAI and NORETTA KOERTGE, Introduction to the World of Women's Studies   79

J. WADE GILLEY, The Distributed University   87

GEORGE D. KUH, JOHN H. SCHUH and ELIZABETH J. WHITT, Some Good News about Campus Life: How "Involving Colleges" Promote Learning outside the University   94

DEBORAH BRANDT, Accumulating Literacy: Writing and Learning to Write in the Twentieth Century   263

DON ADAMS and ARLENE GOLDBARD, Steal This TV: How Media Literacy Can Change the World   286

PAMELA E. KRAMER and SHEILA LEHMAN, Mismeasuring Women: A Critique of Research on Computer Ability and Avoidance   332

LYNN HECHT SCHAFRAN, Is the Law Male?   413

Ethical Values

PHILLIP E. JOHNSON, The Creationist and the Sociobiologist: Two Stories about Illiberal Education   57

GEORGE D. KUH, JOHN H. SCHUH and ELIZABETH J. WHITT, Some Good News about Campus Life: How "Involving Colleges" Promote Learning outside the University   94

REG THERIAULT, Old Blue Collars, Young Blue Collars, and that Little Place You're Going to Get in the Country   133

BENJAMIN SELLS, What Does the Law Want?   350

LEON KASS, Am I My Brother's Keeper? Reflections on Compassion and Justice   360

HADLEY ARKES, Moral Obtuseness in America   433

Family Relationships

LOTTE BAILYN, Two Women at Work: Balancing Work and Family   163

JULIET B. SCHOR, Time Squeeze: The Extra Month of Work   182

MERLISA LAWRENCE CORBETT, Telecommuting: The New Workplace Trend   176

LANA F. RAKOW and VIJA NAVARRO, Remote Mothering and the Parallel Shift   316

DEBORAH BRANDT, Accumulating Literacy: Writing and Learning to Write in the Twentieth Century   263

Gender Issues

DAPHNE PATAI and NORETTA KOERTGE, Introduction to the World of Women's Studies   79

LOTTE BAILYN, Two Women at Work: Balancing Work and Family   163

JOAN RYAN, Little Girls in Pretty Boxes   152

MERLISA LAWRENCE CORBETT, Telecommuting: The New Workplace Trend   176

LANA F. RAKOW and VIJA NAVARRO, Remote Mothering and the Parallel Shift   316

PAMELA E. KRAMER and SHEILA LEHMAN, Mismeasuring Women: A Critique of Research on Computer Ability and Avoidance   332

LYNN HECHT SCHAFRAN, Is the Law Male?   413

Justice System in the United States

LEON KASS, Am I My Brother's Keeper? Reflections on Compassion and Justice   360

ALBERT W. ALSCHULER, Our Faltering Jury   376

CRAIG HOROWITZ, Law and Disorder: How the Juvenile Justice System is Letting Kids Get Away with Murder   386

MARK HANSEN, Final Justice: Limiting Death Row Appeals   403

Language and Style

DAVID M. HUMMON, College Slang Revisited: Language, Culture, and Undergraduate Life   106

RICHARD WEISBERG, From Jefferson to the Gulf War: How Lawyers Have Lost Their Golden Tongue   443

Theories of Law

BENJAMIN SELLS, What Does the Law Want?   350

LYNN HECHT SCHAFRAN, Is the Law Male?   413

Literacy Issues

MIKE ROSE, Entering the Conversation   22

DEBORAH BRANDT, Accumulating Literacy: Writing and Learning to Write in the Twentieth Century   263

SUSAN B. NEUMAN, Television and Reading in the Lives of Young Children   292

CHARLES MCGRATH, The Internet's Arrested Development   252

RICHARD WEISBERG, From Jefferson to the Gulf War: How Lawyers Have Lost Their Golden Tongue   443

Mass Media

NEIL POSTMAN, The Medium Is the Metaphor   242

MICHAEL C. BERTHOLD, *Jeopardy!*, Cultural Literacy, and the Discourse of Trivia   274

DON ADAMS and ARLENE GOLDBARD, Steal This TV: How Media Literacy Can Change the World   286

CHARLES MCGRATH, The Internet's Arrested Development   252

Multiculturalism (and Race Relations)

    CHESTER E. FINN, JR., and BRUNO V. MANNO, Behind the Curtain   44
    PHILLIP E. JOHNSON, The Creationist and the Sociobiologist: Two Stories about Illiberal Education   57
    DAPHNE PATAI and NORETTA KOERTGE, Introduction to the World of Women's Studies   79
    MARK HANSEN, Final Justice: Limiting Death Row Appeals   403
    ALBERT W. ALSCHULER, Our Faltering Jury   376

Popular Culture

    DAVID M. HUMMON, College Slang Revisited: Language, Culture, and Undergraduate Life   106
    NEIL POSTMAN, The Medium Is the Metaphor   242
    CHARLES MCGRATH, The Internet's Arrested Development   252
    SUSAN WILLIS, Public Use/Private State   210
    MICHAEL C. BERTHOLD, *Jeopardy!*, Cultural Literacy, and the Discourse of Trivia   274

Privacy (Public v. Private Interests)

    SUSAN WILLIS, Public Use/Private State   210
    ELLEN ALDERMAN and CAROLINE KENNEDY, The Right to Privacy: High-Tech Monitoring in the Workplace   425

Influence of Television

    SUSAN B. NEUMAN, Television and Reading in the Lives of Young Children   292
    MICHAEL C. BERTHOLD, *Jeopardy!*, Cultural Literacy, and the Discourse of Trivia   274

Time Management

    JULIET B. SCHOR, Time Squeeze: The Extra Month of Work   182
    MERLISA LAWRENCE CORBETT, Telecommuting: The New Workplace Trend   176
    LOTTE BAILYN, Two Women at Work: Balancing Work and Family   163
    LANA F. RAKOW and VIJA NAVARRO, Remote Mothering and the Parallel Shift: Women Meet the Cellular Phone   316

Theories of Work and Play

    STANTON WHEELER, Double Lives   143
    HERBERT APPLEBAUM, Work—Past, Present, and Future   224
    JULIET B. SCHOR, Time Squeeze: The Extra Month of Work   182
    SUSAN WILLIS, Public Use/Private State   210

Workplace Issues

    REG THERIAULT, Old Blue Collars, Young Blue Collars, and that Little Place You're Going to Get in the Country   133
    STANTON WHEELER, Double Lives   143
    MERLISA LAWRENCE CORBETT, Telecommuting: The New Workplace Trend   176
    LOTTE BAILYN, Two Women at Work: Balancing Work and Family   163
    ELLEN ALDERMAN and CAROLINE KENNEDY, The Right to Privacy: High-Tech Monitoring in the Workplace   425

1

Finding Your Place in the Conversation
Becoming an Academic Reader

THE READING-WRITING RELATIONSHIP

Reading and writing are different, but complementary, ways of knowing the world. When we want to know what others think about something, we read what they have written about it. When we want to know more clearly what we think about something, writing is often the best way to clarify those thoughts and to share them with others. The skills you develop as a critical reader will help to make you a more insightful and persuasive writer.

It may help to think of readers and writers as the listeners and speakers in a *textual conversation*. As you read, you are "listening" to what a writer has to say, and you need to listen as carefully and thoughtfully to his or her words as you would to the words of anyone with whom you are engaged in conversation. But in an actual conversation, you don't just listen; you also actively participate, asking questions and raising objections, contributing your own examples or counterexamples. By the end of the conversation, you hope that everyone involved will have both gained insights into how others think *and* refined their own ideas. The best writers, like the best conversationalists, understand fully this constant give and take; they know how to speak *and* how to listen. By learning to listen carefully and thoughtfully to your own ideas and the ideas of others and to ask questions of *all* texts, including your own, you will gain confidence in your ability to understand others' ideas and persuade them of your own skill and expertise.

To become a better reader, then, you need to think like a writer, and to become a better writer, you need to think like a reader. Critical readers and writers must think alike in some crucial ways, because both are engaged in making meaning. It is easy, of course, to think of *writers* as making meaning: putting words together on the page to convey the ideas they have formulated. The idea that *readers* make meaning may be less familiar to you. When people read, however, they are doing more than simply searching for a preexisting meaning that a text reveals. Rather, they are using what they have already learned about language, about sentence structure and style, and even about their own experience with the subject matter in order to actively "construct" a meaning from the words on a page. That is, as readers we participate with the writer in building an explanation of what the words on the page mean.

Does this mean that words can mean anything we as readers want them to mean? Not at all. As readers we are obligated to use the materials and design the writer has provided; we cannot simply construct a whole new edifice. To use a different metaphor, as readers we "perform" a text much as a pianist performs a musical score or an actor performs a play. The resulting concert or play is an interpretation of the author's text, just as our "reading" is an interpretation of the text we encounter as readers. Neither the concert nor the play has life until others interpret the musical score or the dramatic script and *recreate* it. In other words, readers and writers have a symbiotic relationship; neither can survive without the active participation of the other.

This is probably not news to you; you have probably been told before that good readers make good writers. But what exactly is the connection between good reading and good writing? Throughout this book, we emphasize the ways in which the writers move into conversation with one another, and we ask you to think about what you would have to say in such conversations. As soon as you begin to think of yourself as part of these conversations, you are well on your way to finding something to say—and to putting your words down on the page. You are well on your way to becoming a writer.

In this chapter we will look at critical reading as a process—not as a process shrouded in mystery but as one open to analysis and to degrees of mastery. We will also offer some suggestions for approaching the kinds of texts you will encounter not only in this book but in courses across the curriculum. Academic texts sometimes present special challenges. The authors are often experts, and they use language and concepts that are often unfamiliar to those of us who are not experts. As Mike Rose suggests in "Entering the Conversation" in chapter 2, we often have trouble understanding individual concepts or the overall purpose of a text, even when we know what the words themselves mean. Our goal in chapter 1 is to help you begin to cultivate a variety of strategies that will enable you to move beyond simply reading the words on the page toward interpreting complex texts.

WHY DO WE READ?

We say that meanings are "constructed," because readers must systematically arrange and order their perceptions, ideas, and knowledge about any text they read. *Reading*, in the sense we will use it in this chapter, is an act of *interpreting*. In order to understand how the process of interpretation works, we must recognize that all readers do not read all texts in the same way or for the same reasons. The urban commuter, browsing through the daily paper on the morning train; the college student on spring break, reading a spy novel on the beach; the third-grader, reading a long-favorite story for the first time by himself; the science student, reading a textbook to extract methods, theories, and principles; the historian, reading documents in a library archive to supplement her research on nineteenth-century social customs; the lawyer, reading a statute to determine his client's culpability: each of these readers has a different goal and thus reads in a different way. Let's examine more closely each situation and the reader's connection to the text.

The commuter on the train wants merely to pass the time, maybe gleaning some information she will remember and use in a conversation later that day; she does not need to read carefully or to remember much of what she has read, but she most certainly will remember what seems most interesting or relevant at that moment. The college student reading his novel wants to experience vicariously a strange place and unusual people; to enter this new world, he must allow the author to persuade him to believe in this fictional world. The third-grader doesn't need to pay close attention to the story, since he already knows it well. But his pleasure in reading comes from connecting his memories of this story to the words on the page. The science student needs to read her textbook carefully, extracting fundamental and ultimately useful information that she must learn and remember. Thus, she reads carefully, usually with little attention to language or style, but with a clear sense of purpose. The historian, searching for answers to important questions about the past, must read each document closely and carefully, through the lens of her knowledge about history; she looks for ways in which the words on the page, and the context in which they were written, confirm or reveal something about the past. The lawyer must read closely, too, thinking about how other readers might interpret the words on the page and envisioning ways in which the language of the text might apply to the real-life situation that concerns him. In each situation, despite the differences, the reader makes a uniquely significant connection to the text that provides him or her with a purpose for reading and a method for constructing a meaning appropriate to that purpose.

We must remember that the purpose of any reading is not inherent in the text but in the reader in a particular situation. We call that reader's situation a *role* (and people may have many different roles during the day as readers). That role, like the reader's purpose, will determine a variety of reading strategies. The historian—or for that matter her colleague in the English Department—may read a novel, not for the pleasure of escaping temporarily into a fictional world, but to discern the ideas or customs of a particular era. She may find something different in the novel than does the reader who reads simply for pleasure. Similarly, works of popular culture, such as films and television programs, although we describe them as entertainment, can be "read" critically and analytically, and their deeper meanings can be unearthed. The lawyer may read the newspaper, but not casually like the commuter. In his role as a lawyer, he searches in the various stories for insight into the relationship between individuals and the legal system. In addition, our roles as readers often shift quickly. When she gets off the train, our newspaper-browsing commuter might be a scientific researcher, closely and carefully reading the latest journal articles to learn about new developments in genetic engineering. Each of us must adapt the reading process to the demands of our current role.

As we contemplate our own roles as readers, we must remember that a writer also brings a particular role to the text. A writer may be an expert on a topic, intent on exploring it for fellow experts or on explaining it for an audience of lay readers. Some writers see themselves as observers, studying a problem from a distance. The writer may bring to the text an attitude of inquiry, seeking to identify and articulate key questions without offering definitive answers. Understanding these distinct roles—expert, teacher, observer, inquirer—helps us to better understand a text.

THE READER'S ROLE IN THE READING PROCESS

As we have suggested, the reader plays an essential role in constructing the meaning of a text. Just as readers decide what they hope to gain from reading a text, they must also identify what they bring to the reading situation. If as readers we fail to recognize and acknowledge our own prejudices as well as our familiarity with or ignorance of a topic, we risk closing our minds to what a text really says. Each of us brings something unique to each text we read.

For example, our commuter on the train has presumably been reading the morning paper for some time and brings with her a knowledge of current events and of the city in which she lives. She also brings political and social values to her reading, as well as her own personal experience, all of which color her responses to what she reads. Reading the paper for her is different than for our third-grader, who may soon begin to try his developing reading skills on the front page, but whose understanding of the world is simple and relatively uninformed. The lawyer, the historian, and the scientist each bring considerable knowledge and training to the vast literature that makes up the body of knowledge in their disciplines, but even the novel-reading college student may already know something about law or history when he takes a course that requires him to read in that discipline.

Whether we realize it or not, we always form expectations about what we think a text will say. To become better critical readers we must articulate more clearly what these expectations are. For example, we may more readily challenge what a writer has to say if we have prior knowledge of a subject or the author; conversely, when we lack prior knowledge or even feel ignorant about a topic, we may be less critical and more accepting of what a writer says about the subject. We may expect a text to be difficult and feel surprised when it is more accessible or more interesting than we thought it might be. In the process of reading we confirm, challenge, or even reverse our expectations about what we read. If as readers we can consciously identify our expectations and biases, each reading experience will be more fruitful and illuminating. For example, if we ask ourselves what we already know, think, or believe about a topic before we read something else about it, we will read more closely and consider the text as a whole rather than as many distinct parts. This ability to balance the parts and the whole is essential to successful critical reading.

With a clear understanding of our purpose, knowledge, and expectations as readers, we are ready to look more closely at the text. When we read, we balance our freedom as readers to construct from any text a meaning of our own against the restrictions that a particular text places on the range of possible interpretations. Obviously, it would be ridiculous to say that something means whatever we as readers say it means. So how do we come to identify that range of possible meanings? Understanding the various forces that come together to produce a text will allow us, in turn, to understand more fully the restrictions a text places on our ability to construct our own meaning.

UNDERSTANDING RHETORICAL CONTEXT

When we talk about *rhetoric* here, we are mainly discussing the various ways in which messages get communicated between listeners and speakers, between readers and writers. Ordinary experience shows us that we can convey the same meaning with different words, tones, and emphasis. Rhetoric focuses our attention not just on what a text says but on how that meaning is presented. As readers, we can place any text in a rhetorical context by asking a few important questions. Answers to these questions may come from our prior knowledge, from information we glean from editors or critics of the text, and from information provided in the text itself. Just as we place the pieces of a jigsaw puzzle together, watching the image emerge, we can ask and answer these questions in any order, until a clear idea of the rhetorical context emerges. The answer to one question may also help us to more fully understand the answer to another question.

What Role or Identity Does the Author Establish?

Just as we identify our own knowledge and expectations of a text, we must understand the author's expertise, knowledge, and possible biases about the subject matter of the text. When we talk about the author's perspective, we are referring to the "distance" between the author and the text and to the author's relationship to the events or information described. That distance might be geographical, temporal, cultural, political, or emotional. Knowingly or unknowingly, every author creates a *persona* in the text. This persona is not quite the same thing as the author, a real human being, but rather an *image* of that author that emerges from the words on the page. When the author consciously creates a persona, it represents how that author wants to appear to the readers, whether or not that characterization is true or valid. For instance, certain authors may try very hard in a text to assert their objectivity, but what we know about those authors may suggest that they are anything but objective. A persona may emerge accidentally from a text. Sometimes authors seem pretentious or condescending, hardly qualities that any of us would want to project.

By constructing an image of the author based on both textual and *extratextual* information—in other words, from what appears in the text and what we learn about the text from other sources, we can begin to add to our understanding of the text. The facts about an author's experience—for instance, that he is a member of an ethnic or other minority group or that she holds politically conservative views—may often cause us to revise our initial impressions of what a text means.

Who Are the Readers of the Text?

When we ask this question, we are thinking not only about who has actually read or will read this text at any point in time but also about how the text reflects attitudes toward its intended audience. Again, we should look for clues about the intended audience from facts outside the text (Where and when was the text published, and was it received favorably or unfavorably by readers?) and from inside the text (What kind of language does it use? Is it technical, or are sophisticated concepts explained in simple terms?).

Knowing something about the intended audience can help us make more sense out of a text—what the author says (or doesn't say) and how it's said. For example, some of the selections in this book were written for specific occasions, such as for a professional conference or as a chapter in a widely published book. The author's sense of his or her intended audience often shapes the form and content of a text. Writers might choose a particular specialized vocabulary because they know their specific intended audience is familiar with it. Similarly, authors might be more specific in articulating their underlying assumptions if they are aware that their intended audience is less familiar with certain concepts and problems. As readers, the more we know about when and why and for whom a text was written, the more easily we can understand many of the author's choices about language, style, organization, and evidence.

What Is the Author's Tone?

Tone refers to the way a text reflects the author's attitudes toward the readers, toward the subject matter, and toward himself or herself as the author. We can perhaps best understand tone if we think of it as the way a text defines (through choices about style and language, what to include, what not to include) various relationships among author, subject, and audience. We often describe the tone as serious, humorous, ironic, or even sarcastic. These words help us to understand the kind of relationship that the text seeks to build with its readers.

By understanding the author's attitudes, as reflected in the text, our understanding of what the author intended to say becomes more precise. For instance, a writer who sees herself as an outsider to a particular community of readers will address issues differently than writers who have no question about their authority on these topics. A writer who considers himself an expert will adopt a different tone than a writer just discovering ideas about a particular topic. Some writers may establish a rather condescending attitude toward readers, while others may try to draw readers along into the process of discovery. Similarly, an ironic or humorous tone may reveal more than the text itself seems to mean, letting us know as readers that the writer senses some foolishness or absurdity about the situation described. As readers we must recognize the clues about their attitudes, some obvious and some more subtle, that writers leave in their texts. A choice as minor as a single word or phrase may tell us much about what authors think about their topics, their readers, and themselves.

What Is the Purpose of the Text?

Just as we asked ourselves what we hoped to gain by reading something, we need to determine what the author hoped to gain by writing the text. We usually want to state this purpose as an active verb, for example, to inform, explain, entertain, or persuade. Although a text may have more than one purpose (to inform *and* to entertain, for example), we can usually say that one goal predominates. By recognizing that dominant purpose, once again using both textual and extratextual information about the text, we devise a strategy of reading appropriate to the strategies the author uses to accomplish the goals of the text.

READING FOR THE INTENDED MEANING

Reading is obviously about what a text means, not just about how or why that meaning is conveyed. We might call this "what" of the text the *message*, and ask ourselves, "What does the text assert as true?" For readers, constructing the meaning of a text is always, in large part, a process we call *linguistic decoding*. We have to decide what the authors meant when they put the words on the page. Remember, after all, that the words on the page are just codes or symbols for meaning, just as the dots and dashes that make up Morse code or the raised symbols of Braille inscription are codes for meaning. If we cannot unscramble the codes, we cannot uncover the meaning, and the experience will remain an unintelligible jumble of sound or of physical sensation. When we learned to read, we gained the ability to assign meaning to codes, which are, after all, arbitrary signs for the ideas that writers want to express.

Reading for a text's intended meaning may be difficult or easy, depending on the situation. For example, our third-grader, reading for himself a story he already knows well, still makes sense out of individual words and puts them into the context of larger units of meaning: sentences, paragraphs, chapters. He knows what the final message will be, but the process of decoding that message remains rewarding anyway. He finds pleasure in the process because he experiences the story once again through the play of language that he is beginning to master for himself. Similarly, when we read for pleasure or escape, we do not usually read any more closely than necessary to keep track of the plot and make sense of the characters' actions. This is why literature students sometimes find it difficult to write a critical essay on a novel that they have read through only once quickly, as if they were reading for pleasure. Critical analysis of any text (including a literary text) often requires multiple readings. Rereading often fills in gaps in our understanding, and we often see larger connections not apparent the first time.

In your academic career, you will want to improve your ability to read with attention to detail, awareness of style and structure, and understanding of a complex theory or argument—skills required of readers in all the various academic disciplines. When a text contains unfamiliar or specialized words, an unusually complex structure or style, or complex concepts and ideas, reading for meaning is obviously more difficult. So what can you do to make sense out of a text that at first seems formidable? The following practical strategies may help you more easily discern the message of complex texts.

Read More Than Once

Almost certainly, any complex or sophisticated text will require more than one reading. One reading, no matter how careful or meticulous, will not provide enough material for you to adequately construct the meaning of the text. Each additional reading, however, requires a different strategy. For instance, you might skim once, looking for the main ideas, and then read again to fill in gaps and flesh out the main ideas. Or you can read once, looking for information to develop your understanding of the rhetorical context, using subsequent readings to identify other aspects of the structure, style, or argument. Several purposeful readings of a text may, in fact, take you less time than a single unfocused reading, however careful.

Break the Text into Smaller Sections

On a first review, what seem to be the main sections or divisions of the text? If the text is short, you might want to break it down into sections consisting of just a few sentences. In longer texts you may need to identify sections that consist of several long paragraphs. You might also want to examine the structure of a text carefully. You can often make an outline, breaking the text down into its various components. As you do so, make good use of any tools, such as subheadings or section headings. By identifying the parts that make up the text as a whole, you can more easily follow an author's theory, questions, and argument and thus understand how the text builds from that main idea. Identifying the key components in the structure of a piece gives you a better sense of how the author put the argument together. The structure that a writer uses is often a very important clue to the purpose and message of the text.

Put the Meaning of Each Section of the Text into Your Own Words

To translate an author's words into our own is to *paraphrase;* to condense the meaning of a longer text into fewer of our own words is to *summarize*. When we put the ideas of others into our own words, we make certain that we know what the author tried to say. Paraphrasing or summarizing helps you to more easily compare your expectations of a text to what you actually find. The process of paraphrasing or summarizing a complex text will also help you to identify sections of the text that remain unclear even after a close reading. Those sections may require even more detailed analysis; you may need to look up the meanings of words, research a reference or allusion in the text, reconsider the section in the context of the work as a whole, or even ask for help from another reader to understand what a section says. As you become a more confident reader, you will learn to identify the source of your confusion about difficult passages and devise a strategy to better understand such passages.

Identify Key Terms and Concepts in the Text

Often a text depends on your understanding of a few key ideas. Let's say you are reading a text that talks about the difference between various economic concepts. After identifying key concepts such as capitalism and socialism, try to define them. Next determine what you already know about them and then explore their meaning in context. You may then need to use a reference book, such as a dictionary or encyclopedia, to help you understand these concepts more fully. Sometimes specialized reference books, available in your academic library, will be required.

Pay close attention to connotation; this is often an important clue to meaning in a text. *Connotation* is concerned not just with what a dictionary tells us about a word, but with associations and feelings words create among users of a language. If a word has very negative connotations—if, for instance, a writer refers to the payments that a welfare recipient receives as "handouts"—we have a pretty clear idea of that writer's position. In this case, the writer implies that the welfare system is unfair and welfare recipients undeserving. We need to assume as readers that writers make conscious or unconscious choices about which of several possible words to use, and we can use those choices to understand the meaning of a text more fully. If we fail to understand that a word has negative or positive connotations or that an author uses sarcasm, we may completely misunderstand the thesis of the text.

Identify Inferences and Implications

Because a complex text may mean more than the words on the page actually say, critical reading often requires us to draw inferences in order to fully understand the meaning of a text. An *inference* is a conclusion that we reach about something a writer says. When we draw inferences, we are moving beyond what a text says and making sense out of what it hasn't said. By using logical reasoning, as readers we can take the facts and evidence that a writer presents and draw our own conclusions about a topic.

Similarly, authors often suggest more than they say directly in a text. Such suggestions are called *implications,* and recognizing them allows us to create a richer meaning than we could if we failed to move beyond the explicit level of the text. For example, an author may imply without saying it that a certain situation involves dire consequences. Without discerning this implication, we may not fully understand what the author wants to say. As readers we want to be alert to implications that may be present in the words chosen by a writer or in the way an idea is emphasized, and ready to draw appropriate inferences from the opinions and facts a writer provides. We want to identify those places in the text that call upon us to expand on implications or to draw inferences as we construct a meaning.

USING GENRE CONVENTIONS TO CONSTRUCT MEANING

Genre in writing usually refers to ways of classifying texts according to certain properties of form and style and giving groups of similar texts a common name or label. To understand this notion of genre better, think about how an antique dealer classifies furniture according to different styles or designs on a piece: curved legs might place a table in the Queen Anne style or genre, while an ornate carved pediment at the top of a cabinet might distinguish it as Chippendale. Knowledge of the characteristics of these genres allows the dealer to interpret a piece of furniture by judging its age, workmanship, and value, in short, the social conditions that produced it. As readers, we can similarly classify texts according to their formal properties—such as diction, style, order of ideas, paragraph length and structure, citation of sources, and use of quotation—and by classifying them we can better understand their meanings. Similarly, as writers we learn to produce texts that conform to the rules and expectations of particular genres.

But genre is not just about classifying forms or being able to recognize certain patterns; it is also about understanding why those patterns are important. Recent ideas about genre have emphasized the way that understanding genre conventions—and why they develop—can help us to anticipate how writers in particular situations will respond. Thinking about genre is, in fact, thinking about how people in certain social or rhetorical situations make meaning. We know that identifying the audience and the author's role and purpose can help us construct the meaning of a text. Genre allows us to see how these factors, along with form, function on a larger scale—not just in a particular text, but in a whole category of texts.

Anyone who creates a work of art, music, or literature recognizes—by following or rejecting—the rules of the genre to which a work belongs. Both the artist and the audience need to have experience with a genre in order to fully appreciate it. We would be unlikely to write a song, for example, if we had never heard one; also, if we had never heard a song before, we would have difficulty appreciating its style or meaning. Similarly, you probably cannot become a good academic writer until you have had considerable experience with the rules and conventions of academic writing. By reading and writing—that is, by participating in a particular social or rhetorical community, or what we might call a discourse community—you can become familiar with the genre conventions.

Perhaps the easiest way to understand generic differences is to think of a playwright, a novelist, a poet, a biographer, and a sociologist each writing about the same topic, say, a tragic death in a family. The playwright may want to dramatize the dynamics of family relationships; the novelist may want to explore the individual psychology of grief; the poet may want to evoke in readers feelings of loss and consolation; the biographer may want us to see circumstances that led to the tragedy; and the sociologist may want to explore the larger social implications of this specific tragedy. The message of each text might be essentially the same: that a family triumphs over tragedy to achieve a greater closeness. Each writer has chosen the form most compatible with his or her purpose, and each genre or type of text will use different strategies of language, style, and organization to develop this similar message.

The academic reading you do as a student represents a number of different genres, each of which may require you to read in different ways. For example, we call any short, speculative, or personal piece an *essay,* and we refer to a short work of fiction in this book as a *story.* Many selections in this book have been excerpted from academic journals, and we usually refer to them as *research articles.* An article that summarizes, evaluates, and synthesizes texts in a particular field is called a *review article.* We call any piece that originated as a text spoken before an audience—whether it seeks to inform or persuade—a *speech.* Where an author seeks to persuade readers that a particular point of view is correct, we call the text an *argument* or even a *position paper.*

We have already said that a writer has a purpose in writing, a purpose that we can ascertain by looking closely at the text and any extratextual information we have. For the writer, that purpose dictates choices about form, including organization, structure, style, and methods of development. The writer then follows certain conventions, or rules, determined by this choice of form. As readers we can learn to assess genre conventions and use the author's adherence to or violation of those conventions to understand more about what we have read.

The concept of genre can almost always help to explain formal differences among texts. If you understand how a text might be classified, you can usually devise an appropriate strategy for reading it. In part, genre conventions speak to readers' expectations about what they read. For instance, someone writing a grant or research proposal will need to place different pieces of information in different sections of the proposal, because such forms contain specific defined fields of information that readers expect to find in the text. Likewise, laboratory reports in the sciences follow a certain format, and readers expect to find the necessary information in certain categories in a certain order. Someone reading an essay expects to find a structure and organization that is looser and more exploratory. In reading an argument by a law student, you would probably find a more tightly woven argument than you would in reading an argument by a graduate student or a professor in the humanities.

Form and content are always related, and the rules of a genre are not arbitrary. If writers fail to follow the formal rules of the genre, they may not communicate effectively with their readers, whose expectations are determined by their own understanding of that genre. Readers may similarly fail to follow the clues that genre provides. If readers look to a personal essay for an explicit thesis, they may not be able to interpret the text. As readers, we expect lab reports to analyze the researcher's methodology, and a grant proposal to include a section on the project's goals. If this sort of information is missing or incomplete, we may not be able to adequately interpret or evaluate the text. What we know about the rules of genre comes from two sources: our own experience of reading widely in a genre and discerning the relevant and consistent patterns in works classified in that genre, and what other readers tell us about the patterns and conventions. As you gain more experience with a particular genre—for example, the kind of researched argument common in academic journals—you will be better able to construct meaning from those texts.

USING THE RULES OF ARGUMENT TO INTERPRET TEXTS

Once we have learned as readers to identify genre conventions and the conditions that produce them, we can use that knowledge to develop an interpretation of what we read. Academic writing (especially that produced by undergraduate students) is often described as *expository,* that is, it seeks to present information clearly, to expose ideas. But the different kinds of writing described generally as expository may have distinct goals. Much academic writing—including many of the examples we have assembled here in this book—can be classified generically as *researched argument*. Remember that the goal of most academic writing is to create or reflect the creation of new knowledge through research. So even when an academic writer's goal is not specifically to persuade, he or she may be concerned with the theories and opinions of other writers, summarizing and synthesizing theories and opinions. Thus by examining more carefully the generic properties of arguments—in other words, the rules of argument—you will be better able to understand many of the texts encountered in your academic career. The following techniques will help you identify the various parts of an argument and more effectively construct meaning from complex academic texts.

Identify the Thesis

By *thesis* we mean the position that the writer seeks to support in the text. The thesis may be a theory that the author will explain and defend, a claim that the writer wants to develop with evidence and logic, a response to another theory or claim, or even an exploration of a problem. Because most academic writing is about the creation of knowledge (writers write to say something new or to say something old in a new way), you might think of the thesis as simply the writer's attempt to articulate the knowledge that he or she wishes to convey by writing. What does the writer wish to contribute to the wider conversation about the topic at hand? Even a textbook, which may purport not to offer an argument but to provide its readers with facts about a subject, has a particular relationship to the theories and discoveries of that discipline. That relationship to the wider discipline is part of what constitutes a writer's thesis.

Distinguish between Facts and Opinions

A *fact* is an assertion that the writer expects all readers to accept as true because it is based on experience or observation, or because all reasonable people accept it. An *opinion* is an assertion that requires proof before a reader will accept it as true. We have a fact if we cannot imagine someone reasonable disagreeing with an assertion; we have an opinion if we can imagine a reasonable alternative to the assertion. As readers we need to think of fact and opinion not as separate, easily identifiable categories, but as two ends of a spectrum along which we are likely to find varying degrees of fact and opinion. What was once considered an opinion or theory may over time be proved so often that it acquires in the minds of most people the status of fact. Many assertions that we find in texts (or that we make ourselves as writers) lie somewhere between indisputable fact on one end of the spectrum and barely provable opinion on the other. If you are a novice writer working with an unfamiliar topic, you will probably be most comfortable working with facts or with opinions that seem almost like facts. As a result, your early drafts may not go as far as they can toward establishing your own views. As you gain confidence as a writer and learn more about a topic, you will probably be willing to take a chance, moving toward assertions that seem more controversial and that require more proof. Later drafts of your paper will tend to present your own views more forcefully.

If you have ever been asked to provide your own interpretation of a literary text, you have probably made the distinction between fact and opinion, even if you did not realize you were doing so. For example, all readers of Shakespeare's *Romeo and Juliet* agree that both characters are dead at the end of the play. Thus, the assertion "Romeo and Juliet die at the end of the play" is a fact. In contrast, opinions vary about how and why they die. Assertions such as "An ancient, unresolved feud causes Romeo and Juliet's death" or "Romeo and Juliet die because they made foolish mistakes" are both opinions, each offering quite a different insight into facts with which most readers agree. Significantly, both opinions seem reasonable, and we can imagine a writer finding proof from the play to justify either opinion. On the other hand, an assertion like "Friar Lawrence orchestrates the deaths of both Romeo and Juliet to end the Montague-Capulet feud" is not as conventional an interpretation of the play. A writer might be able to marshal a persuasive case for this explanation, but it remains considerably farther from fact than the other two explanations offered.

When we distinguish between fact and opinion in a text we read, we are making sense out of what needs to be proved and what can be accepted as true already. We are also able to define the edge of the controversy that a writer addresses. In addition, distinguishing fact from opinion can help us recognize the questions that a writer is attempting to answer.

Determine the Role of Underlying Assumptions in the Argument

Sometimes writers ask readers to accept as true something that cannot be easily proved. An assumption is often the starting point for building an argument. Unless we accept the assumption as true, it is unlikely that an argument will persuade. For example, an argument opposing affirmative action policies in the workplace might have an underlying assumption that individual merit should be the sole criterion in employment decisions. In contrast, an argument supporting affirmative action policies might assume that other criteria are as important in making such decisions. These assumptions, like what we ordinarily call "beliefs," do not really need to be proved, though they may need to be explained or supported in order to make an argument credible. Readers need to bear in mind that writers frequently do not express their assumptions directly. The best way to elicit any assumptions from a text in which the writer has not identified them is to ask, "Is there anything I need to know or accept before I can be persuaded by this argument?"

Identify the Claims That Support the Thesis

In order to develop a thesis, a writer usually divides the larger problem represented in the thesis into smaller parts. These smaller parts can take several forms: an assertion that defends the position stated in the thesis; an assertion that qualifies or clarifies some aspect of the thesis; a refutation of an opposing argument; or a concession to an opposing argument. By identifying not only what the supporting opinions say, but how each opinion functions in the larger argument, we provide a basis on which any text can be viewed as part of a larger conversation about the central issue. Thus, we begin to understand the ways in which authors synthesize facts and opinions from a variety of sources.

Evaluate the Evidence and the Logic

As you examine the message and function of each supporting opinion, look at the way in which each claim is developed. Does the writer use evidence, that is, facts such as observations, statistical analyses, case studies, or testimony? Is this evidence appropriate to the context and is it reliable? Why should we trust this evidence?

Once we evaluate the evidence, we must examine the logic that a writer uses. Does the writer use logical reasoning to reach conclusions, creating new facts from other accepted facts? The two most common kinds of logical reasoning are *induction,* in which a writer connects two or more specific facts to reach a more general conclusion, and *deduction,* in which a writer begins with an accepted generalization and extracts from that generalization a more specific conclusion. For example, a police investigator may approach a crime inductively: that is, postponing conclusions until all the evidence has been gathered. In contrast, the prosecuting attorney must approach the same crime deductively, using the available evidence to support the conclusion that the individual on trial committed the crime. When we determine how logical reasoning has been used, we can then judge the validity of the steps the writer followed to reach that conclusion.

Determine the Role of Ethics and Emotion in Arguments

While it is somewhat unusual in academic writing, where authority and objectivity are important, some arguments are based less on evidence or logic than on an appeal to the readers' sense of right and wrong or their emotional responses to an issue. As readers we need to determine whether a writer has made an ethical or emotional appeal to an audience and, more important, whether such an appeal is both effective and appropriate given the subject and purpose of the text.

Be Aware of Style

A text often reveals much of its meaning through *style*, that is, through decisions the writer makes about word choice, tone, and sentence structure. As readers learn to recognize the stylistic features of a text, they not only gain a better appreciation for the power of eloquent language, but construct a meaning that is richer than it would be if style were not considered.

Many readers pay little attention to style, "reading through" it to the general meaning. This is especially true of academic writing, in which style seems inherently less important than it does in, say, a literary text, such as a short story or even an essay. But by learning to look closely at what makes the style of any passage unique, we can gain greater insight into a text's meaning. Once you have gathered some observations about a writer's style, you can begin to evaluate its success, given the rhetorical context and the author's purpose. As you read, ask yourself: Are the stylistic features effective? How might the writer have expressed the ideas more effectively? How does an awareness of stylistic features help you elicit more meaning from the text?

As you learn to read for style, you will need to ask different kinds of questions than you have asked before.

- What kinds of words does the writer use—abstract or concrete, general or specific? Do the words paint pictures, give sensory impressions, or present ideas? Do the words help you visualize an idea or event, or make you think about it more intellectually?
- Does the writer use everyday language—colloquialisms, slang—or more formal language—maybe even technical language? Is the writer's vocabulary extensive or ordinary? Would you describe the diction as high, middle, or low? How do these choices affect your response to the text?
- How are words organized into sentences—long, intricate sentences or short, concise ones? Are the sentences simple and direct, or complex and deliberately ambiguous? Is there a rhythm to the prose when you read it aloud?
- Is the writer's organization direct or indirect? Are the ideas stated explicitly in the beginning, or does the writer challenge the reader to discover the meaning in the process of reading? Is the structure inductive or deductive?
- Does the writing reveal emotions—such as anger, joy, humor, pride, fear, or apprehension? Do these emotions add to or detract from the writing? Is the writer satirical or ironic, and do these attitudes contribute to the success of the work? How does the writer seem to feel about the subject and audience?
- Do you notice any repeated or typical patterns of language or sentence structure? What makes this writer's voice unique or special?

How do these stylistic qualities contribute to our experience of the text as readers?

When asking these questions about the texts you read, you can understand them more deeply and completely. Perhaps most important, as you become more aware of the stylistic choices made by other writers, you'll realize that reading for style can help you build a repertoire of stylistic choices for your own writing.

SOME FINAL THOUGHTS ABOUT ACADEMIC READING AND WRITING

Reading is a complex process during which readers balance what they bring to a text with what they uncover in it. In the world of academic discourse—and in your role as maturing scholars and writers—you will want to do more than extract information as you read. Your skill as a reader will improve as you begin to understand the role of the reader in the reading process and the rhetorical context of all readings, and as you begin to develop an awareness of the ways in which writers assemble their ideas into coherent texts.

As you read each of the articles collected in this anthology, experiment with the reading strategies presented in this chapter. Remember that writing and reading are complementary acts, and the skills you are developing as a critical reader will help to make you a more insightful and persuasive writer. As your reading skills improve, you will be more sensitive to your own purpose and to the strategies most effective for accomplishing it. You will become more attuned to the power of language to both reveal and conceal meaning. By learning to identify stylistic characteristics and seeing their relationship to the message of a text, you can make your own style more versatile and flexible and more suited to your purpose in any particular writing situation. And as you improve your ability to express in writing your responses to what you read, you will find that your experience of reading is greatly enhanced.

For example, keeping a writer's journal can help you organize your thoughts about what you have read, and it will help you remember readings when you need to discuss or write about them. A writer's journal can also help you to connect your own experience to what you are reading. It can be a place where you identify key questions about the texts you read and where you explore in writing possible answers to those questions. If you can learn to ask questions about your reading, and if you can begin to integrate the complementary experiences of reading and writing, you will be better able to participate in the various conversations that occur throughout the curriculum.

Although many writer's guides and composition textbooks talk about the steps and stages of writing, at its best, writing is a *recursive process* in which the writer discovers, rethinks, refines, and revises ideas as they are seen in the light of other developing ideas. By continually asking questions like those we've posed here, you'll find yourself remaining open to new ideas and new approaches.

In the early stages of writing an essay—much as when you first pick up an unfamiliar text to read—it may also help to remind yourself that you're about to join a conversation that has been going on for some time. When you read a text, you try to place it in a larger context. Likewise, when you write, you are not expected to create a wholly original topic and approach; all writers and thinkers rely upon and respond to those who have entered the conversation before them. So think about what you've read in various classes, in newspapers and magazines, in your pleasure reading. How would the authors of those pieces respond to your topic? How would your friends respond? And, if all of these people were in the room with you, how would you address the points they make and answer the questions they ask?

Finally, we want to assure you that becoming a better reader—and a better writer—is not merely a straightforward process of learning all the right moves. Students have told us that writing courses are often frustrating because the grades they receive may not reflect the amount of time they have invested in an assignment. They may be doing everything they have been told to do, but they still may not see a significant change in their ability to read and write well because the changes in their reading strategies haven't yet had a lasting effect on them. It takes time and effort and patience to cultivate the habits of mind that allow you to read critically and write effectively about what you have read. You will see improvement as part of a growing process of intellectual maturity and sophistication. As you grow more familiar with the concerns and conventions of academic writing, and as you begin to see the value of your own ideas and opinions, you will become an active participant in the conversations that engage our colleges and universities today. Let's begin, then, in chapter 2, with the questions of what brings you to college and how our institutions of higher education influence the wider community in which we live.

2

The Campus and the Wider Community

If you were to ask your fellow students why they have chosen to pursue a college or university degree at this time and in this place, you would probably find a range of individual responses: personal growth, improved career opportunities, a desire for intellectual exploration, family expectations, training for a specific profession, increased availability of social and cultural advantages. As diverse as these responses are, they only begin to describe the influence of US colleges and universities in today's world.

Throughout US history, higher education has served a variety of social and personal needs, and our institutions of higher learning have evolved and adapted as our society has grown and changed. For example, just as many early American communities had their origins in a desire for religious freedom, our earliest colleges existed to meet the needs of religious as well as professional training. These early American colleges were established to produce leaders for the church and for the professions, and they emphasized a moral education based on a strict code of discipline. But as US society became more diverse, its colleges and universities took on other roles. Not only did aspiring scholars come from more diverse backgrounds, but the curriculum expanded to include a wider range of courses. By the mid-nineteenth century, a "new university" had evolved, devoted not just to training students, but to creating knowledge. Despite its new research mission, the new university still emphasized serving community needs. In 1862, the Morrill Act established a system of land grant colleges and universities designed to promote scholarship that would, quite simply, improve society. Because nineteenth-century America was essentially an agricultural nation, land grant universities devoted much energy to agricultural research, teaching, and outreach. This new partnership between land grant universities and the agricultural community led to new practices in crop production, farm management, and animal husbandry. Colleges and universities now played a larger role in the wider community.

However, not until the mid-twentieth century would a college or university education become widely available to many Americans. Following World War II (1939–1945), the GI Bill of Rights funded higher education for the soldiers returning from service. These older, nontraditional students, who might never have even considered a higher education without the financial assistance now available, transformed the landscape of the university with their maturity and their ethnic and class diversity. The economic boom of the postwar years enabled many states to build extensive systems of publicly subsidized and low-cost higher education, which, along with affirmative action policies and recruitment of racial and ethnic minorities in the 1960s, made a college education available to more of the American population than ever before. This diverse student body forced changes in the curriculum in order to reflect a new image of American culture. Programs in women's studies, ethnic studies, and other interdisciplinary areas of inquiry evolved, requirements changed, and new areas of research developed. Furthermore, where once universities and colleges maintained strict rules for student behavior, this role *in loco parentis* ("in the place of parents") has been virtually abandoned. The Vietnam War student generation raised many questions about the ties between universities and the government, especially with regard to weapons research, and subsequent generations have protested the investment policies and hiring practices of both large universities and small colleges. The university of the late twentieth century bears little resemblance to those small colonial colleges created to make leaders for the churches and courtrooms of early America.

As we approach a new century, technology is once again reshaping the landscape of the American university. In a postindustrial society, where fewer financial resources are available, our institutions of higher learning now seek new ways of providing access to information and instruction. Most libraries use electronic data retrieval, the computer has replaced the typewriter, and what are called *distance-learning* technologies are redefining the concept of the classroom. For example, various kinds of computer, video, and satellite connections can enable students living hundreds of miles from campus to confer with senior faculty, observe lectures, or even participate in class discussions. Logging on to the information superhighway now transports you to almost any college or university in the country. You can check out course offerings, review a professor's lecture notes, browse the library "shelves," or read the mission statements in which administrators try to articulate a vision of the future. As technology continues to change the way we work and learn, the university's relationship to the community must also change if it is to continue to provide leadership in the wider community.

In the readings that follow, we ask you to explore the challenges of the university as we enter the twenty-first century. Just as the university in American society reinvented itself in earlier centuries, clearly our institutions will need to adapt to social, economic, and political changes in the coming century. What does a higher education mean in a postindustrial, service-oriented economy? Have colleges and universities gone too far in designing a curriculum that is "politically correct" and "relevant" to students? What is the legacy of the student movements of the 1960s? Will technology be a positive influence in higher education, making colleges' and universities' resources available to more people, or a negative influence, breaking down a sense of community and leaving students isolated and alienated?

As you begin to examine these questions and others suggested in the readings, bring your own experiences into the conversation. Do the readings confirm your own experience as a student in today's society? In what ways does the college or university in your community differ from the institutions described in the readings? How might you redefine our institutions of higher education to meet the needs of individual students and to respond to the challenges that the authors of these readings identify?

ENTERING THE CONVERSATION

Mike Rose

> "Entering the Conversation" comes from Mike Rose's well-received book Lives on the Boundary, *a mixture of autobiography and argument. In* Lives, *Rose, now a professor at the University of California, Los Angeles, tells of his own and his students' struggles to move among the educated, to acquire their knowledge and their ways of thinking, and to find pleasure in the play of ideas. In the following excerpt, Rose describes his first year at the university, a year in which he felt both uncomfortable with and unprepared for the challenges before him. But he also describes the mentors he had along the way, men who guided him with passion and understanding and who helped him "enter the conversation." Because it describes some of the anxiety with which most of us enter into conversations about ideas we do not know well—and because it reveals the joy that comes when those feelings of anxiety disappear—Rose's piece seems an especially appropriate place for us to begin this book.*

If you walked out the back door of 9116 South Vermont and across our narrow yard, you would run smack into those four single-room rentals and, alongside them, an old wooden house-trailer. The trailer had belonged to Mrs. Jolly, the woman who sold us the property. It was locked and empty, and its tires were flat and fused into the asphalt driveway. Rusted dairy cases had been wedged in along its sides and four corners to keep it balanced. Two of its eight windows were broken, the frames were warped, and the door stuck. I was getting way too old to continue sharing a room with my mother, so I began to eye that trailer. I decided to refurbish it. It was time to have a room of my own.

Lou Minton had, by now, moved in with us, and he and I fixed the windows and realigned the door. I painted the inside by combining what I could find in our old shed with what I could afford to buy: The ceiling became orange, the walls yellow, the rim along the windows flat black. Lou redid the wiring and put in three new sockets. I got an old record player from the second-hand store for five dollars. I had Roy Herweck, the illustrator of our high school annual, draw women in mesh stockings and other objets d'redneck art on the yellow walls, and I put empty Smirnoff and Canadian Club bottles on the ledges above the windows. I turned the old trailer into the kind of bachelor digs a seventeen-year-old in South L.A. would fancy. My friends from high school began congregating there. When she could, my mother would make us a pot of spaghetti or pasta fasul'. And there was a clerk across the street at Marty's Liquor who would sell to us: We would run back across Vermont Avenue laughing and clutching our bags and seal ourselves up in the trailer. We spun fantasies about the waitress at the Mexican restaurant and mimicked our teachers and caught touchdown passes and, in general, dreamed our way through adolescence. It was a terrible time for rock 'n' roll—Connie Francis and Bobby Rydell were headliners in 1961—so we found rhythm and blues on L.A.'s one black station, played the backroom ballads of troubadour Oscar Brand, and discovered Delta and Chicago blues on Pacifica's KPFK:

> I'm a man
> I'm a full-grown man

As I fell increasingly under Mr. MacFarland's spell, books began replacing the liquor bottles above the windows: *The Trial* and *Waiting for Godot* and *No Exit* and *The Stranger.* Roy sketched a copy of the back cover of *Exile and the Kingdom,* and so the pensive face of Albert Camus now looked down from that patch of wall on which a cartoon had once pressed her crossed legs. My mother found a quilt that my grandmother had sewn from my father's fabric samples. It was dark and heavy, and I would lie under it and read Rimbaud and not understand him and feel very connected to the life I imagined Jack MacFarland's life to be: a subterranean ramble through Bebop and breathless poetry and back-alley revelations.

In 1962, John Connor moved into dank, old Apartment 1. John had also grown up in South L.A., and he and I had become best friends. His parents moved to Oregon, and John—who was a good black-top basketball player and an excellent student—wanted to stay in Los Angeles and go to college. So he rented an apartment for forty dollars a month, and we established a community of two. Some nights, John and I and Roy the artist and a wild kid named Gaspo would drive into downtown L.A.—down to where my mother had waited fearfully for a bus years before—and roam the streets and feel the excitement of the tenderloin: the flashing arrows, the blue-and-orange beer neon, the burlesque houses, the faded stairwell of Roseland—which we would inch up and then run down—brushing past the photos of taxi dancers, glossy and smiling in a glass display. Cops would tell us to go home, and that intensified this bohemian romance all the more.

About four months after John moved in, we both entered Loyola University. Loyola is now coeducational; its student center houses an Asian Pacific Students Association, Black Student Alliance, and Chicano Resource Center; and its radio station, KXLU, plays the most untamed rock 'n' roll in Los Angeles. But in the early sixties, Loyola was pretty much a school for white males from the middle and upper middle class. It was a sleepy little campus—its undergraduate enrollment was under two thousand—and it prided itself on providing spiritual as well as intellectual guidance for its students: Religion and Christian philosophy courses were a required part of the curriculum. It defined itself as a Catholic intellectual community—promotional brochures relied on phrases like "the social, intellectual, and spiritual aspects of our students"—and made available to its charges small classes, a campus ministry, and thirty-six clubs (the Chess

Club, Economics Society, Fine Arts Circle, Debate Squad, and more). There were also six fraternities and a sports program that included basketball, baseball, volleyball, rugby, soccer, and crew. Loyola men, it was assumed, shared a fairly common set of social and religious values, and the university provided multiple opportunities for them to develop their minds, their spirits, and their social networks. I imagine that parents sent their boys to Loyola with a sigh of relief: God and man strolled together out of St. Robert Bellarmine Hall and veered left to Sacred Heart Chapel. There was an occasional wild party at one of the off-campus fraternity houses, but, well, a pair of panties in the koi pond was not on a par with crises of faith and violence against the state.

John and I rattled to college in his '53 Plymouth. Loyola Boulevard was lined with elms and maples, and as we entered the campus we could see the chapel tower rising in the distance. The chapel and all the early buildings had been constructed in the 1920s and were white and separated by broad sweeps of very green grass. Palm trees and stone pines grew in rows and clumps close to the buildings, and long concrete walkways curved and angled and crossed to connect everything, proving that God, as Plato suspected, is always doing geometry.

Most freshman courses were required, and I took most of mine in St. Robert Bellarmine Hall. Saint Robert was a father of the church who wrote on papal power and censored Galileo: The ceiling in his hallway was high, and dim lights hung down from it. The walls were beige up to about waist level, then turned off-white. The wood trim was dark and worn. The floor combined brown linoleum with brown and black tile. Even with a rush of students, the building maintained its dignity. We moved through it, and its old, clanking radiators warmed us as we did, but it was not a warmth that got to the bone. I remember a dream in which I climbed up beyond the third floor—up thin, narrow stairs to a bell tower that held a small, dusky room in which a priest was playing church music to a class of shadows.

My first semester classes included the obligatory theology and ROTC and a series of requirements: biology, psychology, speech, logic, and a language. I went to class and usually met John for lunch: We'd bring sandwiches to his car and play the radio while we ate. Then it was back to class, or the library, or the student union for a Coke. This was the next step in Jack MacFarland's plan for me—and I did okay for a while. I had learned enough routines in high school to act like a fairly typical student, but— except for the historical sketch I received in Senior English—there wasn't a solid center of knowledge and assurance to all this. When I look back through notes and papers and various photographs and memorabilia, I begin to remember what a disengaged, half-awake time it really was. I'll describe two of the notebooks I found. The one from English is a small book, eight by seven, and only eleven pages of it are filled. The notes I did write consist of book titles, dates of publication, names of characters, pointless summaries of books that were not on our syllabus and that I had never read ("*The Alexandria Quartet*: 5 or 6 characters seen by people in different stages of life"), and quotations from the teacher ("Perception can bring sorrow."). The notes are a series of separate entries. I can't see any coherence. My biology lab notes are written on green-tint quadrille. They, too, are sparse. There is an occasional poorly executed sketch of a tiny organism or of a bone and muscle structure. Some of the formulas and molecular models sit isolated on the page, bare of any explanatory discussion. The lecture notes are fragmented; a fair number of sentences remain incomplete.

By the end of the second semester my grades were close to dipping below a C average, and since I had been admitted provisionally, that would have been that. Jack MacFarland had oriented me to Western intellectual history and had helped me develop my writing, but he had worked with me for only a year, and I needed more than twelve months of his kind of instruction. Speech and Introductory Psychology presented no big problems. General Biology had midterm and final examinations that required a good deal of memorizing, and I could do that, but the textbook—particularly the chapters covered in the second semester—was much, much harder than what I read in high school, and I was so ill-adept in the laboratory that I failed that portion of the class. We had to set up and pursue biological problems, not just memorize—and at the first sign of doing rather than memorizing, I would automatically assume the problem was beyond me and distance myself from it. Logic, another requirement, spooked me with its syllogisms and Venn diagrams—they were just a step away from more formal mathematics—so I memorized what I could and squirmed around the rest. Theology was god-awful; ROTC was worse. And Latin, the language I elected on the strength of Jack MacFarland's one piece of bad advice, had me suffocating under the dust of a dead civilization. Freshman English was taught by a frustrated novelist with glittering eyes who had us, among other things, describing the consumption of our last evening's meal using the images of the battlefield.

I was out of my league.

Faculty would announce office hours. If I had had the sense, I would have gone, but they struck me as aloof and somber men, and I felt stupid telling them I was . . . well—stupid. I drifted through the required courses, thinking that as soon as these requirements were over, I'd never have to face anything even vaguely quantitative again. Or anything to do with foreign languages. Or ROTC. I fortified myself with defiance: I worked up an imitation of the old priest who was my Latin teacher, and I kept my ROTC uniform crumpled in the greasy trunk of John's Plymouth.

Many of my classmates came from and lived in a world very different from my own. The campus literary magazine would publish excerpts from the journals of upperclassmen traveling across Europe, standing before the Berlin Wall or hiking through olive groves toward Delphi. With the exception of one train trip back to Altoona, I had never been out of Southern California, and this translated, for me, into some personal inadequacy.

Fraternities seemed exclusive and a little strange. I'm not sure why I didn't join any of Loyola's three dozen societies and clubs, though I do know that things like the Debate Squad were way too competitive. Posters and flyers and squibs in the campus newspaper gave testament to a lot of connecting activity, but John and I pretty much kept to ourselves, ragging on the "Loyola man," reading the literary magazine aloud with a French accent, simultaneously feeling contempt for and exclusion from a social life that seemed to work with the mystery and enclosure of the clockwork in a music box.

It is an unfortunate fact of our psychic lives that the images that surround us as we grow up—no matter how much we may scorn them later—give shape to our deepest needs and longings. Every year Loyola men elected a homecoming queen. The queen and her princesses were students at the Catholic sister schools: Marymount, Mount St. Mary's, St. Vincent's. They had names like Corinne and Cathy, and they came from the Sullivan family or the Mitchells or the Ryans. They were taught to stand with toe to heel, their smiles were inviting, and the photographer's flash illuminated their eyes. Loyola men met them at fraternity parties and mixers and "CoEd Day," met them according to rules of manner and affiliation and parental connection as elaborate as a Balinese dance. John and I drew mustaches on their photographs, but something about them reached far back into my life.

Growing up in South L.A. was certainly not a conscious misery. My neighborhood had its diversions and its mysteries, and I felt loved and needed at home. But all in all there was a dreary impotence to the years, and isolation, and a deep sadness about my father. I protected myself from the harsher side of it all through a life of the mind. And while that interior life included spaceships and pink chemicals and music and the planetary moons, it also held the myriad television images of the good life that were piped into my home: Robert Young sitting down to dinner, Ozzie Nelson tossing the football with his sons, the blond in a Prell commercial turning toward the camera. The images couldn't have been more trivial—all sentimental phosphorescence—but as a child tucked away on South Vermont, they were just about the only images I had of what life would be without illness and dead ends. I didn't realize how completely their message had seeped into my being, what loneliness and sorrow was being held at bay—didn't realize it until I found myself in the middle of Loyola's social life without a guidebook, feeling just beyond the superficial touch of the queen and her princesses, those smiling incarnations of a television promise. I scorned the whole silly show and ached to be embraced by one of these mythic females under the muted light of a paper moon.

So I went to school and sat in class and memorized more than understood and whistled past the academic graveyard. I vacillated between the false potency of scorn and feelings of ineptitude. John and I would get in his car and enjoy the warmth of each other and laugh and head down the long strip of Manchester Boulevard, away from Loyola, away from the palms and green, green lawns, back to South L.A. We'd throw the ball in the alley or lag pennies on Vermont or hit Marty's Liquor. We'd leave much later for a movie or a football game at Mercy High or the terrible safety of downtown Los Angeles. Walking, then, past the *discotecas* and pawnshops, past the windows full of fried chicken and yellow lamps, past the New Follies, walking through hustlers and lost drunks and prostitutes and transvestites with rouge the color of bacon—stopping, finally, before the musty opening of a bar where two silhouettes moved around a pool table as though they were underwater.

I don't know what I would have found if the flow of events hadn't changed dramatically. Two things happened. Jack MacFarland privately influenced my course of study at Loyola, and death once again ripped through our small family.

The coterie of MacFarland's students—Art Mitz, Mark Dever, and me—were still visiting our rumpled mentor. We would stop by his office or his apartment to mock our classes and the teachers and all that "'Loyola man' bullshit." Nobody had more appreciation for burlesque than Jack MacFarland, but I suppose he saw beneath our caustic performances and knew we were headed for trouble. Without telling us, he started making phone calls to some of his old teachers at Loyola—primarily to Dr. Frank Carothers, the chairman of the English Department—and, I guess, explained that these kids needed to be slapped alongside the head with a good novel. Dr. Carothers volunteered to look out for us and agreed to some special studies courses that we could substitute for a few of the more traditional requirements, courses that would enable us to read and write a lot under the close supervision of a faculty member. In fact, what he promised were tutorials—and that was exceptional, even for a small college. All this would start up when we returned from summer vacation. Our sophomore year, Jack MacFarland finally revealed, would be different.

When Lou Minton rewired the trailer, he rigged a phone line from the front house: A few digits and we could call each other. One night during the summer after my freshman year, the phone rang while I was reading. It was my mother and she was screaming. I ran into the house to find her standing in the kitchen hysterical—both hands pressed to her face—and all I could make out was Lou's name. I didn't see him in the front of the house, so I ran back through the kitchen to the bedroom. He had fallen back across the bed, a hole right at his sideburn, his jaw still quivering. They had a fight, and some ugly depth of pain convulsed within him. He left the table and walked to the bedroom. My mother heard the light slam of a .22. Nothing more.

That summer seems vague and distant. I can't remember any specifics, though I had to take care of my mother and handle the affairs of the house. I probably made do by blunting a good deal of what I saw and navigating with intuitive quadrants. But though I cannot remember details, I do recall feelings and recognitions: Lou's suicide came to represent the sadness and dead time I had protected myself against, the personal as well as public oppressiveness of life in South Los Angeles. I began to see that my escape to the trailer and my isolationist fantasies of the demimonde would yield another kind of death, a surrender to the culture's lost core. An alternative was somehow starting to take shape around school and knowledge. Knowledge seemed . . . was it empowering? No, that's a word I would use now. Then I felt freed, as if I were untying fetters. There simply were times when the pain and confusion of that summer would give way to something I felt more than I knew: a lightness to my body, an ease in breathing. Three or four months later I took an art history course, and one day during a slide show on Gothic architecture I felt myself rising up within the interior light of Mont-Saint-Michel. I wanted to be released from the despair that surrounded me on South Vermont and from my own troubled sense of exclusion.

Jack MacFarland had saved me at one juncture—caught my fancy and revitalized my mind—what I felt now was something further, some tentative recognition that an engagement with ideas could foster competence and lead me out into the world. But all this was very new and fragile, and given what I know now, I realize how easily it could have been crushed. My mother, for as long as I can remember, always added onto any statement of intention—hers or others'—the phrase *se vuol Dio*, if God wants it. The fulfillment of desire, no matter how trivial, required the blessing of the gods, for the world was filled with threat. "I'll plant the seeds this weekend," I might say. "Se vuol Dio," she would add. *Se vuol Dio.* The phrase expressed several lifetimes of ravaged hope: my grandfather's lost leg, the failure of the Rose Spaghetti House, my father laid low, Lou Minton, the landscapes of South L.A. *Se vuol Dio.* For those who live their lives on South Vermont, tomorrow doesn't beckon to be defined from a benign future. It's up to the gods, not you, if any old thing turns out right. I carried within me no history of assurances that what I was feeling would lead to anything.

Because of its size and because of the kind of teacher who is drawn to small liberal arts colleges, Loyola would turn out to be a very good place for me. For even with MacFarland's yearlong tour through ideas and language, I was unprepared. English prose written before the twentieth century was difficult, sometimes impossible, for me to comprehend. The kind of reasoning I found in logic was very foreign. My writing was okay, but I couldn't hold a candle to Art Mitz or Mark Dever or to those boys who came from good schools. And my fears about science and mathematics prevailed: Pereira Hall, the Math and Engineering Building, was only forty to fifty yards from the rear entrance to the English Department but seemed an unfriendly mirage, a malevolent castle floating in the haze of a mescaline dream.

We live, in America, with so many platitudes about motivation and self-reliance and individualism—and myths spun from them, like those of Horatio Alger—that we find it hard to accept the fact that they are serious nonsense. To live your early life on the streets of South L.A.—or Homewood or Spanish Harlem or Chicago's South Side or any one of hundreds of other depressed communities—and to journey up through the top levels of the American educational system will call for support and guidance at many, many points along the way. You'll need people to guide you into conversations that seem foreign and threatening. You'll need models, lots of them, to show you how to get at what you don't know. You'll need people to help you center yourself in your own developing ideas. You'll need people to watch out for you. There is much talk these days about the value of a classical humanistic education, a call for an immersion in the humanities, a return to the great books. These appeals raise lots of suspicions, for such curricula have traditionally served to exclude working-class people from the classroom. It doesn't, of necessity, have to be that way. The teachers that fate and Jack MacFarland's crisis intervention sent my way worked at making the humanities truly human. What transpired between us was the essence of humane liberal education, and it enabled me to move far beyond the cognitive charade of my freshman year.

From the midpoint of their freshman year, Loyola students had to take one philosophy course per semester: Logic, Philosophy of Nature, Philosophy of Man, General Ethics, Natural Theology, and so on. Logic was the first in the series, and I had barely gotten a C. The rest of the courses looked like a book fair of medieval scholasticism with the mold scraped off the bindings, and I dreaded their advent. But I was beginning my sophomore year at a time when the best and brightest of the Jesuit community were calling for an intellectually panoramic, socially progressive Catholicism, and while this lasted, I reaped the benefits. Sections of the next three courses I had to take would be taught by a young man who was studying for the priesthood and who was, himself, attempting to develop a personal philosophy that incorporated the mind and the body as well as the spirit.

Mr. Johnson could have strolled off a Wheaties box. Still in his twenties and a casting director's vision of those good looks thought to be all-American, Don Johnson had committed his very considerable intelligence to the study and teaching of philosophy. Jack MacFarland had introduced me to the Greeks, to Christian scholasticism, eighteenth-century deism, and French existentialism, but it was truly an introduction, a curtsy to that realm of the heavens where the philosophers dwell. Mr. Johnson provided a fuller course. He was methodical and spoke with vibrance and made connections between ancients and moderns with care. He did for philosophy what Mr. MacFarland had done for literary history: He gave me a directory of key names and notions.

We started in a traditional way with the Greek philosophers who preceded Socrates—Thales, Heraclitus, Empedocles—and worked our way down to Kant and Hegel. We read a little Aquinas, but we also read E. A. Burtt's *The Metaphysical Foundations of Modern Science,* and that gave me entry to Kepler, Copernicus, Galileo (which I was then spelling *Galelao*), and Newton. As he laid out his history of ideas, Mr. Johnson would consider aloud the particular philosophical issue involved, so we didn't, for example, simply get an outline of what Hegel believed, but we watched and listened as Don Johnson reasoned like Hegel and then raised his own questions about the Hegelian scheme. He was a working philosopher, and he was thinking out loud in front of us.

The Metaphysical Foundations of Modern Science was very tough going. It assumed not only a familiarity with Western thought but, as well, a sophistication in reading a theoretically rich argument. It was, in other words, the kind of book you encounter with increased frequency as you move through college. It combined the history of mathematics and science with philosophical investigation, and when I tried to read it, I'd end up rescanning the same sentences over and over, not understanding them, and, finally, slamming the book down on the desk—swearing at this golden boy Johnson and angry with myself. Here's a typical passage, one of the many I marked as being hopeless:

> We begin now to glimpse the tremendous significance of what these fathers of modern science were doing, but let us continue with our questions. What further specific metaphysical doctrines was Kepler led to adopt as a consequence of this notion of what constitutes the real world? For one thing, it led him to appropriate in his own way the distinction between primary and secondary qualities, which had been noted in the ancient world by the atomist and skeptical schools, and which was being revived in the sixteenth century in varied form by such miscellaneous thinkers as Vives, Sanchez, Montaigne, and Campanella. Knowledge as it is immediately offered the mind through the senses is obscure, confused, contradictory, and hence untrustworthy; only those features of the world in terms of which we get certain and consistent knowledge open before us what is indubitably and permanently real. Other qualities are not real qualities of things, but only signs of them. For Kepler, of course, the real qualities are those caught up in this mathematical harmony underlying the world of the senses, and which, therefore, have a causal relation to the latter. *The real world is a world of quantitative characteristics only; its differences are differences of number alone.*

I couldn't get the distinction that was being made between primary and secondary qualities, and I certainly didn't have the background that would enable me to make sense of Burtt's brief historical survey: from "atomist and skeptical schools [to] . . . Campanella." It is clear from the author's italics that the last sentence of the passage is important, so I underlined it, but because Burtt's discussion is built on a rich intellectual history that I didn't know, I was reading words but not understanding text. I was the human incarnation of language-recognition computer programs: able to record the dictionary meanings of individual words but unable to generate any meaning out of them.

"What," I asked in class, "are primary and secondary qualities? I don't get it." And here Don Johnson was very good. "The answer," he said, "can be found in the passage itself. I'll go back through it with you. Let's start with primary and secondary qualities. If some qualities are primary and others secondary, which do you think would be most important?"

"Primary?"

"Right. Primary qualities. Whatever they are. Now let's turn to Kepler, since Kepler's the subject of this passage. What is it that's more important to Kepler?"

I pause and say tentatively, "Math." Another student speaks up, reading from the book: "Quantitative characteristics."

"All right. So primary qualities, for Kepler, are mathematical, quantitative. But we still don't know what this primary and secondary opposition really refers to, do we? Look right in the middle of the paragraph. Burtt is comparing mathematical knowledge to the immediate knowledge provided by—what?"

My light bulb goes on: "The senses."

"There it is. The primary-secondary opposition is the opposition between knowledge gained by pure mathematical reasoning versus knowledge gained through our five senses."

We worked with *The Metaphysical Foundations of Modern Science* for some time, and I made my way slowly through it. Mr. Johnson was helping me develop an ability to read difficult texts—I was learning how to reread critically, how to tease out definitions and basic arguments. And I was also gaining confidence that if I stayed with material long enough and kept asking questions, I would get it. That assurance proved to be more valuable than any particular body of knowledge I learned that year.

For my second semester, I had to take Philosophy of Man, and it was during that course that Mr. Johnson delivered his second gift. We read Gabriel Marcel and Erich Fromm, learning about phenomenology and social criticism. We considered the human animal from an anthropological as well as philosophical perspective. And we read humanistic psychologist Abraham Maslow's *Toward a Psychology of Being*. Maslow wrote about "the 'will to health,' the urge to grow, the pressure of self-actualization, the quest for one's identity." The book had a profound effect on me. Six months before, Lou Minton's jaw quivered as if to speak the race's deepest sorrow, and through the rest of that summer I could only feel in my legs and chest some fleeting assurance that the world wasn't a thin mask stretched over nothingness. Now I was reading an articulation of that vague, hopeful feeling. Maslow was giving voice to some delicate possibility within me, and I was powerfully drawn to it. Every person is, in part, " 'his own project' and makes himself." I had to know more, so I called Mr. Johnson up and asked if

I could visit with him. "Sure," he said, and invited me to campus. So one Saturday morning I took a series of early buses and headed west.

Mr. Johnson and the other initiates to the priesthood lived in an old white residence hall on the grassy east edge of campus, and the long walk up Loyola Boulevard was quiet and meditative: Birds were flying tree to tree and a light breeze was coming in off Playa del Rey. I walked up around the gym, back behind Math Engineering to his quarters, a simple one-story building with those Spanish curves that seem simultaneously thick and weightless. The sun had warmed the stucco. A window by the door was open, and a curtain had fluttered out. I rang the bell and heard steps on a hardwood floor. Mr. Johnson opened the door and stepped out. He was smiling and his eyes were attentive in the light . . . present . . . there. They said, "Come, let's talk."

Dr. Frank Carothers taught what is generally called the sophomore survey, a yearlong sequence of courses that introduces the neophyte English major to the key works in English literary history. Dr. Carothers was tall and robust. He wore thick glasses and a checkered bow tie and his hairline was male Botticelli, picking up somewhere back beyond his brow. As the year progressed, he spread English literary history out in slow time across the board, and I was introduced to people I'd never heard of: William Langland, a medieval acolyte who wrote the dream-vision *Piers Plowman;* the sixteenth-century poet Sir Thomas Wyatt; Elizabethan lyricists with peculiar names like Orlando Gibbons and Tobias Hume (the author of the wondrous suggestion that tobacco "maketh lean the fat men's tumour"); the physician Sir Thomas Browne; the essayist Joseph Addison; the biographer James Boswell; the political philosopher Edmund Burke, whose prose I could not decipher; and poets Romantic and Victorian (Shelley and Rossetti and Algernon Charles Swinburne). Some of the stuff was invitingly strange ("Pallid and pink as the palm of the flagflower . . ."), some was awfully hard to read, and some was just awful. But Dr. Carothers laid it all out with his reserved passion, drew for us a giant conceptual blueprint onto which we could place other courses, other books. He was precise, thorough, and rigorous. And he started his best work once class was over.

Being a professor was, for Frank Carothers, a profoundly social calling: He enjoyed the classroom, and he seemed to love the more informal contacts with those he taught, those he once taught, and those who stopped by just to get a look at this guy. He stayed in his office until about four each afternoon, leaning back in his old swivel chair, hands clasped behind his head, his bow tie tight against his collar. He had strong opinions, and he'd get irritated if you missed class, and he sometimes gave quirky advice—but there he'd be shaking his head sympathetically as students poured out their troubles. It was pure and primary for Frank Carothers: Teaching allowed him daily to fuse the joy he got from reading literature—poetry especially—with his deep pleasure in human community. What I saw when I was around him—and I hung out in his office from my sophomore year on—was very different from the world I had been creating for myself, a far cry from my withdrawal into an old house trailer with a silent book.

One of Dr. Carothers's achievements was the English Society. The English Society had seventy-eight members, and that made it just about the biggest organization on campus: jocks, literati, C-plus students, frat boys, engineers, mystics, scholars, profligates, bullies, geeks, Republicans—all stood side by side for group pictures. The English Society sponsored poetry readings, lectures, and card games, and best of all, barbecues in the Carotherses' backyard. We would caravan out to Manhattan Beach to be greeted by Betsy, the youngest of the seven Carothers children, and she'd walk us back to her father who, wrapped now in an apron, was poking coals or unscrewing the tops from jugs of red wine.

Vivian Carothers, a delicate, soft-spoken woman, would look after us and serve up trays of cheese and chips and little baked things. Students would knock on the redwood gate all through the late afternoon, more and more finding places for themselves among flowers and elephant ears, patio furniture, and a wizened pine. We would go on way past sunset, talking to Dr. Carothers and to each other about books and sports and currently despised professors, sometimes letting off steam and sometimes learning something new. And Frank Carothers would keep us fed, returning to the big, domed barbecue through the evening to lift the lid and add hamburgers, the smoke rising off the grill and up through the telephone lines stretching like the strings of Shelley's harp over the suburbs of the South Bay.

When I was learning my craft at Jack MacFarland's knee, I continually misused words and wrote fragments and run-on sentences and had trouble making my pronouns agree with whatever it was that preceded them. I also produced sentences like these:

> Some of these modern-day Ramses are inherent of their wealth, others are self-made.

> An exhibition of will on the part of the protagonist enables him to accomplish a subjective good (which is an element of tragedy, namely: the protagonist does not fully realize the objective wrong that he is doing. He feels objectively justified if not completely right.).

I was struggling to express increasingly complex ideas, and I couldn't get the language straight: Words, as in my second sentence on tragedy, piled up like cars in a serial wreck. I was encountering a new language—the language of the academy—and was trying to find my way around in it. I have some more examples, written during my first year and a half at Loyola. There was inflated vocabulary:

I conjectured that he was the same individual who had arrested my attention earlier.

In his famed speech, "The American Scholar," Ralph Waldo Emerson posed several problems that are particularly germane to the position of the young author.

There were cliches and mixed and awkward metaphors:

In 1517, when Luther nailed his 95 theses to the door of Wittenburg Cathedral, he unknowingly started a snowball rolling that was to grow to tremendous reprocussions.

And there was academic melodrama:

The vast realm of the cosmos or the depths of a man's soul hold questions that reason flounders upon, but which can be probed by the peculiar private insight of the seer.

Pop grammarians and unhappy English teachers get a little strange around sentences like these. But such sentences can be seen as marking a stage in linguistic growth. Appropriating a style and making it your own is difficult, and you'll miss the mark a thousand times along the way. The botched performances, though, are part of it all, and developing writers will grow through them if they are able to write for people who care about language, people who are willing to sit with them and help them as they struggle to write about difficult things. That is what Ted Erlandson did for me.

Dr. Erlandson was one of the people who agreed to teach me and my Mercy High companions a seminar—a close, intensive course that would substitute for a larger, standard offering like Introduction to Prose Literature. He was tall and lanky and had a long reddish brown beard and lectured in a voice that was basso and happy. He was a strong lecturer and possessed the best memory for fictional detail I'd ever witnessed. And he cared about prose. The teachers I had during my last three years at Loyola assigned a tremendous amount of writing. But it was Ted Erlandson who got in there with his pencil and worked on my style. He would sit me down next to him at his big desk, sweep books and pencils across the scratched veneer, and go back over the sentences he wanted me to revise.

He always began by reading the sentence out loud: "Camus ascented to a richer vision of life that was to characterize the entirety of his work." Then he would fiddle with the sentence, talking and looking up at me intermittently to comment or ask questions: "'Ascent'. That sounds like 'assent', I know, but look it up, Mike." He'd wait while I fluttered the dictionary. "Now, 'the entirety of his work' . . . try this instead: 'his entire work.' Let's read it. 'Camus assented to a richer vision of life that would characterize his entire work.' Sounds better, doesn't it?"

And another sentence. "'Irregardless of the disastrous ending of *Bread and Wine,* it must be seen as an affirmative work.' 'Irregardless' . . . people use it all the time, but 'regardless' will do just fine. Now, I think this next part sounds a little awkward; listen: 'Regardless of the disastrous ending of *Bread and Wine,* it . . . 'Hear that? Let's try removing the 'of' and the 'it': 'Regardless of the disastrous ending, *Bread and Wine* must be seen as an affirmative work.' Hmmm. Better, I think."

And so it would go. He rarely used grammatical terms, and he never got technical. He dealt with specific bits of language: "Try this here" or "Here's another way to say it." He worked as a craftsman works, with particulars, and he shuttled back and forth continually between print and voice, making me breathe my prose, making me hear the language I'd generated in silence. Perhaps he was more directive than some would like, but, to be truthful, direction was what I needed. I was easily frustrated, and it didn't take a lot to make me doubt myself. When teachers would write "no" or "awkward" or "rewrite" alongside the sentences I had worked so hard to produce, I would be peeved and disappointed. "Well, what the hell *do* they want?" I'd grumble to no one in particular. So Ted Erlandson's linguistic parenting felt just right: a modeling of grace until it all slowly, slowly began to work itself into the way I shaped language.

When Father Albertson lectured, he would stand pretty much in one spot slightly to the left or right of center in front of us. He tended to hold his notes or a play or a critical study in both hands, releasing one to emphasize a point with a simple gesture. He was tall and thin, and his voice was soft and tended toward monotone. When he spoke, he looked very serious, but when one of us responded with any kind of intelligence, a little smile would come over his face. Jack MacFarland had told me that it was Clint Albertson's Shakespeare course that would knock my socks off.

For each play we covered, Father Albertson distributed a five- to ten-page list of questions to ask ourselves as we read. These study questions were of three general types.

The first type was broad and speculative and was meant to spark reflection on major characters and key events. Here's a teaser on *Hamlet:*

> Would you look among the portrait-paintings by Raphael, or Rembrandt, or Van Gogh, or El Greco, or Rouault for an ideal representation of Hamlet? Which painting by which of these men do you think most closely resembles your idea of what Hamlet should look like?

The second type focused on the details of the play itself and were very specific. Here are two of the thirty-eight he wrote for *As You Like It:*

Act I, Scene 2

> How is Rosalind distinguished from Celia in this scene? How do you explain the discrepancy between the Folio version of lines 284–287 and Act I, scene 3, line 117?

Act II, Scenes 4–6

It has been said these scenes take us definitely out of the world of reality into a world of dream. What would you say are the steps of the process by which Shakespeare brings about this illusion?

The third kind of question required us to work with some historical or critical study. This is an example from the worksheet on *Romeo and Juliet:*

> Read the first chapter of C. S. Lewis's *Allegory of Love,* "Courtly Love." What would you say about Shakespeare's concept of love in relation to what Lewis presents as the traditional contradictory concepts in medieval literature of "romantic love" vs. "marriage."

Father Albertson had placed over 150 books on the reserve shelf in the library, and they ranged from intellectual history to literary criticism to handbooks on theater production. I had used a few such "secondary sources" to quote in my own writing since my days with Jack MacFarland, but this was the first time a teacher had so thoroughly woven them into a course. Father Albertson would cite them during lectures as naturally as though he were recalling a discussion he had overheard. He would add his own opinions and, since he expected us to form opinions, would ask us for ours.

I realize that this kind of thing—the close, line-by-line examination, the citing of critical opinion—has given rise to endless parodies of the academy: repressed schoolmen clucking along in the land of lost language. It certainly can be that way. But with Clint Albertson, all the learning furthered my comprehension of the play. His questions forced me to think carefully about Shakespeare's choice of words, about the crafting of a scene, about the connections between language and performance. I had to read very, very closely, leaning over the thin Formica desk in the trailer, my head cupped in my hands with my two index fingers in my ears to blot out the noise from the alley behind me. There were times when no matter how hard I tried, I wouldn't get it. I'd close the book, feeling stupid to my bones, and go find John. Over then to the liquor store, out into the night. The next day I would visit Father Albertson and tell him I was lost, ask him why this stuff was so damned hard. He'd listen and ask me to tell him why it made me so angry. I'd sputter some more, and then he'd draw me to the difficult passage, slowly opening the language up, helping me comprehend a distant, stylized literature, taking it apart, touching it.

I would then return to a classroom where a historically rich conversation was in progress. Other readers of Shakespeare—from Samuel Johnson to the contemporary literary critic Wylie Sypher—were given voice by Father Albertson, and we were encouraged to enter the dialogue, to consider, to take issue, to be seated amid all that potentially intimidating shoptalk. We were shown how to summarize an opinion, argue with it, weave it into our own interpretations. Nothing is more exclusive than the academic club: its language is highbrow, it has fancy badges, and it worships tradition. It limits itself to a few participants who prefer to talk to each other. What Father Albertson did was bring us inside the circle, nudging us out into the chatter, always just behind us, whispering to try this step, then this one, encouraging us to feel the moves for ourselves.

Those four men collectively gave me the best sort of liberal education, the kind longed for in the stream of blue-ribbon reports on the humanities that now cross my desk. I developed the ability to read closely, to persevere in the face of uncertainty and ask questions of what I was reading—not with downcast eyes, but freely, aloud, realizing there is no such thing as an open book. My teachers modeled critical inquiry and linguistic precision and grace, and they provided various cognitive maps for philosophy and history and literature. They encouraged me to make connections and to enter into conversations—present and past—to see what talking a particular kind of talk would enable me to do with a thorny philosophical problem or a difficult literary text. And it was all alive. It transpired in backyards and on doorsteps and inside offices as well as in the classroom. I could smell their tobacco and see the nicks left by their razors. They liked books and ideas, and they liked to talk about them in ways that fostered growth rather than established dominance. They lived their knowledge. And maybe because of that their knowledge grew in me in ways that led back out to the world. I was developing a set of tools with which to shape a life.

I continued to take courses from my four mentors, and as I moved through my last two years, I found other teachers who kept the fire going as well: the progressive theologian Paul Hilsdale, the psychologist Carlo Weber, Father Trame—a historian who had us writing papers and exams every other week—the philosophers Gary Schouborg and Norbert Rigali. It was an exciting time for me, full of hope and promise. But I would not be telling the whole story if I didn't admit that with the deep satisfaction of growth came a mix of disturbance and fear.

I began noticing dates of birth and of death. Keats wrote "Ode to a Nightingale" when he was twenty-four. F. Scott Fitzgerald had two novels under his belt by his thirtieth year. A writer's best work, Fitzgerald once said, was produced by the time he was thirty. I became obsessed with impossible comparisons. Jacques Barzun started writing the 375-page *Darwin, Marx, Wagner* in his late twenties. Maslow published his first articles when he was twenty-four. And on. And on. As long as I stayed half-awake intellectually, there was no tension, no failed attempts at mastery, no confrontation with my limits. But now I was trying hard, and I could see how limited I was. It would be quite a while before I could relax into the gifts I did possess, but in the meantime, birthdates, printings, and copyrights all ticked off like some ruthless gauge of my own dim ability.

I lived a life of choice and possibility during the weekdays and then returned every evening to South Vermont. One day in the middle of my junior year, I lay down on the couch in the living room and could not get up. The TV and the table, John and my mother seemed distant, and I was cold and afraid, as if there were some indeterminate sickness all through me. I pulled my knees to my chest. My mother didn't know what to do, so she brought me blankets and a pillow. I stayed there for two days, getting up only to eat, returning quickly to keep the fear at bay, curling up again, bringing the blankets close again. Finally, I asked John to drive me out to see Dr. Metzger, the young Kaiser physician who had ministered to my father during his last year.

Dr. Metzger sat across from me and listened, ten or so years older than me, round faced, a goatee, serious. I couldn't express what it was that was making me feel cold and shaky, just that I was scared and didn't know what to do about it. He encouraged me to talk, and I did—talked about the last few years and Lou Minton and my own imagined infirmity. He leaned forward and told me that I had to move, that my mother would be okay, that she was strong and could manage. It was simple: Move. I would have to move away from South Vermont.

By the time John and I got home, I was feeling better, and within a few days I was back to normal. Dr. Metzger had released something, and eventually I would move. . . . I knew that I had to. I thought maybe I could move once I finished up at Loyola.

Those last years saw a gradual shift from the somnambulance and uncertain awakenings of my earlier time in college. I was involved, and I was meeting with success. And success carried with it its own challenges and threats, its own fears and its own further promises. Perhaps the best way to give you a sense of the texture of these years is to offer a few vignettes, a few clips from the footage that runs through my mind as I sit at my typewriter. I'll begin with one that occurred a month or so after I returned from Dr. Metzger's office.

The third course I took from Mr. Johnson was General Ethics. I was a junior and the class was a mix of juniors and seniors. One of the seniors was Brian Kelly. Brian was Loyola's pride—he was handsome, reflective, and gifted, and, by the time he graduated, he would win the triple crown of graduate fellowships: the Woodrow Wilson, the Danforth, and the Rhodes. A remarkable feat.

A course like General Ethics turns on the question of the existence of universal needs and values, and Mr. Johnson's bent was to look to anthropologists rather than theologians to provide the base for the course. He thought it might be a good idea to introduce the class to the issues by setting up a mock debate, one in which the first speaker would argue for the presence of ethical universals (like incest taboos) and the other speaker would support a strict cultural relativism. He asked me and Brian to conduct this piece of pedagogical theater, each of us collaborating beforehand and presenting the two sides of the argument.

Brian and I worked for two or three weeks, sharing materials and agreeing on methods of presentation. The debate came, and I went first, setting out the various anthropological evidence I could find in favor of ethical universals. Then I turned the podium over to Brian and sat down. He rose to the podium and knocked me flat. He couldn't check his combative instincts and discharged a formidable debater's arsenal: He spoke condescendingly. He questioned my sources and the way I reasoned with them. He brought in material I hadn't seen before. I was dumbstruck. This was big-time, no-holds-barred academic debate; and I was going down for the count. When it came my turn to respond to Brian, I repeated mechanically some of the things I had said earlier, but I couldn't reason with any flair. I was flushed with anger and humiliation, and my mouth dried up and my tongue felt as if it belonged to someone else.

More than a year after the debate with Brian, I won the Blenkiron Award for excellence in English—a plaque and a hundred dollars from one of Loyola's benefactors. Ted Erlandson was by then the chairman of English, and he presided over the ceremony. My name was called, and I walked to the podium. He shook my hand and offered me the plaque. As I was walking back and reading the inscription, I saw that the engraver had made a mistake: *Rose* was spelled *Ruse*. Ruse. A wily subterfuge. A trick. The plaque was returned and made right, of course, but the joke still went down. A peek from behind the curtain. A wink in the hall of mirrors. Was I the real thing or not?

One of the many people I met at the crossroads of Frank Carothers's office was Mike Casey. Casey was usually clad in strong opinion and a thin corduroy jacket. He edited *El Playano,* the campus literary magazine John and I used to lampoon in the old Plymouth. But I started liking Casey, and when he asked me to join the magazine, I put sarcasm behind me and signed on. I worked as an assistant for a semester, and that was fun. Casey promoted me to associate editor, and, at the end of my junior year, he and Dr. Carothers—the magazine's faculty advisor—chose me to be editor. They took a chance. Unlike the other two candidates, I had no experience with high school newspapers or annuals, and all I had done at Loyola was publish, at Casey's suggestion, a stuffy essay on Samuel Beckett and an intellectual exercise that passed for a poem.

El Playano had a small office on the second floor of the student center and was published three times a year. I learned about editing, and, because the magazine had a staff of six, I learned something about management. Students submitted stories and poems, and my editors and I would sit around an old wooden desk and make our decisions. I would then meet with the writers, trying to articulate things about style or plot that I was just coming to understand myself. Then came preparation of manuscripts, paste-up, design, printing, and proofreading, and the exciting day when my assistant editors and I drove to the printers to pick up boxloads of magazines.

We distributed *El Playano* across the campus: walking into the student union, the bookstore, the library, into departments and offices, into solemn places, given entrance with our magazines, probably too loud, like miners back from a long dig slapping bundles onto the assayer's counter. I had responsibilities: timetables, deadlines. I instituted subscriptions for alumni. I made pronouncements, this from my first issue: "Good writing is essential to good learning." I got us an interview with Ray Bradbury. I scouted and found some talented freshman writers. I was on the inside oiling a few gears:

Now I'm a man
I made 21

Every year Loyola sponsored a lecture for the faculty and the alumni. Students were not invited. The speaker for 1965–66 was the distinguished French philosopher and playwright, Gabriel Marcel. Mr. Johnson had told me about Marcel's *Homo Viator,* man the traveler, and I wanted to hear him speak. I sneaked into the auditorium through the exit at the north corridor and nestled in about halfway down the aisle. Mr. Johnson was just finishing his introduction. He turned to the left wing and announced Gabriel Marcel. The applause began, and a tiny, bent man scuttled out across the stage. He used a cane and tried to walk fast and his hips bobbed like pistons gone awry. He was white haired and looked to be seventy. Several times from wing to a desk at center stage he glanced out at the audience to acknowledge the applause. He was smiling—a happy smile, a smile that counterposed his body, all missteps and wild angles.

The auditorium was fairly small, so I could see Marcel's face clearly. I understood only bits and pieces of his speech—which was an attempt to distinguish his philosophy from existentialism—but it was not the text of the speech that pulled me in, it was the delivery. Once this old and crippled man settled into the safe confines of chair and desk, age and infirmity receded. His voice was strong and steady and his eyes were bright. He spoke with conviction and wit, and, for those moments anyway, it seemed that I was witnessing the pure mind that Yeats longed for. When Marcel hobbled out, he was "a tattered coat upon a stick," but when he spoke I saw a body transformed, a promise that an aged person need not be "a paltry thing"— that a life of the mind can bring with it at least momentary deliverance, an athletics of the spirit.

After my poor freshman year, my grades started their ascent. I did increasingly well through my sophomore year and managed to get all A's as a junior. That sort of rise, combined with my work on the campus literary magazine, made me a contender for a fellowship to graduate school. Loyola had a faculty committee charged with preparing promising seniors for fellowship applications, and they contacted me.

I could get strong letters from my teachers, but the committee believed that a further letter from an influential nonacademic—an industrialist or a judge or a legislator—would help my case, particularly with the more prestigious awards. I didn't know any such person, so they set out to have me meet a few people who were part of the wealthy Catholic network.

The first man who interviewed me was the president of an oil company with a branch in Los Angeles. His office was on Wilshire Boulevard near downtown, and when the secretary escorted me in, I entered a world of dark wood and leather and brass. I sat in a chair that took me deep into it. Across a wide expanse of mahogany sat a man in his fifties. He was pale and his white hair was perfectly trimmed and he wore a navy blue suit. He began asking me about my studies, speaking slowly and seemingly from someplace very far away. There was an ornate rifle mounted on the wall behind him. I talked about literature and philosophy and about the literary magazine, and he watched me. He asked several other questions and then shifted in his chair to ask me what I thought of the currently volatile Free Speech Movement. I said a few things in favor of the movement—academic bureaucracy, relevance, the kind of thing you'd expect—and something very quick happened to his face. The next question—one about a priest he knew at Loyola—was asked while he looked into his hands, which were lying, palms up and crossed, on his desk top. Then he thanked me, and the secretary—as if by magic—came through the door, smiled, and walked me out.

A week or so later, I was invited to join the dean and several faculty members at their lunch with a visiting speaker, a former member of the State Department under Jack Kennedy. I was seated across from the man just as the salads were arriving. I introduced myself, and he acknowledged the introduction and began to eat. He leaned over his plate, looking up when spoken to. I asked a few things about the Kennedys—superficial questions, for at that time in my life I had a *Reader's Digest* knowledge of the particulars of working politics. He answered briefly—not rude but not engaged—and returned to his food. Separate body parts were energized—an arm moving up and out from his side, fingers working away like a typist's on chicken amandine—but his face remained jowly and passive. His eyes were flat. When the watermelon arrived, he cut wedges with the knife in his right hand and spit the seeds into the fist of his left. Then he slowly opened his fist to run the palm over the edge of his plate, depositing the seeds.

I have no idea if either man wrote me a letter.

But this is a story with a happy ending. Not all my encounters with the world of academic gamesmanship were so chilly. Father Albertson encouraged me to play a long shot and apply for the big three—the Wilson, Danforth, and Rhodes—and I was lucky enough to get an interview for the Danforth. The Danforth Foundation, a philanthropic organization based in Saint Louis, leaned toward candidates who were planning a career in college teaching. The fellowships were prestigious: Your college had to nominate you, and 120 winners would be chosen from the 2,000 or so nominees.

My interview was set for nine o'clock in the Statler Hilton near downtown L.A. The buses were running late, and I had to transfer twice and sprint through the faded opulence of the Hilton's broad lobby. David Tyack was a historian from Reed College, and he greeted me at the door of his room and we sat by a window in the sun. Just the two of us. Tyack was a young man, academic, tweedy, but humane and engaging. We talked for over an hour about the philosophy I had been reading for Mr. Johnson, about the literary magazine, about my difficult first year at Loyola. I remember one moment particularly: me leaning forward into a stream of sunlight, my elbows on my knees, hands out, describing Gabriel Marcel's walk across the stage.

One year of good grades could never stack up against the best of the Danforth applicants, but Tyack wrote a strong report, and I received an honorable mention from the Danforth Foundation. A month or so later I got word from UCLA that I was awarded full support for three years of graduate study. Like those red A-minuses on Jack MacFarland's papers, the Danforth honorable mention read like a certification of ability. And I'd be going to UCLA. Good Lord. Four years before, I couldn't have shaken out their doormat.

I had promised to meet some friends at Mr. Pockets, a pool hall and pizzeria on Lincoln Boulevard close to Loyola. It was late in the evening, and I was finishing up the layout on the last issue of the magazine. I locked up the office and walked out of the student center into a thick fog. The lights from St. Robert's were out, and the lamps on Loyola Boulevard looked like big tufts of cotton stuck high up on invisible poles. I walked along the boulevard past the library; with its foyer lights left on, it seemed a glowing, fuzzy block floating back in the trees.

I was thinking about the magazine. About particular stories and how much I liked it, felt part of it, how hard it was going to be to leave it. A song lyric started drifting in and out of my thoughts:

Me and my cat named dog.
We're walking high against the fog . . .

I couldn't see more than a few feet in front of me, but the air was moist and it felt good to breathe it. The magazine. I started singing the lyric aloud, its silliness blending with the bittersweetness of parting. I was well past the library when my foot caught something. A white cloth on the ground. I bent over and picked a large pair of men's undershorts off the tip of my shoe. What story is this? I wondered, and kept walking, thinking, finally, about the bar and the friends waiting for me there, finding the song again, singing it louder now and twirling the underwear in rhythmic snaps over my head.

Questions for Discussion

1. Mike Rose says that when he looks back at his notes from his first year of college he can find no coherence to them. Look at your own notes for the courses you're taking this year. What have you written down? Why? How much sense do you think the notes will make ten years from now? How much of a sense of coherence do they have for you now?

2. Rose writes, "It is an unfortunate act of our psychic lives that the images that surround us as we grow up—no matter how much we may scorn them later—give shape to our deepest needs and longings" (paragraph 13). How do later parts of the chapter substantiate this claim? Is this true of the relationship between your own past and your present needs and longings?

3. In what way does Rose support his statement that the "many platitudes about motivation and self-reliance and individualism . . . are serious nonsense" (paragraph 22)? Do you agree with his statement? What evidence can you give for your point of view?

4. Rather than tell us of a single influential teacher, Rose describes several who contribute to his education and help him shape his self. How effective do you find these descriptions? Why did Rose think he needed all of them? What, in other words, does each vignette contribute that the others do not?

Questions for Research and Writing

1. Rose believes that in order to "journey up through the top levels of the American educational system," students—especially those from depressed communities—will need "people to guide [them] into conversations that seem foreign and threatening" (paragraph 22). Write an essay in which you show how you've been guided into those conversations. If you still feel uncomfortable entering into academic conversations, how has your earlier training proved insufficient? How do you hope your present training will prepare you for such conversations in the future?

2. Interview a fellow student who seems an unlikely candidate for college admission. How did this person overcome the financial, emotional, sociological, educational, or linguistic barriers in his or her way?

BEHIND THE CURTAIN

Chester E. Finn, Jr., and Bruno V. Manno

> *Originally published in the Winter 1996 edition of* The Wilson Quarterly, *an opinion journal, the following article argues that colleges and universities are hastening their decline by refusing to limit their spending and to set academic standards, by luring under-qualified students, and by pampering their faculty. In an age of shrinking resources, this argument is increasingly familiar as colleges—both public and private, both two-year and four-year—raise tuition and compete for their share of state and federal budgets. "Behind the Curtain" raises a number of the issues central to raging debates about the future of higher education. Its authors are an assistant secretary of education in the Reagan administration and his counterpart in the Bush administration. They offer an assessment of the problems and a set of solutions to which many readers in academia will respond strongly, whether positively or negatively. Whatever your reaction, the article will, we hope, encourage lively debate.*

During the half-century since World War II, American colleges and universities have been education's Emerald City, not only for Americans but for millions of others who have followed the yellow brick road from abroad. No matter what ups and downs have afflicted the economy, no matter that the stunning mediocrity of our primary and secondary schools has been recognized as a national crisis—through all this and more, higher education has grown in scale, in wealth, in allure and, at least until the very recent past, in stature.

That growth has been a marvel to behold. Before World War II, 1,700 institutions enrolled 1.5 million students, employed 147,000 faculty, and spent $675 million, or about $450 per student per year. After the war, the GI Bill of 1944 underwrote a huge expansion, and the postwar economy's appetite for skilled labor placed an ever-greater premium on a college degree. Regional colleges went national. Community colleges—an American innovation—spread like the ivy that seldom graced their walls. Dozens of new (mostly state) campuses were opened.

No longer was the university merely a place of teaching and learning. Now it was an engine of economic growth and a source of technological and scientific progress. It was looked to for defense preparedness, cultural enrichment, and policy ideas about everything from poverty to air pollution. Corporate investment and high-tech jobs gravitated to communities with research facilities and a supply of educated people. By 1960, there were 2,000 institutions; by 1980, 3,150. Still the growth continued. Today, the United States is indisputably the world's postsecondary superpower.

There are nearly 3,700 colleges and universities in the United States. They enroll 14.4 million people, about 22 percent of all "tertiary" students on the planet. (The student body includes some 440,000 citizens of other countries, an "export" that adds about $7.1 billion to the plus side of our annual balance of payments.) The faculty has ballooned to 833,000. Higher education in America is a $213 billion industry, roughly equal in size to the gross national product of Belgium.

But it is an increasingly troubled enterprise. Except at the top, it has grave quality problems. Nearly 50 percent of the freshmen in the California state university system are enrolled in remedial English and mathematics classes. Higher education's problems are beginning to receive the attention of government officials at the highest levels of power and influence. Speaker of the House (and ex-professor) Newt Gingrich writes that higher education "is out of control [and] increasingly out of touch with the rest of America."

The American public has always had mixed feelings about the university, sneering at the "ivory tower" life while according the professoriate an exaggerated respect. Now, however, a new combination of factors is tilting the balance of opinion against higher education. While among policymakers there is growing concern about the shoddy quality of much higher education, the broader public feels increasingly oppressed by soaring prices. During the 1980s, health care costs increased 117 percent and there was talk of a national crisis. The price of new cars rose 37 percent. But the average cost of attending a public college increased by 109 percent, and the price of an education at a private college jumped by 146 percent. Every other major purveyor in the United States, from Bethlehem Steel to Wal-Mart, has been forced in recent years to hold down or even cut prices. But higher education has done practically nothing to end its decades-long spree of escalating charges and expenditures.

Today, annual tuition and fees at public four-year institutions equal nine percent of the median American family income; the proportion for private institutions is 38 percent. As recently as 1991, the comparable figures were six percent and 27 percent. (In 1980, they were four percent and 17 percent.) Obviously, this can't continue forever.

One saving grace of the "ivory tower" idea was always the public's sense that, however alien university life might seem to an outsider and however much it might cost, it was redeemed by the higher purposes that informed its existence. But the university is losing that precious public trust. There is a sense, in the mad proliferation of course offerings, the embarrassing deficiencies of many graduates, and higher education's embrace of political correctness and other politically inspired assaults on its own ideals, that perhaps the university has lost sight of its higher purposes. Fifty-four percent of Americans believe that higher education in their state needs a "fundamental overhaul," according to a 1993 poll conducted by the Public Agenda Foundation. By margins of seven or eight to one, the public says that college is not a good value for the money—and is fast pricing itself out of reach.

It is impossible to underestimate the power of bad ideas, and certainly the looming crisis of the American university has a great deal to do with the institution's profound confusion over its own functions and purposes. More mundane forces are also at work, however, and these have to do with the political economy of modern higher education.

The American university is a curiously inflexible institution. One of its chief peculiarities is that the only changes it can comfortably handle are tied to growth. Colleges and universities are subject neither to the discipline of a true market nor to any powerful internal constraints on spending. They are in a position to define what "higher education" is, and therefore what their costs and prices will be. Consumers have little choice but to pay. Meeting a new student yearning, accommodating a community request, luring a star professor, improving the football team, acceding to the faculty's yen for doctoral students (and reduced teaching loads), pursuing the latest developments in microbiology, strengthening the gender studies program, giving professors incentives for better teaching—you name it—all are treated as incremental costs of education.

If it were a corporation (or even a government agency), the institution would fund many of these changes internally, by cutting back elsewhere. But universities don't function that way. The combination of tenured faculty, unionized nonteaching staff, protest-prone students, nostalgic alumni, reverence for traditional practices, make-no-waves administrators, remote governing boards, and "collegial" decision making all block that sort of approach.

As a result, the culture of higher education is expansion oriented. Even in this time of crushing tuition costs, colleges are more apt to compete for students by *adding* elaborate recreation centers, dining options, cable television in the dorms, and all manner of new counseling and advising services, rather than by becoming leaner and cheaper. Some call this the "Chivas Regal strategy," boosting sales by marketing one's product as the premium brand.

Whatever it's called, the economics of higher education often seem surreal. The late Howard Bowen, perhaps the leading analyst of the economics of universities, concluded that these institutions simply spend all they can take in. They determine their own costs. They set their own prices—and sometimes collude over them. They are more likely to buff their appeal by raising prices than by slashing them. They aren't really answerable to anyone for their performance. Indeed, they have no clear goals or measurable indicators of effectiveness. They insist that what they teach cannot be tested by outsiders, demand that the work of scholars be evaluated only by their peers, and use academic freedom as a shield against scrutiny and accountability.

Thus constructed, higher education is a perpetual growth machine. Such a machine requires a steady flow of new revenues. Since enrollments produce the lion's share of income (except at a handful of research-centered campuses), attracting more students and charging more for each one are the surest ways to get it. Thus, the average U.S. postsecondary institution enrolled 535 more students in 1993 than in 1974.

Once a university grows, it must maintain its new base. Above all, it must keep its lecture halls and dorms full. Admissions offices today will do almost anything to attract enough students: discount tuition charges, scramble to boost the school's rank in consumer guides such as the annual *U.S. News and World Report* ratings, even fib about the quality of their institution's students. The *Wall Street Journal* recently reported, for example, that for years New College of the University of South Florida deliberately inflated the average SAT scores of its entering class by simply lopping off data on its poorest performers.

The imperative of keeping enrollments up is a powerful contributor to the quality problems that beset the American campus. Seen from afar, the Emerald City's tallest academic pinnacles still gleam. Nobody is really surprised that nearly half of the Nobel laureates in physics and medicine since World War II have been members of American faculties, as have two-thirds of those in economics. This distinction spills over into graduate education in the arts and sciences and extends to major professional schools such as medicine. But intellectual rigor can fall off drastically even at the postgraduate level. Upward of 90,000 master's degrees in education are awarded each year, for example, including 60 (in 1993) in driver education and 3,000 in physical education and coaching. These (and many of the 7,000 education doctorates conferred each year) have more to do with the credentialism of American public schools than with higher learning.

At the undergraduate level, the problems are much the same. While yuppie parents will do anything to get their offspring into Brown or Berkeley, their impulse has more to do with careerism and status than with academic quality. It is true that a degree from such an institution is a marketable asset; it is not altogether clear that students learn a lot—at least academically—during their time on campus. Thus the familiar joke about why Harvard is a great repository of knowledge: its students enter with so much and leave with so little.

Descending from the institutions whose names are household words to those attended by the great majority of American students, the deficiencies become painfully apparent. The recruitment and admission of ill-prepared students is common, though often justified in the name of diversity and social justice. Many schools try to "remediate" underperformers on campus. Others turn a blind eye and pass them along with a degree. Remedial courses in reading, writing, and math are offered on 75 percent of U.S. campuses, and 30 percent of entering students enroll in at least one such course.

(Even at MIT, which has no shortage of attractive applicants, only 17 percent of freshmen passed the entry-level writing appraisal in 1995.)

Many degree recipients never get near a history, math, or literature course. More than half avoid instruction in foreign languages. As a result of student demand for vocational courses and institutions' need to keep classrooms filled, the liberal arts are being pushed aside. Barely a third of 1993 bachelor's degrees were in the arts and sciences. Degrees in home economics outnumbered those in mathematics; more baccalaureates were awarded in "protective services" than in the physical sciences, more in theater than in German and French combined.

Rather than add stimulating courses in math, literature, and other elements of a classic liberal education, administrators and faculty have pandered to some of the worst impulses of students, encouraging (and sometimes requiring) them to take "courses" that indulge the contemporary trend toward self-absorption. At the University of Maryland, freshmen earn credits for a "course" called "The Student and the University," which examines such matters as date rape, cultural diversity, the use of highlighting pens, and fitting a career plan to the contours of one's personality. At Florida A&M, there are seminars on dating relationships. "American higher education," concludes the Wingspread Group, a panel chaired by former U.S. secretary of labor William Brock, "now offers a smorgasbord of fanciful courses in a fragmented curriculum that accords as much credit for 'Introduction to Tennis' . . . as it does for 'Principles of English Composition,' history or physics, thereby trivializing education—indeed, misleading students by implying that they are receiving the education they need for life when they are not."

To keep the customers moving, moreover, U.S. colleges and universities have been willing to confer degrees on people who have not learned much. A 1993 federal survey found that few graduates of four-year campuses reached the highest level of literacy—which involved such things as interpreting a substantial news article. Only about half were capable of writing a brief letter explaining an error made on a credit card bill. Some of the particulars would be funny if they weren't so alarming. As the Wingspread Group noted, "56.3 percent of American-born, four-year college graduates are unable consistently to perform simple tasks, such as calculating the change from $3 after buying a 60-cent bowl of soup and a $1.95 sandwich." [20]

Besides increasing the number of students, the obvious way to boost university revenues is to raise the fees collected from each of them. Every autumn brings word that tuition increases have again outpaced inflation. The 1995–96 school year brought with it a six percent increase—about double the inflation rate—at four-year schools, pushing tuition and fees to an average of $2,860 at public campuses and $12,432 at private ones. At Ivy League-style universities, the price of a bachelor's degree (including room and board) approaches $120,000. In most of the country, one can buy a substantial house for that kind of money.

It is important to note, however, that in the peculiar world of higher education finance, tuition charges both understate and overstate the actual cost of a college education. They understate it because virtually every institution also draws substantial revenues from other sources. The average private campus now spends $28,000 annually per (full-time equivalent) student, more than twice its posted charge for an undergraduate education. Yet the tuition levels that make headlines also exaggerate what most students actually pay for higher education, particularly in the private sector. In a year (1989) when the average "sticker price" of U.S. private universities was $11,735, tuition revenue per student averaged $9,071, some 23 percent less. That difference represented widespread discounting, undertaken partly in the name of equal opportunity but increasingly in an effort to draw in enough students to fill those classrooms and dorms. One veteran analyst of higher education finances compares the way colleges "sell" student places to airline marketing practices—i.e., filling the available seats with people who pay sharply differing prices.

Tufts University, for example, which now charges $21,000 annually for tuition and fees (and $6,000 more for room and board), aids 40 percent of its students, with sums averaging $15,000 each. The 60 percent who pay full price, of course, help underwrite this Robin Hood-style resource transfer. But the bazaar-style pricing policy breeds further unhappiness among consumers, both those forced to pay the full freight and those who sense they could have gotten a better "deal" if they had shopped longer or bargained harder.

Rising tuition and fees are still the overriding reality, and it is extraordinary how long they have been growing. Terry Hartle of the American Council on Education, higher education's top Washington lobbyist, estimates that college charges have risen by an average of two percent more than inflation throughout the 20th century. Yet the demand for higher education has remained strong. Most of its appeal stems from the sizable economic payoff of a college education—although the opportunity it provides for a prolonged spell of unbridled hedonism ought not to be ignored. In the age group 25 to 34, men with college degrees earned $12,000 more in 1994 than those who ended their education with a high school diploma. Women with degrees enjoyed an income premium of $13,000.

Over the course of a career, according to U.S. Census Bureau projections, a person who graduated from college in 1992 can expect $600,000 more income (in constant dollars) than a person of the same age with only a high school diploma. A master's degree adds nearly $200,000 more to lifetime earnings. And unemployment is much lower for college graduates.

Lately, however, a bit of the economic bloom seems to have faded. Real median earnings of young male college graduates actually dropped

4.4 percent from 1989 to '93. Although the earnings of those with no college plunged further (13.7 percent), the "return" on an investment in college may have peaked, at least for men. (It continues to rise for women.)

In a country where high school diplomas mean next to nothing, it is possible that employers have been using the college degree as a simple screening device to identify people likely to possess at least minimal skills and work habits. As access to college becomes nearly universal, however, as low university standards are exposed, and as more radical school reform strategies start to bear fruit at the secondary level, it is likely that the degree's economic edge will narrow.

Amid all these growing signs of educational degradation, life on campus has grown more pleasant for those who live and work there. Between 1976 and 1991, a period when most other enterprises were slashing middle management and substituting technology for labor, the university continued to add poundage. By 1991, there were only 8.3 students per (professional) staff member, compared to 9.8 in 1976.

Salaries are comfortable. The average full professor at a state university earned $62,000 in 1994–95 for what is typically an eight- or nine-month year. At private universities, full professors averaged $73,160. Even at lower-status two-year colleges, the typical professor drew a salary of $51,070. Moreover, some 64 percent of the nation's full-time faculty enjoy the extraordinary job security that comes with tenure.

Course loads have fallen and school years have shrunk. Instruction now consumes only 40 percent of the average university budget. Senior faculty typically spend about 10 hours a week in the classroom and no more than eight hours advising students, according to a study by the Higher Education Research Institute at the University of California, Los Angeles. Michigan State's 2,038 professors (a tenth of whom earn more than $100,000 a year) spend an average of 5.5 hours a week in the classroom during the academic year. That presumably leaves ample time for research and writing. Yet the UCLA study also shows that, from 1991 to '93, 41 percent of American professors published not a single word in professional journals. (Others are more prolific, raising the average output for full-time faculty to about one article, a third of a book review, and two "professional presentations" every year.)

Despite a hundred solemn studies urging that faculty pay be tied more to teaching and less to research, the "publish or perish" imperative endures. A federal survey found that professors' publications correlate positively with their earnings but that teaching has an *inverse* relationship. Faculty whose teaching made up less than half their total work load earned far more ($62,000) in 1988 than those who spent most of their time in the classroom ($41,000).

The consequences are predictable: slipshod instruction, particularly of undergraduate students; constant pressure from faculty for less teaching and more time for research; and tons of research that serves the career needs of the professoriate (and bloats budgets) without significantly enlarging human knowledge. More than 400 new scholarly journals in modern languages and literature, most of them obscure and some bordering on the frivolous, were founded in the 1970s alone. Hundreds of so-called "electronic journals" are also appearing each year.

Many observers predicted that this peculiar industry would suffer a shakeout during the 1980s, but it escaped. National prosperity underwrote increases in enrollment, tuition, and subsidies from state governments. A vibrant stock market boosted endowment returns and encouraged alumni giving. And the federal government chipped in with the Middle Income Student Assistance Act of 1978, which broadened eligibility for federal grants and extended loans to students regardless of financial need. This led to unprecedented increases in student aid. Total aid (from all sources) ballooned to $46.8 billion in 1994–95. The federal taxpayer supplied or—by guaranteeing loans—backstopped three-quarters of this sum. Today, nearly half of all students pay for college and graduate school with Washington's help.

There are, however, several reasons to believe that higher education's day of reckoning can no longer be put off. First, there just are not many more students waiting to be recruited. Postsecondary institutions increased enrollments in the past by opening their doors to older students, encouraging people to return for additional training, and recruiting overseas. But like veins of coal that have been mined for decades, these "nontraditional" populations will eventually provide dwindling yields. There are now more students enrolled in colleges and universities than in high schools.

Moreover, there is widening recognition of the pernicious effects of "open admissions" at the postsecondary level on school standards and pupil performance in secondary schools. Only about 50 of the nation's 3,600 colleges and universities are highly selective, turning away more applicants than they accept. Perhaps 200 more campuses admit 50 to 90 percent of their applicants. The rest, desperate to fill their classrooms, welcome essentially anyone who applies, sometimes not even requiring a high school diploma. Young people therefore are well aware that they can get into college no matter what their transcripts and test scores look like. For them, the incentive to study hard in high school is virtually nonexistent. School reformers can talk about raising standards until they turn blue; rational 16-year-olds know that in their "real world" it simply doesn't matter.

This unpleasant reality is contributing to changes that may make life more difficult for universities. The California state university system is on the verge of barring entry by freshmen who cannot handle college-level math or English. (Three-fifths of new students now fail one or both of the tests.) The City University of New York and the state universities of Massachusetts are moving in the same direction.

Elected officials are also beginning to put pressure on state universities. "The higher education community thinks they're above it all. They don't like to be told what to do," says Ohio legislator Wayne Jones, a senior member of his state assembly's finance committee. "But if they want us to be their sugar daddy, there are going to be some rules." Jones has successfully pressed his colleagues to impose some. Ohio now requires professors in state-supported colleges to spend at least 10 percent more time teaching undergraduates than they did in 1990.

Most ominous of all for universities, money is getting scarce—and consumers and taxpayers more cost conscious. Though state funds for higher education continue to increase in absolute terms, appropriations per student, adjusted for inflation, have dropped. Yet institutional spending is still rising faster than inflation, forcing state universities to increase tuition rapidly. The federal gravy train is no longer a reliable source of income, either. Washington supplied 15 percent of higher education revenues in 1980 and only 12 percent in 1993, and the drive to shrink the federal deficit, curb Uncle Sam's intrusiveness, devolve obligations to states, and make people shoulder greater responsibility for themselves has only begun.

Some of the least popular agencies in Washington—the Department of Education, the national endowments for the arts and humanities—have been the spigots through which much of higher education's federal largesse has flowed. As their budgets are nipped and their programs curbed, universities will feel it. So will students. Budget savings now being exacted from federal loan programs, for example, will boost the cost of borrowing, thereby making hundreds of thousands of students even more keenly aware of—and harder pressed to afford—the price of higher education. The level of federal scientific research support is rising more slowly than inflation at many agencies. Even the reduction in defense spending—a goal dear to the ideological hearts of many academics—is apt to affect university budgets. (One large exception: federal dollars still gush into biomedical research.)

If neither state nor federal government will come to the academy's financial rescue, its one remaining large source of additional funding is, of course, its own students. But tuition payers are also growing more oppressed by—and resistant to—rising prices. Because many people nowadays simply cannot pay for college out of current income, the debt burden is mounting fast. Between 1992—when Congress invited even more middle- and upper-income students to obtain federally guaranteed loans—and 1994, borrowing under the federal loan programs rose 57 percent. Students typically emerge from college with a debt burden of $8,000 or $9,000, and horror stories—families that owe $50,000 after putting two or three youngsters through school—are often heard. What is more, the prospect of hefty monthly payments after college intensifies the pressure on students to major in "practical" fields, thus exacerbating the vocationalism that already afflicts higher education.

In response to all of these challenges, a little belt-tightening has begun. Mostly, administrators do the easy (sometimes shortsighted) things first. They hand out more tuition discounts to maintain enrollments. (On the margin, a student doesn't have to produce a great deal of net income in order to be more valuable to the institution than an empty slot.) They defer maintenance on aging buildings. They may meet new teaching needs with untenured and low-paid part-time or "gypsy" faculty members.

State legislatures are forcing some changes through budget cuts and efforts to mold university behavior. Ohio's mandatory increase in undergraduate teaching is being emulated by other states, as is Tennessee's practice of tying a small portion of its campus funding formula to institutional performance. Signs of entrepreneurialism are also visible, at least in realms where the faculty is not directly affected. Colleges are contracting out the management of such things as bookstores, dormitories, and janitorial work. A few are even turning the Chivas Regal strategy on its head and offering bargains. The University of Rochester now gives an across-the-board $5,000 discount to incoming freshmen from New York State.

Controlling costs—and prices—is plainly vital if American higher education is to get itself into shape, but a proper fitness regimen must go further. There is a long list of possibilities, from making campus amenities optional, so that budget-conscious students can buy the academic equivalent of "basic transportation" rather than the "fully-loaded" model, to imposing real assessments on students so that academic "value added" can be measured (and compared by quality-minded shoppers). The curricular smorgasbord needs to be edited and more "core" requirements instituted; faculties need better incentives to emphasize teaching rather than ersatz research. (How many of today's 833,000 faculty will ever produce "new knowledge" of real significance? Ten percent?) This list could be extended.

But fiscal fitness is not all that U.S. higher education needs to work at. It must renew its moral authority. Particularly if the economic advantage of a degree shrinks, the university's future stature and allure will have more to do with the intrinsic worth of what it does—as perceived by ordinary people, not by academics—and less to do with the personal wealth to be reaped by enduring the process.

Moral capital is not easy to build. It seems to us that the most promising ways by which higher education can regain public trust are by committing itself to the principle of value for money, demonstrating that a college degree truly denotes solid skills and knowledge, and curbing the excesses of political correctness and campus misbehavior.

Are these dreams like the Cowardly Lion's wish for courage and Dorothy's desire to get back to Kansas? Perhaps. But just as the lion and

Dorothy turned out to contain within themselves the essential elements for realizing their hopes, so American higher education has residual strengths that it can tap in a quest for self-renewal.

There are on a few campuses trustees and presidents who are showing signs of reform leadership, and several reform-minded groups have been formed, including the Wingspread Group, the American Academy for Liberal Education (a new accrediting body), and the National Association of Scholars. Inner resources may not suffice, however, unless accompanied by an external shock. Perhaps this will be supplied by restive taxpayers, rebellious tuition payers, change-minded voters, and the demands of employers who need to hire truly educated people if their firms—and the nation's economy—are to remain strong.

Will that be shock enough? We would have greater confidence if state and national leaders were to become as serious about the performance of universities as they are about that of the primary and secondary schools, where bold changes are finally being made in basic ground rules and operating assumptions. This has not yet happened at the tertiary level, but the new crew of legislators, members of Congress, and governors—people who do not share the hoary assumptions or political ties of their predecessors—do show signs that they are prepared to open the curtain and see what the higher education wizard really looks like.

There is risk, to be sure, that something of value may be lost in the process of reforming higher education. But leaving the enterprise as it is carries greater risks. The changes may not make all our wishes come true, but we might at least find American higher education pointed, like Dorothy and Toto, back to the real world.

Questions for Discussion

1. Chester Finn and Bruno Manno argue that too many students are attending college for the wrong reasons: to advance their careers or enhance their earning power. This trend toward vocationalism is, they say, detrimental to both the students and the standards of the institution. To what extent were you drawn to college by the appeal of a good job and a high income? How have you or your peers' interests in career potential and advancement affected your choices of school, major, and particular courses? To what extent has vocationalism affected the quality of the education offered at your institution?

2. Finn and Manno frequently cite statistical studies in support of their arguments. Examine their use of statistics. Where—and why—do you find it convincing? Where—and why—would you like more information about the studies from which the statistics are taken? Where—and why—do you find the statistical evidence incomplete or misleading?

3. Finn and Manno begin and end their article with references to *The Wizard of Oz*. How effective is their comparison of the world and characters of higher education to those of the Emerald City?
4. Examine the use of diction and of metaphor in "Behind the Curtain." How does the tone of the piece (for example, its word choices and its characterizations of the various players in the higher education debate) contribute to or detract from the argument? How does it reflect the authors' political stance? How effectively does the style maintain your interest?
5. If you were to design the ideal college curriculum, what courses would you include? Which ones would you require of all students?
6. Finn and Manno sometimes assert their ideas without taking their opposition's viewpoints into full account. Where do you think opponents would find fault with their argument? What evidence and counterarguments would opponents supply?

Questions for Research and Writing

1. Finn and Manno deplore higher education's willingness to replace a "classic liberal education" with a broader, less clearly academic curriculum. As you think about their reasons for faulting less traditional curricula, examine the course offerings in your college's catalogue and class schedule and gather sample course descriptions and course syllabi. How true are Finn's and Manno's accusations of your institution?
2. "Behind the Curtain" begins with a brief history of higher education in the United States, pointing to the dramatic increases in enrollment since the introduction of the GI Bill of 1944. Interview someone from an earlier generation who did not attend college. What factors led to his or her decision not to attend? How many of those factors affect today's students?

OR

Interview a first-generation college student. What factors entered into that person's decision to attend college? What obstacles did he or she have to overcome? How did this student's family and friends respond to his or her desire to attend college?
3. Finn and Manno say that "the American public has always had mixed feelings about the university, sneering at the 'ivory tower' life while according the professoriate an exaggerated respect" (paragraph 5) and that "fifty-four percent of Americans believe that higher education in their state needs a 'fundamental overhaul'" (paragraph 7). Design a questionnaire to test these assertions. How dissatisfied are Americans with the system of higher education? What are the sources of their satisfaction and dissatisfaction?

4. As evidence of the declining quality of higher education, Finn and Manno mention that the numbers of remedial courses are on the rise and that too many students are enrolled in remedial math and English classes. Research the presence of such courses on your campus. When and why were the courses instituted? What percentage of students are enrolled in such courses? Who are those students and what has led to their need for remediation?

THE CREATIONIST AND THE SOCIOBIOLOGIST
Two Stories about Illiberal Education

Phillip E. Johnson

> *Causing quite a stir when it appeared in the early 1990s, Dinesh D'Souza's book* Illiberal Education: The Politics of Race and Sex on Campus *argued that higher education has fallen victim to the politics of race and gender and that, as a result, it no longer serves either the students or the greater community. In the following review article, originally published in 1992 in the* California Law Review *(a journal edited by the students of Boalt Hall School of Law, University of California, Berkeley), Phillip E. Johnson, law school professor and author of* Darwin on Trial, *explores D'Souza's ideas by examining two different cases where attitudes about "political correctness" influenced what university professors could say in their classrooms. As you read, try to identify the questions that Johnson raises about "what may and may not be said in the contemporary university." What do the experiences of these two professors tell us about tolerance and authority in higher education today?*

Illiberal Education. By Dinesh D'Souza*
*Reviewed by Phillip E. Johnson**

There is a mad reductionism at work [in the universities]. God is not a proper topic for discussion, but "lesbian politics" is. . . . In the famous "marketplace of ideas," where all ideas are equal and where there must be no "value judgments" and therefore no values, certain ideas are simply excluded, and woe to those who espouse them.[1]

In a liberal culture, it is a great rhetorical advantage to appear in a dispute as the champion of free speech against the forces of repression. The left has held this advantage for a long time. The student revolt of the 1960s opened with a "Free Speech Movement," and the bumper sticker that directs us to "Question Authority" implies that the left's politics is a matter of raising questions rather than imposing answers. Recently, however, academic traditionalists like Dinesh D'Souza have seized the moral high ground by describing a left-imposed atmosphere of "political correctness"

---

*B.A. 1983, Dartmouth College.
**Jefferson E. Peyser Professor of Law, Boalt Hall School of Law, University of California, Berkeley. A.B. 1961, Harvard University; J.D. 1965, University of Chicago Law School.

in the universities that leads to "illiberal education." In effect, they have captured the bumper sticker and turned its message around.

The "PC left" under attack is post-Marxist, and its philosophy is post-Modernist. A brief pause for definitions is necessary. In post-Marxism, racial minorities, feminists, and gays have assumed the mantle of the proletariat; the oppressor class is heterosexist white males rather than the bourgeoisie; and the struggle is for control of the terms of discourse rather than the means of production. Post-Modernism challenges the objective validity of academic traditions by starting from the premise that knowledge comes in texts whose meaning and value are determined by communities of interpreters. According to certain cultural critics (post-Liberals?), post-Modern nihilism and post-Marxist political fanaticism have combined to create a university atmosphere that is both anti-intellectual and intolerant.

A successful argument is not one that convinces everybody, because that never happens, but one that captures the terms of a debate and places opponents on the defensive. Judged by this standard, Dinesh D'Souza has been spectacularly successful. It is not only that approving reviews have appeared from prominent writers and journals usually identified with left or liberal politics—including Eugene Genovese in *The New Republic*[2] and C. Vann Woodward in *The New York Review of Books*.[3] More important, the trend-setting media have taken up the debate in D'Souza's terms. The ultimate endorsement came in June 1991, when *The MacNeil/Lehrer NewsHour* featured an entire week of "conversations about political correctness," with the title "The Big Chill."[4]

Of course, the left has tried hard to take back the rhetorical initiative. Duke University law professor Katharine Bartlett stated the main objections to D'Souza's thesis succinctly in the *Wall Street Journal*.[5] Bartlett's institutional identification is important, because the English Department at Duke is a famous center of post-Modernism. Duke's Stanley Fish, a literary critic who also has a law school appointment, is one of the major villains of D'Souza's book. Rebuttal from a feminist scholar with personal knowledge of the situation at Duke was thus particularly appropriate.

The academic traditionalists are still firmly in charge at Duke as elsewhere, wrote Bartlett, and Shakespeare and Milton are being taught as before. The critics from the multiculturalist left are not politicizing the curriculum; rather, they are exposing a long-standing political bias that previously was unquestioned. According to Bartlett, the traditional political philosophy course that begins with Aristotle and ends with John Rawls is just as politically loaded as the new alternative offerings in feminist theory or ethnic studies. The only difference is that the bias inherent in the "western civilization" courses went unrecognized because it reflected the dominant (Eurocentric male) point of view.[6]

Bartlett reclaimed title to that "Question Authority" bumper sticker for the multiculturalists. As she put it, those who have been labelled "PC" "are not trying to stifle debate. We are trying to begin one—a difficult one that challenges perspectives that are taken for granted in the university and in society."[7] The traditionalists, on the other hand, are using the PC charge as a "smoke screen" to avoid "a genuine debate . . . about academic quality and diversity."[8] Their exaggerated complaints about violations of academic freedom are a strategy to "shield themselves from criticism of classroom remarks that some students find racist or sexist."[9]

My purpose in this Review Essay is not to evaluate Dinesh D'Souza's book, but rather to explore a question that is implicit in the PC debate but rarely addressed directly. Everyone writes as if universal tolerance were a virtue, but everyone also seems to assume that there are ideas and expressions that a university should not tolerate, or at least should not encourage. Some, like Katharine Bartlett, will say that racist and sexist remarks are out of place in the classroom, and assume that the offended women and minorities are the proper judges of what is racist and sexist. Others, like Dinesh D'Souza, will deplore the excesses of multiculturalism, insisting that universities should not give writers like Franz Fanon and Rigoberta Menchu an undeserved intellectual status by placing their writing in survey courses that used to be devoted to the likes of Plato, Milton, and Rawls. The real dispute is not so much about tolerance as it is about what ideas a university ought to *value*. Is it more important for students to learn to appreciate John Milton's excellence as a poet or to deplore his views on the role of women? Should an instructor feel free to *defend* Milton's opinions on women or other subjects, including theology? Is Rawls an important thinker and Fanon a mere propagandist, or might it be the other way around? Above all, who ought to have authority to decide questions like these?

I agree with Katharine Bartlett that we ought to have a genuine debate about academic quality and diversity that challenges perspectives that have been taken for granted in the university and society. As an opening move in that debate—with the purpose more of sparking further discussion than of resolving the points in dispute—I offer two true stories. Let's see what they tell us about what may and may not be said in the contemporary university.

I THE CREATIONIST[10]

Phillip Bishop teaches classes in exercise physiology to graduate and undergraduate students in the College of Education at the University of Alabama. Like many other college teachers, he considers it appropriate to tell his students something about himself and what he values. In his case, this personal disclosure involved saying that he believes that "God came to earth in the form of Jesus Christ and he has something to tell us about life which is crucial to success and happiness."[11] Because of this belief, Bishop prefers to invest his time in people rather than in publishing "a stack of technical papers."[12] He presented this view as his own "bias" and told students that "[i]f that is not your bias, that is fine."[13] He also urged students to keep in mind that whatever he said probably reflected his Christian bias and urged them to tell him if his behavior fell short of his Christian ideals.[14]

Courts that later reviewed his conduct agreed that Bishop was otherwise very restrained. "He never engaged in prayer, read passages from the Bible, handed out religious tracts,"[15] or arranged for guest lectures on any religious topic during class. On the other hand, Bishop made no secret of his skepticism about the orthodox doctrine that the human body evolved by purely naturalistic and material processes such as random mutation and natural selection. He did not discourse on this subject in class, but he did invite students and others to a voluntary, after-hours meeting at which he lectured on "Evidences of God in Human Physiology."[16] Bishop is not a Biblical literalist or opponent of evolution in some broad sense, but he believes that materialistic forces alone could not have created the wonderfully complex organs of the human body.

The head of Bishop's academic unit, Dr. Westerfield, later testified that students (whose names he could not remember) complained about Bishop's statements and the optional lectures.[17] Dr. Westerfield himself worried that Bishop's statements might hurt the University's academic reputation, because "other professional colleagues around the nation consider this the 'Bible belt' and [think] that . . . a lot of this type of activity goes on in the University."[18] He shared his anxiety with the Dean of the School of Education, and the two went to see the University counsel to decide whether Bishop's remarks amounted to an unconstitutional establishment of religion. Counsel assumed that what a state university professor says in a classroom is tantamount to an act of state government, and so is governed by the famous three-part test of *Lemon v. Kurtzman*.[19] Applying that standard, counsel thought the University had a duty to "control this kind of activity"[20] because Bishop's remarks had no secular purpose and created an excessive entanglement between government and religion.[21]

Westerfield then ordered Bishop not only to cease referring to his religious beliefs during class time but also to discontinue "the optional classes where a 'Christian perspective' of an academic topic is delivered."[22] The University's rationale for forbidding even after-hours discussions of this nature was that students might feel coerced to agree with Bishop's religion in hopes of gaining some favorable treatment.[23]

Bishop challenged the restrictions in federal court, with initial success. The district court observed that the University's restrictions were aimed not at coercive speech, or irrelevant speech, but only at religious speech. According to the opinion:

> Numerous undisputed affidavits filed indicate University policy does not prohibit faculty members from engaging in non-religious classroom speech involving personal views on other subjects. Such discussions are the norm used to establish rapport between faculty and students. There is no University policy attempting to control

the statements of faculty members as long as they do their job. Nor is there a University policy prohibiting faculty members from organizing after-class meetings if discussions are not from a religious perspective. The University has no policy proscribing professor involvement in extracurricular academic discussions with students.[24]

The district court held that a policy excluding only religious expression from the classroom is unconstitutional under *Widmar v. Vincent*.[25] In *Widmar*, the Supreme Court held that a state university must allow religious student groups to use campus facilities on the same terms as other student groups, on the theory that the First Amendment prohibits discrimination against speech on the basis of its religious content.[26]

A panel of the Court of Appeals for the Eleventh Circuit disagreed, and unanimously reversed the district court's judgment.[27] The opinion by Judge Gibson[28] said that the relevant Supreme Court precedent was not *Widmar* but *Hazelwood School District v. Kuhlmeier*.[29] *Kuhlmeier* had held that a high school principal may censor arguably offensive material from the school newspaper.[30] Like a high school newspaper, reasoned Judge Gibson's opinion, the university classroom is not an "open forum" but rather a restricted venue dedicated to a specific educational purpose.[31] To carry out that purpose, university administrators may exercise "editorial control over the style and content of student [or professor] speech in school-sponsored expressive activities so long as their actions are reasonably related to legitimate pedagogical concerns."[32] This broad authority apparently applies to professorial speech of any kind, whether religious or not.

That a professor in a university classroom has no greater freedom of expression than the student editor of a high school newspaper, and much less than a high school student who wears an armband protesting the Vietnam War,[33] might be surprising to those who recall the strong statements of support for academic freedom in Supreme Court opinions of the loyalty-oath era. For example, Justice Brennan's opinion for the Court in *Keyishian v. Board of Regents* said:

> Our Nation is deeply committed to safeguarding academic freedom, which is of transcendent value to all of us and not merely to the teachers concerned. That freedom is therefore a special concern of the First Amendment, which does not tolerate laws that cast a pall of orthodoxy over the classroom.[34]

Judge Gibson's opinion actually quoted that statement, but only to hold that it "cannot be extrapolated to deny schools command of their own courses," because "[f]ederal judges should not be ersatz deans or educators."[35] Academic freedom is protected not by the judiciary, wrote Judge Gibson, but by the presumed sensitivity of administrators to conditions in the academic labor market. "University officials are undoubtedly aware that quality faculty members will be hard to attract and retain if they are to be shackled in much of what they do."[36]

The district court had been particularly impressed by the selectivity of the University's policy, which did not exclude the *subject* of religion, but permitted only one kind of opinion on that subject to be discussed. The policy "would allow groups of young philosophers to meet to discuss their skepticism that a Supreme Being exists, or a group of political scientists to meet to debate the accuracy of the view that religion is the 'opium of the people.'"[37] The district judge noted that the University even offers courses in religion and theology, but prohibits instructors in those courses (but not in other subjects) from stating their personal views about the subjects they teach.[38] How can the First Amendment permit, much less require, that the content of speech be so selectively restricted?

The court of appeals answered that selectivity was entirely justified, because Bishop's viewpoint was particularly likely to cause "apprehension":

> [T]he University asks only that [Bishop] separate his personal and professional beliefs and that he not impart the former to his students during "instructional time" or under the guise of the courses he teaches in so-called optional classes.
>
> ... Dr. Bishop has tried to make much of the fact that the University has no policy for limiting the speech of its professors only to their subject areas.... [He] has filed numerous affidavits by other instructors at the University describing their extracurricular speech in the classroom as efforts to reach out to students. These attempts at professor-student affinity are laudable. But plainly some topics understandably produce more apprehension than comfort in students. Just as women students would find no comfort in an openly sexist instructor, an Islamic or Jewish student will not likely savor the Christian bias that Dr. Bishop professes.
> ... There is no suggestion that any other professor has produced student complaints or struck constitutional chords.[39]

Although the court of appeals insisted that it was for administrators to decide which opinions were too unsettling to be uttered in the classroom, the administrators themselves were under the impression that they were obligated to silence Bishop on legal grounds. In court, the University defended its position on the theory that Bishop's remarks violated the First Amendment's Establishment Clause.[40] The court of appeals did not formally decide the Establishment Clause question, but left little doubt as to what its decision would have been. "Dr. Bishop's optional class was particularly suspect," remarked the opinion, because the "creation/design aspect of his lecture could have lent itself to an analysis as found in *Edwards v. Aguillard*, 482 U.S. 578 (1987)."[41]

If the First Amendment forbids a state university to allow any mention of creation even in voluntary, after-class sessions, then freedom of expression must be a very subtle doctrine. If the legality of unorthodox speech turns on whether it has any educational value, then it may conceivably benefit students to hear an argument for an opinion that is pervasively denigrated in the rest of the curriculum. Professor Bishop holds such a disfavored opinion about his subject, the human body. He thinks that the body was produced by an intelligent designer rather than by an unguided naturalistic process. He therefore rejects the neo-Darwinistic theory of evolution, which is taught in most universities as fact. According to Darwinism, the appearance of intelligent design in biology is misleading. No designer was involved, because scientific investigation has established that a combination of random genetic changes and natural selection actually crafted the biological wonders that creationists have cited to support the argument from design. As George Gaylord Simpson, one of the most authoritative proponents of neo-Darwinism, put the point in his book *The Meaning of Evolution*: "Man is the result of a purposeless and natural process that did not have him in mind."[42]

Apparently, a statement like Simpson's is professional, scientific, and secular. To contradict that statement, on the other hand, is private, unscientific, and nonsecular. The state practices neutrality on religious questions by privileging statements like Simpson's and relegating opposing statements to the closet of private life. Here is how the court of appeals explained the matter:

> Dr. Bishop has expressed certain personal (perhaps even professional) opinions about his work that happen to have a religious source. The University has concluded that those opinions should not be represented in the courses he teaches at the University. The University has not suggested that Dr. Bishop cannot hold his particular views; express them, on his own time, far and wide and to whomever will listen; or write and publish, no doubt authoritatively, on them; nor could it so prohibit him. The University has simply said that he may not discuss his religious beliefs or opinions under the guise of University courses.[43]

But why forbid free discussion of "perhaps even professional" opinions on a controversial subject that is pervasively addressed in the University's curriculum? Why can the professor write, "no doubt authoritatively," but not talk? Would the University—or the Constitution—forbid him to assign those writings to a class that also considered the writings of George Gaylord Simpson?

At this point I should declare a personal interest. I am the author of a book, *Darwin on Trial*,[44] which supports Bishop's heretical opinion. In the book I argue that the neo-Darwinist theory is a myth, and specifically that an impartial interpretation of the scientific evidence does not support the claim that natural selection has the vast creative power that Darwinists claim for it. What is worse, I propose that unbiased people, including scientists, should "consider the possibility that life is what it so evidently seems to be, the product of creative intelligence."[45] In the opening chapter, I disclose my personal religious viewpoint, "because I do not exempt myself from the general rule that bias must be acknowledged and examined."[46] I have even assigned some of my writing on this subject to law students at the University of California. Have I violated all three prongs of the *Lemon* test?

Judge Gibson's opinion becomes much easier to understand if we infer that he regarded Bishop's opinions as absurd and offensive, and therefore deserving of censorship, but did not want to say so directly. Implicit in the opinion is a thinly veiled contempt that comes out unmistakably in the choice of language. Dishonesty is implied in that Bishop presents his notions "under the guise" of legitimate course work or in "so-called" optional classes. Only a tin ear could miss the sarcasm in the condescending remark that Bishop may publish "no doubt authoritative[]" opinions that the University properly forbids him to utter in class. Finally, the opinion implies that Bishop's acknowledgment of "Christian bias" was as offensive as if he had proudly declared himself to be a bigot.

If that view of Christianity is widespread in elite university and judicial circles, it is easy to see why Bishop was such an embarrassment to administrators concerned about their place in the academic pecking order. Agnostic fashion had to be enforced without departing from the law's famous neutrality on religious matters, of course. The time-honored way of doing that sort of thing is to employ the religious/secular dichotomy, which (ever so respectfully) silences the disfavored opinion in the name of First Amendment freedoms.

II THE SOCIOBIOLOGIST[47]

Vincent Sarich is a physical anthropologist at Berkeley who pioneered in the use of molecular evidence to measure the relative degree of biochemical similarity between humans and various other animals. Employing the "molecular clock hypothesis," Sarich (with Berkeley biochemist Allan Wilson) estimated that the last common ancestor of chimps and humans lived much more recently than had previously been thought. After a period of fierce resistance from fossil experts, the Wilson/Sarich date and methodology became widely accepted. The accomplishment established Sarich's reputation as a major figure in human evolution studies and as a formidable controversialist.

Sarich came to the attention of a different audience when he published a paper in the *California Monthly* (Berkeley's alumni magazine) with the provocative title "Making Racism Official at Cal."[48] His thesis was that Berkeley's undergraduate admissions policies systematically discriminate against whites. Whites comprise about 60% of high school graduates and 65% of those academically eligible for admission to the University of California, but they comprised only 34% of fall 1989 freshman registrants at Berkeley. For Asians the corresponding numbers were 8%, 20%, and 23%; for Hispanics, 20%, 7%, and 23%; and for Blacks, 8%, 2.5%, and 12%.[49] In plain language, Asians were hugely overrepresented in the freshman class in comparison to their share of the general population; Hispanics and Blacks were hugely overrepresented in comparison to their representation in the population deemed academically qualified on the basis of high school performance; and Whites were underrepresented in comparison to both their share of the general population and of the population deemed academically qualified.

The social and political factors that produced these figures are no mystery. Like other universities, Berkeley has been under strong moral and legal pressure to increase the percentage of Black and Hispanic students at least to their level in the population. At the same time, Asian-American groups have vigorously and effectively protested the "discrimination" Berkeley has practiced by not admitting Asians on the basis of their academic performance. This mix of pressures has produced a tacit policy of population parity (generously measured) for Blacks and Hispanics, and admission by grades and test scores for Asians. Somebody has to pay the price.[50]

Sarich argued that the admissions policy had created a two-tiered student body, "separable on racial/ethnic grounds, and increasingly divergent from one another academically, socially, and in ethos."[51] The consequences include increased racial tension, discouragement of the pursuit of excellence among all groups, and the decay of a great public educational institution. Sarich concluded that the costs of Berkeley's racial policy "are obvious and large; the benefits, if any, difficult to perceive, and certainly undocumented."[52] Dinesh D'Souza made similar arguments, using Berkeley as the prime example of race-based admissions policies.[53]

Sarich provoked hostility not just because he concluded that the costs of the university's admissions policy outweigh its benefits but because he insisted publicly that real academic costs exist. The university's official position is that policies aimed at achieving (racial) diversity do not sacrifice (academic) excellence.[54] Berkeley officials in particular insist that the mean Scholastic Aptitude Test score for entering freshmen has steadily increased, arguing that this figure establishes that academic quality and racial diversity have improved in tandem.[55] Advocacy groups that support affirmative action are still more vehement in disputing any suggestion that less qualified students are being admitted to meet racial targets. Anyone who wants a relatively peaceful life in Berkeley does not seek occasions for asserting a different interpretation of the facts.

Sarich's admission paper did not spark that genuine debate over academic quality and diversity desired by Katharine Bartlett.[56] Instead, it led to a retaliatory demonstration directed at disrupting his teaching in the introductory anthropology course.[57] As a scientist who made his reputation studying molecules rather than tribes, and as a political conservative (by university standards), Sarich is hardly in the mainstream of anthropology. Moreover, he teaches an "advocacy course," in which students get a heavy dose of the Sarich viewpoint. In a nutshell, the Sarich viewpoint is that the logic of evolutionary biology should be extended to questions of human nature and social policy.[58] This approach is highly controversial because the political left regards anything reminiscent of "social Darwinism" as pseudoscientific propaganda for the status quo. Although Sarich's teaching was popular with many students, there were also continual complaints, articulated especially in courses in Women's Studies.[59] The publicity given the admissions paper suggested to these critics that Sarich's philosophy might have tangible political consequences. Since Anthropology I is a required course for majors in a field that appeals to many students having intense interests in the politics of race and gender, the mix was explosive.

The explosion came in November 1990, when more than fifty students invaded Sarich's classroom to demonstrate against his "racist, sexist, and homophobic" opinions. The opinions in question were culled from the admissions paper and from lecture transcripts that Sarich made available to students as a study guide. The most frequently quoted statement was Sarich's comment in the admissions paper that excellence and diversity are at cross purposes because "unfortunately, the levels of qualification, preparation, or motivation are not randomly distributed with respect to race and ethnicity."[60] Sarich had added that he attributed relatively poor academic performance by Blacks and Hispanics to cultural influences, not genetic differences, but this important qualification did not seem to mitigate the offense and was subsequently ignored.

Sarich had also said in his lectures that human brain size steadily increased as human intelligence evolved. A correlation of brain size and intelligence in the remote past is uncontroversial and probably an essential premise of the theory that humans evolved from small-brained apes,[61] but Sarich offended contemporary sensitivities by arguing that the correlation might still exist.[62] He went so far as to suggest that it would be appropriate to conduct research on whether differences in male and female mental capabilities are related to the smaller average size of women's brains.[63] Finally, Sarich had said in his lectures that homosexuality in humans is culturally rare and not genetically determined because natural selection would not foster a gene for a nonreproductive sexual orientation.[64]

The demonstration was resisted by many of the students actually enrolled in the class,[65] who defended Sarich (or at least their right to hear him teach) vigorously. The point at issue between the enrolled students and the demonstrators was nicely captured in an exchange reported in the campus disciplinary report:[66] One student yelled, "How can you argue about his teachings if you don't really know what he says?"[67] to which a demonstrator responded, "How can we have intelligent discussion if he doesn't believe we belong in school?"[68] The demonstrators denounced minority students in the class as traitors for listening to Sarich. A teaching assistant tried to mollify the demonstrators by proposing a debate, but they shouted down the invitation, with one remarking that "FDR wouldn't debate Hitler."[69] There was no physical violence, but the uproar and distraction finally forced Sarich to give up his attempt to finish the class.

Berkeley's newly installed Chancellor Chang-Lin Tien issued a statement saying that the disruption would be investigated with an eye towards disciplinary action, but also that there would be an investigation of Sarich's teaching if allegations of discriminatory remarks were made in a proper manner. Members of the leaderless Anthropology Department also took tentative steps in the direction of investigating Sarich.[70] Faculty senate committees were horrified that responsible authorities reacted to a classroom disruption by proposing an investigation of the victim[71] and issued statements deploring the demonstration as a violation of academic freedom. In the end the demonstrators received only meaningless warnings as punishment, and nobody investigated Sarich.

The principal aftermath of the incident was a public forum a month later, at which Sarich defended his views against criticism from other faculty members. On this occasion the diversity issue became entwined with an ongoing debate among Berkeley's biochemistry professors concerning the materialist reductionism that dominates this branch of science. Biochemistry Professor Richard Strohman complained that "the lay public is under the impression that DNA controls everything."[72] Strohman threw cold water on this scientific hubris, implying that speculation about genetic causes of human behavior goes way beyond what science can establish.

Sarich defended his emphasis on the genetic role in human behavior by pointing out that most other anthropologists slight genetics and attribute everything to culture. He also added his own voice to the criticism of reductionism, complaining that "[s]cientists act like people are controlled by a puppeteer.... They tend to argue, 'Is the puppeteer your genes or is the puppeteer society?' You never hear about an individual's will."[73] The reason we never hear about it is that free will is a meaningless concept to a materialist reductionist, who (by definition) assumes that all events have material causes. If Sarich really means that people have the power to change their traits of character by an exercise of free will, then to that extent he is, by his own definition, a creationist.[74]

The ultimate judgment on Sarich from the anthropological left was delivered at the public forum by his departmental colleague, Professor Nancy Scheper-Hughes. Asserting the need to protect students from false teaching because of their "impressionable minds,"[75] she dismissed Sarich's theories from the realm of science in precisely the language Sarich would use in speaking of creationism: "[I]t isn't bad science, it isn't science at all."[76] Professor Sarich, meet Professor Bishop.

EPILOGUE

The moral of my stories is not that there are pressures to conform in the university. Of course there are such pressures, as there always were. A university is not Hyde Park Corner, where cranks of every description hold forth from their soap boxes. It is meant to be a place where knowledge is gained through research and then transmitted in classrooms. It is also a place where ideas and ideologies are taken seriously, which implies that they may be expounded passionately. Expression of opinion is on the whole free in most universities, in the strictly formal sense that disciplinary action against either faculty or students for offensive statements is rare. This does not mean, however, that all opinions or theories are treated equally. First, freedom of expression itself can be used against dissidents, in the form of protest demonstrations, hecklers, and strident editorials in campus newspapers. Students may apply political standards when rating the teaching quality of their professors on forms which administrators use in deciding who gets rehired or promoted.

The most important pressures towards conformity, however, arise from the very nature of the academic enterprise. Any academic institution endorses some fundamental doctrines that its ruling authorities consider to be true and works mightily to transmit these doctrines to the minds of students as *knowledge*. The Evolutionary Biology Department teaches that the Darwinian theory of evolution is *true,* not just that it appeals to some people who speak for the interpretive community that calls itself "science." The liberal arts departments teach—or used to teach—that something called Western Civilization has a literary and intellectual tradition of unique excellence. Persons who are skilled at propagating knowledge are given good grades, graduate fellowships, and tenured professorships. Persons who try to advance beliefs that are contrary to received knowledge are considered to be ignorant, and so they face heavy discouragement. The established academic authorities consider it their duty to cure ignorance, not to reward it.

This encouragement of knowledge and discrimination against ignorance is proper and even inevitable in principle, but it may be oppressive in practice. Unconventional theories might be true, or at least stimulating, and they might offend by rousing the more conventional members of the university community from their dogmatic slumbers. Wherever we find power, we also find prejudice. Aspiring scholars who consider themselves to be victims of prejudice are not necessarily helpless, however. If they have influence of one kind or another, they might persuade the university's ruling bodies to give them academic departments of their own, in which they will have the power to decide what qualifies as knowledge and what should be disqualified as prejudice. If their influence grows, they might eventually be able to transform the university itself.

The battle to control the university's intellectual agenda is no recent innovation. For much of the nineteenth century most universities were church-sponsored, and as such they did not willingly give a platform to atheists or sponsors of free love. Later in the nineteenth century, scientific naturalism began to replace Christian theism as the governing ideology. One consequence of this development was that Darwinian evolution acquired the status of knowledge, and students who did not accept it as such were classified as ignorant. That a professor of science would tell a class that he did not believe in naturalistic evolution became unthinkable, and a university that tolerated that sort of nonsense would have cause to fear a loss of academic status. This fear explains the determination of University of Alabama administrators to exclude Phillip Bishop's mild dissent.

Ironically, the prestigious institutions to which the Alabama administrators looked for approval are themselves in turmoil and possibly on the verge of another transformation in their governing philosophy. Scientific naturalism still reigns supreme among senior faculty and in the natural science departments, but in the liberal arts and social sciences a relativistic pluralism is gaining ground. The historian Page Smith, whose description of the university's selective open-mindedness began this Review Essay, wrote that the nonscientific departments in the recent past suffered from "physics envy." No more. The newly fashionable post-Modernist model of knowledge is not based on scientific empiricism, but on literary criticism, and its philosopher kings are Richard Rorty, Stanley Fish, and Jacques Derrida. Knowledge in this model is relative to culture, and no single picture of reality has absolute authority over rival cultural understandings.

As new groups have begun to assert themselves, the philosophy of cultural relativism has made it easy to justify the institution of advocacy departments, in subjects like ethnic studies, women's studies, and now gay and lesbian studies. The premise of these departments is that the groups in question have been silenced and stigmatized, and therefore they need to find their own voices and assert their own theories of knowledge. This premise implies a certain homogeneity of ideological approach. One does not expect to find many professors of women's studies who favor restrictions on abortion, although many women take that position. Just as the Evolutionary Biology Department by definition rejects the creationist, women's studies by definition excludes the antifeminist.

The Sarich incident is an example of how a theory of knowledge that has wide support in the university can generate bitter conflict if it is taken to its logical conclusion before the wrong audience. The theory in question is that scientific investigation is the basis of all real knowledge and that science ought to be free to investigate all subjects. But what if the investigation seems to point in directions that many consider to be profoundly offensive? Is it a violation of academic freedom to discourage a professor from conducting research into the relationship between brain size and intelligence, or from trying to convince a class of undergraduates that such research is likely to lead to interesting and controversial conclusions? Scientific naturalism presupposes a fundamental distinction between fact and value, which implies that the results of scientific research will not necessarily be pleasing to any group's cherished values, be they religious or political. But the conclusions of scientific researchers might be erroneous and might cause tangible harm before their error is exposed. Should a university community require its scientists to exercise restraint when dealing with sensitive subjects, in view of this potential for harm?

No one can answer such questions adequately in the abstract. They are especially difficult to answer in the context of a contemporary university, where the nature and even the very existence of objective knowledge is in question. If the university is dedicated both to the pursuit of knowledge and to the realization of equality, which goal has priority in the event of a conflict? The founding document of our national tradition states that "all men [we would now say all persons] are created equal." This means that, despite their differing abilities and attainments, all persons are of equal importance in the sight of their creator, who is the author of values. Human equality in the Declaration of Independence sense is a sacred dogma, and as such it can never be discredited by any scientific discovery or rationalistic argument.

But suppose men and women are not created, and instead evolved by some haphazard process from animals. Suppose that dogmas exist no more, because the author of values has been exposed as an imposter and all persons must now decide for themselves what they will believe. On what foundation, then, can human equality rest? Is equality a fact everyone can see, a scientific hypothesis open for testing, or a story that appeals to certain kinds of listeners? It isn't easy to see how either literary theory or unfettered scientific research into human capacities can be trusted to support the ideals of equality to which the contemporary university is formally dedicated. People still have their sacred dogmas, of course, even if they do not call them that. They just do not know what makes them sacred.

The status of human equality is not a puzzle for me. That is because I still believe that humanity was *created,* and therefore I understand that there are moral axioms that take precedence over the temporarily alluring products of rationalistic disciplines. To me, the most interesting problem in philosophy is how we are to recognize the axioms, so we know what to protect from the indiscriminate corrosiveness of skeptical analysis. It is a tough problem, even when you understand how to ask the question. If you think you can build values on reason, and have adopted a model of reason that consigns value judgments to the realm of subjective belief, you do not have a prayer.

Notes

1. PAGE SMITH, KILLING THE SPIRIT: HIGHER EDUCATION IN AMERICA 5 (1990). Page Smith, the author of a famous multivolume history of the United States, retired in 1974 from his professorship at the University of California at Santa Cruz. He was one of many persons, formerly regarded as very liberal critics of American society and its universities, whose voice sounds conservative in today's atmosphere.
2. *See* Eugene D. Genovese, *Heresy, Yes—Sensitivity, No.* THE NEW REPUBLIC, APR. 15, 1991, at 30.
3. *See* C. Vann Woodward, *Freedom & the Universities,* N.Y. REV. BOOKS, July 18, 1991, at 32.
4. *The MacNeil/Lehrer NewsHour: The Big Chill* (PBS television broadcast, June 17–21, 1991) (transcripts Nos. 4056–4060), *available in LEXIS*, Nexis Library, SCRIPT File.

5. *See* Katharine T. Bartlett, *Some Factual Correctness About Political Correctness,* WALL ST. J., June 6, 1991, at A19.
6. See *id.*
7. *Id.*
8. *Id.*
9. *Id.*
10. Except when otherwise noted, the source for the facts relating to the "creationist" story is the opinion by Judge Guin in *Bishop v. Aronov,* 732 F. Supp. 1562 (N.D. Ala. 1990) [hereinafter *Bishop I*], rev'd, 926 F.2d 1066 (11th Cir. 1991), *cert. denied,* 112 S. Ct. 3026 (1992). Although the Court of Appeals reversed Judge Guin's legal conclusions, it adopted his findings of fact, which were based upon stipulations and undisputed affidavits. *See Bishop v. Aronov,* 926 F.2d 1066, 1068 (11th Cir. 1991) [hereinafter *Bishop II*], *cert. denied,* 112 S. Ct. 3026 (1992). Professor Michael McConnell of the University of Chicago Law School filed a petition for certiorari in the case which refers to some other details from the undisputed record that are not mentioned in the district court and court of appeals opinions. *See* Petition for a Writ of Certiorari at 2-9, *filed sub nom. Bishop v. Delchamps,* 112 S. Ct. 294 (1991) (No. 91-286), *cert. denied,* 112 S. Ct. 3026 (1992) [hereinafter *Delchamps* Petition].
11. *Bishop II,* 926 F.2d at 1068.
12. *Id.*
13. *Id.*
14. *Id.*
15. *Bishop I,* 732 F. Supp. at 1563.
16. *Id.* at 1564.
17. The facts in this paragraph are taken from the undisputed record in the case as summarized by Professor Michael McConnell in *Delchamps* Petition, *supra* note 10, at 2–9.
18. *Id.* at 6.
19. In *Lemon v. Kurtzman,* 403 U.S. 602 (1971), the Supreme Court set out a famous three-part test for determining whether a state statute is consistent with the First Amendment's Establishment Clause. "First, the statute must have a secular legislative purpose; second, its principal or primary effect must be one that neither advances nor inhibits religion; finally, the statute must not foster 'an excessive government entanglement with religion.'" *Id.* at 612–13 (citations omitted).
20. *Delchamps* Petition, *supra* note 10, at 6.
21. *See Bishop I,* 732 F. Supp. at 1564.
22. *Id.* (quoting the disciplinary memorandum sent by Westerfield to Bishop).
23. *See id.* Bishop used a blind grading system, and so in theory the student's identity would have no effect on grading. The district court conditioned its approval of Bishop's practices on the requirement that he continue to use a blind grading system. See *id.* at 1569. Of course, no similar requirement was imposed upon professors who express personal opinions of other kinds that students might also be tempted to mimic in order to get a good grade.
24. *Id.* at 1564.
25. *See id.* at 1565 (citing *Widmar v. Vincent,* 454 U.S. 263 (1981)).
26. *See Widmar v. Vincent,* 454 U.S. 263, 276 (1981). Although the district court was apparently unaware of it, another state university had followed the *Widmar* principle in a controversy very similar to the *Bishop* case. University of Georgia Professor Henry F. Schaefer, an internationally famous quantum chemist, gave voluntary,

after-hours lectures on campus for students at which he explained his Christian faith and his doubts about Darwinism. Other faculty members demanded that the University stop allowing Schaefer to use its facilities for religious speech, but the University's President ruled that Schaefer had freedom to express his thoughts on campus property since the lectures were not university-sponsored. The ruling was not challenged in court, and Schaefer has continued to speak freely. *See* Motion for Leave to File Brief Amici Curiae and Brief of Dr. Henry F. Schaefer III, Dr. Gerald R. Bergman, Dr. Clinton H. Graves, and Dr. Byron R. Johnson as Amici Curiae in Support of the Petition for Certiorari at 2, *Bishop v. Delchamps*, 60 U.S.L.W. 3292 (U.S. Oct. 15, 1991) (No. 91-286), *cert. denied*, 112 S. Ct. 3026 (1992).
27. *Bishop II*, 926 F.2d at 1078.
28. Senior Circuit Judge Floyd R. Gibson of the Eighth Circuit was sitting on the Eleventh Circuit by designation.
29. 484 U.S. 260 (1988).
30. *See id.* at 276.
31. *See Bishop II*, 926 F.2d at 1071.
32. *Id.* at 1074 (quoting *Kuhlmeier*, 484 U.S. at 273) (bracketed phrase "[or professor]" added in *Bishop II* opinion).
33. In *Tinker v. Des Moines Independent Community School District*, 393 U.S. 503, 514 (1969), the Supreme Court held that school authorities could not forbid a student to wear a black armband (protesting the Vietnam War) to school, absent a showing that the forbidden conduct would substantially interfere with the work of the school or impinge upon the rights of other students.
34. 385 U.S. 589, 603 (1967).
35. *Bishop II*, 926 F.2d at 1075.
36. *Id.* The United States District Court for the Southern District of New York took a different position on the judicial protection of academic freedom in *Levin v. Harleston*, 770 F. Supp. 895 (S.D.N.Y. 1991). Michael Levin is a philosophy professor at the City College of the City University of New York who has published various provocative statements on racial issues, in particular claiming that "on average, blacks are significantly less intelligent than whites." *Id.* at 902. As a consequence his classes were disrupted by demonstrators, the college president appointed a committee to investigate his writings with a view to possible disciplinary action, and administrators wrote to students in his introductory philosophy class that they would create a "shadow section" for students who wished to take the course but avoid Professor Levin. *Id.* at 903-8. District Judge Conboy held that appointment of the investigating committee and the institution of "shadow sections" violated Levin's free speech and tenure rights. *See id.* at 919-25. The court permanently enjoined the college from investigating Levin's writings and also ordered the administrators to take reasonable steps to prevent disruption of his classes. *See id.* at 927. The *Levin* case is distinguishable from the case discussed in this Review Essay, however, because it did not involve the authority of academic administrators to control what a professor says in the classroom. Levin apparently did not introduce his views on racial issues into his philosophy courses. The controversy involved solely his out-of-class writings. *See generally id.* at 899-903.
37. *Bishop I*, 732 F. Supp. at 1568 (quoting *Widmar v. Vincent*, 454 U.S. 263, 281 (1981) (Stevens, J., concurring)).
38. *See id.* at 1567-68.
39. *Bishop II*, 926 F.2d at 1071-72 (citation omitted).

40. *Bishop I,* 732 F. Supp. at 1565.
41. *Bishop II,* 926 F.2d at 1077. *Edwards v. Aguillard* held unconstitutional a Louisiana statute requiring balanced treatment in science classes for "creation-science" and "evolution-science" on the ground that the Legislature's purpose "was clearly to advance the religious viewpoint that a supernatural being created humankind." 482 U.S. at 591.
42. GEORGE G. SIMPSON, THE MEANING OF EVOLUTION 345 (rev. ed. 1967).
43. *Bishop II,* 926 F.2d at 6 (footnote omitted).
44. PHILLIP E. JOHNSON, DARWIN ON TRIAL (1991).
45. *Id.* at 110.
46. *Id.* at 14.
47. Except where otherwise indicated, the source for information about Vincent Sarich and the class disruption at Berkeley is Paul Selvin, *The Raging Bull of Berkeley,* 251 SCIENCE 368 (1991).
48. Vincent Sarich, Making Racism Official at Cal, CAL. MONTHLY, Sept. 1990, at 17.
49. *Id.*
50. Berkeley Chancellor Ira M. Heyman apologized publicly in April 1989 for pursuing admissions policies aimed at increasing minority representation that had the unintended effect of disadvantaging Asians who obtained high scores on aptitude tests and high grades in high school. Berkeley promised to stop discriminating against high-aptitude Asians without otherwise abandoning its goal of ensuring racial balance in the student body. *See* DINESH D'SOUZA, ILLIBERAL EDUCATION 30 & n.30 (1991) [hereinafter cited by page number].
51. Sarich, *supra* note 48, at 18.
52. *Id.*
53. *See* pp. 24–58 (detailing admissions policies and their effects on individual students and the campus at large).
54. *See, e.g.,* Letter from Vincent Sarich, Professor, University of California at Berkeley, to William French Smith, Regent, University of California 3 (Apr. 4, 1990) (on file with author) (quoting university administration officials as having said "these achievements are not at the expense of quality" and "everyone admitted to the school is 'University of California-eligible'").
55. *See* Committee on Admissions and Enrollment, Freshman Admissions at Berkeley: A Policy for the 1990's and Beyond (Karabel Report) (May 1989) (committee report, on file with author). The Karabel Report states that "[t]he great accomplishment of the overall admissions policy has, in our view, been its capacity to continue the process of diversification of Berkeley's student body at the same time it has maintained and even raised the academic level of the freshman class." *Id.* at 26, *quoted in* Letter from Vincent Sarich to William French Smith, *supra* note 54, at 5. Sarich's article in the *California Monthly* attributed the rise in mean SAT scores to a continuing rise in scores of admitted whites and Asians (about 60% of admittees) during the 1980s. In other words, the rise in mean academic indicator scores does not contradict Sarich's claim that the class is increasingly composed of distinct groups whose academic qualifications barely overlap. On the other hand, former Berkeley Chancellor Ira M. Heyman in a letter of response noted among other things that Sarich presented no evidence about how well various categories of students perform once admitted. *See* Letter from Ira M. Heyman, Chancellor, University of California at Berkeley, to William French Smith, Regent, University of California 5 (May 9, 1990) (on file with author). Heyman cited figures to

support the conclusion that "the GPAs of underrepresented students are much higher than one would expect from Professor Sarich's observations." *Id.*

56. *See supra* text accompanying notes 5–9. Ideally, such a debate would not be limited to the relatively sterile issue of whether efforts at racial diversity in admissions are in principle a good thing. In the contemporary social climate an institution like the University of California simply must use its resources for the benefit of all the major racial and ethnic groups of the state. The use of race as a factor in admissions is like the use of medicine: taken for the right purpose and in the right amount, medicine alleviates illness without devastating side effects. To determine the right medicine and the right dosage, it is necessary to discuss honestly the underlying illness and the actual effects of the treatment.

57. *See* T. Christian Miller, Students Clash in Anthro, THE DAILY CALIFORNIAN, Nov. 8, 1990, at 1.

58. Professor Sarich generously provided me with transcripts of his Anthropology I lectures and other material relating to the course content. His central thesis is that, while most educated people agree that Darwinian evolution is responsible for the human body, they refuse to acknowledge the implications of Darwinian theory in the area of human behavior, politics, and ethics. Most left/liberal intellectuals, including even leading evolutionary biologists, are essentially "creationists" when it comes to human affairs. They have merely substituted human society for God as the creator of human nature. In other words, they deny that evolution has formed human nature in important ways and imagine instead that our nature is a blank slate upon which culture can write at will.

Specifically, these humanistic creationists refuse to acknowledge that human *in*equality rather than equality is the norm, because "the evolutionary process continues to run on variation and that variation must be functionally significant." Vincent Sarich, Notes, Lecture No. 3, at 1 (Aug. 29, 1990) (on file with author). This leads them into absurdities such as imagining that male/female behavioral differences have no biological bases, or that it is possible to achieve an artificial equality of outcomes by social coercion. Such utopian projects end in unfreedom (and also inequality) because they ignore the constraints imposed by evolution. Specific applications of this general theme are addressed throughout the course.

59. Sarich's teaching materials include a paper that was written in 1986 by a freshman woman who was taking Women's Studies 10 and Anthropology I (with Sarich) at the same time and naively wrote a paper for the former course defending Sarich against charges of sexism. The teaching assistant who graded the paper could not restrain her fury that anyone would say anything good about Sarich and covered the paper with heavy-handed political comments. *See* Vincent Sarich, Lecture Materials 27–34 (1990) (on file with author).

60. *See, e.g.,* Miller, *supra* note 57, at 11 (quoting Sarich, *supra* note 48, at 18).

61. Here is what Darwin himself wrote on the subject:

> As the various mental faculties were gradually developed, the brain would almost certainly have become larger. No one, I presume, doubts that the large size of the brain in man, relatively to his body, in comparison with that of the gorilla or orang, is closely connected with his higher mental powers. . . . On the other hand, no one supposes that the intellect of any two animals or of any two men can be accurately gauged by the cubic contents of their skulls. . . .
>
> The belief that there exists in man some close relation between the size of the brain and the development of the intellectual faculties is supported by the compar-

ison of the skulls of savage and civilised races, of ancient and modern people, and by the analogy of the whole vertebrate series.

Charles Darwin, *The Descent of Man* 145–46 (photo reprint, Princeton University Press 1981) (1871).

62. In one lecture Sarich made his point about brain size with a pungent review of Stephen J. Gould, *The Mismeasure of Man* (1981):

This book received the Pulitzer Prize and was spoken of approvingly by just about everyone except Professor Sarich who thinks that the book is mostly nonsense. It is particularly nonsensical in its extensive castigation of his professional ancestors in the 19th and early 20th centuries who were fascinated with the idea [of] variation in brain size of human beings and its significance. These individuals measured heads both externally and (after death) internally. . . . Gould spends about half of his book denigrating this activity as at best useless and at worst intensively racist and sexist. . . . [I]f you read only that book . . . you would never know that the human brain had increased (tripled) in size over the last [two] million years. There is not a hint in that book that that happened. Why? Professor Sarich thinks that that fact is not mentioned because the only way that the human brain could have increased in size over time is if somehow larger brains (conferred) . . . fitness on their possessors. If they conferred greater fitness on their possessors in the past, then they would also (presumably) do so in the present. This would invalidate the entire thesis of Gould's book.

Vincent Sarich, Notes, Lecture No. 16, at 4 (Oct. 3, 1990) (on file with author) (significant typographical errors in original transcript corrected by author).

63. Offensive or not, studies of male/female differences in brain size and structure are very much in the scientific mainstream. For example, a 1991 article in *Science* by Ann Gibbons observes that:

[T]here is now a solid body of data indicating sex differences in the brains of almost every mammalian family examined so far: rodents, birds, monkeys, and— most recently and most intriguingly—human beings. . . . Men's brains are on average larger than women's by 15%—about twice the difference in average body size between men and women.

Ann Gibbons, The Brain as "Sexual Organ," 253 *Science* 957, 957–58 (1991). Attempts to explain behavioral differences between men and women on the basis of brain anatomy are controversial, but researchers "speculate that [brain differences] have roots in strong evolutionary pressures on the sexes during prehistory when the brain was expanding rapidly." *Id.* at 958. A companion article by Constance Holden began with the observation that "a large body of evidence, accumulated over many decades, suggest[s] that there are some differences in cognition and perception between men and women." Constance Holden, Is "Gender Gap" Narrowing?, 253 *Science* 959, 959 (1991). The subject is "something of a political minefield," however, and all specific claims are disputed and doubtful. *Id.*

64. The Sarich viewpoint on homosexuality is that heterosexuality promotes reproduction, and therefore is more natural in evolutionary terms. Homosexuality is therefore unlikely to have a genetic cause. In other cultures it is rare as an exclusive adult predisposition, although adolescent homosexual experimentation is common. Sarich explained contemporary male homosexuality as growing out of the fact that some males are more inclined to the feminine side of the spectrum of male/female

differences. Males having relatively more feminine emotional natures might feel less need to complement themselves with a heterosexual relationship, and might experience greater difficulty in fulfilling culturally imposed models of masculine behavior. In most cultures adolescents tend to grow out of homosexual tendencies because "[s]ocial completeness as an adult requires complementation," and "[i]t is set up evolutionarily and biologically that that complementation is set up with an individual of the opposite sex." Vincent Sarich, Notes, Lecture No. 16. at 1 (Oct. 3, 1990) (on file with author).

65. See Miller, *supra* note 57, at 11.
66. The source for the facts related in this paragraph is the unpublished report of Alan T. Kolling, the Administrative Analyst who officially investigated the disruption. See Report of Alan T. Kolling, Principal Administrative Analyst, University of California at Berkeley, to Francisco J. Hernandez, Dean of Student Life, University of California at Berkeley (Feb. 26, 1991) (on file with author) [hereinafter Kolling].
67. Kolling, *supra* note 66, at 3. The Kolling report amplified this statement:

> Interestingly, almost all of the students claimed to have some disagreement with Sarich and his teachings, and said they enjoyed challenging him in his optional study sections or during office hours. This was apparently one of the major reasons why the demonstrators won few converts in the class: the students taking the course felt that the demonstrators neither understood what Sarich said in class nor realized the extent to which they disagreed with his material. All seemed disappointed that the parties failed to engage in a debate because they were interested in knowing what the demonstrators really had to say and because they believed that Sarich was quite open to participating in such a debate.

Id. at 7.
68. *Id.* at 3.
69. *Id.* at 5.
70. The Anthropology Department at Berkeley is so divided and opposed to hierarchy that it has no chairperson. The Vice-Chancellor advised the Department that the Academic Senate's Committee on Courses was the appropriate body to investigate complaints against teaching, much to the surprise of the Committee on Courses, which did nothing.
71. Experienced faculty members did not take seriously the Chancellor's promise to take disciplinary action against the demonstrators. It is notorious at Berkeley that threats of disciplinary action against demonstrations are so much hot air, because substantial punishment is never imposed. Students will not testify against demonstrators, and aggressive lawyers know how to stymie the overjudicialized campus disciplinary proceedings. When misdemeanor criminal charges are brought, Berkeley jurors will not convict. In some circumstances administrators might have a legal obligation to take reasonable steps to prevent disruption of classes, however. See *supra* note 36.
72. T. Christian Miller, Faculty Challenge Sarich, THE DAILY CALIFORNIAN, Dec. 7, 1990, at 1.
73. *Id.* at 1.
74. See *supra* note 58.
75. Miller, *supra* note 72, at 1.
76. *Id.* The official report by analyst Allan Kolling contains an interesting reference to this confrontation:

> Many of the students who attended the . . . debate between Sarich and other anthropologists expressed anger at the way Sarich was treated by his colleagues, especially Nancy Scheper-Hughes. Some expressed admiration for Sarich's 'bravery' while at least one student felt that Scheper-Hughes' behavior at the forum was as 'disruptive' as some of that exhibited by the demonstrators. This particular student expressed some apprehension about testifying against demonstrators since *faculty members had behaved in an equally outrageous manner towards Sarich and would not be held accountable.* It bears repeating that many of these same students stressed their disagreement with Sarich's material during my interview.
>
> Kolling, *supra* note 66, at 7.

Questions for Discussion

1. How would you characterize Johnson's tone in "The Creationist and the Sociobiologist"? Where does it seem most neutral and objective? Where is it most sarcastic or ironic? How do you know?
2. The debate about "political correctness" finally comes down to a debate about what a university should *be*. If the university is an open "marketplace of ideas," presumably *all* ideas—no matter how repugnant to some people—should be allowed a place. But is that either realistic or, finally, even desirable? Where would *you* draw the line between the free expression of *all* ideas and the desire, maybe even the need, to limit offensive or dangerous speech? (How do you define "offensive" and "dangerous"?)
3. Critics of all kinds have long debated the question of whether art has a moral side. Is it possible, they ask, to admire as fine art (or literature or music) a piece whose values we deplore? In Johnson's terms, can we appreciate Milton's art if we are repelled by his ideas about women? What do *you* see as the relationship between art and morality? And, if you were to design a course syllabus, how would you deal with the fact that ideas of morality shift across time and across cultures?
4. To what extent should instructors reveal possible biases, as Phillip Bishop did? If you had been in Bishop's classroom, how would you have responded to his revelations about his personal beliefs? Would you have felt differently if the instructor had expressed beliefs about politics? About sexual preference? About race or gender?
5. Were you surprised to learn that Johnson holds some of the same beliefs that Bishop does and that, as a professor, he has been in a position similar to Bishop's? If you were not surprised, what clues did you find that indicated Johnson's own bias? If you were surprised, why do you think Johnson delayed revealing this information?
6. Like art critics, scientists often debate about the extent to which their work should be held to moral standards. If science exists independent of culture and morality, what are we to do with scientific investigations

that may lead to truths repugnant to us? Think, in other words, about how you would have responded if you were a student in Sarich's class.

7. The two stories Johnson tells raise big questions about the nature of the university and the obligations it has to its students and the larger society. Consider the assumptions behind Bishop's and Sarich's ideas and their teaching. To what extent do you agree with their notions of good teaching and the ideal university?

Questions for Research and Writing

1. Citing evidence from the history of the 1960s and the bumper stickers of the present, Johnson begins his review by asserting that the political left has long held a rhetorical advantage insofar as it has seemed to promote free speech and to encourage the questioning of authority. Examine the political rhetoric of earlier decades. To what extent does the rhetoric of those on the political left reveal that they have what Johnson (and others) calls the "moral high ground"? (Be careful to focus on the *rhetoric* of the political writings and speeches; it's possible to disagree with someone who has, nevertheless, built his or her foundation on the moral high ground.)

2. Do some research on "academic freedom." Where did the concept originate? Where have individual instructors, departments, universities, and the courts drawn the line between academic freedom and the needs of the institution or the greater community? To what extent do students, instructors, university administrators, and the general public agree about where those lines should be drawn?

3. Johnson's questions about how our universities should respond to scientific investigations into sensitive areas (the correspondence between brain size and intelligence in men and women, for instance) find an echo in questions scientists have been forced to ask frequently. Investigate the response that faced one of the following scientists who proposed a theory that shook his society's values and beliefs: Copernicus, Galileo, Darwin, or Einstein. How welcome would these scientists and their theories be in the universities Johnson describes?

4. Locate a copy of Sarich's "Making Racism Official at Cal" and analyze its use of logic and language. How effective are Sarich's language and logic? How justified are his critics in their criticisms of him?

INTRODUCTION TO THE WORLD OF WOMEN'S STUDIES

Daphne Patai and Noretta Koertge

> *What follows is the first chapter in Professors Patai and Koertge's book,* Professing Feminism: Cautionary Tales from the Strange World of Women's Studies. *Avowed feminists, Patai and Koertge take an unusual approach to their subject, writing less about the issues that concern feminists than about the methods by which feminists, particularly scholars in women's studies programs, approach their subject and interact with each other, the campus community, and the society at large. Why, they ask, are the debates within women's studies programs often so rancorous? What is the proper relationship between scholarship and politics? Although their focus is on women's studies programs, the issues raised here are central to understanding the role of the university as a whole. To what extent are scholars and teachers obligated to keep their scholarly and ideological lives separate? To what extent is that possible?*

Changes in the status of women are undoubtedly among the most important social developments of the twentieth century. Each demand for equality has been contested; each step has made a vivid impression on the women who lived through it; each advance has become part of the birthright of the next generation. Despite the apparent lull in—and to some extent, even reversal of—women's gains during the 1950s, the contemporary feminist movement in the United States, now in its fourth decade, has carried the redefinition of women and their roles steadily forward.

In important ways, both intellectual and practical, this movement's agenda was shaped by the work of feminist scholars in the academy. The result of their efforts has been an enormous flowering of Women's Studies programs, feminist scholarship, and women's culture, as well as an increasing public awareness of job discrimination, domestic abuse, sexual assaults, and other impediments placed on women in the public and private spheres. Complementing all this attention, albeit on a more modest scale, have been political and economic gains for at least some women.

Women's Studies, which began in the late 1960s as individual courses typically offered through humanities departments, proliferated throughout the United States during the 1970s and 1980s. Now, after two and a half decades, there are more than six hundred undergraduate and several dozen graduate programs at colleges and universities. This success drove, and in turn was driven by, a spate of scholarly publications in various fields. During this time, too, the use of gender as a powerful conceptual tool and a key category of analysis in the humanities and social sciences transformed entire fields, of which feminist literary criticism was the first to attain national prominence and respectability.

Why, after these successes, have Women's Studies programs turned into such a combat zone? Some reasons are fairly ordinary. One is their anomalous position, which made them simultaneously contest and exploit established institutional structures. Another is frustration not only over the difficulty of getting more faculty positions but also over the slow pace of material change generally. Paradoxically, discontent and infighting also reflect the great achievement of Women's Studies. The study of gender is no longer news, and thus Women's Studies may seem to have lost some of its revolutionary appeal. Incoming students are no longer astonished to find Women's Studies programs in place; they take such programs for granted and are either attracted or hostile to them in advance.

Then, too, given the current economic and political climate, there is less optimism that the academic study of women and gender is itself an effective agent of change. Women's Studies programs also continue to experience conflicts over their acceptance in academe, and it is hard, over the long run, to sustain feminism's moral presuppositions and activist style unless new issues can be found around which to crusade.

But the deeper and far more disturbing reasons for the problems currently visible are, we believe, to be sought elsewhere: they are the direct result of self-destructive habits and assumptions that have grown up within Women's Studies itself. Long before the term "political correctness" gained currency in its present conservative/ironic sense, ideological policing was a common feature of Women's Studies programs. Women appraised one another; and, too frequently, found reason to judge others deficient, undeserving of the accolade "feminist."

Whereas feminists originally argued for a loosening of gender roles, now there is great pressure from within for conformity. Feminists used to urge women to explore their own sexuality freely, but now there is a figurative policing of the bedroom. At an early stage of second-wave feminism, consciousness-raising groups helped women work toward self-actualization and develop a nonstigmatized identity, but now women are pressured to conform to the microstereotypes of identity politics. In feminist pedagogy, the new valorization of women's modes of communication and interaction has led to the use of sentiment as a tool of coercion. Many feminist classrooms cultivate an insistence on "feeling," which, on examination, turns out to be the traditional split between intellect and emotion recycled, with the former still assigned to men and the latter to women. The characterizations of male and female have not changed; instead, the plus and minus signs associated with each gender have been reversed.

In yet another significant area of feminist endeavor, the early assumptions about women's "commonality" gave way to crucial realizations that not only gender but a variety of other important factors such as race, ethnicity, and sexual identity shape women's private and public selves and their life opportunities. In particular, "minority" women have increasingly entered feminist debates, which had too often neglected the problems these women face. But this valuable corrective now threatens to degenerate into a host of particularisms that could turn feminism into little more than a gathering of competing narrow "identities," each hotly promoted. Such wars have already been fought over sexual orientation, and we know how destructive they can be.

In each of these instances—as in many other aspects of contemporary feminism that we will explore in this book—we are witnessing the progressive deterioration of a vital movement. This has now reached the point that, today, distinctions between style and substance are blurred, escalation of rhetoric replaces real gains, and ostentatious posturing is taken for achievement. In the process, many women have come to feel marginalized by the coercive treatment received at the hands of some feminists and, as a result, are increasingly alienated from—and puzzled by—a movement they once embraced.

What troubled us most was that many of the aspects of Women's Studies that distanced, and in some cases drove away, women were the very features in which advocates took particular pride. The still-hopeful supporters of Women's Studies with whom we spoke often revealed, through their own accounts, the same landscape as that portrayed by the disillusioned. Where critics objected to emotional coercion in the classroom, advocates talked about the importance of transforming students' consciousness. Where dissenters saw feminist ideology distorting scholarship, advocates praised the virtues of research guided by political commitments. Where exiles complained about an atmosphere rife with hypocritical avoidance and shunning, advocates claimed to have found a sanctuary from patriarchal strife in groups based on the cultivation of women's "difference."

From the outset, Women's Studies occupied an unusual position in academe. It was not just multidisciplinary but had a dual agenda: educational (the study first of women and then of gender) and political (the correction of social injustice). As stated in the constitution of the National Women's Studies Association (NWSA):

> Women's Studies is the educational strategy of a breakthrough in consciousness and knowledge. The uniqueness of Women's Studies has been and remains its refusal to accept sterile divisions between the academy and community . . . between the individual and society. Women's Studies, then, is equipping women to transform the world to one that will be free of all oppression . . . [and is] a force which furthers the realization of feminist aims.[1]

Inevitable tensions have resulted from this grand, not to say grandiose, vision. As a brave new field that sprang up from grassroots efforts—first motivated by the student movement of the 1960s, and later spurred by the example of Black Studies programs—Women's Studies faced many obstacles within the university. The legitimation of any new academic field is a long process, but feminists believed that the challenges they faced were invariably manifestations of sexism. This sense of vulnerability contributed to the development of a siege mentality.

At the same time, Women's Studies was always allied with university reform: affirmative action, offices of women's affairs, and so on. Commitment to good causes meant that Women's Studies, in order to be effective, could not withdraw but had to play academic politics. This entailed a constant negotiation between feminist ideals (even assuming all feminist faculty agreed about what these were—which was hardly the case) and the pragmatics required to build a program in an academic setting. In the post-1960s atmosphere where in-your-face political activism was valorized above all else, feminist academics were often accused of being ivory-towered recluses, far removed from the barricades, and many academics accepted this characterization and felt guilty. Today, women "in the movement" are still leveling such charges against feminists in academe.

Confronting competing demands and pressures, Women's Studies adopted two self-defeating practices: academic separatism and a deference to political activism. These two strategies, as we shall see, are closely connected and reinforce each other.

Separatism has been a dominant theme since the inception of Women's Studies. The biblical injunction to "set yourself apart and be a separate people" describes a time-honored method for building group solidarity and is undoubtedly an effective way for a minority community to resist assimilation. But it cannot be a good long-term strategy for changing the ambient culture, and it is certainly incompatible with creative intellectual inquiry.

Today, separatism in Women's Studies is readily and graphically illustrated by the widespread exclusion of male authors from course syllabi, assigned reading lists, and citations in scholarly papers. In particular cases, there can, of course, be practical reasons for mentioning only female sources, and probably scholars in every field tend to overcite close colleagues and allies. But a systematic refusal to read or respond to male authors harms feminist scholarship in many ways. In addition, the separatist agenda has caused many Women's Studies programs not to seek collaboration with and support from male colleagues, as if mere association with men would contaminate feminist purity. Such moves are debilitating to the cause of feminism, and they may lure female students into the—obviously false—belief that all intellectual work produced by males is irrelevant to, or in conflict with, feminist projects.

Some feminists would argue that they were forced to set up their own programs, found their own journals, and form their own intellectual networks because the academic mainstream (or "malestream") would have nothing to do with them. This may well be so. But even if academic separatism was necessary in the past, it seems clearly counterproductive today, for gender analyses and the study of women have succeeded in making widely acknowledged contributions to the humanities and, increasingly, to the social sciences as well. In the hard sciences, feminist scholarship has been less influential, but the best way of gaining recognition there is by engaging in open dialogue with both male and nonfeminist female scholars. Separatism unavoidably discourages such dialogue. Instead, it favors dogmatic assertion, a standard tactic of ideologically inflamed movements, whether religious or political.

While academic feminism has tried to keep the rest of the university at bay, it has energetically fostered an intimate relationship with feminist political initiatives, both inside and outside the academy. Arguably, some forms of participation in these initiatives have been appropriate. For example, a professor might give her textbook order to the local feminist bookstore, thus offering financial support to a woman-owned business while also ensuring that her students are exposed to the novels, T-shirts, records, buttons, and periodicals of feminist popular culture.

But at other times academic feminism has made itself subservient to activist agendas. Consequently, in many programs, the appointment of faculty has hinged on the candidates' commitment to community organizing or other forms of feminist activism, rather than on the strength of their academic credentials. Some programs have adopted course and instructor evaluation forms that encourage students to judge the quality of their education in terms of its direct relevance to a rather narrowly defined and constantly shifting political agenda. It is not uncommon for students to be urged to engage in nonscholarly internships and practicums, for which they are able to earn academic credit. The degree of supervision of these internships, like the extent to which they include academic components (such as writing a final paper), varies enormously from program to program.

The American university accommodates many academic units that, like professional schools, provide intellectual service to various constituencies in the "real world." But these units typically maintain a certain critical distance from their practical objectives. Schools of education, for example, train teachers, but they also theorize about pedagogy and school policies. Forensic science departments offer courses of use to police officers and probation counselors, but they also scrutinize the operations of the criminal justice system. The ivory-tower model of inquiry has always been recognized as freeing the scholar from the need to demonstrate practical relevance, and the whole point of academic freedom and tenure is to protect the scholar from political pressure.

An unfortunate reversal of these tenets occurs when a program sees itself as a site of correct political action and therefore promotes not independent inquiry but adherence to a particular line of analysis and to the activities that follow from it. In such cases—as we find in some Women's Studies programs that attempt to minimize the difference between themselves and groups engaged in feminist activism outside the university—educational aims are made entirely subordinate to political goals.

Academic units that manage to balance these internal and external values do so by maintaining high intellectual standards while also using as texts some material selected for its political utility. Thus, a sociology department, for example, may have a Marxist orientation while insisting on excellent scholarship and publication records from its faculty and all-around competence in sociology from its majors and graduate students. Such a department sees its mission as providing a solid education shaped, but not outweighed, by a political commitment that many (but rarely all) faculty in the department share. But Women's Studies has never even acknowledged that achieving such a healthy balance is a worthwhile goal as well as an inherently difficult feat. Instead, both academics and activists have tended to repudiate the very desirability of such a balance and have agreed that "Women's Studies is the theory and activism the practice"—as if the relationship between the two were both comfortable and obvious. And because "activism" has had the brighter luster in feminist rhetoric, many Women's Studies programs have felt compelled to embrace and promote an activist stance.

The yearly NWSA conferences have always dramatically exhibited the uneasy mingling of academic and nonacademic concerns within Women's Studies—and this quite apart from the charges of racism that nearly destroyed the organization at its 1990 meeting in Akron, Ohio. Thus, the typical NWSA program includes not only symposia on Emily Dickinson or on the depiction of women in Hindu temple art, but also panels on how feminist organizations can get tax-exempt status or on how lesbian couples can practice do-it-yourself artificial insemination. Publishers' displays of academic books stand side by side with booths featuring crystals, drums, massage oils, and the other paraphernalia of "women's culture." Over time, the nonacademic components of the annual meetings have come to predominate, perhaps because activists outside the academy provide an important portion of the market for books in Women's Studies. Not surprisingly, many serious scholars stopped attending the annual NWSA meeting because (so they told us) they felt it was no longer a worthwhile professional endeavor. Here, too, people could, after all, vote with their feet—the "exit option," as some political scientists call it.

Activism as a legitimate goal of Women's Studies has certainly been communicated to students. When we put the question "What do you think Women's Studies is all about?" to approximately 150 undergraduates in Women's Studies courses at two contrasting institutions—one a large research university in the Northeast with a twenty-year-old, highly political program, the other a former teacher's college, now a university, in the Southwest, whose Women's Studies program is less than ten years old and quite unpoliticized—most answers touched only the practical side. Students wrote: To "raise women's self-esteem," "create a less patriarchal society," "break down sexism," "empower women," "lessen discrimination against women," "help women find a career centering on improving women's lives," and so on. When we asked "What do you think *other* students at your school think Women's Studies is all about?" the vast majority of the respondents answered with some form of the notion of "male bashing"; and a few added "a touchy-feely class," "militant," and "raging militant feminists." This negative image, too, should be of concern to those responsible for Women's Studies.

The twin tendencies toward academic separatism and deference to activism have developed in concert. Academic feminists who either felt rebuffed by the established disciplines or wanted to develop a radically different approach often turned to the welcoming audience of cultural feminists and activists. As they elaborated their writings in response to the concerns of this largely nonacademic audience (an important market even for university press books), much of their research tended to become both less accessible and less acceptable to colleagues in the mainstream disciplines. Traditional academics, moreover, could readily be denounced for their "elitism" and narrowly academic concerns. As a result, those Women's Studies faculty whose own research remained connected to the conventional disciplines have come under increasing pressure from activist students to base their courses on more radical or less scholarly texts.

In such an atmosphere, scholarship itself becomes suspect as faculty members feel constant pressure not to betray the cause. One result is the rhetorical assertion that scholarship *is* politics, an insistence that only signals the devaluation that scholarship has already undergone. A feminist professor who says, "My scholarly work is my form of activism," or even, "Teaching is my form of activism," is thus inevitably affirming that "activism" is indeed the correct measure of all aspects of Women's Studies.

Women's Studies, in its early phases, had a choice. Its justified critique of much traditional knowledge as biased and limited (if not overtly misogynist), and therefore ultimately erroneous, could have led it to claim the high ground by insisting on broader, more balanced, less biased curricula and research. But this is not the choice many programs and Women's Studies faculty made. Instead, at every juncture at which feminist bias emerged, it was justified by reference to the prior bias of men—as if emulation of the thing being rejected had, unconsciously, become the feminist agenda. Such inconsistencies are unworthy of a feminism that hopes to have a future. By capitulating to them, Women's Studies has become the defender of the faith within the academy's walls.

Notes

1. Cited in Adena Bargad and Janet Shibley Hyde, "Women's Studies: A Study of Feminist Identity Development in Women, *Psychology of Women Quarterly* 15 (1991): 181.

Questions for Discussion

1. Patai and Koertge note, "Incoming students are no longer astonished to find Women's Studies programs in place; they take such programs for granted and are either attracted or hostile to them in advance" (paragraph 4). When you entered your college or university, were you attracted, hostile, or indifferent to women's studies? Why?
2. How do you define "feminist"? What are the word's connotations? Are they the same for women as for men? For Generation X-ers as for Baby Boomers?
3. Patai and Koertge say that many in women's studies still identify "feeling" as the province of women and "intellect" as the province of men. How real is this gender distinction? How much is it biologically or culturally determined?
4. What is the appropriate relationship between a gender studies or ethnic studies program and the community outside the university?

Questions for Research and Writing

1. If your campus has a women's studies program, examine its course offerings and their descriptions in the campus catalogue. What do the offerings and descriptions suggest about the courses' political orientation, if any? Their interest in academic or activist agendas?
2. Interview members of a women's studies program and/or students and faculty members interested in studying gender issues. Do they agree with Patai and Koertge about the current state of gender studies? What do they see as the likely future of such studies? How much consensus about such issues is there among those who call themselves feminists?
3. Conduct a survey similar to the one Patai and Koertge conducted in the women's studies programs at two institutions (paragraph 24). Then use your survey either to argue for a revision of the women's studies curriculum or to analyze the ways in which respondents' backgrounds (for example, their genders, their political orientation, their knowledge or ignorance of the women's studies program) have influenced their responses.
4. Some argue that women and men think and even write differently. Test this notion by devising a study to determine how accurately respondents can discern writers' genders on the basis of seeing only their written material. You might, for instance, present your respondents with a series of written passages on the same subject, one whose content is not gender-specific. What stylistic, tonal, organizational, and philosophical signposts do your respondents look for in trying to determine a writer's gender? Do male respondents look for different signposts, or come to different conclusions, than do female respondents?

THE DISTRIBUTED UNIVERSITY
J. Wade Gilley

> With the widespread use of computer technology in the workplace and the home, it is not surprising that many see the computer as a promising educational tool. Some have even argued that it is now possible to have universities or classrooms "without walls," that is, universities and classrooms unbounded by geographical limitations. J. Wade Gilley, an environmental engineer and university president, looks into this future in his book Thinking about American Higher Education: The 1990s and Beyond. *In the following article, which first appeared in that book, he links the Jeffersonian concept of a university distributed across geographical regions to the more modern concept of a networked university. As you read, think about how different your education would be if you were to converse with professors and other students over a computer network or if you were to take classes via an interactive audio-video connection that would allow you to see and hear colleagues miles, even continents, away.*

The year is 2003. On a crisp morning, you leave your home in Manassas for the nearby Prince William Institute, one of several institutes in the George Mason University network. You attend a class in your urban systems engineering program, an interdisciplinary degree that has brought together experts in several areas, including urban planning, real estate development, public policy, and civil engineering.

Your next class is held at the Fairfax (Virginia) campus, but that's no problem for you; there's a video room down the hall that allows you to participate in the lecture without leaving Prince William. After class, you use one of the institute's computers to have a library book sent to you from the Arlington Institute. Heading home you realize that you forgot to drop off a paper, so you send it through your personal computer when you get home.

Sound hard to believe? Such a scenario may become a reality in George Mason's future. The university is now embarking on a plan to create a network of George Mason institutes, known as the "distributed university," throughout Northern Virginia. In this model, each institute, like nodes on a computer network, is linked by telecommunications systems that can access the facilities of all the institutes on the network. This massive undertaking is an attempt to provide education of equal quality to all areas of the region, and to develop interdisciplinary research and programs aimed at solving the region's—and the nation's—most timely problems.

From "The University of the Future" by Maureen Mayer

The idea of a distributed university is not new. Thomas Jefferson is said to have suggested a set of colleges within a day's ride of each Virginian, all tied to the state's capstone institution, the University of Virginia. It is highly unlikely that Jefferson ever used the word "network," but his concept describes just such an educational system. Later, the land grant college, through its network of county agents, emerged as a special type of American institution designed to distribute knowledge from the university to the agriculture industry. In addition, some of the many universities and colleges that established branch campuses during the last seventy-five years have from time to time taken on the appearance of a network, especially multicampus community colleges, such as the system in Dallas County, Texas.

But none of these illustrations exemplifies an educational network that allows individuals to access the complete range of courses and other services (including library, computing, campus mail, course advising, and registration) characteristic of the modern American university. Today, however, technology and the knowledge age requirement that each person participate in the educational process for life, demand such educational services, giving new force to the idea of a distributed university. Because of changing demographic patterns, large numbers of people now live in urban villages. Increasing numbers of others live in areas of decreasing density. All require lifelong education. Obviously, higher education must look for new forms and approaches to address these twenty-first-century needs.

HISTORICAL HIGHER EDUCATION

Originally, American colleges were founded in remote areas, free from distractions, where it was hoped learners and scholars could evolve into an ideal residential and intellectual community. One early Harvard University president believed so strongly in the educational value of such communities that he once remarked that he would rather build dormitories than classrooms. Of course, the residential colleges situated (or distributed) around the great English universities Oxford and Cambridge provided an early example of effective education resulting from students and teachers living in community. Even that American invention, the land grant college, was usually placed in remote locations within each state in the interest of creating a similar cloistered learning environment.

After industrialization (1879–1920), however, city colleges and universities emerged. These institutions reflected the urban development of the time, i.e., a core city surrounded by suburbia and exurbia. City colleges began in central city areas, and later, as populations spread, established branch campuses and extension centers. But none of these offshoots were considered part of a network, or even a real part of the main institution. Rather, these campuses and extension centers bore the stigma of second-class institutions.

CHANGING EDUCATIONAL DEMAND

But the world is changing. Urban development has abandoned the central city/suburbia/exurbia concept in favor of urban villages, multiple concentrations of office, shopping, residential, and recreational facilities. Tied together by telecommunications and transportation, these large enclaves are heavy consumers of information and education.

Because of work hours, traffic congestion, and other logistic factors characteristic of urban villages, however, main university campuses are becoming less convenient, therefore less accessible, to the learner. Yet, second-class operations such as branch campuses or extension centers are increasingly unacceptable to the sophisticated new American knowledge worker. Thus, the idea of a distributed university is gaining popularity in many fast-growing areas around the country, particularly in Washington, D.C., Atlanta, Southern California, South Florida, and other postindustrial locations where the urban village concept is developing.

The distributed university theory can find applications in other settings as well. Far from the teeming urban villages, areas with sparse and widely-distributed populations also face the fundamental question of how to effectively distribute high quality educational services. In Alaska, for example, low college attendance rates among native Alaskans, who represent the bulk of that state's dispersed population, imply a disinclination toward higher education, making it doubly imperative to deliver high quality, accessible education to potential students where they live. Realistically, only highly motivated learners can be expected to travel great distances for educational services.

The distributed university concept can also meet the growing need for lifelong education. Engineers, for example, now require continuing advanced education throughout their productive careers. Yet, not all industrial locations can offer a full range of graduate engineering or continuing education opportunities. To fill this gap, a new institution was born in 1985. The National Technological University, a consortium of several renowned engineering colleges, is headquartered at Colorado State University. Its goal is to offer first-rate master's level courses and engineering degrees via satellite television. In addition, many other engineering schools are now offering advanced work by means of interactive television—one-way video and two-way audio. This experiment is apparently working well.

Other forces affecting the organization and delivery of high quality educational programs and services that argue for the distributed university concept include the impending faculty shortage and, most importantly, the force of technological development. Most knowledgeable educators agree that in time technology will transform the way people teach and learn. The continuing advancement of computers, telecommunications, and other products of the information age is destined to impact higher education. The challenge for colleges and universities is to learn to maximize technology before new institutions and forms emerge to meet the educational needs of the twenty-first-century and learning flees the academy.

THE THEORY OF DISTRIBUTION

Theoretical discussion of the distributed university has been around for decades. For years academicians have discussed and debated the merits of the centralized versus the decentralized library. Which is best, they question, one major library facility or a core library supporting several strategically-located branch libraries around campus? The fundamental question in this ongoing debate is how to create a critical mass of learning resources while at the same time distributing those resources to the users.

This same debate has surfaced from time to time in regard to computers and computing. In this case, however, the development of the microchip has made it possible to centrally amass major computing capability while distributing significant capabilities to individual users via ever-more-powerful microcomputers. The major challenge in computing now is networking, i.e., how to unite both centralized and decentralized computing into one powerful communications and computing network.

Another recent advancement in distribution is the use of the facsimile (fax) machine, a phenomenon that has grown dramatically in the past few years. Universities with only one fax machine five years ago now employ hundreds of faxes in cross-campus mail networks. Engineering firms, too, are using the fax machine and other telecommunications devices to coordinate work from several locations hundreds of miles apart as easily as from offices just down the hall. In fact, one big-city engineering firm with huge backlogs of work found it simpler and more cost-effective to buy a smaller engineering firm in another city and fax designs back and forth than to hire a sufficient number of engineers at the home office. Such recent quantum leaps in computing and networking are illustrative of the technological advances that make the idea of a distributed university thinkable.

A REAL LIFE MODEL: BELL LABS

As technology advances and becomes more commonplace, the potential for its use in education becomes more practical, even mandatory; the idea of distributing a university over a geographical area becomes more feasible. In fact, there is already an example of a distributed knowledge age institution that provides a good model for colleges and universities—AT&T's Bell Laboratories.

Those who know of Bell Labs recognize this prestigious enterprise as America's premier research institution, the workplace of Nobel laureates and the birthplace of many now ubiquitous inventions, including the transistor, the laser, the solar cell, the communication satellite, and sound motion pictures.

But what is Bell Labs? A large building filled with busy scientists running around in white coats? Or, perhaps, a campus of laboratory buildings? In reality, Bell Labs is a distributed network of research facilities with several major laboratories located in New Jersey and other states. There is no main building versus branch labs. Scientists who have won Nobel prizes for work done at Bell Labs have operated from several different facilities. Bell Labs is, in fact, a working network of research facilities or nodes tied together with modern communications. This network provides each person at each location with access to the same resources and the same information. In reality, Bell Labs is a distributed institution that can serve as an excellent model for institutions of higher education looking to the twenty-first-century.

CANDIDATES FOR THE DISTRIBUTED UNIVERSITY

Which American institution will become the nation's first distributed university? There are currently several candidates, including the University of Alaska and George Mason University in Fairfax, Virginia.

In Alaska, the state university has been restructured from a system of three university branch campuses and eleven community colleges plus other facilities into three university centers. Each center offers multiple sites and a broad range of programs, and each bears responsibility for remote sites. In reality, each of these three university centers is a distributed network of educational sites. Given the proper context and the appropriate use of technology, these centers could take the form of a twenty-first-century distributed university.

Whether or not this evolution occurs rests on questions of strategy and will. Alaska is a frontier where the limits and possibilities of distribution theory can be tested; with its great distances and its sparse, dispersed population, it is a state whose very future depends on solving the educational problems the distributed university theory is designed to address. Alaska is an obvious candidate for a great educational experiment.

Across the continent in Virginia, George Mason University stands at the other extreme. Surrounded by 1.4 million people living within a thirty-mile radius of its main campus, George Mason is challenged to overcome problems of transportation and community organization as they affect the delivery of educational programs and services. The Northern Virginia region that George Mason serves now includes eight major urban villages, with more sure to develop during the twenty-first-century. Severe transportation problems make it difficult for this area's education-hungry populace to commute to the university's main campus in Fairfax.

The George Mason plan for a distributed university includes creating a parallel academic organization consisting of institutes—located both on and off the Fairfax campus—that combine departments, schools, colleges, and centers. Thus far, an institute for the arts has been organized on the Fairfax campus to replace the performing arts departments. This institute has assumed the additional responsibilities of managing the university's new $30 million Center for the Arts and of implementing an innovative university wide-arts education program. Also located on the Fairfax campus are the Robinson Professors Program, consisting of twenty endowed professorships for distinguished scholars committed to teaching undergraduates and building a modern university, and the Krasnow Institute for Advanced Study, an endowed interdisciplinary research institute.

George Mason's Arlington, Virginia campus houses the Institute for International Transactions, headed by economist John Moore, former deputy director of the National Science Foundation. Also sharing the Arlington site is the university's law school and its noted Center for Law and Economics. Twenty miles to the west of Fairfax, George Mason is currently working with Prince William County to establish the Prince William Institute, designed to offer an array of degree and credential programs, including a school for urban systems engineering, an executive MBA, plus graduate and undergraduate courses and programs as needed. Other institutes, to be located both on the Fairfax campus and elsewhere, are under consideration. All will be tied together in a communications and service network, with faculty stationed at one site, but carrying responsibilities for other sites and programs as well.

The nature of these institutes raises many concerns: Where does a faculty member involved at several centers receive tenure? How does a distributed university achieve the degree of nodal democracy evident at Bell Labs? Can these different nodes be tied together electronically? Can the educational establishment make the adjustments necessary to maximize emerging technologies in the interest of better education for all Americans?

Whatever the ultimate answer to these questions, clearly a major educational experiment is underway at Virginia's George Mason University. If nothing else, this experiment will test the validity and accepted context of traditional American higher education.

In summary, demographics, technology, and the empowerment offered by education in the new science-driven economy will come together into one powerful force destined to restructure higher education in America. The main question to be answered as this scenario unfolds is: Will colleges and universities lead America into the future with innovation, experiments, and pilot programs, or will they be painfully forced into the new century?

Questions for Discussion

1. Gilley is clearly an advocate of the distributed university. What are your responses to his arguments? What questions would you like to see him answer more fully? What concerns do you think an opponent might raise?
2. Gilley mentions several universities that he thinks are clear candidates for the implementation of the concept of the distributed university. Some are candidates because they or their potential student populations

reside in remote areas; others are candidates because they lie in areas that are so densely populated that it's impossible for a single campus to serve everyone. What of the vast number of colleges between these two extremes? To what extent should they, too, participate in the move toward distributed universities?

3. Gilley's most specific examples come from the world of engineering, though he gives examples from the arts and the professional schools as well. Which disciplines and ways of teaching and learning are most consistent with the methods and goals of the distributed university?

Questions for Research and Writing

1. In writing about the uses of technology that make a distributed university a possibility, Gilley says that many engineering schools are offering courses through interactive television, thus making them available to students at some distance from the physical location of the campus. He goes on to say that "this experiment is apparently working well," but he is not specific about how students and instructors are responding. Interview students and instructors who have participated in such a "distance-learning" project (or who are discussing a future possibility of it), asking them what they see as its advantages and drawbacks. If your own campus is involved in such a project, you can conduct some of the interviews face-to-face, but you may also want to use the resources of the Internet to interview students and instructors at other institutions. (Begin perhaps by attempting to contact faculty and students at the universities Gilley mentions in his article.) Then write an essay arguing for or against the implementation of a particular distance-learning project on your campus.

2. Certain types of distance learning are controversial, perhaps more so than Gilley acknowledges. Survey students and instructors on your own campus to determine their reactions to various modes of distance learning. (Ask questions about distributed libraries, interactive television, distance learning via computer networks, and so on.) In analyzing your data, determine the extent to which the respondents' fields of study, knowledge of technology, theories of learning, and so on, influence their attitudes toward distance learning.

3. As Gilley notes, the distributed university is not an entirely new concept. Since the late 1950s, educators have often seen in new forms of technology—from television and audio-lingual tapes to calculators and computers—the promise of educational innovations or the threat of educational ruin. Take one such technological innovation and trace its introduction into the schools. What were the predictions that accompanied its introduction? What were the actual results? (You'll need to remember, of course, that even years after its introduction, we may still be debating its consequences.)

SOME GOOD NEWS ABOUT CAMPUS LIFE
How "Involving Colleges" Promote Learning outside the Classroom

George D. Kuh, John H. Schuh, and Elizabeth J. Whitt

> *The media often portray colleges and universities in a negative light: News reports emphasize racial tension, alcohol abuse, date rape, and questionable teaching practices. But a more positive side of campus life has received relatively little attention. This article, which appeared in the Fall 1991 edition of* Change, *a periodical published by the American Association of Higher Education, identifies a number of institutions, called "involving colleges," which have created climates that cultivate and encourage what the authors, all college professors and administrators, call "educationally purposeful behavior." As you read the article, try to identify the values and attitudes that such institutions share. Clearly, the authors imagine an audience of faculty and administrators. From your perspective as a student, how significant or important are the out-of-class learning opportunities that the authors identify in their analysis of these fourteen colleges and universities?*

Bad news about the quality of campus life seems to be everywhere. Alcohol abuse, hate crimes, physical assaults, and an absence of civility on campus have become routine stories in the press. Some of the stories make for sensational journalism; in other cases, the public reads simplistic descriptions of the inevitable acting out on campus of complex societal problems. Whatever the case, the incidents that make news, the ones behind "the erosion of campus life," have one thing in common: they occur most often outside the classroom. This fact contributes to their visibility, of course, but also to a sense that they are somehow out of the control of the administrators and faculty—except through the enforcement of rules and regulations.

There are some institutions, however, that have been able to create and maintain campus climates that promote educationally purposeful behavior on the part of their students. During the 1988–89 academic year, we identified and visited 14 colleges and universities that provide unusually rich out-of-class learning opportunities for their undergraduates.

We spent the equivalent of a week on most of these campuses, talking with nearly 1,300 students, faculty members, administrators, and graduates, reviewing hundreds of documents and observing the routines of campus life. Many of our findings we share here, confident that many of the properties of these "Involving Colleges" merit consideration by other institutions seeking ways to foster student learning and a climate of civility.

The properties of Involving Colleges work together in different ways toward different ends, depending on the institution's mission, size, location, and student characteristics. Across the 14 institutions, however, three factors have a profound influence on encouraging students to participate actively in campus life: 1) a clear, coherent philosophy that sets expectations for student behavior and guides the development of campus policies and practices; 2) a campus culture that encourages student participation and loyalty; and 3) people committed to student learning who appreciate the importance of out-of-class experiences to the aims of the institution.

PHILOSOPHY

An institution's philosophy determines "how we do things here"; it is the rationale for the means (policies, practices, standard operating procedures) by which an institution conducts its business and pursues its mission. A college rarely describes its philosophy in writing; indeed, faculty and administrators at most institutions are unaware of the assumptions and beliefs about human potential, teaching, and learning that drive institutional practices. But a college's philosophy can be discovered by examining what people say and do in various settings and circumstances.

Although the philosophies of Involving Colleges differ, they share three themes: 1) high expectations for student performance; 2) interpersonal distinctions (or their absence) consistent with the institution's educational purposes and student characteristics; and 3) an unwavering commitment to multiculturalism.

Great Expectations

An Involving College's mission and student characteristics dictate how students are expected to behave, both in and out of the classroom. The vast majority of students at Earlham, Grinnell, Miami, Mount Holyoke, Stanford, and UC Davis matriculate with well-developed academic skills. Other Involving Colleges, particularly the metropolitan universities, attract a high proportion of students whose academic skills need to be sharpened. Student preparation and ability notwithstanding, faculty members and others at Involving Colleges send a clear message to all their students: "You are here because we believe you can succeed."

For example, Xavier University was described in the 1989 edition of *Selective Guide to Colleges* as "a school where achievement has been the rule, and beating the odds against success a routine occurrence." The Xavier yearbook proclaims that "Xavier is a no-excuse school. You take what you have, do the best with it, and don't make any excuses." African-American and white faculty and staff model and reinforce the importance of hard work in order to attain one's aspirations. Display cases in the academic buildings feature pictures and brief biographies of recent graduates who attend graduate and professional schools.

Socialization During Recruitment. An Involving College assumes that new students need a lot of information about how to act at college. Between the time a prospective student first expresses interest in attending the college and matriculation, the institution describes, in plain language, what it values and is trying to accomplish, what students can expect from the college, and how they are expected to behave. For example, during the summer, Stanford University sends 15 mailings to incoming students including letters from a resident fellow (a faculty member living in the student's dorm or house), a resident assistant, the president, the provost, the dean for undergraduate studies, and the dean of student affairs. One of the mailings, a pithy, light-hearted publication produced by Stanford sophomores, describes the cycles, extremes, and challenges first-year students are likely to encounter. Sprinkled throughout are student quotes, many of which poke fun at Stanford. But more important, the themes that characterize Stanford's philosophy—acting as a responsible adult, exercising mature judgment, making one's own choices—are stated over and over again.

Orientation Activities and Events. After new students arrive, orientation programs are used to explain standards and expectations for academic and social behavior. Concerted efforts are made to help newcomers feel welcome and to unequivocally affirm them as full members of the campus community. Students also learn what to expect and how to behave through informal orientation activities. For example, the night new students arrive at Earlham College, each "hall" (groupings of 12–15 students) meets to set social and community standards. For most students, this is their first experience in using consensus to make decisions, the way things are done in this Quaker community. These and other orientation activities are integral to encouraging responsible behavior and bonding students to the institution and to one another.

Ladders to Success. The ability of students to make responsible judgments varies considerably. Therefore, to encourage the development of both independence and an affirming community, Involving Colleges provide different amounts of structure. At Berea, Xavier, Miami, and Iowa State, more rules are provided than at Earlham, Grinnell, Mount Holyoke, and Stanford. The Xavier "ladder" includes a sequence of programs and activities (summer programs, a required semester-long orientation course, tutoring) to help students get involved, feel supported, and succeed academically. In effect, the institution says to students: "These are the steps you must take if you are to be successful here." As one student said, "when you enter Xavier University, you need a crutch of study skills." Students at Earlham, Grinnell, Mount Holyoke, and Stanford are responsible for determining and monitoring community standards. The Honor Codes at Mount Holyoke and Stanford are a strong statement of trust in students, and students behave accordingly.

Programs and administrative structures at the metropolitan institutions guide and, in some instances, "hold students in place" until they are capable of navigating the collegiate experience on their own. Wichita State has a transition semester to assist new students—many of whom have not been in a classroom for years—in meeting the university's academic standards. If a student's grade point average is below 2.0 at the end of their first semester, they may request that any grade below C be reflected on their transcript as "no credit." The following semester, the student may not enroll for more than 12 hours and must earn a grade point of at least 2.0 to remain in good standing.

An Ethic of Care. At the core of an Involving College's philosophy are values and assumptions that communicate caring and belonging to students and the importance of respecting all individuals as persons of worth and dignity. When an institution acknowledges basic human needs for social and psychological comfort, students sense they are full and valued members of the campus community, even in larger institutions. For example, Miami University students and faculty speak of the "great dissonance between the size we really are and the way we behave." A staff member described the ambience to be more like a liberal arts college "because of the attention and support for freshmen, the small-town setting, the small residence halls, and the architecture." Miami *feels* like a small college even though it is a state university with 16,000 students.

It is almost impossible for a student at an Involving College to be anonymous. This is not to say that tragedies do not occur or that debilitating personal behaviors always are checked immediately by peer pressure, or that no one ever feels lonely. More often than not, however, the change in disposition of a roommate is noted and help is requested from one or more people who make up the "safety nets" that "catch" students having difficulty. These safety nets are more or less invisible, depending on the needs of students. At Mount Holyoke College, for example, sources of support are many and apparent, ranging from groups for daughters of alcoholics and for women with eating disorders to counseling by peers and professionals to residence hall programming on a variety of topics related to student problems. At Stanford, however, extensive support is available but not obvious; students can find help if they want it and look for it.

Interpersonal Distinctions

Status differences among individuals and groups are either accentuated *or* minimized at Involving Colleges, depending on the institution's mission and educational purposes. Earlham, Grinnell, Mount Holyoke, Stanford, and The Evergreen State College are democratic communities with egalitarian aspirations. Virtually anyone can become a member of any group or organization. Egalitarianism in this context suggests a level playing field free from the influence of political, social, and economic differences. Distinctions made on the basis of status or title, such as "doctor," "president," or "professor" are eschewed because titles often place someone in a dependent, lower-status role and make people seem more different from one another than they really are. For example, at Stanford, institutional memoranda carry only individuals' names, not titles. Undergraduates can enroll in any course or major; there are no policies to regulate the flow of students, such as differential grade point averages for admission to popular majors. All campus housing costs the same, regardless of how old or new, worn or plush.

Other Involving Colleges are meritocracies: Policies and practices regulate status attainment and academic achievement. At Miami, competition among students is particularly intense for membership and leadership positions in most prestigious groups. Typically, systematic reviews of credentials and interviews determine appointments to student and university committees. At Xavier, titles are used without apology, students are addressed by their surnames, and professional dress is expected. These are deliberate efforts to instill a sense of pride and raise the hopes, expectations, and confidence of students whose backgrounds do not predict success in college. The message conveyed is that with achievement comes respect.

Commitment to Multiculturalism

Embedded in the philosophy of an Involving College is an unwavering commitment to multiculturalism. Statements about the value of individual and group differences are made consistently and are supported by the development of subcommunities of students with similar interests or backgrounds. Some subcommunities are formal, such as living units organized according to cultural or ethnic background or academic interest (e.g., the theme houses at Earlham, Stanford, and UC Davis) or student organizations based on gender, race, ethnicity, or sexual orientation (e.g., the Lesbian-Bisexual-Gay Persons Union at Earlham). Others are informal groupings, such as older adult students at Wichita State and Louisville, international students at Iowa State, and students of color at any of the predominantly white institutions.

The rationale for enabling multiple subcommunities is educationally purposeful. For students to be successful and feel valued, they must have their interests and backgrounds acknowledged, legitimated, understood, and—as a longer-term goal—appreciated. Although subcommunities can be found at any of the 14 institutions, Stanford offers a particularly powerful example. About 35 percent of Stanford undergraduates are African-American, Asian-America, American Indian, Native Alaskan, or Mexican-American. Four of Stanford's residences are cross-cultural: Casa Zapata, the Mexican-American theme house; Okada, the Asian-American theme house; Muwekma-tah-ruk, the American-Indian theme house; and

Ujamaa, the African-American theme house. In addition to providing support, these houses also expose students who are not members of those groups to cultures different from their own.

Of course, an Involving College's aspiration to become a multicultural learning community keeps racial and ethnic differences at the forefront. It is somewhat ironic that the institutions fostering multiculturalism are also potentially the most explosive because they have opened themselves to the conflicts inherent in differences and high expectations. It is likely that difficult times are ahead for these and other institutions committed to multiculturalism. Their long-term prospects for understanding and learning will, however, help to keep their commitment firm despite the turmoil.

CAMPUS CULTURE

There is a special quality about an Involving College, an intangible "something in the woodwork" that sustains the community. This "something special" is rooted in the institutional culture and dominant subcultures that promote involvement and a sense of ownership among members. Some of the most powerful cultural influences on student involvement are found in institutional history, traditions, language, and symbols.

History

The circumstances leading to an institution's founding as well as the ways in which the institution has responded to crises and the upheaval of change send messages about where it places the importance of student learning and participation in the life of the campus community. The mission of Xavier, the only black Catholic university in the Western Hemisphere, was to serve persons of color who were denied educational opportunities. All newcomers—students and faculty alike—hear the story of how Mother Katharine Drexel and the Sisters of the Blessed Sacrament started the institution in 1915; a videotaped reenactment of Mother Katharine's audience with the Pope, during which he encouraged her to create Xavier, is shown in orientation classes. Pictures of Mother Katharine are found in almost all Xavier buildings—on every floor in some. Celebration of religious holidays, the continuing presence of members of the religious order on the faculty, and an active campus ministry program keep the Catholic influence alive.

The founder of Berea College, John Fee, came from Oberlin College to establish an institution to serve persons of all races and poor backgrounds from Appalachia. The college's commitment to the youth of Appalachia remains firm. Although black students were prohibited from attending Berea for a time because of the Kentucky Day Law (passed in the early 1900s), blacks were enthusiastically welcomed by the Berea College community as soon as the law was repealed in the early 1950s.

Various programs and services offered by Iowa State put the university in contact with more than 500,000 Iowans annually. Even though a small percentage of students major in agriculture, the spirit of the ISU's agricultural roots permeates campus life. A "pitch-in-and-help" spirit, a legacy of the university's beginnings as a land-grant institution, continues to influence the student culture; more than 5,000 students hold leadership positions in the more than 400 special interest and department-sponsored organizations.

Traditions

Traditions communicate important institutional values, maintain and renew the community by binding past and present lives with shared meanings and actions, and reinforce expectations for taking an active part in campus life. Although The Evergreen State College is relatively young, it boasts a set of traditions as distinctive as its history. Students and graduates describe with affection the potlucks, a time when students and faculty become acquainted. Often held in the homes of faculty members, these informal gatherings provide the initial "glue" for the bonding that characterizes student and faculty groups engaged in interdisciplinary explorations into topics of mutual interest, the basic building blocks of the Evergreen curriculum.

Reunion and Commencement at Mount Holyoke link past and present generations of students, evoking a timeless sense of sisterhood. Graduating seniors, dressed in white, march to the amphitheater bearing chains of laurel leaves that symbolize achievement and continuity. They are preceded by scores of alumnae (some from as far back as 60 years), also wearing white with touches of their class colors, carrying signs with statements about their student adventures and their lives after graduation. The effect is a human chain of history, with each woman and each class unique, and yet all having shared the experience of Mount Holyoke, the experience of being "uncommon women."

Metropolitan Involving Colleges have fewer distinctive traditions than their residential counterparts, due in part to their relative youth and limited numbers of full-time, traditional age students. For example, Wichita State has undergone dramatic changes in structure and mission in the last 70 years—from a Congregational liberal arts college to a municipal university to a Kansas Regents institution with an urban mission. As WSU's "natural rivalries" in intercollegiate sports have evolved, so have some meaningful traditions. However, even without a football game, Homecoming remains popular with residents of the city of Wichita, many of whom are WSU graduates. Another Wichita campus-city tradition is the Fourth of July celebration held in the football stadium. The 1989 rendition, the 14th annual, included a performance by "Up with People," recognition of people who have made significant contributions to the community, an aircraft flyover, and a fireworks display. These traditions exemplify the importance of strong, mutually enhancing relationships between metropolitan Involving Colleges and the citizens they serve.

Language

Many Involving Colleges have an extensive vocabulary specific to the institution—what we call "terms of endearment." At Miami University, the phrases "Mother Miami," "cradle of coaches," and "mother of fraternities" connote nurturance and a sense of family; the university is a source of life (of the mind) and nourishment (for the spirit), and is a sheltering home for all her "children." Similarly, the "Miami Bubble" implies that the university is a safe place, a protected seat from which to observe, and occasionally experience, the "real" world. "Miami memos" are the calendars that students keep in order to organize their time "by the hour." The message of "Miami memos" is that students are so involved in so many activities, they must live by precise schedules in order to get everything done. "Miami mergers" are marriages between Miami students; these couples annually receive Valentines from the university symbolically commemorating their membership in the Miami family.

The language of Evergreen implies a place that refuses to take itself too seriously, yet is very serious about the qualities that set it apart from traditional institutions. Roughly translated, the college's motto—*Omnia Extares*—means "let it all hang out," an accurate description for a place fervently committed to personal freedom. Students are known, and refer to one another, as "Greeners," a label connoting political activism, social consciousness, and liberal attitudes. We were told that the collegiality and egalitarianism permeating the college's philosophy are reflected in how students and faculty view their roles: "At Evergreen, many of the things that separate students and faculty [at other institutions] just don't exist. Here there are only younger learners and older learners."

Symbols

Institutional symbols call attention to important values and elicit feelings of pride and identification with the institution. Various members of the campus community (presidents, senior faculty, upper-class students) bring institutional symbols into focus for members of the community, calling to mind the ideals to which they aspire. For example, at Iowa State University and College orientation sessions, the deans of academic units make a point of urging new students to participate in out-of-class activities. The message to students is clear: It is important (and expected!) that you become fully involved in all aspects of campus life.

At UC Davis, themes of environmental preservation and egalitarianism are symbolized by the ever-present bicycle. A network of bike paths and roads form the principal conduits by which students, faculty, and staff move about the campus, virtually free from interference from cars. Bicycles are both a "California thing to do" and a symbol of the belief that "we're all in this together"; even the chancellor rides a bike.

All the cultural elements described above and more, such as the shaping influences of regional and local cultures, work together to help students create a shared understanding of how the institution works, what is valued, and how to get things done.

PEOPLE

People are the heart and soul of any enterprise, including an Involving College. Administrators, faculty, and other institutional agents are indispensable in creating a variety of positive out-of-class learning opportunities.

Administrators

Presidents communicate the importance of student involvement in campus life by explaining events in the institution's history that demanded students take responsibility for the quality of campus life and their own learning and personal development. They acknowledge the importance of, and assiduously maintain, relationships with students and student affairs staff—relationships that are characterized by trust, loyalty, and mutual respect. Last, but certainly not least, they encourage faculty to spend time with students outside of class and model this behavior by participating in orientation events and eating an occasional meal with students.

The role of the president in setting the tone for out-of-class life is mediated by institutional features such as size. For example, small college presidents tend to be more knowledgeable about student life than their counterparts at large universities. Also shaping the president's role are previous experience, length of tenure at the institution, personal interests, and personality. For example, Donald Kennedy, the Stanford University president, was a resident assistant at Harvard; he witnessed first-hand the power of the residential experience in attaining the institution's educational purposes. That experience has influenced his commitment to the residential aspects of undergraduate life at Stanford and his ability to articulate that commitment in powerful ways.

At most Involving Colleges, the chief academic officer readily acknowledges the importance of a mutually enhancing relationship between out-of-class life and the curricular goals of the institution. Some are more articulate about out-of-class experiences than others. Some are more sensitive to the symbolic power of their role, particularly those at residential institutions. But all recognize that everything happening on a college campus either contributes to or competes with a college's educational goals. Consider how James Rosse, the Stanford provost, describes the importance of residential education:

Many faculty have a romanticized recollection of the quality of the intellectual experience they had as undergraduates. Not all students will have the same level of intensity as far as their intellectual experience is concerned. However, it is Stanford's responsibility to give all students an opportunity; the out-of-class experience—particularly through residential education—can enhance the possibilities that students will be challenged intellectually at various places and times.

Presidents and academic administrators point to student life staff as the campus experts on students. To many faculty members, student affairs is a black box, a set of functions about which little is understood and even less is noticed. At Involving Colleges, however, faculty members are quick to acknowledge and compliment the quality of their work. As faculty members spend less time with students outside of class, student affairs staff have become the de facto caretakers of the collegiate culture, assisting students through academic, social, emotional, and physical difficulties and creating such links between the academic program and out-of-class life as internships (UC Davis), cooperative education (Louisville), and community service (UNC–Charlotte). Through their contacts with students—often at odd hours, when many "teachable moments" occur—they explain to students how their behavior is consistent or conflicts with the institution's philosophy and educational purposes.

Faculty

Although more faculty-student interaction may take place at Involving Colleges than many other institutions, contacts between faculty and students are usually student-initiated. Student-faculty interaction—when it occurs—is often related to academic issues, such as discussions immediately following class to pursue points raised during class, or in departmental clubs. Even at Involving Colleges, changes in expectations and reward systems have altered faculty roles and priorities. As a result, two faculty cultures now exist as far as out-of-class life is concerned: student-centered faculty members—those who are committed to involvement with undergraduates (they tend to be older, tenured faculty)—and those who are not involved with undergraduates (often younger faculty or cosmopolitan scholars). However, those institutions with salient images as teaching colleges (Berea, Earlham, Grinnell, Evergreen, Xavier) continue to attract faculty willing to invest considerable time with students and participate fully in community governance and other activities.

Much more could be said about the role of institutional agents in encouraging students to take responsibility for the quality of their lives and to become actively involved in the campus community. Moreover, the whole of the contributions of institutional agents is greater than their individual parts. The complementarity among the priorities of faculty and student affairs staff, the blending of academic and student life objectives, and the compatibility of both within the institutional philosophy help to create a campus with rich out-of-class learning opportunities.

Involving Colleges have a clear, coherent philosophy that communicates high but reasonable challenges for students, buttressed by an ethic of care. They deliberately accentuate or minimize status distinctions and espouse a clear, unwavering commitment to multiculturalism by enabling subcommunities, such as ethnic or academic theme houses, to flourish. A complicated web of cultural artifacts (history, myths, traditions, rites and rituals, language) underscores the importance of involvement and communicates to students "how the institution works." Thus, in some subtle and some not-so-subtle ways, faculty, staff, and others promote student participation in educational out-of-class activities.

Partitioning a college or university into what appear to be separate properties does violence to the holistic nature of an institution of higher education as a learning enterprise. Philosophy, institutional cultures, and people work together to enact policies and practices that encourage students to take responsibility for their learning and the quality of campus life. To isolate one for emphasis is to overlook the symbiotic relationship among the parts of the whole.

Involving Colleges offer some good news about campus life at a time when higher education seems to be overwhelmed by the bad news. But they do not provide blueprints for ensuring a high quality undergraduate experience for every student nor are they models to be emulated by every college or university. Because something—a symbol, assumption, program, or policy—works (or seems to work) in one setting does not mean it will be effective in another. Nonetheless, administrators, faculty, and staff at other colleges and universities would do well to reflect on how the characteristics of Involving Colleges could be adapted to their campuses to foster learning and civil behavior outside the classroom.

Questions for Discussion

1. Kuh, Schuh, and Whitt list a good orientation program as one of the characteristics of an "involving college." How helpful were the orientation materials and meetings at your college or university? If the administrators, faculty, and student leaders at your school were to redesign the orientation program, what changes would you suggest they make?

2. At some involving colleges, we are told, status differences are deliberately minimized; at others, they are emphasized, as long as those status differences are based upon merit. How easily recognized are differences in academic, professional, and intellectual status at your institution? How obvious do you think they should be?

3. How important are campus history and traditions at your school? How do they help establish (or, for that matter, prevent) the feelings of community the authors describe?

Questions for Research and Writing

1. The headnote to and first paragraph of this reading say that news media often emphasize the bad news about college life. For the next several weeks, systematically keep a clipping file of articles about campus life that appear in your local newspaper and national newsmagazines and newspapers. Describe the news media's characterization of campus life. Given your own knowledge of campus life, to what extent do those characterizations seem justified?
2. Imagine that you have been asked to write the kind of "pithy, light-hearted publication" that Stanford sophomores write to prepare first-year students for Stanford life. What would you tell a prospective student about the "cycles, extremes, and challenges first-year students are likely to encounter" at your school? What would you tell them about the traditions and history of your campus? About its symbols and what they represent? About faculty/student relations?

COLLEGE SLANG REVISITED
Language, Culture, and Undergraduate Life
David M. Hummon

> *In this article from the January–February volume of* The Journal of Higher Education, *anthropology and sociology professor David M. Hummon studies the linguistic patterns of college undergraduates. Looking at slang, a subject that most of us probably don't consider the stuff of academic analyses, Hummon puts undergraduates under an analytical microscope and uses his statistical data to form conclusions about their lifestyles and values. As you read through the article, ask yourself whether Hummon's methodology seems valid, whether you agree with the conclusions he draws, and whether your language is revealing something important about your lifestyle and values.*

"Kansas University Slang" by Dundes and Schonhorn [9] stands as a landmark in the study of college slang. The immediate goal of the article was to replicate a 1926 study of college slang at the University of Kansas and, by doing so, to document continuity and change in undergraduate speech. Yet, Dundes and Schonhorn certainly envisioned more than this. By the 1960s, they noted, college slang had been an object of study for more than a century. Compendiums of student language and customs appeared as early as 1851 [15]; more serious surveys of student language followed by the turn of the century [1]. In the three decades following the First World War, students of American slang published more than thirty compilations of student expressions from a wide range of institutions: Brown and Stanford, Annapolis and The Citadel, the Universities of Florida and Nebraska, Bryn Mawr and Smith. Now, by offering a scholarly, comparative study of campus slang, Dundes and Schonhorn wished at once to affirm the significance of this research tradition and to call for renewed, systematic analyses of "the vital idiom of American college youth" [9, p. 177].

"Kansas University Slang" did elicit a flurry of responses; some were based on new research on student slang at Ohio State [2] and the University of California at San Francisco [24], while others challenged the study of college slang on theoretical grounds [18, 25, 26]. As the decade closed, however, articles on campus slang largely disappeared from scholarly journals. "Kansas University Slang," rather than signal the beginning of a new wave of college slang studies, marked the end of a century's fascination with undergraduate speech.[1]

This article takes a fresh look at undergraduate slang by examining the slang identities that students use to characterize peers. Based on the results of a systematic comparison of such terms at two institutions, I conclude that undergraduate speech draws from both the general slang of the larger culture and from a subcultural vocabulary of college slang terms, of which some are broadly shared as part of a national collegiate subculture and others are part of more provincial regional or institutional subcultures. I also propose that college slang, as opposed to general slang, plays a specific role in undergraduate life, providing terms that are particularly appropriate to undergraduate conceptions of college life. In short, I argue that college slang remains a significant subcultural idiom, yet one complexly situated in the multiple social worlds of contemporary undergraduate life.

COLLEGE SLANG: A WORKING PERSPECTIVE

In their classic article, Dundes and Schonhorn [9] never defined college slang, but simply referred to the "characteristic diction of the American undergraduate" [p. 163] and "the vital idiom of American college youth" [p. 174]. To some extent, this may be a result of method: the classification of particular expressions as college slang was preordained in the very enterprise of replication. Thus, they directly elicited slang terms from K.U. undergraduates by providing denotative phrases for both academic and social life—for instance, asking for terms for "a studious classmate" or "an unpleasant male date." These solicited terms were then compared with previously documented slang. Yet, this omission also suggests that the definition of what constituted college slang was relatively unproblematic. That undergraduates spoke with a distinct style and expressive vocabulary, that this undergraduate speech was peculiar to college life, and that such slang focused primarily on academic and social concerns—all these observations were largely taken for granted.

Critics of Dundes and Schonhorn immediately challenged several of these assumptions [see, especially, 2, 18, 25]. Most often, they raised questions about slang usage. Was *college* slang best conceptualized as any slang used by undergraduates, slang used exclusively by undergraduates, or slang learned by undergraduates while at college? Was it limited to terms commonly shared by undergraduates, or did it include more specialized vocabularies within the student world—for instance, those of a fraternity or an engineering school? Less often, they raised concerns about language style and diction. Were student terms for formal curricula really *slang* terms; were there other important facets of college speech that were not slang?

These queries suggest a need for a working definition of college slang, however difficult such a definition may be.[2] Following Flexner's classic statement, I regard slang as language that is "not accepted as good, formal usage" by the majority of the public and that is largely part of oral, rather than written, expression [12]. Stylistically, such informal discourse is often highly expressive, rich in metaphor. It also often "lacks dignity": its insertion in more formal speech or writing will destroy the gravity of the statement [8]. Socially, slang terms are frequently ephemeral in usage, but this is not always the case. Many, characterized as *general slang,* are widely recognized in the culture; others—*subcultural slang*—are intelligible only within a smaller social world.

In this context, *college slang* can be defined as *oral, informal, highly expressive language that is created and used primarily by students as part of undergraduate life.* As such, college slang is distinctly *subcultural in usage,* spoken within the bounded social worlds of undergraduate life and used to symbolize identification with other undergraduates [10]. Not all slang spoken by undergraduates is college slang; much, in fact, draws on general slang terms that students appropriate from the broader culture. Similarly, college slang is *subcultural in meaning,* more often than not communicating the values of undergraduates rather than the concerns of other adults in and outside of the academy. With its informal style and student orientation, college slang is the expressive medium of student life, often unknown, sometimes offensive to those not part of the subculture.

COLLECTING SLANG IDENTITIES

To study college slang, I have focused on slang terms that students use to characterize their peers. Such *slang identities* are primarily used to typify others rather than self. As social identities, they enable undergraduates to categorize people and to infer both personal and social attributes on the basis of such placement [14].

Such a focus on slang identities is particularly fruitful for an analysis of college slang for several reasons. First, college slang identities are a central and enduring part of student culture, reported in historical studies of both American and English undergraduate life [17, 21].[3] Second, the slang identities used by undergraduates are drawn from both the larger culture (for example, *jock, yuppie, barbie doll*) and the subculture of student life (for example, *dork, party animal, blade*). By collecting slang identities, it becomes possible to compare the relative usage of general and college slang and to examine the range of meanings conveyed by each type of slang. Finally, slang identities provide an inclusive system of classification for all facets of undergraduate life, thus facilitating an analysis of the role of slang in such different domains of undergraduate life as academics, extracurricular activity, and informal sociability.

The primary sample of slang identities was collected at Holy Cross College, a private, Jesuit, liberal arts college in Massachusetts. Its 2,500 undergraduate students come predominantly from New England (54 percent) or the Mid-Atlantic states (33 percent). Eight out of ten reside on campus, and most of the remainder live in neighborhoods adjacent to the campus [5]. These slang epithets were collected *by* undergraduates through peer interviews and participant observation, thus providing direct access to student culture. Between the fall semesters of 1985 and 1988, students in seven introductory sociology classes were invited to participate in this project as part of their research paper assignment. Student researchers, both men and women, completed a minimum of four focused interviews with peers who differed in gender and academic class. Using a standard interview form, they asked respondents to volunteer "labels" that students "use to identify different types of students at Holy Cross" and to suggest a definition for each identity offered. For part of a day, student researchers also observed slang use among peers, recording the place of usage, the referent of usage (self/other), and the apparent meaning of the term.

A secondary sample of slang identities was collected at the University of California at Davis. Davis's 16,000 undergraduate students are predominantly Californians (95 percent), less than one-third of whom reside in university housing [5].[4] In 1988 undergraduates in a social psychology class were given the opportunity to list and define student identities that "you know are used by students at U.C., Davis."

At Holy Cross 137 student researchers collected 465 slang identities. At Davis, 51 students volunteered 239 different epithets.[5] All terms, even when similar in meaning and language, were treated as distinct identities for purposes of analysis (for example, *crewbie and crewton; jocksniff and jocklover*). They were recorded, defined by using student definitions, coded for both usage and meaning, and analyzed using a database program.

COLLEGE SLANG: USAGE

Michael Moffatt's recent ethnography of undergraduate life at Rutgers [23] makes two important points about undergraduate speech. Contemporary undergraduates spend a considerable portion of their day talking informally and "hanging-out" with their peers, devoting as much of their day to such "friendly fun" and "verbal banter" as to academic pursuits. Much of this talk at Rutgers is sprinkled with slang terms, including slang identities for academic concerns (*grind, bio-sci, computer nerd, hot shot, throat, blow-it-off, study-holic*), social competence (*nerd, Poindexter, airhead*), unfriendliness (*phoney, asshole, wimp, bitch, scumbag, faggot*), drug use (*burnout*), clothing styles (*prep, punk, gay, GQ, jock*), ethnic and racial epithets (*spics, nigger, Sambo*), women as sex-objects (*chicks, broads, sluts*), and sexual prowess (*scorers*).[6]

To what extent can these slang terms spoken by contemporary undergraduates be considered *college* slang—that is, terms and expressions that are part of a distinct undergraduate subculture? Several forms of indirect evidence suggest that at least some of this slang is transmitted as part of a culture of undergraduate life. A few slang terms—like *grind* and *crib*—have remarkably long histories, indicating intergenerational transmission of campus culture for more than a century [9, 17]. Moreover, studies of student recognition of slang terms at Ohio State and Princeton indicate that knowledge of slang terms increases between the first and fourth years, providing further evidence that undergraduates are socialized to a distinct language of college life [2, 13].

TABLE 1 Slang Usage: Social and Geographic Diffusion

Social Diffusion	Geographic Diffusion	
	National	*Local*
All adults	general slang	regional slang
Undergraduates only	national collegiate slang	local college slang

Somewhat more direct evidence can be obtained by examining the extent to which slang identities voiced by college students are diffused across *social* and *geographic* boundaries (see table 1). Following Fine's study of preadolescent slang [11], such social diffusion can be estimated by comparing slang identities spoken by college students with those listed in a contemporaneous dictionary of American slang [6], thus distinguishing terms that are generally known to the public from those that are subcultural. Such geographic diffusion can be estimated by comparing slang usage at widely separated undergraduate campuses. If the slang used by undergraduates is part of a distinct undergraduate culture, some such college slang should be shared by undergraduates at different institutions (*collegiate slang*) as opposed to being known only at single institutions (*local college slang*).

Table 2 provides simple estimates of the extent to which slang identities used by students at Holy Cross and U.C., Davis are general slang, collegiate slang, or local college slang. Column 1 shows that approximately one third (30.5 percent) of the 642 slang identities voiced at one or the other campus are general slang—identities that are present in *The New Dictionary of American Slang* [6] with identical or similar meanings to those offered by students. Conversely, approximately two-thirds of the identities used by students might be designated college slang—identities that were absent from *The New Dictionary*, or if present, (a) had a substantially different meaning, or (b) were explicitly noted to be college or high-school slang.

Column 2 indicates that 62 slang identities—approximately one in ten—were *volunteered* at both the liberal arts college and the university campus on opposite coasts. (Had students been directly asked about stated terms, this proportion would undoubtedly be higher.) Two out of three of these terms, however, are also found in *The New Dictionary of American Slang*, suggesting that widely known slang identities used by students are also likely to be general American slang—terms such as *babe, bitch, brown noser, dick, jerk, jew, womanizer,* and *yuppie.* Nevertheless, some terms qualify as collegiate slang, both widely known and socially bounded: terms such as *dork, dweeb, god, god squad, granola, monger, party animal.*

Finally, columns 3 and 4 indicate that the use of college slang may well vary by institution. In this comparison, students at Holy Cross volunteered a significantly higher proportion of college slang identities than

TABLE 2 Slang Identity Usage: Simple Estimates
of Social and Geographic Diffusion

Social Usage	Geographic Diffusion			
	Term volunteered at:			
	College or University	College and University	College	University
General slang[1]	30.5%	66.1%	27.7%	45.2%
College slang[2]	69.5	33.9%	72.3	54.8%
	100.0%	100.0%	100.0%	100.0%
	(642)	(62)	(465)	(239)

[1] An identity was classified as general American slang if it was recorded in *The New Dictionary of American Slang* [6] and if it had an identical or similar meaning to that offered by students.
[2] An identity was classified as subcultural slang if it was either absent from *The New Dictionary of American Slang* or, if present: (a) it had a substantially different meaning from that of the dictionary or (b) it was explicitly noted by the dictionary to be high-school or college-student slang.

did undergraduates at U.C., Davis. Though this may be an artifact of method, the relative density of college slang terms at Holy Cross is certainly consistent with a subcultural interpretation of college slang, if one assumes that the small, private, socially homogeneous residential college provides a more coherent and exclusive social context for the elaboration and transmission of student culture. This assumption receives partial confirmation from a South African study of student slang in private and public high schools. There, students of private institutions have more extensive knowledge of adolescent slang than do those in government schools [7].

In sum, table 2 indicates a complex pattern of slang usage, but one suggestive of the presence of significant college slang. Though undergraduate students, as members of the larger society, draw upon general slang identities to categorize and interpret other students, they also appropriate slang epithets from student subculture, a subculture that is in part national in scope, in part provincial, known only within regional or institutional contexts.[7]

The relatively high proportion of college slang identities that appear to be local rather than collegiate terms, however, raises one final question about college slang usage. Are local college slang terms broadly shared by undergraduates at an institution or are they part of distinct *idiocultures* [11] within the undergraduate subculture? Though undergraduates share a social world as part of their collective experience as students, they, in turn, are certainly divided by idiocultures that cross-cut that undergraduate subculture. Such idiocultures may take highly varied forms, ranging from the traditional symbolic worlds of fraternities, varsity athletics, and student rebels [17] to the complex, ever-changing world of dormitory cliques [23].

TABLE 3 Holy Cross Slang Identities:
Detailed Social and Geographic Usage

Usage	All Identities		College Slang Identities	
	Percent of Identities	Percent of Reports	Percent of Identities	Percent of Reports
General slang[1]	27.7	35.5	—	—
College slang[2]	72.3	64.5	—	—
Collegiate[3]	(4.5)	(11.4)	6.3	17.7
Institutional[4]				
↑ Reports > 10%	(2.4)	(19.0)	3.3	29.4
Reports 5–10%	(3.0)	(6.1)	4.2	9.4
↓ Reports < 5%	(62.4)	(28.0)	86.3	43.4
Idiocultural				
	100.0%	100.0%	100.1%	99.9%
	(465)	(1416)	(336)	(914)

[1] See table 2 for definition. Examples: *airhead, artsy-fartsy, barbie doll, B.P., brown-noser, cutthroat, druggies, fag, goober, jock, loser, prep, stud.*
[2] See table 2 for definition.
[3] An identity was classified as collegiate slang if it was college slang and it was volunteered at Davis as well as Holy Cross. Examples: *dork, dweeb, flake, geek, god squad, granola, homeboy, hosebag, monger, nerd, new wave girl, partier, party animal, sleeze, study hound, wench.*
[4] An identity was classified as institutional slang or idiocultural slang if it was college slang and not reported at Davis. These terms are subdivided into three groups: (a) those reported by more than 10 percent of student researchers, (b) 5 to 9 percent of researchers, and (c) fewer than 5 percent of researchers. Examples: (a)—*blade, fatneck, jocksniff, band fag, RA Woorat* [Worcester resident], *O.C., Amazon, pre-med*; (b)—*blow-off artist, choir fag, crats, theater fag, tool, FICNAB, married, Beavenite, grind, moussehead, normal, pre-wed*; (c)—*8th grader, book fag, cherub, dorm potato, football wench, heathen, make-up gods, nuns, shellak head, scooping machine, chem geek, orgo-blade.*

Table 3 offers an initial answer to this question by providing a finer breakdown of slang identity usage at Holy Cross, based upon the relative frequency with which identities were *reported* by student researchers. (At Holy Cross, the 465 identities were reported 1416 times, some only once, a few as many as fifty times). As noted above, slang identities at Holy Cross were much more likely to be college slang (72 percent) than general slang (28 percent). Such college slang terms may well be used somewhat less frequently than general slang terms, for they make up only 65 percent of the total identity reports. Of college slang identities, *collegiate terms* like *dork, dweeb, geek, nerd, party animal* make up a relatively small proportion of slang epithets (6 percent). However, these epithets are used often, composing nearly 18 percent of identity reports. Of local college slang identities, a relatively small number of slang terms qualify as *institutional slang*, known by most undergraduates at Holy Cross. Words like *blade, fatneck, jocksniff, RA* 'resident assistant,' *Woorat* 'Worcester resident,' *amazon*, though composing only a small proportion of college slang identities (3 percent), account for nearly 30 percent of the identity reports of college slang terms. Conversely, the substantial majority of college slang terms may well be *idiocultural*, words like *8th grader* 'student who acts immature,' *cherub* 'overweight young woman with a great personality,' *make-up god* 'young woman with excessive, unnatural make-up,' *sci-lib* 'student who spends much time in the science library.'[8]

In sum, tables 2 and 3 document a highly layered, complex pattern of slang usage among undergraduates, ranging from general slang usage on the one hand to the highly localized, socially circumscribed idiographic terms of small-group culture on the other. This intricate pattern of language use reflects the complex and stratified world of contemporary undergraduates, a world firmly embedded in the larger society, yet also shaped by the shared interests of college life, the immediate experiences of the local institution, and the volatile, intimate concerns of peer group sociability.

COLLEGE SLANG: MEANINGS

If college students spend much of their time in informal conversation with their peers, if much of their speech makes use of slang terms that are used and recognized primarily within the social worlds of undergraduate life, then we might also expect that the meanings of such slang will be expressive of the student subculture. To the extent that this is the case, college slang should symbolize reality in a manner that is consistent with undergraduate experience and values [22]. In particular, college slang should provide a rich vocabulary for those facets of experience that are important or unique to undergraduate life. Also, college slang should facilitate a student perspective on college life, interpreting daily life in a manner consistent with student, as opposed to institutional, interests.[9]

These functions of college slang can be explored by examining the patterns of meaning conveyed by undergraduate slang identities in general and by college slang identities in particular. To undertake this analysis, I constructed a system of classification for the meanings of slang identities, using the 642 epithets volunteered at Holy Cross and Davis and the definitions for these terms supplied by students. Table 4 provides a summary of this coding system along with illustrative identities for the 52 basic categories of meaning.[10]

When viewed as a whole, this coding system indicates that students collectively use slang to talk about a wide range of matters. Slang epithets can be used to characterize peers in terms of daily campus life, including matters of academics, social life, and the more formal extracurriculum. They enable the discrimination of classmates in terms of more personal attributes, including aspects of personality, physical demeanor, and values. They even provide typifications for placing students within the broader social strata of the society and the fine-grained groupings of private life.

TABLE 4 Coding Categories and Illustrative Identities

CAMPUS LIFE: ACADEMIC		PERSONAL ATTRIBUTES: PERSONALITY, continued	
Academic subject	chemhead, premie		
Study, +/−	blade/blow-off artist	Self-centered	snob, actress, wise guy
Teacher-student	brown-noser, the hand	Stingy	leech, jew, mooch, sponge
		Unreliable/ reliable	flake/(good man, normal)★
CAMPUS LIFE: EXTRACURRICULAR		Follower	groupie
Art & theater & music	artsy-farts, band-fag	Well-rounded/ narrow	Joe Holy Cross/ (geek)★
Athletics	jock, crewton, fatneck	PERSONAL ATTRIBUTES: PHYSICAL DEMEANOR	
Campus locale	Beavenite, O.C., shut-in		
Institutional-ties	alumni brat	Attractive/ugly	babe/butt ugly
Involvement, +/−	gung-hos/room potato	Body, good/bad	golden girl/ (mega-moo)★
Military	jarhead, Nazi-rotc	Clumsy	gomer, spaz, bozo
Other organizations	Keyer, frat rat	Dress	JAPS, pure prep
Campus jobs	Kimbalite, Kimball rat	Grooming & make-up	wind-tunnel chick
		Weak/strong	wuss-wimp/ (Marlboro man)★
CAMPUS LIFE: SOCIAL			
Alcohol, +/−	beerchugger, alkie	PERSONAL ATTRIBUTES: VALUES	
Drugs	heads, burnout, stoner	Liberal/conservative	commie/cookie cutter
Party life, +/−	party animal/polly purity	Nature	granola
		Politics	martyr
Recreation, other	coach potato, gameroom rat	Religion +/−	god squad/heathen
Sex activity, +/−	sleezebag, sex monger	SOCIETAL GROUPS	
PERSONAL ATTRIBUTES: PERSONALITY		Age, +/−	eighth grader/fossil
		Class	beautiful person, crat
Social competence, +/−	dweeb, gweeb, loser	Gender	
		Female id	barbie doll, jocksniff
Easy-going/intense	mellow/monger	Male id	dude, stud, wimp
Dumb/smart	airhead, bonehead/ brain	Generation	sixties dude
		Race or ethnicity	'rican, spicks, niggers
Enthusiast/ complainer	Mrs. Holy Cross/ wanta be	Rural/urban	hick, aggie
Inauthentic	plastic person	Sexual orientation	dyke, fag, flamer, homo
Individualist	deviant, freak, rebels	PRIMARY GROUPS	
Lazy	sloth, waste product		
Nice/nasty	peach, saint/jerk, dink	Couples & dating	appendage, marrieds
		Friend	homeboy, homegirl
Crazy/normal	gocher/wicked-good-kid	MISCELLANEOUS	
Exclusive	(crats, P. R.)★		cigarette group

★Illustrations in parentheses have this meaning for a secondary connotation.

What, however, do slang terms enable students to talk about with ease, providing multiple terms to communicate the same meaning? What meanings are most easily communicated by general slang and college slang? What meanings are communicated most frequently through general and college slang?

Tables 5 and 6 shed light on these questions. Both focus on the primary meaning communicated by an identity.[11] Table 5 summarizes the *proportion of identities* collected at Holy Cross or Davis that communicate a given meaning. As such, it indicates the relative *density* of slang terms with a given meaning, indicating areas of student life for which there are relatively many or few terms to communicate a given meaning. Table 6 provides a summary of the *relative frequency with which slang identities with a given meaning were reported* at an institution, based on 1,416 reports of 465 identities at Holy Cross and 405 reports of 239 identities at Davis. As such, it offers a simple estimate of the relative *frequency* with which slang identities are used to communicate a given meaning.

Campus Life

Undergraduates at both schools use slang epithets to characterize peers in terms of campus life. They are substantially more likely to do so at Holy Cross, where 33 percent of identities and 44 percent of reported usages address campus life, compared to 18 percent for both identities and usages at Davis. Notably, a higher proportion of college, as opposed to general, slang terms typify students in terms of campus life, though some notable exceptions to this pattern do exist for subcategories of meaning.

Academic life. Slang epithets that classify peers in terms of academic life make up a modest but significant proportion of terms (7 percent) and usages (13 percent) at Holy Cross, but are relatively infrequent at Davis (4 percent, 5 percent). The over-all scarcity of such slang terms is, itself, notable: this domain of undergraduate life is the most controlled by faculty and administrative policy and the least segregated by age [compare 10, 23]. Of such identities, those dealing with study habits are prevalent at both schools, and distinctively college slang terms contribute disproportionately to this vocabulary. More often than not, these identities stigmatize students who study excessively in terms of student subcultural norms (*grind, blade, book fag, book worm, curve buster, druid, gunner, mole, Myrons, study hound, Chemical gweeps, Dinand rat, computer heads, pseudo blade, blade-geek, study monger, cut-throat*), but some terms exist for those who study appropriately (*Joe Average College*) or too little (*blow-off artist, pseudo student; 3D loser, padders*).* Relatively few terms exist for identifying students in terms of their

---

*Unless noted otherwise in the text, I have included examples of slang epithets from both institutions, listing college slang terms first, then those classified as general slang: (college slang, a, b, c, d; general slang, a, b, c, d).

TABLE 5 Primary Meanings of Identities
by Institution and Type of Slang

	INSTITUTION					
	Holy Cross Slang Type			U.C., Davis Slang Type		
	All	General	College	All	General	College
	%	%	%	%	%	%
Campus Life	(33.7)	(30.3)	(35.4)	(18.1)	(14.0)	(21.6)
Academic Life	(7.3)	(4.6)	(8.4)	(4.2)	(2.8)	(5.4)
Study habits	4.7	2.3	5.7	2.5	0.9	3.8
Academic subject	1.5	0.0	2.1	0.4	0.0	0.8
Student-teacher	1.1	2.3	0.6	1.3	1.9	0.8
Extracurricular Life	(17.5)	(14.8)	(18.9)	(4.6)	(1.8)	(6.9)
Athletics	4.1	4.7	3.9	0.4	0.9	0.0
Campus locale	3.2	0.8	4.2	0.0	0.0	0.0
Art & music & theater	3.0	2.3	3.3	1.7	0.9	2.3
Involved in campus life	2.6	3.9	2.1	0.4	0.0	0.8
Military	1.7	3.1	1.2	0.0	0.0	0.0
Other organizations	1.7	0.0	2.4	2.1	0.0	3.8
Campus jobs	0.6	0.0	0.9	0.0	0.0	0.0
Institutional ties	0.6	0.0	0.9	0.0	0.0	0.0
Social Life	(8.9)	(10.9)	(8.1)	(9.3)	(9.4)	(9.3)
Party life	3.0	0.8	3.9	2.1	1.9	2.3
Drugs	2.4	5.4	1.2	1.7	2.8	0.8
Alcohol	1.3	2.3	0.9	1.3	1.9	0.8
Sexual activity	1.3	0.8	1.5	2.1	1.9	2.3
Recreation	0.9	1.6	0.6	2.1	0.9	3.1
Personal Attributes	(27.8)	(35.2)	(25.5)	(40.1)	(47.2)	(34.4)
Personality	(17.1)	(26.5)	(13.8)	(26.4)	(29.7)	(23.7)
Nice/nasty	3.2	5.4	2.4	6.7	8.3	5.3
Individualist	3.2	3.1	3.3	0.4	0.0	0.8
Dumb/smart	2.8	6.2	1.5	7.1	6.5	7.6
Social competence	1.9	2.3	1.8	2.5	2.8	2.3
Normal/crazy	1.1	1.6	0.9	2.1	2.8	1.5
Authentic/inauthentic	0.9	0.8	0.9	1.7	1.9	1.5
Self-centered/others	0.9	0.8	0.9	1.3	1.9	0.8
Share/stingy	0.9	3.1	0.0	0.4	0.9	0.0
Easy-going/intense	0.4	0.8	0.3	2.1	3.7	0.8
Enthusiast/complainer	0.4	0.0	0.6	0.4	0.0	0.8
Follower	0.4	1.6	0.0	0.0	0.0	0.0
Lazy	0.4	0.0	0.6	0.0	0.0	0.0
Well-rounded/narrow	0.4	0.8	0.3	0.0	0.0	0.0
Reliable/unreliable	0.2	0.0	0.3	1.3	0.9	1.5
Open/exclusive	0.0	0.0	0.0	0.4	0.0	0.8
Physical Demeanor	(7.1)	(6.3)	(7.5)	(12.1)	(15.7)	(9.1)
Dress	2.6	2.3	2.7	2.1	2.8	1.5
Grooming & make-up	1.9	0.8	2.4	0.4	0.9	0.0
Attractive/ugly	1.1	1.6	0.9	5.0	4.6	5.3
Clumsy	0.9	1.6	0.6	0.8	1.9	0.0
Body	0.4	0.0	0.6	1.3	0.9	1.5
Weak/strong	0.2	0.0	0.3	2.5	4.6	0.8

TABLE 5 Primary Meanings of Identities by Institution and Type of Slang, *continued*

	INSTITUTION					
	Holy Cross Slang Type			U.C., Davis Slang Type		
	All	General	College	All	General	College
	%	%	%	%	%	%
Personal Attributes, *continued*						
Values	(3.6)	(2.4)	(4.2)	(1.6)	(1.8)	(1.6)
Religion	2.2	1.6	2.4	0.8	0.9	0.8
Liberal/conservative	0.6	0.8	0.6	0.4	0.9	0.0
Nature	0.6	0.0	0.9	0.4	0.0	0.8
Politics	0.2	0.0	0.3	0.0	0.0	0.0
Societal Groups	(35.4)	(34.2)	(35.7)	(40.1)	(38.1)	(42.0)
Gender:						
Female	17.2	11.6	19.3	16.7	17.6	16.0
Male	8.2	10.1	7.4	12.6	8.3	16.0
Social class	3.0	2.3	3.3	0.8	1.9	0.0
Race & ethnicity	2.2	1.6	2.4	1.7	1.9	1.5
Sexual orientation	2.2	7.0	0.3	3.3	4.6	2.3
Community & region	1.5	0.8	1.8	0.4	0.0	0.8
Age	0.9	0.8	0.9	2.5	1.9	3.1
Generation	0.2	0.0	0.3	0.0	0.0	0.0
Rural/urban	0.0	0.0	0.0	2.1	1.9	2.3
Primary Relations	(2.1)	(0.8)	(2.7)	(1.6)	(0.9)	(2.3)
Couples & dating	1.9	0.8	2.4	0.8	0.9	0.8
Friend	0.2	0.0	0.3	0.8	0.0	1.5
Miscellaneous	0.9	0.0	1.2	0.0	0.0	0.0
	99.9%	99.7%	100.5%	99.9%	100.2%	100.3%
	(465)	(129)	(336)	(239)	(108)	(131)

relations with teachers; those that do are always pejorative and more often general slang terms (*ass-kisser, brown-noser, kiss-ass*) than not (*heroes, the hand, butt-sniff*). Identities communicating academic major or subject area, though relatively uncommon, are exclusively college slang terms (*bio-sci, chemhead, eco-acc, orgo-blade, pre-med, premie, chem geek*).

Extracurricular life. Slang identities based on formal extracurricular life are relatively common as terms (17.5 percent) and usages (24 percent) at Holy Cross, but are infrequent at Davis (4.6 percent, 6.4 percent). Of such terms at Holy Cross, slang identities for athletes are most common, with general slang (*jock, musclehead, no neck*) and college slang (*crewfag, crewton, F.B.P.* 'football player,' *fatneck, hooper, intramural all star, crewbies*) contributing similar proportions of such epithets. Terms identifying peers through campus locales are also notable at Holy Cross and are very much the stuff of local college slang. Such terms include dormitory identities

TABLE 6 Frequency of Reports of Primary Meanings of Identities by Institution and Type of Slang

	INSTITUTION					
	Holy Cross Slang Type			U.C., Davis Slang Type		
	All %	General %	College %	All %	General %	College %
Campus Life	(44.4)	(40.0)	(46.6)	(18.0)	(20.7)	(15.0)
Academic Life	(12.8)	(11.0)	(13.8)	(4.7)	(5.8)	(3.5)
Study habits	9.9	6.6	11.7	1.5	0.5	2.5
Academic subject	1.1	0.0	1.8	0.2	0.0	0.5
Student-teacher	1.8	4.4	0.3	3.0	5.3	0.5
Extracurricular Life	(23.6)	(20.4)	(25.2)	(6.4)	(7.7)	(5.0)
Athletics	10.4	12.2	9.4	3.7	7.2	0.0
Campus locale	2.8	1.6	3.4	0.0	0.0	0.0
Art & music & theater	4.7	3.8	5.1	1.0	0.5	1.5
Involved in campus life	1.6	1.6	1.5	0.5	0.0	1.0
Military	0.8	1.2	0.7	0.0	0.0	0.0
Other organizations	1.8	0.0	2.8	1.2	0.0	2.5
Campus jobs	0.5	0.0	0.8	0.0	0.0	0.0
Institutional ties	1.0	0.0	1.5	0.0	0.0	0.0
Social Life	(8.0)	(8.6)	(7.6)	(6.9)	(7.2)	(6.5)
Party life	3.2	0.2	4.8	1.2	1.0	1.5
Drugs	2.0	4.4	0.8	1.5	2.4	0.5
Alcohol	1.0	1.8	0.5	1.0	1.0	1.0
Sexual activity	1.2	1.2	1.2	1.5	1.4	1.5
Recreation	0.6	1.0	0.3	1.7	1.4	2.0
Personal Attributes	(21.3)	(26.0)	(18.7)	(38.4)	(41.6)	(36.3)
Personality	(13.6)	(17.6)	(11.2)	(27.5)	(27.0)	(28.8)
Nice/nasty	2.3	3.4	1.8	6.4	7.7	5.1
Individualist	1.6	2.0	1.3	0.2	0.0	0.5
Dumb/smart	2.1	3.4	1.4	9.1	7.7	10.6
Social competence	4.3	4.6	4.2	5.4	5.3	5.6
Normal/crazy	0.4	0.4	0.3	1.2	1.4	1.0
Authentic/inauthentic	0.4	0.2	0.4	1.2	1.0	1.5
Self-centered/others	0.4	0.2	0.5	0.7	1.0	0.5
Share/stingy	0.7	2.0	0.0	0.2	0.5	0.0
Easy-going/intense	0.1	0.2	0.1	1.2	1.9	0.5
Enthusiast/complainer	0.3	0.0	0.4	0.2	0.0	0.5
Follower	0.3	0.8	0.0	0.0	0.0	0.0
Lazy	0.3	0.0	0.4	0.0	0.0	0.0
Well-rounded/narrow	0.2	0.4	0.1	0.0	0.0	0.0
Reliable/unreliable	0.2	0.0	0.3	1.5	0.5	2.5
Open/exclusive	0.0	0.0	0.0	0.2	0.0	0.5
Physical Demeanor	(5.4)	(7.6)	(4.3)	(10.0)	(13.6)	(6.5)
Dress	2.3	4.8	1.0	1.7	1.9	1.5
Grooming & make-up	1.6	0.2	2.4	0.2	0.5	0.0
Attractive/ugly	0.8	1.8	0.3	4.9	6.3	3.5
Clumsy	0.5	0.8	0.3	0.5	1.0	0.0
Body	0.1	0.0	0.2	0.7	0.5	1.0
Weak/strong	0.07	0.0	0.1	2.0	3.4	0.5

TABLE 6 Frequency of Reports of Primary Meanings of Identities by Institution and Type of Slang, *continued*

	INSTITUTION					
	Holy Cross Slang Type			U.C., Davis Slang Type		
	All	General	College	All	General	College
	%	%	%	%	%	%
Personal Attributes, *continued*						
Values	(2.3)	(0.8)	(3.2)	(0.9)	(1.0)	(1.0)
Religion	1.8	0.6	2.5	0.5	0.5	0.5
Liberal/conservative	0.2	0.2	0.2	0.2	0.5	0.0
Nature	0.2	0.0	0.3	0.2	0.0	0.5
Politics	0.1	0.0	0.2	0.0	0.0	0.0
Societal Groups	(32.2)	(34.2)	(31.1)	(40.9)	(36.8)	(45.3)
Gender:						
Female	13.5	8.2	16.4	12.6	12.1	13.1
Male	7.3	6.4	7.8	20.2	15.9	24.7
Social class	5.9	11.8	2.7	0.5	1.0	0.0
Race & ethnicity	1.2	0.6	1.5	1.0	1.0	1.0
Sexual orientation	2.3	6.4	0.1	3.7	4.8	2.5
Community & region	1.4	0.2	2.1	0.2	0.0	0.5
Age	0.5	0.6	0.4	1.5	1.0	2.0
Generation	0.1	0.0	0.1	0.0	0.0	0.0
Rural/urban	0.0	0.0	0.0	1.2	1.0	1.5
Primary Relations	(1.8)	(0.2)	(2.6)	(1.9)	(1.0)	(3.0)
Couples & dating	1.7	0.2	2.5	0.7	1.0	0.5
Friend	0.1	0.0	0.1	1.2	0.0	2.5
Miscellaneous	0.3	0.0	0.4	0.0	0.0	0.0
	100.0%	100.4%	99.4%	99.2%	101.1%	99.6%
	(1416)	(502)	(914)	(405)	(207)	(198)

(*Beavenite, Healy boy*), terms for off-campus apartment complexes (*Cambridge Crew, Caro Street girls*), as well as more general terms (*O.C.* 'off-campus,' *hall rat, sci-libs, shut-ins*). Students associated with the theater, band, or other artistic activities are often labeled (*band fag, band-uh, choir fag, band geek, play fag, rasta, theater jocks; artsy, art freaks, artsy fartsy, rocker*), as are students identified with other campus organizations. At Holy Cross such identities ranged from terms for students affiliated with officer training programs (*bullethead, rambo, squid, nazi-rotc; fly boys, jarhead, skinhead*) to the clique associated with the campus radio station (*WCHC people, radio-station punk*). At Davis, such epithets focused on fraternity life (*frat rat, frat-brat, frat dweeb, Greek child*).

Campus social life. Slang epithets concerned with informal peer sociability and leisure make up a modest but notable proportion of terms and usages at both schools (Holy Cross, 9 percent, 8 percent; Davis, 9 percent, 7 percent). Subcultural slang, particularly, provides a range of terms for those who "party" a good deal (*party animal, party-people, party hound, party monsters, screw-up, festive people, fun bunch, general party guys, grunchies, cool heads, hot babe, mad-man; wild*) or don't (*polly purities, squirrel, dud*). Alcohol and drug-related identities are present, with general slang terms contributing disproportionately to such epithets (alcohol: *beer chugger, drinking crowd, headbanger, lush, zonk, alkie, hammered;* drug use: *hoofhead, dopeheads, burnout, loadie; heads, deadhead, pothead, drughead, stoner, druggie*). Identities denoting recreational sexuality also occur, but are relatively uncommon as primary meanings (*micro wave girl, sex monger, sleeze, sleezebag, perv, public maker* versus *prude; tease, scammer, smoocher*). However, such terms are quite common as secondary or tertiary meanings of gender identities (see below).

Personal Attributes

Slang epithets that can be used to characterize the personal qualities of individuals are common in undergraduate speech. Such identities are substantially more prevalent at Davis, where they account for 40 percent of the identities and 38 percent of the reported usages (versus 28 percent and 21 percent at Holy Cross). Unlike identities concerned with campus life, these epithets constitute a greater proportion of general than college slang identities.

Personality. Most often, such terms denote facets of an individual's personality or interactional style—26 percent of the terms at Davis; 17 percent, at Holy Cross. At Davis and Holy Cross, identities commonly convey whether a person is nice (*good man, saint; peach*) or, more often, nasty (*backstabber, butt-head, butt-wipe, dick ball, dick lick, neo-maxi-zoom-dweebi, nimrod, master of unknown facts, S.S.C.* 'serious social climber,' *saccharin sweet, scum, tool; asshole, jerk, jerk-off, dink, douche* or *douche-bag, mouth, scumbag, shit-head, slime, turd, weasel, wienie*). Similarly rich vocabularies exist for persons that are smart (*god, smack; brain*) or less intelligent (*blondie, clueless, dork, dupahead, hair-brain, id, poozer, queeb, sketch, slow leak, wog, zippy; airhead, bonehead, chump, dufus, knob, knobhead, lame, loonie, pudding head, space case, space cadet, tard, zoner*). At Davis, other relatively common slang epithets for personality characterize people in term[s] of social competence (*fab; cool*) or incompetence (*dweeb, neanderfuck; goober, loser*); "craziness" (*nut-bucket, weenie-1; case, F.U.B.A.R.* 'Fucked-Up Beyond All Recognition,' *psycho*); and whether a person's outlook is easy-going ([none listed; *freak, puppet*) or intense (*monger; boner, pigheaded, tight ass*). At Holy Cross, terms describing students in terms of highly individualistic personality are also notable (*outcases, deviants, revolutionaries, the fringe, real people, rebels; freak, funky people, radicals, rads*).

As a group, these personality identities are unusual for their relative variety of meanings, enabling the communication of a wide range of qualities. Though rare, slang identities are even reported for people who are inauthentic (*credit card people, politicians, hoodsie, bleeder, poser; plastic, bull-*

shitter); self-centered (*actress, snob, snaughty, righteous; stuck-up, ego-tripper, wise guy*); stingy ([none listed]; *jew, leech, mooch, sponge*); or lazy (*sloth, waste product*); or unreliable (*flake, weak tit; fuck-up*).

Physical demeanor. Identities that classify peers in terms of physical demeanor are relatively common as terms (12 percent) and usages (10 percent) at Davis, and are notable, if less common at Holy Cross (7 percent, 5 percent). Of such terms, identities denoting styles of dress are relatively common at both Davis and Holy Cross (*pseudo prep, new wave girl, sack, young republican, Madonna wanna bees, pure prep, bombarded; JAPS, prep, mod, slob*). At Davis, terms characterizing physical beauty (*awesome, hella fine, sweet meat; babe, dollface, sweet*) or ugliness (*butt ugly, heinous, Herman, quasi-heinous; fugly*) are also common, as are those conveying weakness (*gimp; candy-ass, noodle, puss, pussy, whipped*).

Values. Slang identities for general value orientations are relatively rare among slang epithets at both campuses. At Holy Cross, only terms characterizing religious views and involvements are notable (*heathen, god squad, holly roller, religious nerds, religious fanatics, Euch Min; religious freaks, religious buffs*). Terms for politics (*martyr*), a liberal/conservative outlook (*young democrat, cookie cutter; commie*), and environmental commitment (*earthy-crunchie, granola*) are infrequent at both campuses.

Societal Groups

Students use slang identities to locate classmates in terms of the broad social positions of contemporary American society, such as gender, class, and race. Such terms are very common at Davis, where they compose 40 percent of terms and 41 percent of usages, and common at Holy Cross (35 percent, 32 percent). Such epithets may be either subcultural or general slang, depending on their particular focus.

Gender identities. Of such status identities, those of gender—characterizing an individual as a particular type of man or woman—are by far the most common at both campuses. In fact, they are the most frequent form of identity observed of all types, accounting for approximately one quarter of all slang epithets. As Holland and Skinner have recently noted, the abundance of such identities on campus may well be indicative of youth culture in general, an age-graded culture "devoted to the elaboration of gender relationships" [16, p. 106]. Yet, their prevalence may well be heightened by the college subculture, where dorm and campus life promote informal sociability and where students define "fun," including sexual fun, as an integral feature of college life [23].

Some sense of the variety and structure of gender identities can be gained by briefly examining several forms of such identities, based on the secondary meaning that such identities communicate. For both women and men, identities that address sexual activity are prevalent. A few college slang terms exist for women who are sexually inactive (*nuns, virgins, freaks*); a great many epithets for women who are considered promiscuous, most of which are pejorative and subcultural terms (*flinger, hose monster, hose bag, hoser, hugger, queenie, scooper, scrumper, slam piece, sled dog, slut, whore, shiksa, yut, bouff queen, donut, skank or scank, slut muffin; pig, gash or gasher, ho-bag, nympho*). For men, no terms mention sexual inactivity, and male sexual identities are likely to be favorable (*scoop king, schema, scooping machine, scoop master, scoop monster, user, abuser, queerbaits, gigolo; womanizer, cat, casanova*).

Gender identities denoting exceptional physical beauty are also relatively common for both women and men. An attractive woman may be described as *snapper, burger supreme, rocket, Wheeler blond; goddess, hot chick*; a handsome man, as a *calendar boy, G.Q. man, chunk, god, P.D.M.* 'Potential Date Material', *fine guy, tenda, Tommy, squala; doll, flash, hunk, stud*. Conversely, terms that stigmatize women who are unattractive in terms of subcultural norms are also relatively common (*smear, troll patrol, moose, women's movement, sixpack beauty queen; dog*), though no comparable terms are reported for men.

At both institutions, types of women are also classified in terms of grooming and make-up styles, sometimes with a neutral or favorable orientation (*Vogue girl, Farrah, Fawcett Flipper, sunflower chick; barbie doll*); more often with an unfavorable posture (*boof, buffonts, mousse patrol, puff heads, bifs, peroxide head, bitch head*). Body styling and shape also are typified (*aerobic queen*), nearly always in unfavorable terms (*hoss, mega-moo, F.U.B.* 'Fat Ugly Bitch,' *cherub, F.I.C.N.A.B.* 'Fat Irish-Catholic No-Action Broad,' *moo-moo, B.P. as bouncy poon* 'large-breasted bra-less woman,' *faked baked; fat chick, cow*). Finally, at Holy Cross, a set of college slang terms exists for women who are identified by their dependent relationship to male athletes (*jocksniff, sniff, crew sniff, rugby sniff, hockey pucks, football wenches, rugby queen, jocklover; football chick, jockettes, rugby groupie*).

Other statuses. Several other forms of status identities are notable in terms of their relative occurrence. At both campuses, slang identities stigmatizing nontraditional sexual orientation are reported, though these terms are most always general (*butch, dykes, fag, flamer, gay, homo, pretty boy, queer, fem*) rather than subcultural slang (*salad bar, queen, B. P. as bumping poon* 'lesbian', *butt pirate*). At Holy Cross, terms designating social class are also fairly common, particularly in terms of relative usage of general slang terms (*coolies, crats, gold card club, normals, phonies, pretty people, social climber, socialites, aristocrat, elitist; B. P. as beautiful people, rich bitch, yuppie*). Racial and ethnic epithets are reported, though usage is infrequent (*'rican, guido, P.R.* 'Puerto Rican', *united nations, spanish connection, little Spain; niggers, spicks*). At Davis, terms denoting age (*skipper, younglings, antique, wrinkled; jailbait, fossil*) and rural-urban background (*aggie, agr type, backward-ass-country-fuck; hick, redneck*) are also notable, but such terms are not reported frequently.

Primary Relations

As a group, slang identities for friends and other more private relations are uncommon at both Holy Cross (2.1 percent, 1.8 percent) and Davis (1.6 percent, 1.9 percent). Nevertheless, slang identities denoting friendship do exist (*homeboy, homegirl*), as well as several terms for labeling couples and romantic others (*appendages, husband-wife team, married, pre-wed, wuss, twins, lupe dobe; main squeeze, spoon*).

DISCUSSION

This analysis of the slang identities spoken by undergraduates provides several basic lessons for the study of college slang and undergraduate culture. First, because contemporary undergraduate life is socially complex, undergraduate slang is inevitably complex. Some is drawn from the general slang of the national culture; some, from a national collegiate culture of undergraduate life. Some is appropriated from regional or institutional sources; some has its origins in the ephemeral idiographic cultures of small-group experience. Such a pattern of slang usage suggests the continuing importance of college slang as a unique form of subcultural discourse. Yet, it also indicates that undergraduate speech is simultaneously open both to the changing fashions of national discourse and to the privatization of culture so common to late twentieth-century life [3].

Second, because college slang is part of a subculture of undergraduate life, it provides a vocabulary of terms that is particularly useful for characterizing important facets of college experience. Relative to general slang spoken on campus, college slang at both institutions is rich in epithets for campus life (parties, campus organizations, campus locales) and matters of academic life (study habits, academic subjects). Conversely, with the exception of relations with faculty, general slang terms are disproportionately concentrated around matters of sexual orientation, personal attributes (nastiness, stinginess, intensity), and alcohol and drugs—matters that cross-cut the particular interests of undergraduate life or are tied to national youth culture.

Third, because college slang is part of the undergraduate subculture, many of its terms express important values of undergraduate life, values that are often in tension with the institutionalized values of higher education as articulated by administrators and faculty. This is clear in the simple preponderance of terms that are devoted to nonacademic life. As Moffatt [23] has recently argued, contemporary undergraduates value college social life for its personal autonomy, dorm life, informal sociability, fun, and sexuality, regarding it as equally important to academic life. Much college slang, thus, speaks to—and for—these domains of undergraduate life [compare 10].

Ironically, the reinforcement of student values by college slang is also apparent in slang identities that do address academic life. More often than not, such epithets stigmatize students who work "too hard" or are "too friendly" with faculty. As such, these slang terms function as a means of social control within the subculture, regulating the academic behavior of peers in and outside of the classroom. This may well be the case in several other areas, where terms to stigmatize peers who deviate from shared norms seem particularly abundant: in matters of personal demeanor, of dress, and of physical attractiveness. In this light, the very abundance of slang terms that can be used to stigmatize peers who deviate from dominant norms may indicate the significant value of conformity itself within the peer-centered, undergraduate subculture.

Finally, because much student slang is transmitted within the context of a particular institution, the social and cultural organization of the institution also shapes the slang of undergraduates. In some cases, such differences may arise from the historical traditions of the school. For instance, Davis's agricultural roots still nourish epithets concerning rural background; Holy Cross's Jesuit presence fosters religious slang identities. In other cases, compositional differences in student populations may influence vocabularies of status identities. Though racial and ethnic identities are relatively rare, at Holy Cross such epithets currently focus on Puerto Rican students, while at Davis, such terms include Asian and Middle Eastern terms [compare 4]. It is even possible that institutional differences in college slang reflect deeper, systematic variation due to institutional structure. In this study, slang use at the small, residential liberal arts college differs significantly from that of the large university. Students at Holy Cross are significantly more likely to use college slang than students at Davis. Whether college or general slang, Holy Cross undergraduates also identify peers in terms of academic and extracurricular aspects of campus life more often than do their counterparts at Davis. Conversely, Davis students characterize peers in terms of personal attributes. Such differences in usage and meaning are at least suggestive of distinct institutional cultures rooted in social structure, the one expressive of a traditional, campus-centered college experience, the other of a more individualized, open, privatized university experience.

At the same time, this study of undergraduate slang clearly suggests the need for further research and conceptual work. Studies of undergraduate slang at different types of institutions are certainly in order—for example, at junior colleges and nonresidential, "commuter" schools. Such work would enable us to trace the effects of an increasingly diversified college experience on undergraduate culture and language. Research on different groups within the undergraduate subculture is also needed to document internal variation in college speech. Some differences in slang use are certainly grounded in traditional dimensions of social organization, such as gender [see, for instance, 16, 19, 27]. Others may well be expressive of conflicting, traditional subcultures *within* student life—those of the student rebel, of the career-oriented student, or of the worlds of fraternities and varsity athletics [17]. Still others are grounded in the intimate worlds of peer-group sociability in the dormitory and the shared apartment [23]. Such work is critical to a sophisticated understanding of college slang, sensitive at once to the continuing importance of this subcultural idiom and to its complex relations to undergraduate life and the larger society.

Notes

1. The causes of this shift in scholarly interest are certainly complex, rooted in cultural changes among students, intellectual movements among the professoriate, and the emergence of a national youth culture. With respect to undergraduate culture itself, Horowitz [17] argues that the sixties ended a century-long dominance of a college-life subculture that emphasized peer loyalty, pleasure, anti-intellectualism, and sports—a fertile ground for subcultural slang. That such change did not eradicate college slang is apparent from this study. Yet, it may well have decreased the visibility of traditional forms of undergraduate cultural display, including language use, and it certainly increased the complexity of slang usage among college students. With respect to changing professorial interests it is worth noting that college slang reappears in the '70s and '80s as a secondary concern in studies of gender stereotypes [16, 19, 27]. A notable exception to this shift away from studies of college slang is Connie Eble's work on undergraduate slang at the University of North Carolina at Chapel Hill which spans the last two decades [10].
2. See Dumas and Lighter [8] for a general discussion of definitions of slang; de Klerk [7] for a recent account with specific reference to student slang among adolescents.
3. Eble [10] notes that the first recorded slang term dates from the beginnings of European university life, when medieval students used the Latin term, *lupi* or wolves, to refer to students who informed on other students for speaking the vernacular rather than Latin.
4. Many Davis students do reside in the community, making for a "college town" atmosphere. Davis students are more ethnically and racially diverse than Holy Cross's predominantly Catholic student body, and they are much more likely to come from public school backgrounds (95 percent versus 53 percent). Though both schools are strong academically, Holy Cross students matriculate with stronger academic preparation, as indicated by standardized test scores [5].
5. Members of the college community often express initial surprise at hearing the number of terms collected. To a substantial degree, this surprise is a function of the fact that these terms differ dramatically in the breadth of their usage, ranging from terms known by students at campuses on opposite coasts to terms that are the creation of a single clique at one institution. At the same time, students initially underestimate slang terms in their own speech because these identities are part of the taken-for-granted reality of their own culture [cf. 16]. Faculty and administrators, socially segregated from the informal interaction of student life, remain relatively ignorant of this language.
6. These identities and their attributed meanings can be found throughout Moffatt's account of student life [for example, 23, pp. 15, 18, 34, 51, 56, 89, 137, 149, 166, 183, 188, 278, and 295].

7. A third dimension might well be added to this analysis—that of membership within the world of higher education. Certainly, some of the terms used nationally by college youth that are not general slang are also used by noncollege youth, and hence are part of youth culture rather than a distinct collegiate subculture (for example, drug terms, such as *pothead, stoner*). Such patterns of diffusion could be investigated by comparing the slang use of college with noncollege youth, a worthwhile enterprise but beyond the scope of this article.
8. I expect the relatively high proportion of idiographic terms is partially an artifact of method on two accounts. Similar terms (*chemhead* and *chem geek, crewhead* and *crewbies, scoopmaster* and *scoopmonster*) were analyzed as separate identities, though their similarity of meaning suggests institutional rather than idiographic slang. Slang terms were collected by observation or by asking students to volunteer terms, rather than by directly asking students whether they recognized or used a given term.
9. For an excellent ethnographic description of what one such undergraduate "voice" might entail, see Moffatt's characterization of "Undergraduate Cynical" [23, pp. 90–95]. This distinct way of speaking about college life, which is situated and normatively expected within student culture, symbolizes the official motives of college administrators and faculty as highly self-interested and base, hence legitimating student action that deviates from college policy.
10. Although these categories were derived inductively from the slang terms, their construction is, to some extent, arbitrary. For instance, I have in some cases combined meanings that are relatively similar but might well be treated separately in another study—for example, categorizing slang identities that have to do with the theater (*theater-fag*) with those related to music (*band-fag*). Nevertheless, these fifty-two categories are nearly exhaustive of the highly varied connotations communicated by these slang identities (99 percent of the terms can be placed within this framework), and they provide a relatively rich and discriminating system of units for characterizing slang vocabularies.
11. Each slang identity was coded for its most salient meaning and, where appropriate, its secondary and tertiary meanings. For instance, the term, *blade,* is used at Holy Cross for a particularly studious peer (study), though it can also connote someone who "doesn't party" much (party life) and is hence "narrow" (well-rounded/narrow). With the exception of my discussion of gender identities, I have focused on primary meanings because the samples are more comparable across institutions for such meanings: Holy Cross identities are more likely to connote multiple meanings, which may simply be a function of the more intensive and long-term manner in which they were collected.

References

1. Babbitt, E. H. "College Slang." *The Chautauquan,* 31 (1900), 22–24.
2. Banchero, L., and W. Flinn. "The Application of Sociological Techniques to the Study of College Slang." *American Speech,* 42 (1967), 51–57.
3. Bellah, R., et al. *Habits of the Heart.* Berkeley: University of California Press, 1985.
4. Bruner, E., and J. P. Kelso. "Gender Differences in Graffiti: A Semiotic Perspective." In *The American Dimension,* edited by S. Montague and W. Arens, pp. 139–56. Sherman Oaks, California: Alfred Publishing Co., 1981.
5. Cass, J., and M. Birnbaum, eds. *Comparative Guide to American Colleges,* 14th ed. New York: Harper and Row, 1989.

6. Chapman, R. L., ed. *New Dictionary of American Slang*. New York: Harper and Row, 1986.
7. De Klerk, V. "Slang: A Male Domain?" *Sex Roles*, 22 (1990), 589–606.
8. Dumas, B. K., and J. Lighter. "Is Slang a Word for Linguists?" *American Speech*, 53 (1978), 5–17.
9. Dundes, A., and M. Schonhorn. "Kansas University Slang: A New Generation." *American Speech*, 38 (1963), 163–77.
10. Eble, C. *College Slang 101*. Georgetown, Conn.: Spectacle Lane Press, 1989.
11. Fine, G. A. *With the Boys: Little League Baseball and Preadolescent Culture*. Chicago: The University of Chicago Press, 1987.
12. Flexner, S., and H. Wentworth, eds. *Dictionary of American Slang*, rev. ed. New York: Thomas Y. Crowell, 1975.
13. Friendly, M. L., and S. Glucksberg. "On the Description of Subcultural Lexicons: A Multidimensional Approach." *Journal of Personality and Social Psychology*, 14 (1970), 55–65.
14. Goffman, E. *Stigma*. New York: Touchstone Books, 1963.
15. Hall, B. H. *A Collection of College Words and Customs*. Cambridge: Published by John Bartlett, 1856. Republished by Gale Research Company, Detroit, 1968.
16. Holland, D., and D. Skinner. "Prestige and Intimacy: The Cultural Models behind Americans' Talk about Gender Types." In *Cultural Models in Language and Thought*, edited by D. Holland and N. Quinn, pp. 78–111. Cambridge: Cambridge University Press, 1987.
17. Horowitz, H. L. *Campus Life: Undergraduate Cultures from the End of the 18th Century to the Present*. New York: Knopf, 1987.
18. Kratz, H. "What is College Slang?" *American Speech*, 39 (1964), 188–95.
19. Kutner, N. G., and D. Grogan. "An Investigation of Sex-Related Slang Vocabulary and Sex-Role Orientation among Male and Female University Students." *Journal of Marriage and the Family*, 36 (1974), 474–83.
20. Lehman, A., and E. Suber, eds. *Peterson's Guide to Four-Year Colleges*, 19th ed. Princeton, N.J.: Peterson Guides, 1989.
21. Marples, M. *University Slang*. London: no publisher given, 1950.
22. Maynard, D. "Language, Interaction, and Social Problems." *Social Problems*, 35 (1988), 311–34.
23. Moffatt, M. *Coming of Age in New Jersey: College and American Culture*. New Brunswick: Rutgers University Press, 1989.
24. Olesen, V., and E. Whittaker. "Conditions under which College Students Borrow, Use, and Alter Slang." *American Speech*, 43 (1968), 222–38.
25. Poston, L., III. "Some Problems in the Study of Campus Slang." *American Speech*, 39 (1964), 114–23.
26. Poston, L., III, and F. J. Stillman. "Notes on Campus Vocabulary, 1964." *American Speech*, 40 (1965), 193–95.
27. Risch, B. "Women's Derogatory Terms for Men: That's Right, 'Dirty' Words." *Language in Society*, 16 (1987), 353–58.

Questions for Discussion

1. Hummon suggests that the slang used by college students reflects their sense that the "fun" that college life offers is at least as important as the academic rewards. How well does his evidence support that argument?

How true is it that college students value the socializing that is a part of college life as much as they do the academics?
2. To what extent are you aware of having learned a new slang when you entered college? With whom are you most likely to use that slang? When are you least likely to use it?
3. Analyze Hummon's methodology. Would you suggest any changes? How convincing do you find his study and the conclusions he draws from it?

Questions for Research and Writing

1. Replicate Hummon's study on your own campus by asking students to list as many slang terms as possible. Then, grouping these terms as Hummon does, write an analysis of what your peers' slang tells us about the campus culture and values.
2. If you live in an area with more than one college or university—or if you have access to the Internet—study the slang used on two or more campuses. Do the students on the different campuses use different kinds of slang? Do the differences in language reflect differences in campus culture? In the ethnic or socioeconomic make-up of the student bodies? In the students' political or religious orientations?
3. Hummon doesn't attempt to break down his data according to the respondents' genders, ethnic or cultural backgrounds, ages, economic classes, political or religious orientation, and so forth. Conduct a study similar to his, asking students on your campus to list the slang terms they most often use. Then analyze the extent to which their background identities influence their use of slang.
4. Slang is often used by the members of a group to establish a group identity and, at the same time, to exclude outsiders from the group. Thus, for example, men are likely to use slang *about* women that they would not use *with* women. Studious students are likely to have heard some of the slang labels applied to them but are unlikely to use the terms themselves. Select a cluster of slang terms used to label a particular group of people and analyze its implications. As part of your analysis, interview both those who use the slang and those who are labeled by it. What does each group think of the implications and connotations of the slang terms being used?

CROSSCURRENTS
Questions for Connecting the Readings in Chapter 2

1. In several essays in this chapter, various writers debate the merits or flaws of affirmative action policies and of a "traditional" or "classical" education. How do you think Mike Rose would respond to the opin-

ions expressed by Phillip Johnson and by Chester Finn and Bruno Manno, for instance?

2. Imagine a conversation between Rose and Finn and Manno. Where would they agree? Where would they disagree? To what extent do they bring common assumptions to the issues involved?

3. How do you think that the authors in this chapter describe the proper relationship between the university and the community? On what points would different authors agree and on what points would they disagree?

4. How would Daphne Patai and Noretta Koertge respond to Johnson's claim that "[p]ersons who try to advance beliefs that are contrary to received knowledge are considered to be ignorant"?

5. J. Wade Gilley sees in the success of AT&T's Bell Laboratories and of the use of "distribution" in various engineering firms an argument for similar kinds of success in the university. Looking at the assumptions behind such an argument, how do you think Finn and Manno would respond to Gilley's sense of the connections between the university and the world outside it? How might George Kuh, John Schuh, and Elizabeth Whitt see the role of the university in the wider community?

6. If Hummon is right that a great deal about undergraduates' lifestyles and values can be learned from their slang, other authors in this chapter might see in that slang evidence for their own beliefs about the current state of the university. What might Rose say about the undergraduates whom Hummon studied? What would Patai and Koertge say? Johnson?

3

Work and Play

"What do you want to be when you grow up?" Most of us started hearing that question when we were about four or five years old. *Then* it was an exciting question. It was fun to play at working, and secretly we knew that we were just trying out the possible occupations of our future; tomorrow we could decide to fashion an entirely new working self. As we grow older, and the questions get more insistent and serious, it's sometimes hard to feel the same joy at the prospect of work.

We think of the way that others have spoken of the world of work: they tell us that it's a "jungle out there," "a grind," "a rat race," and a "dog-eat-dog world." We know that Mondays, the start of the work week, are "blue Mondays" and that Fridays, the end of the work week, are welcomed with a weary sigh (or a joyful exclamation) of "TGIF"—Thank God It's Friday! The weekends, we know, are always much too short. It's no wonder, then, that many Americans, those about to enter the work force and those who have become accustomed to its pressures, are daunted by the prospect of spending as many as forty to sixty or more hours a week earning a living.

College students often have a particularly practical outlook on work, of course. Worried less about finding *fulfilling* work than about finding *any* work, many students choose their college majors with an eye toward marketability and the promise of a high income. (If you've read the selections in chapter 2, you know that some find the trend toward "careerism" in college disheartening, while others see it as both necessary and understandable in today's market-driven society.) Critics of "Generation X" complain that today's students see work largely as the means toward a shallow end: the purchase of more consumer goods. They complain that Generation X-ers feel no craftsman's pride in what they make or do and that, selfishly interested only in getting ahead, they feel no need to contribute to the larger social good. According to this view, Generation X-ers are sloppy and lazy in their work habits, interested only in doing as little as possible for as much money as they can get. Work, according to this way of thinking is only the unpleasant means toward the ultimate goal of living a life entirely for one's own pleasure.

Sociologists and historians tell us that work does not have to be like this. It is possible, they say, to see work as a kind of play, to bring creativity and joy to the job, and to find self-fulfillment in the work world, the same self-actualization—the complete and passionate fulfillment of one's potential—that Mike Rose tells us is the purpose of education (see chapter 2, "Entering the Conversation"). The blending of work and play is what interests us here. While many Americans would place the two at opposite ends of the spectrum, viewing work as the antithesis of play, others look for ways to bring the two into closer proximity or, at least, to bring them into equilibrium.

Several authors in this chapter argue that such an equilibrium can be achieved only if we rethink the nature of work itself. We need, they say, to move away from our "service" economy, an economy in which we devote our lives to buying and selling services in the worlds of finance, entertainment, and consultation, and to return to the ethic of earlier times, when workers took pride in their crafts and products and when they traded tangible goods (not merely services). People need to rediscover the joy of labor and to work for the fulfillment of essential needs, not for the power to purchase unnecessary consumer goods that keep afloat an economy based on consumerism and artifice. These authors argue that in an economy where image and the desire for financial gain become paramount, the creative impulse weakens and we are left with mediocrity on the job and in our recreation. So divorced are we from the tangible product and so unwilling to expend our own energy that, some say, we can no longer even play; our amusement parks and sports events testify to our inability to embrace spontaneity and escape the traps of corporate and individual greed.

Many of the following articles present visions of a world in which we *can* find the appropriate intersection of work and play. For Stanton Wheeler that means our finding a way to lead a "double life," to find outside the workaday world a passion that will sustain and define us in our nonworking hours. For Juliet Schor, it means bringing to the work world a sense of play that will emancipate workers and enliven their hearts and minds, thereby freeing them to bring to their jobs a sense of commitment and community that will help all of us prosper.

As you read these selections, consider your own attitudes toward work and play. How fair are the stereotypes about "lazy," "selfish," and "uncommitted" Generation X-ers? How much do you look forward to leaving the world of the university and entering the world of work (including the work of maintaining a home)? What are your priorities in your job search? Are you looking mainly for a job that will bring a high income and prestige? Or one that will excite and interest you? How much time and emotional energy do you expect to devote to your job? When considering your options, how much weight will you give to the work's social value? As you read through the following pieces, we hope you will bring your own thoughts, observations, and experiences into the conversation and, finally, that you will think about how you hope to find the balance that will enable you to work *and* play with passion, energy, and commitment.

OLD BLUE COLLARS, YOUNG BLUE COLLARS, AND THAT LITTLE PLACE YOU'RE GOING TO GET IN THE COUNTRY

Reg Theriault

> Most of us have heard the lament that people just aren't working as hard as they used to. Usually that lament comes from an older person who has either reconciled himself to a life of hard work or has retired altogether. Or at least so it appears to the young people who still dream of moving beyond their current jobs and finding a way to spend less time working and more time pursuing leisure. In the humorous piece that follows, Reg Theriault helps us see work from the perspectives of both older and younger workers and of workers representing a variety of cultural and ethnic backgrounds. In the process, he helps us see not only what we do but what we value. Theriault prides himself on providing the "worker's" perspective in this book, drawing on his own experiences of working as a fruit packer, a longshoreman, and a truck driver. "Old Blue Collars, Young Blue Collars" originally appeared in his 1995 book, How To Tell When You're Tired: A Brief Examination of Work.

"Kids don't want to work nowadays." I hear this statement made every day I work. Naturally, it is made by some old-timer. I think it is generally true, but I have mixed feelings about it. In the first place, why the hell should they? Why should anyone want to harness himself all day long to something that is hard, or monotonous, or dirty, and frequently all three? The statement has probably always been with us, voiced over the centuries by older workers since God knows when. On the other hand, nothing comes free in the world, and if you aren't carrying your own weight it simply means that someone else is packing it for you. The old-timer has a point here. Why should it be him?

Leaving aside the man with a work ethic—that is, the type of guy who works hard because he thinks hard work is virtuous and he feels good only when is he tired—there really isn't much to argue about here between the old-timer and the kid. When an old-timer says of some younger man that he doesn't want to work, he is usually complaining that the kid hasn't picked up *his* work habits yet. Who needs them, maybe. But if the kid really isn't doing enough work, that is an argument that should probably take place between the kid and the man who signs his checks.

Of course, this does not hold true if the kid and the old-timer are working at some job together and the kid is not doing his share, or the kid has contrived things so that the old-timer is doing more than he is. Then the old-timer has a legitimate complaint. For instance, suppose that the two of them are throwing coffee together, one on each end of the sack, and the kid is taking a slight jump on his partner and lifting up his end first, putting the bulk of the coffee beans, and the weight, down at the old-timer's end of the sack—a practice known as giving someone "the Portagee Lift." In a situation like this, I am on the side of the old-timer. But most kids won't do this. At least not more than once. There is a countermove to the Portagee Lift known as "the Dago Stall." (In northern Europe I am sure there are equally insulting terms featuring Finns and Swedes.) Moves and countermoves can get very involved, and if the situation goes on long enough it will usually end up with a series called the left jab and the right cross. The best solution is to separate the team before it goes this far and give the kid a new partner who works just like him. Then everyone can be entertained watching them work against each other all day long.

But young workers do approach labor differently from old workers. I have worked with black men, orientals, Latinos, and just about every European ethnic group found in America; inside the work scene itself, if there is a split, it is as pronounced along generational lines as any other. The slow loss of vitality that takes place over the years is certainly a factor that bonds older workers together, but it is insufficient as an explanation if you consider the lively old men you encounter here and there. They are more likely to share the attitudes of their own age group than those of the lively young.

As I grow older, I have noticed in myself and in the older men I work with an acceptance that it is easier to *do* the job than to fight it. As you grow older working, work becomes your "thing," and you do it with somewhat less resistance. When they are young and first go to work, most people, especially if they are white and they live in America, do not accept work as their fate. If they aren't angling to rise to a boss's job, then they frequently have some scheme in the backs of their heads to start a business for themselves, however small, or buy a little farm in the country. Some of them make it. Most do not. The man who starts a small business invariably finds that he is working about eighteen hours a day for the same income he made back at the factory working eight. The worker who becomes a small farmer usually ends up even worse off, since agro-economics is not learned working on the assembly line.

Years ago, chicken ranches were popular, and I know several men who ventured in that direction. "What happened?" I asked one would-be chicken farmer I knew who showed up on the job after an absence of a few years.

"Feed," he said. "It cost more to feed them than they were worth."

This was literally true. Being a small operator he was unable to buy feed in large tonnage lots and had to pay top price for it. Although he was getting thirty-six cents a pound for his fryers, it was costing him forty cents a pound to bring them to market. Even though he kept track of costs, economic reality wasn't brought home to him until one day a virus swept his flock when it was young and all the little chicks died. He "made" more money, as he put it, off that batch of birds than any other.

His wife had worked at the telephone company all during this time to keep their heads above water. She had pitched right in, working Mondays through Fridays in town and then helping to clean out the chicken pens on the weekend. After they quit raising chickens, she kept her job. Now that they were both making wages they were fairly well off, and I had expected them to be enjoying their new affluence. But I was wrong. He was still driving the same old banged-up pickup truck.

"When you going to get a new car?" a mutual friend asked him. The three of us were eating lunch.

"No way," the former chicken rancher said, shaking his head and biting into a peanut butter sandwich. "We're saving our money."

"What for?" I asked.

"Calves."

"What?"

"I can buy drop calves from the dairies for fifteen bucks apiece," he explained. "Soon as we save enough money, I'm quitting my job and we're going to raise beef. Sell them as yearlings. There's a lot of money in it."

"What about feed?" I asked.

"I've looked into that. They eat mostly hay."

"What does your wife think of it?" the other man asked him.

"She's all for it," he replied with enthusiasm. "She's happy about it. She'll go for anything to get away from all that chickenshit."

She may have gotten away from *some* of that chickenshit, as the other man observed later, but she wasn't getting away from all of it. To get away from *all* that chickenshit, she would have to get a divorce.

Although this would-be cattle baron was not young, his schemes are typical of those of a lot of young workers. It seems not to occur to them that the work they are doing now is the work they will be doing for the rest of their lives. It takes a while for that understanding to sink in. Sometimes it never does. Without the attitudes and values of a workingman, the man working is something else.

The one group of American workingmen who learned this earliest and know it most completely, it seems to me, are older blacks, especially if they are from the South. Given their start, it would be pretty foolish of them to look forward in life to anything but work. These men have taught me a lot when it comes to hard, physical labor. The work is going to be there tomorrow. But if *you* are important, what you do today is important, so do it right.

Black people are separated along generational lines just as much as any other group, and the gap takes the same form as with whites. But the civil rights movement has increased opportunities and has had a tremendous impact on young blacks. Blue-collar work is not the only course open to them anymore, and now they have their schemes too. Their dreams may not be of chicken ranches, but they are pretty much the equivalent. Furthermore, personal drive and ambition seem to me to be more pronounced among the young black workers that I know than among the white. The myth of the lazy black may persist in some quarters, but among those workers I know who are moonlighting at other jobs, blacks far outnumber whites. Not only does the black worker often work two jobs himself, but his wife is usually employed. Also, blacks are among the hardest hitters when it comes to going after overtime.

Curiously, the two groups of workers that are farthest apart in all other respects—young blacks and older whites—have one thing in common. When it comes to their kids, young blacks are ambitious as hell in the old-fashioned sense. They are just as high on education for their young as the older white workers ever were, and for the same reason—they think education will get their children away from manual labor and into white-collar work or the professions.

I do not know what the end result of this ambition will be in the young black worker, but in the older white man it has frequently left him disappointed and confused. If you work all your life but raise your kids to avoid it, you have made an obvious criticism of your own life spent working. If you are a trade unionist and along the way you have helped to raise the wages and working conditions of yourself and other working people, everything you have done in this direction you can be proud of. Without exception, all old-timers are. Still, they want their kids out of it, which means getting them into the white-collar middle class.

It is true that workers, older workers in particular, have extremely naive ideas of what white-collar people do for a living. They see them as going through life staying clean, sitting on their butts, and making a lot of money doing it. They also see them gaining a great deal of status and respect that they feel are denied them as blue-collar workers. That is what they want for their kids. From listening to the complaints of my white-collar friends, however, I get the impression that though white-collar people may stay clean and may spend much of their time sitting down, they all seem to put in a pretty full, hard day. As for prestige, they may not be on the bottom of the totem pole, but there is always someone above them, and if that person is a petty tyrant the underdog is not protected by a trade union. To cap it off, most of them make less money than I do.

The fact that all white-collar workers are not enjoying a picnic occasionally filters down to the ranks of blue-collar workers, even if they have no white-collar friends. Many years ago in San Francisco, the longshoremen opened their ranks to take in six hundred new men, and there were fourteen thousand applicants for those few hundred jobs. Almost half of the applicants were schoolteachers, and a big hunk of the remainder were in white-collar occupations. When I asked an older longshoreman, who had two kids in college, what he made of this, he just shook his head. His confusion left him with no response. White-collar people, apparently in large numbers, would eagerly trade places with him. Maybe in the case of these white-collar men it was simply an instance of the grass appearing greener, but most older longshoremen I know would not accept that explanation. This attitude is not as persistent among the younger blue-collar workers; but among the old-timers, the grass *has* to be greener over there in the white-collar fields.

A lifetime of hard work and perhaps childhood memories of the depression combined to solidify the older blue-collar worker's attitude. Poverty and hard work are twin plagues; education is the vaccination against them, and, by God, his kid is going to have one. Education is the one thing he did *not* have, so it must be the answer, he feels, and it is pretty hard to shake him out of it. And the kid had better not blow it, either. I once came upon an old winch driver, a father whose son had gone to work on the waterfront the same time as I had. The son was working below in the lower hold of the ship in the same gang as I was, palletizing two-hundred-pound sacks of coffee. The old man was so angry he was dancing up and down.

"Look at him," he said to me. "Look at him! He wouldn't have to be doing that. No! Goddammit, he could have gone to college! If he hadn't knocked up that little twist and had to get married, he could've gone to college."

As I looked down to where the work was being done, I did not know whom to sympathize with. It was very hard work. I knew because I had been doing it myself all day. I had come up on deck to take a leak, and now I was going back down below to throw coffee for a couple hours more. As I watched I realized the son was not merely tired, but in trouble. He was young and he had not done much of that kind of work, and as yet he was not very good at it. He and his partner were having to lift the sacks up almost head high to top off the load, and they were getting the coffee from down around their shoelaces. Both the son and his partner were just barely making it.

The old man understood. He had done a lot of hard work in his time and he knew what it was like. Over the years he had worked himself up to a job where all he had to do was manipulate a couple of handles up and down, and now, with rage and frustration, he was reliving all that hard work through watching his son do it, which was probably worse, to him anyway. Watching your son go through a cruel form of torture is cruel torture too, and I could sympathize, seeing it through the old man's eyes. Even more, it seemed a bitter punishment for someone whose crime, at the age of about nineteen, had been making love.

Finally, however, you always see things from where you are standing, and everything has a way of sorting itself out. On deck beside the old man I had to turn away so as not to witness his agony. Going down the ladder to the lower hold, however, my viewpoint changed. Perhaps I should not have said it, but I could not help myself

"What about me, asshole?" I yelled up at him. "I've been to college, and it doesn't make those sacks any lighter."

I cherish old-timers, however. Most of what I know about work, the ways of the world, who the enemy is, I learned from old-timers. On your first day on a new job, it is usually an old-timer who makes the first overture of friendship. When you are a kid just starting out, it is a rare old-timer who won't show you the ropes, not just on how to get along on the job and how to do your work, but what the score is generally—what bars and saloons to stay away from, and so forth. I started out working as a kid in the late thirties, and my head is still full of information of this sort that I treasure. Although I never had occasion to put much of it to use and most of it is now obsolete, I will never forget it:

When you are on the bum, watch out for those tin cans you find under bridges. Don't step on them and smash them just for the hell of it. Guys cook *food* in those cans. And if you use a can yourself, leave it clean for the next guy. And be sure you dry it out good and turn it upside down so it doesn't get rusty.

Do not hobo through the southern states in the late springtime. That is when they repair the flood damage, and you might end up on a road gang. Worse, next month the sheriff might pass you on to the next county and you are liable to spend all summer down there on the end of a long-handled shovel. However, they *will* let you go in the fall. If there is no work to be done, they don't want to feed you.

If you land in jail, don't accept any gift, not even a candy bar, from *anyone!* I haven't seen anyone roll a handmade cigarette in twenty years, and I don't smoke myself anymore, but I know that if you land in jail you're supposed to throw your Bull Durham into the common pot—usually a coffee can—with everybody else's tobacco. And you shouldn't hold out. That way not only will you show everyone that you're okay, but later on when you might not have any money left to buy tobacco yourself you will have established the right to dip into the common pot. Incidentally, if I take up smoking again and I am broke and getting toward the end of the pack, I will never smoke my last cigarette. That way I will never run out.

If you are sleeping in a park, or anywhere in or close to a city, don't take off your shoes. If they are any good, most likely they will be stolen. And no one is going anywhere without shoes.

Here's a really obsolete tip. If you're picking cotton, if you have no intention of returning at the end of the day to that particular field in the morning, make the last row you pick a long one. Forget the cotton—leave it on the bush—and when you get to the end of the row, keep going, and make sure you take the cotton sack with you. In the old days you picked cotton by hand, dragging the sack between your legs, stuffing it as you went. The farmer furnished the sack. You were paid, by the pound, right there in the field. As soon as the sack was full, you dragged it over to wherever the farmer had his scales set up, it was weighed, and your money was placed in your pocket right then and there. Empty, a cotton sack is about six feet long, and it is supposed to be just about the best thing in the world to sleep inside of.

I say *supposed* to be because although I have picked a lot of things, I have never picked cotton. I never *had* to. Over the years I was led to believe that this was a mark of achievement—never having had to pick cotton—since in the American West that occupation was just about the lowest rung on the job ladder. Compared to cotton, picking hops, pears, apples, and cherries practically made you an aristocrat.

Now I realize that I missed something. There was a world out there in those cotton patches in western America that was unique. Now that cotton is no longer picked by hand (all cotton is now picked by machine), the stories are beginning to come out. In addition to a lot of excruciatingly hard work, a whole life existed among the cotton pickers. People were born in those cotton patches and people died in them, sometimes violently. And some fell in love—"I met my wife in a cotton patch," one man told me. Everything in the world at large was to be found, out there in that cotton, and sometimes under it. However, I missed it, and when I go back among my fruit tramp friends and the subject of picking cotton comes up, I have to confess I am not an authority on the matter.

"What? You never picked no cotton?" The question is always put to me incredulously.

"No." I have to shake my head. "I never picked cotton." Invariably someone will crane his head around somebody else to get a better look at me.

"No *shit?* You never picked any cotton?"

"No."

After a general shaking of heads, I am forgotten and the stories begin.

"Where did you pick cotton?"

"Where *didn't* I pick cotton!"

"Ever pick cotton in Tulare?"

"Hell, yes, I picked cotton in Tulare. Why Tulare?"

"I picked cotton in Tulare one time coming right out of jail. They turned me out early in the morning, no breakfast or nothing, and there was this farmer waiting down at the end of the block. That's probably why they turned me loose. He and the cops probably fixed it up between them. Anyway, the farmer said he needed cotton pickers, I was broke and hungry, so I climbed into the back of his pickup truck along with a number of others and we rode out to his cotton patch. It was the second picking and there wasn't much cotton *there,* but all I wanted to do was make enough money to buy some groceries and then I was going to be on my way. I started down the first row just a-snatching and a-grabbing, but the picking was so bad that it was after midmorning before my sack began to fill up. Then, just as I was about to weigh in, I heard somebody say, 'Hello, honey.' I'd been working away at that cotton so hard that I hadn't noticed her, but when I looked up there was this little gal sitting in the dirt at the end of my row with her legs spread wide, wide apart.

"'Hello,' I said.

"'Hello, yerself,' she said. 'How'd you like a little lovin'?' I'd been in jail nearly a month and I was pretty hard up, but I knew she wasn't giving it away for free, so I told her right out that I didn't have any money.

"'Sure you do, honey,' she said. 'You've got money right there between your legs.' She meant my sack full of cotton, of course. They only paid about a cent a pound in those days, but I must have had sixty, maybe seventy pounds in my sack, and that was something.

"'It's a deal,' I said, and I laid her right there between the rows on top of my cotton sack, soft as a mattress. When we were done, she rolled me off, dropped her empty sack, and grabbed hold of my full one. I laid there and watched her drag my breakfast and my lunch off to the weigh station.

"Pretty soon I commenced to realize that if I was going to eat that day I was going to have to pick some more cotton, so I got up and went back to work. Even though I worked all through the noon hour it wasn't until midafternoon that I had my sack close to full again. God, I was hungry. My stomach was growling and the only thing I'd had to chew on all day was a couple of wild turnip roots. Finally, my sack was almost full. I was getting on toward the end of a row and about to call it a day when sure enough I hear someone say, 'Hello, honey.' There she was, a different gal this time, sitting there at the end of the row with her legs apart.

"'Nope, not this time,' I said, hearing my stomach growl.

"'Are you sure, honey?' she said, pulling back her skirt and rubbing her crotch.

"'You're on!' I yelled, feeling my pecker get hard, and we went at it, bouncing up and down on top of the cotton sack.

"I was the last person out of that cotton patch. It was almost sundown when I came dragging ass in. The farmer was about to fold up his scales and go home.

"'Where the hell have you been?' he said. 'I haven't seen you all day.'

"'Here,' I said, giving him my cotton sack. 'Weigh it and give me my money.'

"'Why, you son of a bitch!' he said. 'There ain't thirty-five pounds of cotton here. What have you been doing all day?'

"'Never mind,' I said. 'Just weigh my cotton and pay me my money.'

"'Pay you? Why, I've got two skinny little ol' gals out there who've picked almost five hundred pounds apiece. Pay you? You lazy bastard, I ought to take you back to jail where you belong.'

" 'Mister,' I said, 'weigh my cotton and give me my money. I haven't eaten all day. I need that thirty-five cents for a couple of cans of pork and beans.'

"He flipped me a quarter. Two bits. 'Get off my property,' he said. 'And don't come back tomorrow. I don't even want you tromping up and down my cotton patch.'

"That farmer didn't know it and I didn't tell him, but he had some cotton patch. There was pussy growing out of the end of almost every row. I learned something from it, however. A young gal with an active snatch can make more money in a cotton patch than a strong man with a hard-on. And it don't matter if he's hungry or not."

After hearing an account like this, no one would conclude, of course, that spending a month in jail only to be freed to work your ass off all day in total hunger is a lot of fun. But these stories always bring forth bursts of laughter all around. And they always have a point to make, a moral, I guess. In this case, I suppose, it is to illustrate how impossible it is sometimes for a young man to keep his pecker in his pants. But they are best appreciated if you have shared that world of work. I, and perhaps the reader, have never put in time in a cotton patch, and a picking machine has ensured that we never will. But there is still a lot of work out there in the working world. I am certain there always will be. Those doing that hard work do not see themselves as victims seeking pity. They are simply fleshing out their lives with something more than meager wages for a lot of sweat. And they never fail, I have found, to temper irony with laughter.

Questions for Discussion

1. Theriault begins with an adage that most of us have heard from our parents and grandparents and others of their generation: "Kids don't want to work anymore." How true is that? How different are your generation's attitudes toward work from those of your parents and grandparents? From those your parents and grandparents had when they were your age?

2. Characterize Theriault's tone and diction in this piece. How does his colloquial language affect your response to what he has to say? How would your response—and his message—change if the chapter were rewritten in a more formal style?

3. Examine Theriault's use of one of the following anecdotes: the anecdote about the chicken farmer/would-be cattle baron and his wife, or the anecdote about the cotton picker. What is the purpose of the anecdote? How effectively does it help Theriault advance his ideas about the nature and function of work?

4. "Without the attitudes and values of a workingman, the man working is something else," Theriault tells us. What *is* that "something else"? What is Theriault's attitude toward the "workingman" and the "man working"?

5. Toward the end of his essay, Theriault records some advice he was given in the late 1930s by old-timers. He has, he tells us, "never had occasion to put much of it to use and most of it is now obsolete. I will never forget it." What makes the advice memorable, do you suppose? And, if it's obsolete, why does Theriault include it for us to read sixty years later?

6. Some readers will be offended by Theriault's diction and anecdotes, arguing that they are unnecessarily vulgar. Were you offended? If so, what do you think Theriault intends to accomplish by using vulgarity? In your opinion, why don't his diction and anecdotes help him meet his goals? However, if you were *not* offended, how would you defend Theriault against those who might question his approach?

Questions for Research and Writing

1. Theriault contends that people's attitudes toward work change as they grow older, that older people approach work with less resistance than do younger workers. Interview someone who has been working for at least ten years, asking that worker to chronicle the changes in his or her attitude toward work in general and the job in particular. Consider asking questions not only about the work ethic but also about the dreams and hopes with which the worker began and continues a career.

2. Surveying an equal number of older and younger workers, test Theriault's notions that older and younger workers hold different attitudes toward work and about the function of work in their present and future lives. To what extent does each group believe in a work ethic? To what extent do the two groups have similar dreams and hopes about their working lives? Do both groups look for the same kinds of fulfillment in their jobs? What, in other words, does each group see as the function of work in the worker's life?

3. The blue-collar workers about whom Theriault writes often exaggerate the prestige and ease of a white-collar job. Undoubtedly, white-collar workers often hold similarly false ideas about those who work in blue-collar jobs. Interview someone who holds a job you could never imagine yourself doing, either because you lack the interest or skill or because you consider the job demeaning, too physically or intellectually demanding, or limiting. To what extent does your interviewee substantiate your impressions of and stereotypes about the job?

4. Many workers in the United States have what Theriault calls "some scheme in the backs of their heads to start a business for themselves, however small, or buy a little farm in the country." Spend a day (or, even better, several days) observing and interviewing a small business owner at work. Then write an essay presenting your argument for why you would or would not want to own a small business of your own. (You may discuss a type of business different from the one you observed.)

DOUBLE LIVES

Stanton Wheeler

> *Published in 1990 in a collection entitled* The Nature of Work: Sociological Perspectives, *"Double Lives" was presented earlier as a paper before the American Sociological Association's 1985 meeting. In response to the theme of that meeting—"Working and Not Working"—Yale Law Professor Stanton Wheeler redefines a particular kind of "not working" moment, those moments when we are engaged in a kind of "play" that is so profoundly important to us that it helps us define who we are. That kind of play is, for Wheeler, a kind of work. In the following selection, a revision of his earlier paper, he examines the ways in which many of us, dissatisfied with the workaday world in which we earn our livings, enrich ourselves after hours with what we consider to be our more important, and more "real," work.*

"His failures as a reporter and a practicing attorney were behind him, and he found his vocation in the insurance world, where he was to stay for the rest of his life." But for this gentleman, being a lawyer for an insurance company didn't really capture his sense of self. Shortly after he began this vocation, he wrote to a new girlfriend, "I should like to make a music of my own, a literature of my own, and I should like to live my own life." And he did so. In fact, two of them. For the rest of his life, the person we know as the poet Wallace Stevens led a double life. The money that made life comfortable came from the offices of insurance companies. The quality that gave it richness and joy came from writing poetry.

Like many who lead double lives, Wallace Stevens was troubled by the condition. He complained that working for the American Bonding Company made it impossible to get away, even on Saturday afternoons, to visit J. P. Morgan's collection of manuscripts on display at Columbia University's library, where he wanted to study the work of John Keats. At one point he said, "It seems insincere, like playing a part, to be one person on paper and another in reality."

But which was the reality? He had this to say about working in the insurance business: "I certainly do not exist from nine to six when I am at the office. Today was the anniversary [his first year with a new firm]; but tonight I could not write a single verse. There is no everyday Wallace, apart from the one at work—and that one is tedious. At night, I strut my individual state once more."

Wallace Stevens is one of a number of illustrious people who have led double lives. William Carlos Williams, a contemporary of Stevens, was a physician by day, a poet by night. Charles Ives left music to earn a living, like Stevens, through insurance. (Maybe something about the field of insurance encourages double lives.) But he gained a sense of self and later recognition from his music compositions. The actor Paul Newman is another—we know him through his films, but he expresses much of his self and his being through race car driving.

But double lives are not only for the illustrious. Let me describe a fellow I shall call George, a janitor at a school for children with learning disabilities. We met as I was moving from one house to another. He answered an ad I had placed announcing a refrigerator and stove for sale. But his interest was not alone in kitchen appliances. He asked of my new abode: "Have you gone completely through the attic and the basement?" When I expressed some curiosity at the question, he said that it quite often happened that people left old model trains or parts of trains when they moved from one house to another.

George, it turned out, spent his evenings and weekends on model railroading. On a janitor's salary, he had filled his basement with what he estimated to be $50,000 to $60,000 worth of model railroading equipment. He was also an officer in the model railroading society, and when he and his wife went on vacation they frequently went to model railroading conventions. During the workday his mind was often on model railroading, and he spent most evenings in the basement with his son. They were engaged in what some might have called playing with trains, but it clearly had a larger significance than that for him. It was a way of being special, of mastering a particular niche in the universe. It was perhaps his chief source of identity, the thing that made him distinctive as a human being. And it also organized his social life. He observed, apropos the model railroading conventions: "You meet the nicest people."

George and Wallace Stevens are only two examples of a phenomenon I believe to be important and increasingly familiar. Virtually any human activity has the capacity to become enough of a preoccupation for someone to consider it a core part of their life. You will all have your own examples, but I'll give you a handful simply to fill out the range. I have known a high school teacher so deeply into birding—searching out and identifying the names and call of birds—that many dawns and virtually all weekends are consumed with the activity. I know a Jewish lawyer who describes himself as "an Israel person." His time and identity are very tied up with the fate of Israel as a nation and a culture, and he sees his work as a necessary interference with that commitment. I know a secretary in New York who spends virtually all her savings beyond the necessities of life in attending a wide array of musical events. Her work is in a Manhattan office tower, but her life and her heart are at Lincoln Center. I also know a bailiff who sings operatic arias on the job and who is committed to the study of opera. The morning paper tells of a policeman who, much to the surprise of his colleagues, has just published a first book of poetry. I know a woman in Vermont whose gardens are so well known that people come from around the town to admire them. Her life is made full by the flowers she grows during the hours and hours she spends in the garden. And, of course, the world of games and sports, like the world of art and music, provides many examples: while for most these activities are mere pastimes, for a few they become the central, organizing focus of their lives. This has been true of tennis and golf, of rock climbing and deep sea diving, of bridge and chess. And those who love old things can often turn that love into a double life. There are persons whose evenings and weekends are consumed repairing and displaying antique automobiles.

The key idea here—and the keystone of my topic—is that work, if it ever did, no longer provides a full sense of vocation. The special calling, the investment in something for its own sake, the commitment, constrained only by the demands of work and family, to an activity that is its own reward—that is my central concern.

It is important to be absolutely clear about what the subject is not. It is not what is normally thought of as "leisure studies," the study of hobbies or avocational pursuits. It bears a close family resemblance to be sure, for one and the same activity may serve some as a diversion or a time filler and others in the much more significant role I am interested in here. Rather than hobbies, these activities may be thought of as *preoccupations*—things so important to the self that it is hard to get them off one's mind and out of one's thoughts. But I admit that it is not easy to find a clear and sharp boundary. My criterion would be a social-psychological one: If the person himself or herself does not think of the activity in question as truly central to their life and their well-being, then it doesn't qualify as a preoccupation and won't necessitate a double life.

Do the activities from which double lives are constructed have any special attributes? I think they do. They must have enough complexity and enough detail to be able to capture one's interest and hold one's commitment. But that, of course, is a relative matter. The level of complexity is a function of the starting point—it perhaps depends on one's own level of intelligence. If the starting point is fairly low it may not require a great deal of complexity to leave plenty of room for most of us to expand our horizons without exhausting the material at hand.

I am thinking of central life interests (Dubin 1956) that fall outside the sphere of the family, the workplace, and religion. Clearly for some people it may be enough to express one's self through these major institutions. The mother or father of the year awards that are given in some communities may indeed go to those who have made their families a preoccupation, devoting all free time to family time. And there are many we know as workaholics, for whom work is not only an occupation but a preoccupation. And I am not talking, at least for these purposes, about those whose other life or double life is essentially a deviant one matched with a conventional cover—the classic double agent, the quiet officeworker by day who is a sneak thief at night, or those doing conventional jobs whose lives are preoccupied with deviant sexual practices of one kind or another. I am talking about the enormous variety of ways of giving individuality and distinctiveness to the self through pursuits that are legitimate, though not ones that every neighbor is going to be interested in. These are the activities that add infinite variety and color to life, that add diversity and range to human experience.

Double lives are not a new phenomenon. They can probably be found in some number in virtually every civilization, but certainly not in the same rates or numbers. For all but the leisure classes, preindustrial societies pretty much ruled out the level of involvement that is required to sustain a double life. Work was too hard and there was too much of it. One had to define one's self in relation to one's work because it consumed such a large portion of the waking hours. But a number of conditions have changed so as to make double lives a more prevalent phenomenon now than in the past.

Most important is the changing nature of work. Work for most people is less backbreaking than it used to be and less time-consuming as well. When the forty-hour work week replaced the forty-eight- or sixty-hour week, when clean and light industry replaced heavy industry, and when mechanical tools were developed and took much of the burden off the human body, both time and energy were freed up and available for allocation elsewhere. Sometimes, of course, this time and energy went into a second or even a third job, the economic pressures remaining despite improvements in the workplace. But often they were available for preoccupations.

Changes in values may have occurred as well. When a production society becomes a consumption society, there may be increased demand for goods and activities that allow more opportunity for individual self-expression.

Double lives may grow in importance as institutional networks weaken. If people have fewer children, weaker extended kinship systems, and less of a sense of rootedness in family or religion, they have lost important sources for the construction of social identity, and they may have as a result greater need for the kinds of identity I am describing.

If one of the important attributes of preoccupations is that they allow persons to develop a distinctive sense of self—a special identity and a special niche in life—then there are two further conditions of modern society that tend to favor the emergence of double lives. The first is sheer population density. It is easier to sustain the preoccupation or double life when others are doing it too. But if distinctiveness comes in part from the fact that few other people do it, only the largest areas may have enough of a population base to sustain the culture of the preoccupation. To take a distinctly nonrandom example, those who currently pursue jazz music as a serious preoccupation will find a culture of jazz in New York and to some degree in a handful of other major cities, but the number of talented professionals to listen to and learn from as well as the number of amateurs who share a high level of commitment is likely to be too small in out-of-the-way places. So cities, those breeding grounds of diversity and specialization, become a favorite home for those with a passionate commitment to activities other than work and family.

A second condition is the emergence of the photocopying machine and similar tools of communication. Many who don't live in large urban areas nevertheless sustain a strong preoccupation, in part through special-interest newsletters. Only a few preoccupations have such a mass following as to allow the regular appearance of articles about them in daily newspapers, though bridge, chess, and coin and stamp collecting may get attention in the largest dailies. But it is the inexpensive, do-it-yourself newsletter, now made much cheaper and easier to produce by xerography, that enables networks of those consumed with a given preoccupation to stay in touch and keep the network going. We might also expect that as television increases the potential for diverse programming made possible by cable, it may be possible for some preoccupations to be encouraged and reinforced through that medium.

When all of these conditions are present we have the potential for a flourishing of preoccupations—and of double lives. But it remains only a potential until individuals actually become preoccupied. What determines whether they will become preoccupied and what their preoccupation will be? It is too early to support generalizations in this area, and perhaps there won't be any. Perhaps the fact of a preoccupation and the object of the preoccupation are both functions of so many situational contingencies that it will be hard to generalize about them. Certainly some people simply fall into a side interest and don't realize until much later that it has become a preoccupation. Others may feel a lack in their lives, a real need for a deeper involvement, and may consciously throw themselves into the activity in question. It may be enough for some folks to dabble in this and that, giving the appearance of well-roundedness, but not letting any one thing or activity grow to the point of becoming a preoccupation. Others may find they have an all or nothing at all attitude: either the thing is worth doing wholeheartedly so that it becomes a major part of the self or it is to be dropped altogether, it being less painful to drop it than to sustain the activity at unsatisfactorily low levels of involvement.

All those preconditions, being expressed, it is nonetheless true that many preoccupations seem to have their roots in events of childhood or adolescence. They are often activities first undertaken at an early age. Not a lot of research has been done on the topic, but Dale Dannefer's study of old car enthusiasts lends support to this view.

Dannefer studied those who organize their lives around collecting, restoring, showing, and touring in antique automobiles, and they are a fine example of the phenomenon I am talking about. Here is his description:

> The consciousness and the round of activities that typify the social world of old cars are sustained by a genuine and intense subjective attraction that can accurately be described as passionate. From the standpoint of participants, it is clear that the social network of car people exists for the sake of this passion. When the enthusiast—

most often a male—climbs into his old car, it envelops him and insulates him from the world. When he settles back into the seat, it comforts him. When he turns the key and the engine responds, it submits to him. When he puts it in gear and drives away, it serves and glorifies him. If it's a dependable car, it is anthropomorphized as a benevolent friend. If it is of massive size, it appears "damn near omnipotent"—especially if it is loud, or fast, or both. If it contains an engineering innovation, its cleverness is regarded as the product of superior knowledge. For many, it is a point of contact for treasured memories of the past and, so long as it is taken care of, it will remain so for the foreseeable future. These are some of the reasons that people find to become passionate about cars. (Dannefer 1980)

Half of the old car enthusiasts that Dannefer studied said they had been fascinated by cars since their childhood and youth. Their interest appears to have been a distinctly individualistic and private one. Only after becoming strongly committed did many of them learn of the existence of a world of car people with similar interests. Others in Dannefer's sample were late bloomers who often had a strong interest in cars when very young but did not pursue them as collectors until years later.

It seems at least plausible to me that all those special extracurricular activities that occur in the more affluent school systems—the camera clubs, language clubs, nature clubs, and the like that are offered sometimes to spell relief from training in the three r's—may also provide early experience in what may become the locus of a more lasting commitment.

The enormous range and variety of possible preoccupations make any classification scheme both much needed and much in doubt. How are we to know what the central qualities are, and what dimensions it is most important to isolate and identify?

The second dimension is whether the activity in question is privatizing, in the sense that it must be pursued essentially on one's own and may require isolation from others—poetry is a good example—or whether the activity throws one into the company of others, as do bridge and team sports. Many provide a mix of both, as when amateur musicians practice alone but get together with others for performances.

This dimension of range of involvement may be particularly important in the relationship between the person with the preoccupation and his most significant others. Some preoccupations may bind families, as all members join in the same activity. There are skiing families, golfing families, bowling families, singing families. But sometimes the preoccupation pulls one away from significant others. It may be what makes the person special *to* the family rather than *with* the family. And it may, indeed, be a source of aggravation to those outside the activity. The person's heart may be seen as not really lying with the others but with the preoccupation.

Another obvious basis of classification is cost. People who are poor may be able to afford a preoccupation, but they won't have much choice, for most of the activities we have discussed require a degree of financial as well as emotional investment. A relatively high level of affluence in a society will enable the kind of cost commitments that allow expensive preoccupations to flourish. But here again it is a relative matter. Those whose lives are lived through music can stand at the back or sit in the fifth balcony if necessary, and those who are invested in old cars don't have to work on the most expensive models.

I began this paper by discussing double lives, and I have drifted into talking about preoccupations. There is obviously an intimate relationship between the two, and I should like to end the paper by discussing that relationship. For some people, of course, work *is* their preoccupation, and they have no double life in the sense that I'm using it here. For others, work bears a variety of relationships to the preoccupation in question. Sometimes the work is chosen precisely because it fits in with the preoccupation that one is hoping to convert into an occupation: the legions of young actors, dancers, musicians, and writers who wait on tables in New York and Los Angeles are examples.

More commonly, people bend their occupation to fit their preoccupation. I've known firemen who love golf more than family life and who work nights in order to have the daylight hours free to pursue that passion. And there are, of course, many whose sense of identity is linked to place and who can move only so far because of it. Sailors and body surfers come to mind. In arranging their place of work, some place a high premium on access to their preoccupation. Is it only one subway ride away or does it require a change?

Many allow their preoccupation to become an occupation, as they leave what they do for money for what they think they love. When the preoccupation is turned into a way to make a living, it may well be a mixed blessing. One is then required to do what before one really loved doing for its own sake. Still, there are lawyers who have become professional photographers and stamp collectors, and art collectors who have become professional art dealers. I know a former pharmacist who loved books and book collecting and gave up pharmacy for it. He now owns two used book stores in New England, and summers find him on the roads of Vermont and New Hampshire, selling books out of an old car at various flea markets and small town celebrations. He says it's not as good a living, but he's happier selling books than packaging pills.

I have meant to do no more than raise a series of questions and observations about the passionate interests I have called preoccupations that for many lead to the living of double lives. The traditional image of a double life is that of a Doctor Jekyll and Mr. Hyde. I am suggesting that double lives need not be organized in that stark a manner but may be the principal means by which people give expression to the self while doing paid work that provides only limited meaning and shape to their lives. If I'm right, double lives may increase in frequency as more people have more time away from work and find less meaning in work. A double life is an answer of a sort to the notion of worker alienation.

Perhaps my main theme is simply to suggest that although we know a great deal about how the world is divided up into levels of stratification, we still know little about how the world is divided into functional interests and pursuits. There is research on the so-called situs dimension as it applies to occupations, but that barely scratches the surface. If we spend relatively less time studying what people do and more studying what they really care about, we may come closer to learning how people construct workable identities. For Wallace Stevens, for George, and for legions of others, work and the workplace are not enough. What makes them distinctive and gives their life substance and character are activities they pursue elsewhere. These are labors of love in the truest sense.

References

Dannefer, Dale. 1980. "Rationality and Passion in Private Experience: Modern Consciousness and the Social World of Old-Car Collectors." *Social Problems*, 27, no. 4: 392–93.

Dubin, Robert. 1956. "Industrial Workers' Worlds: A Study of the Central Life Interests of Industrial Workers." *Social Problems* 3.

Questions for Discussion

1. "It seems insincere, like playing a part, to be one person on paper and another in reality," Wallace Stevens says. But many of us adopt different personae in the different roles we play. How similar are your work, home, and school selves? Why do you feel the need to create different selves for different situations? Can you envision a work life that would enable you to integrate your work and home selves?

2. Wheeler says that the emergence of the photocopy machine has encouraged the development of special-interest newsletters, and that the proliferation of cable channels has led to an increase in special-interest programming. The result, he says, is that aficionados of any kind can easily find others with whom to share their enthusiasm and exchange information. The same can, no doubt, be said about the growing use of the Internet and its forums. What forums and lists have you joined? What connections have you established over the computer that you might not otherwise have made?

3. Throughout "Double Lives," Wheeler makes a distinction between *vocation*—what we do for money—and *avocation*—what we do for love. How similar are your vocational goals and your avocation? If you had

no concerns about making a "good living," what avocation would you pursue? What does it offer that your intended vocation may not? What keeps you from making your avocation into your vocation?
4. What accounts for the kinds of "double lives" that Wheeler describes here? Why do people feel the need for these "extracurricular activities"? What does Wheeler see as the difference between the activities of these double lives and other leisure activities?

Questions for Research and Writing

1. Many preoccupations begin, Wheeler tells us, in childhood or adolescence, and they often represent a nostalgic desire to return to an earlier time. Interview several people who lead "double lives." When and how did their preoccupations begin? What causes them to remain passionate about their preoccupations? Finally, to what extent do they deliberately keep their two lives separate? Why?
2. Wheeler mentions several well-known people who have led double lives: Wallace Stevens, William Carlos Williams, and Paul Newman. Others are Geoffrey Chaucer and Nathaniel Hawthorne, both of whom worked as city officials. Use the World Wide Web or ask your reference librarian for help in locating a biography on one of these people (or on another well-known person with a double life). Read more than the biographical facts about your subject; look also at some of that person's work. When you examine that work, what conclusions can you draw about why your subject felt compelled to lead a double life?
3. Sometimes people make a conscious decision *not* to lead a double life but, instead, to pursue their dreams and turn their backs on the professional lives they know would bring them a comfortable lifestyle. Research the work and life of someone like Michael Crichton, who trained as a doctor but decided to pursue his dream of being an author, writing about medicine rather than practicing it. Or investigate the work and life of author-lawyer John Grisham or someone else—famous or not—who consciously decided to *avoid* living a double life. How do you think Wheeler would respond to such a decision?

LITTLE GIRLS IN PRETTY BOXES

Joan Ryan

> *The following selection was originally the introduction to Joan Ryan's book,* Little Girls in Pretty Boxes. *Published in 1995, this book is an exposé of women's gymnastics and figure skating, two sports that require very young girls to commit themselves to hard and often dangerous physical training. Ryan, a sports columnist for the* San Francisco Chronicle, *argues in* Little Girls in Pretty Boxes *that America's obsession with thinness and infatuation with little-girl cuteness has often prompted young athletes and their parents and coaches to cross the line from athletics to abuse. As citizens who revel in the ceremony and elegance of these Olympic sports, should we recognize that joy may have turned to obsession, that the love of grace may have been replaced by the need for money and recognition? When we watch the skaters pirouette gracefully on the ice and the gymnasts spin and soar on the uneven parallel bars, it seems jarring to compare them to the children in the factories and mines of the nineteenth century. But Ryan asks us to do so—and, in the process, to think about the dark side of the intersection between sport and work.*

The little girls marched into the Atlanta arena in single file, heads high, shoulders back, bare toes pointed. Under hair ribbons and rouged cheeks, their balletic bodies flowed past bleachers where expectant fathers craned forward with videocameras. Small and pretty in their shimmery leotards, the girls looked like trinkets from a Tiffany box. They lined up facing the crowd, and when the announcer summoned the winners of the Peachtree Classic, the gymnasts stepped forward and bowed their heads as soberly as Nobel laureates to receive their medals. Mothers with scoresheets tucked under their arms clapped until their hands hurt, shooting hopeful glances at the ESPN cameras roving among the girls. Along velvet ropes strung across the base of the bleachers, awestruck seven- and eight-year-olds stretched toward the winning gymnasts clutching programs and gym bags for them to sign.

On the opposite coast, at a skating rink in Redwood City, California, one fifteen-year-old skater—in a ponytail, braces and baby-blue sequins—stood at the edge of the rink, eyes wide, listening to her coach's last-minute instructions as her parents held hands in the bleachers, packed solid for the Pacific Coast Sectional Championships. She glided to the center of the ice. Then, as her music began, she spun like a jewel-box ballerina, executing the intricate choreography of leaps and footwork she had practiced nearly every day for as long as she could remember. On her $1/4$-inch skate blades rode her hopes of qualifying for the U.S. Figure Skating Championships, moving her one step closer to the Winter Olympic Games.

In gyms and rinks across the country, the air is thick with the scent of the Olympics. And the parents, coaches and young athletes chase it like hounds, impatient for the rewards of the sports that captivate American audiences as no others do. Gymnasts and figure skaters hold a unique and cherished place among American athletes. Gymnasts are the darlings of the Summer Games, figure skaters the ice princesses of the Winter Games. Every four years they keep us glued to our televisions for two weeks with their grace, agility, youth and beauty. They land on magazine covers, Wheaties boxes, the "Today" show. Television ratings for Olympic gymnastics and figure skating events rank among the highest for any sport on television. Helped by the Tonya Harding–Nancy Kerrigan saga, the women's technical program at the 1994 Winter Games drew the fourth-highest rating of any show in the history of television, placing it up there with the final episode of "M*A*S*H." But even at the controversy-free 1992 Winter Games, women's figure skating attracted a larger television audience than either the final game of the 1992 World Series or the 1992 National Collegiate Athletic Association basketball championship game between Michigan and Duke. Americans are so enchanted by gymnasts and figure skaters that in a 1991 survey they chose gymnast Mary Lou Retton and skater Dorothy Hamill—both long retired—as their favorite athletes, beating out the likes of Chris Evert, Michael Jordan and Magic Johnson.

Yet while gymnastics and figure skating are among the most-watched sports in the country, the least is known about the lives of their athletes (with the exceptions, of course, of Harding and Kerrigan). We watch thirteen-year-old Michelle Kwan, an eighth grader, land six triple jumps to finish second at the 1994 U.S. Figure Skating Championships. We see sixteen-year-old Shannon Miller soar above the balance beam as if it were a trampoline to win a silver medal at the 1992 Olympics. But we know little about how they achieve so much at such a young age or what becomes of them when they leave their sport.

Unlike women's tennis, a sport in which teenage girls rise to the highest echelon year after year in highly televised championships, gymnastics and figure skating flutter across our screens as ephemerally as butterflies. We know about tennis burnout, about Tracy Austin, Andrea Jaeger, Mary Pierce and, more recently, about Jennifer Capriati, who turned pro with $5 million in endorsement contracts at age thirteen and ended up four years later in a Florida motel room, blank-eyed and disheveled, sharing drugs with runaways. But we hear precious little about the young female gymnasts and figure skaters who perform magnificent feats of physical strength and agility, and even less about their casualties. How do the extraordinary demands of their training shape these young girls? What price do their bodies and psyches pay?

I set out to answer some of these questions during three months of research for an article that ran in the *San Francisco Examiner*, but when I finished I couldn't close my notebook. I took a year's leave to continue my research, focusing this time on the girls who never made it, not just on the champions.

What I found was a story about legal, even celebrated, child abuse. In the dark troughs along the road to the Olympics lay the bodies of the girls who stumbled on the way, broken by the work, pressure and humiliation. I found a girl whose father left the family when she quit gymnastics at age thirteen, who scraped her arms and legs with razors to dull her emotional pain and who needed a two-hour pass from a psychiatric hospital to attend her high school graduation. Girls who broke their necks and backs. One who so desperately sought the perfect, weightless gymnastics body that she starved herself to death. Others—many—who became so obsessive about controlling their weight that they lost control of themselves instead, falling into the potentially fatal cycle of bingeing on food, then purging by vomiting or taking laxatives. One who was sexually abused by her coach and one who was sodomized for four years by the father of a teammate. I found a girl who felt such shame at not making the Olympic team that she slit her wrists. A skater who underwent plastic surgery when a judge said her nose was distracting. A father who handed custody of his daughter over to her coach so she could keep skating. A coach who fed his gymnasts so little that federation officials had to smuggle food into their hotel rooms. A mother who hid her child's chicken pox with makeup so she could compete. Coaches who motivated their athletes by calling them imbeciles, idiots, pigs, cows.

I am not suggesting that gymnastics and figure skating in and of themselves are destructive. On the contrary, both sports are potentially wonderful and enriching, providing an arena of competition in which the average child can develop a sense of mastery, self-esteem and healthy athleticism. But this book isn't about recreational sports or the average child. It's about the elite child athlete and the American obsession with winning that has produced a training environment wherein results are bought at any cost, no matter how devastating. It's about how our cultural fixation on beauty and weight and youth has shaped both sports and driven the athletes into a sphere beyond the quest for physical performance.

The well-known story of Tonya Harding and Nancy Kerrigan did not happen in a vacuum; it symbolizes perfectly the stakes now involved in elite competition—itself a reflection of our national character. We created Tonya and Nancy not only by our hunger for winning but by our criterion for winning, an exaggeration of the code that applies to ambitious young women everywhere: Talent counts, but so do beauty, class, weight, clothes and politics. The anachronistic lack of ambivalence about femininity in both sports is part of their attraction, hearkening back to a simpler time when girls were girls, when women were girls for that matter: coquettish, malleable, eager to please. In figure skating especially, we want our athletes thin, graceful, deferential and cover-girl pretty. We want eyeliner, lipstick and hair ribbons. Makeup artists are fixtures backstage at figure skating competitions, primping and polishing. In figure skating, costumes can actually affect a score. They are so important that skaters spend $1500 and up on one dress—more than they spend on their skates. Nancy Kerrigan's dresses by designer Vera Wang cost upward of $5000 each.

Indeed, the costumes fueled the national fairy tale of Tonya and Nancy. Nancy wore virginal white. She was the perfect heroine, a good girl with perfect white teeth, a 24-inch waist and a smile that suggested both pluck and vulnerability. She remained safely within skating's pristine circle of grace and femininity. Tonya, on the other hand, crossed all the lines. She wore bordello red-and-gold. She was the perfect villainess, a bad girl with truck-stop manners, a racy past and chunky thighs. When she became convinced Nancy's grace would always win out over her own explosive strength, Tonya crossed the final line, helping to eliminate Nancy from competition. The media frenzy tapped into our own inner wranglings about the good girl/bad girl paradox, about how women should behave, about how they should look and what they should say. The story touched a cultural nerve about women crossing societal boundaries—of power, achievement, violence, taste, appearance—and being ensnared by them. In the end, both skaters were trapped, Tonya by her ambition and Nancy by the good-girl image she created for the ice—an image she couldn't live up to. The public turned on Nancy when foolish comments and graceless interviews made it clear she wasn't Snow White after all.

Both sports embody the contradiction of modern womanhood. Society has allowed women to aspire higher, but to do so a woman must often reject that which makes her female, including motherhood. Similarly, gymnastics and figure skating remove the limits of a girl's body, teaching it to soar beyond what seems possible. Yet they also imprison it, binding it like the tiny Victorian waist or the Chinese woman's foot. The girls aren't allowed passage into adulthood. To survive in the sports, they beat back puberty, desperate to stay small and thin, refusing to let their bodies grow up. In this way the sports pervert the very femininity they hold so dear. The physical skills have become so demanding that only a body shaped like a missile—in other words, a body shaped like a boy's—can excel. Breasts and hips slow the spins, lower the leaps and disrupt the clean, lean body lines that judges reward. "Women's gymnastics" and "ladies' figure skating" are misnomers today. Once the athletes become women, their elite careers wither.

In the meantime, their childhoods are gone. But they trade more than their childhoods for a shot at glory. They risk serious physical and psychological problems that can linger long after the public has turned its attention to the next phenom in pigtails. The intensive training and pressure heaped on by coaches, parents and federation officials—the very people who should be protecting the children—often result in eating disorders, weakened bones, stunted growth, debilitating injuries and damaged psyches. In the last six years two U.S. Olympic hopefuls have died as a result of their participation in elite gymnastics.

Because they excel at such a young age, girls in these sports are unlike other elite athletes. They are world champions before they can drive. They are the Michael Jordans and Joe Montanas of their sports before they learn algebra. Unlike male athletes their age, who are playing quarterback in high school or running track for the local club, these girls are competing on a worldwide stage. If an elite gymnast or figure skater fails, she fails globally. She sees her mistake replayed in slow motion on TV and captured in bold headlines in the newspaper. Adult reporters crowd around, asking what she has to say to a country that had hung its hopes on her thin shoulders. Tiffany Chin was seventeen when she entered the 1985 U.S. Figure Skating Championships as the favorite. She was asked at the time how she would feel if she didn't win. She paused, as if trying not to consider the possibility. "Devastated," she said quietly. "I don't know. I'd probably die."

Chin recalled recently that when she did win, "I didn't feel happiness. I felt relief. Which was disappointing." Three months before the 1988 Olympics, Chin retired when her legs began to break down. Some, however, say she left because she could no longer tolerate the pressure and unrelenting drive of her stern mother. "I feel I'm lucky to have gotten through it," she said of skating. "I don't think many people are that lucky. There's a tremendous strain on people who don't make it. The money, the sacrifices, the time. I know people emotionally damaged by it. I've seen nervous breakdowns, psychological imbalances."

An elite gymnast or figure skater knows she takes more than her own ambitions into a competition. Her parents have invested tens of thousands of dollars in her training, sometimes hundreds of thousands. Her coach's reputation rides on her performance. And she knows she might have only one shot. By the next Olympics she might be too old. By the next *year* she might be too old. Girls in these sports are under pressure not only to win but to win quickly. They're running against a clock that eventually marks the lives of all women, warning them they'd better hurry up and get married and have children before it's too late. These girls hear the clock early. They're racing against puberty.

Boys, on the other hand, welcome the changes that puberty brings. They reach their athletic peak after puberty when their bodies grow and their muscles strengthen. In recent years Michael Chang and Boris Becker won the French Open and Wimbledon tennis titles, respectively, before age eighteen, but in virtually every male sport the top athletes are men, not boys. Male gymnastics and figure skating champions are usually in their early to mid twenties; female champions are usually fourteen to seventeen years old in gymnastics and sixteen to early twenties in figure skating.

In staving off puberty to maintain the "ideal" body shape, girls risk their health in ways their male counterparts never do. They starve themselves, for one, often in response to their coaches' belittling insults about their bodies. Starving shuts down the menstrual cycle—the starving body knows it cannot support a fetus—and thus blocks the onset of puberty. It's a dangerous strategy to save a career. If a girl isn't menstruating, she isn't producing estrogen. Without estrogen, her bones weaken. She risks stunting her growth. She risks premature osteoporosis. She risks fractures in all bones, including her vertebrae, and she risks curvature of the spine. In several studies over the last decade, young female athletes who didn't menstruate were found to have the bone densities of postmenopausal women in their fifties, sixties and seventies. Most elite gymnasts don't begin to menstruate until they retire. Kathy Johnson, a medalist in the 1984 Olympics, didn't begin until she quit the sport at age twenty-five.

Our national obsession with weight, our glorification of thinness, have gone completely unchecked in gymnastics and figure skating. The cultural forces that have produced extravagantly bony fashion models have taken their toll on gymnasts and skaters already insecure about their bodies. Not surprisingly, eating disorders are common in both sports, and in gymnastics they're rampant. Studies of female college gymnasts show that most practice some kind of disordered eating. In a 1994 University of Utah study of elite gymnasts—those training for the Olympics—59 percent admitted to some form of disordered eating. And in interviewing elites for this book, I found only a handful who had not tried starving, throwing up or taking laxatives or diuretics to control their weight. Several left the sport because of eating disorders. One died. Eating disorders among male athletes, as in the general male population, are virtually unknown.

"Everyone goes through it, but nobody talks about it, because they're embarrassed," gymnast Kristie Phillips told me. "But I don't put the fault on us. It's the pressures that are put on us to be so skinny. It's mental cruelty. It's not fair that all these pressures are put on us at such a young age and we don't realize it until we get older and we suffer from it."

Phillips took laxatives, thyroid pills and diuretics to lose weight. She had been the hottest gymnast in the mid-1980s, the heir apparent to 1984 Olympic superstar Mary Lou Retton. But she not only didn't win a medal at the 1988 Summer Games, she didn't even make the U.S. team. She left the sport feeling like a failure. She gained weight, then became bulimic, caught in a cycle of bingeing and vomiting. Distraught, she took scissors to her wrists in a botched attempt to kill herself. "I weighed ninety-eight pounds and I was being called [by her coach] an overstuffed Christmas turkey," Phillips said in our interview. "I was told I was never going to make it in life because I was going to be fat. I mean, in *life*. Things I'll never forget."

Much of the direct blame for the young athletes' problems falls on the coaches and parents. Obviously, no parent wakes up in the morning and plots how to ruin his or her child's life. But the money, the fame and the promise of great achievement can turn a parent's head. Ambition gets perverted. The boundaries of parents and coaches bloat and mutate, with the parent becoming the ruthless coach and coach becoming the controlling parent. One father put gymnastics equipment in his living room and for every mistake his daughter made at the gym she had to repeat the skill hundreds of times at home. He moved the girl to three gyms around the country, pushing her in the sport she came to loathe. He said he did it because he wanted the best for her.

Coaches push because they are paid to produce great gymnasts. They are relentless about weight because physically round gymnasts and skaters don't win. Coaches are intolerant of injuries because in the race against puberty, time off is death. Their job is not to turn out happy, well-adjusted young women; it is to turn out champions. If they scream, belittle or ignore, if they prod an injured girl to forget her pain, if they push her to drop out of school, they are only doing what the parents have paid them to do. So, sorting out the blame when a girl falls apart is a messy proposition; everyone claims he was just doing his job.

The sports' national governing bodies, for their part, are mostly impotent. They try to do well by the athletes, but they, too, often lose their way in a tangle of ambition and politics. They're like small-town governments: personal, despotic, paternalistic and absolutely without teeth. The federations do not have the power that the commissioners' offices in professional baseball, football and basketball do. They cannot revoke a coach's or an athlete's membership for anything less than criminal activity. (Tonya Harding was charged and sentenced by the courts before the United States Figure Skating Association expelled her.) They cannot fine or suspend a coach whose athletes regularly leave the sport on stretchers.

There simply is no safety net protecting these children. Not the parents, the coaches or the federations.

Child labor laws prohibit a thirteen-year-old from punching a cash register for forty hours a week, but that same child can labor for forty hours or more inside a gym or an ice skating rink without drawing the slightest glance from the government. The U.S. government requires the licensing of plumbers. It demands that even the tiniest coffee shop adhere to a fastidious health code. It scrutinizes the advertising claims on packages of low-fat snack food. But it never asks a coach, who holds the lives of his young pupils in his hands, to pass a minimum safety and skills test. Coaches in this country need no license to train children, even in a high-injury sport like elite gymnastics. The government that forbids a child from buying a pack of cigarettes because of health concerns never checks on the child athlete who trains until her hands bleed or her knees buckle, who stops eating to achieve the perfect body, who takes eight Advils a day and offers herself up for another shot of cortisone to dull the pain, who drinks a bottle of Ex-Lax because her coach is going to weigh her in the morning. The government never takes a look inside the gym or the rink to make sure these children are not being exploited or abused or worked too hard. Even college athletes—virtually all of whom are adults—are restricted by the NCAA to just twenty hours per week of formal training. But no laws, no agencies, put limits on the number of hours a child can train or the methods a coach can use.

Some argue that extraordinary children should be allowed to follow extraordinary paths to realize their potential. They argue that a child's wants are no less important than an adult's and thus she should not be denied her dreams just because she is still a child. If pursuing her dream means training eight hours a day in a gym, withstanding abusive language and tolerating great pain, and if the child wants to do it and the parents believe it will build character, why not let her? Who are we to tell a child what she can and cannot do with her life?

In fact, we tell children all the time what they can and cannot do with their lives. Restricting children from certain activities is hardly a revolutionary concept. Laws prohibit children from driving before sixteen and drinking before twenty-one. They prohibit children from dropping out of school before fifteen and working full-time before sixteen. In our society we put great value on protecting our children from physical harm and exploitation, and sometimes that means protecting them from their own poor judgment and their parents' poor judgment. No one questions the wisdom of the government in forbidding a child to work full-time, so why is it all right for her to train full-time with no rules to ensure her well-being? Child labor laws should address all labor, even that which is technically nonpaid, though top gymnasts and figure skaters *do* labor for money.

In recent years the federations have begun to pay their top athletes a stipend based on their competition results. The girls can earn bonuses by representing the United States in certain designated events. Skaters who compete in the World Figure Skating Championships and the Olympic Games, for example, receive $15,000. They earn lesser amounts for international competitions such as Skate America. They also earn money from corporate sponsors and exhibitions. The money might not cover much more than their training expenses, which can run $75,000 for a top skater and $20,000 to $30,000 per year for a top gymnast, but it's money—money that is paid specifically for the work the athletes do in the gym and the skating rink.

The real payoff for their hard work, however, waits at the end of the road. That's what the parents and athletes hope anyway. When Mary Lou Retton made millions on Madison Avenue after winning the gold medal at the 1984 Olympics, she changed gymnastics forever. "Kids have agents now before they even make it into their teens," Retton says. Now the dream is no longer just about medals but about Wheaties boxes and appearance fees, about paying off mom and dad's home equity loans and trading in the Toyota for a Mercedes. It doesn't seem to matter that only six girls every four years reach the Olympics and that winning the gold once they get there is the longest of long shots. Even world champion Shannon Miller didn't win the all-around Olympic gold in 1992.

Figure skating, even more than gymnastics, blinds parents and athletes with the glittering possibilities, and for good reason. Peggy Fleming and

Dorothy Hamill are still living off gold medals won decades ago. Nancy Kerrigan landed endorsements with Reebok, Evian, Seiko and Campbell's soup with only a bronze medal in 1992. With glamorous and feminine stars like Kerrigan and Kristi Yamaguchi to lead the way, the United States Figure Skating Association has seen the influx of corporate sponsorship climb 2000 percent in just five years. Money that used to go to tennis is now being shifted to figure skating and gymnastics as their popularity grows. The payoff in money and fame now looms large enough to be seen from a distance, sparkling like the Emerald City, driving parents and children to extremes to reach its doors.

I'm not suggesting that all elite gymnasts and figure skaters emerge from their sports unhealthy and poorly adjusted. Many prove that they can thrive under intense pressure and physical demands and thus are stronger for the experience. But too many can't. There are no studies that establish what percentage of elite gymnasts and figure skaters are damaged by their sports and in what ways. So the evidence I've gathered for this book is anecdotal, the result of nearly a hundred interviews and more than a decade of covering both sports as a journalist.

The bottom line is clear. There have been enough suicide attempts, enough eating disorders, enough broken bodies, enough regretful parents and enough bitter young women to warrant a serious reevaluation of what we're doing in this country to produce Olympic champions. Those who work in these sports know this. They know the tragedies all too well. If the federations and coaches truly care about the athletes and not simply about the fame and prestige that come from trotting tough little champions up to the medal stand, they know it is past time to lay the problems on the table, examine them and figure out a way to keep their sports from damaging so many young lives. But since those charged with protecting young athletes so often fail in their responsibility, it is time the government drops the fantasy that certain sports are merely games and takes a hard look at legislation aimed at protecting elite child athletes.

It is also my hope that by dramatizing the particularly intense subculture of female gymnastics and figure skating, we can better understand something of our own nature as a country bent on adulating, and in some cases sacrificing, girls and young women in a quest to fit them into our pretty little boxes.

Questions for Discussion

1. In her opening to "Little Girls in Pretty Boxes," Joan Ryan compares the young gymnasts and skaters to "trinkets from a Tiffany box" and "jewel box ballerina[s]." What does she imply by using such metaphors? Are they effective? Finally, consider the use of these metaphors, and others like them, as a structural device. How do they help Ryan both support her thesis and tie her ideas together?

2. Consider the tone, the use of metaphors, and the word choices in paragraph 3, which begins "In gyms and rinks . . .". How does Ryan *imply* her criticisms of our approach to the Olympics without making her disapproval explicit?

3. Ryan says that once the skaters and gymnasts become women, once their bodies look less like boys' bodies, their careers are over. Other writers and scholars have made similar claims about all girls, arguing that, with puberty, their sense of themselves changes and their self-esteem often plummets. If you are a woman, was this true in your experience? If you are a man, do you think Ryan is right that "boys . . . welcome the change that puberty brings" because they achieve more athletic prowess after puberty? Finally, think about the ways your friends and siblings responded to puberty. Did you notice any difference between the ways the boys and the girls reacted emotionally and psychologically to its onset?

4. We have here only the introduction to Ryan's book, but already it is clear that Ryan is making a strong case against current training and treatment of young skaters and gymnasts. How convincing is the argument so far? If you have had experience with either of these sports—or with any other sport or activity to which you became devoted at a very early age—how fully do your observations and experiences accord with those Ryan describes?

Questions for Research and Writing

1. Ryan claims that our interest in both figure skating and gymnastics is "anachronistic" because it recalls a "simpler time when girls were girls, when women were girls for that matter: coquettish, malleable, eager to please" (paragraph 9). She says that in these athletes we admire, are young women who hide their womanhood, who perform in little girls' bodies and look like the girl next door. Test this notion by examining the portrayal of women athletes in the sports pages of your local newspaper and popular magazines. If you have access to videotapes of sporting events (especially the Olympics), examine them also. As you read and watch, pay particular attention to what the women wear and say, to how their body language helps them create a particular image, and to how others—writers and the public—respond to them. To what extent do your reading and observation bear out Ryan's notion about what we most want and admire in women athletes?

2. Young gymnasts and skaters risk doing permanent damage to their bodies, Ryan warns, but others might counter that all sports bring particular risks. Basketball players risk knee injuries, tennis players risk elbow and shoulder injuries, boxers face serious brain damage, and so on. Do some research—in the library, in your local newspaper and

sports magazines—about sports injuries. Then survey ten or fifteen of your peers who have played sports seriously in high school or college. What dangers are associated with particular sports? To avoid simply reporting about and listing injuries and risks, address the implications of your findings. What particular remedies would you propose to the problems you've uncovered? Think about coaching techniques, attitudes toward sports, equipment and rule changes, medical solutions, and so forth.

TWO WOMEN AT WORK: BALANCING WORK AND FAMILY

Lotte Bailyn

> *The following selection originally appeared in Swarthmore Management Professor Lotte Bailyn's book* Breaking the Mold: Women, Men, and Time in the New Corporate World, *published in 1993. Printed as "interludes" to Bailyn's more argumentative and analytical discussion of the relationship between work and family, the stories of Nancy Wright and Elizabeth Gray give human faces to the debate about the assumptions that employees and employers make about the appropriate balance between corporate demands and family needs. In earlier generations, when traditional families included a stay-at-home mother, there was little need to balance family and work: men worked outside the home; women took care of the children and household. Whereas men may often have wanted to spend more time with their families, and women may often have wanted to find a different kind of fulfillment in the workplace, the separation of roles made for less overt tension between work and family. In today's world, many employees—usually women, but often men, too—find the work/family relationship a little more difficult to define, and a comfortable balance a little more difficult to find. In this selection, Bailyn explores the choices two women and their employers made. As you read, imagine yourself in both the employer's and the employee's roles. Would you have made the same choices?*

NANCY WRIGHT: SUCCESS?

Nancy Wright is among the first women to have reached the executive level at a large, progressive, dynamic, and successful company. She is an excellent performer, and the company has rewarded her efforts. She loves her work and has succeeded far more than she ever expected. But now, looking back, she expresses some concerns. Why?[1]

The Story

Nancy Wright has been with the company for more than fifteen years. She joined it when her previous job with a bank required more travel than she thought she could manage: "I love to travel, thought it was exciting. But as I started to think about planning a family, I realized that having a family plus the amount of traveling I had to do were sort of mutually exclusive." At that point she was not thinking about a career. "What I really thought about was a job and an interesting job."

Nancy married immediately after college; after five years of work at the bank, when she began to think of having children, she felt that a change made sense. Negotiations took a long time, and by the time she was offered a job at her present company she was pregnant:

> So I turned down the job, saying that it didn't make sense to join [the company] because I was pregnant. . . . The person that I was interviewing with said, "Well, what difference should that make?" I said I really hadn't decided on whether I wanted to work. He said, "Even if you only work at the company six months, I'll feel lucky that we got you for those six months." So I thought, why not? My husband was supportive. . . . So anyway, I wound up joining the company. I was three months pregnant.

Before taking the job, Nancy asked for and got agreement that she could have a three-month leave of absence once the baby was born. Company policy at the time was flexible (though all leave was unpaid), but normally there was a requirement to return to work after eight weeks. About the added leave Nancy said, "I had negotiated that right up front as part of the decision to come. Because, after all, I knew I was pregnant, and I knew my due date and all that."

Nancy was attached to the company because she felt that "the corporate world tended to attract bright, aggressive people, and you tended to get ahead based on your abilities rather than time in the job." It was different from the bank, which was "conservative, not the best and brightest, no fast-track kind of potential—they didn't single people out and deal with them separately. It was sort of a 'wait your turn' environment."

The baby came early, and Nancy worked until the day she delivered. "I came back after three months, and as it turns out, I had a very difficult baby and was more than happy to flee the house and come back to work. I went through some difficult child care arrangement times." She and her husband wanted a live-in au pair, but they had difficulty finding someone who was reliable and would stay. "There just simply wasn't anybody I could turn to. Nobody I knew worked and had children, let alone had live-in help." Nancy's parents and in-laws lived in the area but were not very supportive of her going back to work.

> It's not that they were deliberately working against me, but they just felt that my place was home with the baby, that my husband was a successful attorney, what do you need to work for? That was their attitude. Just simply not understanding why, having chosen to have a child, I would choose to go back to work.

Her husband, however, was very supportive: "Whatever would make me happy he would be willing to do."

After a particularly harrowing experience with a baby-sitter, and because her father had fallen ill, Nancy almost quit work. But her boss (the same man who had hired her) said, "Why don't you take as much time as you need, get through your father's illness, straighten up the child care situation, and let me know if I can be of help." Nancy took a few weeks off, during which time her father died and her mother-in-law found an older woman to take care of the child.

> It was a very stressful time. . . . It was stressful having a child that was very colicky, very difficult. It was stressful going through all of these rotating baby-sitters . . . and feeling totally inadequate and also feeling that I wasn't doing a good job at work because of all this stress. But anyway, I found a woman, and my husband and I agreed that either it worked this time or I would quit. And it worked! The woman was an older woman, she had raised a number of kids of her own, she needed a job, and she was with us for five and a half years. She, in effect, raised my son and was there when, three and a half years later, I had another child, and brought up that child until she was two.

Nancy nursed the second child, a girl, by going home two to three times a day. And she also had to leave at times to drive her son to preschool, since the caretaker could not drive.

> So there was a period of time, I would say during the first five to six years that I was at the company, that my loyalties were very divided—where my heart wasn't always in my work and I clearly was not giving work my all. . . . Also, shortly after I got the child care situation straightened out, my boss changed. And the second boss was far less sympathetic and far less patient with my coming and going to the house to nurse my daughter or to take my son to preschool or whatever, and he and I really got along very poorly. We were at loggerheads all the time over the time away from the office.

Nonetheless, Nancy was given more and more responsibility, including more travel. During her daughter's first year, Nancy was in Europe seven times (for between one and two weeks each time) and took a trip to the Far East:

> Although there were times where the tradeoff meant my family came first or my responsibilities at home came first, there were also times where I just simply said, so my son can't go to preschool, or he goes in a taxi. Or I get friends to do it. But again, in those days, it was very unusual for a woman to be working, a woman who lived in the suburbs and who had other forms of livelihood. It was unusual.

When the Wrights' caretaker finally left, they got another older woman, who stayed with them for two years. During this time Nancy went off to a residential executive training program, the only woman among more than one hundred men. This program took her out of the home for many weeks except for Saturday night and Sunday. Her husband, who had been consistently supportive until then, found this a difficult period.

> I really enjoyed the school experience. [But] for the first time, the trade-off that I was making caused friction between my husband and myself. He could clearly tell that I was enjoying school—I made no secret about it, that I enjoyed being away from home . . . so that I think there may have been some jealousy. There may have been some resentment that there she is, having a great time with all of these guys, and I'm left at home with the burden of the responsibility. . . . I think it didn't help that people said to me—our friends, or people at work, or his family—"Oh, it must be so tough on you being at school." No one said to him, "And look at the wonderful thing you're doing taking care of the home front while she has this great opportunity." Everyone was somehow saying what a tough thing it was for me, and it wasn't at all. I was having a grand old time. I was working hard, but I was having a great time. I think that was, of all the years of work/home trade-off, the most stressful time, because of the fact that my husband's support wasn't really there emotionally. . . . It was a stressful time recovering from it as well. So we went through about a good year of relationship difficulty over the whole thing, which we have weathered and got through.

On the whole, Nancy has had very supportive managers, people with families of their own who understood her needs, "understood that there would be times when I was here 150 percent of what was required, and other times when it was only 50 percent of what was required." In part, Nancy educated her managers to be understanding.

> I think [I succeeded] mainly because I was in touch with it and confronted them with the fact that there were trade-offs to be made. I wasn't in touch with it in the very beginning, but over time, as I became aware of what was causing me stress, I was able to verbalize it and share it with my manager and able to say, "Look, it's 5:30 and I've got to go," . . . or "I'll be in late tomorrow because my daughter's in the school play."

The Wrights still have live-in help, now mainly someone to handle car pools and "cook and keep our life organized and on track—arrange for plumbers, arrange for electricians, that kind of thing. It's not so much primary day care provider any more as it is sort of chief cook and bottle washer." Nancy has no sense that her family concerns ever put her at a disadvantage at work or in competition with peers. Indeed, she has been extremely successful in her career, and she now has one of the highest positions of any woman in the company. Nor does she feel that being a woman played any part in her career or in the reaction that people had to her. "One of the sort of coping mechanisms that I've had over the years is to not recognize any difference between myself and my male counterparts." So she is the model of the woman who did it all, achieving exceptional things in the professional world and having a family as well. But she is not interested in progressing any further up the ladder or in "moves that would prepare me developmentally for the next promotion or the next assignment," a feeling she has shared with her boss. In fact, she has asked her boss to let her know if he ever wants her to move out of the position she is in, at which point she would probably leave the company.

As Nancy reflects back on her career, things begin to take on a different look. She recognizes that her life has indeed been different from that of her male peers. "I now see that I have had to make trade-offs and I am different in a lot of ways, that women in general are different than men in a lot of ways. I'm more in touch with that now than I used to be. But at the time . . . I didn't think of it that way." She realizes that though she had a family, hers was "not a very demanding home life, or at least a home life where I could pass it off, trade it off without a lot of hassle."

In hindsight, Nancy regrets some of the choices and trade-offs she made. Over the years, she says, she chose to escape into her work. She found it easier to deal with the problems at work than the problems her children had in school. She drew more satisfaction from work and advanced by following the rules of an environment in which children, child care, and parenting were devalued. Indeed, for most of her career the notion of placing family above work was so foreign to her professional world that the choice did not even seem to exist. She did not feel aware of the costs, the long-term implications of her decisions. Despite this, Nancy feels that her decisions were entirely her own. But she does not at this point feel good about them.

> If I had it to do all over again, I think I would do things very differently. . . . I think I probably would have taken off several years instead of choosing to go right back to work. I think with the benefit of hindsight, which of course is real easy for me to say given my position, the security of having achieved where I am, it's easy to look back and say, "That's how I would do it." I'm not sure I'd have the guts to do it that way, but my relationship with my son to this day is mediocre to poor and I think it's traceable back to [the fact that] I had an escape valve. There were many years in which after dinner—which I didn't eat with the children; the children were always fed before I got home, so I had dinner with my husband—I went up to my study and I sat and did work for the office and I was unavailable for my young children, to play with, to parent, to put to bed, because I was all-consumed with responsibilities at work because I really enjoyed it and I didn't enjoy [and] never had to get used to doing the mothering tasks of reading to them.

I can't even count on one hand the number of times I sat down and read them a book. Or played a game with them. Though I think I have a good relationship with my daughter, it is not the quality of the relationship that I think I would have been enjoying if the foundation had been there for her as a young child, or even as a not-so-young child. . . . I put a lot more of my emotional energy and a lot more of my *self* into work than I did into being a parent.

Such a lament has frequently been heard from male executives at a similar stage in their lives, and Nancy has followed a "male" route to career success. But her actions also have implications for women and for the company's hope of achieving gender equity in its management ranks, for she is an active voice inside the company encouraging young mothers to consider taking time off from work to be with their children, and to think hard about the choices they are making. She tells them:

> No one's going to write on my tombstone, "Nancy Wright, senior executive of [company]." Hopefully someone will write on my tombstone, "Loving wife and mother." No one will remember, hopefully, when I die at eighty-five, that I even worked here. But hopefully my children, who I haven't done a real terrific job raising, will get through whatever resentment they feel about that and we will have been able to establish a relationship where they will care to write on my tombstone, "She was a loving mother."

What is complicated about this reaction is that Nancy limits her concerns to the women in the company. She thinks "there should be a place in every company for women to be able to take the slower track for a while, to work part-time, or to take off a couple years, and to be able to come back to work and give of themselves 150 percent of the time once they are through some of those early child-raising years, which are the most demanding timewise." But if one makes special arrangements only for women, it will not be possible to provide gender equity in the work place. Women will have been singled out for needs that make them less fully members of the organization, and the real needs of many men will have been neglected.

Thus Nancy's story illustrates two clear costs that occur when the work organization remains unchanged and individuals self-select into the most ambitious roles. The personal costs are evident; the guilt and self-recrimination Nancy feels are painful. But the organization pays a cost as well. Investing as it does in the training and development of women managers and striving for gender equity at all levels of the organization, the company is now faced with the fact that a woman such as Nancy, who has succeeded by conventional standards and who should be the role model for younger women, is actively encouraging them (and not men) to take time off from work. Because of this, the organization's initiatives toward achieving a more balanced management team are frustrated.

Comment

Is Nancy Wright a success? Yes, but by a narrow set of rules that govern only one part of her life. And paradoxically, the personal cost she has had to pay for this success is now having unintended organizational ramifications. Not only is she herself no longer available for advancement, but her advice to younger women makes their progress problematic. Her well-meaning attempts to alert younger female employees to possible future regret presumes that the issues she faced are only women's issues. By ignoring the role of general workplace demands—or by assuming that these are given and not subject to change—she falls into the "mommy track" view of organizational life. As such, her interventions inadvertently undermine the stated desire of her company to move women into the upper ranks of management. True gender equity requires not special (and inevitably invidious) distinctions, however benignly meant, but general provisions for flexibility in career paths that will benefit men as well as women.

ELIZABETH GRAY: FAILURE?

Elizabeth Gray works in a progressive company, a company that prides itself on giving its employees great flexibility in their work. Yet when Elizabeth wanted to arrange a part-time schedule after the birth of her child, the negotiations collapsed. Why?[2]

The Story

Elizabeth Gray graduated from business school in 1983. Interested in both marketing and human resources, she took a position in the internal management consulting group of a rapidly growing, innovative company. While she was drawn to the organization for geographic and job content reasons, she was also impressed by the stated human resources philosophy of the company. It was a company that valued diversity, valued its employees, and actively sought ways to create an environment in which employees could perform at peak capacity.

Elizabeth worked in the management consulting group for two and a half years. She was a strong performer, earning the respect and trust of her clients in the organization. A high-level executive in the marketing group was particularly impressed with her talent and brought her into his group in early 1986. When he left the company only a few months later, he asked Carol Peters, his colleague, to provide Elizabeth with the mentoring and guidance she needed.

Elizabeth worked in this group for about a year, but it was a difficult and unsettling year. First, both of the women with whom she was mostly associated—Carol Peters and Susan Carey—were absent on maternity leave during her first summer, leaving Elizabeth with a somewhat vague set of reporting relationships in a new work group. Second, Elizabeth herself became pregnant in the spring of the same year. Carol and Susan returned to work full-time in the fall, and Elizabeth left (two weeks early) at Thanksgiving. When she left, Elizabeth expected to return to a full-time position; as the time neared to return, however, she decided a part-time schedule made more sense. In the following spring, the three women tried to work out an arrangement whereby Elizabeth could administer the program she had previously run, but now on a part-time basis.

Elizabeth's husband Mark fully supported her decision to return to work. They had met in college. After graduation, Mark worked in retail before taking a position with a government agency. When he and Elizabeth decided to get married, they moved to the city where Elizabeth wanted to get her MBA. Mark arranged a transfer to that city in order to accommodate Elizabeth's plans but felt the move was good for his career as well, as it permitted him to get more field experience.

Elizabeth and Mark initially patterned their lives together according to unconventional rules. Mark was content to work a standard workweek of forty hours and was supportive of Elizabeth's extremely ambitious career aspirations. They had always thought that Mark would be the primary caretaker for their children, and Elizabeth would be the partner with the heavy career commitment. Mark described the situation as follows:

> For a long time we pictured ourselves in the role that Elizabeth is going to this hot business school, she's got an MBA, it's important for her to have a lot of job success. And I thought that was fine. She was making more money than me, and I liked the role of "OK, I'll do more stuff around the house, and you can go do crazy hours at work."

After Elizabeth graduated and began working, Mark started thinking about going to law school, "since all I ever did was work with attorneys anyway." Initially Mark saw law school as something to open new possibilities or give him some flexibility. He felt that he was at a "stagnant point" in his career and needed something to help him go further in his organization or in other public service jobs. Elizabeth was very supportive of this idea.

For four years Mark maintained his job full-time while going to school at night. He enjoyed a great deal of success, which opened up opportunities to him that he had not really expected when he entered law school. He had expected to return to the public or nonprofit sector upon graduation, but midway through the process he started eyeing jobs in large private law firms. While he characterized his first year in law school as one in which he was motivated by fear of failing, his attitude changed after he found out that he could potentially place at or near the top of his class. Able to see the top (and thinking that being at the top would "open up a lot more opportunities"), he started to work to achieve it. In the second year, he started engaging in such extracurricular activities as moot court and trying out for law review. His efforts paid off, and after graduation he was hired by a large law firm. At the time of being interviewed, he was in his third year of the partnership track (expected to take about nine years) and worked seven days a week, often till 10:00 P.M. each night.

This was the situation that faced Elizabeth as she approached her return to work. In some ways, it seemed a good context in which to negotiate a flexible work schedule. The organization was one committed to workplace diversity; several women had arranged part-time work schedules with their managers. Elizabeth had an excellent track record, with several letters of commendation in her personnel file from satisfied clients. She was negotiating with two women who had each recently given birth to their first child, and who were sympathetic to the emotional and scheduling strains infants could introduce to the work-family equation. And she had a husband who completely supported her in her professional decisions.

The arrangement did not, however, come to fruition. While Susan and Carol were able to identify a piece of work they estimated would take approximately twenty-four hours per week, negotiations over the more subtle terms of their working relationship broke down. Elizabeth ended up resigning from the company, and Susan hired a new person to do the work she had hoped Elizabeth would do.

What Elizabeth tried to negotiate was a discrete piece of work for which she would assume full responsibility, but which would allow her the time she wanted to be with her child. The specific job identified by Susan and Carol seemed to fit the bill. But the attempt to negotiate a viable arrangement failed because Elizabeth was unwilling to subscribe to the belief that her work involved not simply responsibility for the defined task but also an open-ended availability to the organization whenever called upon. When she sat down with Carol and Susan to negotiate the terms of her return to a part-time job, this was the issue on which the three were unable to agree: whether Elizabeth would guarantee that job demands would take precedence over her family arrangements. All three believed that Elizabeth could limit her tasks. But they differed on whether she was entitled also to limit and bound her availability to meet all standard company demands.

As the time to return to work had drawn near, Elizabeth had begun to draw boundaries around her personal life and family responsibilities. Knowing that Mark was going to be very busy, she took steps to make sure that she would be able to provide the necessary parenting to her son. She wanted to work part-time, but she did not want the work to "get out of control" and start eroding the boundaries she felt she needed. Elizabeth did not see this as an unworkable situation. She wanted to work and to do a good job at what she did, but she did not want to commit to more than she was capable of delivering. She wanted assurances that twenty-four hours per week of excellent work were going to be enough to maintain her standing in the organization.

In the early stages of the negotiations, Carol and Susan sought a verbal commitment from Elizabeth that she would do whatever was necessary to make sure the work got done. For example, Carol asked her: "What about meetings? Will you be able to come whenever there's a meeting?" When Elizabeth asked about planning meetings for the days she was in the office, Carol said, "Well, sometimes we can, but sometimes we won't be able to;

then you'll have to have your day care person be more flexible." When verbal exchanges such as these failed to convince Elizabeth's managers that she would rearrange her schedule whenever they thought it necessary, they presented her with a written document outlining the terms of her arrangement as they understood them. The letter said, in essence, that the managers had a right to increase Elizabeth's hours at any point to make sure the work got done, that she had to be "totally flexible," and that she would be expected to attend all meetings scheduled during her days off. Elizabeth refused to work under these conditions.

> You have to trust that I'm going to get the job done. It's to my benefit to get the job done well, too. I certainly would not want to do the job unless I could do it well. It's been my policy, it's the way I've always done things and the way I always intend to do things.... I'll do the job for you, but I don't want a letter, a contract stating that you have the right to do whatever you want and demand whatever you want from me.

It is important to note that the impression Susan and Carol had developed about Elizabeth's shifting priorities was accurate. The problem arose because Susan and Carol interpreted the new ordering of priorities as threatening to the organization. They were no longer able to see Elizabeth as "committed to the work" in the way that employees in this organization were supposed to be committed, and without this demonstration or "proof" of commitment, they were concerned that the work would not get done.

Ultimately, their suspicions that Elizabeth was unwilling to place work before her family responsibilities were confirmed when she refused to work under the written terms they drew up. The conflict over priorities was finally brought out into the open. Elizabeth made it clear that she would not allow organizational demands to encroach on her personal life past a certain point; she would not agree to subjugate her other interests to the demands of the work. Even in this progressive and flexible working world, the violation of the norm that work should take precedence in one's life rendered a resolution of the conflict impossible. Given this fundamental difference in approach to the link between the organization and private life, there was nothing for Elizabeth to do but to leave, even though she was only a few months from having her pension vested.

Three years later, when we interviewed Susan, Carol, and Elizabeth, they all still harbored a great deal of anger and resentment over the incident. Carol commented, "It isn't the way I would have liked it to go. There was something underneath not right about it." Susan recalls feeling Elizabeth was an excellent candidate for the position, and was significantly inconvenienced when Elizabeth turned it down.

> She had already done the job when I was gone. She was familiar and I didn't have to teach someone else, which took me a lot of

time. So she had already done it, and I was here again and I didn't want to do it. I ended up hiring someone and . . . doing a lot of the work, but she was a perfect candidate for it.

All three commented that they were surprised they still felt so much emotion and anger around the memory.

Shortly after making the decision to leave, Elizabeth was hired to work in administration at a local university. Though the job was originally designed as a full-time position, Elizabeth was able to negotiate a flexible part-time schedule as a condition for accepting the job. An agreement was made only after she visited with and obtained approval from her manager and her peers.

> I had to fight for myself. I had to really step back and think about what my priorities are and—you know, in the long run, if I take some time off from my career or if I slow down, that's OK, because what's important to me now . . . and I would not have said this when I graduated from business school . . . there's just more important things to me in life right now than my career. That's the kind of thing I'm not sure I want anyone else at [this job] to know . . . but you know, I think they know that about me. I actually think I made that pretty clear when I interviewed.

Thus Elizabeth is still ambivalent about the propriety of her new priorities, even in an employment situation in which she made them explicit. It is a feeling or set of values she continues to experience, on some level, as deviant. Her view of herself as a competent professional who produces quality work and her view of herself as a mother who values motherhood above her career are difficult to reconcile.[3] She still feels that her reputation with her coworkers may be tarnished if they know of the precedence she gives to her family life.

We see in Elizabeth's remark a conflict between her ideas about professionalism and work and her personal feelings about taking care of herself and her family. Her comment illustrates the dissonance between the prevailing ideology about professionalism—that work can and should take precedence in one's life—and the conflicting belief in the ultimate value of family and children. Elizabeth at one time enjoyed feelings about work and the role of work in her life that were congruent with organizational norms. But as she attempted to adjust her priorities, she found that her feelings about her private life created tension in the workplace, where a dominant value on family is marginalized and not easily accommodated to organizational life.

Comment

Is Elizabeth Gray a failure? Not in her eyes, though she may represent a failure to the company that lost the benefit of her competence. But her story brings up a number of issues. All three women involved in Elizabeth's work situation think of what went wrong in terms of the specific people and personalities involved; none of them sees it in terms of larger social and ideological issues. Their interpretation thus reinforces the status quo.

This reading of the situation also has personal implications. Elizabeth and Mark seem to think in terms of trade-offs between one career and the other. The idea that both could pursue a high-profile career did not seem viable once children entered the picture. But if the only margin for adjustment is one's own career, or one's spouse's, then tension becomes focused on the trade-offs. Thus one might argue that organizational policies that encourage an all-or-nothing level of commitment generate family stress because they implicitly deny the possibility that the work situation could provide a margin for adjustment. What in fact is a societal issue driven by inflexibility in career structures becomes a private issue between husband and wife in which the only possible solution is for one of them to "sacrifice."

Notes

1. This case study is based on an interview conducted by Amy Andrews, who contributed greatly to the analysis. It is a stand-alone case, for we have no information from her spouse or her coworkers or managers.

2. This case study is written jointly with Amy Andrews. The story is based on her interviews and her analysis of the situation. See Amy Andrews, *Flexible working schedules in high commitment organizations: A challenge to the emotional norms?*, Sloan School of Management Working Paper #3329-91-BPS, MIT, 1991.

3. I recently heard of a female professor and her female Ph.D. student, both of whom had small children, who had a close personal relationship but *never* discussed the issues they faced in dealing with their families while pursuing their professional work.

Questions for Discussion

1. Compare Nancy Wright and Elizabeth Gray. What assumptions and values does each bring to her situation? To what extent are their supervisors or husbands responsible for what happens to them?

2. The case of Elizabeth Gray raises important questions about the relationship between work and family life and about one's obligations to each. Where would you place the appropriate boundaries between the responsibilities to family and to job? Are those boundaries different for men and women? Are they different for blue-collar and white-collar workers? For parents of young children and of older children?

3. The conflict in Elizabeth Gray's case arises over her unwillingness to sign a contract that she believes would obligate her to put work needs over family needs and her supervisors' unwillingness to give her the trust and flexibility she feels she needs. Look again at the conversations Elizabeth has with Carol and Susan. What causes the negotiations to

stall? What leads to defensiveness on each side? How might both sides have maintained their positions but worded them differently so as to avoid threatening and alienating the other side?

4. In her book, Bailyn titles these interludes "Nancy Wright: Success?" and "Elizabeth Gray: Failure?" Her use of question marks invites us to define for ourselves the extent of Wright's and Gray's success or failure. Do you see these women as successes and/or failures? What assumptions about the relationship between work and family underlie your own answer?

Questions for Research and Writing

1. Nancy Wright chooses a different path than Elizabeth Gray and, in the end, says that she regrets having distanced herself from her children. Survey some children of double-income families. How do they describe their relationships with their parents? How much did their parents' working affect that relationship? Ask respondents to consider not only their own needs and desires but their parents' needs and desires. Finally, you might ask them about their own career choices and decisions about the appropriate balance between work and family. Will those decisions differ from those of their parents?

2. Like Elizabeth Gray, many parents who work outside the home find it difficult to reconcile professional and domestic obligations. Interview a number of parents who have faced the kinds of problems Elizabeth Gray has faced. What balance have they found between professional obligations and family responsibilities? How satisfied are they and their employers with that balance? As you analyze your results, consider whether the following groups make different assumptions about the appropriate balance between work and family: employers and employees, men and women, and blue-collar and white-collar workers. Finally, if you were an employer, what provisions would you make for working parents?

TELECOMMUTING: THE NEW WORKPLACE TREND

Merlisa Lawrence Corbett

> *How will the new technologies influence the way that we work? The following short article appeared in June 1996 in* Black Enterprise, *a magazine whose readership includes African-American professionals. The author, a journalist and frequent contributor to the magazine, outlines some advantages of what has come to be called "telecommuting." By working from home, many professionals can better balance work and home responsibilities. Clearly, telecommuting works best for certain kinds of work and certain kinds of workers. In talking to both workers and managers, the writer has discovered several conditions that contribute to successful telecommuting arrangements, as well as possible pitfalls that telecommuters and their employers will want to avoid. As you read this article, ask yourself whether you would want to telecommute—and whether you would want to have grown up in a household with telecommuter parents.*

Rush hour traffic may be a thing of the past as more workers find that their new workplace is as close as home.

It's Monday, 8 A.M., and Chandra Pikes begins her daily commute to work. She strolls from her bedroom to her dining room-cum-office and turns on her computer. As it boots up, she heads to the front door for the newspaper. Fifteen minutes later, showered and dressed in shorts and a T-shirt, Pikes is in front of her computer—her commute complete.

The 29-year-old software architect used to wake up at 7 A.M. and fight 20 minutes of traffic to get to her office at the Texas Department of Human Services. Now, working from her Austin apartment, Pikes has joined the growing legion of telecommuters who are connected to their offices by a computer. Fueled by new technology and the tremendous growth of the information industry, telecommuting is predicted to become the office environment of the future.

Yet, telecommuting is nothing new, according to Jack Nilles, author of *Making Telecommuting Happen: A Guide for Telemanagers and Telecommuters* (Van Nostrand Reinhold, New York, $24.95). "Before the industrial revolution, everyone worked from home," he says. Back then, industry brought workers into major cities and America's workforce became centralized. Today, the tide is turning again as computer sales rival those of televisions. As more people flock to the suburbs and more rural landscapes, working outside of the office is now commonplace.

While companies have to absorb the installation and training costs associated with telecommuting (in some cases even buying the computers), they're also reaping long-term benefits, such as reduced operating expenses and office leasing fees. More importantly, telecommuting can result in greater productivity, allowing employees the flexibility and comfort of working from the environment of their choice. Telecommuting is also environmentally friendly since it means less traffic.

According to a recent survey by IDC/Link, a New York-based consulting and market research firm, nearly 8 million people telecommuted last year, making them the fastest growing segment of home workers. Nilles, who coined the term "telecommuting" in 1973, estimates that by the end of the century some 20 million employees will telecommute.

EMPLOYEE FLEXIBILITY

Why telecommuting? One main reason is the flexibility it gives employees. When her co-workers found out that Pikes would be telecommuting, some of them wondered aloud, "How do we know you'll really be working from home?" Pikes shot back, "How do you know I'm working at work?" Pikes was one of 10 employees selected to participate in a telecommuting pilot program. Six months into the program, she was wondering why she hadn't done it sooner.

"I love it," says Pikes. "I was amazed at how much I could get done. I am so much more focused. There are fewer distractions." There are also results. Last year, Pikes was assigned to develop software for pharmaceutical vendors with a deadline of July 1996; by early February, the project was finished.

Charles Holley, project leader for the pilot program, say it's important to evaluate a person before offering them the option of telecommuting. "We tried to limit it to the type of jobs suitable to telecommuting," says Holley, who decided the best candidates were workers who didn't need a lot of person-to-person contact. "Generally telecommuting is better geared to people like computer programmers. People who have to attend a lot of meetings wouldn't make good telecommuters," he explains.

According to Nilles, the occupations most suitable for full-time, home-based telecommuting include architect, data entry clerk, graphic artist, journalist, telemarketer, civil engineer, realtor, stock broker, applications programmer and financial analyst. "It should be done on a volunteer basis," he advises. "No one should be forced into it, and the moment someone wants to stop telecommuting, they should be allowed to."

Yet, there are some drawbacks to telecommuting. Although it offers workers the privilege of choosing their own work environment, it can also produce feelings of isolation. A young, single person may require a more social environment than someone in their mid-30s with a family. For Pikes, conquering the isolation hurdle means being actively involved with her sorority and church. She also takes a two-mile walk in the middle of the day.

Working from home often means being confined to one space. "I have to get out of the house. If I didn't, I'd go crazy," says Pikes, who also guards against overworking. "At work you take breaks: walking breaks, lunch breaks, snack breaks. At home, if I don't get up from my computer for my walk at noon, I'd work straight through lunch without realizing it."

Sometimes, she also returns to her computer at midnight when an idea pops into her head. "You wouldn't think about driving to the office at midnight to do some work, but I figure I'm here."

One thing Pikes doesn't miss is office gossip and meetings at the water cooler—permanent fixtures of corporate America. However, telecommuting doesn't mean cutting ties with the office. In fact, Holley encourages employees in his pilot program to maintain a buddy system. "There should be someone in their group they can contact regularly," he says. "It's important that they remain an interactive part of the group." To stay connected, Pikes places a telephone call to her supervisor and various co-workers daily. She also goes into the office every Thursday for a team meeting. By showing up only one day a week, Pikes saves $60 a month in clothing, dry-cleaning and gasoline costs.

For Atlanta-area resident William B. Hill, Jr., a litigation attorney with Paul, Hastings, Janofsky & Walker, telecommuting is a godsend. With the view of the Olympic Village from his 23rd floor office window, Hill says getting to work during the Games will be nearly impossible. Olympics' officials estimate that some 2.5 million people will converge on the area this July. Add that to the more than 2 million people who live there and you have a commuter's nightmare.

The 44-year-old Hill is no stranger to telecommuting. Last year, before Hill left his job as Fulton County superior court judge, he often conducted legal research in the wee hours of the night from home. "It was great. The only problem was that I kept finding myself up until 2:30 in the morning. Once you get into something, you just want to keep going," he says. "I found my productivity went way up. The telephone wasn't ringing, and I didn't have attorneys coming in and asking me questions."

Nonetheless, Hill doesn't plan to be a full-time telecommuter. A self-described "people person," Hill says he thrives on interoffice relationships. As a trial attorney, he has to make frequent trips to the courthouse. But Hill won't hesitate to telecommute when there is an ice storm or something special such as the Olympics.

SECURE SKILLED EMPLOYEES

Another reason why telecommuting is so attractive is that it allows employers to hold on to highly skilled workers. "Many companies, if they want a person bad enough, are willing to make concessions," says Linda Giavia, manager of commercial services at Productive Data Systems, a computer and information services consulting group in Denver. One Omaha, Nebraska-based company, she recalls, was having trouble attracting quality employees until Giavia suggested they use a staff of telecommuters based in Denver. In talent-starved areas, telecommuting can dramatically increase productivity and reduce operation costs for companies, she says.

While many firms are still experimenting with telecommuting, Atlanta will move to the forefront during this summer's Olympic Games.

"We're getting a lot of calls every day from corporations asking for help," says Frank Boyd, president of the Metro Atlanta Telecommuting Advisory Council and head of the telecommuting project at Georgia Power.

Boyd is ready to offer short-term solutions, but he encourages companies to take a long-term look at telecommuting. "There's always going to be something. Whether it's the Super Bowl, political or other business conventions, we're going to continue to have these types of events in town," he says.

COST-BENEFIT ANALYSIS

Georgia Power, which received the 1995 Innovation Award from the National Telecommuting Advisory Council, first implemented a telecommuting project in 1992 to reduce air pollution. The project, which began with 14 development employees working from home, resulted in annual savings of more than $100,000 in leased office space.

Today, Georgia Power has about 80 telecommuting employees who take their office computers home or to a satellite work center. The main cost to Georgia Power was the one-time installation of second telephone lines. This price was minimal compared with the benefits. Not only does office space now cost less, but there's been a reduction in sick leave, parking requirements and employee turnover.

Small businesses and start-ups save as well, says Marcel Leonard, project manager for Marco Design Group, an environmental engineering firm in Detroit. Leonard applauds telecommuting. For the past two years, many of his employees who own laptop computers have been working out of the office, communicating via e-mail and attached files. This has worked out so well that Leonard plans to purchase 15 NEC 2000D laptops, at a bulk-rate discount of $1,500 each, for his other employees.

"The venture capital needed to start a design consulting business can be $50,000 and up," says Leonard. Through telecommuting, start-ups save the money they would otherwise spend on leased office space, maintenance and support staff. "Telecommuting not only gives me mobility, but it levels the playing field," Leonard adds. He and a team of other civil engineers in other areas are able to work together on a project without being together under one roof. With such talent at his fingertips, Leonard is better able to compete with larger firms for projects.

OUT-OF-SIGHT MANAGEMENT

Yet, despite the high acclaim for telecommuting, many employers are apprehensive. The traditional style of management doesn't work with telecommuting, and many managers fear letting go of the reins. There's often a lack of trust. "Managers are afraid of the increasing flow of information. They don't want to give up control," Leonard says.

Managers must start to think outside the box, Nilles agrees. "The fundamental barrier to telecommuting is between managers' ears. We have to train telecommuters and telemanagers," he says. There is no room for the "out-of-sight-out-of-mind" theory of management. If you trust your employees, Nilles points out, they will do their jobs, whether or not you are physically there. Employees expect managers to provide competent direction and guidance, reward them for work well done—and penalize them for work poorly performed. That's why it's best to have only the more established workers telecommute.

When it comes to telemanaging, it's also important to consider the work site and equipment. If someone's home environment is not set up for telecommuting, there's another option—a telework center, an office site designed for telecommuters. Check with local city officials to see if these sites are available near you.

Another key point for proper telemanaging is quality communication—and that's more than just placing a daily telephone call, says Nilles. One tried-and-true communications instrument is electronic mail. With e-mail, managers and telecommuters can exchange precise instructions and maintain a dialogue. Regardless of how you do it, the bottom line is that you must maintain frequent communication so that the telecommuter still feels like part of the team. "You have to have the full support of the manager, or it just won't work," warns Holley.

What managers shouldn't do, says Boyd, is try to use telecommuting as positive discipline. "If a person is struggling or not getting the job done, a manager shouldn't offer them telecommuting, thinking this might help turn things around," he says.

After selecting workers you believe fit the profile of a telecommuter, and who have expressed a willingness to do so, you need to set up performance criteria. This criterion should be determined by the managers and telecommuters. "They should build a business case and sign an agreement on what to expect," says Boyd. "That agreement should say that if at any time either party, the manager or the employee, says it's not working, then the telecommuter should come back into the office."

Questions for Discussion

1. Corbett clearly finds telecommuting exciting and efficient, and she conveys her enthusiasm for the idea not only through her content but also through her style. How does her rhetorical style—the connotations of the words she chooses, the images she employs, even her sentence structures—signal to you that she thinks telecommuting is a good idea? (You might ask yourself how early in the piece you suspect that she'll begin arguing in favor of telecommuting. Does that moment of realization come before you get to an explicit statement of the argument?)

2. Among those Corbett believes might find their jobs suitable for telecommuting are architects, data entry clerks, graphic artists, journalists, telemarketers, civil engineers, realtors, stock brokers, applications

programmers, and financial analysts. Why might those employees find telecommuting convenient and productive? For what other kinds of jobs might telecommuting seem suitable?

3. Corbett is careful to say that telecommuting should probably be voluntary, that some people—whatever their profession—would find telecommuting beneficial while others would find it burdensome. In your opinion, what character traits (or life circumstances) would make for the ideal telecommuter? What character traits (or life circumstances) might make telecommuting problematic?

4. Much of Corbett's article focuses on the business side of telecommuting, rather than the personal side. Do you think telecommuting is more likely to appeal to employers or employees? Do you think it is more likely to appeal to large businesses or smaller ones? To businesses in cities or in suburbs?

5. If given the chance, do you think you would prefer to work at home or in another location? What do you see as the advantages of working at home? The disadvantages? Describe your ideal work environment.

6. Some teleworkers complain that they are looking at "the same four walls" all the time, that there's no one to talk to and too little variety in their physical environment. Many who live with teleworkers complain they require too much quiet and privacy.

If you work and study at home, consider your own habits. How often do you move around? Talk to other people? Deliberately allow yourself to be distracted by others' conversations? By the television?

If you have lived with a teleworker—perhaps one of your parents—how did that person's working at home affect your relationship?

Questions for Research and Writing

1. Interview someone who has engaged in "telework." Why did that employee choose to work at home? What does he or she see as the advantages and drawbacks of such work? How did he or she prevent distractions from eating away at work time?

2. Television situation comedies have occasionally portrayed work-at-home parents: the fathers on *The Bill Cosby Show, The Donna Reed Show, The Brady Bunch,* and *Growing Pains* could all be seen working out of home offices and solving their families' problems. Look at some episodes of these or other television shows to get a sense of how the entertainment media portray work-at-home life. How does it compare to the telework described in this article?

TIME SQUEEZE:
THE EXTRA MONTH OF WORK

Juliet B. Schor

> *Originally published as the second chapter in Juliet Schor's* The Overworked American: The Unexpected Decline of Leisure *(1992), the following piece explodes some of the myths with which many of us grew up: time-saving devices will save us time, and increased prosperity means increased leisure. Schor, a professor of economics at Harvard, raises a number of questions about the way we spend time. Consider, for instance, some of the modern machines we now take for granted. For example, we might assume that a mother used to washing clothes by hand would find the washing machine an amazing labor- and time-saving device, or that those who can microwave a complete dinner in seven minutes would marvel at the time they have saved and find in that saved time an opportunity for contemplation and leisure. But Schor examines those assumptions and finds surprising evidence of just how much time our devotion to technology and consumption has cost us. As you read "Time Squeeze," ask yourself whether you've already entered the "squirrel cage" and whether you see any way out of it.*

Time squeeze has become big news. In summer 1990, the première episode of Jane Pauley's television show, "Real Life," highlighted a single father whose computer job was so demanding that he found himself at 2:00 A.M. dragging his child into the office. A Boston-area documentary featured the fourteen- to sixteen-hour workdays of a growing army of moonlighters. CBS's "Forty-Eight Hours" warned of the accelerating pace of life for everyone from high-tech business executives (for whom there are only two types of people—"the quick and the dead") to assembly workers at Japanese-owned automobile factories (where a car comes by every sixty seconds). Employees at fast-food restaurants, who serve in twelve seconds, report that the horns start honking if the food hasn't arrived in fifteen. Nineteen-year-olds work seventy-hour weeks, children are "penciled" into their parents' schedules, and second-graders are given "half an hour a day to unwind" from the pressure to get good grades so they can get into a good college. By the beginning of the 1990s, the time squeeze had become a national focus of attention, appearing in almost all the nation's major media outlets.[1]

The shortage of time has also become a staple of women's magazines and business publications. The subject is covered in major newspapers, such as the *New York Times*, the *Wall Street Journal*, and *USA Today*, as well as in the regional dailies. *Time* magazine devoted a cover story to the fact that "America has run out of time."[2] How-to books on time management have proliferated. Even Madison Avenue has discovered time poverty. In a 1990 commercial, statistics on the decline of leisure time flashed across the screen; then General Motors hawked its wares by promising to get the customer in and out of the showroom faster than the competition.

The time squeeze surfaced with the young urban professional. These high achievers had jobs that required sixty, eighty, even a hundred hours a week. On Wall Street, they would regularly stay at the office until midnight or go months without a single day off. Work consumed their lives. And if they weren't working, they were networking. They power-lunched, power-exercised, and power-married. As the pace of life accelerated, time became an ever-scarcer commodity, so they used their money to buy more of it. Cooking was replaced by gourmet frozen foods from upscale delis. Eventually the "meal" started disappearing, in favor of "grazing." Those who could afford it bought other people's time, hiring surrogates to shop, write their checks, or even just change a light bulb. They cut back on sleep and postponed having children. ("Can you carry a baby in a briefcase?" queried one Wall Street executive when she was asked about having kids.)[3]

High-powered people who spend long hours at their jobs are nothing new. Medical residents, top corporate management, and the self-employed have always had grueling schedules. But financiers used to keep bankers' hours, and lawyers had a leisured life. Now bankers work like doctors, and lawyers do the same. A former Bankers Trust executive remembers that "somebody would call an occasional meeting at 8 A.M. Then it became the regular 8 o'clock meeting. So there was the occasional 7 A.M. meeting. . . . It just kept spreading."[4] On Wall Street, economic warfare replaced the clubhouse atmosphere—and the pressure forced the hours up. As women and new ethnic groups were admitted into the industry, competition for the plum positions heightened—and the hours went along. Twenty-two-year-olds wear beepers as they squeeze in an hour for lunch or jogging at the health club.

What happened on Wall Street was replicated throughout the country in one high-income occupation after another. Associates in law firms competed over who could log more billable hours. Workaholics set new standards of survival. Even America's sleepiest corporations started waking up; and when they did, the corporate hierarchies found themselves coming in to work a little earlier and leaving for home a little later. As many companies laid off white-collar people during the 1980s, those who remained did more for their monthly paycheck. A study of "downsizings" in auto-related companies in the Midwest found that nearly half of the two thousand managers polled said they were working harder than two years earlier.[5]

At cutting-edge corporations, which emphasize commitment, initiative, and flexibility, the time demands are often the greatest. "People who work for me should have phones in their bathrooms," says the CEO from one aggressive American company. Recent research on managerial habits reveals that work has become positively absorbing. When a deadline approached in one corporation, "people who had been working twelve-hour days and Saturdays started to come in on Sunday, and instead of leaving at midnight, they would stay a few more hours. Some did not go home at all, and others had to look at their watches to remember what day it was." The recent growth in small businesses has also contributed to overwork. When Dolores Kordek started a dental insurance company, her strategy for survival was to work harder than the competition. So the office was open from 7 A.M. to 10 P.M. three hundred and sixty-five days a year. And she was virtually always in it.[6]

This combination of retrenchment, economic competition, and innovative business management has raised hours substantially. One poll of senior executives found that weekly hours rose during the 1980s, and vacation time fell. Other surveys have yielded similar results.[7] By the end of the decade, overwork at the upper echelons of the labor market had become endemic—and its scale was virtually unprecedented in living memory.

If the shortage of time had been confined to Wall Street or America's corporate boardrooms, it might have remained just a media curiosity. The number of people who work eighty hours a week and bring home—if they ever get there—a six-figure income is very small. But while the incomes of these rarefied individuals were out of reach, their schedules turned out to be downright common. As Wall Street waxed industrious, the longer schedules penetrated far down the corporate ladder, through middle management, into the secretarial pool, and even onto the factory floor itself.[8] Millions of ordinary Americans fell victim to the shortage of time.

The most visible group has been women, who are coping with a double load—the traditional duties associated with home and children and their growing responsibility for earning a paycheck. With nearly two-thirds of adult women now employed, and a comparable fraction of mothers on the job, it's no surprise that many American women find themselves operating in overdrive.[9] Many working mothers live a life of perpetual motion, effectively holding down two full-time jobs. They rise in the wee hours of the morning to begin the day with a few hours of laundry, cleaning, and other housework. Then they dress and feed the children and send them off to school. They themselves then travel to their jobs. The three-quarters of employed women with full-time positions then spend the next eight and a half hours in the workplace.

At the end of the official workday, it's back to the "second shift"—the duties of housewife and mother. Grocery shopping, picking up the children, and cooking dinner take up the next few hours. After dinner there's clean-up, possibly some additional housework, and, of course, more child care. Women describe themselves as "ragged," "bone-weary," "sinking in quicksand," and "busy every waking hour." For many, the workday rivals those for which the "satanic mills" of the Industrial Revolution grew justly infamous: twelve- or fourteen-hour stretches of labor. By the end of the decade, Ann Landers pronounced herself "awestruck at the number of women who work at their jobs and go home to another full-time job. . . .

How do you do it?" she asked. Thousands of readers responded, with tales ranging from abandoned careers to near collapse. According to sociologist Arlie Hochschild of the University of California, working mothers are exhausted, even fixated on the topic of sleep. "They talked about how much they could 'get by on': . . . six and a half, seven, seven and a half, less, more . . . These women talked about sleep the way a hungry person talks about food."[10]

By my calculations, the total working time of employed mothers now averages about 65 hours a week. Of course, many do far more than the average—such as mothers with young children, women in professional positions, or those whose wages are so low that they must hold down two jobs just to scrape by. These women will be working 70 to 80 hours a week. And my figures are extremely conservative: they are the lowest among existing studies. A Boston study found that employed mothers *average* over 80 hours of housework, child care, and employment. Two nationwide studies of white, married couples are comparable: in the first, the average week was 87 hours; in the second, it ranged from 76 to 89, depending on the age of the oldest child.[11]

One might think that as women's working hours rose, husbands would compensate by spending less time on the job. But just the opposite has occurred. Men who work are also putting in longer hours. The 5:00 Dads of the 1950s and 1960s (those who were home for dinner and an evening with the family) are becoming an "endangered species." Thirty percent of men with children under fourteen report working fifty or more hours a week. And many of these 8:00 or 9:00 Dads aren't around on the weekends either. Thirty percent of them work Saturdays and/or Sundays at their regular employment. And many others use the weekends for taking on a second job.[12]

A twenty-eight-year-old Massachusetts factory worker explains the bind many fathers are in: "Either I can spend time with my family, or support them—not both." Overtime or a second job is financially compelling: "I can work 8–12 hours overtime a week at time and a half, and that's when the real money just starts to kick in. . . . If I don't work the OT my wife would have to work much longer hours to make up the difference, and our day-care bill would double. . . . The trouble is, the little time I'm home I'm too tired to have any fun with them or be any real help around the house."[13] Among white-collar employees the problem isn't paid overtime, but the regular hours. To get ahead, or even just to hold on to a position, long days may be virtually mandatory.

Overwork is also rampant among the nation's poorly paid workers. At $5, $6, or even $7 an hour, annual earnings before taxes and deductions range from $10,000 to $14,000. Soaring rents alone have been enough to put many of these low earners in financial jeopardy. For the more than one-third of all workers now earning hourly wages of $7 and below, the pressure to lengthen hours has been inexorable. Valerie Connor, a nursing-home worker in Hartford, explains that "you just can't make it on one job." She and many of her co-workers have been led to work two eight-hour shifts a day. According to an official of the Service Employees International Union in New England, nearly one-third of their nursing-home employees now hold two full-time jobs. Changes in the low end of the labor market have also played a role. There is less full-time, stable employment. "Twenty hours here, thirty hours there, and twenty hours here. That's what it takes to get a real paycheck," says Domenic Bozzotto, president of Boston's hotel and restaurant workers union, whose members are drowning in a sea of work. Two-job families? Those were the good old days, he says. "We've got four-job families." The recent influx of immigrants has also raised hours. I. N. Yazbek, an arrival from Lebanon, works ninety hours a week at three jobs. It's necessary, he says, for economic success.[14]

This decline of leisure has been reported by the Harris Poll, which has received widespread attention. Harris finds that since 1973 free time has fallen nearly 40 percent—from a median figure of 26 hours a week to slightly under 17. Other surveys, such as the 1989 Decision Research Corporation Poll, also reveal a loss of leisure. Although these polls have serious methodological drawbacks, their findings are not far off the mark. A majority of working Americans—professionals, corporate management, "working" mothers, fathers, and lower paid workers—*are* finding themselves with less and less leisure time.[15]

THEORIES OF THE TIME SQUEEZE

Although the symptoms of time squeeze are relatively uncontroversial—an acceleration in the pace of life, a rise in time-saving innovations, increasing stress, and role overload—analysts differ sharply in how they understand these phenomena. Social critic Jeremy Rifkin believes that what has changed is our perception of time itself. Everything is speeding up, and the culprit is technology. "The computer introduces . . . a time frame in which the nanosecond is the primary temporal measurement. The nanosecond is a billionth of a second, and though it is possible to conceive theoretically of a nanosecond . . . *it is not possible to experience it*. Never before has time been organized at a speed beyond the realm of consciousness." Once people become acclimated to the speed of the computer, normal human intercourse becomes laborious. Programmers get irritable and impatient. Children complain that their teachers talk too slowly, in comparison with Nintendo or Atari. And even the machines can be too slow. Sue Alstedt, a former AT&T manager, became impatient with the computer she bought to save her time at home: "I couldn't stand to wait for it, even though it was coming out at the rate of speech."[16]

Not everyone blames technology. A second theory is that we are merely victims of our own aspirations. We have become more demanding in terms of activities, goals, and achievements. And today's life styles "offer people more options than ever before," according to John P. Robinson, one of the nation's leading chroniclers of how people spend their time. This theme is echoed by another time-use expert: "We have become walking résumés. If you're not doing something, you're not creating and defining who you are." Since the time available to us to do and to define ourselves cannot increase, we are naturally frustrated. While some have suggested that this is merely a "baby-boom" problem, the evidence suggests it is more widespread.[17]

The idea of rising aspirations echoes views put forward more than twenty years ago by economists Gary Becker and Staffan Linder.[18] Becker's work was based on the simple observation that consuming takes time. As people get richer, and own more and more consumer goods, there is less and less time to spend with each item. Unavoidably, use of the Walkman, the VCR, the camcorder, and concert tickets gets crammed into the space once occupied by the lone record player. Linder also believed that leisure time would eventually become hectic as people tried to keep up with the use of an accumulating mountain of possessions. In *The Harried Leisure Class,* he predicted that growing affluence would lead people to switch to those activities that can be done quickly. Long courtships, leisurely walks on the beach, or lingering over the dinner table were destined for extinction. People would do more things at once and do them faster. Even if the amount of leisure time itself did not change, it would become much more harried.

At first blush, events appear to have borne out Linder's ingenious argument. The *New York Times* has already chronicled the quiet death of the dinner party, as he prophesized. ("Most people I know have turned their ovens into planters," notes one professional woman.) Life *has* become more harried—but probably not so much for the reasons Linder and Becker predicted. They anticipated that rising incomes would cause the frenzy. But for many workers, earning power reached a high point just after Linder's book was published, and has been declining since. By this analysis, their lives should have become *less* harried. What Linder did not foresee was that the growing demands of work would lead to a decline in leisure time itself.[19]

There is undoubtedly truth in the ideas that technology and aspirations have led to an accelerated sense of time. But both these explanations have missed a much more obvious force operating in our lives. Time has become more precious because people have less of it to call their own. We have become a harried *working,* rather than leisure, class, as jobs take up an ever larger part of ever more Americans' lives.[20]

DOING MORE FOR THE PAYCHECK

Behind the mushrooming of worktime is a convergence of various trends. These include an increase in the number of people who hold paying jobs; a rise in weekly hours and in weeks worked each year; and reductions in paid time off, sick leave, and absences from work.

More People Working

The mythical American family of the 1950s and 1960s was comprised of five people, only one of whom "worked"—or at least did what society called work. Dad went off to his job every morning, while Mom and the three kids stayed at home. Of course, the 1950s-style family was never as common as popular memory made it out to be. Even in the 1950s and 1960s, about one-fourth of wives with children held paying jobs. The nostalgia surrounding the family is especially inaccurate for African-American women, whose rates of job holding have historically been higher than whites'. Even so, in recent years, the steady growth of married women's participation in the labor force has made the "working woman" the rule rather than the exception. By 1990, two-thirds of married American women were participating in the paid labor market (see figure 2.1).[20]

Female employment has justifiably received widespread attention: it is certainly the most significant development afoot. But the expansion of work effort in the American family is not occurring just among women. American youth are also working harder in a reversal of a long decline of teenage job holding, the result of increased schooling and economic prosperity. The likelihood that a teenager would hold a job began to rise in the mid-1960s, just as adult hours began their upward climb. By 1990, the labor

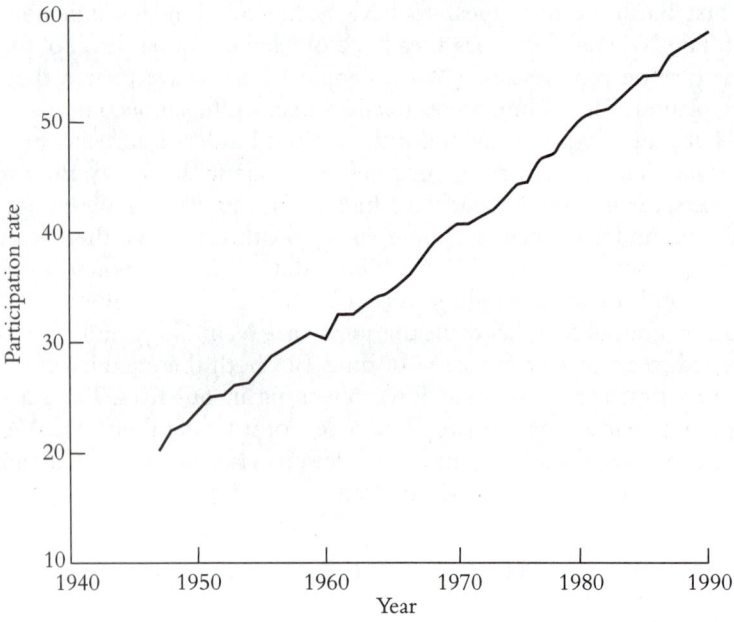

SOURCE: Bureau of Labor Statistics, Special Labor Force Data.

FIGURE 2.1 *Married Women's Labor Force Participation Rates*

force participation rate of teens had reached 53.7 percent, nearly 10 points higher than it had been twenty-five years earlier (see figure 2.2).

Not only are more of the nation's young people working, but they are working longer hours. A 1989 nationwide sweep by government inspectors uncovered widescale abuses of child labor laws—violations of allowable hours, permissible activities, and ages of employment. Low-wage service sector establishments have been voracious in their appetite for teen labor, especially in regions with shortages of adult workers. In middle-class homes, much of this work is motivated by consumerism: teenagers buy clothes, music, even cars. Some observers are worried that the desire to make money has become a compulsion, with many young Americans now working full-time, in addition to full-time school. A New Hampshire study found that 85 percent of the state's tenth- to twelfth-graders hold jobs, and 45 percent of them work more than twenty hours a week. At 10 P.M. on a school night, Carolyn Collignon is just beginning hour eight on her shift at Friendly's restaurant. Teacher's report that students are falling asleep in class, getting lower grades, and cannot pursue after-school activities. Robert Pimentel works five days a week at Wendy's to pay off loans on his car and a $5,600 motorcycle, the purchase of which he now describes as a "bad move." Pimentel averages "maybe six hours of sleep a night. If you consider

SOURCE: Bureau of Labor Statistics. Sixteen- to nineteen-year-olds.

FIGURE 2.2 *Teenage Labor Force Participation Rates*

school a job, which it pretty much is, I put in a long day." He wants to go to college, but his grades have suffered.[21]

This is the picture in suburban America. In large urban centers, such as New York and Los Angeles, the problem is more serious. Inspectors have found nineteenth-century-style sweatshops where poor immigrants—young girls of twelve years and above—hold daytime jobs, missing out on school altogether. And a million to a million and a half migrant farmworker children—some as young as three and four years—are at work in the nation's fields. These families cannot survive without the effort of all their members.[22]

There is one ironic exception to the general trend of rising labor force participation: Dad, the mainstay of the 1950s family, is more likely to be out of the labor force than ever before. As women's rates of job holding have risen, men's have fallen. The male decline is somewhat less, from 89 percent in 1948 to 78 percent in 1987, but still substantial (see figure 2.3). This pattern for men should give us pause. Does it contradict our picture of overwork in America? Does it represent a trend toward increasing leisure, albeit among only half the population?

There can be little doubt that many men, especially the elderly, are experiencing a newfound leisure. In 1948, almost half of all men aged sixty-five and above were in the labor force; by 1987, the figure had fallen to 16

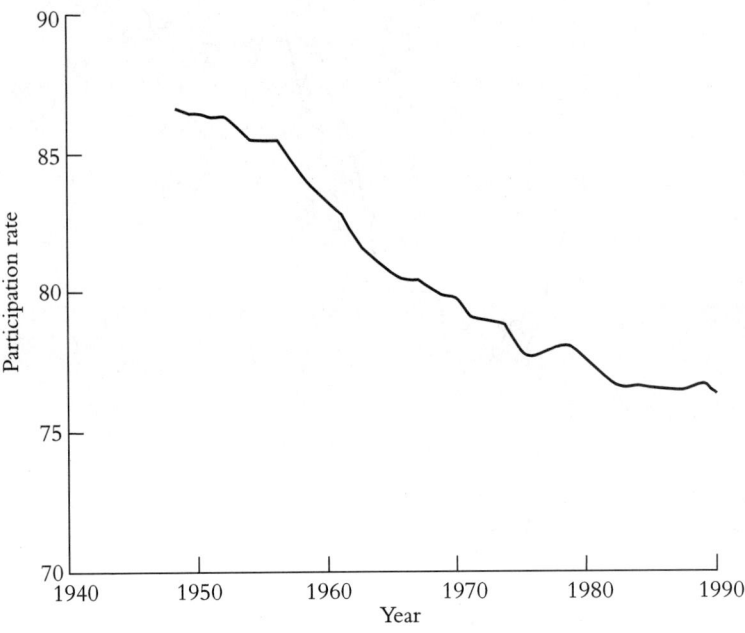

SOURCE: Bureau of Labor Statistics.

FIGURE 2.3   *Male Labor Force Participation Rates*

percent. Social security, private pension plans, and prosperity have made possible a longer period of leisure at the end of life than ever before.[23]

Yet it would be a serious mistake to characterize as "at leisure" all the men who are out of the labor force. Among young males, schooling—which counts as productive activity and cannot be properly measured as leisure time—has been a major cause of labor force withdrawal. The underground economy is also a source of unmeasured work for young men. A closer look than the standard statistics provide will reveal that much of the "leisure" of older males is involuntary, particularly for the substantial numbers now leaving the labor force before age sixty-five. According to a 1990 survey of men between the ages of fifty-five and sixty-four who are out of the labor force, almost half (45 percent) would prefer to have jobs, a far larger percentage than has previously been recognized. Mandatory retirement and pressures to take early leave have led many unwillingly out of the world of work. Plant closings, corporate restructuring, and ageism have contributed to their difficulties in finding re-employment. Among African-American men, the unemployment situation is about twice as bad as for whites, and participation rates have fallen far more.[24]

More Hours of Work

My estimates—the first comprehensive calculations of worktime spanning the last two decades—confirm not only that more people are working, but that they are working more. (Data are not available for earlier years.) These statistics solve several problems associated with most measures: These are annual, rather than simply weekly, figures. They account for changes in jobs and hours worked which are made within any one year. They are calculated at comparable points in the business cycle to avoid spurious trends. And perhaps most important, they correct for the growth of unemployment and underemployment which artificially reduces the uncorrected figures.

According to my estimates, the average employed person is now on the job an additional 163 hours, or the equivalent of an extra month a year (see table 2.1). Hours have been increasing throughout the twenty-year period for which we have data. The breakdown for men and women shows

TABLE 2.1 Annual Hours of Paid Employment, Labor Force Participants[a]

	1969	1987	Change 1969–87
All participants	1786	1949	163
Men	2054	2152	98
Women	1406	1711	305

Source: Author's estimates.

[a]Includes only fully employed labor force participants.

lengthening hours for both groups, but there is a "gender gap" in the size of the increase. Men are working nearly one hundred (98) more hours per year, or two and a half extra weeks. Women are doing about three hundred (305) additional hours, which translates to seven and a half weeks, or 38 added days of work each year. The research shows that hours have risen across a wide spectrum of Americans and in all income categories—low, middle, and high. The increase is common to a variety of family patterns—people with and without children, those who are married, and those who are not. And it has been general across industries and, most probably, occupations.[25]

The extra month of work is attributable to both longer weekly schedules and more weeks of work, as table 2.2 indicates. As long as work is available, people are on the job more steadily throughout the year. This factor accounts for over two-thirds of the total increase in hours. It has been especially important for women, as they are increasingly working full-time and year round. Women now take less time off for the birth of a child and are not as likely to stop working during the summer recess in order to care for children.[26] For better or worse, the pattern of women's employment is getting to look more and more like men's.

Weekly schedules are also getting longer, by about one hour per week (54 minutes, to be exact). This is the first sustained peacetime increase in weekly hours during the twentieth century. What is especially surprising is that it is not just women whose days are getting longer, but men as well. And after twenty years of increase, the proportion of employees on long schedules is substantial. In 1990, one-fourth of all full-time workers spent forty-nine or more hours on the job each week. Of these, almost half were at work sixty hours or more.[27]

Frequently, trends in weekly hours of work are caused by changes in a country's occupational or industrial makeup. Because doctors tend to have

TABLE 2.2 Hours Worked per Week, Labor Force Participants[a]

	1969	1987
All participants	39.8	40.7
Men	43.0	43.8
Women	35.2	37.0

Weeks Worked per Year, Labor Force Participants[a]

	1969	1987
All participants	43.9	47.1
Men	47.1	48.5
Women	39.3	45.4

Source: Author's estimates.
[a]Includes only fully employed labor force participants.

longer hours than teachers, an employment shift toward doctors and away from teachers will cause average hours to rise. Surprisingly, recent changes in the relative sizes of industries have on balance had no impact on hours. The growth in "short-hour" service jobs, such as those in retail trade, have been offset by rising numbers in "long-hour" areas, such as those that hire large numbers of professional or managerial workers, all of whom have above-average hours. My analysis shows that the shifts in industries have just about canceled each other out.[28]

So what's pushing up hours? One factor is moonlighting—the practice of holding more than one job at a time. Moonlighting is now more prevalent than at any time during the three decades for which we have statistics. As of May 1989, more than seven million Americans, or slightly over 6 percent of those employed, officially reported having two or more jobs, with extremely high increases occurring among women. The real numbers are higher, perhaps twice as high—as tax evasion, illegal activities, and employer disapproval of second jobs makes people reluctant to speak honestly. The main impetus behind this extra work is financial. Close to one-half of those polled say they hold two jobs in order to meet regular household expenses or pay off debts. As one might expect, this factor has become more compelling during the 1980s, with the disappearance of stable positions that pay a living wage and the increase of casual and temporary service sector employment.[29]

A second factor, operating largely on weekly hours, is that Americans are working more overtime. After the recession of the early 1980s, many companies avoided costly rehiring of workers and, instead, scheduled extra overtime. Among manufacturing employees, paid overtime hours rose substantially after the recession and, by the end of 1987, accounted for the equivalent of an additional five weeks of work per year. One automobile worker noted, "You have to work the hours, because a few months later they'll lay you off for a model changeover and you'll need the extra money when you're out of work. It never rains but it pours—either there's more than you can stand, or there isn't enough." While many welcome the chance to earn premium wages, the added effort can be onerous. Older workers are often compelled to stretch themselves, because many companies calculate pension benefits only on recent earnings. A fifty-nine-year-old male worker explains:

> Just at the point in my life where I was hoping I could ease up a little bit on the job and with the overtime, I find that I have to work harder than ever. If I'm going to have enough money when I retire, I have to put in five good years now with a lot of overtime because that is what they will base my pension on. With all the overtime I have to work to build my pension, I hope I live long enough to collect it.

[Apparently he didn't—he was diagnosed with incurable cancer not long after this interview.][30]

The Shrinking Vacation

One of the most notable developments of the 1980s is that paid time off is actually shrinking. European workers have been gaining vacation time—minimum allotments are now in the range of four to five weeks in many countries—but Americans are losing it. In the last decade, U.S. workers have gotten *less* paid time off—on the order of three and a half fewer days each year of vacation time, holidays, sick pay, and other paid absences. This decline is even more striking in that it reverses thirty years of progress in terms of paid time off (see figure 2.4).

Part of the shrinkage has been caused by the economic squeeze many companies faced in the 1980s. Cost-cutting measures often included reductions in vacations and holidays. DuPont reduced its top vacation allotment from seven to four weeks and eliminated three holidays a year. Personnel departments also tightened up on benefits such as sick leave and bereavement time. As employees became more fearful about job loss, they spent less time away from the workplace. Days lost to illness fell dramatically. So did unpaid absences—which declined for the first time since 1973.[31]

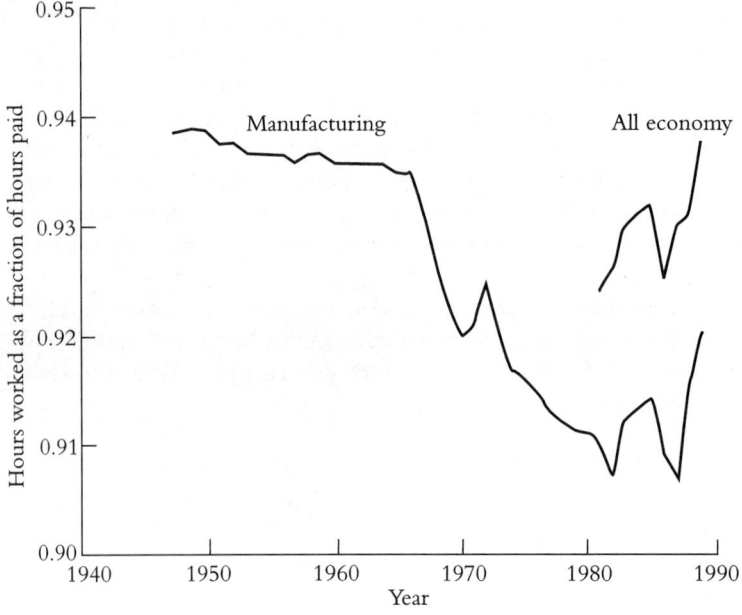

SOURCE: Bureau of Labor Statistics.

FIGURE 2.4 *Hours Worked as a Fraction of Hours Paid*

The other factor reducing vacations has been the restructuring of the labor market. Companies have turned to more "casual" work forces—firing long-term employees and signing on consultants, part-timers, or temporaries. Early retirements among senior workers also reduced vacation time. Because the length of vacations in this country is based on duration of employment, these changes have all contributed to lowering the amount of time off people actually receive. The growth of service sector occupations, where the duration of employment tends to be shortest, has also been a factor.[32]

Since my data exclude paid time off and commuting, and thus may be biased in one direction or another, I have made a rough calculation of these two factors. The prevailing view is that paid time off has risen substantially. Indeed, business has expressed concern about what one researcher, in 1984, dubbed "the gradual erosion of the annual workyear." Particularly in view of recent reductions in paid time off, this assessment appears to have been premature. By my calculations, the net change in paid time off has been minimal during the period covered by the data (1969–87). The two methods I have used yield estimates of increases in paid time off of between only three and twelve hours a year.[33]

Increases in commuting time have eliminated even this modest gain. Travel time to and from work began rising after 1975, for an overall increase of about three days (23 hours) a year. Together with the change in paid time off, I find an additional rise in worktime of between eleven and twenty hours—or one and a half to two and a half days. If anything, my figures appear to have slightly understated the real increase in working time.[34]

THE TIME SQUEEZE AT HOME

Along with the work people are paid for—time spent at "regular jobs"—almost an equal amount of work is done every year which is not paid for—most of it housework, child care, and other "domestic labor." To get the full story on changes in leisure time, we need estimates of this labor, too. However, as one might expect, calculating hours of household work is not a simple matter. The major difficulty is that the government does not provide any information—despite requests from scholars for official household record keeping which date back more than a hundred years. A second problem is that household labor tends to be less regimented than many forms of paid work. There are no time clocks to punch, and schedules can be erratic. Partly for this reason, researchers have found that the most accurate method for measuring household labor is through minute-by-minute records—or diaries—of people's activities. But this procedure is expensive. Because diary surveys have been carried out exclusively by university-based research institutes, the expense has kept their efforts small and sporadic; and the data are not always representative of the U.S. population.[35]

To ameliorate these drawbacks, I carried out a statistical procedure that combines the time diaries with the large-scale data set on which my earlier calculations are based. In essence, I have constructed estimates of how much household labor each person in my sample is doing, on the basis of information taken from the diaries.[36] This procedure allows one not only to predict trends in household labor but also to identify those factors that determine how much of this work is done at any point in time. The margin of error with these data is, however, greater than with the earlier figures.

Accounting for household labor does not reverse the upward trend in worktime. On average, employed people are doing the same amount of household work they did twenty years ago (I find only a one-hour difference per year!). There have been big changes: women are doing much less at home and men are doing more. But on balance these changes exactly cancel out. *In terms of total hours—that is, market plus household—the extra month of work remains* (see table 2.3).

While employed people have maintained their hours of domestic labor, the population as a whole is doing less. The social changes of recent decades—women's employment, reduced marriage rates, lower births, and changes in gender roles—have substantially decreased women's ability, need, and willingness to perform household work. Men are doing more, but they haven't fully compensated for the reduction by women.

To explore these developments, I turn to a second set of estimates— hours worked per adult American (rather than per employed person). This measure (table 2.4) allows me to capture worktime changes caused by movements in and out of the workforce, as well as what's happening with those who are out of the labor force altogether. The hours-per-person measure has another advantage: it shows, succinctly, the total quantity of work required for a society to sustain its standard of living. On the other

TABLE 2.3 Total Annual Hours, Labor Force Participants[a]

	1969	1987	CHANGE 1969–87
Market Hours			
All participants	1786	1949	163
Men	2054	2152	98
Women	1406	1711	305
Household Hours			
All participants	889	888	−1
Men	621	689	68
Women	1268	1123	−145
Total Hours			
All participants	2675	2837	162
Men	2675	2841	166
Women	2674	2834	160

Source: Author's estimates.
[a]Includes only fully employed labor force participants.

TABLE 2.4 Total Hours Worked per Year, Entire Population

	1969	1987	CHANGE 1969–87
Market Hours			
All Persons	1199	1316	117
Men	1759	1680	–79
Women	723	996	273
Household Hours			
All Persons	1227	1157	–70
Men	683	834	151
Women	1689	1440	–249
Total Hours			
All Persons	2426	2473	47
Men	2442	2514	72
Women	2412	2436	24

Source: Author's estimates.

hand, it is an average measure, which does not account for the distribution of either work or income among the population. Because it includes those who are not employed, it yields far lower figures than those I have been considering so far.[37]

These figures show that Americans as a whole have also experienced a decline in leisure time. If I correct (once again) for the growth in unemployment and underemployment, leisure time has fallen by 47 hours a year.[38] On average, hours of employment are up, and hours of domestic labor are down. But men and women have had very different experiences. Among women, the labor market has been the driving force. In general, the more work women do for pay, the less work they do without it. A major change has been the disappearance of the full-time housewife and the rise of the "working woman." During this period, the fraction of married women who were housewives fell from 30 percent to 15 percent of the adult female population. This exodus from the home has had a large impact on the quantity of household labor currently being done. Each additional hour a woman puts into her paid job reduces her household work by nearly half an hour. She spends less time with her children, cooks fewer meals, and does less cleaning. There is also a one-time, extra reduction of up to four hours per week when a woman initially joins the labor force. According to my calculations, of the 223-hour decline in women's household labor, slightly over half is due to increased hours of employment.

To some extent, women have been able to substitute commercial services for their own labor, using their newly earned paychecks to pay the bill. Expenditures on precooked food—either at restaurants or from the neighborhood deli—professional child care, and dry cleaning have risen rapidly in recent years. Indeed, there is a self-reinforcing nature to this process, as the growing demand for commercially produced products draws more women into service sector employment. But the buying-out of domestic responsibilities has limits. For both two-earner families and single mothers, the reduction in women's time at home has led to a painful cutback in "household services." Children are left in the care of others or even by themselves, there are shortcuts in cooking and cleaning, and the extras provided by 1950s-type "Moms" disappear. Unless husbands are willing and able to pick up the slack, these changes are virtually inevitable: employed women just do not have the time. Their workloads have already climbed above virtually all other groups.[39]

The changing labor market of the 1970s and 1980s has had just the opposite effect on patterns of men's labor. Their market hours have fallen—by 79—and hours of domestic work have increased—by 151. But men's trends have been slightly more complicated. As I showed earlier, employed men are working more, not less. But for the whole population, men's market hours have fallen because there are far fewer of them in the labor force (see table 2.4). Each man who drops out of the labor force reduces his hours so substantially that this effect has outweighed the longer hours of men who are employed. Overall, a smaller proportion are working longer hours, and a larger proportion are without jobs.

The lower market hours of men have been partially replaced by more work at home, thereby making up for some of women's vanishing labor. The average man is doing just under three additional hours a week. A detailed breakdown of activities shows that men are occupying themselves not only with traditional male tasks such as outdoor work and home repairs, but with cooking and cleaning as well. They are also taking on a larger proportion of child care. This combination of more domestic work by men and less by women means that men are now doing almost 60 percent as much as women, up from 40 percent two decades ago.[40]

Despite this rise, it is premature to conclude that we are on the fast track to gender equality with regard to household labor. Most of the increase in men's domestic labor has been caused by the fact that many more men are out of the labor force. Quite naturally, they do more at home (approaching twice as much) than their counterparts with paying jobs. This has been true for decades. Among men who are employed, the increase is far less—amounting to slightly more than one additional hour per week. For the great majority of employed women who also have working husbands, their spouses have provided only partial relief.

The labor market is not the only factor causing a decline in domestic labor. Housewives' hours have finally started to fall. According to my estimates a middle-class, married mother of three is putting in two fewer hours of work a week than she was in 1969. There are also far fewer women who fit this once common demographic profile. Women (and men) are having fewer children and are far less likely to be married. Both these factors have further reduced domestic hours. The influence of children should be obvious: they require tremendous amounts of time, especially when they are young. With marriage, which I define as the presence of a spouse in the household, the effect is more subtle. It turns out that the acquisition of a spouse (especially a husband) leads to more work: homecooked meals, and bigger houses and apartments to care for. Married people also try to save more (to buy those houses or raise their children), which cuts down on the purchasing of services. For women, gaining a husband adds 4.2 hours of domestic work per week. (The case of men is a bit ambiguous; not until the 1980s did they do more when they married.)

During the last twenty years, the married proportion of the adult population fell from about 70 percent to 60 percent. At the same time, the average number of children declined, from one child per person in 1969 to slightly over one-half child today. By 1987, only one-third of the population had children under eighteen years of age, a ten-percent fall. These factors together reduced domestic labor in the neighborhood of one hundred hours a year for women. Of course, declining birth and marriage rates are not independent of the growth of work. Women's employment has also been a cause of fewer births and even later and shorter marriages.[41]

INVOLUNTARY LEISURE: UNDEREMPLOYMENT AND UNEMPLOYMENT

There is at least one group of Americans for whom time squeeze is not a problem. These are the millions who cannot get enough work or who cannot get any at all. They have plenty of "leisure" but can hardly enjoy it. One of the great ironies of our present situation is that overwork for the majority has been accompanied by the growth of enforced idleness for the minority. The proportion of the labor force who cannot work as many hours as they would like has more than doubled in the last twenty years. Just as surely as our economic system is "underproducing" leisure for some, it is "overproducing" it for others.

Declining industries provide poignant illustrations of the coexistence of long hours and unemployment. The manufacturing sector lost over a million jobs in the 1980s. At the same time (from 1980 to 1987), overtime hours rose by fifty per year. Many of those on permanent layoff watch their former co-workers put in steady overtime, week after week, year after year. Outside manufacturing, unemployment also rose steadily. At the height of each business expansion (1969, 1973, 1979, and 1987), the proportion of the labor force without a job was higher—rising from only 3.4 percent in 1969 to almost twice that—6.1 percent—in 1987.

Enforced idleness is not just confined to those who have been laid off. Underemployment is also growing. The fraction of the labor force working part-time but desiring full-time work increased more than seven times. The fraction employed only part of the year, but wanting a job year-round, nearly doubled. Those who had neither full-time nor full-year work, but wanted both, rose four times. All told, in the first year of my study, 7 percent of the labor force were unable to obtain the work they wanted or needed. Twenty years later, this category had more than doubled—and stood at almost 17 percent (see table 2.5).

The trend toward underemployment and unemployment signals a disturbing failure of the labor market: the U.S. economy is increasingly unable to provide work for its population. It is all the more noticeable that growing idleness is occurring at a time when those who are fully employed are at their workplaces for ever longer hours. Like long hours, the growth of unemployment stems from the basic structure of the economy. Capitalist systems such as our own do not operate in order to provide employment. Their guiding principle is the pursuit of profitability. If profitability results in high employment, that is a happy coincidence for those who want jobs. If it does not, bottom-line oriented companies will not take it upon themselves to hire those their plans have left behind. . . . [Schor covers the relationship between the pursuit of profits, unemployment, and long working hours in chapter 3 of *The Overworked American*.]. Full employment typically occurs only when government commits itself to the task.

In the last twenty years, full employment has become ever more elusive as a result of high interest rates, declining investment, sluggish productivity, takeovers and mergers, increased market uncertainty, and stiffer foreign competition. At the same time, Washington has abdicated its responsibility for maintaining jobs. The "golden age" of Western capitalism is over, and with it went the promise of high employment. The rise and fall of the golden age is a long story in itself, which I, along with others, have told elsewhere.[42] What is important here is that the pressures on businesses have spurred a search for cost-cutting measures. Rather than hire new people, and pay the extra benefits they would entail, many firms have just demanded more from their existing workforces. They have sped up the pace of work and lengthened time on the job. In an atmosphere of high unemployment and weak unions, workers have found it difficult to refuse. The result has been a labor market characterized by a glaring inequity.

As unemployment rose in the 1970s, some labor economists and educators began to advocate shorter hours. Harking back to the labor move-

TABLE 2.5 Fraction of Labor Force Experiencing Unemployment and Underemployment

	1969	1973	1979	1987
Total unemployed and underemployed	7.2	9.8	16.2	16.8
No Work All Year	0.4	0.7	0.8	1.6
Part Year/Part-Time	1.0	1.8	4.0	4.4
Full Year/Part-Time	0.2	0.3	0.9	1.5
Part Year/Full-Time	5.6	7.0	10.5	9.3

Source: Author's estimates from *Current Population Survey*.

ment's longstanding traditions, they argued that reductions in weekly hours would put millions of people back to work. But despite their obvious appeal, these proposals received little serious attention. Even as the unemployment problem worsened during the 1980s, work sharing continued to be virtually ignored. Yet if "spreading-the-work" is a sensible and humane solution to a clear irrationality of our economic system, why has it failed? The ostensible rationality of workweek reductions fails to come to terms with a "larger" capitalist logic. Employers have strong incentives to keep hours long. And these incentives have been instrumental in raising hours and keeping them high. In retrospect, the reformers underestimated the obstacles within capitalism itself to solving both the nation's shortage of jobs and its shortage of time.[43]

Notes

1. "All Work, No Play," on "Real Life with Jane Pauley," NBC, 17 July 1990.
   "Overworked and Out of Time," on "Our Times," WHDH-TV, Boston, 14 April 1990.
   Transcript of "Fast Times," Show 97, "48 Hours," CBS News, 8 March 1990. All these examples are from the script.
2. Nancy Gibbs, "How America Has Run Out of Time," *Time,* 24 April 1989, p. 59.
3. Anne B. Fisher, *Wall Street Women: Women in Power on the Street Today* (New York: Alfred A. Knopf, 1990), 152, 150.
4. Quoted in Brian O'Reilly, "Is Your Company Asking Too Much?" *Fortune,* 12 March 1990, p. 39.
5. See Amanda Bennett, *The Death of the Organization Man* (New York: William Morrow, 1990).
   On downsizings, see O'Reilly, "Is Your Company," 41.
6. Evidence on the increased commitment in what she calls "post-entrepreneurial" firms can be found in Rosabeth Moss Kanter's *When Giants Learn to Dance* (New York: Simon and Schuster, 1989), chap. 10, p. 275. The quote is from Thomas Bolger, CEO of Bell Atlantic.
   Kanter, *When Giants Dance,* 273.
   Dolores A. Kordek, personal interview, 5 January 1991. Kordek followed this schedule for twelve years, rarely seeing her family, eating either in the office or the car, and eventually "burning out."
7. A poll by Korn/Ferry International in 1985 found that among Fortune 500 and Service 500 companies, senior executives' hours rose from 53 to 56 between 1979 and 1985; vacation days fell from 16 to 14. A poll of CEOs by Heidrick and Struggles found that the percentage who worked more than 60 hours per week rose between 1980 and 1984, from 44 percent to 60 percent. Cited in Ford S. Worthy, "You're Probably Working Too Hard," *Fortune,* 27 April 1987, p. 136. The Harris Poll reports consistent findings for managers. Sixty-two percent of CEOs also report that their subordinates are putting in longer hours. See Sally Solo, "Stop Whining and Get Back to Work," *Fortune,* 12 March 1990, p. 49.
8. See Bennett, *Death,* and Kanter, *When Giants Dance,* for evidence from case-study research on individual companies.

9. Labor force participation rate of adult women from Current Population Survey, author's estimates. Rates of labor force participation for mothers (of own children under eighteen) from "Marital and Family Characteristics of the Labor Force from the March 1990 Current Population Survey," unpublished Bureau of Labor Statistics mimeo, October 1990, p. 4, table 15.
10. These quotes are from Ann Landers's column, *Boston Globe*, 26 February 1990. "Busy every waking hour" is from Laurie Sheridan, "Interviews on Working Hours," unpublished mimeo.

    Arlie Hochschild, *The Second Shift: Working Parents and the Revolution at Home* (New York: Viking Penguin, 1989), 9.
11. Boston study is Dianne S. Burden and Bradley Googins, *Boston University Balancing Job and Homelife Study,* mimeo (Boston University, 1987), 18, table 10.

    Shelley Coverman, using the Quality of Employment Survey, found an average workweek of 87.4 hours for white, currently married, employed women. See "Gender, Domestic Labor Time, and Wage Inequality," *American Sociological Review,* 48 (October 1983): 623–37, table 1, p. 629. A second study, based on the Panel Survey of Income Dynamics, found that in white, married couples, mothers who worked full-time had a workweek ranging from 76 hours (if the oldest child was 4 to 13 years old) to 89 (oldest child 0 to 3 years). See Cynthia Rexroat and Constance Shehan, "The Family Life Cycle and Spouses' Time in Housework," *Journal of Marriage and the Family,* 49, 4 (November 1987): 739–50, fig. 1, p. 746. A nationwide magazine survey by the 9to5 union found that women respondents had an average workweek of 84.3 hours. See *The 9to5 National Survey on Women and Stress* (Cleveland, Ohio: 9to5, 1984), estimates calculated from appendix C; however, this was not a statistically representative survey.
12. Anna Quindlen, "Men at Work," in "Public and Private," *New York Times,* 18 February 1990, p. 19, on "endangered species" and 50-plus hours.

    Weekend data from Harriet Presser, "Can We Make Time for Children? The Economy, Work Schedules, and Child Care," *Demography,* 26 (November 1989): 523–44, table 1.
13. Sheridan, "Interviews."
14. One-third figure calculated from table 3.5 in Lawrence Mishel and David M. Frankel, *The State of Working America,* 1990–91 ed. (Armonk, N.Y.: M. E. Sharpe); hourly wage figure for 1988, p. 77.

    Valerie Connor (pseud.), personal interview, 23 December 1990.

    Bill Meyerson, Service Employees International Union, Hartford, Connecticut, personal interview, 30 November 1990.

    Dominic Bozzotto, personal interview, December 1990.

    I. N. Yazbek, personal interview, 11 December 1990.
15. The Harris Poll question on leisure is the following: "About how many hours each week do you estimate you have available to relax, watch TV, take part in sports or hobbies, go swimming or skiing, go to the movies, theater, concerts, or other forms of entertainment, get together with friends, and so forth?" Louis Harris, *Americans and the Arts,* Study 871009 (New York: Louis Harris and Associates), January 1988, Appendix C. The Decision Research Corporation question is: "Compared to a few years ago do you feel you have more leisure time, less leisure time or the same amount of leisure time?" Decision Research Corporation, *Decision Research Corporation's 1990 Leisure Study: Trends in America's Leisure Time and Activities* (Lexington, Mass.: D.C. Heath, February 1990), 6, table 1.

For the Harris Poll, the most serious problem is that it reportedly has a very low response rate. A second issue, for both the Harris and Decision Research Corporation polls, is the accuracy of estimates that are based on respondent recall. For a critique of this method, see John P. Robinson, "The Validity and Reliability of Diaries versus Alternative Time Use Measures," in F. Thomas Juster and Frank P. Stafford, eds., *Time, Goods, and Well-Being* (Ann Arbor: Institute for Social Research, University of Michigan, 1985), 63–91. Because time diaries are expensive to administer, most surveys of time use are based on the recall method; therefore, it is difficult to avoid reliance on it altogether.

16. Jeremy Rifkin, *Time Wars* (New York: Henry Holt, 1987), 14–15.
    On Nintendo, ibid., 26.
    Alstedt quote from Trish Hall, "Why All Those People Feel They Never Have Enough Time," *New York Times,* 2 January 1988, p. 1.
17. John P. Robinson, "The Time Squeeze," *American Demographics,* 12, 2 (February 1990): 30–33. Results from Robinson's 1985 survey show that rising numbers of people feel rushed in other age groups besides the "baby boomers." The walking résumé quote is from Geoffrey Godbey of Pennsylvania State University, in Hall, "Why All Those People."
18. Gary Becker, "A Theory of the Allocation of Time," *Economic Journal,* 75, 299 (1965): 493–517; and Staffan B. Linder, *The Harried Leisure Class* (New York: Columbia University Press, 1970).
19. Trish Hall, "The Dinner Party Quietly Bows to More Casual Alternatives," *New York Times,* 24 February 1988, p. C1.
    Linder, following standard neoclassical economic theory, has no prediction about whether a wage increase will lead to more or less leisure time. There is also a logical question about Linder's theory: If the income effect for leisurely activities is large, demand for them may increase. See William J. Baumol, "Income and Substitution Effects in the Linder Theorem," *Quarterly Journal of Economics,* 87 (1973): 629–33.
20. One-fourth from Bureau of Labor Statistics, *Labor Force Statistics Derived from the Current Population Survey, 1948–1987* (Washington, D.C.: Government Printing Office, 1988), 801, table C–12, 804, table C–14. The percentage was rising over this period; one-quarter is a rough figure.
    Bureau of Labor Statistics, "Marital and Family Characteristics," 4, table 15.
21. Bruce D. Butterfield, "Long Hours, Late Nights, Low Grades: In Labor-Short Towns Across America, Teen-agers Are Overworked," *Boston Globe,* Children at Work series, 24 April 1990.
22. Bruce D. Butterfield, "The New Harvest of Shame: For Farm Workers' Children, Cycle of Poverty and Work Unbroken," *Boston Globe,* Children at Work series, 26 April 1990.
23. Bureau of Labor Statistics, *Labor Force Statistics Derived from the Current Population Survey, 1948–1987,* 153, table A–10.
24. One study of older male (aged 45–65) nonparticipants indicates that these men have relatively little income that suggests voluntary retirement—namely, pensions, rental income, interest, or dividends. Instead, their support comes much more from government disability payments, indicating that physical and mental impairments are preventing them from working. The inability to find jobs is also correlated with disability rates. For white men, disability payments alone made up about 30 percent of total family income; for black men, these payments were roughly half.

Donald O. Parsons, "The Decline in Male Labor Force Participation," *Journal of Political Economy*, 88, 11 (1980): 117–34. Since these data were collected before the Reagan administration's attack on disability programs, the figures may be lower during the 1980s.

1990 survey is in The Commonwealth Fund, *Americans Over 50 at Work Program*, Research Reports 1 and 2 (New York: The Commonwealth Fund, 25 January and 8 March 1990).

See Bennett, *Death,* for a discussion of pressures to take early retirement among white-collar workers. For evidence on the effects of plant closings or job loss on older workers, see Paul O. Flaim and Ellen Sehgal, "Displaced Workers of 1979–83: How Well Have They Fared?" *Monthly Labor Review* (June 1985): 3–16. Their figures show that about 34 percent of males aged fifty-five and above dropped out of the labor force after being displaced (calculated from table 1, p. 4).

African-American men face rates of unemployment more than twice those of white men. They have also been disproportionately hit by plant closings, industrial decline, and suburbanization. Once they suffer job displacement, African-Americans have a 42-percent chance of becoming unemployed, nearly twice the rate for whites, and are more likely to drop out of the labor force altogether. Data on job displacement are from a special Bureau of Labor Statistics survey for 1979–83. See Flaim and Sehgal, "Displaced Workers," p. 4, table 1. For a discussion of the long-term picture, see William J. Wilson, *The Truly Disadvantaged: The Inner City, the Underclass, and Public Policy* (Chicago: University of Chicago Press, 1987), 100–101.

25. More information on these categories can be found in Laura Leete-Guy and Juliet B. Schor, "Is There a Time Squeeze? Estimates of Market and Non-Market Hours in the United States, 1969–1987," *HIER Working Paper* 1525, Harvard University, November 1989. The occupational data are difficult to construct due to changes in the occupational codes between 1969 and 1987; however, a rough test confirmed the generality of the rise. The results for industries are also likely to be somewhat correlated with those for occupations.

26. Earl F. Mellor and William Parks II, "A Year's Work: Labor Force Activity from a Different Perspective," *Monthly Labor Review* (September 1988): 13–18.

27. The decline in average weekly hours registered in the establishment data is spurious because it double-counts moonlighters and excludes the informal sector and many of the self-employed.

Figures on long schedules are from Bureau of Labor Statistics, *Employment and Earnings,* August 1990, p. 32, table A-27, calculated as a percentage of full-time workers only, all industries (49+ hours are 25 percent, 60+ hours are 11 percent).

28. See Leete-Guy and Schor, "Assessing the Time Squeeze Hypothesis: Estimates of Market and Non-Market Hours in the United States, 1969–1987," unpublished mimeo, Harvard University, June 1990.

29. Bureau of Labor Statistics Press Release, "Multiple Jobholding Reached Record High in May 1989," 89–529, 6 November 1989.

See Sar A. Levitan and Richard S. Belous, *Shorter Hours, Shorter Weeks: Spreading the Work to Reduce Unemployment* (Baltimore: Johns Hopkins University Press, 1977), 12 on under-reporting.

See Bureau of Labor Statistics News release, 89–529, 6 November 1989, table 6; and Daniel E. Taylor and Edward S. Sekscenski, "Workers on Long Schedules, Single and Multiple Jobholders," Research Summary, *Monthly Labor Review*, 105, 5

(May 1982): 47–53 for data on reasons for multiple jobholding and the differences between 1980 and 1989.
30. Average annual overtime hours per job were 204.5 in 1987:4, which on the basis of a 40-hour week is equivalent to five weeks. Overtime data are from Ray Fair, of Yale University, whose original source is *Employment and Earnings*. They are the variable HO, as defined in his *Specification, Estimation, and Analysis of Macroeconomic Models* (Cambridge, Mass.: Harvard University Press, 1984), table A-4. Data are not available outside the manufacturing sector.

Quotes from Sheridan, "Interviews."
31. Bennett, *Death,* 140–41, on DuPont and other large corporations.

Illness data from author's calculations from Current Population Survey data.

Absences from Bruce W. Klein, "Missed Work and Lost Hours, May 1985," *Monthly Labor Review,* 109, 11 (November 1986): 26–30.
32. Max L. Carey, "Occupational Tenure in 1987: Many Workers Have Remained in Their Fields," *Monthly Labor Review,* 111, 10 (October 1988): 3–12.
33. "Gradual erosion" quote from Theresa Diss Greis, *The Decline of Annual Hours Worked in the United States Since 1947* (Philadelphia: Industrial Relations Unit, Wharton, University of Pennsylvania, 1984), 1.

I have used two methods to estimate paid time off. The first used unpublished Bureau of Labor Statistics estimates of hours paid relative to hours worked. The drawback to these data is that they are only available for the manufacturing sector earlier than 1981. Therefore, I have relied on manufacturing sector data for the period 1969 to 1981. These data show a rise in time off of three days. After 1981, I have all-economy data to 1989, which indicate a decline equivalent to three and a half days per year. There is, therefore, a net decrease in total paid time off between 1969 and 1989 of one-half day, or about four hours. If I calculate these figures only until 1987, the year my data end, I get a net increase in paid time off of one and a half days, or about twelve hours. (The difference is due to the decline in paid time off between 1987 and 1989.)

A second method is to use direct estimates of the major forms of paid time off—vacations, holidays, and sick leave. Because the Current Population Survey does not provide the information to enable me to calculate vacations and holidays, I have used BLS estimates. They calculate that in 1968 paid vacation and holidays totaled seventeen days per year. In 1983–86, they estimate 19.5 days per year, or an increase of 2.5 days (or 20 hours). Against this, I have calculated sick leave from the Current Population Survey (the variable is available only for full-time workers). Total hours lost to illness for full-time workers fell between 1969 and 1987 from 58 per year to 41, a decline of 17 hours. (Notably, between 1969 and 1979 there was little change; all of the decline happened after 1979.) Combining the vacation, holiday, and sick leave yields a net figure of 3 hours per year in additional paid time off. For Bureau of Labor Statistics estimates, see Janice Hedges and Daniel E. Taylor, "Recent Trends in Worktime: Hours Edge Downward," *Monthly Labor Review,* 103, 3 (1980): 3–11; and John E. Buckley, "Variations in Holidays, Vacations, and Area Pay Levels," *Monthly Labor Review,* 112, 2 (February 1989): 24–30.
34. Commuting times calculated from John P. Robinson, "Trends in Americans' Use of Time: Some Preliminary 1965–1975–1985 Comparisons," mimeo, 1986 University of Maryland, Survey Research Center, p. 36, table 5.

A development my calculations do not fully capture is the growth of the underground economy. The underground economy consists of economic production that is not reported to the government and does not show up in official statistics—either because the activity itself is illegal (drugs, prostitution, gambling) or because those engaging in it wish to avoid paying taxes on the income it generates. It is difficult to know exactly how these considerations affect people's responses to the CPS; however, it is probable that some percentage will not acknowledge hours of work that are "underground." The fact that the underground economy has increased tremendously over the period I am considering means that my calculations are biased downward. In effect, I am counting a shrinking percentage of the total economy. It is impossible to calculate with any accuracy how much it is shrinking and how many hours I am missing. This problem is common to all estimates of worktime.

35. There is no single, convenient term for unpaid work done in the home. Some terms commonly in use are *domestic labor, unpaid labor, household work,* and *work done in the home.* The latter is somewhat confusing because some work for pay is physically located in the home (transporting family members, purchasing food, etc.). *Domestic labor* and *unpaid labor* are somewhat arcane. The economist's preferred terminology is *market* and *nonmarket work,* but these have little meaning in common parlance. I try to avoid these terminological minefields by using most of these terms interchangeably. Some readers may have their doubts about whether such household activities as food preparation, child care, and house cleaning should be considered work. . . .

Officers of the Association for the Advancement of Women wrote to the U.S. Congress in 1878, requesting changes in Census procedures that would allow enumeration of household workers. See Nancy Folbre and Marjorie Abel, "Women's Work and Women's Households: Gender Bias in the U.S. Census," *Social Research,* 56, 3 (Autumn 1989): 545–69.

The diary studies originating at the University of Michigan are biased upward in terms of income and the percentage of whites, two factors that raise domestic hours. A second problem is that the Michigan surveys were done during recessions (1975–76 and 1980–81), which distorts their estimates of market work.

36. . . . My colleague, Laura Leete-Guy, and I predicted hours of domestic labor for our CPS sample based on a multiple regression model using data from the University of Michigan surveys in 1975–76 and 1980–81. The independent variables included marital status, number of children, age, number of hours worked in paid employment, and so forth. The 1975–76 survey was used to predict hours for 1969 and 1973. The 1980–81 follow-up survey was used for 1979 and 1987. See Victor Fuchs, "His and Hers: Differences in Work and Income, 1959–79," *Journal of Labor Economics,* 4, 3 (1986): pt. 2, S245–72, for an earlier example of this methodology. One drawback to this method is that we cannot pick up any post-1981 trends occurring due to excluded factors, such as men's increased willingness to do work around the house. A more recent survey was carried out in 1985; however, these data were not available except in summary form.

37. In the contemporary United States, hours per working-age person is a superior measure to a second, often-cited statistic—namely, hours per capita, which includes children and teenagers. There are at least two reasons for this. First, since child labor has been legally restricted and for some ages prohibited, including children as part of the potential labor force is somewhat suspect. Inclusion of child labor would also be hampered by the lack of adequate data, given that it is often illegal. (As noted earlier, however, child labor is on the rise.) Second, there has been

a sharp decline in the number of children per adult during the last twenty years, which artificially inflates the hours-per-capita figure.

The standard of living will also be affected by the extent to which income flows in and out of the country on the basis of assets held abroad by U.S. citizens and domestic assets owned by foreigners. The hours-per-capita measure also does not account for consumption that occurs by running down stocks of previously produced goods and services, or for the labor of children.

38. I am here defining leisure time as whatever is left over after household and market work are accounted for. The uncorrected figures show a more modest decline of 25 hours per year. See Leete-Guy and Schor, "Assessing the Time Squeeze."
39. Researchers have not yet provided an estimate of how much domestic production is being replaced by marketed goods and services; however there is no doubt that this substitution is taking place.
40. John P. Robinson, "Who's Doing the Housework?" *American Demographics,* 10, 12 (December 1988): 24–28.
41. See James P. Smith and Michael Ward, "Time-Series Growth in the Labor Force," *Journal of Labor Economics,* 3, 1 (January 1985): 559–590, and Elaine McCrate, "Trade, Merger, and Employment: Economic Theory on Marriage," *Review of Radical Political Economics,* 19 (1987): 73–89.
42. For a comprehensive discussion of the decline of macroeconomic performance and the resulting unemployment, the reader is referred to Stephen A. Marglin and Juliet B. Schor, eds., *The Golden Age of Capitalism: Reinterpreting the Postwar Experience* (Oxford: Clarendon Press, 1990). For more on changes in unemployment itself, see Jukka Pekkarinen, Matti Pohjola, and Bob Rowthorn, *Social Corporatism: A Superior System?* (Oxford: Clarendon Press, 1991). Both these volumes were produced by the Macroeconomic Policies Project of the World Institute for Development Economics Research.
43. See, among others, Levitan and Belous, *Shorter Hours;* Martin J. Morand and Ramelle Macoy, eds., *Short-time Compensation: A Formula for Work Sharing* (New York: Pergamon Press, 1984); and William McGaughey, Jr., *A Shorter Workweek in the 1980s* (White Bear Lake, Minn.: Thistlerose Publications, 1981).

These proposals also overestimated the impact workweek reductions were likely to have on the demand for labor. . . . there is strong evidence that workweek reductions are accompanied by rising productivity, which largely negates the positive employment effect. Recent European experience provides strong support for this conclusion. See Wouter van Ginneken, "Employment and the Reduction of the Work Week: A Comparison of Seven European Macro-economic Models," *International Labour Review,* 123, 1 (January/February 1984): 35–52.

Questions for Discussion

1. Juliet Schor describes the United States as a time-starved society: none of us has enough time to do what we need or want to do. How rushed do you feel? What demands on your time make you feel rushed? How do you apportion work/study time and leisure time? When—and how—do you relax?
2. Some critics have argued that Americans feel rushed not so much because they have more to do than they once did but because they

allow themselves to be controlled by the "time-saving devices" that were meant to free them. Think about the technological devices you use—perhaps a beeper, a computer, or even a microwave or VCR. Are there any ways in which these devices force upon you a greater sense of urgency and pressure than you need to feel?

3. Schor says that the "5:00 Dads of the 1950s and 1960s" have almost disappeared and that working mothers are weary to the point of exhaustion. How true was this in your family? How much of your parents' time was spent either working at a job or working around the house? How much of their time was spent with you? Finally, how much time did they have that was free from work, home, or childcare responsibilities?

4. Did you work while you were in high school? If so, why? How many hours a week did you work? What did you do with the money you earned? Finally, what do you see as the educational, social, and financial advantages and disadvantages of your having worked in high school?

5. Given the choice between working overtime for extra money or having leisure time, which would you choose? If you'd choose to work, what would you do with the extra income? In what ways would you compensate for the loss of time? If you would choose to have leisure time, how would you spend it?

6. Some critics worry that if Americans worked less, they would just waste the free time they gained. We are, they say, either too lazy or too enamored of work to use our free time well. If you had more free time, how would you want to use it? How do you think you would actually use it?

Questions for Research and Writing

1. According to one poll that Schor cites, many workers feel they are working harder today than they were two years ago. Survey people who have been working in the same job for at least two years. Do their responses substantiate the responses Schor cites? Over the past two or three years, how have the following changed: their job, their job performance, their job satisfaction, and their relationship with their employer?

2. Schor raises a familiar question: How much of the work around the house is being done by men and how much by women? Survey your peers about the work done around the house in which they grew up. How much of it was done by the men and boys of the household? How much by the women and girls? Ask your respondents to consider also the *kinds* of tasks each member of the household performed.

3. Interview someone who is working part-time. Is that person working part-time by choice? What does that person see as the benefits and drawbacks of part-time work?

4. In a later section of her book, Schor proposes several ways out of the "squirrel cage" in which we have entrapped ourselves: Require employ-

ers to define the standard number of weekly hours for which even professional employees would be paid *and* pay them—in time, not money—for any overtime hours; require employers to give their workers the option of future paid time off instead of a pay increase; and require employers to grant minimal vacation leaves (she suggests four weeks per year) and parental leaves even to employees in low-wage jobs.

Interview employers and employees about the benefits and drawbacks of these proposals. Then write an essay arguing for or against their implementation. (You may accept some arguments and reject others.)

5. Conduct a survey on the use of free time. How much free time do most of your respondents have? How do they spend that free time? If they had more free time, would they spend it differently than they do now? If they had less, what activities would they be most likely to give up? As you design your survey, you might include some questions about respondents' cultural, ethnic, and socioeconomic backgrounds. How important are those factors in determining one's attitude toward leisure time and activities?

PUBLIC USE/PRIVATE STATE

Susan Willis for The Project on Disney

> "Public Use/Private State" originally appeared in Inside the Mouse: Work and Play at Disney World *(1995)*, an examination by the Project on Disney of the ways in which we attribute meaning to Disney World and the ways Disney World structures our understanding of work, play, and reality. In the following chapter from Inside the Mouse, Susan Willis, an English professor at Duke University, explores the intersections between public and private space and between play and amusement; she concludes that Disney World offers its visitors a kind of ordered fantasy that makes impossible real imagination and creativity. Hiding behind the pretense of play at Disney World lies a world structured on the principles of consumerism and white, middle-class values that is averse to fanciful spontaneity. Willis argues that, despite its outward appearance, Disney World is closer than we might think to the regulated world of work. See if you agree.

At Disney World, the erasure of spontaneity is so great that spontaneity itself has been programmed. On the "Jungle Cruise" khaki-clad tour guides teasingly engage the visitors with their banter, whose apparent spontaneity has been carefully scripted and painstakingly rehearsed. Nothing is left to the imagination or the unforeseen. Even the paths and walkways represent the programmed assimilation of the spontaneous. According to published reports, there were no established walkways laid down for the opening-day crowds at Disneyland.[1] Rather, the Disney Imagineers waited to see where people would walk, then paved over their spontaneous footpaths to make prescribed routes.

The erasure of spontaneity has largely to do with the totality of the built and themed environment. Visitors are inducted into the park's program, their every need predefined and presented to them as a packaged routine and set of choices. "I'm not used to having everything done for me." This is how my companion at Disney World reacted when she checked into a Disney resort hotel and found that she, her suitcase, and her credit card had been turned into the scripted components of a highly orchestrated program. My companion later remarked that while she found it odd not to have to take care of everything herself (as she normally does in order to accomplish her daily tasks), she found it "liberating" to just fall into the proper pattern, knowing that nothing could arise that hadn't already been factored into the system. I have heard my companion's remarks reiterated by many visitors to the park with whom I've talked. Most describe feeling "freed up" ("I didn't have to worry about my kids," "I didn't have to think about anything") by the experience of relinquishing control over the complex problem-solving thoughts and operations that otherwise define their lives. Many visitors suspend daily perceptions and judgments altogether, and treat the wonderland environment as more real than real. I saw this happen one morning when walking to breakfast at my Disney resort hotel. Two small children were stooped over a small snake that had crawled out onto the sun-warmed path. "Don't worry, it's rubber," remarked their mother. Clearly only Audio-Animatronic simulacra of the real world can inhabit Disney World. A real snake is an impossibility.

In fact, the entire natural world is subsumed by the primacy of the artificial. The next morning I stepped outside at the end of an early morning shower. The humid atmosphere held the combination of sun and rain. "Oh! Did they turn the sprinklers on?" This is the way my next-door neighbor greeted the day as she emerged from her hotel room. The Disney environment puts visitors inside the world that Philip K. Dick depicted in *Do Androids Dream of Electric Sleep?*—where all animal life has been exterminated, but replaced by the production of simulacra, so real in appearance that people have difficulty recalling that real animals no longer exist. The marvelous effect of science fiction is produced out of a dislocation between two worlds, which the reader apprehends as an estrangement, but the characters inside the novel cannot grasp because they have only the one world: the world of simulacra. The effect of the marvelous cannot be achieved unless the artificial environment is perceived through the retained memory of everyday reality. Total absorption into the Disney environment cancels the possibility for the marvelous and leaves the visitor with the banality of a park-wide sprinkler system. No muggers, no rain, no ants, and no snakes.

Amusement is the commodified negation of play. What is play but the spontaneous coming together of activity and imagination, rendered more pleasurable by the addition of friends? At Disney World, the world's most highly developed private property "state" devoted to amusement, play is all but eliminated by the absolute domination of program over spontaneity. Every ride runs to computerized schedule. There is no possibility of an awful thrill, like being stuck at the top of a ferris wheel. Order prevails particularly in the queues for the rides that zigzag dutifully on a prescribed path created out of stanchions and ropes; and the visitor's assimilation into the queue does not catapult him or her into another universe, as it would if Jorge Luis Borges fabricated the program. The Disney labyrinth is a banal extension of the ride's point of embarkation, which extends into the ride as a hyper-themed continuation of the queue. The "Backstage Movie Tour" has done away with the distinction between the ride and its queue by condemning the visitor to a two-and-a-half-hour-long pedagogical queue that preaches the process of movie production. Guests are mercilessly herded through sound stages and conveyed across endless back lots where one sees the ranch-style houses used in TV commercials and a few wrecked cars from movie chase scenes. Happily, there are a few discreet exit doors, bail-out points for parents with bored children. Even Main Street dictates programmed amusement because it is not a street but a conduit, albeit laden with commodity distractions, that conveys the visitor to the Magic Kingdom's other zones where more queues, rides, and commodities distinguish themselves on the basis of their themes. All historical and cultural references are merely ingredients for decor. Every expectation is met programmatically and in conformity with theme. Mickey as Sorcerer's Apprentice does not appear in the Wild West or the exotic worlds of Jungle and Adventure, the niches for Davy Crockett and Indiana Jones. Just imagine the chaos, a park-wide short circuit, that the mixing of themed ingredients might produce. Amusement areas are identified by a "look," by characters in costume, by the goods on sale: What place—i.e., product—is Snow White promoting if she's arm in arm with an astronaut? The utopian intermingling of thematic opportunities such as occurred at the finale of the movie *Who Framed Roger Rabbit?*, with Warner and Disney "toons" breaking their copyrighted species separation to cavort with each other and the human actors, will not happen at Disney World.

However, now that the costumed embodiment of Roger Rabbit has taken up residence at Disney World, he, too, can expect to have a properly assigned niche in the spectacular Disney parade of characters. These have been augmented with a host of other Disney/Lucas/Spielberg creations, including Michael Jackson of "Captain EO" and C3PO and R2D2 of *Star Wars,* as well as Disney buyouts such as Jim Henson's Muppets and the Saturday morning cartoon heroes, the Teenage Mutant Ninja Turtles. The Disney Corporation's acquisition of the stock-in-trade of popular culture icons facilitates a belief commonly held by young children that every popular childhood figure "lives" at Disney World. In the utopian imagination of children, Disney World may well be a neverending version of the finale to *Roger Rabbit* where every product of the imagination lives in community. In reality, the products (of adult imaginations) live to sell, to be consumed, to multiply.

What's most interesting about Disney World is what's not there. Intimacy is not in the program even though the architecture includes several secluded nooks, gazebos, and patios. During my five-day stay, I saw only one kiss—and this a husbandly peck on the cheek. Eruptions of imaginative play are just as rare. During the same five-day visit, I observed only one such incident even though there were probably fifty thousand children in the park. What's curious about what's not at Disney is that there is no way of knowing what's not there until an aberrant event occurs and provokes the remembrance of the social forms and behaviors that have been left out. This was the case with the episode of spontaneous play. Until I saw real play, I didn't realize that it was missing. The incident stood out against a humdrum background of uniform amusement: hundreds of kids being pushed from attraction to attraction in their strollers, hundreds more waiting dutifully in the queues or marching about in family groups—all of them abstaining from the loud, jostling, teasing, and rivalrous behaviors that would otherwise characterize many of their activities. Out of this homogenous "amused" mass, two kids snagged a huge sombrero each from an open-air stall at the foot of the Mexico Pavilion's Aztec temple stairway and began their impromptu version of the Mexican hat dance up and down the steps. Their play was clearly counterproductive as it took up most of the stairway, making it difficult for visitors to enter the pavilion. Play negated the function of the stairs as conduit into the attraction. The kids abandoned themselves to their fun, while all around them, the great mass of visitors purposefully kept their activities in line with Disney World's prescribed functions. Everyone but the dancers seemed to have accepted the park's unwritten motto: "If you pay, you shouldn't play." To get your money's worth, you have to do everything and do it in the prescribed manner. Free play is gratuitous and therefore a waste of the family's leisure time expenditure.

Conformity with the park's program upholds the Disney value system. Purposeful consumption—while it costs the consumer a great deal—affirms the value of the consumer. "Don't forget, we drove twenty hours to get here." This is how one father admonished his young son who was squirming about on the floor of EPCOT'S Independence Hall, waiting for the amusement to begin. The child's wanton and impatient waste of time was seen as a waste of the family's investment in its amusement. If a family is to realize the value of its leisure time consumptions, then every member must function as a proper consumer.

The success of Disney World as an amusement park has largely to do with the way its use of programming meshes with the economics of consumption as a value system. In a world wholly predicated on consumption, the dominant order need not proscribe those activities that run counter to consumption, such as free play and squirming, because the consuming public largely polices itself against gratuitous acts which would interfere with the production of consumption as a value. Conformity with the practice of consumption is so widespread and deep at Disney World that occasional manifestations of boredom or spontaneity do not influence the compulsively correct behavior of others. Independence Hall did not give way to a seething mass of squirming youngsters even though all had to sit through a twenty-minute wait. Nor did other children on the margins of the hat dance fling themselves into the fun. Such infectious behavior would have indicated communally defined social relations or the desire for such social relations. Outside of Disney World in places of public use, infectious behavior is common. One child squirming about on the library floor breeds others; siblings chasing each other around in a supermarket draw others; one child mischievously poking at a public fountain attracts others; kids freeloading rides on a department store escalator can draw a crowd. These playful, impertinent acts indicate an imperfect mesh between programmed environment and the value system of consumption. Consumers may occasionally reclaim the social, particularly the child consumer who has not yet been fully and properly socialized to accept individuation as the bottom line in the consumer system of value. As an economic factor, the individual exists to maximize consumption—and therefore profits—across the broad mass of consumers. This is the economic maxim most cherished by the fast-food industry, where every burger and order of fries is individually packaged and consumed to preclude consumer pooling and sharing.

At Disney World the basic social unit is the family. This was made particularly clear to me because as a single visitor conducting research, I presented a problem at the point of embarkation for each of the rides. "How many in your group?" "One." The lone occupant of a conveyance invariably constructed to hold the various numerical breakdowns of the nuclear family (two, three, or four) is an anomaly. Perhaps the most family-affirming aspect of Disney World is the way the queues serve as a place where family members negotiate who will ride with whom. Will Mom and Dad separate themselves so as to accompany their two kids on a two-person ride? Will an older sibling assume the responsibility for a younger brother or sister? Every ride asks the family to evaluate each of its member's needs for security and independence. This is probably the only situation in a family's visit to Disney World where the social relations of family materialize as practice. Otherwise and throughout a family's stay, the family as nexus for social relations is subsumed by the primary definition of family as the basic unit of consumption. In consumer society at large, each of us is an atomized consumer. Families are composed of autonomous, individuated consumers, each satisfying his or her age- and gender-differentiated taste in the music, video, food, and pleasure marketplace. In contrast, Disney World puts the family back together. Even teens are integrated in their families and are seldom seen roaming the park in teen groups as they might in shopping malls.

Families at Disney World present themselves as families, like the one I saw one morning on my way to breakfast at a Disney resort hotel: father, mother, and three children small to large, each wearing identical blue Mickey Mouse T-shirts and shorts. As I walked past them, I overheard the middle child say, "We looked better yesterday—in white." Immediately, I envisioned the family in yesterday's matching outfits, and wondered if they had bought identical ensembles for every day of their stay.

All expressions of mass culture include contradictory utopian impulses, which may be buried or depicted in distorted form, but nevertheless generate much of the satisfaction of mass cultural commodities (whether the consumer recognizes them as utopian or not). While the ideology of the family has long functioned to promote conservative—even reactionary—political and social agendas, the structure of the family as a social unit signifies communality rather than individuality and can give impetus to utopian longings for communally defined relations in society at large. However, when the family buys into the look of a family, and appraises itself on the basis of its look ("We looked better yesterday"), it becomes a walking, talking commodity, a packaged unit of consumption stamped with the Mickey logo of approval. The theoretical question that this family poses for me is not whether its representation of itself as family includes utopian possibilities (because it does), but whether such impulses can be expressed and communicated in ways not accessible to commodification.

In its identical dress, the family represents itself as capitalism's version of a democratized unit of consumption. Differences and inequalities among family members are reduced to distinctions in age and size. We have all had occasion to experience the doppelgänger effect in the presence of identical twins who choose (or whose families enforce) identical dress. Whether chosen or imposed, identical twins who practice the art of same dress have the possibility of confounding or subverting social order. In contrast, the heterogeneous family whose members choose to dress identically affirms conformity with social order. The family has cloned itself as a multiple, but identical consumer, thus enabling the maximization of consumption. It is a microcosmic representation of free market democracy where the range of choices is restricted to the series of objects already on the shelf. In this system there is no radical choice. Even the minority of visitors who choose to wear their Rolling Stones and Grateful Dead T-shirts give the impression of having felt constrained not to wear a Disney logo.

Actually, Disney has invented a category of negative consumer choices for those individuals who wish to express nonconformity. This I discovered as I prepared to depart for my Disney research trip, when my daughter Cassie (fifteen years old and "cool" to the max) warned me, "Don't buy me any of that Disney paraphernalia." As it turned out, she was happy to get a pair of boxer shorts emblazoned with the leering images of Disney's villains: two evil queens, the Big Bad Wolf, and Captain Hook. Every area of Disney World includes a Disney Villains Shop, a chain store for bad-guy merchandise. Visitors who harbor anti-Disney sentiments can express their cultural politics by consuming the negative Disney line. There is no possibility of an anticonsumption at Disney World. All visitors are, by definition, consumers, their status conferred with the price of admission.

At Disney World even memories are commodities. How the visitor will remember his or her experience of the park has been programmed and indicated by the thousands of "Kodak Picture Spot" signposts. These position the photographer so as to capture the best views of each and every attraction, so that even the most inept family members can bring home perfect postcard-like photos. To return home from a trip to Disney World with a collection of haphazardly photographed environments or idiosyncratic family shots is tantamount to collecting bad memories. A family album comprised of picture-perfect photo-site images, on the other hand, constitutes the grand narrative of the family's trip to Disney World, the one that can be offered as testimony to money well spent. Meanwhile, all those embarrassing photos, the ones not programmed by the "Picture Spots," that depict babies with ice cream all over their faces or toddlers who burst into tears rather than smiles at the sight of those big-headed costumed characters that crop up all over the park—these are the images that are best left forgotten.

The other commodified form of memory is the souvenir. As long as there has been tourism there have also been souvenirs: objects marketed to concretize the visitor's experience of another place. From a certain point of view, religious pilgrimage includes aspects of tourism, particularly when the culmination of pilgrimage is the acquisition of a transportable relic. Indeed, secular mass culture often imitates the forms and practices of popular religious culture. For many Americans today who make pilgrimages to Graceland and bring home a mass-produced piece of Presley memorabilia, culture and religion collide and mesh.

Of course the desire to translate meaningful moments into concrete objects need not take commodified form. In Toni Morrison's *Song of Solomon,* Pilate, a larger-than-life earth mother if there ever was one, spent her early vagabondage gathering a stone from every place she visited. Similarly, I know of mountain climbers who mark their ascents by bringing a rock back from each peak they climb. Like Pilate's stones, these tend to be nondescript and embody personal remembrances available only to the collector. In contrast, the commodity souvenir enunciates a single meaning to everyone: "I was there. I bought something." Unlike the souvenirs I remember having seen as a child, seashells painted with seascapes and the name of some picturesque resort town, most souvenirs today are printed with logos (like the Hard Rock Cafe T-shirt), or renderings of copyrighted material (all the Disney merchandise). The purchase of such a souvenir allows the consumer the illusion of participating in the enterprise as a whole, attaining a piece of the action. This is the consumerist version of small-time buying on the stock exchange. We all trade in logos—buy them, wear them, eat them, and make them the containers of our dreams and memories. Similarly, we may all buy into capital with the purchase of public stock. These consumerist activities give the illusion of democratic participation while denying access to real corporate control which remains intact and autonomous, notwithstanding the mass diffusion of its logos and stock on the public market. Indeed the manipulation of public stock initiated during the Reagan administration, which has facilitated one leveraged buyout after another, gives the lie to whatever wistful remnants of democratic ownership one might once have attached to the notion of "public" stocks.

Disney World is logoland. The merchandise, the costumes, the scenery—all is either stamped with the Disney logo or covered by copyright legislation. In fact, it is impossible to photograph at Disney World without running the risk of infringing a Disney copyright. A family photo in front of Sleeping Beauty's Castle is apt to include dozens of infringements: the castle itself, Uncle Harry's "Goofy" T-shirt, the kids' Donald and Mickey hats, maybe a costumed Chip 'n Dale in the background. The only thing that saves the average family from a lawsuit is that most don't use their vacation photos as a means for making profit. I suspect the staff of "America's Funniest Home Videos" systematically eliminates all family videos shot at Disney World; otherwise prize winners might find themselves having to negotiate the legal difference between prize and profit, and in a larger sense, public use versus private property. As an interesting note, Michael Sorkin, in a recent essay on Disneyland, chose a photo of "[t]he sky above Disney World [as a] substitute for an image of the place itself." Calling Disney World "the first copyrighted urban environment," Sorkin goes on to stress the "litigiousness" of the Disney Corporation.[2] It may be that *Design Quarterly,* where Sorkin published his essay, pays its contributors, thus disqualifying them from "fair use" interpretations of copyright policy.

Logos have become so much a part of our cultural baggage that we hardly notice them. Actually they are the cultural capital of corporations. Pierre Bourdieu invented the notion of cultural capital with reference to individuals. In a nutshell, cultural capital represents the sum total of a person's ability to buy into and trade in the culture. This is circumscribed by the economics of class and, in turn, functions as a means for designating an individual's social standing. Hence people with higher levels of education who distinguish themselves with upscale or trendy consumptions have more cultural capital and can command greater privilege and authority than those who, as Bourdieu put it, are stuck defining themselves by the consumption of necessity. There are no cultural objects or practices that do not constitute capital, no reserves of culture that escape value. Everything that constitutes one's cultural life is a commodity and can be reckoned in terms of capital logic.

In the United States today there is little difference between persons and corporations. Indeed, corporations enjoy many of the legal rights extended to individuals. The market system and its private property state are "peopled" by corporations, which trade in, accumulate, and hoard up logos. These are the cultural signifiers produced by corporations, the impoverished imaginary of a wholly rationalized entity. Logos are commodities in the abstract, but they are not so abstracted as to have transcended value. Corporations with lots of logos, particularly upscale, high-tech logos, command more cultural capital than corporations with fewer, more humble logos.

In late twentieth-century America, the cultural capital of corporations has replaced many of the human forms of cultural capital. As we buy, wear, and eat logos, we become the henchmen and admen of the corporations, defining ourselves with respect to the social standing of the various corporations. Some would say that this is a new form of tribalism, that in sporting corporate logos we ritualize and humanize them, we redefine the cultural capital of the corporations in human social terms. I would say that a state where culture is indistinguishable from logo and where the practice of culture risks infringement of private property is a state that values the corporate over the human.

While at Disney World, I managed to stow away on the behind-the-scenes tour reserved for groups of corporate conventioneers. I had heard about this tour from a friend who is also researching Disney and whose account of underground passageways, conduits for armies of workers and all the necessary materials and services that enable the park to function, had elevated the tour to mythic proportions in my imagination.

But very little of the behind-the-scenes tour was surprising. There was no magic, just a highly rational system built on the compartmentalization of all productive functions and its ensuing division of labor, both aimed at the creation of maximum efficiency. However, instances do arise when the rational infrastructure comes into contradiction with the onstage (park-wide) theatricalized image that the visitor expects to consume. Such is the case with the system that sucks trash collected at street level through unseen pneumatic tubes that transect the backstage area, finally depositing the trash in Disney's own giant compactor site. To the consumer's eyes, trash is never a problem at Disney World. After all, everyone dutifully uses the containers marked "trash," and what little manages to fall to the ground (generally popcorn) is immediately swept up by the French Foreign Legion trash brigade. For the consumer, there is no trash beyond its onstage collection. But there will soon be a problem as environmental pressure groups press Disney to recycle. As my companion on the backstage tour put it, "Why is there no recycling at Disney World—after all, many of the middle-class visitors to the park are already sorting and recycling trash in their homes?" To this the Disney guide pointed out that there is recycling, backstage: bins for workers to toss their Coke cans and other bins for office workers to deposit papers. But recycling onstage would break the magic of themed authenticity. After all, the "real" Cinderella's Castle was not equipped with recycling bins, nor did the denizens of Main Street, U.S.A., circa 1910, foresee the problem of trash. To maintain the image, Disney problem solvers are discussing hiring a minimum-wage workforce to rake, sort, and recycle the trash on back lots that the environmentally aware visitor will never see.

While I have been describing the backstage area as banal, the tour through it was not uneventful. Indeed there was one incident that underscored for me that dramatic collision between people's expectations of public use and the highly controlled nature of Disney's private domain. As I mentioned, the backstage tour took us to the behind-the-scenes staging area for the minute-by-minute servicing of the park and the hoopla of its mass spectacles such as firework displays, light shows, and parades. We happened to be in the backstage area just as the parade down Main Street was coming to an end. Elaborate floats and costumed characters descended a ramp behind Cinderella's Castle and began to disassemble before our eyes. The floats were alive with big-headed characters, clambering off the superstructures and out of their heavy, perspiration-drenched costumes. Several "beheaded" characters revealed stocky young men gulping down Gatorade. They walked toward our group, bloated Donald and bandy-legged Chip from the neck down, carrying their huge costume heads, while their real heads emerged pea-sized and aberrantly human.

We had been warned *not* to take pictures during the backstage tour, but one of our group, apparently carried away by the spectacle, could not resist. She managed to shoot a couple of photos of the disassembled characters before being approached by one of the tour guides. As if caught in a spy movie, the would-be photographer pried open her camera and ripped out the whole roll of film. The entire tour group stood in stunned amazement; not, I think, at the immediate presence of surveillance, but at the woman's dramatic response. In a situation where control is so omnipresent and conformity with control is taken for granted, any sudden gesture or dramatic response is a surprise.

At the close of the tour, my companion and I lingered behind the rest of the group to talk with our tour guides. As a professional photographer, my companion wanted to know if there is a "normal" procedure for disarming behind-the-scenes photographic spies. The guide explained that the prescribed practice is to impound the camera, process the film, remove the illicit photos, and return the camera, remaining photos, and complimentary film to the perpetrator. When questioned further, the guide went on to elaborate the Disney rationale for control over the image: the "magic" would be broken if photos of disassembled characters circulated in the public sphere; children might suffer irreparable psychic trauma at the sight of a "beheaded" Mickey; Disney exercises control over the image to safeguard childhood fantasies.

What Disney employees refer to as the "magic" of Disney World has actually to do with the ability to produce fetishized consumptions. The unbroken seamlessness of Disney World, its totality as a consumable artifact, cannot tolerate the revelation of the real work that produces the commodity. There would be no magic if the public should see the entire cast of magicians in various stages of disassembly and fatigue. That selected individuals are permitted to witness the backstage labor facilitates the word-of-mouth affirmation of the tremendous organizational feat that produces Disney World. The interdiction against photography eliminates the possibility of discontinuity at the level of image. There are no images to compete with the copyright-perfect onstage images displayed for public consumption. It's not accidental that our tour guide underscored the fact that Disney costumes are tightly controlled. The character costumes are made at only one production site and this site supplies the costumes used at Tokyo's Disneyland and EuroDisney. There can be no culturally influenced variations on the Disney models. Control over the image ensures the replication of Disney worldwide. The prohibition against photographing disassembled characters is motivated by the same phobia of industrial espionage that runs rampant throughout the high-tech information industry. The woman in our tour group who ripped open her camera and destroyed her film may not have been wrong in acting out a spy melodrama. Her photos of the disassembled costumes might have revealed the manner of their production—rendering them accessible to non-Disney replication. At Disney World, the magic that resides in the integrity of childhood fantasy is inextricably linked to the fetishism of the commodity and the absolute control over private property as it is registered in the copyrighted image.

As I see it, the individual's right to imagine and to give expression to unique ways of seeing is at stake in struggles against private property. Mickey Mouse, notwithstanding his corporate copyright, exists in our common culture. He is the site for the enactment of childhood wishes and fantasies, for early conceptualizations and renderings of the body, a being who can be imagined as both self and other. If culture is held as private property, then there can be only one correct version of Mickey Mouse, whose logo-like image is the cancellation of creativity. But the multiplicity of quirky versions of Mickey Mouse that children draw can stand as a graphic question to us as adults: Who, indeed, owns Mickey Mouse?

What most distinguishes Disney World from any other amusement park is the way its spatial organization, defined by autonomous "worlds" and wholly themed environments, combines with the homogeneity of its visitors (predominantly white, middle-class families) to produce a sense of community. While Disney World includes an underlying utopian impulse, this is articulated with nostalgia for a small-town, small-business America (Main Street, U.S.A.), and the fantasy of a controllable corporatist world (EPCOT). The illusion of community is enhanced by the longing for community that many visitors bring to the park, which they may feel is unavailable to them in their own careers, daily lives, and neighborhoods, thanks in large part to the systematic erosion of the public sector throughout the Reagan and Bush administrations. In the last decade the inroads of private, for-profit enterprise in areas previously defined by public control, and the hostile aggression of tax backlash coupled with "me first" attitudes have largely defeated the possibility of community in our homes and cities.

Whenever I visit Disney World, I invariably overhear other visitors making comparisons between Disney World and their home towns. They stare out over EPCOT's lake and wonder why developers back home don't produce similar aesthetic spectacles. They talk about botched, abandoned, and misconceived development projects that have wrecked their local landscapes. Others see Disney World as an oasis of social tranquility and security in comparison to their patrolled, but nonetheless deteriorating, maybe even perilous neighborhoods. A recent essay in *Time* captured some of these sentiments: "Do you see anybody [at Disney World] lying on the street or begging for money? Do you see anyone jumping on your car and wanting to clean your windshield?—and when you say no, they get abusive?"[3]

Comments such as these do more than betray the class anxiety of the middle strata. They poignantly express the inability of this group to make distinctions between what necessarily constitutes the public and the private sectors. Do visitors forget that they pay a daily use fee (upwards of $150 for a four-day stay) just to be a citizen of Disney World (not to mention the $100 per night hotel bill)? Maybe so—and maybe it's precisely *forgetting* that visitors pay for.

If there is any distinction to be made between Disney World and our local shopping malls, it would have to do with Disney's successful exclusion of all factors that might put the lie to its uniform social fabric. The occasional Hispanic mother who arrives with extended family and illegal bologna sandwiches is an anomaly. So too is the first-generation Cubana who buys a year-round pass to Disney's nightspot, Pleasure Island, in hopes of meeting a rich and marriageable British tourist. These women testify to the presence of Orlando, Disney World's marginalized "Sister City," whose overflowing cheap labor force and overcrowded and underfunded public institutions are the unseen real world upon which Disney's world depends.

Notes

1. Scott Bukatman, "There's Always Tomorrowland: Disney and the Hypercinematic Experience," *October* 57 (Summer 1991): 55–78.
2. Michael Sorkin, "See You in Disneyland," *Design Quarterly* (Winter 1992): 5–13.
3. "Fantasy's Reality," *Time,* 27 May 1991, 54.

Questions for Discussion

1. What do you think of when you hear the words "Disneyland" or "Disney World"? Look again at the way Susan Willis describes Disney World. How would your own description differ from hers? What is your response to her characterization of Disney World?
2. Consider Willis's distinction between "amusement" and "play." Then characterize your own recreational behavior: is it amusement or play?
3. "Just imagine," Willis teases, "the chaos, a park-wide short circuit, that the mixing of themed ingredients might produce." Take Willis up on her dare. Imagine a Disney World or Disneyland in which the Sorcerer's Apprentice *does* find his way into the Wild West or Indiana Jones *does* find himself in Davy Crockett's world or Snow White *does* walk arm-in-arm with an astronaut. What would such a theme park, such a world, be like?
4. Willis contends that "As we buy, wear, and eat logos, we become the henchmen and admen of the corporations, defining ourselves with respect to the social standing of the various corporations." What logos

do you "buy, wear, and eat"? What does that tell people about you? About your relationship to consumer and corporate culture?
5. Disney World is, Willis tells us, a place for the family, a place where people outside the family unit—single people or people traveling alone, for instance—might feel uncomfortable. In your experience and observation, how does Disney World (or another theme park) encourage people—parents, young children, even teenagers—to remain in their family groups? Are there other settings that, through their physical layout, the consumer products they sell, or their advertising, make similar assumptions about the family and its values?
6. Elsewhere in *Inside the Mouse,* Willis argues that the eternal sunshine that is supposedly part of the Florida and California landscapes made those states especially appropriate locations for the two Disney utopias. But other theme parks thrive in less sun-filled areas of the country. How are those theme parks less utopian than the two worlds of Disney?

Questions for Research and Writing

1. Earlier in *Inside the Mouse,* Willis says that her students have had difficulty answering her request that they "name the public places or publicly defined activities that had shaped their daily lives," they had difficulty finding an answer. Ask a similar question of ten or fifteen of your peers. How much have publicly funded places and activities influenced their lives? What part have privately funded, corporate places and activities played in their lives? Do they see a danger in what Willis calls the growing privatization?
2. Willis contends that intimacy and imaginative play are rare in Disneyland and Disney World. Observe the behavior of people in several places where crowds gather. How do those places encourage or discourage intimacy and imaginative play?
3. Consider the concept of a "Kodak Picture Spot," a place where perfect photo opportunities are guaranteed and where families memorialize not so much their memories but the fact that they have spent their money well. With this concept in mind, look through your own photo albums and analyze the kinds of pictures you, your friends, and your family have taken. Talk, too, to others who make picture taking part of any trip. What are their reasons for taking pictures? What are yours? What kinds of events and scenes are you most likely to photograph?
4. Willis says that Disney World is largely a middle-class white person's world. To test this hypothesis, survey people of different ethnic, cultural, and socioeconomic groups. Do social class, ethnicity, and cultural background influence one's experience in and response to Disney World or Disneyland? Does one's political ideology influence the experience?

5. Elsewhere in *Inside the Mouse,* Willis writes that "Disney tends to redefine and remarket itself every five or ten years." Examine five or ten years of Disney history—the films Disney and its subsidiaries produce, the products Disney markets, and the changes Disney makes to Disney World and Disneyland. Do you notice the redefinition and remarketing upon which Willis comments? If you do detect a redefinition, what changes in image or philosophy does that redefinition reflect?

WORK—PAST, PRESENT, AND FUTURE

Herbert Applebaum

> *In the following selection, which concludes his book* The Concept of Work: Ancient, Medieval, and Modern *(1992), Herbert Applebaum, who has worked in the construction industry and edited scholarly texts on work, gives us a brief history of how work has been viewed over the centuries. During some periods of world history, the farmer performed the most respected work, for he brought forth life (and thus emulated God) and made himself strong for the time when he might need to offer himself in military service to protect his city and his own land. In other eras, the artisan earned the most respect, using his skills to craft a product of beauty or utility. Today, Applebaum asks us to consider, whom do we most admire? Who is it that most embodies our sense of what work should be? As he looks at the changing attitudes toward work, Applebaum invites us to think about what we value and look for in the workplace. As you read, ask yourself how your views of work compare to those of your predecessors. Does work represent for you primarily a means toward an income? A means of gaining respect or establishing your identity? A chance to contribute to today's society and the future? In comparing your own attitudes toward work to those of earlier times, ask yourself what you've lost or gained.*

Those who worked through the ages have left us the results of their work, not their conceptualizations. A Hesiod and his plow, a Sturt and his wheelwright shop (1974), a Benjamin Franklin and his printing shop were rare and exceptional. It is only in the recent period—and they are still the exception—that we have had workers writing about their work and their thoughts in the form of full participant ethnographies. Mostly, work has been analyzed from outside the workplace and conceptualized by philosophers and social thinkers, whether sympathetic or otherwise.

Starting with Homeric society, we find the unusual phenomena of nobles and aristocrats working with their hands. Odysseus challenges the suitors to a plowing contest, builds his own bed chamber, and constructs a raft to carry him home. Even the great Achilles and the noble Hector perform work, as do the deities, including Athena herself and Hephaistos. Under such social conditions, work is esteemed even if commoners are not. Later, the work ethic is expressed with great poetic and religious force by Hesiod. These early concepts and reflections of work relate to small-scale cultures based on family, religion, and decentralized social and political authority.

In the fifth and fourth centuries, and with the development of centralized city-states, the concept of work underwent fundamental changes with a developed division of labor, specialization of trades, and a widespread use of slavery. These changes are discussed in Plato's *Republic,* (1968: 369a–1373b) in which he explains that the basis on which the city-state is created is the division of labor and the exchange of products. At the same time an ideology developed of aristocratic disdain for engaging in work and the necessity for the abstention from work as the precondition for a good life, with the *good life* defined as the life of leisure to develop mind and body. This was Aristotle's concept which he articulated for the rest of the aristocracy (Politics 1946, 133:66–1334a). There was no contempt for work that was natural, and farming was considered to be natural in that while the farmer grew his own products for his own consumption, there was no exchange. Socrates thought that farmers made the best citizens and soldiers since their training predisposed them for fighting, and that, as owners of land, they would defend the city. There was contempt for all those who worked for others, wageworkers as well as slaves, for those persons were not free. There was also contempt for the manual trades. Socrates said that such trades ruined the bodies by sitting indoors in workshops or by the fire for metallurgy. For example, Hephaistos—the god who worked, the god of metallurgy—is significantly deformed and crippled.

But this is not the whole story. Burford, studying the craftsmen of Greece and Rome, found much objective evidence of self-pride of craftsmen, including tombstones, which announced with pride their occupations as miner, cobbler, baker, carpenter, or mason. Craftsmen had their collegia in Rome, and in Greece craftsmen had their own deity, Athena. Many objects of craft, particularly pottery, were also signed by potters and painters.

Roman society reflected similar patterns to those of Greece. Cincinnatus, the Roman farmer/general, was the ideal hero—the farmer who worked on the land, who was called to fight for the city, and, when his military duties were done, returned to work his farm with his own hands. Again, this is the ideal. Virgil extolled the farmer, but Cato saw farming as the exploitation of slaves for the glory and power of the wealthy landowner. Burford found Roman craftsmen even more conscious of their own self-respect than the Greeks. They formed *collegia,* so powerful at times that they were outlawed by Augustus. Roman craftsmen also left monuments to themselves, on which they identified their trades and signed their works. Still, the attitude of the powerful and wealthy, as it has always been the case, was prejudicial against the manual trades and work in general. In Roman culture, it was expressed clearly by Cicero in *De Officiis,* (Book I:XLII.150–151) where he lists the honorable professions and considered working for others to be a form of slavery.

Hebrew and Christian ideology introduced a new element into the concept of work. God was portrayed as a worker, laboring six days to make the world and resting on the seventh from his labors. What could be clearer to show work as divinity? But work was also associated with sin when

Adam was punished and had to earn his living by the sweat of his brow. Work was also treated by Christians and Jews as an honorable activity against the sin of idleness and sloth. Saint Paul said that he who does not work neither shall he eat. Saint Augustine and Saint Benedict founded the monastic movement on the principle and the morality of work as means to combat sin, and work as honorable in the image of God, the master craftsman and architect of the world. There is an entire literature presenting the thesis that the monastic movement and its ideology have provided the basis for the positive evaluation of work in Western society (Ovitt 1987; Benz 1966; Mumford 1967–1970; White 1940).

During the Middle Ages, medieval civilization was founded on an agricultural economy, and its society was composed, for the most part, of small, local, fairly self-sufficient communities. Agricultural work was valued and was based on a protective system of dependency and obligation. Service and work was returned for protection. The concept of the three orders—namely, *orators* (clergy), *bellatores* (warriors/nobles), and *laboratores* (workers)—was promulgated by bishops such as Adelbero and Gerard. In general, the three orders were those who prayed, those who fought and those who worked. The *laboratores* were the lowest order on the social scale, but they were accorded a place in society, and the Church did what it could, although unsuccessfully, to protect them through the Peace of God and other means. The respect for work was nowhere more eloquently presented than in the capitulary of Charlemagne, De Villis (1936). However, both the Church and the nobility put into place a system of management of work which made the peasants and serfs subordinate to the interests of the Church, the manor and the developing state.

The network of obligations, rights and protections were such as to stress, not zeal or initiative, but the simple performance of work necessary to ensure the survival of the family and as a tax due to the lord or the Church. There was little point in working harder or more productively since the market was rudimentary and there was nothing one could do with a surplus. Nature was the taskmaster on the land, compelling those who would wrest a living from the earth to adhere to the rhythms and cycles of the seasons.

As did the Bishops, Thomas Aquinas, the greatest of the Christian philosophers, constructed a conception of the Christian universe based on human law wedded to divine law. Following Aristotle, Aquinas saw society as based on a mutual exchange of services for the sake of the good life. The farmer and the artisan supplied the material goods of life, the priests provided prayer and moral leadership, and the nobility provided protection. Human society was seen by Aquinas as governed by the same principles of reason and order that permeated the whole universe. This participation in the eternal law by rational creatures was natural law. Human law derived from eternal law and all callings, that of the ruler as well as that of the worker, was needed to maintain the common good. Aquinas regarded

Christian society as an interdependent and interlocking community, a rational scheme of God, nature, and man within civil authority that was resistant to change, and existed in a closed system of eternal, stable equilibrium.

It was mainly in the cities where change took place and where manual work—other than farm work—received its recognition through the guilds. To go to the city made one free. Cities received charters from the state or the Church and set up communes. The guilds were powerful forces in the early cities, providing forces for military duty, civic projects, and goods for the local market. The guilds created the handicraft tradition, establishing respect for masters and its system of apprenticeships and journeymen. While they later became constraints on expansion and industrial development, during their period of ascendancy, guilds brought respect for the manual trades and established a tradition of quality and standards of workmanship which is still held up as an ideal. The apprenticeship system is still used in skilled trades in printing, construction, and many of the manual arts. We also still revere the handicraft tradition whereby the worker has control over his tools and materials, creating his own product in an atmosphere of joy and independence.

With Luther and Calvin, we have the beginnings of the modern work ethic, starting with the concept of *calling* as a Christian duty, and the admonition to be successful in commercial enterprise, something which was looked down upon in the ancient and medieval world. As with many other great books, Weber's *Protestant Ethic and the Spirit of Capitalism* (1950) has been misinterpreted to read that his thesis established a causal relationship between Protestantism and capitalism. The spirit of capitalism, according to Weber, as well as others such as Tawney, which was upheld by Protestantism, viewed economic acquisition as an end in itself, not subordinated to man as the means for the satisfaction of his material needs. It was Calvin, even more than Luther, who supplied the interpretation of a calling into a Protestant ethic of work. Weber singles out Puritanism and Richard Baxter as exemplars of this new ethic, which emphasized work and gave religious sanction to the pursuit of profit. At the same time, it discouraged the enjoyment of wealth and preached the limitation of consumption. This, combined with the acquisitive activity, resulted in savings and the accumulation of capital. Weber also ascribed to the Puritan outlook the development of a rational bourgeois outlook.

The new Protestant ethic took two directions. One was the direction of hard work and business enterprise, stressing thrift and business success. The other was the direction of radical ideology, such as that of the levellers and diggers, who also stressed the need to work hard, but wanted to bring respect for the working man, common ownership of land, and redistribution of goods and services so that none would suffer from want. The one direction led to the success of capitalism and became the more dominant, while the other laid some of the seeds for a socialist outlook (Anthony 1977, 49).

The seventeenth century witnesses the appearance of the English Enlightenment, represented by Bacon, Hobbes, and Locke. Francis Bacon starts a new thrust in human knowledge and development with his insistence that human knowledge be based on scientific methods (1967). He was followed by Hobbesian materialism (1939) and Locke's theory of human understanding based on perceptions of the objective world (1939). Locke becomes important for the concept of work with his theory that labor is the basis for property, and which anticipates Smith's labor theory of value (1967).

The eighteenth century is the century of the French Enlightenment—the century of Diderot, Rousseau, and Voltaire. Diderot championed the mechanical arts, wishing to wed them to science and viewing the manual worker as having something to contribute to the knowledge of the material world (1953). Voltaire concluded his great satire, *Candide,* with the philosophy that work in one's own garden was the ultimate answer to man's search for meaning in life (1959). Ferney was Voltaire's practical expression of this philosophy, in which he created a villager of watchmakers, built decent housing for workmen, and created a model community. Rousseau had a first-hand taste of work, being apprenticed to an engraver at the age of twelve. He never lost his respect for the skilled crafts, and, in his theory of education embodied in his book, *Emile,* he advocated the teaching of a skilled trade for all youngsters, in addition to other subjects (1953). An American, Benjamin Franklin, was also a man of the Enlightenment, who was greatly influenced by both the English and French Enlightenment thinking. Franklin was a worker/printer, an entrepreneur, scientist, public servant, political figure, and a signer and framer of the American Declaration of Independence. Franklin was a member of both the British and French Academies of Science. All his life, particularly in his *Poor Richard's Almanac,* he preached the value and dignity of work (1987:1181–1304). He was singled out by both Weber and Marx as a prime representative and teacher of the work ethic.

In 1776, Adam Smith, professor of Moral Philosophy at Glasgow University, published his great work, *Wealth of Nations*. In that seminal study—which many regard as the firm foundations for the science of economics—Smith developed a labor theory of value. Smith also clearly considered that the people who perform productive work, rather than gold, are the chief foundation for any society. Smith also saw the division of labor as the key to increased productivity. In addition, the division of labor, with its consequent specialization and reduction of skills to simple tasks, laid the basis for the introduction of machinery to the production process, which further led to the enormous increase in the productivity of labor. Smith believed in a society based on self-interest (1937:14) and minimum government interference in economic affairs, but he was not an apologist for manufacturers and merchants, reserving some of his most biting irony for this class of people. He was far in advance of his time in his belief that the difference between the common working man and the philosopher was more a matter of habit, custom, and education than it was from nature or heredity (1937:15).

With the nineteenth century—and following Adam Smith's principle that society works best through everyone following their own self-interests by rational calculation, along with the developing science and technology based on quantification—a new set of values and ethics was put into place. It treated all matters, including individuals, in terms of quantification, profit, and loss. The utilitarian principle of liberals such as Jeremy Bentham, of the greatest good for the greatest number, was a matter of summing up figures (Bentham 1948:2). It is true that a number of reforms were put into place which advanced the cause of democratic principles, but the calculating ethos of profit and loss was rapidly replacing the traditional, religious principles of community, family, and individuals as ends in themselves. Work and workers were now a means to an end. The change was not an easy one, and it took a long time to adapt the work force to the factory system, the discipline of time, and the necessities of the wage system and the market. The handicrafts persisted throughout the nineteenth century, but were ultimately and inevitably replaced by the machine which was largely tended by unskilled hands.

Marx established work as being of prime importance, philosophically asserting that man created his world and, therefore, himself through his work. Work was elevated by Marx to a position of absolute importance. As a result of this elevation, the worker was accorded dignity, as man's essential activity is his work. For Marx, production is the fundamental foundation of society—along with its laws and institutions—and work is of fundamental importance in the whole historical process.

Marx argues that the worker has become alienated from his work because industrial society—and capitalism in particular—has dehumanized his relationship to work (1844). Marx argues—as others, including Pope John Paul II, did after him—that the worker has become an object of work, an instrumental part of the work process, which has led to his/her alienation. This alienation results from the rational, calculating, self-interested, and totally economic motives associated not only with work, but with almost all aspects of industrial cultures. Alienation in work represents the triumph of material, calculable, and self-interested values in industrial society (1971).

Marx also saw the increasing domination of machinery, technology, and social knowledge over living labor. This was particularly expressed in the *Grundrisse* (1971:284–285). He predicted an enormous increase in the productivity of capital through the increased use of automatic machinery and a virtual disappearance of the living portion of the work process—that of the worker. For Marx, the solution to the problem of alienated labor, which he saw as a necessary and inevitable part of capitalist and industrial work, was to reduce the necessary portion of the labor process—namely that which was necessary to sustain all workers—and to increase the free time or leisure portion of one's life. Thus, there is the paradox that the ideology of work, so necessary for the enlarged productivity of industrial society, leads to an ideology in which work ceases to be the central interest in life. Thus, Marx envisioned a society in which general production would be so high and so regulated that one could do one thing today and another thing tomorrow. In addition, one could hunt in the morning, fish in the afternoon, rear cattle in the evening, and criticize after dinner (1959, 254). If there is one aspect of Marx's theories which has proven to be true, it is that alienation from work and the problem of motivation of work have been a constant problem in industrial society, and continues to be a matter of great concern today to those who continue to worry about the decline of the "work ethic."

The nineteenth century was the century when the ideology of the work ethic was fostered by religious, social, and political leaders, as well as the leaders of industry and commerce. But it was also a century during which handicrafts were still strong—and even predominated—in certain industries. Many of the workers in the skilled trades resisted the onslaught of industrialized, and factory and machine technology, while owners of business and industry complained about the lack of discipline among their employees.

By the beginning of the twentieth century, it was evident that the management of the industrial working class was a problem if work was to be properly organized to fit the needs of the expanding industrial society. Taylorism and scientific management was one answer from the human side of the equation, and assembly-line and continuous-process production was the answer from the technology side (Taylor 1947). Taylorism led to the deskilling of the workers and reduction of work tasks to simple, repetitive, and monotonous tasks that took the joy out of work, as de Man saw it.

Other social thinkers noted the growing problem of the work ethic. Veblen saw a contradiction between the instinct of workmanship and the goals of business enterprise (1914), as well as between the desires of owners for profit and the outlook of engineers for rational organization of work (1983). Later thinkers, such as Hannah Arendt, (1958) saw the contradictions between work as a creative and satisfying process, and labor which was nothing more than an instrumental activity. Pope John Paul II noted that workers had become the objects of what they produced rather than the subjects.

The scientific management movement of the early twentieth century was followed by the Human Relations movement in industry. The Human Relations movement tried to address some of the more subtle aspects of the management of work, such as the communal control exercised by workers in opposition to the goals of management (Roethlisberger & Dickson 1939). Burawoy and Roy found workers struggling to maintain some autonomy over their work, but fighting a losing battle (1979). Studs Terkel in his book *Working* (1972), and the Health, Education & Welfare Dept.

report on *Work in America* (O'Toole 1975), found widespread dissatisfaction with work in industrial society. The basic dimension of work in the twentieth century is that it is seen as an instrumental activity, as a means for acquiring income for subsistence and consumption, and that there is little or no satisfaction or meaning to be found in the workplace. Whereas, in the nineteenth century, work was largely seen as central to the lives of individuals and families, this no longer seems to be true, or at least this attitude is being questioned. There is debate over whether the educational system should prepare people for work, or for life. There are attempts to introduce new methods in the factory, such as quality circles and autonomous work teams, to increase work satisfaction, along with productivity. There is debate over whether automation will increase or decrease work skills. And there is the continuing problem in the twentieth century of the management of work, as manufacturing, construction, and blue-collar sectors of industrial society decrease in favor of increases in service, financial, retail, government, and leisure and play sectors. Attempts by governments to integrate labor through the government—such as in the Soviet Union and Eastern communist countries and others, including Fascist Germany—have proved to be failures. Thus, the question of the meaning of work and the management of work continues to be a central concern for industrial cultures.

Whether work has the same central meaning to people's lives as in the past, it is, nevertheless, still true that work is probably the most important single factor in status and self-respect for the individual. The kind of work one performs, one's occupation, and one's employer are all indicators of the type of power and income which one can command and, with that, the type of consumption goods one can command. Work is still a major arena for social interaction, and, therefore, for social prestige and power—all of which affect one's self-esteem. Whether people find satisfaction in the work they perform, many still enjoy the social contacts at work. For some occupations, they constitute the most important contacts, affecting out-of-work friendships as well as friendships on the job. Many trade, professional, technical, and middle managerial jobs carry life-long interests and contacts associated with the type of work performed. Even when people have boring and unsatisfying jobs, there is still attachment to organizations and institutions. As Abbott has suggested, organization attachments are replacing trade attachments, so that one associates his future and interests, not with other auto workers, for example, but with the particular automobile company for which he works (1989). This is less true for professionals, but, even with professionals, there is attachment to the firm or institution. Finding meaning in work and believing that work constitutes meaning in life may not have the same hold on people that it did in the nineteenth century, but it still plays a central role in determining one's station in life, as well as the possibilities for the quality of one's own life and that of one's family and offspring.

In order to get people to work with some degree of effort, intelligence, skill, and motivation, some type of ideology is necessary for people to justify to themselves that what they are doing is the right thing. If not, then the work force will be passive, obstructive, nonproductive, and cynical about the goals of their work and the organizations that employ them. Basically, the dominant culture of industrial societies continues to be (1) economic rationality—the calculated utility of choices, money as the measure of value and maximizing behavior in economics; (2) the measurement of the success of nations as growth in the gross national product; and (3) the necessity of technological progress. This ideology has historically been strongest among those who manage and own the industrial organizations which employ the work force. There are some indications that this dedication has waned in recent decades (Anthony 1977, 291–300). If this is true then the modern ideology of work faces serious problems because, as the group finding the greatest challenges and satisfactions in work, managers and professionals have been especially dedicated to their work.

The twentieth century has witnessed enormous increases in industrial productivity and in the standard of living for a majority of populations in industrial society, in spite of continuing sectors of poverty in these countries. With increases in the standard of living, consumerism, and leisure activities, the work ethic must compete with the ethic of the quality of life based on the release from work. The Human Relations movement of the 1930s and 1940s and the Quality of Work movements in recent times have not resulted in any tangible results to date with regard to increasing the dedication to work. Mainly it has been directed to blue-collar and white-collar jobs, in which absenteeism, poor discipline, and low productivity reflect the lack of success in instilling a strong work ethic among industrial occupations. The service industries, which absorb a large number of the decreasing jobs in industry and office sectors, are plagued by dead-end jobs and work characterized by rote and void of meaning or even utility.

One of the major problems facing industrialized nations—along with pollution, environmental protection, political repression, and wars—is the need to find work for people being replaced by new, high technologies so as to prevent massive amounts of unemployed and unemployable people. If only 25 percent of our work force now produces all of our material needs, it is conceivable that, by 2010, only 10 percent of our work force will be needed to create our material wealth because of continuing use of microprocessors, computers, automation and robots.

What will we do with the rest of the population? What types of choices will be made with regard to the quality of life—more work or more leisure? How will we define work under these new conditions? Can a society be created which is based on leisure time rather than work time? How will the resources of industrial society be distributed since a small elite of 10 percent is now producing all of its material wealth? And how will all the other institutions of society be affected—including education, health, politics, government, and private enterprises?

A number of proposals have been made based on the industrial society achieving a level of output and productivity that would permit a drastic reduction of the workyear, the workweek, and the workday. Such proposals are usually linked with some form of guaranteed income for everyone, whether they work or not. Tom Stonier argues that we can reduce the work week so as to become an education-oriented society (1989). He would have industrial societies double and triple their education budgets, and to, eventually, have 50 percent of the work force employed in education. Gorz talks about redefining work, reducing it to one thousand hours per year for paid work, and then developing a series of institutions to permit people to make free choices whether to work for more income, or engage in leisure and self-fulfilling activities (1982, 1985, 1986).

Since everyone would be guaranteed the necessities of life people would have such choices. This type of society was envisioned by Karl Marx, Charles Fourier, Henri Saint-Simon, and William Morris (1946), who sought to have society develop to the point where necessity gave way to freedom, as well as where work became the precondition for leisure and could be redefined within the framework of the quality of life based on other than economic necessity.

It is as if all the past history of work was the necessary part associated with providing for the necessary sustenance of life, and that we are now approaching the juncture of history at which the necessary part of life can give way to the start of true human freedom and human choice based on self-fulfillment of one's total human capabilities. Thus, we come full circle from Aristotle's concept of the good life as the leisured life (1946), based on the active development of the total human being, to the modern theories of people, such as Stonier (1989) and Gorz (1985) who have a similar view. The big difference is that Aristotle's vision was based on a small elite minority, while the modern theorists see a restructuring of society based on the free choice of work and being available to the mass of citizenry. Whether this vision is a realistic goal or realizable in the future will depend on political and social choices, and the development of a new set of values in modern, industrial cultures.

Concluding with a positive summarization of the concept of work, we can say that, regardless of how work has been conceptualized in the past, or, how it is viewed in the present, work has to be performed. Our man-made environment, our institutions, and our very survival as a species is based on the need to work, regardless of how work may be conceptualized or regardless of whether the work ethic is strong or even accepted.

Work is a cooperative effort of mankind, requiring some degree of voluntary cooperation among those who work, and between those who work and those who supervise work. Work requires some degree of effort, skill, care, dexterity, mental application, and physical energy requiring commitment to the object of work, no matter how minimal. Mankind's need to cooperate, no matter what type of society, gives legitimacy to the concept of work. For most people, work is necessary for their self-respect and their psychological well-being. Work is thought of as being necessary for social progress and the quality of life, even if it is seen only as an instrumental and necessary activity serving as the precondition for other pursuits. Work can be satisfying, especially for those who can combine mental and manual work, such as craftworkers and professionals; skilled, scientific, and technical workers; and managers and supervisors. Even manual workers can gain satisfaction from the pure physical pleasure of working hard and well at a task. All people who work can also derive pleasure from social relationships in the work place and gaining the respect of their coworkers.

There is no simple relationship between work and satisfaction in life, nor between work and self-fulfillment. The subject of work is complex, because work is intertwined with all aspects of human existence. Work is associated with maturity, discipline, and all the moral values of societies, as well as with its economic and political institutions.

If the work ethic has been recently challenged, it does not mean that work is no longer important. We have now reached the stage where people need to know what they should be working for rather than just working. The advance of technology now provides industrial cultures with the possibilities of choice—choice of work and choice of what useful things to make, so as to restore work to its human dimensions and meanings.

References

Abbott, Andrew (1989). "The New Occupational Structure." *Work and Occupations* 16:3, August: 273–291.

Anthony, P. D. (1977). *The Ideology of Work*. London: Tavistock Publications.

Arendt, Hannah (1958). *The Human Condition*. Chicago: University of Chicago Press.

Aristotle (1946). *The Politics,* translated by Ernest Barker. New York: Oxford University Press.

Bacon, Francis (1967). *Novum Organum*. Modern Library Edition. New York: Random House.

Baxter, Richard (1925) (1673). *Chapters from a Christian Directory,* edited by Jeanette Tawney. London: G. Bell & Sons.

Bentham, Jeremy (1948). *An Introduction to the Principles of Morals and Legislation*. New York: Hafner Publishing.

Benz, Ernst (1966). *Evolution and Christian Hope: Man's Concept of the Future from the Early Fathers to Teilhard de Chardin*. Garden City, N.Y.: Doubleday.

Burawoy, Michael (1979). *Manufacturing Consent*. Chicago: University of Chicago Press.

Burford, Allison (1972). Craftsman in Greek and Roman Society. Ithaca, N.Y.: Cornell University Press.

Calvin, John (1964). *A Compend of the Institutes of the Christian Religion,* edited by Hugh T. Kerr. Philadelphia: The Westminster Press.

Cato, Marcus Porcius. (1936) *On Agriculture*. Loeb Library Edition, translated by William D. Hooper, revised by Harrison Boyd. London: William Heinemann, Ltd.

Charlemagne (1936). "De Villis." In *A Source Book for Medieval Economic History*, edited by R. Cave and H. H. Coulson. New York: Bruce Publishing Co.

Cicero (1938). *De Officiis*. Loeb Library Edition, translated by Walter Miller. London: William Heinemann, Ltd.

de Man, Henri 1929. *Joy in Work*, translated by Eden Paul and Cedar Paul. London: George Allen & Unwin.

Diderot, Denis (1953) (1751–1765). "Article on Art." *The Encyclopaedia*. In *French Thought in the Eighteenth Century*, edited by Romain Rolland, Andre Maurois, and Edouard Herriot. London: Cassell & Co., Ltd.

Fourier, Charles (1971). *Harmonian Man: Selected Writings of Charles Fourier*, edited with an introduction by Mark Posten, translated by Susan Hanson. Garden City, N.Y.: Doubleday & Co.

Franklin, Benjamin (1987). *Writings*. New York: The Library of America.

Gorz, Andre (1982). *Farewell to the Working Class*. London: Pluto Press.

——— (1985). *Paths to Paradise: On the Liberation from Work*. Boston: South End Press.

——— (1986). "The Socialism of Tomorrow." In *Telos* 67, Spring: 199–205.

Hobbes, Thomas (1939). *Leviathan*. Modern Library Edition. New York: Random House.

Locke, John (1939) (1690). "An Essay Concerning Human Understanding." In *The English Philosophers from Bacon to Mill*. Modern Library Edition. New York: Random House.

——— (1967) (1690). *Two Treatises of Government*. Cambridge: Cambridge University Press. Introduction and Analysis by Peter Laslett.

Marx, Karl (1844). "The Economic and Philosophical Manuscripts." In *Karl Marx, The Essential Writings*, edited by Frederic L. Bender. Boulder, Colo.: Westview Press.

——— (1971). *The Grundrisse*, translated by David McLellan. New York: Harper & Row.

Marx, Karl, and Friedrich Engels (1959). *Basic Writings*, edited by Lewis S. Feuer. Garden City, N.Y.: Doubleday and Co.

Morris, William (1946). Edited by G. D. H. Cole. London: Nonesuch Press.

Mumford, Lewis (1967–1970). *The Myth of the Machine*. Two volumes. New York: Harcourt, Brace and World.

O'Toole, James (1975). *Work in America. Report of a Special Task Force to the Secretary of Health, Education and Welfare*. Cambridge, Mass.: Massachusetts Institute of Technology Press.

Ovitt, George, Jr. (1987). *The Restoration of Perfection, Labor and Technology in Medieval Culture*. New Brunswick: Rutgers University Press.

Plato (1968). *The Republic*, translated with notes and interpretive essay by Allan Bloom. New York: Basic Books, Inc.

Pope John Paul II (1982). "Laborem Exercens." In *The Priority of Labor*, edited by Gregory Baum. New York: Paulist Press.

Roethlisberger, F. J., and W. J. Dickson (1939). *Management and the Worker*. Cambridge, Mass.: Harvard University Press.

Rousseau, Jean-Jacques (1953) (1765). "Emile: ou De l'education." In *French Thought in the Eighteenth Century*, edited by Romain Rolland, Andre Maurois, and Edouard Herriot. London: Cassell & Co., Ltd.

Roy, Donald F. (1952.) "Quota Restricting and Goldbricking in a Machine Shop." In *American Journal of Sociology* 57, March: 427–442.

Saint-Simon, Henri 1975. *Selected Writings on Science, Industry and Social Orgainization,* edited by Keith Taylor. New York: Holme and Meyer Publishers, Inc.

St. Augustine 1950. *The City of God.* Modern Library Edition, translated by Marcus Dods. New York: Random House.

Smith, Adam (1937) (1776). *Wealth of Nations.* Modern Library Edition. New York: Random House.

——— (1961) (1776). *Wealth of Nations,* edited by Edwin Cannan. London: Methuen.

——— (1986). *The Theory of Moral Sentiments and the Wealth of Nations,* edited with an introduction by Robert L. Heilbroner, with the assistance of Laurence J. Malone. New York: W. W. Norton.

Stonier, Tom (1989). "Technological Change and the Future." In *Freedom and Constraint: The Paradoxes of Leisure,* edited by Fred Coalter. New York: Routledge.

Sturt, George (1974) (1923). *The Wheelwright's Shop.* Cambridge: Cambridge University Press.

Tawney, R. H. 1947. *Religion and the Rise of Capitalism.* New York: Penguin Books.

Taylor, Frederick W. (1947). *Scientific Management.* New York: Harper & Row.

Terkel, Studs (1972). *Working.* New York: Random House.

Veblen, Thorstein (1914). *The Instinct of Workmanship.* New York: The Macmillan Co.

——— (1983) (1921). *The Engineers and the Price System,* with an introduction by Daniel Bell. New Brunswick, N.J.: Transaction Books.

Virgil 1987. *The Georgics.* Penguin Classics Edition, translated by L. P. Wilkinson. New York: Viking/Penguin.

Voltaire, Francois Marie Arouet (1959). *Candide,* translated by Lowell Blair, with an appreciation by Andre Maurois. New York: Bantam Books.

——— (1953). "Voltaire." In *French Thought in the Eighteenth Century,* edited by Romain Rolland, Andre Maurois, and Edouard Herriot. London: Cassell & Co., Ltd.

Weber, Max (1950). *The Protestant Ethic and the Spirit of Capitalism,* translated by Talcott Parsons, with a foreword by R. H. Tawney. New York: Charles Scribner's Sons.

White, Lynn, Jr. (1940). "Technology and Invention in the Middle Ages." In *Speculum.* 15:141–159.

Questions for Discussion

1. Applebaum takes some of his examples from works considered more a part of literature than history (Homer's *Odyssey,* for example). How effective is the use of evidence from fictional works? What do works of contemporary American fiction, including television shows and films, tell you about our concepts of work?

2. Eighteenth-century economist Adam Smith believed that "the difference between the common working man and the philosopher was more a matter of habit, custom, and education than it was from nature or heredity." Do you agree that the common working man has the potential for more philosophical thought? What is the relationship between people's jobs and their willingness to think philosophically?

Questions for Research and Writing

1. In this selection, Applebaum gives us a brief history of the world's attitudes toward work. Virgil admired farmers; Cato held them in some

contempt. Consider a profession that has existed for at least 100 years, and examine the history of people's attitudes toward its practitioners, for example, doctors or dentists, bankers or money lenders, farmers, attorneys, or teachers. You might draw your evidence from historical documents, from literature, and, of course, from discussions with current practitioners and their clients.

2. As Appelbaum says, Karl Marx believed that the introduction of more and more machines into the workplace causes workers to feel alienated from their work and to lose their creativity and independence. Interview a worker whose job has been changed by the introduction of a machine (or machines). How has the machine's presence changed the worker's job? How has it changed the worker's attitude toward the job?

3. Applebaum envisions a future in which our standard of living, our desire for consumer goods, and our leisure time all continue to spiral upward. Recently, some economists—and some young Americans—have argued that the spiral has begun to reverse itself, and that, for the first time in U.S. history, young adults are likely to face a standard of living *lower* than that enjoyed by their parents. Do some research on the average salaries and on the costs of various commodities when your parents were your age. How do they compare to today's salaries and costs?

CROSSCURRENTS
Questions for Connecting the Readings in Chapter 3

1. In his brief history of work, Herbert Applebaum identifies a number of reasons for working and shows us how what we value about work has changed over the centuries. Look again at Reg Theriault's "Old Blue Collars, Young Blue Collars." How much do the workers whom Theriaut describes seem to subscribe to the modern concepts of work? In what ways do their attitudes and values reflect the attitudes and values of earlier societies?

2. Applebaum notes that there is some debate about whether education should prepare students for work or for life. On which side of the debate should the authors in chapter 2 find themselves? How would their proposed curricula prepare students for the worlds of work described in Applebaum's history and throughout this chapter?

3. Many of the authors in this chapter—Theriault, Applebaum, and Stanton Wheeler among them—consider the often problematic connection (or separation) between creativity, on the one hand, and work, on the other. In a debate about the relationship between work and creativity, how would each define the problem? What solutions would they propose?

4. Although the two authors have very different styles and methodologies, the title of Juliet Schor's book—*The Overworked American*—has a great

deal in common with the title of Theriault's book—*How to Tell When You're Tired: A Brief Examination of Work*. What viewpoints, if any, do the two authors share? What solutions to the problem of overwork would the two propose?

5. In "Double Lives" Wheeler accounts for the increased frequency of double lives by remarking that we spend less time at work than we used to and that the increased use of machines has freed us from hard physical labor. In "Time Squeeze," Schor argues that time-saving devices don't save us time for leisure. How would Schor and Wheeler respond to the distinction between "amusement" and "play" Susan Willis makes in "Public Use/Private State"? How might other authors in this chapter respond?

6. Compare the vision of "telework" presented in Merlisa Lawrence Corbett's article to the vision of "distance learning"—what might be called "telelearning"—presented in J. Wade Gilley's "The Distributed University" (chapter 2). How do you think the authors of the two pieces would respond to each other's arguments? Which of the two visions presented do you find more convincing? Why? Do the same impulses and motives drive the desire for telelearning and telework? To what extent do the different purposes and environments of the workplace and the college or university affect our response to the use of distance technology?

7. Like other uses of technology, telework (Corbett) and distance learning (Gilley) raise the issue of Americans' relationship with their machines. Imagine a conversation between Gilley, Corbett, Applebaum, and Schor. How would each define the relationship between people and their machines? What do they see as the consequences of that relationship in terms of our use of time, our attitudes toward our jobs, and our emotional lives?

8. Although both men and women feel the tensions between the obligations to the workplace and obligations to the family, many associate such tensions primarily with working women. For that reason, these tensions become the center of many "feminist" discussions. Look at Daphne Patai and Noretta Koertge's "Introduction to the World of Women's Studies" (chapter 2) and at Lotte Bailyn's "Two Women at Work" (chapter 3). To what extent do either Elizabeth Gray's or Nancy Wright's beliefs and behaviors seem similar to those of the feminists described by Patai and Koertge?

4

Media, Technology, and Literacy

The readings in this chapter all share a common concern: What does it mean to be "literate"? Earlier in our nation's history, literacy might have meant simply the ability to read and write. But, clearly, today's more complex world requires more sophisticated skills. One estimate suggests that 80 percent of all new jobs require more than a high school education, while 21 million American adults cannot read at the fourth-grade level. Given these startling statistics, what must our schools teach in order to ensure a qualified and competent work force?

As we discussed in chapter 1, it is not enough merely to read for information; people must be able to assess that information, judge its value, question its validity. Our sources of information have become much more diverse than they were even a generation ago. It is not sufficient to know how to read and analyze the written word alone; we must "read" messages in many media: photographs, films, videos, sound recordings, and radio transmissions. As students, workers, and citizens, we must understand the implications in our lives of all the new communications technologies, including computers, photocopy machines, fax machines, and electronic mail. Thus, we need to talk not just about literacy in the singular, but about the myriad "literacies" needed in a technological society: critical literacy, cultural literacy, media literacy, visual literacy, workplace literacy, computer literacy. Eventually, as Brazilian educator Paolo Freire has said, we need to be able "to read the world."

These new technologies have undoubtedly altered our sense of what it means to be literate. A three-year-old says he is "reading" when he pushes a blue button that activates a sound recording of the words on the blue page of his book. We know he isn't really reading—but why not? How is his experience of the book really different from our own? The buttons, with their embedded microchips, are a kind of code that the child uses to construct the message, just as an adult uses the words on the page to construct the message that the book conveys. The child's task is certainly easier than the adult's and requires less training, but does that alone make it inherently less valuable or less meaningful? In what ways does his "reading" produce less understanding of the text than our own reading would?

Computer technology is also transforming the traditional practices of printing and publishing. Some people have speculated that books as we know them may become obsolete. A reasonably sophisticated personal computer with a modem and the appropriate software allows access to millions of pages of published and unpublished information. Hundreds of volumes of great literature can be reduced to a slim, portable, key-word-searchable compact disc. Encyclopedias and other reference works are no longer just heavy, dusty books languishing on bookshelves, they have been transformed into interactive, multimedia texts that reproduce not just words but photos, sounds, even video clips, and have almost instantaneous cross-referencing capabilities. To disseminate our views on any topic, we no longer need to convince a publisher that our work merits the company's investment in time, energy, and money. Instead, we can learn a relatively simple computer language that allows us to publish any document on that part of the Information Superhighway known as the World Wide Web.

As exciting as technological developments may be—and as promising for teaching and learning, working and playing—it is important to remember that people who lack the skills or the machines to tap into this information are in much the same position as those a century ago who could not read or had no access to books.

Mass media, too, have changed the way we read our world. Not surprisingly, many of the selections in this chapter focus on the role of television in developing literacies. The controversy about the effect of television persists. As Don Adams and Arlene Goldbard explain in their article on media literacy education, we can adopt the position that television "destroys brain cells and deadens our spirits" or the position that television has the "potential to expand minds and lift spirits." Regardless of where our own sympathies lie in this debate, it is virtually impossible to talk about literacy without trying to assess the influence of the "black box" that is turned on in some American homes for as many as twelve hours a day. Children in particular learn about the wider world mainly from television, which brings the most remote corners of the planet into their living rooms. But do most people—again, children in particular—possess the skills to analyze and interpret the sounds and images that fill their homes? Many experts emphasize the need for literacy education that will enable people to analyze, evaluate, and even produce media messages.

As America's founders recognized when they created our government, a literate and informed citizenry is essential to participatory democracy. Technology, by enabling communication over vast distances and giving a voice to more people, can facilitate democracy. The town meeting of a simpler day has been replaced by what Lawrence K. Grossman, former president of PBS and NBC, calls in his new book "the electronic republic." But if many citizens are unequipped to participate critically and analytically in the conversations generated by new technologies, how can they constitute the kind of informed electorate upon which broad-based democracy depends? Opportunities to influence and shape public policy have increased dramatically with technical change. But is our ability to understand and evaluate those policies undermined, simply because the media's presentation has become so complex?

Several selections in this chapter provide stories of the literacy experience. How do people learn to read and write, and how has that process changed over time? As you read, consider carefully how technology influences this learning process. As you reflect on these literacy stories, think about your attitudes toward learning to read and write. How would your "literacy narrative" read? What experiences have shaped your reading and writing practices? What are your stumbling blocks when it comes to achieving "functional literacy" in a high-tech world?

Finally, just as technology shapes our culture, so our own dreams and desires influence technological change. In a market economy, inventions must find consumers; thus new developments typically respond to perceived consumer needs. Where will our dreams and desires drive the technology of the future? And how will the new technologies change the definition of functional literacy and affect our struggles to achieve it?

THE MEDIUM IS THE METAPHOR

Neil Postman

> *In this opening chapter to his widely read book,* Amusing Ourselves to Death: Public Discourse in the Age of Show Business *(1988), Neil Postman argues that most aspects of American life have been "transformed into congenial adjuncts of show business." Postman, a well-known author and Chair of the Department of Cultural Communication at New York University, says that as a result, public discourse has become trivial and insubstantial. He uses this chapter to explore not so much the consequences but the causes of this situation. Drawing on sources from Plato to the Bible to Marshall McLuhan, Postman suggests that what we have to say as a culture is deeply influenced by the tools we have for conducting such "conversations." Postman tries to show how throughout history new technologies have had the power to transform our ways of thinking.*

At different times in our history, different cities have been the focal point of a radiating American spirit. In the late eighteenth century, for example, Boston was the center of a political radicalism that ignited a shot heard round the world—a shot that could not have been fired any other place but the suburbs of Boston. At its report, all Americans, including Virginians, became Bostonians at heart. In the mid-nineteenth century, New York became the symbol of the idea of a melting-pot America—or at least a non-English one—as the wretched refuse from all over the world disembarked at Ellis Island and spread over the land their strange languages and even stranger ways. In the early twentieth century, Chicago, the city of big shoulders and heavy winds, came to symbolize the industrial energy and dynamism of America. If there is a statue of a hog butcher somewhere in Chicago, then it stands as a reminder of the time when America was railroads, cattle, steel mills and entrepreneurial adventures. If there is no such statue, there ought to be, just as there is a statue of a Minute Man to recall the Age of Boston, as the Statue of Liberty recalls the age of New York.

Today, we must look to the city of Las Vegas, Nevada, as a metaphor of our national character and aspiration, its symbol a thirty-foot-high cardboard picture of a slot machine and a chorus girl. For Las Vegas is a city entirely devoted to the idea of entertainment, and as such proclaims the spirit of a culture in which all public discourse increasingly takes the form of entertainment. Our politics, religion, news, athletics, education and commerce have been transformed into congenial adjuncts of show business, largely without protest or even much popular notice. The result is that we are a people on the verge of amusing ourselves to death.

As I write, the President of the United States is a former Hollywood movie actor. One of his principal challengers in 1984 was once a featured player on television's most glamorous show of the 1960's, that is to say, an astronaut. Naturally, a movie has been made about his extraterrestrial adventure. Former nominee George McGovern has hosted the popular television show "Saturday Night Live." So has a candidate of more recent vintage, the Reverend Jesse Jackson.

Meanwhile, former President Richard Nixon, who once claimed he lost an election because he was sabotaged by makeup men, has offered Senator Edward Kennedy advice on how to make a serious run for the presidency: lose twenty pounds. Although the Constitution makes no mention of it, it would appear that fat people are now effectively excluded from running for high political office. Probably bald people as well. Almost certainly those whose looks are not significantly enhanced by the cosmetician's art. Indeed, we may have reached the point where cosmetics has replaced ideology as the field of expertise over which a politician must have competent control.

America's journalists, i.e., television newscasters, have not missed the point. Most spend more time with their hair dryers than with their scripts, with the result that they comprise the most glamorous group of people this side of Las Vegas. Although the Federal Communications Act makes no mention of it, those without camera appeal are excluded from addressing the public about what is called "the news of the day." Those with camera appeal can command salaries exceeding one million dollars a year.

American businessmen discovered, long before the rest of us, that the quality and usefulness of their goods are subordinate to the artifice of their display; that, in fact, half the principles of capitalism as praised by Adam Smith or condemned by Karl Mark are irrelevant. Even the Japanese, who are said to make better cars than the Americans, know that economics is less a science than a performing art, as Toyota's yearly advertising budget confirms.

Not long ago, I saw Billy Graham join with Shecky Green, Red Buttons, Dionne Warwick, Milton Berle and other theologians in a tribute to George Burns, who was celebrating himself for surviving eighty years in show business. The Reverend Graham exchanged one-liners with Burns about making preparation for Eternity. Although the Bible makes no mention of it, the Reverend Graham assured the audience that God loves those who make people laugh. It was an honest mistake. He merely mistook NBC for God.

Dr. Ruth Westheimer is a psychologist who has a popular radio program and a nightclub act in which she informs her audiences about sex in all of its infinite variety and in language once reserved for the bedroom and street corners. She is almost as entertaining as the Reverend Billy Graham, and has been quoted as saying, "I don't start out to be funny. But if it comes out that way, I use it. If they call me an entertainer, I say that's great. When a professor teaches with a sense of humor, people walk away remembering."[1] She did not say what they remember or of what use their remembering is. But she has a point: It's great to be an entertainer. Indeed, in America God favors all those who possess both a talent and a format to amuse, whether they be preachers, athletes, entrepreneurs, politicians, teachers or journalists. In America, the least amusing people are its professional entertainers.

Culture watchers and worriers—those of the type who read books like this one—will know that the examples above are not aberrations but, in fact, clichés. There is no shortage of critics who have observed and recorded the dissolution of public discourse in America and its conversion into the arts of show business. But most of them, I believe, have barely begun to tell the story of the origin and meaning of this descent into a vast triviality. Those who have written vigorously on the matter tell us, for example, that what is happening is the residue of an exhausted capitalism; or, on the contrary, that it is the tasteless fruit of the maturing of capitalism; or that it is the neurotic aftermath of the Age of Freud; or the retribution of our allowing God to perish; or that it all comes from the old stand-bys, greed and ambition.

I have attended carefully to these explanations, and I do not say there is nothing to learn from them. Marxists, Freudians, Lévi-Straussians, even Creation Scientists are not to be taken lightly. And, in any case, I should be very surprised if the story I have to tell is anywhere near the whole truth. We are all, as Huxley says someplace, Great Abbreviators, meaning that none of us has the wit to know the whole truth, the time to tell it if we believed we did, or an audience so gullible as to accept it. But you *will* find an argument here that presumes a clearer grasp of the matter than many that have come before. Its value, such as it is, resides in the directness of its perspective, which has its origins in observations made 2,300 years ago by Plato. It is an argument that fixes its attention on the forms of human conversation, and postulates that how we are obliged to conduct such conversations will have the strongest possible influence on what ideas we can conveniently express. And what ideas are convenient to express inevitably become the important content of a culture.

I use the word "conversation" metaphorically to refer not only to speech but to all techniques and technologies that permit people of a particular culture to exchange messages. In this sense, all culture is a conversation or, more precisely, a corporation of conversations, conducted in a variety of symbolic modes. Our attention here is on how forms of public discourse regulate and even dictate what kind of content can issue from such forms.

To take a simple example of what this means, consider the primitive technology of smoke signals. While I do not know exactly what content was once carried in the smoke signals of American Indians, I can safely guess that it did not include philosophical argument. Puffs of smoke are insufficiently complex to express ideas on the nature of existence, and even if they were not, a Cherokee philosopher would run short of either wood or blankets long before he reached his second axiom. You cannot use smoke to do philosophy. Its form excludes the content.

To take an example closer to home: As I suggested earlier, it is implausible to imagine that anyone like our twenty-seventh President, the multi-chinned, three-hundred-pound William Howard Taft, could be put forward as a presidential candidate in today's world. The shape of a man's body is largely irrelevant to the shape of his ideas when he is addressing a public in writing or on the radio or, for that matter, in smoke signals. But it is quite relevant on television. The grossness of a three-hundred-pound image, even a talking one, would easily overwhelm any logical or spiritual subtleties conveyed by speech. For on television, discourse is conducted largely through visual imagery, which is to say that television gives us a conversation in images, not words. The emergence of the image-manager in the political arena and the concomitant decline of the speech writer attest to the fact that television demands a different kind of content from other media. You cannot do political philosophy on television. Its form works against the content.

To give still another example, one of more complexity: The information, the content, or, if you will, the "stuff" that makes up what is called "the news of the day" did not exist—could not exist—in a world that lacked the media to give it expression. I do not mean that things like fires, wars, murders and love affairs did not, ever and always, happen in places all over the world. I mean that lacking a technology to advertise them, people could not attend to them, could not include them in their daily business. Such information simply could not exist as part of the content of culture. This idea—that there is a content called "the news of the day"—was entirely created by the telegraph (and since amplified by newer media), which made it possible to move decontextualized information over vast spaces at incredible speed. The news of the day is a figment of our technological imagination. It is, quite precisely, a media event. We attend to fragments of events from all over the world because we have multiple media whose forms are well suited to fragmented conversation. Cultures without speed-of-light media—let us say, cultures in which smoke signals are the most efficient space-conquering tool available—do not have news of the day. Without a medium to create its form, the news of the day does not exist.

To say it, then, as plainly as I can, this book is an inquiry into and a lamentation about the most significant American cultural fact of the second half of the twentieth century: the decline of the Age of Typography and the ascendancy of the Age of Television. This change-over has dramatically and irreversibly shifted the content and meaning of public discourse, since two media so vastly different cannot accommodate the same ideas. As the influence of print wanes, the content of politics, religion, education, and anything else that comprises public business must change and be recast in terms that are most suitable to television.

If all this sounds suspiciously like Marshall McLuhan's aphorism, the medium is the message, I will not disavow that association (although it is fashionable to do so among respectable scholars who, were it not for

McLuhan, would today be mute). I met McLuhan thirty years ago when I was a graduate student and he an unknown English professor. I believed then, as I believe now, that he spoke in the tradition of Orwell and Huxley—that is, as a prophesier, and I have remained steadfast to his teaching that the clearest way to see through a culture is to attend to its tools for conversation. I might add that my interest in this point of view was first stirred by a prophet far more formidable than McLuhan, more ancient than Plato. In studying the Bible as a young man, I found intimations of the idea that forms of media favor particular kinds of content and therefore are capable of taking command of a culture. I refer specifically to the Decalogue, the Second Commandment of which prohibits the Israelites from making concrete images of anything. "Thou shalt not make unto thee any graven image, any likeness of any thing that is in heaven above, or that is in the earth beneath, or that is in the water beneath the earth." I wondered then, as so many others have, as to why the God of these people would have included instructions on how they were to symbolize, or not symbolize, their experience. It is a strange injunction to include as part of an ethical system *unless its author assumed a connection between forms of human communication and the quality of a culture.* We may hazard a guess that people who are being asked to embrace an abstract, universal deity would be rendered unfit to do so by the habit of drawing pictures or making statues or depicting their ideas in any concrete, iconographic forms. The God of the Jews was to exist in the Word and through the Word, an unprecedented conception requiring the highest order of abstract thinking. Iconography thus became blasphemy so that a new kind of God could enter a culture. People like ourselves who are in the process of converting their culture from word-centered to image-centered might profit by reflecting on this Mosaic injunction. But even if I am wrong in these conjectures, it is, I believe, a wise and particularly relevant supposition that the media of communication available to a culture are a dominant influence on the formation of the culture's intellectual and social preoccupations.

Speech, of course, is the primal and indispensable medium. It made us human, keeps us human, and in fact defines what human means. This is not to say that if there were no other means of communication all humans would find it equally convenient to speak about the same things in the same way. We know enough about language to understand that variations in the structures of language will result in variations in what may be called "world view." How people think about time and space, and about things and processes, will be greatly influenced by the grammatical features of their language. We dare not suppose therefore that all human minds are unanimous in understanding how the world is put together. But how much more divergence there is in world view among different cultures can be imagined when we consider the great number and variety of tools for conversation that go beyond speech. For although culture is a creation of speech, it is recreated anew by every medium of communication—from painting to hieroglyphs to the alphabet to television. Each medium, like language itself, makes possible a unique mode of discourse by providing a new orientation for thought, for expression, for sensibility. Which, of course, is what McLuhan meant in saying the medium is the message. His aphorism, however, is in need of amendment because, as it stands, it may lead one to confuse a message with a metaphor. A message denotes a specific, concrete statement about the world. But the forms of our media, including the symbols through which they permit conversation, do not make such statements. They are rather like metaphors, working by unobtrusive but powerful implication to enforce their special definitions of reality. Whether we are experiencing the world through the lens of speech or the printed word or the television camera, our media-metaphors classify the world for us, sequence it, frame it, enlarge it, reduce it, color it, argue a case for what the world is like. As Ernst Cassirer remarked:

> Physical reality seems to recede in proportion as man's symbolic activity advances. Instead of dealing with the things themselves man is in a sense constantly conversing with himself. He has so enveloped himself in linguistic forms, in artistic images, in mythical symbols or religious rites that he cannot see or know anything except by the interposition of [an] artificial medium.[2]

What is peculiar about such interpositions of media is that their role in directing what we will see or know is so rarely noticed. A person who reads a book or who watches television or who glances at his watch is not usually interested in how his mind is organized and controlled by these events, still less in what idea of the world is suggested by a book, television, or a watch. But there are men and women who have noticed these things, especially in our own times. Lewis Mumford, for example, has been one of our great noticers. He is not the sort of a man who looks at a clock merely to see what time it is. Not that he lacks interest in the content of clocks, which is of concern to everyone from moment to moment, but he is far more interested in how a clock creates the idea of "moment to moment." He attends to the philosophy of clocks, to clocks as metaphor, about which our education has had little to say and clock makers nothing at all. "The clock," Mumford has concluded, "is a piece of power machinery whose 'product' is seconds and minutes." In manufacturing such a product, the clock has the effect of disassociating time from human events and thus nourishes the belief in an independent world of mathematically measurable sequences. Moment to moment, it turns out, is not God's conception, or nature's. It is man conversing with himself about and through a piece of machinery he created.

In Mumford's great book *Technics and Civilization,* he shows how, beginning in the fourteenth century, the clock made us into time-keepers, and then time-savers, and now time-servers. In the process, we have learned irreverence toward the sun and the seasons, for in a world made up of seconds and minutes, the authority of nature is superseded. Indeed, as Mumford points out, with the invention of the clock, Eternity ceased to serve as the measure and focus of human events. And thus, though few would have imagined the connection, the inexorable ticking of the clock may have had more to do with the weakening of God's supremacy than all the treatises produced by the philosophers of the Enlightenment; that is to say, the clock introduced a new form of conversation between man and God, in which God appears to have been the loser. Perhaps Moses should have included another Commandment: Thou shalt not make mechanical representations of time.

That the alphabet introduced a new form of conversation between man and man is by now a commonplace among scholars. To be able to *see* one's utterances rather than only to hear them is no small matter, though our education, once again, has had little to say about this. Nonetheless, it is clear that phonetic writing created a new conception of knowledge, as well as a new sense of intelligence, of audience and of posterity, all of which Plato recognized at an early stage in the development of texts. "No man of intelligence," he wrote in his Seventh Letter, "will venture to express his philosophical views in language, especially not in language that is unchangeable, which is true of that which is set down in written characters." This notwithstanding, he wrote voluminously and understood better than anyone else that the setting down of views in written characters would be the beginning of philosophy, not its end. Philosophy cannot exist without criticism, and writing makes it possible and convenient to subject thought to a continuous and concentrated scrutiny. Writing freezes speech and in so doing gives birth to the grammarian, the logician, the rhetorician, the historian, the scientist—all those who must hold language before them so that they can see what it means, where it errs, and where it is leading.

Plato knew all of this, which means that he knew that writing would bring about a perceptual revolution: a shift from the ear to the eye as an organ of language processing. Indeed, there is a legend that to encourage such a shift Plato insisted that his students study geometry before entering his Academy. If true, it was a sound idea, for as the great literary critic Northrop Frye has remarked, "the written word is far more powerful than simply a reminder: it re-creates the past in the present, and gives us, not the familiar remembered thing, but the glittering intensity of the summoned-up hallucination."[3]

All that Plato surmised about the consequences of writing is now well understood by anthropologists, especially those who have studied cultures in which speech is the only source of complex conversation. Anthropologists know that the written word, as Northrop Frye meant to suggest, is not merely an echo of a speaking voice. It is another kind of voice altogether, a conjurer's trick of the first order. It must certainly have appeared that way to those who invented it, and that is why we should not be surprised that the Egyptian god Thoth, who is alleged to have brought writing to the King Thamus, was also the god of magic. People like ourselves may see nothing wondrous in writing, but our anthropologists know how strange and magical it appears to a purely oral people—a conversation with no one and yet with everyone. What could be stranger than the silence one encounters when addressing a question to a text? What could be more metaphysically puzzling than addressing an unseen audience, as every writer of books must do? And correcting oneself because one knows that an unknown reader will disapprove or misunderstand?

I bring all of this up because what my book is about is how our own tribe is undergoing a vast and trembling shift from the magic of writing to the magic of electronics. What I mean to point out here is that the introduction into a culture of a technique such as writing or a clock is not merely an extension of man's power to bind time but a transformation of his way of thinking—and, of course, of the content of his culture. And that is what I mean to say by calling a medium a metaphor. We are told in school, quite correctly, that a metaphor suggests what a thing is like by comparing it to something else. And by the power of its suggestion, it so fixes a conception in our minds that we cannot imagine the one thing without the other: Light is a wave; language, a tree; God, a wise and venerable man; the mind, a dark cavern illuminated by knowledge. And if these metaphors no longer serve us, we must, in the nature of the matter, find others that will. Light is a particle; language, a river; God (as Bertrand Russell proclaimed), a differential equation; the mind, a garden that yearns to be cultivated.

But our media-metaphors are not so explicit or so vivid as these, and they are far more complex. In understanding their metaphorical function, we must take into account the symbolic forms of their information, the source of their information, the quantity and speed of their information, the context in which their information is experienced. Thus, it takes some digging to get at them, to grasp, for example, that a clock recreates time as an independent, mathematically precise sequence; that writing recreates the mind as a tablet on which experience is written; that the telegraph recreates news as a commodity. And yet, such digging becomes easier if we start from the assumption that in every tool we create, an idea is embedded that goes beyond the function of the thing itself. It has been pointed out, for example, that the invention of eyeglasses in the twelfth century not only made it possible to improve defective vision but suggested the idea that human beings need not accept as final either the endowments of nature or the ravages of time. Eyeglasses refuted the belief that anatomy is destiny by putting forward the idea that our bodies as well as our minds are improvable. I do not think it goes too far to say that there is a link between the invention of eyeglasses in the twelfth century and gene-splitting research in the twentieth.

Even such an instrument as the microscope, hardly a tool of everyday use, had embedded within it a quite astonishing idea, not about biology but about psychology. By revealing a world hitherto hidden from view, the microscope suggested a possibility about the structure of the mind.

If things are not what they seem, if microbes lurk, unseen, on and under our skin, if the invisible controls the visible, then is it not possible that ids and egos and superegos also lurk somewhere unseen? What else is psychoanalysis but a microscope of the mind? Where do our notions of mind come from if not from metaphors generated by our tools? What does it mean to say that someone has an IQ of 126? There are no numbers in people's heads. Intelligence does not have quantity or magnitude, except as we believe that it does. And why do we believe that it does? Because we have tools that imply that this is what the mind is like. Indeed, our tools for thought suggest to us what our bodies are like, as when someone refers to her "biological clock," or when we talk of our "genetic codes," or when we read someone's face like a book, or when our facial expressions telegraph our intentions.

When Galileo remarked that the language of nature is written in mathematics, he meant it only as a metaphor. Nature itself does not speak. Neither do our minds or our bodies or, more to the point of this book, our bodies politic. Our conversations about nature and about ourselves are conducted in whatever "languages" we find it possible and convenient to employ. We do not see nature or intelligence or human motivation or ideology as "it" is but only as our languages are. And our languages are our media. Our media are our metaphors. Our metaphors create the content of our culture.

References

Cassirer, Ernst. *An Essay on Man*. Garden City, N.Y.: Doubleday Anchor, 1956.
Frye, Northrop. *The Great Code: The Bible and Literature*. Toronto: Academic Press, 1981.

Notes

1. As quoted in the *Wisconsin State Journal,* August 24, 1983, Section 3, page 1.
2. Cassirer, p. 43.
3. Frye, p. 227.

Questions for Discussion

1. What examples does Postman use to show how different aspects of American society—for example, politics, religion, journalism—have been influenced by the attitudes of the entertainment industry? Can you think of other, more recent examples of the same phenomenon?
2. What does Postman say specifically about the way that visual media have influenced our attitudes toward politicians and other leaders? Do you agree or disagree with his views?
3. Postman's chapter title, "The Medium Is the Metaphor," is a twist on Marshall McLuhan's famous assertion from the 1960s that "the medium is the message." Do these two aphorisms say the same thing or something different about how the use of a particular medium affects the message we present? What does Postman mean by "metaphor"?

4. Postman argues that writing and speech are fundamentally different—"another voice altogether." What evidence or explanation does he present for this claim? Do you agree with this assertion?
5. Toward the end of the selection, Postman notes that to a purely oral people, writing seems "strange and magical"—"a conversation with no one and yet with everyone." What is your sense of the difference between oral and written conversations? How does moving from speech to writing change the way you explore ideas?
6. Describe Postman's tone in this piece. Do you think it is appropriate to his purposes? Why or why not? In what ways do metaphors help him present his ideas?

Questions for Research and Writing

1. Postman argues that print and television are "so vastly different" that they "cannot accommodate the same ideas." Test this hypothesis. Choose a topic, issue, or event that appears in both the daily newspapers and on television. Compare the presentations of this topic for a period of several days. What is different about the discussion in print and the discussion on television? What might account for these differences?
2. Try to imagine our culture without some of the technological inventions that we take for granted today. How would American culture be different today without the radio, television, telephone, or computer? What have we gained and what have we lost as a result of technology?
3. As a way of testing the impact of mass media and media technology in your own life, try eliminating all newspapers, magazines, television, radio, movies, faxes, computers, and telephone communications from your life for two days. (You may read and write for class assignments, but for no other reason.) At the end of this "deprivation" period, write about how you felt without this media connection to the rest of the world. In what ways did the absence of media change your perceptions of the world?

THE INTERNET'S ARRESTED DEVELOPMENT

Charles McGrath

> *What does it really mean that we live in what some have called the Information Age? How do the new technologies influence the way that we read, write, and experience the world around us? Clearly, new media require new forms and styles. The following article first appeared in* The New York Times Magazine *in December 1996. Journalist Charles McGrath, editor of the* New York Times Book Review, *here explores some of the characteristics of communication on the Internet. While much of what one finds on the Internet is new and exciting, McGrath believes that the Internet has not yet developed beyond a kind of adolescent phase. As he says in the closing line, it has yet to become "a place you wouldn't be ashamed to have your parents visit." As you read the article, decide whether McGrath's criticisms of the medium are fair and reasonable. If you have experience with the Internet, how do McGrath's impressions compare to your own?*

A couple of weeks ago, during a long afternoon surfing the Internet, I experienced an overload. First I checked my E-mail (messages from the kids, from a former colleague setting up a lunch date and from someone in an electronic discussion group I joined a few months ago, talking about the Battle of Trafalgar). Then I made a brisk electronic tour of the Uffizi and the Louvre. I read some valuable tips on lockpicking written by someone named Ted the Tool. I checked out the standings on the College Hockey home page. I browsed through the various on-line journals—Slate, Salon, Hotwired, Suck, Feed and Swoon. I consulted a weather map customized for my neighborhood. I visited the poetry archive at the University of Toronto and ran a little search on the number of times the word "thistle" turns up in Byron. I window-shopped—screen-shopped—for a yacht in the Buzzards Bay classifieds. I stopped by the Kraft Interactive Kitchen and watched the dancing utensils for a while. I went to the Timothy Leary home page and read some of the gibberish posted there by fans of the doctor. I also went to the Internet cemetery, a place where people leave testimonials to their departed loved ones. And then somehow I found myself by the pool at the Cybercity Hotel, sipping my third or fourth virtual martini.

Or, rather, it wasn't me exactly; it was my Net self. Let's call him Chuck. He's 23, 6 foot 4, 220 and has an amazingly sculptured hard body combined with the creativity and passion of an artist. Around me—him, I mean—were, I recall, Zak, jamhead, Texas Honey, Budda, Mako, Nikki, Endorphin Man, Naughty Nancy and several others, most of them also in their early 20s, also with amazingly sculptured hard bodies and also very generously endowed sexually, with large penises or large, firm breasts. The endowment was fortunate because all these people were preparing to go upstairs to one of the Cybercity Hotel's six floors of rooms and have sex. Dozens of others, including Elron, marigold, Coolbreeze, Wifey, Big Papa and Clocker, were already hotly engaged and having on-screen orgasms that looked like this: "OHHHHHHHhhhh," "ARRRRRghhhh," "yessssssssss!" Up in room 401, Sven and Elsa were about to get it on in Swedish. "Joda, var ar du nagonstans?" she was saying. "Hej hur mar du? Mycket bra!"

I sat there for a while, until my brain began to click softly, the way my computer does when it's getting ready to undergo the process known as "cache cleanup"—a kind of self-purging intended to relieve an overtaxed memory. All those chattering cyberbeings! All that writhing and longing! All that bad spelling! (Amazingly few people on the Internet know the correct way to write "masturbate.") I reached over and with my left hand pressed the control and command keys on my keyboard. And then with my right index finger I hit the nuke button. There was a pause, followed by a single, Mahleresque "boing," and my screen went silently, blessedly blank.

Like most people of my generation—people who grew up in the 1950's and 60's, with books and typewriters—I began exploring the Internet partly out of curiosity but mostly out of fear. If, as the techies and the zealots keep telling us, the Net is the world of the future, the place where we will work and play and think and socialize, I wanted to know what this brave new world was like. What I discovered, not really to my surprise, is that the Net is all too much like the world we already live in. It's essentially a vast, ever-sprawling shopping mall, anchored, as they say, by a great many upscale emporiums but also cluttered by countless tacky storefronts that are the electronic equivalent of fast-food joints, video arcades and those places that sell incense and earrings. And some of the most conspicuous people on the Internet tend to be just like the people you run into at the mall: proselytizers and leafleteers and all those sullen young people shuffling along aimlessly.

Or think of a labyrinthine and cosmically cluttered basement. If you shine your flashlight over here by the stairs, you find all the bric-a-brac for grown-ups: the gateways to the world's museums and the archives of countless libraries and research centers; the Web sites maintained by I.B.M., Time Warner, the A.C.L.U. and just about every other corporation or important organization you can think of. Over here are the tools, useful stuff to know about. Poke around a little and you can read the paper (including this paper, among many others), you can place bets, you can buy insurance, you can look for a spouse, you can even buy airline tickets and groceries. Over here, lounging on the old sofas and spring-bursting easy chairs, are the devotees of the chat rooms—the freewheeling conversations devoted to every subject imaginable, from home construction to bird watching to record collecting to investing to bomb building. But keep going, past the coal chute

5

and the sump pump, and you come upon a corner of the basement that Mom and Dad don't know about: an immense trove of trivia, trash and pornography—the aspect of the Net that's a monument to idleness and wasted time. Here's an entire site cheerfully devoted to fecal matter; over here are dozens that recycle feeble jokes and gags and still more that specialize in extreme sexual practices. And, while we're rummaging through this stuff, let's not overlook all the home pages lovingly maintained by individuals. Move your cursor here if you want to see a picture of Larry's grad-student apartment, here for a list of his favorite rock groups, here for a synopsis of "Good Chemistry," his last semester's term paper on De Quincey, Coleridge and Burroughs.

To make matters worse, there's no map to all this clutter, not even a promontory where you can stand and get your bearings. You have to either trust yourself to a Virgil, someone who's been here before, or else, like a character in a Beckett novel, you have to grope and delve and sift your way along, learning by trial and error. Snaking beneath the rubble, you quickly discover, are invisible cables connecting one part of the Net with another, so that if you click on a highlighted word or phrase on one site you are instantly transported to another, related site. This is the much-vaunted link feature, the one that is supposed to have transformed the Net from a linear medium to one of infinite and serendipitous multi-dimensionality. In fact, the links are merely an elaborate footnoting device, and their serendipity is serendipity that is preordained; what the mechanism really creates is not multiple coexisting levels of connection but a series of forking paths all, alas, on a single undifferentiated plane, so that it is almost impossible, for example, to take short cuts—you have to follow every twist in the path— and it is all too easy to forget the way home.

Something the Net surfers, with their quick-firing synapses and non-linear thought patterns, don't like to tell you is that the Internet is *slow*. If you're trying to get on via modem, through one of the consumer E-mail providers, like Compuserve or America Online, good luck. Even if you have a state-of-the-art hookup, with an Internet browser like Netscape, say, and a direct connection, you can expect maddening pauses, interminable delays and even sudden crashes as, first, the "host" is contacted and then your screen fills up with pixels sifting down line by line. This is partly because our home computers are already outmoded; they're Model T's, as the Net groupies like to say: balky, hand-cranked flivvers compared with the turbocharged limos, with cable modems, accelerated circuitry and high-resolution screens that even now are idling in high-tech garages all over Silicon Valley. But there is also just too much traffic on the information highway. With the number of new loggers-on growing at the rate of about 2,300 percent a year, the data pipes have already become sclerotic. Like many people, I've learned never to venture onto the Net without equipping myself the way I do when I set out for the doctor's office: I bring along something to read while I wait.

It's customary in Net-speak to make a distinction between "r/t," or real time—the time in which all these delays and jam-ups occur—and "v/t," or virtual time, which is time on the Net: a kind of eternal present in which it is neither day nor night and the clock never ticks. V/t is time without urgency, without priority. One factor contributing to the Internet traffic jams, in fact, is that the system makes no distinction between the electrons carrying your Elle MacPherson photos and those carrying the verification codes for my six-figure stock transaction; it devotes exactly the same amount of attention, and at the same pace, to each. V/t is also time without subjectivity. It affords neither those moments of speeded-up intensity when everything seems to be happening at once nor those moments of deep immersion when you sink so thoroughly into a project or activity that afterward you can't recall where the time went.

V/t is shallow time, surface time—time elongated in such a way that to me it most resembles that skittering, half-suspended state that occurs just before sleep, when random circuits begin firing in your brain, initiating loops of thought that never quite connect and causing your body every now and then to twitch in slow motion. But the main thing that has to be said about v/t is that it is an enormous waster of r/t, which is a problem if, instead of hanging out at the computer mall, you happen to have a full-time job. Most people I know who have embarked even halfheartedly upon the Net say they have no time anymore to read, watch TV, visit with their friends—no time to do all the things they used to like to do.

There would be fewer delays on the Net if there was less graphic material—fewer pictures and illustrations and animated icons; this stuff uses more bandwidth, or channel capacity, and takes much longer to load. But who in his right mind would want fewer graphics? A Net without pictures would be a boring Net indeed. At the moment, most of the really interesting and sophisticated material, and certainly most of the fun, is visual. This is probably because the challenges of getting graphic material onto the Net appeal more to the kinds of people now working there—people who grew up with computers and animation—than do textual challenges. The writing on the Net will get better, you keep hearing, when writers, and not techies, start writing for it.

Actually, there's some pretty good writing on the Net already, much of it in Salon, a lively on-line magazine financed by Borders, the bookstore chain, and featuring interviews, book reviews and brief social and political commentaries. Salon has evolved an on-screen style that is smart and literate and inflected with sufficient attitude and irreverence so as not to seem a mere print journal recycled onto the screen. This, for example, is what Salon had to say when Slate, the much-heralded but (by Net standards) somewhat staid publication edited by Michael Kinsley and bankrolled by Microsoft, finally came on line in June:

After a buildup only slightly exceeded in length, fervor and stick-twirling bombast by the interminable drum solo on Iron Butterfly's "In-A-Gadda-Da-Vida," Slate, the Great Web Legitimizer, has finally made its entrance before a gaping world. Not even the most epochal of publications could have lived up to this not-since-amoebas-crawled-from-the-ooze-hype.... Before donning surgical mask and gloves, therefore, we will pause for a brief moment of commiseration with our new Web colleagues. Pause. O.K., nurse, hand me that chain saw.

Slate, for its part, has maintained consistently high literary standards and has also experimented with a feature, at once old-fashioned and state-of-the-art, in which writers are asked to keep an on-line diary for a week, updating it daily. Among the contributors are Muriel Spark and Cynthia Ozick.

But it remains to be seen whether in the long run the Internet will really prove hospitable to writing. The problem in part is that technology isn't particularly hospitable to reading right now. The typical computer screen doesn't offer anything like the degree of clarity and resolution achieved with ink and paper. Even in the classiest, most sophisticated presentations, type that is on screen has an undifferentiated, flyspeck quality, and though some of us have taught ourselves how to look at this stuff long enough and carefully enough even to make our livings from doing so, few people, I think, would do this for pleasure. As far as the editors of Slate can determine, their publication, by far the brainiest and least gimmicky of the on-line offerings, is still being read the old-fashioned way; many people are printing it out, that is. (A paper version is also distributed at many of the Starbucks cafes—a throwback, come to think of it, to those London coffeehouses where Boswell and Dr. Johnson used to go to read the newspaper.)

And then there's the disorienting business of scrolling, as opposed to simply turning a page. The old technology is still more satisfying—that mounting stack of paper, slightly splayed, imprisoned gently under your left thumb, while the first and second fingers of your right hand eagerly (or sadly, as the case may be) riffle ahead, feeling the heft of what's to come before decisively flicking over the next sheet, instantly turning recto into verso. Page turning is actually faster and more flexible. By taking away many of the visual and tactile clues we use to measure our progress through a text—by making it harder to find our place—scrolling helps render those texts shapeless.

But there's another, deeper limitation, one that has less to do with screen technology than with the value-free nature of on-line writing. Electronic communication prizes content over form, information over style, immediacy over proofreading and fact-checking; it tolerates an ungrammatical, misspelled sentence as happily as a correct one, and, by instantly storing a muddled thought in memory or displaying it on a screen, it can make that thought seem as shapely and permanent as a profound one.

The Internet also lets anyone become a publisher, literate or not. If you read enough stuff that's been written for or on the computer, in fact, you can at times find yourself thinking that what you're seeing is nothing less than the dumbing down of writing itself—the dilution of prose into a gruel that's thinner and far less nourishing than what we grew up on. What works best in this new writing—or what's most effective, at any rate, and what is imitated most often—is not subtlety but cuteness: emoticons, as those ubiquitous happy and sad faces are called — :) and :(— and all the in-group acronyms and abbreviations that make up so much of what passes for discourse in the discussion groups: "lol," "f2f" and so on. Loudness works, too—lots of CAPITAL LETTERS, that is—and so does rudeness and incivility.

Who owns the Internet and who controls it? No one at the moment, and for many of its users that's precisely the point. They see in the Net our last great avenue to freedom—a place where everyone can say and be what he likes. Perhaps the highest-minded champion of this philosophy is Jon Katz, who writes "The Netizen" column for Hotwired. He has argued that the Net, free of the corruptions of advertising, the pettiness of Government, the moralism of the right and the rigidities of religious fundamentalism, can enable a kind of free, open and rational discourse that will instill in us nothing less than a new Enlightenment. Elsewhere on the Net this strain of thought is snarlier and less exalted; every now and then you stumble on a user group or a chat room that seems an extension of those aggrieved, establishment-baiting conversations whipped up by early-American firebrands like Daniel Shays or Nathaniel Bacon—except that these sessions, as often as not, are about freedom in the abstract rather than about the whisky tax or landlord-tenant relations. They're about the freedom to be free.

The philosophers and the cranks alike are united in their opposition to censorship on the Net. The issue is more than just a First Amendment one; it has to do with the very nature of the Net and of their hopes and dreams for it. The Net, its champions believe, needs to be free—in every sense of the word—and free, in particular, from the restraints imposed by editors, publishers, cultural policemen and standard-bearers or authority figures of any sort. Some of the Net patriots even resist, on principle, the notion that it might make sense for the various networks, services and providers to get together and agree on a few protocols that might speed up the traffic flow. The way to keep the Net egalitarian, they say, is to keep it decentralized.

You wonder what A. J. Liebling, who said that freedom of the press belongs to whoever owns one, would make of this. In a way, the Net is just such a forum—the electronic newsstand for millions of private presses—and yet the result is often cacophony rather than wisdom, a form of expression that follows not parliamentary principles but the Hobbesian law of the boring dinner party: it belongs, that is, to the person who talks loudest, logs on most often. At the moment, at least, discourse in cyberspace seems to favor lengthy, reasoned arguments less than it does dialogue or, more often, statement and riposte, declaration and put-down. Because everyone must be free to speak to what is on his or her mind, everyone is also presumed to have something worthwhile to say. The Net is full of ranters standing on invisible soapboxes, and a great many exchanges essentially come down to: Enough about you. Let's hear from me.

There is even a movement on the Net to liberate us from the tyranny of the author and from texts that mean only one thing. The hotbed of this effort has been the Hypertext Fiction Workshop at Brown University, which has assembled dozens and dozens of novels, and even autobiographical and critical texts, that operate according to the principles of those "Choose Your Own Adventure" books. At different points along the way, you click on this or that character or location or plot development and thus shape—help create, even—the very story you are reading. Some of the Brown texts are so complicated, with proliferating links and options, that they have probably never been read the same way twice. Accompanying the hypertexts, needless to say, is an outpouring of faddish theory and philosophy—about the erotics of cyberspace, the ontology of cyberspace and the role of the Leibnizian monad in same, all of which argues that hyperreading is immeasurably superior, more faithful to ourselves and the nature of the world, than the unhypered version.

In truth, though, this whole enterprise seems for now little more than an electronic parlor game—partly because the hypertexts themselves are so dreary. Take away the bells and whistles, and they're snippets of undistinguished prose, usually about thinly characterized folks wandering about in cyberspace, naturally. But the hypertext philosophy—and some of the libertarianism on the Net—also ignores that at a certain level reading is not about freedom at all but about submission, about stifling your own voice, stilling your mind and yielding fully to the designs (in every sense) of another. If I'm going to read "Villette," say, I don't want to choose my own Bruges, I want Charlotte Brontë to do it for me. Similarly, I don't want to tell Conor Cruise O'Brien what I think about Thomas Jefferson. I want him to tell me what to think. I want him, that is, to temporarily take over my mind and make use of it. Ultimately, reading is about what happens between a writer and me; it's not a community activity.

Many of the censorship battles on the Net are being fought on the shabby ground of pornography. The best that can be said for all the porn on the Net is that most of it is presented in a straightforward, businesslike fashion. And though it is a heaven-sent gift—a daydream come true—for legions of horny youths, most of it is ostensibly aimed at mature, consenting adults. Unlike sex in the rest of our culture, sex on the Internet doesn't assault you. You don't have to look hard for it, but you do have to look. (And you usually have to click in a little box to certify that you're 18 or older and don't object to explicit material.) The worst that can be said is that Internet pornography is far more accessible to young children than all those low-tech magazines and tapes, and that the sheer volume of it is astounding: countless pictures and even little film clips depicting human beings (and sometimes animals) in every form of sexual activity that you've ever heard of or imagined, and in some that you probably haven't.

You don't have to be a member of the religious right to think that most of this stuff is highly inappropriate for kids—though the real danger, I think, is less that they will be corrupted by it, turned into lust-crazed monsters, than that they will be de-eroticized, their natural curiosity sated too quickly and easily, and that they will eventually become bored, or even turned off, by this endless display of naked grown-ups carrying on in such weird and embarrassing ways. Needless to say, most of the sexual material on the Internet is not particularly erotic; it's not really concerned with sex at all, in fact, but with sexual imagery, devoid of even the filmy peignoir of narrative or context that usually accompanies the cheesiest of magazine spreads, the most low budget of videos. Context and narrative, you discover in their absence, are no small part of what makes sex sexy.

The one exception to this general blight of almost contentless sexual imagery is the kind of fantasy and role playing that prevails in the various chat rooms and electronic hot-pillow joints, like the Cybercity Hotel and a popular hangout called bianca's Smut Shack, where people go to have on-line sex with one another—or, to put it bluntly, where they pretend to have sex in v/t, while in r/t they sit at their computers and masturbate. Typically in these encounters, the participants introduce themselves, describe what they look like and what they're wearing and then exchange back-and-forth descriptions of what they're doing to each other. The language in these transactions is invariably the ripely clichéd, overheated language popularized by Penthouse Forum, among others, and they follow a plot as ritualized and unvarying as that of a Japanese tea ceremony. True variety or innovation is not in fact a particularly desirable commodity in on-line relationships; what's valued, oddly, is familiarity.

If you're a "lurker," as those who prefer to watch but not join in are known, the spectacle of all this transparent loneliness and longing, of all this second-rate and secondhand fantasy life is more than a little depressing. Who *are* these people, you wonder. To judge from what they say about themselves, they're college kids, lonely housewives, bored office workers (a lot of computer sex seems to happen on company time), or people who want to explore the possibilities of bisexuality, say, in a safe, unthreatening way. But of course what they say may not be true. A frequent annoyance reported in the chat rooms, for example, is the problem of men posing as women on screen. And in the land of computer sex you rarely come across anyone who is middle-aged or has a weight problem or difficulty with hair loss, and you certainly never meet anyone who is slow to become aroused or has trouble maintaining an erection. These cyberselves are always available, always turned on. And they're amazingly free of self-consciousness: there's almost never a wink, a parenthesis or an exclamation mark, to indicate that everyone knows this is just a game. It's too simple, obviously, to conclude that these electronic heavy breathers inhabit a world that, in "Alice in Wonderland" fashion, is a mirror image of the real one, and yet clearly there is an enormous amount of wish projection going on. The subtext—or antitext—of all these humid, feverish encounters is not bliss but its opposite: solitariness and frustration.

The other striking thing about Net sex is that, for all the emphasis on physical description, it actually suggests a deep-seated wish to shuck off the body altogether; it's sex-in-the-head. And the same tendency toward disembodiment can be found in less steamy areas of the Net, in the many "virtual communities" that have sprung up—places where you, or a three-dimensional icon of you, your avatar, can go and live full time if you'd like. One of them, Sherwood Forest Towne, has an elaborate form of town or community government that sets policy, passes laws, figures out how to deal with intruders. It also has gardens, glades, communal rooms with glowing hearths—places where you can kick back and share your innermost thoughts with other three-dimensional icons. The implicit assumption behind this and other movements on the Net may represent something like a major philosophical shift: the assumption that virtual is better than real. Virtual, or virtually, used to be a loophole, a term of elastic qualification: your new car is virtually maintenance free, your refund check is virtually in the mail. Now it's reality that has been qualified; virtual is newer, cooler and far less fuss and trouble.

The Internet, we should recall, had its origins in the cold war—as a way of decentralizing communications and making them less vulnerable to attack—and its greatest virtue may still be in its capacity to become a repository for our more presentable side. If the Net is a basement in need of cleaning, it's also the library at Alexandria rebuilt or a permanent, distortion-proof version of that archive maintained by the band of outlaws at the end of Ray Bradbury's "Fahrenheit 451," who have each undertaken to learn a book by heart in case the printed texts are burned. The Net contains, in accessible, searchable form, all of Greek tragedy, for example, and the full texts of most of the classics of English literature. It is also an unparalleled research tool—even if at the end of your search you still wind up turning to a book.

And then there's E-mail, the one feature that everyone seems to love—young and old, Flintstone and Jetson alike. Where would we be without this reliable, unobtrusive courier, swiftly toting hither and yon—to the next apartment or to an office across the world—our memos, our business correspondence, our mash notes, our holiday greetings, our chain letters, our missives of complaint or of thanks, our news about our families and ourselves. You type, you click and—blip!—your message is on its way.

It's already there, in fact. *Too* swiftly sometimes. Most of us have either sent or received an electronic jolt that would have benefited from the cooling-down period afforded by the traditional drawer-yanking search for an envelope and fumble for a stamp. But these occasional melt-downs are a small price to pay for such a benign and transforming invention, one that, if you allow it to, pleasingly combines the virtues of ease and immediacy with those of contemplation, of forethought. The great advantage that E-mail has over the telephone is not just that the line is seldom tied up but that it forces you, literally, to compose yourself—to create a text that presents you in your own best version.

If nothing else, the Internet has made pen pals of us all, and sometimes, sitting at my computer, I really do feel connected, part of a vast interlocking web. Once in a while, I even feel a twinge of the excitement and adventure that the Net pioneers are always writing about. All that virgin space, unspoiled and unclaimed—a gleaming ethereal vista brimming with the promise of freedom, adventure and possibility. Sometimes I can almost believe that we have embarked on a brand-new mode of being, one in which our minds are free to travel anywhere. And then I think, nah.

To me, the Internet for now more often recalls that black-lit, book-stuffed, beer-sticky, hemp-smelling, hormone-raging grotto that was my college dorm room back in 1968. Think of it: a place where, at any hour of the day or night, you can order a pizza, shoot the breeze, skim through library books, utter profundities, listen to music, look at pictures of naked girls, read poetry, watch movies and deliver tirades against the Government and the professoriat—all without the bother of having to get dressed up, as Truman Capote once said about another solitary activity or, indeed, without budging from your chair. No one, I suspect, would choose to dwell in the grotto, but it was fun to hang out there for a while—oh, to have been hot-wired back then!—and there are worse places to be reminded of and even to drop by from time to time. Eventually, the Internet will grow up, or maybe we will. We will know that this has happened when the Net becomes invisible and we can finally stop talking about it—when it has become a place you wouldn't be ashamed to have your parents visit.

Questions for Discussion

1. How would you characterize McGrath's tone and style? How, for instance, does his introduction prepare you for both the tone and content that follow?
2. McGrath says that "virtual time" on the Internet wastes "real time" spent doing the things we "used to like to do." If you and your friends have access to the Internet, how much time do you spend surfing the Net? What do you spend your virtual time doing? To what extent has time spent on the Internet replaced time spent on work? On school? On other forms of leisure?

3. People have sometimes argued that computers will someday—perhaps soon—make books obsolete, because we'll simply be able to download whatever reading material we want. McGrath disagrees. What do you see as the advantages and disadvantages of book reading as opposed to screen reading?
4. At one point, McGrath compares the Internet to a basement full of forgotten treasures and paraphernalia better kept hidden; at another, he compares it to a college dorm room where fantasies and profundities gain life. Imagine your own metaphor for the Internet. To what place might you compare it?

Questions for Research and Writing

1. McGrath argues that the Internet values "content over form, information over style, immediacy over proofreading and fact-checking." If you have access to the Internet, put McGrath's assertions to the test by looking at the kinds of ideas and writing that find their ways onto the Internet and that seem to be most valued by Internet users.
2. As McGrath notes, free speech issues rage around the use of the Internet. Obviously, the Internet wasn't a medium for expression the writers of the Constitution had in mind when framing the Bill of Rights. Do some research into free speech laws that govern television and radio. How would you modify those laws to apply them to Internet use?

ACCUMULATING LITERACY
Writing and Learning to Write in the Twentieth Century

Deborah Brandt

> *The following selection includes excerpts from a long article in the October 1995 issue of* College English, *a journal published by the National Council of Teachers of English. By looking at three generations of the same Wisconsin family, University of Wisconsin English Professor Deborah Brandt is able to trace differences in what it means to read and write at different moments in American social history. Changes in literacy learning have resulted not only from rising standards of what it means to be literate but from a growing need to "amalgamate new reading and writing practices in response to rapid social change." Brandt's essay helps us put a human face on the effects of technological change.*

Genna May was born in 1898 on a small dairy farm in south central Wisconsin, the eighth of nine children of Norwegian immigrants. She spoke no English when she enrolled at the age of seven in a one-room schoolhouse built on land donated to the school district by her parents. Although Genna May would eventually go on to complete high school (as one of a graduating class of thirteen) by boarding in a town ten miles from her farm, she started school at a time when Wisconsin required only that young people ages seven to fifteen attend a local grammar school for twelve weeks a year (Landes and Solomon 56). As a student in "the grades," as she calls them, Genna May wrote spelling lessons on slates, erasing with a wet cloth to go on to arithmetic lessons. She remembers a home with few books and little paper, and she said she would have had no reason to write as a girl except to compose an occasional story assigned by her teacher. After high school graduation in 1917, she enrolled for several months in a private business college in the state capital, just long enough to learn typing and shorthand and win a certificate in penmanship before being placed by the college in the office of a local business that was manufacturing disinfectants for dairy farms. In 1994, Genna May was using writing to record recipes, balance her checkbook, and send holiday and birthday greetings to family members.

Genna May's great-grandson Michael May was born in 1981 in a sprawling suburb east of Wisconsin's state capital. In the early 1990s he was attending a middle school equipped with computers. The first of four children in his family, Michael remembered that his earliest composing occurred at two years old, when his parents helped him form simple words with magnetic letters on a metal easel and chalkboard in the family's TV room. As a participant in a grade-school enrichment program called Future Problem Solvers, he wrote a letter to his principal arranging to correct erosion on the school playground. In the bedroom of his eight-year-old sister Rhonda was a manual typewriter that their father had bought and used while attending a local technical school, a typewriter that Rhonda was now using recreationally. One weekend Michael's mother brought home a personal computer from her job as a data processor at a national insurance company so that she could learn a new program, and Michael remembered, she allowed him and his sister to type messages back and forth to each other on it. Asked what made writing important to him, Michael responded that "it has a lot to do with speaking," with "seeing correct words."

These accounts by two members of the same family capture many of the economic and social transformations of twentieth-century America: population movements from farms to urban centers to suburbs; shifts in the economic base from agriculture to manufacturing to information processing; the rise of big business; a rapid escalation in educational expectations; revolutions in communication technology; and the growth of a print culture so saturating that it has become a principal means by which some children learn to talk. Against that backdrop we see the dramatically different social contexts in which Genna May and her great-grandson learned about literacy and its relationship to the world. In the sparse setting of Genna May's prairie farmhouse, paper, hard to come by, was reserved for her father's church work. In Michael May's print-cluttered suburban ranch home, his parents introduced him to writing and reading amid the background chatter of network television. For members of the community in which Mrs. May grew up, the ability to write the words of everyday life often marked the end of formal schooling, while for Michael May these same experiences served as a preparation for kindergarten. In the social dynamic of the rural school district of the 1890s, it would not have been unusual for a teacher to board with her students' families while school was in session. Three generations later, in a twenty-five room middle school, students learned to address their principal by formal letter as a lesson in bureaucratic action.

These accounts complicate the argument that the demand now is simply for more people to achieve a kind of literacy that used to be achieved only by a few—or, as Lauren Resnick has put it, that everyone now has to develop reading and writing skills that used to belong only to an elite. (See Randall Collins for a critical treatment of rising educational standards.) However, to say merely that social changes dictate that Michael May achieve a higher level of literacy and education than his great-grandmother is to miss how the same social changes that demand higher eventual skills are already tangibly present at the scene of his literacy learning, part of the way a two-year-old in the 1980s learned what literacy is.

Not even elites of the past have encountered the current contexts in which literacy in its many forms is being practiced and learned.

In fact, these accounts suggest that what is unprecedented about literacy learning (and teaching) in the current climate is not so much a demand for literacy that seems chronically to outstrip supply, but rather the challenges faced by all literacy learners in a society whose rapid changes are themselves tied up so centrally with literacy and its enterprises. If Genna May carved out an early life amid a scarcity of print, her great-grandson must carve one out amid a material and ideological surplus. The setting in which Michael May first encountered the ABCs is layered with discarded and emergent forms of literacy and their histories. With his magnetic slate, he recapitulates in eerie ways a rudimentary ritual of the nineteenth-century schoolhouse at the same time that he must absorb from his parents the meanings that literacy and education have for middle-class families of the late twentieth century....

The piling up and extending out of literacy and its technologies give a complex flavor even to elementary acts of reading and writing today. Contemporary literacy learners—across positions of age, gender, race, class, and language heritage—find themselves having to piece together reading and writing experiences from more and more spheres, creating new and hybrid forms of literacy where once there might have been fewer and more circumscribed forms. What we calculate as a rising standard of basic literacy may be more usefully regarded as the effects of a rapid proliferation and diversification of literacy. And literate ability at the end of the twentieth century may be best measured as a person's capacity to amalgamate new reading and writing practices in response to rapid social change....

"IT WAS ALL DONE WITH WORDS:" LITERACY LEARNING BETWEEN THE WORLD WARS

To consider what these dynamics of accumulating literacy actually have meant to ordinary Americans, we now rejoin the May family, this time focusing on Sam May, the son of Genna May and grandfather of Michael. At the time of our interview, Sam May was nearing retirement from his position as an electronics technician in a science laboratory in a large state university. Born in 1925 and raised as part of an extended family in his mother's rural homestead, Sam May attended the same sparsely equipped schoolhouse as his mother through the eighth grade. He also attended the same high school as his mother had (this time making the ten-mile trip by carpool) and graduated in 1942, at a time when graduation rates in American high schools were doubling with each generation (Cremin 230; also see Daniel Resnick).

At home, Sam May was raised into a literacy of gentility and upward mobility promoted especially by his aunt, an invalid and autodidact, who had left school after the eighth grade yet wrote columns and editorials for a local newspaper. She had taken classes through the Palmer School in Iowa, becoming "famous for her fancy hand," and gave Sam and his two siblings penmanship lessons on rainy Saturday afternoons. "My mother's sister was always chiding us to read better books and practice more writing," he explained.

In many of Sam May's recollections of early literacy learning, one detects still influential associations between language correctness and good breeding so prevalent in nineteenth-century ideologies of the upwardly mobile middle class—a literacy that was also designed to express a local identity and community ethos. Above all, literacy learning was part of acquiring manners. "We had to have manners," Mr. May explained. "If the minister was to be at the table on Sunday we all were supposed to be able to talk a little bit to anyone who was there, or if someone important was there." Mr. May described the impression made on him by the language habits of older, wealthy people who lived in his village, people for whom he would do occasional yard work:

> I was exposed to some pretty high class people early in life—people who had thousands of bucks and mansions—and they took me in. They used proper grammar in their talking, their speech, and their actions were geared such that you felt comfortable with them. It all had to do with words. If they wrote a note for you, it was beautiful handwriting, and, gosh, I wish I could have done that. [They] had a cultured way about them which we little farm boys would try to emulate. At the time. I've since given it up!

While early school experiences seemed to reinforce many of these values ("spelling and neatness were very important to the teachers"), other influences pressed in—and were brought in by new technologies. Sam May recalled frequent writing in connection with outdoor boyhood play, such as leaving messages for his friends on the sides of their forts and developing a "code machine" ("two papers that slid around"), inspired by the decoder rings promoted on the radio show "Little Orphan Annie." He also recalled collaborating with large groups of children on "sideshows" that they wrote and performed in connection with weekly outdoor movie nights that started up in the village during the warm months. The children would charge people a few cents each to watch their skits, which were organized in circus-like or vaudeville fashion yet were also inspired by the celluloid action:

> When I was from the age of ten on they had weekly outdoor movies. On Thursday night five hundred people would come into this little town, sit down on the grass, and watch a western. It was

> put on by the businesses. So it was like carnival night.... Well, there weren't any live people up there so [we figured] let's make a sideshow. We had to write these flyers, and we would have to write these scripts, and there had to be a master of ceremonies [who would] have to organize this thing, and maybe even write down what he had to say, at least the order in which the show was going to come off. Then we'd have a little dance and there would be someone singing. It was all fun. It was great.

As Mr. May explained, with the Depression, large families were moving to rural communities like his, where vegetable gardens could be grown and barter was more acceptable. Composing skits, plays, circus routines, and secret messages was a way for children to build and maintain community during this transient time. Collaborative writing developed as a necessity ("If you had a neighborhood play and there was only one person organizing it all," Mr. May explained, "the rest of the kids would quit!").

Yet Mr. May's memories also address in interesting ways how intrusions of new technologies of film and radio stimulated writing and altered recreational literacy. For example, the converging of farm families to watch westerns on Thursday nights created a new, public audience beyond family or school for whom Sam May and his playmates could perform, as well as new visual genres to fuel their imaginations. The film nights also created an economic niche in which children could write and perform for money.

New technology stimulated writing in other ways, too. Radio shows such as "Little Orphan Annie" and "Jack Armstrong" encouraged Sam May and his siblings to write letters to distant radio stations to acquire decoder rings. And the radio became an additional forum for communicating standards of correct or finer speech—a matter that continued to draw Mr. May's attention:

> So to listen to those stories of "The Shadow" or "Orson Welles Theatre" or "Mercury Theatre." God, you could get right in. I mean, you could picture this whole thing going on and it was all done with words. In our neighborhood plays we would try to reconstruct that or if you were entertaining some relatives or a friend. Or if you got a little poem that your mother wants you to read in front of them, a dozen relatives, because they think it's good and you want to show off. And you read this dumb thing and you realize how really limited you are compared to Orson Welles. You were always comparing yourself to Orson Welles.

We can gauge in Mr. May's recollections a more complicated, even contradictory literacy landscape in comparison to what his mother remembered. In a period of rapidly rising educational expectations and painful economic dislocations, Sam May was still being oriented to a legacy of nineteenth-century rural literacy practices based on oral performance, piety, manners, and communal expression—a legacy transmitted principally through the self-education of a member of the previous generation. This legacy in turn was mixing with the influences of new media that to some extent were incorporated into the conservative aims of this genteel literacy, but also, as we shall see, foreshadowed a radical transformation in society and in Sam May's literacy development. Initially, for the young Sam May and his associates, the arrival of radio and film inspired and enhanced writing for purposes of local, oral performances that resembled the old-fashioned circus ("there weren't any live people up there"). At the same time, though, technological innovations brought into the village from the outside new, more abstract genres, new audience configurations, new channels of communication, and new ways of hearing oneself ("You were always comparing yourself to Orson Welles").

As a teenager Sam May set up a "little workshop" in an abandoned garage where he began to build crystal radio sets and where he often recorded thoughts and ideas for inventions in a notebook that he carried with him constantly. Radio was taking on yet another kind of meaning for Sam May—and the country. In 1941, only seventeen days after the attack on Pearl Harbor, a correspondence school called the Army Institute was established nearby in Madison, Wisconsin, as part of what Harold F. Clark and Harold S. Sloan describe as an "explosive" growth in technology and military education brought on during and just after the war (22). In a span of a few years, the development of radar, the jet airplane, the first digital computer, and the transistor (not to mention the atomic bomb) created nearly instant need for new knowledge and skill, much of it literacy-based. (See Ginzberg and Bray [39ff.] for an account of how male illiteracy was constructed as a social problem at the outbreak of World War II.)

Graduating from high school in 1942 and planning to enlist, Sam May took courses through the Army Institute, becoming a certified radio repairman by the time he was eighteen. Soon after, he joined the armed services and was assigned to the Army Signal Corps, but, because of a surplus of radio repairmen, he eventually became a fourth-echelon radar technician stationed in Europe. Like other military veterans I have interviewed, Mr. May described his service years as a period of intensified writing, a period especially when learners of new technologies quickly turned around and became the teachers. (See Clark and Sloan for descriptions of classroom education in the military during and after World War II.)

For Mr. May's part, he began writing service manuals and also weekly reports back to the factory where radar equipment was being manufactured. These reports described changes he was making to the equipment. "We were engineering out the mistakes," he explained. While confident of his technical ability, Sam May said he was less satisfied with his ability to write reports, describing his efforts as "perfunctory." "I'd say 'I changed this resistor to that.' [The form] would ask, 'What was the reason for the change?' and I'd write, 'Because this other one is a mistake.'"

Sam May then went on to describe a strategy he developed for acquiring a new kind of technical literacy that his position was demanding. Just as he often had to improvise to keep the radar equipment working, Sam May improvised a method of learning report writing, modeled in fact on his earlier ways of approaching "manners" in boyhood:

> Other people used to ask my advice a lot, people who were better at phrasing things than I was, and I'd listen to them, especially the officers, I'd listen to them. Or I'd have to discuss what I wanted to do with, say, a lieutenant or a captain. I was just a mere sergeant. These were all college guys and I was, of course, just a high school brat. So I'd listen to how they'd talk with each other and how they would talk to their peers and their minions. So you could sense the correctness of how they phrased things and how they put things. They always knew how to stay on the subject, not get sidetracked. That had something to do with writing.

Sam May eventually became a "college guy," enrolling for four years under the G.I. Bill in the engineering school of his state university. Now an electronics technician, Mr. May said he devotes about 30 percent of the work day to writing, mostly making circuit diagrams (often on blackboards) and writing footnotes or captions for science reports produced in the labs to which he is assigned. At the time of our interview, sixty-seven-year-old Mr. May indicated he did not use a computer available to him a work. "I haven't had time to learn but I plan to," he said, "because it is very useful. Saves a lot of drafting time."

This partial account of one man's literacy learning between the 1920s and 1940s shows in very particular ways how transformations in literacy accompany large-scale economic, technological, and cultural changes and how these transformations are felt within individual lives. We can gauge this change most interestingly in the two episodes in which Sam May recalls emulating the language of the elite: the first, as a farm boy in a context of manners and noblesse oblige in a socially stratified rural village; the second, as a subordinate army officer in an emerging military-industrial context beginning to require even of "mere sergeants" an ability to render technical know-how in professional prose. These scenes speak to the enduring power of dominant classes to define language standards (a power Pierre Bourdieu has explored in detail); they predict the emerging power of a highly educated, technocratic elite after the war. Most interesting, these accounts also indicate how much the meaning of education and educated language had begun to change by mid-century—shifting from the cultivated talk of the well-bred to the efficient professional prose of the technocrat—thereby altering the paths of upward mobility for people like Sam May.

Many of the materials and strategies that Sam May identifies as part of his literacy learning also appear frequently in the stories of others I have interviewed. The accounts suggest that while a society's older forms of literacy may be superseded by new ones, the old ones don't disappear. Print lasts and artifacts accumulate—that is their appeal and power—littering the material sites of subsequent literacy learning and shaping future interpretations of reading and writing.

This holding on or holding over of older literacies is actually an integral part of the way that one generation passes on the fruits of its education to subsequent generations, a process that is at the center of what we think of as the educational advances of the twentieth century and a process that can have both a conservative and a propelling effect. Schooling typically brings into a family's possession books, manuals, typewriters, and the like that then become the first forms of literacy that the next generation encounters. So Sam May recalled how he would "beg a book" from his aunt's collection and how she would reenact her Palmer School handwriting lessons around the dining room table of the family farm. In an interview Sam May's son, Jonathan, indicated that some of the first books he recalled encountering as a boy were the college textbooks and technical manuals of his parents. The influence of other people's literacy and artifacts of their literacy move back and forth across generations, sometimes from younger to older. At the time of our interview, for instance, seventy-nine-year-old Emily Staubach had recently acquired the first personal computer of her life, a "hand-me-up" from her professional son, which she was using to write family memoirs. She in turn had passed her old manual typewriter on to her grandchildren to play with. When I asked thirty-four-year-old Jonathan May to recall how he learned to write reports, he replied, "Well, I think I'm learning more now with my own kids going through school."

It is through such material channels that literacy traditions of previous times appear in the present and that formal education accumulates as a resource in middle-class and working-class households. Reading and writing strategies acquired from older (or younger) generations are then reinterpreted and transformed for use in new and different circumstances—as Sam May's search for writing "manners" demonstrated. In fact, the transformation of literacy obtained in one context for use in another was a principal strategy of literacy learning among the people I interviewed and a hallmark of advancing literacy. Sometimes I think what I am seeing and trying to describe are merely diffusions of education and upward mobility in action, the means by which those resources and aspirations translate into specific experiences with literacy. I also think what I am seeing and trying to describe are the things that bring such complexity to contemporary literacy acquisition. Whereas at one time literacy might have been best achieved by attending to traditional knowledge and tight locuses of meaning, literacy in an advanced literate period requires an ability to work the borders between tradition and change, an ability to adapt and improvise and amalgamate. . . .

ACCUMULATING LITERACY: IMPLICATIONS FOR THEORY

In *The Importance of Illiteracy,* a wise little book written at mid-century, M. M. Lewis suggested that sharply rising concerns about illiteracy around that time were actually indications of the success of literacy in spreading and escalating in value. He pointed out how the social significance of literacy is itself a contributing factor in illiteracy, as spiraling expectations for achievement contribute to the shame and frustration of those who fall below the standard (98). Lewis's book is intriguing because it draws attention to the effects created by a surplus of literacy in this century, even when contemplating the phenomenon of illiteracy. That is, Lewis asks that we entertain the paradoxes that an advancing literacy presents, including the possibility that achievements *and* failures in reading and writing are caused in some ways by the same conditions. . . .

Especially important is the ideological potency of literacy materials that come into people's lives and into the scenes of their learning. Materials to some degree always will reflect how individuals, including students, are intersecting at a certain time with the ongoing, official history of mass literacy and the institutions that have controlled it. Because written materials tend to accumulate as household possessions, as forms of inheritance, and because they accumulate as well in the form of remembered readings or writings, these intersections with the history of literacy can be quite complex processes of projection and retrospection. And, while written materials always carry traces of the grand history of official literacy, they also can be infused, as we have seen, with family histories and autobiographical constructions.

Important too is the realization that the history of literacy at any moment is always carrying along a complex, sometimes cacophonous mix of fading and ascending materials, practices, and ideologies. Literacy is always in flux. Learning to read and write necessitates an engagement with this flux, with the layers of literacy's past, present, and future, often embodied in materials and tools and just as often embodied in the social relationships we have with the people who are teaching us to read and write. Indeed, as changes in literacy have speeded up in the twentieth century, literate ability has become more and more defined as the ability to position and reposition oneself amidst literacy's recessive and emergent forms.

This essay has only begun to scratch the surface of accumulating or advancing literacy. Yet to be treated, among other things, are the profound effects of electronic media, including television and computers, as well as the meanings of language diversity and immigration in an advanced literate society. But at this point in the investigation I lean, with M. M. Lewis, toward the proposition that problems with reading and writing are less about the lack of literacy in society than about the surplus of it. Being literate in the late twentieth century has to do with being able to negotiate that burgeoning surplus.

References

Beniger, James R. *The Control Revolution: Technological and Economic Origins of the Information Society.* Cambridge: Harvard UP, 1986.
Bourdieu, Pierre. *Language and Symbolic Power.* Cambridge: Harvard UP, 1991.
Clark, Harold F., and Harold S. Sloan. *Classrooms in the Military: An Account of Education in the Armed Forces of the United States.* New York: Teachers College, 1964.
Cochran-Smith, Marilyn. *The Making of a Reader.* Norwood, NJ: Ablex, 1984.
Collins, Randall. *The Credential Society: An Historical Sociology of Education and Stratification.* New York: Academic P, 1979.
Cremin, Lawrence A. *American Education: The Metropolitan Experience.* New York: Harper and Row, 1988.
Ginzberg, Eli, and Douglas W. Bray. *The Uneducated.* New York: Columbia UP, 1953.
Heath, Shirley Brice. *Ways with Words.* New York: Cambridge UP, 1984.
Landes, William, and Lewis Solomon. "Compulsory Schooling Legislation." *Journal of Economic History* 32 (1972): 54–91.
Lewis, M. M. *The Importance of Illiteracy.* London: Harrap, 1953.
Resnick, Daniel. "Historical Perspectives on Literacy and Schooling." *Literacy: An Overview by 14 Experts.* Ed. Stephen R. Graubard. New York: Noonday P, 1991.

Questions for Discussion

1. What are the most striking differences in the learning experiences of the three generations of the May family that Deborah Brandt portrays here? Which circumstances most clearly seem to dictate the need for a different approach to literacy learning? Describe your own literacy learning process.

2. Brandt talks about social and psychological "incentives" for learning to read and write. What are some of those incentives in the stories she presents? What have been your most important incentives in learning to read and write?

3. What do Brandt's interviews tell us about the connection between literacy learning and a desire for upward mobility? How is learning related to other social or community values?

4. Brandt notes that older forms of literacy do not simply disappear when new forms emerge. How does she use Sam May's experience to illustrate this conclusion? What are the effects of holding on to older forms of literacy? How have older forms of literacy influenced your own learning experiences?

5. Based on changes Brandt describes here, what do you suppose it will mean to be literate in ten years? In fifty years?

Questions for Research and Writing

1. Using the same kinds of questions that Brandt uses to gather information from her sources, interview a friend, roommate, or classmate about his or her experience of learning to read and write. How does the literacy narrative created from your subject's experience differ from the narratives of Brandt's subjects? Also, interview someone from a different generation (or a different cultural, ethnic, or socioeconomic background) and compare that person's literacy narrative to yours. How do differences in age, sex, race, ethnicity, or class influence learning experiences?
2. Find Brandt's original article in the October 1995 issue of *College English*. Read the section on Charles Randolph, an African American born in Mississippi in 1948. What seems most important about this story, and how does it relate to your experiences of literacy learning?

JEOPARDY!, CULTURAL LITERACY, AND THE DISCOURSE OF TRIVIA

Michael C. Berthold

> *When it was first published in 1988, E. D. Hirsch's book* Cultural Literacy *raised widespread concerns about what Americans know and why they need to know it. In Hirsch's opinion, a body of knowledge common to a people or society ensures national cohesion. The following article from* Journal of American Culture *(1990) by Villanova University English Professor Michael C. Berthold argues, in effect, that television may be a major force in transmitting the kind of cultural literacy for which Hirsch clamors. The argument raises even broader questions about how knowledge and culture are defined. Why are certain kinds of information valued over others?*

It may come as some surprise to Merv Griffin that *Jeopardy!*, his popular television game show, is strikingly analogous to *Cultural Literacy*, E. D. Hirsch's recent educational manifesto. In this article I will examine some of the implications of this probably inadvertent alliance. Mark Crispin Miller, in his analysis of the culture of TV, has described the way in which television is not only "on the air," but has become "the very air we breathe."[1] If Miler is correct in this assumption about TV's diffuse and determinant role in the construction of our environment, it seems to me to be necessary to evaluate Hirsch's program within the context of the video culture that inevitably contains it. That is, what kind of transmission of Hirsch's cultural literacy does TV allow? And what kind of validation of cultural literacy does TV allow? The pertinence of a game show like *Jeopardy!* to these questions is that its quiz format makes explicit the facts that are known and perpetuated in a cultural environment dominated by TV. Conversely, to read *Jeopardy!* against *Cultural Literacy* is a way to clarify the cultural work that a show like *Jeopardy!* is, and is not, doing.

A brief summary of the premises of each program is helpful at this point. On *Jeopardy!*, players are given answers in various categories for which they provide the questions. The categories range from the bookish "Ancient History" to the more visceral "Potent Potables" or contemporary "Tough TV Trivia;" there are five "answers" per category. The show is comprised of a Single Jeopardy round (of six categories), a Double Jeopardy round (also of six categories, double the monetary value), and Final Jeopardy (all three contestants, having decided how much of their winnings to wager, write their questions to a single answer). Final Jeopardy determines the day's winner, the only contestant who actually keeps the cash he or she has tallied. Although some strategy and luck are involved in playing the game, gimmickry and glitz are minimal, and knowledge is rewarded. As a *TV Guide* review panegyrizes, the show is nothing if not "classy."[2]

Beneath *Jeopardy!*'s formalism, however, there is a vigilant edginess. The very title *Jeopardy!* adumbrates danger, risk, and the threat implicit in not having the right information or knowing the right answer; on *Jeopardy!*, as Pynchon wrote in *The Crying of Lot 49,* "possibilities for paranoia become abundant." The urgent exclamation point that dots the title and the show's inexorable movement towards a "final" jeopardy further suggest a game show plot whose basic configuration is apocalyptic.

Subtitled "What Every American Needs to Know," Hirsch's book focuses on "the background knowledge necessary for functional literacy and effective national communication.["][3] "Cultural literacy," according to Hirsch, is a whole "network of information" that enables a "competent" reader to generate the "unstated context" (2) which gives words and texts their meaning. The breadth of this basic information is "great, extending over the major domains of human activity from sports to science;" it is not confined to "'culture' narrowly understood as an acquaintance with the arts" (xiii). Ideally, cultural literacy for Hirsch insures political liberalism by enabling all Americans, whatever their age, ethnicity, or region, to communicate with one another and to participate in the country's larger political discourse.[4] But Hirsch's book, like *Jeopardy!,* also has a telos of materialism; one of Hirsch's great worries is the erosion of "our competitiveness in the world" (5), and he proclaims that "only highly literate societies prosper economically" (1). If *Jeopardy!* is something of an allegorical apocalypse, *Cultural Literacy* is a good American jeremiad; it is a sermon built around baleful facts of educational backsliding and cultural decline that nevertheless heralds a renewed national faith and prosperity. Hirsch himself imagines cultural literacy to be a "civil bible" (100).

Hirsch's very definition of "culture" suggests parallels with *Jeopardy!*. The game show too assumes a "breadth" of information that extends over "the major domains of human activity;" in fact, Hirsch's examples of "sports" and "science" are two favorite *Jeopardy!* categories. Further analogies are suggested by the "Appendix" to *Cultural Literacy* on "What Literate Americans Know."[5] In this list of nearly 5000 entries from "Aaron, Hank," to "Zurich," Hirsch not only codifies his program of cultural literacy, but authors a virtual script for a TV quiz show. The back of the Vintage paperback edition of *Cultural Literacy,* for example, offers this challenge: "Test your cultural literacy. Can you put the following in context?" (Sample entries from the appendix—Homestead Act, penis envy, Valhalla—follow). Similarly, an ad for the book from the Quality Paperback Book Club urges the reader to "Find out how culturally literate you are by taking the illuminating 'self-test' . . . in this provocative best seller." Simon and Schuster, finally, have actually published a text entitled *Test Your Cultural Literacy* that was recently advertised in the *New York Times Book Review.*

Hirsch, of course, is not necessarily responsible for these seeming bastardizations of his project. But I think it is more important to suggest that *Cultural Literacy* is hardly demeaned by its similarities to a *Jeopardy!*'s trivial pursuits. The very intimacy of cultural literacy and trivia is instructive—instructive both of the relativism underlining all cultural agendas, Hirsch's included, and of the latent seriousness informing much that is dismissed as trivial. *Jeopardy!*, to borrow Wilde's subtitle from *The Importance of Being Earnest*, is "trivial" theater "for serious people." Hirsch himself, in the course of his very brief comments on television in *Cultural Literacy*, admits that we cannot blame television for the state of our literacy and that "in some respects, such as its use of standard written English, television watching is acculturative" (20). As a television analogue to *Cultural Literacy*, *Jeopardy!* dramatizes how deeply acculturative TV watching can be.

Closer examination of *Cultural Literacy* and *Jeopardy!* reveals how congruent their ideologies are. *Jeopardy!*, essentially, validates the central tenets of Hirsch's program. One of these tenets has to do with the individual's actual relationship with Hirsch's daunting list of what literate Americans "know." For "knowing," as Hirsch himself readily acknowledges, is a fundamental misnomer; rather, recognition and association are much more crucial to cultural literacy than knowledge *qua* knowledge. Hirsch, for example, explains:

> Very few specific titles appear on the list, and they usually appear as words, not works, because they represent writings that culturally literate people have read about but haven't read. *Das Kapital* is a good example. Cultural literacy is represented not by a *prescriptive* list of books but rather by a *descriptive* list of the information actually possessed by literate Americans. (xiv)

In prefatory remarks to the appendix, Hirsch continues in a similar vein:

> The information about literature that exist in the minds of literate people may have been derived from conversation, criticism, cinema, television, or student crib sheets like *Cliff Notes* . . . Only a small proportion of literate people can name the Shakespeare plays in which Falstaff appears, yet they know who he is. They know what *Mein Kampf* is, but they haven't read it. (146)

The unflinching pragmatics of Hirsch's cultural literacy are reminiscent of the truism that Americans look deeply into the surface of things. In fact, the ingenuity by which Americans find out about books without actually reading them may itself be quintessentially American. Cultural literacy privileges intellectual alacrity and well-informed glibness. The very attainment of "cultural literacy" implies a certain insouciance; the culturally literate never let others see them sweat.

Jeopardy! embodies this same pragmatics of knowing in which recognition is more important than profundity, in which hearing about a book is more important than reading it. In a gracious and informative letter to me, Kathy Easterling, one of *Jeopardy!*'s writers, described the process by which the show's questions are constructed.⁶ Staff writers try to have two sources for every item of information used; the very reference books the writers rely on—*Encyclopedia Americana, Encyclopedia Brittanica, The Reader's Encyclopedia, The Oxford Companion to English Literature, Bartlett's Familiar Quotations*—order and distill knowledge in a fashion similar to Hirsch's. A larger philosophy of recognition underlines *Jeopardy!*'s construction of its questions. According to Easterling,

> We try to write only questions that are possible to answer. We HATE it when the contestants just stand and stare at a question; we want them to guess even if they aren't sure of the answer.

Thus, even a $1000 question in Double Jeopardy, technically the most esoteric questions the show asks, "should require more of a thought process and be more difficult, but not impossible." At another point in her letter, Easterling makes the affinities between *Jeopardy!* and *Cultural Literacy* even more explicit: *Jeopardy!*'s writers "assume" that the show's contestants "have heard of the books we write questions about, even if they haven't read them." A fundamental credo of the game show, like *Cultural Literacy*, is that "we try not to be too obscure." An "obscure novel" by a "famous author" might be the basis of a question, but "never an obscure book by an obscure author." Like *Cultural Literacy*, *Jeopardy!* is informed by principles of familiarity and recognition that endorse the common cultural idiom that the literate presumably share.

Even *Jeopardy!*'s sense of its audience is similar to Hirsch's. Easterling, for example, is concerned both with the contestants' *and* the home audience's familiarity with the show's questions:

> Our audience must relate to the material in some way. Our producer wants the audience to relate to every question in some way—even if they haven't heard of Mark Twain's book about Joan of Arc they've heard of both Twain and Joan so we can use a question about it.

As individual "texts," both *Jeopardy!* and *Cultural Literacy* not only mirror a larger cultural field and consensus, but also enact virtual rites of initiation and participation for that culture.

Sample questions from *Jeopardy!* further demonstrate how entwined the modes of the game show and Hirsch are. For example, the answer to one Final Jeopardy category on "Books & Authors" posed the following: "Born in Bengal in 1903, this author's most famous book was set 81 years later." As a prime example of *Jeopardy!*'s tactics of familiarity, the correct "question" to the "answer" here is intimated by the clue itself. The answer's numerics ("1903," "81 years later") presumably lead the contestant to the crucial number "1984," immediately suggesting George Orwell as the author in question. Actual reading knowledge of *1984* is irrelevant; what matters is the recognition of the significance of the date itself, and the ability to associate that date with Orwell and, typically, his most "famous" work. The way that this Final Jeopardy round played itself out is also interesting. Two of the contestants arrived at the correct question. But the third, an adept *Jeopardy!* player who had already won three games, outsmarted himself. He first guessed "Kipling" as the question to the answer, crossed it out, and then wrote down "Naipaul." Pursuing the red herring of "Born in Bengal," he overlooked the clue's pivotal coded information about 1984. On *Jeopardy!*, in short, too much knowledge is a dangerous thing. It is also not surprising that "Orwell" is an item in *Cultural Literacy*'s appendix, and that Hirsch lists "1984" as one of only seven pivotal dates the literate should recognize.

Another telling *Jeopardy!* illustration comes from a category on "K in Literature" in a Double Jeopardy round. Again, the clue itself generates its correct response, and no hard knowledge either of the author or the literature is required: "He wrote odes on so many subjects, he may have been the most 'ode'ious poet in English literature." Arriving at the correct question, "Who is John Keats?," involves no intimacy with British Romanticism; merely keying on the amusingly egregious pun on "ode" and associating the ode with Keats suffice. Again, not surprisingly, both "Keats" and "ode" are items in Hirsch's appendix.

One last set of examples should serve to underscore how deeply committed *Jeopardy!* is to recognition over knowledge. The answers to an entire category devoted to F. Scott Fitzgerald read as follows:

$100   Fitzgerald moved to this city in 1937 and began an unsuccessful career as a screenwriter.

$200   Like several of his main characters, Fitzgerald was an army officer in this war.

$300   In *The Beautiful and the Damned,* Fitzgerald's marriage to her is fictionally described.

$400   Reportedly saying it began on May Day 1919, Fitzgerald wrote "Tales" of this era.

$500   Uncompleted, this was Fitzgerald's "Last" novel.

The day's contestants had no problems with any of these clues ("What is Hollywood?," "What is World War I?," "Who is Zelda?," "What is the Jazz Age?," "What is *The Last Tycoon*?), perhaps because not a single one of them demands any real knowledge of Fitzgerald's work. Even the "poser" here, the $500 answer, is a fill-in-the-blank clue about an only slightly obscure Fitzgerald title. Fitzgerald's currency is a function of his status as belletristic icon and cultural hero—his stint in Hollywood, his romance with Zelda, his chronicling of the Jazz Age. The category provides a version of literary history via *People* magazine. As such, it is a parable of the perils of cultural literacy.

Both Hirsch and *Jeopardy!* encode programs of "extensive but limited" (127) information that finally reflect a larger conservatism. Hirsch admits that "The body of background knowledge that is taken for granted in literate national communication changes very slowly" (xi). Although he attempts (I think unconvincingly) to dissociate the conservatism of literacy from any political conservatism and himself preaches a political liberalism, he confesses that the "materials in the list that are of recent origin constitute less than 20 percent of the total" (xii). Moreover, in an observation he emphasizes by italicizing it, Hirsch notes that "Eighty percent of the listed items have been in use for more than a hundred years!" (xii). Hirsch voices his essential conservatism when he explains that his list aims "to represent but not to alter current literate American culture" (136).

It is this business of representing but not altering current literate American culture that holds especially true for *Jeopardy!*'s own conservatism. To focus my consideration of this conservatism, I wish to concentrate on *Jeopardy!*'s treatment of American literature—a species of knowledge that is salient to Hirsch's discussion and that has provoked vigorous academic debate in recent years. *Jeopardy!* advocates a very traditional canon of American literature at a time when Americanists have sought to redefine and extend their sense of what constitutes a national "classic." The traditional canon of American literature tends to center on white, male authors, such as, Emerson, Hawthorne, Poe, Melville, and Hemingway; these figures, the argument goes, are artificers of eternity whose texts are monuments of unageing intellect. The new canon, however, has sought to recover misconstrued figures from America's literary past and to make room for the women, blacks, gays, Native Americans, Mexican Americans, Asian Americans, and other minorities whose work has usually been ignored or marginalized. Thus Emory Elliott, editor of the 1988 *Columbia Literary History of the United States,* argues that "the distinctive features" of American literature are its "diversity of literary materials" and "wide variety of critical voices;" the history of American literature, writes Elliott, "is not one story but many different stories."[7] Sacvan Bercovitch, currently editing a multivolume literary history of America for Cambridge University Press that should be the definitive American literary history for this generation, propounds similar views; Bercovitch questions the presentation of our "literary heritage" as a series of "classic writers" and "major works" authorized by standards that their justifiers regard as "timeless, universal, and inherent in the process of literary creation," and he employs "dissensus" rather than consensus as the governing principle of his history.[8] A reconstructed American literature, thus, will include not only the Emersons, Hawthornes, and Hemingways of our literary tradition, but also the Black Elks, Zora Neale Hurstons, and Anzia Yezierskas.

Jeopardy!'s own consensus ideology commits the show to a traditional canon of American literature. Says Easterling, "American Literature, on *Jeopardy!,* at least, is composed of classics and of excellent modern literature." Although the show does "try to include black authors and women authors," its primary avoidance of obscurity limits such inclusions. Through a closer examination of actual questions from *Jeopardy!*, I would like to demonstrate the show's deep allegiance to traditional American "classics" and to consider some of the ramifications of this conservatism.

For a six-month period, I watched *Jeopardy!* daily and recorded every question related to American literature. These questions appear both in categories devoted strictly to American literature ("American Literature," "American Poetry," "American Authors") and in more general literary categories ("World Literature," "Pulitzer Prize Novels," "Women in Fiction"). Literature categories are staples of *Jeopardy!* and usually appear at least once or twice a week; specific American literature categories appear approximately every other week.

Certain of *Jeopardy!*'s American literature categories reveal nothing but straightforward recapitulations of the traditional canon. One "American Literature" category, for example, built questions around Edward E. Hale's "Man Without a Country," Faulkner's *The Sound and the Fury*, Twain's *Tom Sawyer*, Cooper's Natty Bumppo, and Howell's *The Rise of Silas Lapham*. Hale's story is a hoary high-school favorite. The other four writers are the standard fare of college survey courses in American literature. The Howells' clue perhaps verges on obscurity, but the wording of the clue, as is *Jeopardy!*'s wont, compels a correct response: "In this Wm. Dean Howells novel, the title character 'rises' morally while falling financially."

Jeopardy!'s understanding of an American literary "classic," however, is sometimes dubious. Another "American Literature" category, for example, juxtaposed questions about Henry James and Ambrose Bierce with questions about Frank Buck's *Bring 'Em Back Alive* and (in a particular howler) Norman Vincent Peale's *The Power of Positive Thinking*. Similarly, a category on "American Poetry" set Robert Frost's "Fire and Ice" against such less finely wrought poetic specimens as Longfellow's "Paul Revere's Ride," Clement Moore's "A Visit from St. Nicholas," and "Casey at the Bat." On the basis of these examples, the *Jeopardy!* American literary canon reveals its own idiosyncrasies; its traditionalism co-exists with a strange populism that deems Peale and Moore "literary" and grants their work cultural currency. *Jeopardy!* itself, on the one hand, is an example of populist intellectualism that enforces hierarchies between "high" and "low" culture; says Easterling, for example, "A question on Jackie Collins or Judith Krantz would never be included under 'literature' but under Books and Authors." Yet within a single "Literature" category, the show does not necessarily differentiate between a Peale and a Frost.

A look at questions about American literature in *Jeopardy!*'s broader literature categories further reveals a traditionalism veering towards the middlebrow. For example, Thornton Wilder and Erskine Caldwell both appear twice. Modernist poet *par excellence* Odgen Nash appears *three* times! Writers such as James Thurber, Edgar Lee Masters, Joyce Kilmer, and Vachel Lindsay are also popular. Although Hawthorne, Twain, Faulkner, *et al.* continue to make their obligatory appearances, they share their air-time with figures who are not always included even in traditional American literary canons. I suspect that the source of the *Jeopardy!* middlebrow canon may be the well-intentioned curriculums of traditionalist high schools. I am reminded, say, of the rather antediluvian reading list that the New York State Board of Regents draws up for its high school students, or at least drew up when I was a high school student in the seventies.

Despite some peculiarities, the design of *Jeopardy!*'s canon is consistent with Easterling's claim that American literature on the show is composed "of classics and of excellent modern literature." My specific tabulation of the show's questions about American literature underlines its bedrock conservatism. Almost one hundred questions on American literature appeared on *Jeopardy!* during my six-month survey. The show's preferred authors, with number of appearances in parentheses, are: Poe (8), Fitzgerald (6), Steinbeck (5), Hawthorne (3), Longfellow (3), Faulkner (3), Nash (3). The authors who appear twice are: Holmes, Twain, James, Frost, Hemingway, Cather, Wilder, Caldwell, Edna St. Vincent Millay, Tennessee Williams, Shirley Jackson. Constituting over fifty percent of the show's questions on American literature, these entries alone suggest how *Jeopardy!* combines "classics" and "modern literature" and how it favors a restricted canon of authors. The domination of the "classics" is especially evident in the list of authors who appear three or more times; with the exception of Nash, each of these authors is a white, male, canonical figure, three from the nineteenth century, three from the twentieth. Questions about modern literature are ubiquitous both in these lists of *Jeopardy!*'s privileged authors and throughout my larger sample. Over half the entries from the whole sample, in fact, concern twentieth century works and writers; other favored recent writers include Sandburg, Mencken, Thurber, Styron, and Albee.

The skewed nature of the *Jeopardy!* canon becomes clearer on an examination of the place of women and minorities in it. Only about ten percent of the entries of this sample are devoted to American women writers: Stowe, Alcott, Dickinson, Cather, Millay, Jackson, Helen Keller, Ayn Rand, Carson McCullers. This roster is itself problematic; Keller is really an extra-literary talent, Shirley Jackson appears twice because of her frequently anthologized story "The Lottery," Millay's presence is in part attributable only to the music of her patronymic and its aptness for categories such as "Authors' Middle Names." Regardless, whether the category be "classics" or "excellent modern literature," women are under-represented. Even when *Jeopardy!* devotes an entire category to "Women in Fiction," a category that appeared twice during my survey, the women, in nine out of ten instances, are characters in men's books. In the calculus of *Jeopardy!*, there are eight Poe questions for every one Dickinson question, and such ratios indicate the show's biases. The show fares even less well on the issue of the place of minority writers in the canon. It is particularly disturbing that only one minority writer—Ralph Ellison—appears on the show in six months of literature questions. Although *Jeopardy!* does sometimes employ categories such as "Black America," to deny Black American writers a more solidified place in its literary categories is to deny them deserved aesthetic sanction. If, say, contemporary Black woman writer Gloria Naylor's *The Women of Brewster Place* can serve as the basis for an Oprah Winfrey TV miniseries, perhaps Naylor warrants a place in *Jeopardy!*'s literary categories as well.

I do not mean to cavil about the limitations of a game show that does, after all, propose a near-radical and ever-fearful symmetry between book knowledge and television culture; my cavils are those of a *Jeopardy!* fan. But both *Cultural Literacy* and *Jeopardy!*, in their insistence on representing without altering current American culture, seem not to recognize that mirroring a *status quo* is itself a politicizing gesture. As custodians of a cultural hegemony, both Hirsch and *Jeopardy!* are neglectful of the flux of canons and the variabilities of culture. As Maria Margaronis suggests, Hirsch (and by extension *Jeopardy!*) tends to slight "the common ground of lived experience. You can't join people with disparate histories and unequal power in a more perfect union simply by programming them with the same raw data."[9] Paul Armstrong, in response to Hirsch's "monistic" cultural literacy, has called for a program of "'pluralistic literacy'—the ability to deal effectively with cultural differences and to negotiate the competing claims of multiple ways of reading."[10]

Both *Cultural Literacy* and *Jeopardy!* come to enact certain paradoxes and impasses of democracy and elitism. Hirsch zealously affirms the openness of the idiom of cultural literacy:

> It is, therefore, a very odd cliché that connects literate national culture with elitism, since it is the least elitist or exclusive culture that exists in any modern nation. Literate culture is far less exclusive, for instance, than any ethnic culture, no matter how poverty bound, or pop culture or youth culture. It has no in-group, no generational or geographical preference. It can be mastered in the country or in the city, in a shanty or a mansion, so long as the opportunity is given. (106)

While arguing for the inclusiveness of "literate culture," Hirsch actually shows it to be implacable and polarizing, in continual binary opposition to "ethnic culture," "pop culture," or "youth culture." In a fundamental tension of Hirsch's text, a rhetoric of exclusivity propels his egalitarian program. As a subtext of this passage, moreover, cultural literacy also functions as an implicit vehicle of economic mobility, launching its masters from "shanty" to "mansion."

Jeopardy! might seem to offer a more truly inclusive agenda; the show, at least, does employ categories of pop and youth culture ("The Movies," "Magazines," "Songs of the 80's") along with those of literate culture. But as cavalierly democratic as *Jeopardy!*'s idiom might seem to be, the show itself is perceived quite differently and supports those "clichéd" critics of Hirsch who equate literate culture with elitism. Hirsch imagines cultural literacy as lying "*above* the every day levels of knowledge that everyone possesses and *below* the expert level only known to specialists" (19). But, as *Jeopardy!* dramatizes, the translation of this belief that cultural literacy is a middle ground occupied by the "common reader" belies its figuration. *Jeopardy!* and its contestants are typically regarded as admirable and appealing, but finally remotely cerebral. *Jeopardy!*, argues a *Newsweek* article, is "the thinking man's game show" and "owns the franchise for intellectual challenge."[11] One *TV Guide* review describes the show as "fun" but "mighty humbling"; another applauds the "erudition" of the show's contestants and stands in awe of these players' "startling familiarity with bafflingly obscure information."[12] "Mighty humbling," "erudition," "startling familiarity with bafflingly obscure information"—such phrases hardly conform to any recognizable vernacular of democracy. At work here, perhaps, is a larger American distrust of cerebration; too much smarts is bad manners and bad morals. But actual perceptions and evaluations of the literate, as epitomized by *Jeopardy!*'s contestants, have little to do with Hirsch's formulation of the accessibility of cultural literacy. The contestants who do best on *Jeopardy!* tend to be white, well-educated males. The show's all-time top money winner, Chuck Forrest, was an undergraduate at Yale and studied law at Michigan; last year's winner of the show's Tournament of Champions, Mark Lowenthal, was a History major and English minor in college and now, in a brilliant synecdoche of who actually participates in the country's larger discourse, works for the State Department. The less schooled can always play *Wheel of Future*; both *Jeopardy!* and *Cultural Literacy* are better at perpetuating, rather than extending, an existing *status quo* of cultural literacy.

Hirsch worries that students "will trivialize cultural information without really possessing it" (142); I hope that this argument has shown how deeply trivia inheres in his very project. *Jeopardy!* itself actualizes a sustained discourse of trivia that plays a conserving function in our culture. It is an authoritative discourse that, echoing Hirsch, legitimizes "stability, not change" (29). *Jeopardy!* may flirt with what Russian critic Bakhtin described as the "realities of heteroglossia"—a potentially limitless series of competing languages and epistemologies jostling against one another. But despite the flexibility of *Jeopardy!*'s categories, knowledge within these categories, especially its literary categories, tends to be closed and fixed; the show offers a compartmentalized, rather than dialogic, democracy. *Jeopardy!*'s fundamental conservatism is perhaps most evident in its affirmation of the marketplace that informs it. Television's *raison d'etre,* after all, as Miller points out, "is to sell you to the advertisers."[13] In the commercials that punctuate it, in its generation of winners and losers, and in the big bucks it awards its culturally literate achievers, *Jeopardy!* is an emblem of the economy in which its and *Cultural Literacy*'s discourses take place. Hirsch's *Cultural Literacy* promises a similar ascension out of the "shanties" and into the "mansions;" the rewards of *Jeopardy!* are the ramifications of *Cultural Literacy* writ large.

Notes

1. Mark Crispin Miller, *Boxed In: The Culture of TV* (Evanston: Northwestern UP, 1988) 8.
2. Don Merrill, "Review," *TV Guide* 26 March 1988: 40.
3. E. D. Hirsch, Jr., *Cultural Literacy: What Every American Needs to Know* (New York: Random House, 1988). Subsequent references to *Cultural Literacy* will be from this text.
4. Hirsch's work has provoked significant commentary, much of it antagonistic. See, for example, *Profession 88*, ed. Phyliss Franklin (New York: Modern Language Association of America, 1988) and the January/February 1989 *Voice Literary Supplement* for publications given over to Hirsch, Allan Bloom, and recent debates about education and culture.
5. The appendix has since been expanded into an entire dictionary of cultural literacy. Hirsch himself admits that the list is "provisional:" "we do not seek to create a complete catalogue of American knowledge but to establish guideposts that can be of practical use to teachers, students and all others who need to know our literate culture" (146).
6. I would like to thank Kathy Easterling for her invaluable information about the composition of questions for *Jeopardy!*. I would also like to add that whatever critique I offer of *Jeopardy!* is in no way a reflection of Easterling's own point of view or commitment to the show.
7. Emory Elliott, "General Introduction," *Columbia Literary History of the United States*, ed. Emory Elliott (New York: Columbia UP, 1988) xxi.
8. Sacvan Bercovitch, "America as Canon and Context: Literary History in a Time of Dissensus," *American Literature* 58 (March 1986), 106–7. The projects of Elliott and Bercovitch have themselves been criticized for their ideological biases. For a good summary of responses to new American literary history, see Peter Carafiol, "The New Orthodoxy: Ideology and the Institution of American Literary History," *American Literature* 59 (December 1987), 626–38.
9. Maria Margaronis, "Waiting for the Barbarians," *Voice Literary Supplement*, 14.
10. Paul B. Armstrong, "Pluralistic Literacy," *Profession 88*, 29.
11. H. F. Waters, "What a Deal," *Newsweek* 9 February 1987: 66.
12. "Cheers 'N' Jeers," *TV Guide* 13 August 1988: 39; Merrill, 40.
13. Miller 24.

Questions for Discussion

1. If you have watched *Jeopardy!* on television, do you agree with Michael Berthold's description of it in paragraph 2? How might you describe it differently? How does it differ from other television game shows?
2. According to Berthold, how are the serious and the trivial more closely related than we might have thought? Why?
3. Berthold's comparison of the kind of knowledge *Jeopardy!* elicits and the kind of knowledge Hirsch values in *Cultural Literacy* raises important questions about how we know what we know. What is the main source of your knowledge of American and Western culture? How is your cultural knowledge similar to or different from the questions asked on *Jeopardy!*?

4. The examples that Berthold provides from *Jeopardy!* and *Cultural Literacy* indicate that both value recognition over knowledge. Explain the distinction that Berthold makes here. Why is it so important to the argument he makes in the essay?

5. Do you agree with the assertion that Americans "look deeply into the surface of things" (paragraph 6)? Why or why not?

6. What does Berthold mean by saying that *Jeopardy!* and *Cultural Literacy* represent cultural conservatism?

Questions for Research and Writing

1. Find copies of both the paperback and hardback editions of *Cultural Literacy*. Are there any significant differences in the presentations of Hirsch's ideas in these two editions? Berthold argues that the paperback edition bears an especially striking similarity to the concept behind *Jeopardy!* Do you agree or disagree with Berthold's argument? Why or why not?

2. At one point Berthold asserts that "the ingenuity by which Americans find out about books without actually reading them may itself be quintessentially American." Make a list of titles of recent books from *The New York Times* best-seller list. Ask several people of different ages what they know about the books on the list. How many people have heard about these books? How many people have actually read these books? Where did they learn about them? Do your findings refute or confirm Berthold's assertion?

3. Berthold's essay offers a particular "reading" of a television game show. Choose another game show and, using the same sorts of questions Berthold asks about *Jeopardy!*, illustrate how this show reflects cultural values.

STEAL THIS TV
How Media Literacy Can Change the World

Don Adams and Arlene Goldbard

> *In the following article, Don Adams and Arlene Goldbard, writers and partners in a consulting firm, argue that the proliferation of electronic media requires a public policy of media education. Reading and writing have historically meant power for people who possess those skills, and powerlessness for people who do not. Today, failure to master the electronic media means "we doom ourselves to be forever in the grip of the powerful interests who own and control the mass media." An awareness of the relationship between media and power underlies their proposal for media literacy education. First printed in the August/September 1989 issue of* The Independent Film & Video Monthly, *this excerpt received renewed attention when it appeared in the* Utne Reader *the following year.*

Democracy requires critical thinking. Almost everyone agrees that the ability to read and write should be a fundamental human right, extended to everyone. We understand that a person who cannot read is in thrall to those who can. You cannot enter the developed world as a full human subject unless you can break and master the code of the word. Today, literacy doesn't stop with words and numbers. To enter social and political debates as a full participant one must also break the thrall of the magic box and master its secrets. If we fail to adopt media literacy—a basic knowledge of how and why media images are chosen—as an essential goal of public cultural policy, we doom ourselves to be forever in the grip of the powerful interests who own and control the mass media. This essay explores the question of public policy for media literacy. The global proliferation of electronic mass media has excited deep feeling and passionate debate. Most alarming to observers around the world has been the passivity the mass media seem to breed in most people; it displaces and undermines social life, community activities, and other creative pursuits. We jokingly call it being couch potatoes. As a society, we need to foster a more dynamic relationship between the citizenry and the media, one that does not stop when the program ends and the TV set is turned off. For those who aspire to greater democracy in public life, our greatest challenge is transforming the media into a tool for democratic change.

Achieving this will require starting from square one. People without some special interest in this field find it hard to grapple with the idea that media is a public and political issue. This is not surprising, since one of the things our mass media do best is pound home the inevitability of the way that they are currently organized, ideally suited to their role as the pep squad for our consumer society. Their self-ratifying quality makes it hard even to imagine that the media can be changed in any way.

The massive, interlocking complex of business interests that make up the mainstream media have been allowed to develop pretty much as they wish, in the pursuit of commercial success. Meanwhile, the essential public issue—the media role as our primary public forum, its tendency to erode democratic life—has been pushed further and further into the background.

It is necessary that we think about and promote a public policy that looks at what role media should play in our society and how people can participate in shaping television and the other mass media that affect all of our lives. Such a public policy could counter the imbalances that result from the domination of a country's cultural industries by commercial interests. We cannot expect the commercial arena to accommodate the goals that should be the essence of this public policy: nurturing diversity, stimulating and supporting creativity, and encouraging active participation and interaction in community and political life.

In setting out a selection of practical proposals for a new public policy concerning media and democracy, we want to strike a balance between the practical and the ideal. Improving existing policy is important, but if we allow our thinking about public policy to be constrained by the current arrangements, we'll never be free of them.

The first step to putting any policy proposals for media literacy into practice will be to raise the topic as a broad public issue, to mobilize a constituency for change. There's no point minimizing the effort this will require, though it's encouraging to remember that it has been done in the past in other fields. Social security was a fringe idea before it became law. The environmental impact statement was a notion that went from way out in left field squarely into the mainstream in record time. Any effort to bring about this sort of transformation starts by getting ideas out into the public arena, where they can be examined, debated, and refined. We hope that our proposals will stimulate others to contribute their own ideas and broaden the debate.

Media literacy is a catchy phrase, its precise meaning open to argument. We use it here in a very generous sense. Complete media literacy means mastery of the electronic media: knowledge of how films, tapes, and records are produced, with enough hands-on experience at the lower end of the technological scale to make taking part in more complex media productions an option later on; knowledge of the social, economic, and political characteristics of the media as they're currently organized, including a sense of how they developed; and knowledge of the debates over the media's effects—psychological, physiological, and social—as they've been perceived by diverse interests and competing schools of thought.

These three dimensions of media literacy can describe the education of a third-grader or a Ph.D. candidate. An 8-year-old can hold a camera, understand how *Who Killed Roger Rabbit?* was produced and sold, and talk about how it feels to watch a lot of TV. The graduate student can pursue the same lines of inquiry, taken to a deeper level.

Stormy debates rage over the kind and amount of the media's effects on the individual and on society. It would be easy to let the problem of media education collapse beneath the weight of these controversies. Unable to decide whether to teach that TV is a mechanical device that destroys brain cells and deadens our spirits or that TV is our portal to a communications network embodying human potential to expand minds and lift spirits, we don't teach anything at all. The obvious solution, suggested by educators in other contexts, is to teach the controversies: describe the poles of opinion, investigate, analyze, locate the reasons to care, and, in doing so, vivify a public issue that badly needs a little life.

As part of public education policy, then, a mandate for universal media literacy ought to include at least the following commitments: Every public school should be equipped with closed-circuit audio and video systems and studio facilities, as well as sufficient numbers of recorders, cameras, and other necessary tools to give every child adequate hands-on experience. Every public school should involve students in producing the audio-visual equivalent of school newspapers, yearbooks, and literary magazines, to supplement (but not supplant) these print publications. The curriculum from grade school through high school should acquaint every student with how the media are organized, how they've developed, and what policy measures have been considered and enacted to guide and regulate this public trust.

If media education stops at the schoolhouse door, however, it will be very difficult to bring about universal media literacy. Continuing education policy must encourage the deployment of media resources in many community settings. For instance, where they've existed, community cultural centers have historically played a significant role in making the means of artistic production available—art classes, painting and ceramics studios, drama groups. Many of the oldest such centers in this country were established during Federal One, the arts project of the Roosevelt administration's New Deal, which incorporated the Federal Theater Project, Federal Writers Project, and similar publicly supported programs in all the arts. The New Deal arts programs were based on an understanding that seems to have slipped the minds of our current policymakers: There is a role for the public interest in correcting the imbalances of marketplace culture.

In many ways, conditions today parallel those of the 1930s. Unemployment and homelessness in this country are scandals. Our physical infrastructure is crumbling, and, though less apparent, so is our cultural infrastructure. Community arts groups across the country were put out of business when President Reagan cut the Comprehensive Employment and Training Act (CETA) public service program as one of his first acts in office. But now there's been almost a decade to begin to recoup, this time with the emphasis on surviving in spite of government policies. There are a few inklings that members of Congress are emerging from the long deregulatory snooze of the Reagan era. In 1988, for instance, Congress voted to reinstate the Fairness Doctrine as a policy of the Federal Communications Commission; it also passed laws regulating commercial time and standards for children's TV. Both policies fell to Reagan's axe, but President Bush may not be so successful in overturning similar legislation.

The moment seems right for constituencies of all kinds—artists, employment advocates, people concerned about cultural equity in their own communities—to launch a campaign for a new Federal One. A major national initiative like this could ensure that community cultural centers are situated in every community, staffed with media professionals, and brought into the electronics age with public access facilities linked to cable and broadcast outlets.

We're not suggesting that a steady diet of amateur TV and radio should overtake broadcasts of professional productions. But there must be places within the higher-end media for citizens to tell their own stories in their own ways, without appropriation by the dream machine, without compulsory translation through the omniscient, omnipresent official voice. There are small examples all over the world that hold this kind of promise. Consider the Community Television Station (CTS), incorporated 12 years ago as part of the construction of the Chiba Garden Town housing complex about an hour from Tokyo. Because of high-rise interference, a complete cable system was built into the complex. The CTS studio includes VHS cameras and editing equipment available to residents of all ages, who learn by doing. Children as young as 8 are involved in producing a weekly magazine-style show that is transmitted to every television in the complex. CTS' main show is broadcast several times each week and has a higher rating than anything offered on the main networks. The very interesting discussions on democratization of communication in *One World, Many Voices* (the report of UNESCO's MacBride Commission on a "new world information order") lists dozens of other experiments: a chain of film workshops in France for people who wish to make short films on neighborhood issues; a TV station in the Federal Republic of Germany that helps community groups make films about their work to be broadcast and inspire similar groups to form elsewhere; Yugoslavian information centers that produce stories on local events and workplace issues, some broadcast nationally; and so on. None of these examples is perfect—they are plagued by ham-handed government intervention, self-censorship, underfunding, and other handicaps of all kinds. But this doesn't cancel the fact that model structures for multidirectional communication exist and could be perfected.

Needless to say, projects like these don't spring out of the ether. They are not commercially viable—they will not turn a buck—and must be supported by public or quasi-public authorities with an interest in democratic communications. In turn, that democratic interest must be rooted in public demand. The forces of status quo inertia are too strong to be overcome by anything less than urgent pressure to open democratic dialogue through the media. We have a long way to go before this is the case in the United States. At the federal level, for instance, the public is offered very little opportunity to affect communications policy. Those with passionate interest and commitment can launch letter-writing campaigns to affect broadcasters' programming choices or petition to deny the licenses of particularly egregious broadcasters. Effective campaigns have been mounted to pass new communications legislation (for instance, limiting commercial time). But the issues go much deeper, to the heart of communications policy, to the very definition of the public interest: What do we, as a democratic society, want these essential parts of our cultural commonwealth to stand for and achieve?

We should be working toward communications policies that mandate minimum requirements for locally originated and independent programming for all broadcast and cable outlets. To extend popular media literacy and bring the United States into the international dialogue, a quotient of foreign film exhibition and programming also should be mandated, including programming originating in languages other than English. The most promising direction would be to offer incentives to producers, distributors, and exhibitors of certain kinds of media. For instance, the German Film Advancement Institute taxes commercial film screenings to subsidize native German films (including part of the cost of overseas advertising). But another alternative, which could also be effective in the United States, is to incorporate appropriate requirements into public policy as Canada has done in requiring broadcasters to carry a certain percentage of Canadian-originated program material in their broadcast schedules. Since most of the media we see within the United States already originates here, we'd have to create a workable definition of "independent media content" to substitute for "Canadian content," but it could be done. If exhibitors and programmers were required to use or rewarded for using independent films and tapes, the market would grow and the necessary distribution systems expand. Thus a policy initiative taken in the interest of creating a more dynamic relationship between the media and its publics would also have salutary effects on the incomes of those in the independent media sector.

Broadcast and public exhibition aren't everything, of course. In a media-literate society, small groups and individuals should be able to use audio-visual media precisely as they now use two-dimensional media. They would be used to create expressive works intended for an audience of aficionados. They'd be deployed as a matter of course to tell the story of an organization or cause or movement, just as one might publish a pamphlet or brochure. Multimedia newsletters could evolve to help keep a group's diffuse membership in touch with each other. Electronic media could be used to paint a family portrait or to communicate with the folks back home.

Our proposals posit a public role in media education as significant and powerful as the private sector's. In this country, the debate is really just beginning. We can and should argue about the best way to proceed. But the essential principles seem to us to be self-evident: The media will not be made more democratic by exempting them from the claims of democracy, and without a massive effort to bring about media literacy, our ability to practice democracy will remain critically impaired.

Questions for Discussion

1. Don Adams and Arlene Goldbard begin with the assertion, "Democracy requires critical thinking." Do you think that they prove this or merely ask readers to believe it? Why do you think the assertion might be true? Why not?
2. The authors call for a "more dynamic relationship between the citizenry and the media." What does that mean and how might it be accomplished?
3. What do Adams and Goldbard mean by "media literacy"? What sorts of critical thinking skills would be required to achieve the level of understanding they describe?
4. Identify the various components of the public policy for media education that the authors would like to see implemented. Which of these components seem most feasible? Which seem least feasible? Since the article was first published in 1989, do you think society has become more "media literate"? Why or why not?
5. This article is clearly a call for action and change. What strategies do the authors use to persuade readers? Are these strategies effective? Are you persuaded that the need for media education is as vital as the authors suggest? Why or why not?

Questions for Research and Writing

1. Based on your own knowledge of the subject and on your own reading of the articles in this chapter, formulate a project for developing media literacy among elementary school students, high school students, or adults. What would be the goals of your project and how would you hope to accomplish those goals?
2. Use the World Wide Web to locate information about any kind of media education project anywhere in the United States. Using Adams and Goldbard's criteria, analyze the strengths and weaknesses of the project.

TELEVISION AND READING IN THE LIVES OF YOUNG CHILDREN

Susan B. Neuman

> *Critics of television often deplore the influence it has on the lives of young children, citing the number of hours children spend watching and the passivity that results. In the following excerpt from chapter 7 of her book* Literacy in the Television Age: The Myth of the TV Effect *(1991), Susan Neuman, a Temple University researcher, uses her observations of three families to determine what impact television has on the reading activities of the children in those families. By examining three common assumptions about the relationship of television viewing to cognitive development and creativity, the author seeks to determine whether, in fact, television viewing displaces more worthwhile pursuits.*

COMMON ASSUMPTIONS

Central to the charges against television is its extraordinary hold on children's time and attention. Many theories, as shown in the previous chapters, have proposed different causal mechanisms to account for the potentially deleterious effects on children's developing literacy. Nevertheless, the element common to most of this research has been their reliance on the factor of time. In practice, it may be argued that most of the weight of interpretation for television's effects has rested on some variation of the displacement theory.

As we have seen, however, no direct evidence indicates that the amount of time spent reading has essentially changed since the introduction of television. Still, a great number of critics support the view that television may be indirectly related to reading. Some authorities consider that viewing may harm the acquisition of reading skills by displacing activities thought to be associated with children's emergent reading and writing (Elkind, 1981; Singer & Singer, 1983). Such negative displacement is believed to occur when viewing substitutes for an activity that provides opportunities for skill practice, active participation, and exploration (Gadberry, 1980; Gaddy, 1986). For example, it has been suggested that problem-solving skills may develop more slowly if viewing replaces an ability-enhancing activity such as imaginative play (Singer & Singer, 1983).

Judging from the research (Gadberry, 1980; Roberts, Bachen, Hornby, & Hernandez-Ramos, 1984; Singer & Singer, 1980) as well as theoretical accounts (Beentjes & Van der Voort, 1988; Greenfield, 1984; Hornik, 1981; National Institute of Mental Health, 1982), three common assumptions, reflecting the processes of spending time with television and children's learning to read, are thought to underlie these views:

1. Television stifles children's imagination and creativity: By presenting concrete visual images and fast-paced entertainment, television substitutes for self-generated imaginative activity. This assumption suggests that television is essentially a reactive, passive activity, which may later transfer to a lack of mental effort or incentive in learning how to read.

2. Television takes time away from more worthwhile pursuits: Time given to television displaces out-of-school activities that might otherwise facilitate the development of reading skills. This assumption implies that television may reduce cognitive growth as it displaces more beneficial home-based activities such as drawing, or time spent reading.

3. Television is functionally equivalent to alternative leisure activities: Television displaces activities serving children's needs for novelty, social reinforcement, and information. This assumption suggests that children might favor spending time with the vicarious learning experiences of television rather than become involved in an activity more directly.

Following a description of the participant families. Each of these assumptions are addressed in this chapter. Analyzing issues, however, one should recognize that the goal of this naturalistic inquiry is in the discovery of the meanings of family actions and events, and not at a generalizable explanation of the patterns of all families.

THE PARTICIPANT FAMILIES

Since young children tend to be heaviest consumers of television (National Institute of Mental Health, 1982), the focus of the research was on families with children in the primary grades. A number of studies have suggested that television's effects might be particularly strong at the critical juncture of school entry where children are beginning formal reading instruction (Gadberry, 1974, 1980; Zuckerman, Singer, & Singer, 1980). To examine this potential association, then, families were selected in which one of the children was just about to enter the first grade in the following September. Three families were chosen in an effort to look at the potential differences in family experiences as well as the commonalities among these parents and children.

The Clarkes, living in a well-to-do suburban neighborhood, were the first family selected for the study. At the time, Claire was a full-time homemaker, and Rob, a management consultant. Three of their five children were currently living at home: Harry, Eddie, and Stephanie, ages 6, 8, and 10, respectively.

Also agreeing to participate in the study, Mary Alice Conley, a single parent, lived in what she described as a "Betty Crocker" district in a local suburban area—a mostly white, lower-middle-class rental neighborhood. Mary Alice was chiefly responsible for the two children, Stacey, age 6, and Alex, 2½, even though the father frequently called and spent occasional weekends with the children. As the president of fledgling public relations company, Mary Alice was often busy at meetings and called on her friends to help in taking care of the children. When I first started observing, Robbie, an old acquaintance, was living in the house, because he was "down on his luck." During the year, there were a succession of young women from France who became "au pairs," helping with housework and the children in return for free rent.

In contrast to the Conley family, the Diamonds lived in an older, transitional neighborhood, where large homes were being renovated by young middle-class families. The Diamonds were selected to explore displacement in a home where the children had greater free time available during the day. Having taken a sabbatical year from preschool teaching, Caroline wanted Jennifer, age 5, and Leah, age 2½, to have some time off from day care, and her husband, Peter, a computer salesperson, strongly agreed with the decision. Few extra activities were scheduled for the children; Leah was picked up daily from the preschool at 12:00 and Jennifer usually arrived home by 3:00.

My role in the family was that of a participant observer. As noted by Leichter and her colleagues (Leichter et al., 1985; Taylor, 1983), establishing oneself in a home environment is difficult, involving a process of negotiating how to be perceived by the members of the family. In order to become familiar with each family's natural patterns of interactions, therefore, it seemed most appropriate to become a participating member of the household, helping with chores and the children, babysitting at times, eating meals, and spending time informally chatting with various family members.

Since television viewing time is likely to vary from week to week due to perceptions of available time (Bower, 1985), it was also necessary to make observations over a sufficient time span and over a variety of time periods to obtain a picture of seasonal, weekly and daily cycles of the family's life. Scheduled visits occurred at different time periods on all days of the week except Sunday over a 12-month period. Approximately 314 hours of observation, in all, were conducted.

During these visits, I carried a small notebook which allowed me to note important points, situations, and comments in shorthand form, often using a catch-phrase to get the gist of the account. After each observation, these notes were more fully transcribed, detailing the behaviors and contexts observed, the hours and family members present, the seasonal variations, as well as any personal and theoretical notations.

On occasion, family storybook readings and conversations around the television set were audiotaped. These recordings allowed me to capture the intimacy of the parent-child interactions during storybook reading when observations were intrusive; it also permitted me to examine the typical "family talk" that occurred when the families spent time watching television together.

These ethnographic procedures provided an opportunity to observe young children's television viewing and reading activities within the context of their other daily patterns. In this respect, it was a useful strategy for analyzing the ways in which television is mediated by the family environment and how displacement is thought to occur. But this approach also has its limitations. One, of course, is the number of families. While the types of families selected enable contrasts and comparisons, this discussion rests on young children who may be considered to be broadly within the middle class. In addition, these particular parents, demonstrating considerable skepticism about television, all controlled children's viewing time and to some degree, the type of content to be watched. None of these children would be regarded as excessive viewers. Consequently, the patterns described here reflect moderate viewers and average readers. The basic characteristics of these families are shown in Table 7.1.

AN ETHNOGRAPHIC LOOK AT TELEVISION AND READING

Displacement of Cognitive and Imaginative Activities

It is frequently claimed by some critics that television viewing weakens children's active thought processes, decreasing their imaginativeness and ability to be creative (Singer & Singer, 1980; Winn, 1977). These arguments are largely based on the issue of cognitive overload (Mander, 1978; Singer, 1980; Trelease, 1982). Television's pacing, its constant sensory bombardment is thought to maximize an involuntary form of attention, preventing children from strategically processing or generating hypotheses from televised content. Without the time necessary to assimilate incoming information, it is argued, that children become transfixed by the medium (Singer & Singer, 1983).

Such inactivity is thought to impede the development of reading ability on two grounds: (a) The cognitive passivity of television viewing may be internalized, and later generalized to more demanding processing tasks like reading (Salomon, 1984), and (b) television's concrete visual images may obviate the need for children to spontaneously produce their own mental images (Tower, Singer, Singer, & Biggs, 1979). This may exert a destructive influence on children's imaginative play, considered to be associated with emergent narrative competence (Pellegrini, 1985).

To examine these assertions, observations were analyzed first to examine how children watched television. It seemed fair to assume that if children spent a large proportion of their time passively incorporating television content, with little evidence of cognitive activity, then they might be less prepared to engage in higher level processing tasks, like reading.

Table 7.1. Summary of Characteristics of Participant Families.

CHARACTERISTICS	FAMILIES		
	Claire & Rob Clarke	Caroline & Peter Diamond	Mary Alice Conley
Children in study	Stephanie, 10 Eddie, 8 Harry, 6	Jennifer, 5 Leah, 2 1/2	Stacey, 6 Alex, 2½
Parent's profession			
Mother	Homemaker	Homemaker (on sabbatical from school)	President, public relations
Father	Management Consultant	Computer Salesperson	Salesperson
Housing	Owned home	Owned home but rented out second floor home	Rented two-family
Non-Kin Household Members	None	None	1 (4 different people in year)
Number of TV sets	2	1	2
Videotape owned	yes	yes	yes
Approximate amount of weekly TV viewed by children (varying by season)	21 hours	14 hours	18 hours
Attend public library	Weekly	Weekly	Rarely
Involvement in community activities	Sports Church-related Lessons	None	Sports

The television viewing context. Children did not appear to be cognitively passive at all while watching television. In contrast to the conception of the child just sitting and staring blankly at the television, observations indicated that there were wide variations in the way the children responded to television. Sometimes, these response patterns gave clear indications that children were actively engaged in processing the televised content. For example, Harry tended to be highly participatory, as he responded to television with both physical and verbal activity:

> We are watching The Cosby Show. The story is about Bill Cosby who is trying to fix the plumbing in the bathroom.
>
> Harry: "Maybe he might need the plumber (starts imitating what a plumber might do).
>
> (Some minutes later) Probably that's not real glue, probably they use plastic or something.

(A couple of minutes later)
Most plumbers don't do that—they don't take down a wall.
(later) I know where the sledge hammer is—(that Cosby was using to break down a wall) —it's under the tub."

Other times, however, children made few overt responses while viewing. In the past, this lack of motor involvement has been taken as evidence that little processing occurs (Mates, 1980). Such an interpretation, unfortunately, has not allowed for the alternative explanation that children may be actively processing the content, albeit covertly (see Table 7.2).

Table 7.2. Different Ways of Watching Television

VIEWING STYLES	EXAMPLES
The participatory viewer	Harry is watching a commercial on television and starts singing "Have you driven a Ford, lately."
The reflective viewer	Stephanie is watching a fight from the movie Rocky on TV. "They're not really hitting each other. See they're using water to make it look like sweat, and red stuff to make it look like blood, and false teeth to make it look like their faces are bulging"
The strategic viewer	Stacey watches TV while playing with her new stamp album. She only occasionally looks up at the TV set, as she tells her mother all about her new book.
The zombie viewer	Jennifer is watching a tape of Charlotte's Web. As she turns it on, her mother asks her a question. "Shh, it's now beginning, and never says another word until the end of the show.

Evidence for children's covert involvement was observed through their questions and comments during breaks from their viewing. For example, often annoyed by her brother's running commentaries, Stephanie's viewing style tended to be reflective, as she watched a program intensely without saying a word. Her comments during the commercials or following the show, seemed to belie the conventional view of passivity, as she revealed her attention to even the smallest story details, as well as her inferencing from story content:

Stephanie has just finished watching *A Different World*.

Stephanie: Where is Princeton?
Mother: New Jersey.
Stephanie: Is it warm in New Jersey in February?
Mother: No, but why did you think so?
Stephanie: Because everyone on the show is wearing short sleeves and so I thought it must be warm out.

Similarly, in the Conley home, there were no outward signs to suggest that Stacey comprehended and interpreted story sequences on television.

Displaying a very different style from Harry or Stephanie, Stacey was a strategic viewer, using the music and sounds to key into significant story events. Staring only occasionally at the set, she simultaneously engaged in a host of other activities, as in this example:

> Stacey is sitting on the bed, talking to her Dad on the phone, and then her step-sister Heather. She is discussing her upcoming birthday plans. At the same time, Isabel, the current 'au pair' is yelling at Alex, "it's time to go to bed." She chases him around the room, and he bites her. Stacey continues to talk, occasionally saying in her grown-up voice to Alex, "It's time to go to bed." These events are simultaneously occurring as she watches *Who's the Boss,* and *Growing Pains.* When the programs are over, I ask:
>
> *SBN:* Those programs are pretty sophisticated—I mean what do you think?
> *Stacey:* They both teach you things.
> *SBN:* Oh, like what?
> *Stacey:* Oh, I don't want to tell you. OK. The first, *Who's the Boss* teaches you not to tell a lie because remember how she got caught, and the second, *Growing Pains* that you shouldn't marry too young.

Though monitoring several other events, Stacey was obviously able to comprehend the essence of the plots from each of the television narratives.

In contrast, Jennifer's viewing style often resembled the popular characterization of the "zombie" viewer. She tended to watch as if she were in a stupor, neither responding to comments or questions from anyone in the room. But even this trance-like behavior, suggesting extreme passivity, was somewhat deceptive. For example:

> Jennifer is watching *The Cat in the Hat* on television.
>
> *Mother:* What's he doing?
> No answer.
> *Mother:* What's happening?
> No answer.
> *Mother:* What's that?
> No answer.
> After the show is over,
> *Jennifer:* Now I want to read the book. (She runs upstairs to get *The Cat in the Hat*).

While it was impossible to gauge how much Jennifer was actually absorbing from the program, the outward appearance of passivity may, in this case, have reflected her intense concentration. "Zombie viewing" in Jennifer's situation interacted with program content; during unfamiliar shows, she seemed transfixed, while she was clearly more participatory when watching reruns or tapes.

Jennifer's mother puts on the Winnie-the-Pooh tape that they own.

Jennifer: You've got to watch my favorite part. See—
(Tigger is buried under a big snow drift)
Jennifer: It's old long ears. (She laughs)
I wish I were Roo.
(Someone falls)
Jennifer: That's so funny.
Leah: That's so funny.
Jennifer: I wish I were Roo.

Variations on viewing styles, therefore, suggested that there was no one typical "active" processing style. Children, who were active, were not always physically or verbally participating in the televised action; instead, many times, they were absorbed or gave intense concentration to the television screen. These variations in viewing, however, did not seem closely tied to the children's abilities to predict and interpret television content. Thus, those who have argued that television is a passive cognitive activity may be confounding viewing style with the processing of televised content. In contrast to the assumption that the children are held captive by the set, the pacing of information, nor the multiple stimuli from television did not appear to hinder their ability to generate ideas, nor to prevent different strategies for viewing. In fact, television viewing may have given children opportunities to practice those processing skills.

Outside the television-viewing context. It may be the case, however, that television's impact on children's active thinking processes and imaginative activities takes place on a more long-term basis. Thus, its influence may be only evidenced in a different context apart from the actual viewing of television. Since children's imaginative play activities have been strongly associated with their developing sense of narrative (Heath, 1983; Pellegrini, 1985), observations were examined to analyze the potential linkages between television and children's free play activities at home.

Observations indicated that, rather than inhibit play, television content was often used as a point of departure for children's imaginative play activities. Generally, this occurred over two sages. At the first stage, the children seemed almost to duplicate the televised story in their pretend play. Caroline, for example, found Jennifer actually acting out a favorite *Rainbow Brite* story, assigning specific character roles to her friends, and using the dialogue directly from the show. Once familiar with the characters and themes, the children at the second stage invented whole new adventures of their own, while at the same time, conforming to the underlying story structure.

Not all of children's viewing, however, was a resource for pretend play. Rather, the selection of television content reflected children's already existing play themes. For example, Jennifer incorporated the character of Heidi in a familiar play theme of family after watching only a few minutes of a

Disney cartoon; programs including *Sesame Street* and *Misterrogers' Neighborhood*, for which she devoted many hours, never related to any of her play scenarios. In this respect, television was not just uniformly incorporated in their play; instead, children used its content selectively to satisfy their needs.

Three factors were associated with the television content selected for pretend play: (a) The characters had clearly identifiable behaviors, (b) uncomplicated plot structures, and (c) general familiarity among many children.

Television characters used in pretend play reflected distinguishable character traits, such as "Big Bird" who according to Alex was "always afraid" or "Carebears" who had "magic in their stomachs" and engaged in highly predictable behaviors, such as "Snuffelupiguss" who "always gets into trouble," and "My Little Pony" who had "so much smooze and so much witches and so much monsters." These characters were used in such common play themes as good versus evil, marriage and family, and fear of monsters.

Children selected television content with highly formulaic plot structures for their pretend play. After viewing the program *The Carebears* on television, for example, it became a frequent variation in Jennifer's good versus evil play theme. The plot of the televised version followed a simple formula involving the magical Carebears, living in the land of "Care-a-lot," who fight against the evil spirits that would remove all caring from the world. Retaining the basic theme from the story, Jennifer and her friends created a new story of their own making:

> *Jennifer:* (swinging on a hammock) That cloud—it's a care-a-lot cloud.
> *SBN:* What's that?
> *Jennifer:* The carebears live there. The carebears shaped me. I just jumped from the cloud. I helped take care of the teensie-weensies and kept them away from Dark Heart, who had red eyes and he can turn into anything he wants. He trapped the grown-ups and I have the key. Me and Lara, she had the other key and I had the key to the babies and Lara to the adults. Star and Heart were the helpers. And more and more children came, and the adults were away, and we saved the care-a-lots and flew home.

The basic plot structures from *Rainbow Brite, My Little Pony, Brady Bunch,* and *Family Ties* were among the many television-related pretend play activities observed during the year.

In order to sustain play, it was necessary to be familiar with the televised "script." It was not uncommon for the children to invite particular friends over to play a mutually-shared favorite of *Family Ties* or *Carebears*. On some occasions, the older children invited their younger brother or sister to join in, but only if they were able to follow the story structure. When they did not, play was interrupted, as in the case when Jennifer yelled to her sister "C'mon Leah, remember in Rainbow land you have to have a problem." Such awareness of the implicit rules of a television story argues against the conception that, for Jennifer, viewing was merely reactive.

These observations, both in the television viewing context and in children's pretend play activities, suggest that, rather than stifle their imaginative capacities, television may embellish children's play by offering new variations of content on well-established play themes. In this respect, television as a common cultural experience may serve the important social function of helping children to initiate and interact with others (Anderson & Collins, 1988). James and McCain (1982), in their observational study in preschools, found that when play involved television-related content, more children actually joined in. Thus, in contrast to preventing symbolic play, a moderate amount of viewing age-appropriate content may involve children in the production and comprehension of decontextualized language associated with literate behavior.

Displacement of Worthwhile Pursuits

A central concern of displacement is that the time spent watching television diverts children away from more worthwhile activities (Hornik, 1981). This assumption implies that children's emerging literacy skills may be inhibited by displacing activities, both directly and indirectly, which are thought to facilitate general cognitive development (Gaddy, 1986). Among the activities that are considered to be most likely, and directly, affected is leisure reading. Presumably, if television is taking time away from leisure reading, then the development of reading skills and fluency might suffer. Activities that are thought to indirectly impair children's reading skills might include such ability-enhancing pursuits as drawing, homework, or even resting (Gadberry, 1980; Maccoby, 1954; Schramm et al., 1961).

For television to be displacing more worthwhile activities, it is logical to assume that children must be viewing during the times when they would otherwise be engaged in these valuable activities. To examine this assumption, observations were analyzed focusing on when television viewing and reading occurred most often and for what general purposes they were used by these families.

When television viewing occurs. Observations indicated that, in contrast to displacing organized activities, children's patterns of viewing tended to reflect the times perceived to be free from these other pursuits. Established family routines, indicating parent's educational and social priorities, served as an important mediational influence in structuring children's time. Such routines included formal lessons, as in the case of the Clarke children who were scheduled for a particular activity every afternoon. Or they might simply include care-taking responsibilities, such as the evening bath, or the bedtime reading routine. In either case, however, these routines, consciously or unconsciously, controlled when children were able to view television and what purposes it served for these families.

For the Clarke children, for example, television was turned on immediately after they entered their house around 5:00, following their heavily scheduled day. Soon interrupted by dinner at 5:30, then homework and other responsibilities, viewing was only allowed to be resumed after (or if) other activities of greater priority were completed:

> Rob is giving instructions to the babysitter before he goes out.
>
> R: Stephanie must first go up and do her homework and have it checked. (to Stephanie) Good piano lesson today, sport. Remember you have to practice piano before TV. Otherwise, no Cos. (to babysitter) Then if she has finished she's allowed to watch *Cosby* and *A Different World*.

Television viewing in this family was often used as a reward system, serving to encourage and reward the children for fulfilling their responsibilities.

For the Diamond children, television viewing occurred during the latter part of each afternoon from 4–6 p.m., when the children were either tired or getting fussy after playing with friends. Caroline prepared dinner while the children viewed either a videotape or educational programs, like *Reading Rainbow* or *Sesame Street*:

> I usually have the children watch *Sesame Street* in the afternoon to calm them down when they get a little wild. Or when Jennifer is in a bad mood, when nothing Leah can do is right. Jennifer's a bit too old for it, really. But it puts her out. She doesn't think about it. Television just makes her rest.

> My father gave us a videotape with many of the family occasions together. The tape is filled with family and relatives, and with long segments of Christmas and playing in the backyard of our house. Leah watches "her video" every day, generally falling asleep for a nap on the couch after 15 minutes.

In addition to these functions, television served as a time clock in the Conley family. Children watched *Sesame Street* while dressing every morning for school, came downstairs for breakfast and *Mister Rogers'*, then viewed "whatever was on" following dinner and their evening bath from 8:00–8:30 each night before going to bed. Living in a busy neighborhood, the children either played outside or in the house with friends in the later afternoon; nighttime television was reserved for relaxation and escape:

> Mary Alice: After dinner, it's quiet time. No friends over. The children can play with their coloring books, and watch a bit of TV. Sometimes Alex listens to a music tape before he goes to bed, but no more playing.

Afternoon television was discouraged in all three families for reasons that "the children could be doing something better with their time, like playing." Generally these parental restrictions were followed, as noted by Harry in his school diary:

> The thing I like best about my mother is when she doesn't let us watch TV. It makes me feel happy, because in Spring, I can always go outside to play.

By establishing priorities and routines, parents exercised their influencing potential in helping children structure their time. In doing so, they confined children's choices in selecting television content, and, to a great extent, controlled the time available to watch television. In these homes, television did not replace active involvement in alternative activities; instead, television was used primarily as an activity to mark the end of a busy day. Even with these limitations on time, however, children were able to free approximately 14–21 hours per week for watching television.

When storybook reading time occurs. Associated chiefly as a night time activity, storybook reading typically vied for children's attention at the same time as television viewing, and thus had the greatest potential of all free time activities to be displaced. Observations indicated varying degrees of displacement; to the degree that storybook reading was incorporated as a structured family activity, it was not displaced by television. However, when book reading was regarded by children as an optional activity, it was not only often displaced by viewing, but by other activities as well.

As expected, television viewing, occurring only in the late afternoon, did not compete with the nightly storybook reading in the Diamond home. Here, the nighttime story was a highly ritualized event, beginning right after dinner:

> About 6:00–6:30, the children begin to go upstairs. They put on their PJ's, brush their teeth, and then they both go to Jennifer's room, unless Peter is home and he takes one of them, and I take the other. Then Jennifer either reads to Leah in front of me, or I read about 5 or 6 stories to them. Then I sing a song like "Twinkle twinkle" and Leah goes to bed. After that, I read to Jennifer alone out of a chapter book, and then I sing her a night time song.

Night time, however, was more complicated in the Clarke family. Parent meetings, and varying reading interests among the children, sometimes interfered with the regularly scheduled storybook hour:

> We read almost every single night. But it's getting kind of split up now. I read to Eddie and Harry together, and Stephanie separately, 'cause she's into different stuff. Then the children are allowed to stay up ½ hour past the time they are put into bed to read. Stephanie and Eddie listen to a tape and read along with it—Harry just listens to a tape.

Book reading time, however, was indeed a candidate for displacement when the structured story hour did not take place or when the children had the option to choose between other activities:

> A babysitter is taking care of the children. Checking on the children for bedtime, she sees that Stephanie is watching *The Breakfast Club* on television.
>
> *Babysitter:* Stephanie, it's 8:30. You said you were supposed to read. When are you going to do that?
> *Stephanie:* I'll go to bed at 8:45, and then I'll read until 9:00. I've got to have lights out at 9.00.
>
> The babysitter leaves and comes back at 8:45.
>
> *Babysitter:* You need to go to bed.
> *Stephanie:* Please please, just let me watch one little bit more.
> *Babysitter:* You promised to read.
> *Stephanie:* Please, please.
> *Babysitter:* Why don't you get in your pajamas, brush your teeth, and you can watch 10 more minutes.
> *Stephanie:* OK, only ten more minutes.

Even when television viewing was not possible, during the half hour designated as individual reading time before bedtime, reading was easily replaced by other activities. At night, I often found Eddie playing with his cars in bed, Stephanie sewing a hook rug in her room, and Harry only occasionally listening to a music or *Curious George* audio tape. Yet at the same time, Eddie complained, "I never have any time to read. During the day, I'm too busy, and then at night, I'm too tired."

Unlike the other two families, there was no bedtime story in the Conley home. Having many late business meetings, Mary Alice left the night time routine to the "au pair," who knew little English, and would send the children off to bed following the nightly prime time television program. Even when Mary Alice was home, however, other commitments took precedence before book reading; instead, television was used by her as a substitute for the nighttime story, as described in the following examples:

> Alex brings a book into his mother's room and asks her to read him a story. Mary Alice ignores this, and puts on a *Bill Cosby* videotape.
>
> Mary Alice puts Alex to bed by kissing him and talking to him. She tells Stacey that it's time to go to bed, but Stacey brings in a story about *Madeline* to read. Mary Alice starts making a phone call.
>
> *SBN:* Do you read a story before bed?
> *Stacey:* No—we watch TV. Mom never reads to us because she's too busy. Only when we have babysitters do we read books.

Observations of these episodes suggested that Stacey and Alex did not actively choose to substitute television viewing for book reading. Rather, television was selected in the absence of any book reading opportunities. Given television's accessibility to the very young child, viewing, in this respect, may be conceptualized as a "default option" for those who have a limited set of alternatives during the evening hours.

These observations argue for a more complicated pattern of displacement than has been described in previous research. Unlike television viewing, storybook reading for young children is a dependent activity, one that is facilitated by an adult's encouragement and supervision. Without parental support, it may be that television is watched because it happens to be there when other, even possibly more attractive activities, are not. Thus, in the case of young children, the displacement theory might provide a more accurate description of a parent's behavior rather than his/her child's.

Television viewing, however, did replace book reading on occasion for the older children, who were capable of reading on their own. But, again, these patterns are complicated, revealing a fundamental paradox about book reading. Even when viewing was not possible, other activities such as playing, or music, often displaced reading, suggesting that the very flexibility of the book reading activity, may, at the same time, allow it to be more easily displaced than some other activities. Further, as a relatively effortful activity, books may not be considered "leisure" for young children who are tired at the end of a day.

Concurrent activities. One of the problems in interpreting the displacement of worthwhile pursuits, however, is that some activities are not mutually exclusive with television viewing. Studies involving extensive videotaping of viewing behavior, for example, have indicated a variety of other activities are likely to be time-shared with television (Anderson, Field, Collins, Lorch, & Nathan, 1985; Bechtel, Achelpohl, & Akers, 1972). Beentjes and Van der Voort (1988) have argued that some of these activities may be qualitatively displaced because of the distraction provided by the TV.

Over half of the children's viewing time in this study involved both viewing and other activities, including playing, eating, reading and homework. Observations suggested that, in contrast to qualitative displacement, the children seemed to strategically allocate their attention to television according to the demands of the time-shared activity.

For example, though not allowed to do so, sometimes Stephanie combined viewing and homework activities:

> The Clarkes have given instructions to the babysitter that Stephanie is to complete her homework before watching TV. After her parents leave, however, I find her upstairs watching *Wheel of Fortune* while doing her homework. She is trying to guess at the missing letters.
>
> SBN: Stephanie, I don't think you are allowed to watch and do your homework.
> *Stephanie:* Oh, I only put this on as background. I find something that doesn't bother me when I do it.

For Stephanie, this homework assignment, which was completed by the end of the program, presented little challenge, allowing her to expend more effort on watching the television show.

Contrary to the opinion that these time-shared activities suffer when combined with television, observations indicated that it was often the television that was neglected.

> It is 7:30 on Thursday at the Clarke home, and the children are getting ready for *The Bill Cosby Show*, a family event. Claire makes popcorn and the boys decide to build a fort, with gym mats and large tubes in the TV room. They turn the TV on, watch for a moment, and then continue to play in the fort. Claire turns the TV off, but no one seems to notice, as they are now playing hide and go seek in their fort.

Particularly for the younger children, who were rarely in control of the program selected, these other activities at times drew them away from the TV set when the program was of little interest or comprehensibility:

> Alex and Stacey are watching *Growing Pains* while coloring in their new coloring books. Alex, looking at the TV only occasionally, takes a magic marker, and begins to tell a story about the pictures in the book. "That's my old buddy Burt. Burt is going to catch a ball, and there's me and Stacey. Stacey is hugging me." As he turns each page, he tells a new story about his old buddy, Burt. After about six times, Stacey, who is trying to watch the program, suggests that I read the coloring book to him. Alex comes over to me and continues to tell his stories, ignoring the TV show altogether.

These observations suggest that young children adjust their attention to television and other activities on the basis of their interest and the amount of mental effort required for each activity. Children's differential attention seems to involve a strategy of attending more closely to the activity that demands the higher level of concentration, while investing less effort in the other. This interactive pattern contrasts sharply with the view that the quality of time-shared activities is invariably displaced while viewing. Conceivably, it is possible that in some cases, the viewing environment may even support children's engagement in these other activities.

The enhancement of worthwhile activities. Generally, the displacement theory assumes a negative relationship between viewing and other pursuits; that is, television is thought to take away from these other, more valuable cognitive activities. Only rarely has television been thought to facilitate children's involvement in reading-related activities. Of those few scholars that have supported this view, television's role has alternately been cast as an information-providing experience (Dorr, 1986), a boost to the reading of specific books (Hamilton, 1976), or a strategy for reluctant readers (Potter, 1976).

In these family contexts, however, I observed not a one-way, but a reciprocal, ongoing relationship between viewing and print. Children's interests often crossed media lines as they looked for opportunities to spend time with their favorite characters and stories. For example, Caroline describing Jennifer's current interest:

> Jennifer's just in love with *Charlotte's Web* right now. She tries to read a chapter when she wakes up in the morning. We got the video and I thought, "Oh dear"—here she was reading the book. But the video helped her get back into the book again, which surprised me. It brought her back to the book.
>
> She just loves Templeton. The video makes it so funny. And she laughs about that. And then when she gets in the book, she laughs because she knows what's going to happen. Whereas, I could never get into Templeton—he was the terrible one. So I think the video has given her a new angle on Templeton.

In this case, Jennifer's interest in *Charlotte's Web* first began with her teacher reading the book at school. But at other times, Jennifer became interested in reading as a result of watching television. For example, having seen *Rainbow Brite* on television, she bought a little golden book that she learned to read independently. Later, with her mother's help, she used these resources to write and illustrate her own book. Such similar cross media patterns occurred with *Winnie-the-Pooh, The Cat in the Hat* as well as *The Carebears,* which Jennifer described in a message to her mother: "Carebear my fafrit movie the carebear storybook."

For the Clarkes, television was occasionally used to directly encourage reading. Scanning the Disney Channel guide each week, Claire videotaped a number of classics, including *The Lion, the Witch and the Wardrobe,* and *The Lord of the Rings* that she wanted the children to eventually read. The videos were used as a way of "getting into" the story, which she later read during their evening storyhour.

Cross-media connections were also evident in the Conley's home, where television often substituted for the children's storybook hour. Alex's and Stacey's interest in *The Velveteen Rabbit*, first introduced by their respective teachers, was transferred to the home via a videotape, bought through the school book club. With no one to read the story to him, Alex repeatedly watched the video with intense interest, waiting for his favorite scene, "when all the toys get fired."

In this home, television was often used explicitly by Mary Alice as a catalyst for the children's literacy interactions. Linkages between Alex's interests in *Sesame Street* and print, for example, were seen in a calendar in his room, a primary vocabulary (and picture) learning game, an alphabet videotape, a Big Bird jigsaw puzzle, a subscription to the *Sesame Street* magazine and a Big Bird Cookbook. Similarly, Mary Alice joined the *Fraggles* Book Club for Stacey, who was just beginning to read on her own.

The sheer variety of connections between television and print suggested that children's interests tended not to remain medium-specific. Seeking time beyond the immediate television or reading experience, children pursued their favorite stories and characters through multiple exposures with different media. In fact, the distinctions between media became increasingly blurred, as the children moved freely back and forth from visually oriented media (i.e., television, videotapes, movies) to print-oriented media (books, toy books, advertising circulars). Thus, contrary to displacing worthwhile activities, these observations indicated that television often served as a resource for children's emerging interests. Rather than conflict, there was a complementarity between children's media activities; interests in one medium often sparked similar interests in the other.

In sum, these observations argue that the consequences of television viewing are more complex than are indicated in the hypothesis for displacement. There was no consistent or strong evidence that television viewing displaced valuable cognitive activities. Rather, children often viewed in the absence of stimulating activities. For example, there were indications that children replaced reading with viewing when there was a lack of parental guidance, or when the option for being read to was unavailable.

However, there were also instances when viewing was concurrent with, or facilitated children's involvement with print activities, either directly by encouraging them to read TV-related books or indirectly, by generating or sustaining interests in activities associated with reading. Thus, it was the children who were active agents in their choices of leisure activities: their uses of the media were guided by their interests and their practical assessment of attractive alternatives.

Displacement of Functionally Equivalent Needs

A related assumption of displacement is that television is functionally equivalent to alternative leisure time activities. Here, it is argued that television displaces activities serving children's similar needs, but requiring more effort than viewing. Because it is continuously available and instantly gratifying, television is thought to subsume children's needs for excitement, information and social reinforcement (Gadberry, 1980; Gaddy, 1986). Thus, from this perspective, television may induce children to become mentally and physically lazy, preferring vicarious learning experiences rather than those requiring active exploration. Such an assumption implies that children would be less interested in learning to read and less prepared to invest the mental effort required by reading.

Children's viewing and reading behavior, however, have been shown to be influenced by the models set by their parents (Bryce, 1980; Neuman, 1986b). Such influence may be exercised by parent's attitudes toward each medium or by personal example. Presumably, if parents use television to the exclusion of reading or other activities, it might be reasonable to assume that their children would be likely to follow their model. To examine this assumption, therefore, observations were analyzed for examples of how parents may guide, implicitly or explicitly, their children in the uses of television and reading and how these lessons seem to be internalized by their children.

Lessons about television. Observations indicated that parents' beliefs about television exerted a strong influence in their children's perceptions about the medium. These influences, however, did not tend to be manifested in the amount of time children actually spent on viewing; in all cases, the children's viewing time far exceeded the models set by their parents. Rather, these informal lessons appeared to play a significant role in the way children watched television and in their definition of its uses to serve their needs. In this respect, parent influences served as an important constraining factor in television's capacity to displace other potentially similar activities.

The strong educational orientation in the Clarke and Diamond homes, for example, exerted its influence on their children's attitudes and uses of the medium. In both families, time was regarded as too precious to waste on noneducational activities; television, though sometimes informative and enjoyable, should be used only sparingly to the degree that it is not substituting for more active, worthwhile pursuits.

Different mediational styles, however, were evident in the way these families elected to exercise their influence. For example, with older children, the Clarkes monitored the frequency of their children's viewing, but with the exception of violent programming, not its content:

> I want the children to learn to self-regulate. I rather have them come to see these things in the home rather than somewhere else. When they watch, I answer all their questions even if it's a little embarrassing. I like them to analyze what they see and hear on television. Occasionally, though, if I'm in there reading and Stephanie is watching something like she was last night, I'll say this is trash, this is really stupid, you must have something better to do with your mind!

The children were well-aware of their parents' orientation toward television. In his school diary, Harry drew a picture of a television as an example of an activity he did that grown-ups hated. Similarly, when a teacher-strike disrupted school and Stephanie got caught by her mother watching *The Price Is Right* in the afternoon, she quickly turned it off, then rationalized, "I was just learning how to estimate."

In contrast, viewing in the Diamond home was monitored for both its frequency and content. Here, television was limited primarily to educational fare:

> Time is so valuable. I'd rather the children play or something. But if they're really exhausted they can watch one of the educational programs like *Square 1* or *Reading Rainbow*, something really useful.

Monitoring, however, became more difficult when cable television, along with a remote control panel, was installed in the home. Spot checking, Caroline noticed that Jennifer was changing channels to noneducational daytime television. Arguing that television was "getting out of control," new restrictions were instituted:

> The children can choose anything they want, like *Square 1* or *3-2-1 Contact,* but they can only have it on for one hour. I think they're having more fun doing things as a result of less television.

> *SBN:* Jennifer, what do you think you're doing more of? No answer.
> *Caroline:* Oh, I think the kids are just playing more, playing with their dolls, doing more drawing. Hasn't it been fun Jennifer?
> *Jennifer (playing with her doll):* Yeh.

Television viewing for the Diamonds' children, therefore, was carefully controlled by their parents: the medium was to be used as an enhancement for learning, or it was not to be used at all. Even with educational fare, however, the Diamonds clearly communicated the message that active involvement in playing or other activities was always preferable to viewing.

Unlike the other two families, there was a strong social orientation in the Conley home. Being a single parent, Mary Alice encouraged her friends, relatives, and business associates to stop by or telephone each night. Television often served as a backdrop during these informal social occasions; TV jokes were remembered and repeated to her children and her friends around the kitchen table. Similarly, Stacey used television for social purposes, memorizing jokes from her favorite shows and sharing them with her friends:

> *Stacey:* I've been telling everybody at school these riddles from the *Bill Cosby Show.* Here's one. A boy went into the hospital and the doctor said that it was impossible to operate because the child was family. The doctor was not the father—who was it?
> *Boy next door:* I don't know.
> *Stacey:* It was the mother, get it?

In this family, television did not substitute for social interaction; rather, its content was used as part of their social exchanges with friends. In fact, these jokes were so successful that Stacey later borrowed a *Bill Cosby Joke Book* from the library and started memorizing jokes from *Discovery* magazine. Thus, in contrast to displacement, television content served to enhance this family's social involvement with friends.

Bryce (1980), in an ethnographic analysis of families and television, argued that the uses of the medium are inextricably related to the values and patterns by which family groups organize their lives together. "Television is a new dimension in an old system" (p. 359). In homes, where education and active exploration are valued, television does not replace such ability-enhancing activities; similarly, where social activities are important, television content may be used to provide more opportunities to practice these skills.

Lessons about reading. Parents' beliefs about reading, were similarly transmitted to their children by their attitudes and actions. Though different in their goals, reading held an exalted status in all three families. Children received a very clear and distinct message from their parents that their success in reading was symbolic of their success overall.

While there were books, newspapers, and magazines in all the nooks and crannies of each house, there were variations in the models set by the parents and the functional uses of reading in two of the three families. In the Clarke and Diamond homes, for example, one of the parents in each family was a heavy reader; Claire Clarke read books from 10–12:00 each night, and Peter Diamond was a voracious reader of business-related and more classical fiction.

In these families, reading served an important communication function, as a way for the parents and children to spend time together. On family trips, for example, Caroline and the children made language experience books to remember their favorite vacation activities, then she bound these books for the children's library. Similarly, Rob, who had many late meetings, would use the opportunity of the night-time story to catch up on the children's daily events.

Reading also served as an important source of information; the library was used as a frequent resource when planning gardens, house renovations, and organizing family vacations. By their actions, parents were emphasizing the way they believed their children should be exposed to reading. For example, Caroline, frustrated with Jennifer's reading program at school, remarked:

> The teacher doesn't seem to link ideas together. You see, in our house, if the children see something, like a raccoon, we'll go and open up a book and find out more about raccoons. In this class, Jennifer said they worked on raccoons, but in truth, they only heard a story about raccoons.

The uses of reading for purposes of escape or coping with difficult times was also communicated to the children. Claire sometimes used reading as anesthesia, "I read one murder mystery after another when I'm hurt or angry." Similarly, when Stephanie was going through a difficult period socially in school, Claire bought her "Sweet Valley Twins" books, which addressed and attempted to resolve young children's problems of jealousy, friendships, and sibling rivalry.

The models established by these parents emphasized the multifunctional nature of reading. Books were not confined to school-related activities; rather, by their examples and their own behavior, parents demonstrated the importance and usefulness of reading in their daily activities at home. In this respect, parents used their influencing potential to introduce children to a variety of reading experiences and circumstances for which gratifications from reading might be derived.

In contrast, there was a greater emphasis on "product" in the Conley family. Like the other two families, Mary Alice was keenly aware that reading was central to her children's later success. Just three years old, Alex was formally tested by the school on his prereading skills because she was worried that he was "a little bit behind." Similarly, Mary Alice proudly reported after a conference that Stacey was "at the top of her class, in the top reading group." But not being much of a reader herself, Mary Alice was less interested in the reading process than in Stacey's progress in school, as noted in this example:

> Stacey shows her mother a picture with a language experience story from school.
>
> *MA:* That's great, Stacey, look your teacher says 'lovely'—Stacey you're doing so well in school.
> *Stacey:* Let me tell you how I did it. This poem was written on the board. See, I read it over and over again, and I think about it in my mind. Then I make the pictures that come to my mind.
> *MA:* (as she's cleaning Stacey's lunchbox) Oh, that's great Stacey, that's really nice.

Here, the functions of reading seemed more narrowly defined than in the other two families. There were virtually no observances of Mary Alice's direct guidance or involvement in reading at home with her children. Rather, reading appeared to be regarded as a skill learned in school, one that must be acquired in order to perform well in later life.

Though differing widely in the scope of functions these parental models represented, children in each family received strong messages that reading was important. Accomplishments in reading were highly praised, rewarded, put prominently on display on refrigerator doors, and walls, framed for others to see. In this respect, reading was held separate from all other subjects and leisure activities that children engaged in during their busy day. Thus, in contrast to the assumption of functional equivalence, parents helped to distinguish the importance of various activities and set priorities for their children. Reading, as a result, appeared to be tied to a very different set of needs and gratifications for parents and their children from alternative leisure options, including television viewing.

In sum, according to the displacement of functionally equivalent needs, it has been assumed that given a choice, children may prefer the vicarious experiences of television in favor of alternative activities, requiring greater physical or mental effort. Salomon (1984), in his conceptualization of the amount of mental effort (AIME), for example, argued that the relative ease of watching television may produce a general tendency not to expend much effort in other domains as well.

There was no evidence, however, to suggest that children transferred their notions of the perceived ease of television viewing to other situational demands. Rather, each family through their own values and examples, guided their children in the uses of each medium. Parents made categorical distinctions between these media; above all, reading was equated with successful achievement, while television, with novelty and entertainment. Even at such an early age, there were indications that children internalized these values, if not directly the behaviors associated with them. Maccoby (1954) hypothesized that these internalized models, though failing to be overtly displayed at a young age, may be manifested later in adulthood. As evidence of this argument, Himmelweit and Swift (1976), in a 20-year follow-up of their benchmark television study, found that parents' orientation toward the media appeared to be exhibited in their child's subsequent media behavior in early adulthood.

In contrast to the view that children may substitute television for other activities, observations indicated that in instances where there was a choice between an active, socially related activity, or the more sedentary activity of viewing television, children invariably selected the more active experience. These findings substantiate Schramm, Lyle, and Parker's (1961) classic study indicating that the vicarious pleasures children attain through viewing tend to be hierarchically less satisfying than the ones derived from direct experiences, providing, of course, that these experiences are available. Consequently, it seems fair to assume that the satisfactions children gained from television did not displace their ongoing interests for intellectually stimulating and socially reinforcing activities.

References

Anderson, D. R., & Collins, P. (1988). *The impact on children's education: Television's influence on cognitive development*. Washington, DC: U.S. Department of Education, Office of Educational Research and Improvement, Contract No. 400-86-0055.

Anderson, D. R., Field, D. E., Collins, P. A., Lorch, E. P., & Nathan, J. (1985). Estimates of young children's time with television: A methodological comparison of parent reports with time-lapse video home observation. *Child Development, 56*, 1345–1357.

Bechtel, R. B., Achelpohl, C., & Akers, R. (1972). Correlates between observed behavior and questionnaire responses on television viewing. In E. A. Rubinstein, G. A. Comstock, & J. P. Murray (Eds.), *Television and social behavior: Vol. 4. Television in day-to-day life: Patterns of use* (pp. 274–344). Washington, DC: Government Printing Office.

Beentjes, J. W. J., & Van der Voort, T. H. A. (1988). Television's impact on children's reading skills: A review of research. *Reading Research Quarterly, 23*, 389–413.

Bower, R. (1985). *The changing television audience in America*. New York: Columbia University Press.

Bryce, J. (1980). *Families and television: An ethnographic approach*. Ann Arbor, MI: University Microfilms International.

Dorr, A. (1986). *Television and children*. Beverly Hills, CA: Sage Press.

Elkind, D. (1981). *The hurried child*. Reading, MA: Addison-Wesley.

Gadberry, S. (1974). Television as a babysitter: A field comparison of preschoolers' behavior during playtime and during television viewing. *Child Development, 45*, 1132–1136.

Gadberry, S. (1980). Effects of restricting first graders' TV viewing on leisure time use, IQ change, and cognitive style. *Journal of Applied Developmental Psychology, 1,* 45–57.

Gaddy, G. (1986). Television's impact on high school achievement. *Public Opinion Quarterly, 50,* 340–359.

Greenfield, P. (1984). *Mind and media: The effects of television, video games, and computers.* Cambridge, MA: Harvard University Press.

Hamilton, H. (1976). TV tie-ins as a bridge to books. *Language Arts, 33,* 129–130.

Heath, S. B. (1983). *Ways with words.* New York: Cambridge University Press.

Himmelweit, H. T. and Swift, B. (1976). Continuities and discontinuities in media usage and taste: A longitudinal study. *Journal of Social Issues, 32,* 133–156.

Hornik, R. (1981). Out-of-school television and schooling: Hypotheses and methods. *Review of Educational Research, 51,* 193–214.

James, N., & McCain, T. (1982). Television games preschool children play: Patterns, themes and uses. *Journal of Broadcasting, 26,* 783–800.

Leichter, H. J., Ahmed, D., Barrios, L., Bryce, J., Larsen, E., & Moe, L. (1985). Family contexts of television. *Educational Communications and Technology Journal, 33,* 26–40.

Lyle, J., & Hoffman, H. R. (1972). Explorations in patterns of television viewing by preschool-age children. In E. A. Rubinstein, G. A. Comstock, & J. P. Murray (Eds.), *Television and social behavior, Vol. 4. Television in day-to-day life: Patterns of use* (pp. 275–273). Washington, DC: Government Printing Office.

Maccoby, E. (1954). Why do children watch television? *Public Opinion Quarterly, 18,* 239–244.

Mander, J. (1978). *Four arguments for the elimination of television.* New York: William Morrow.

Mates, B. F. (1980). Current emphases and issues in planned programming for children. In E. Palmer and A. Don (Eds.), *Children and the faces of television* (pp. 19–31). New York: Academic Press.

National Institute of Mental Health. (1982). *Television and behavior: Ten years of scientific progress and implications for the eighties* (DHHS Publication No. ADM 82-1195). Washington, DC: U.S. Printing Office.

Neuman, S. B. (1986). Television, reading and the home environment. *Reading Research and Instruction, 25,* 173–183.

Parker, E. B. (1963). The effects of television on public library circulation. *Public Opinion Quarterly, 27,* 578–589.

Pellegrini, A. D. (1985). Relations between preschool children's symbolic play and literate behavior. In L. Galda & A. Pellegrini (Eds.), *Play, language, and stories* (pp. 79–97). Norwood, NJ: Ablex.

Potter, R. L. (1976). *New season: The positive use of commercial television with children.* Columbus, OH: Charles E. Merrill.

Roberts, D., Bachen, C., Hornby, M., & Hernandez-Ramos, P. (1984). Reading and television: Predictors of reading achievement at different age levels. *Communications Research, 11,* 9–49.

Salomon, G. (1984). Television is "easy" and print is "tough": The differential investment of mental effort as a function of perceptions and attributions. *Journal of Educational Psychology, 76,* 647–658.

Schramm, W., Lyle, J., & Parker, E. (1961). *Television in the lives of our children.* Stanford, CA: Stanford University Press.

Singer, J. L. (1980). The power and limitations of television: A cognitive-affective analysis. In P. H. Tannenbaum (Ed.), *The entertainment function of television* (pp. 31–65), Hillsdale, NJ: Erlbaum.

Singer, J. L., & Singer, D. (1980). *Television, imagination and aggression: A study of preschoolers' play and television viewing patterns.* Hillsdale, NJ: Erlbaum.

Singer, J. L., & Singer, D. (1983). Implications of childhood television viewing for cognition, imagination and emotion. In J. Bryant & D. R. Anderson (Eds.), *Children's understanding of television: Research on attention and comprehension* (pp. 265–296). New York: Academic Press.

Taylor, D. (1983). *Family literacy.* Exeter, NH: Heinemann Educational Books.

Tower, R., Singer, D., Singer, J., & Biggs, A. (1979). Differential effects of television programming on preschoolers' cognition, imagination and social play. *American Journal of Orthopsychiatry, 49,* 265–281.

Trelease, J. (1982). *The read-aloud handbook.* New York: Penguin.

Winn, M. (1977) *The plug-in drug.* New York: Viking Press.

Zuckerman, D. M., Singer, D. G., and Singer, J. L. (1980). Television viewing, children's reading, and related classroom behavior. *Journal of Communication, 30,* 166–174.

Questions for Discussion

1. How effective is the ethnographic approach Susan Neuman uses in her study? Is her approach scientific?
2. What is the "displacement theory" that Neuman addresses in her first section on "Common Assumptions"? Can you draw examples from your experience to illustrate this theory?
3. What do you think are the most important similarities and differences in the three families Neuman examines?
4. The article suggests there are four different ways of watching television. What characterizes each of these approaches, and which approach might we want to cultivate? Why?
5. Did the author find any social or emotional advantages or benefits to television viewing? If so, what are they? How does television seem to affect the imagination and creativity of young children?
6. In what ways did the children that Neuman observed incorporate television plots and characters into their play activities? What is the significance of this behavior? How does Neuman's evidence compare with your own experience of television viewing?

Questions for Research and Writing

1. Interview separately two fellow students, one who enjoys reading and one who does not. What roles did television play in their childhood homes?
2. Watch a film based on a book you have read. How are the two experiences different? Write briefly about your relative activity or passivity in each situation. Which experience did you enjoy more? Why? Do you usually prefer first to see a movie based on a book or read the book? Why?
3. Observe people (either children or adults) as they watch TV. How involved do they become in the program they are watching? What social or emotional functions does television viewing seem to serve?

REMOTE MOTHERING AND THE PARALLEL SHIFT
Women Meet the Cellular Telephone

Lana F. Rakow and Vija Navarro

> *The following article was first published in 1993 in the academic journal* Critical Studies in Mass Communications. *The authors, one an associate vice chancellor and the other a student at the University of Wisconsin-Parkside, analyze data gathered from a United Nations research project exploring the impact of new technologies on women in the United States and Canada. The article suggests that rather than liberating women from political and social conventions, technology may simply reinforce those conventions. Men use their phones for business, but women use the phone to fulfill their domestic obligations. Also, the article argues that technology shapes our relationship with our environment and that the way we use technology shapes new developments and advancements.*

Abstract: New technologies could have a positive impact on women's lives because of their potential to disrupt old social and political conventions. Using the recent development of the cellular telephone as an example, the authors find, however, that gender differences in the acquisition and use of this technology already are reproducing familiar inequities. Women in the authors' study use the cellular telephone to manage creatively their responsibilities for home and children. Their husbands believe the women are in special need of protection.

While communication technologies continue to be developed and marketed at a rapid rate, we know very little about the changes for women that might accompany these new developments. Yet we have ample reason to believe that new communication technologies could or should have an impact on women's lives. New technologies and technological systems—facsimile machines, computers and computer networks and bulletin boards, mobile paging systems, cellular telephones, video disks, electronic imaging, telephone "Caller I.D."—have the potential to disrupt old social and political conventions, to rearrange hierarchies, and to re-configure the boundaries of the public and the private. Will they?

Historically, communication technologies have been developed to generate profit for U.S. businesses and to serve the military; in contemporary times, technological development is a means for U.S. business and the military to compete in a global economic and political order. The need for change in the position of subordinate groups such as women is not a consideration or a public policy issue in making decisions about technological development; the critical relationship of gender to design, purpose, use, and outcome of communication technologies is masked or ignored. But we know that when it comes to technology (as everything else), gender matters

(Rakow, 1988a). Technologies have gendered persona (automobiles and ships as female) and are differentiated by the gender of users (washing machines for women, video cameras for men). In other words, technologies both represent and enact gender ideology, or our belief structure about gender. Feminist theorists have variously argued that men have used technology as a means to dominate and that women have been as active as creators and users of technology as men but without the credit. Feminist theorists also vary in the extent to which they are optimistic or pessimistic that new technologies will somehow be different (Kramarae & Taylor, 1992; van Zoonen, 1992).

We will need to look closely at individual technologies to see both the possibilities and the outcomes for women, a task to which we hoped to make a contribution with this research project on the development of the cellular telephone technology and industry. The cellular telephone has been on the market for only a few years, yet we discovered rather striking gender implications already. According to our research, middle class women and men are establishing a different relationship to cellular telephone technology, and they are making use of it in different ways. We conclude that these differences both stem from and help preserve women's subordinate social position. Women's seemingly "natural" tie to the domestic or private sphere has led to two phenomena for suburban, middle class women—which we identify as remote mothering and working parallel shifts—that distinguish their use of the technology. The belief that women are in need of protection already has led the industry and purchasers to the dubious conclusion that the cellular telephone will solve the problem of women's physical vulnerability. Despite claims to the contrary, cellular telephone service is likely to reproduce gender inequities, albeit with some shifting of public and private ground, under the guise of *solving* those very inequities. If the path taken by this technology is any indication, feminists will need to intervene actively in the formation of technological systems if technological potential is to turn into social reality for women.

WOMEN AND BASIC TELEPHONE SERVICE

To understand the implications for women of the development of cellular telephones, it is first necessary to understand women's relationship to the pre-existing telephone service, or basic service. Up to this point, the telephone is a technology that has been strongly associated with women, at least in the domestic sphere. The manner in which they use it and social evaluations of women's talk on it are indicative of women's social position in the United States. However, in the historic development of basic service, it was not immediately clear that the telephone would acquire a "feminine" association, even though women were among its earliest users.

As with any technology, the telephone had no inherent uses or social destiny when it was first introduced. In fact, the telephone industry played a large role in designing a place for it in American life (see Fischer, 1988).

Initially, the industry promoted it to men by stressing the telephone's business and practical applications. Though customers did use the telephone for interpersonal conversation, the telephone industry discouraged such uses until the late 1920s. While some advertising encouraged women's domestic uses of this technology, they were primarily concerning safety and shopping by telephone (Fischer, 1988, p. 40). A lore about women's talk on the telephone developed in the industry and among the populace, indicative of social disapproval of women's talk. Women's talk on the telephone was trivialized and characterized as gossip (see Rakow, 1988b).

In the late 1920s, AT&T began encouraging purely social uses of the telephone, not only reflecting a marketing strategy designed to increase telephone usage but also indicating a change in industry attitudes about the telephone (Fischer, 1988, p. 48). The telephone initially had been conceptualized in masculine terms, as an instrument of control rather than an instrument of sociability. Then private and public usage of it was distinguished. In the home, the telephone was seen as a domestic appliance for women. In the political and economic world, it was an instrument for men's business, with women employed as clerical workers and receptionists to handle placing and receiving calls, enabling men to compete for hierarchy among themselves (Rakow, 1988b).

Women apparently found important uses for the telephone even in the technology's earliest years and despite telephone industry preferences. It was commonly observed in early popular literature that lonely farm women and housewives found a solution to their loneliness through the telephone, but social observers failed to ask why it was that farm women and housewives were lonely. If the question had been raised, women's use of the telephone might have been more accurately seen as a symptom of women's social place rather than as a solution to it. Women's social and physical location in the home, increasingly distant from city centers and extended families, and women's responsibility for home and children, were integral factors in determining why and how women would come to use the telephone (Rakow, 1986).

One study of women's use of the telephone in a small midwestern community, called Prospect in the study, revealed that women are responsible for using the telephone for household business and for doing family and community work (Rakow, 1992). The telephone in Prospect is strongly associated with women; most men eschew talking on it, requiring their wives to answer and make calls for them. Women, particularly those tied more closely to their homes because of their advanced age or because of small children, use the telephone for what can be otherwise scarce social contact. They arrange school, church, and community functions by telephone. They maintain contact with family and friends, keeping families tied into larger local and distant networks. Their use of the telephone is consonant with an ideology of gender that approves of women's domestic and nurturing responsibilities while claiming those activities are simple reflections of women's natural inclinations. By carrying out their expected responsibilities and by dealing creatively with their social place through the telephone, women seem to prove the correctness of the social definition of being a woman.

A troubling difficulty for women in this community is reconciling two different worlds—the domestic and the economic. Their responsibilities for home and children make it difficult to find work—usually outside of the small community, which has few opportunities—and then to be away at work. Some have developed creative strategies for using the telephone to connect the two, bridging the spatial distance. For example, a realtor used the same telephone line at her home and at her office in order to take work related calls at home or the office. Others created economic opportunities that combine both worlds, such as operating a family business. While gender definitions in the community have shifted sufficiently to make working for payment an option—albeit a difficult one—for women, women still retain primary responsibility for home and child care.

THE RISE OF CELLULAR TELEPHONE SERVICE

The cellular telephone industry only began in the United States in 1983 with a field trial in Chicago, yet the industry has grown rapidly. By January 1991, almost 5.3 million Americans had cellular telephones, a figure that represents half of the world's cellular subscribers (CTIA, 1991). While AT&T had been working on cellular technology since 1947, it was not until 1981 that the Federal Communications Commission released its Report and Order that specified the regulatory scheme that would govern the new technology that uses the broadcast spectrum. The FCC decided that two competing cellular companies would be licensed in each market, one reserved for the local telephone company. Licenses have been determined by a lottery process. All metropolitan markets and half of the rural markets of the country now have service; every market was expected to have at least one cellular system in operation by mid-1992 (CTIA, n.d. "A Brief History of Cellular"). While individual fortunes still are being made and lost in the cellular business, the industry is settling into a familiar pattern in the communication technology business: Two-thirds of the U.S. population now falls under the license areas of only 10 companies—the 7 regional Bell companies, GTE, McCaw, and Centel (Donner, 1991, p. 54).

The technology works by using low power sending and receiving towers to pick up and transmit calls in a small (1 to 20 miles in diameter) geographic "cell." The cells are all linked together through a computerized switching system that passes off calls between cells, if necessary. In this way, a small slice of the radio spectrum (824–849 Megahertz and 869–894 MHz) can have maximum usage (CTIA, n.d. "How Cellular Works"; Berresford, 1989). Three kinds of telephones are available: mobile, which are installed permanently in a vehicle; transportables, which can be carried in a case outside a car; and portables, which are small and lightweight and can be used anywhere cellular service is available.

It is not clear what effect the development of Personal Communication Networks (mobile cordless handsets that operate by microcell technology, licensed for experiment by the FCC in 1990) and the move to digital computer switching from analog (which will reduce the use of airwaves and allow greater capacity) will have on the composition of the industry. Despite these uncertainties, predictions are that the industry will boom. One estimate is that within 10 years, one in every three telephone calls will be placed or received by wireless communication (Donner, 1991, p. 53). Already equipment prices have dropped sharply as a result of competition for new subscribers (see Bennett, 1990). By the end of 1990, average monthly customer bills had dropped to $80.90, while the average length of a cellular call was 2.2 minutes (CTIA, 1991). The decline in price is leading to predictions that a large consumer market is next to be tapped. Business customers still account for over three-fourths of purchases, but it has been predicted that in 1993, one out of every three cellular phones sold will be for personal use (Rosenberg, 1990, p. 65), possibly extending to 5 to 10% of the consumer market by 2005 (Jarratt & Coates, 1990, p. 79).

Initially the industry did almost no marketing of its product, instead relying on pent-up demand from business users of conventional mobile and paging systems (Campbell, 1985; Martin, 1985). Since then, it has marketed the cellular telephone almost exclusively as a business technology. Through its trade association and advertising, it has made a concerted effort to transfer the definition of the office telephone (with its association of masculine power and control) to the cellular telephone (see CTIA, n.d., "Cellular is a 'Can-Do' Tool"), "bundling" the cellular telephone ideologically and technically with other technologies—such as laptop computers, portable facsimile machines, and paging systems—into an imagined (if not yet real) autonomous mobile office. The benefit of cellular telephones for conducting business while out of the office is heralded as liberating for business and professional workers, giving them increased flexibility and more time (see as examples Krotz, 1990; Begole, 1991), as well as an edge over their competition.

The popular press has jumped on the cellular band wagon, making predictions about future uses and effects of the telephone that go beyond its business applications. A *Business Week* cover story in 1987 on the cellular telephone boom claimed that "cellular phones are transforming the way individuals communicate" (Keller, 1987, p. 84). Some writers are beginning to make dire predictions about the consequences of cellular service. One business consultant cautioned against the dangers of driving while operating a telephone and against the dangers of being overheard (Menkus, 1990). Both problems are likely to be lessened with the changeover to voice activated sets and digital computer switching between cells. One popular woman's magazine, unlike others which have heralded cellular telephones (even *Ms.* magazine, see Wartik, 1989) carried a story critical of technologies such as the cellular telephone which are extending work and one's availability into all periods of time and into all places (Reed, 1989).

The possibility of being always available to anyone, whether heralded or bemoaned, is unlikely to come about, however; a cautious approach is advisable in predicting any outcomes for a technology. The same claim of availability was made about basic service, but methods of screening and limiting calls were quickly devised—secretaries and rules of etiquette, for example, followed by answering machines and Caller I.D.—to prevent such access (Rakow, 1988b). Businesses are even now marketing devices to block or screen calls, especially important to cellular subscribers because they must pay for calls they receive as well as make. A variety of hierarchies are likely to be available. For example, as with basic service, an employee's highest superiors may have access to her or him at all times, but the access will not be reciprocal. Access to middle managers by those who report to her or him may increase, however. Access by those outside the chain of command to those inside the chain of command will not. For example, consumers still will not be able to call the chair of the board of directors of a business or industry; citizens still will not be able to call and talk to the country's president.

WOMEN AND CELLULAR SERVICE

While women have not been the primary cellular customers of the industry, marketing to women is on the horizon. Even though the industry claims it has not been marketing to men, the marketing strategy it has used has had that consequence. Even as late as 1988, one company on the East Coast reported that 97% of its customers were men, explained by the rationale that its primary customers are small business owners, who happen to be men (Olsen, 1988, p. 44). By 1989, the overall ratio of men to women was still only 90:10. However, the age, income, and occupational level of the typical male user had dropped from a 55-year-old top manager with an average income of $90,000 to a 39-year-old middle manager with a $44,000 average income (Sextro, 1989, pp. 105–106). Predictions have been made in the past few years that other marketing strategies reaching new markets are likely to come about. The president of Ameritech Mobile Communications in Shaumburg, Illinois—the first online cellular operation in the country—was reported in an industry magazine as claiming that the safety aspect of cellular would be increasingly important to people (Olsen, 1988, p. 49). A vice president for marketing of Centel predicted that the industry would target the "supermom," juggling a career and family (Sextro, 1989, p. 107).

By 1991, the supermom approach was not yet visible, but glimpses of new marketing strategies involving women were. For example the April 1991 issue of *Popular Science* carried a full page advertisement by Radio

Shack for a Tandy cellular telephone. Photographs of two men in business suits, carrying or using a transportable telephone, flank a middle photograph of a woman in casual clothes talking on the phone while golfing. One of the men is a light-skinned black. The other man and the woman are white. The similarity of dress and background lighting for the two men highlight their difference from the women, suggesting that gender and class rather than race are intended by the advertiser to be taken as the category of difference distinguishing use of the cellular telephone. In the same issue, Cellular One ran a full page advertisement for Oki phones with photographs of a businessman at an airport and of a man in a hardhat on location, both speaking on their phones. In a third picture, a woman is speaking on the phone kneeling next to her two children on a soccer field. All are white. Both advertisements demonstrate the manner in which white women representing the domestic or personal are beginning to be linked to the predominantly featured masculine/business application.

Of course, some women already have cellular telephones and they use them for a variety of applications, regardless of a historic industry lack of interest in them. A survey completed in January, 1991, of women and men cellular users, reveals some of those applications. Gallup, for Motorola, surveyed 650 cellular telephone users in a national sample, of which 232 were women. The majority of respondents were between 25 and 54 years of age, worked in professional or managerial, sales or service occupations, had some college education or were college graduates, and had incomes over $45,000 (Gallup Organization, 1991, p. 16). Eighty-nine percent of women compared to 74% of men said use of the cellular phone made them feel more safe and secure; 83% of women compared to 68% of men said it made their personal lives less stressful; 82% of women compared to 72% of men said it helped them make the most of their personal lives; 60% of women compared to 51% of men said it improved their relationship with their spouse; and 46% of women compared to 31% of men said it improved their relationship with their children (Gallup Organization, 1991, p. 7).

Women who participated in the survey said they use their phone for such things as calling if they will be late (87%), making or scheduling appointments (80%), phoning a loved one "just to say hello" (71%), closing a business deal (44%), and calling for assistance for their disabled vehicle (25%) (Gallup Organization, 1991, p. 5).

The Gallup survey makes clear that differences already are developing between middle class women's and men's use of the cellular telephone. What the survey did not make clear is why. We hoped to discover why by analyzing women's use of the cellular telephone in its deeper context of the meanings and consequences of gender in their lives. We conducted telephone interviews with 19 women in the affluent and predominantly white northern and western suburban Chicago area during July of 1991. Women were located for interviewing by a "snowball" method of sampling, where participants are asked for the names of others they know who could be interviewed (Taylor & Bogdan, 1984), in this case, of other women they know who had cellular telephones. Interviewing stopped when no new information was being learned, which had occurred by the time 19 women had been interviewed. Participants were asked a set of general open-ended questions about their background and their use of the telephone.

The women in this study included 17 who are married, 1 who is widowed, and 1 who is single; they range in age from 26 to their 40s; 2 have no children, 2 have 1 child, 11 have 2 children, and 4 have 3 children. Seventeen of the 19 are white, while 2 are black. All identified themselves as middle or upper middle class. Eight work full-time, year-round in sales, management, and professional occupations (1 of the 8 has her own business). Four work full-time during the school year as teachers or child care specialists. Three are full-time homemakers. Three work part-time year-round, 1 as a programmer analyst, 1 as a nurse, and 1 as a secretary. One woman works part-time only during the school year as a substitute teacher. All of the women have a mobile phone in their car or have access to a portable phone to take in the car, one that might also be used by their husbands. They had had their cellular telephones ranging from two weeks to three years.

Despite the cellular industry's focus on business applications and customers, the women in this study were much more likely to have and use their telephones for personal reasons or domestic responsibilities, even if they were employed. In fact, only 5 said the telephone was used primarily for business; the other 14 use it primarily for family and personal reasons. A sales representative who uses her telephone primarily for business said, "If it creates more work, that's good. It's an aid. . . . The bottom line is, it helps me in my job." However, even the women who use it primarily for business find family uses important as well. This emphasis on family usage differs from the way many of them described their husbands' use of the cellular telephone.

Most of the women did not express a great enthusiasm for their cellular phones. In one rare case, a woman did say, "It's wonderful!" Others said they had not been enthusiastic about getting one. In 10 of the cases, husbands actually had made the decision for their wives to get a cellular telephone or had gotten one for her. In 2 of those 10 cases, the husbands had won the telephones and, since the husbands already had cellular telephones, the phones were given to the wives. In another case, a husband wants his wife to get her own—they have a portable that they share—but she does not want one. In the other cases, husbands were sometimes insistent that wives have them. One woman, a realtor, said she got it "For safety reasons. My husband kept getting on me about—that something might happen, you might be out someplace and you might need a phone. He was right." Though she initially did not want one because she did not want people to think she had it as a status symbol, her husband insisted it was for her safety: "He really forced me to get the phone," she said.

Another woman, who is a part-time programmer analyst with two small children, said her husband wanted her to have it because "He just feels better if I have something at my fingertips as opposed to, like, being stuck in the middle of winter with two small children and having to walk somewhere." A woman who is a full-time homemaker said her husband got her the telephone because she travels with her children to sporting events and he feels more comfortable knowing she has a way to get help in the car.

The husband of a woman who had been seriously ill for a time bought her a cellular telephone in case she had a medical emergency and needed help. A woman whose husband is on the road constantly as a sales representative got her one because "He wanted me to have it for safety reasons when he was gone." Another woman said that after a family discussion about how difficult it was to coordinate schedules, "My husband said, that's it. You need a phone in the car."

While husbands seemed more concerned about their wives' safety and security than wives sometimes did, women, too, stressed safety as a reason for having a cellular telephone. As a realtor said, "I don't know the first thing about repairs," a common assessment among the participants. They stressed that it gave them peace of mind or made them feel better to have it. A business manager, who reported she does not use her cellular telephone for business because business calls are too important, has one because "as a woman" she does not want to be driving alone or with her child without some means of communication if something happens to her car.

For women, then, having a telephone in the car provides a means to call for help, reflecting their husbands' and in some cases their own perception that as women they are more vulnerable than men when they are alone, whether it is because they do not have the mechanical skills to handle car trouble or because they are possible victims of assault. As one woman said, "I just think single women or women alone at night should have a car phone." This perception stems from ideological notions that women are less mechanically inclined than men and that women are particularly vulnerable to violence, ideological notions that lead to a conviction that women need the protection of men. Husbands who want their wives to have telephones may be carrying out their gendered roles as protectors (which comes with being husbands and fathers) by providing the cellular telephone. The telephone provides access to him or to other authorities who can rescue her from her situation. One woman said, "It's a real sense of security, knowing that in an emergency, or if I really need him, he's always available."

The role of husband as protector fits an ideological pattern of gender found in most of the marriages. A few of the married women said they and their husbands share household and child care responsibilities equally and some believed it is desirable. It is also true that few of the marriages seem to work that way, a finding that is consistent with what is known about U.S. marriages in general. The kind of jobs wives and husbands in this study have reflect the discrepancy. All of the husbands work full-time, many at jobs that require extensive traveling. Most of the wives who work outside the home do not work full-time or do not work all year round. Their greater responsibility for homes and children make it more likely they will seek jobs that allow them to be closer to home and give them more time there. Then, their closer proximity to home and their greater presence in the home makes it seem "natural" that they should assume more responsibility for the domestic (see Rakow, 1992, ch. 3). The woman in this sample who started her own business in desktop publishing and business consulting explained it by saying she wanted to give her children the kind of home life she had had, with a mother who was not working, a "Kool Aid Mom," she called them. However, she had to work for economic reasons, so she looked for a happy medium that would allow her to combine both worlds.

The desire to be available to their children is a theme that ran through almost every interview, which included those who work outside their homes and those who do not. A middle class gender ideology that specifies that mothers should be the primary caregivers for children and should be constantly available to them (comparable to the ideology that husbands should be the protectors of the family) has been addressed by these women with the technological capabilities presented by cellular technology. Suburban middle class life is complex and necessarily mobile. Increased pressure for children to be active in athletics, music, and other activities which might improve their ability to compete for admission to colleges and careers—as well as a decline in extended family and neighborhood support for child-rearing—means mothering work has taken on new and longer-term dimensions. As children get older, mothering work changes to coordinating and meeting children's schedules and being "on-call," especially if the mother needs to be elsewhere. Children attend schools and extracurricular activities at various locations that require transportation, but for which public transportation is limited or non-existent. Shopping and other family business occur at yet another set of locations. It is no wonder that one woman pointed out, "I live in my car, just being taxi service."

The cellular telephone lets these women practice what could be called "remote mothering." One woman, a high school teacher during the school year, said she likes being always available to her children by having a cellular telephone: "That's my children. I like that. I want them to have that freedom. I think it's more security than it is annoying. I just feel better knowing that if they need me I'm available *all* the time." Women who work at paying jobs—particularly those that require car travel—find the cellular telephone permits them to exist in their domestic and work worlds simultaneously. They may be the harbingers of a trend for women who are trying to bridge the space and time gap between the domestic and work worlds, women working "parallel shifts" rather than what has been described as the "double shift" of work at a paying job followed by work at home (Hochschild, 1989). This interest in connecting the two worlds was foreseen in how some women used the telephone in the Prospect community study (Rakow, 1992). It also may be indicated by the rapidly growing number of women who own their own small businesses: women-owned businesses now account for 30% of all firms in the United States (U.S. Department of Commerce, 1990, p. 4).

Mothers with children who may be at home alone particularly appreciated their ability to reach them or be reached. One woman, a homemaker, described getting caught in traffic and not being home by the time her children arrived from school. She called them on the cellular telephone and talked to them until she drove into the driveway. As she said, "This was security for them but it was also security for me since they'd never been home alone before."

Other women talked about being able to "keep the family in contact with each other," a responsibility that they also assume in their use of home telephones. This finding is consistent with what women reported in Prospect of women's use of the telephone (Rakow, 1992). In this study, one woman said she uses her home telephone to keep in contact with people and to keep relationships going, which her husband does not do. "If it weren't for me, we wouldn't have continued relationships," she observed.

Keeping in contact with family members does not mean the same things when carried over to the cellular telephone, however. Women use the cellular telephone to keep track of children and to be available to them as well as to be available to ill or aged members of their families. They do not use the cellular telephone for other social purposes such as talking to friends. Only two women reported using their cellular telephones in such a way. It was unusual to hear it expressed, as one woman did: "I just use it like another phone. I do [chat on it]." Most others said they would not use it "just to chat" with friends or family. This marks the cellular telephone as different from most of their home telephone use. It suggests that "family business" is considered an appropriate way to use the technology. In part this is due to the cost difference between home and cellular calls. Women described their calls as brief and to the point. One woman used her portable cellular telephone for a social call when her teenager had the home telephone tied up. The size of the bill for her lengthy call caused her husband "to put a stop to that," indicating the authority he has in the family to make those decisions.

Besides the cost, cellular technology is not used in the same way as the home telephone for another reason. The cellular telephone represents a different kind of technology to them than their home telephones. One woman said about it, "I don't consider it an extension of my phone, I consider it a completely different system." Another said her cellular telephone had a "whole different feeling." It was common for women to report that they did not feel comfortable using it because the telephone distracted them from their driving. While newer and more expensive equipment permits hands-free operation, women will not necessarily feel more comfortable with the new equipment. The cellular telephone already sits in an ambiguous position for most of them, between being a feminine and familiar appliance (the telephone), and a masculine machine (a mechanical and/or electronic gadget). One woman reported, for example, that she does not like to use her cellular telephone very much because she is uncomfortable using it while driving. Though her telephone is programmable so that she does not have to manually dial numbers, that feature of the technology moves it into unfamiliar territory that she is unlikely to pursue. As she said, "I'm not real good at anything programmable. I'm not mechanically inclined."

DISCUSSION

In sum, many of these women did not want a cellular telephone nor are they enthusiastic about the technology now that they have it. For more than half of the 19 women, their husbands exerted decision-making authority over acquiring the telephone service, largely out of a desire to protect their wives and children from weather hazards and possible violence. Now that they have use of the service, these women are using it in a creative way to carry out their geographically complicated responsibilities for home, family members, and paid labor. They are able to accomplish mothering responsibilities across time and space; they are able to bring their private world of domestic responsibilities into their public world of work.

Despite the gender differences already apparent with the use of the cellular telephone, it is not clear what gender association cellular telephones eventually will come to have. Since the automobile is so heavily gendered as masculine in the United States, and certain technologies used to exert power or control are gendered masculine, the cellular telephone could remain primarily a technology associated with men and under their decision-making, much as video and computer technology seem to be. The cellular telephone, because it lies in that twilight area between public and private, seems to be an extension of the public world when used by men, an extension of the private world when used by women. That is, men use it to bring the public world into their personal lives. Women tend to use it to take their family lives with them wherever they go. There is nothing inherent in the technology that requires women and men to use it differently. It is gender ideology, operating within a particular political and economic context, that leads to women and men living different lives and using technology differently.

Cellular telephone technology may appear to provide a solution to two important problems faced by middle class, suburban women: the problem of safety and security in a violent and mobile society, and the problem of carrying out family responsibilities across barriers of time and space. It must be remembered, however, that cellular telephones are not available to all economic strata of society, nor are they likely to be. Additionally, individual strategies are unlikely to solve women's social problems. For example, the presence of cellular telephones will not end violence against women, even if some individual women may feel more secure with one present. In point of fact, women are far more likely to be the victims of violence by someone they know than they are to be assaulted by a stranger (Flanagan & Maquire, 1990, p. 248). Nor will turning the double shift into parallel shifts relieve women of their work burdens or raise their economic position.

Solving women's problems will take a large-scale public policy agenda that would include a proactive plan for the development of new communication technologies that would benefit women, rather than a post hoc transfer of technologies to women when certain groups of women present a lucrative market for the industry. While the final configuration of cellular telephone service is not yet established, it appears to be following the route that basic telephone service already has traveled. The story of the cellular telephone may be all too common as the development of new communication technologies continues.

References

Begole, C. (1991, April). Work where you want, when you want. *Working Woman,* pp. 36–37.
Bennett, J. (1990, July 9). Scramble for cellular customers drains phone company's parent. *Crain's Chicago Business,* p. 13.
Berresford, J. W. (1989). The impact of law and regulation on technology: The case history of cellular radio. *The Business Lawyer, 44* (3), 721–735.
Campbell, R. S. (1985, October). Selling small: Personalization is key to opening doors in small markets. In Online International, Inc. (Ed.), *Cellular communications '85: Proceedings of the conference held in New York, October, 1985* (pp. 33–38). New York: Online Publications.
CTIA. (n.d). A brief history of cellular. Washington, D.C.: Cellular Telecommunications Industry Association.
CTIA. (n.d). Cellular is a "can-do" tool. Washington, D.C.: Cellular Telecommunications Industry Association.
CTIA. (n.d). How cellular works. Washington, D.C.: Cellular Telecommunications Industry Association.
CTIA. (1991, March 18). Cellular subscriber count jumps past 5 million. Washington, D.C.: Cellular Telecommunications Industry Association.
Donner, J. F. (1991, July). The future of cellular: An investment perspective. *Mobile Office,* pp. 53–54, 56, 58, 60.
Fischer, C. S. (1988). "Touch someone": The telephone industry discovers sociability. *Technology and Culture, 29* (1), 32–61.
Flanagan, T. J. & Maquire, K. (Eds.). (1990). *Sourcebook of criminal justice statistics 1989.* Washington, D.C.: U.S. Department of Justice, Bureau of Justice Statistics.
Gallup Organization. (1991, May). *The Motorola cellular impact survey.* Princeton, NJ: Gallup Organization, Inc.
Hochschild, A., with Machung, A. (1989). *The second shift: Working parents and the revolution at home.* New York: Viking.
Keller, J. J., with Harris, C. L. & Verity, J. (1987, September 21). Hello anywhere: The cellular phone boom will change the way you live. *Business Week,* pp. 84–86, 90, 92.

Jarratt, J. & Coates, J. F. (1990). Future use of cellular technology: Some social implications. *Telecommunications Policy, 14* (1), 78–84.

Kramarae, C. & Taylor, H. J. (1992). Women and men on electronic networks: A conversation or a monologue? In H. J. Taylor, C. Kramarae, & M. Ebben (Eds.). *Women, information technology, and scholarship* (pp. 59–67). Urbana-Champaign, IL: Women, Information Technology, and Scholarship Colloquium. University of Illinois at Urbana-Champaign.

Krotz, J. L. (1990, March). The ultimate office on wheels. *Money,* pp. 101–102, 108.

Martin, R. C. (1985). Selling techniques—cellular mobile service in large markets. In Online International, Inc. (Ed.), *Cellular communications, '85: Proceedings of the conference held in New York, October, 1985.* New York: Online Publications.

Menkus, B. (1990, August). Cellular telephone use can be dangerous. *Modern Office Technology,* pp. 60, 62.

Olsen, W. (1988, January). Customer profiles. *Cellular Business,* pp. 44–49.

Rakow, L. F. (1986, November). The telephone and women's talk: An ethnographic study. Paper presented at the Speech Communication Association conference, Chicago.

Rakow, L. F. (1988a). Gendered technology, gendered practice. *Critical Studies in Mass Communication, 5* (1), 57–70.

Rakow, L. F. (1988b). Women and the telephone: The gendering of a communications technology. In C. Kramarae (Ed.), *Technology and women's voices: Keeping in touch* (pp. 207–228). New York: Routledge & Kegan Paul.

Rakow, L. F. (1992). *Gender on the line: Women, the telephone, and community life.* Urbana: University of Illinois Press.

Reed, J. (1989, November). Present tense. *Vogue,* pp. 428–429.

Rosenberg, R. (1990). Trends in personal communications. *Telecommunications, 24* (9), 65–66.

Sextro, D. (1989). Analysis: Growing the typical cellular user. *Cellular Business, 6* (1), 104–107.

Taylor, S. & Bogdan. R. (1984). *Introduction to qualitative research methods* (2nd ed.). New York: John Wiley & Sons.

U.S. Department of Commerce. (1990, August). Women-owned businesses. *1987 economic censuses.* Washington, D.C.: U.S. Government Printing Office.

Wartik, N. (1989, November). Life in the fax lane. *Ms.,* pp. 43–44.

van Zoonen, L. (1992). Feminist theory and information technology. *Media, Culture & Society, 14* (1), 9–30.

Questions for Discussion

1. Lana Rakow and Vija Navarro begin by noting that little attention has been paid to the effect of new communication technologies on women. What is your response to their focus on women? What does the article say about how such technology has affected men?

2. Rakow and Navarro tell us that early observers believed women often used the telephone to combat loneliness but failed to ask why the women were lonely. Perhaps other stereotypes similarly allow us to stop short of real analysis. How might you push past these common stereotypes?

1. Housewives watch a lot of soap operas.
2. After returning home from work, men park themselves in front of the TV and don't do anything.
3. Generation X-ers are selfish and apathetic.

Do these stereotypes contain some truth? If so, what do these behaviors tell us about the attitudes, fears, hopes, and positions in society of men, women, and Generation X-ers?

3. Rakow and Navarro make a number of claims about what is likely to happen as cellular phones become more prevalent; for example, there will be more ways to screen out unwanted calls. How convincing are their predictions of the future of cellular technology? Consider not only how their ideas conform to your own but also how well they present and use evidence in support of their ideas.

4. Citing an earlier study, Rakow and Navarro say that "when it comes to technology (as everything else), gender matters." In what ways do you think "gender matters" to your outlook, your observations and experiences, and the way others respond to you? What other hereditary or biological characteristics outside of your control matter to the way you see yourself and the way others see you?

5. Some readers will object that Rakow and Navarro believe so strongly that "gender matters" that they allow their observations about gender to cloud their objectivity. Look at *one* of the following and evaluate its objectivity: the analysis of advertisements in paragraphs 13–19 or the methodology of their July 1991 survey in paragraphs 20–27. How well do the authors use evidence? How fully do they acknowledge and respond to other interpretations of the evidence? How might they strengthen their analysis and argument?

Questions for Research and Writing

1. According to Rakow and Navarro, most technological developments have been in response to the needs of business or the military. Do some research on a particular technological development. Was it born out of corporate and/or military need? To what extent have its original purposes been superseded by more private and personal ones? Finally, has it affected different groups of people differently—for instance, women and men or people of different socioeconomic groups? (Some technological developments you might want to research include the radio, television, satellites, the computer, the microwave, or the fax machine.)

2. Interview owners and potential owners of cellular phones, asking them why they bought (or hope to buy) them, what they see as the advantages or drawbacks of owning a cellular phone. In other words, conduct a study that replicates Rakow and Navarro's. Do your findings mirror

theirs? To what extent does gender predict one's use of and reaction to cellular phones? What other factors—such as age, socioeconomic status, cultural or ethnic background—relate to the use of cellular technology?

3. Survey men and women about their telephone use. For what reasons are they most likely to use the telephone? How long are most of their telephone conversations? Are they more likely to make or receive calls? How would they describe their attitudes toward the telephone (for instance, do they welcome the ringing of a telephone or see it as an interruption)?

4. Examine television and magazine advertisements for cellular phones. Do advertisers make appeals based on gender? How do their marketing techniques reveal their assumptions about the uses and users of cellular technology?

5. Cellular phones have become even more ubiquitous since the authors completed their research. Cell phones can be purchased almost anywhere, and the phones themselves are often given away in exchange for contracts to provide cellular service. Many companies provide "companion plans" in which two people receive a benefit for signing up for service at the same time. Interview someone in the cellular phone industry about why such marketing plans have evolved.

MISMEASURING WOMEN
A Critique of Research on Computer Ability and Avoidance

Pamela E. Kramer and Sheila Lehman

> *Included as part of a special cluster of articles on women and computers published in 1990 in* Signs: Journal of Women in Culture and Society, *the following review article confronts the issue of gender differences in learning and using computers. The authors, both research scholars in social science at Polytechnic University in Brooklyn, are obviously concerned with a number of common views about men, women, and computers. Why do we think of women as less comfortable with the new technology than men are? Why do boys seem to take to computer games more readily than girls do? The authors of this piece focus not only on the answers to these questions but on the ways we go about looking for answers to such questions. As in several other articles in this chapter, the authors are concerned with the influence of "ways of knowing" on attitudes toward technology.*

Among secondary-school-aged children (eleven to eighteen years), boys are at least three times more likely than girls to use a computer at home, participate in computer-related clubs or activities at school, or attend a computer camp.[1] This 3:1 pattern continues through the postsecondary years. In 1985, though approximately fourteen thousand out of twenty-six thousand bachelor's degrees in computer science were awarded to women, women earned only two thousand out of seven thousand master's degrees.[2] Approximately 30 percent of all employed computer specialists are women. This figure has remained constant for the past decade, during which computer fields have become the fastest growing occupational area for both sexes. Yet, there is also evidence that female computer professionals are disproportionately concentrated in lower-paid, less prestigious jobs.[3] Among this population, National Science Foundation figures for 1986 show less than 5 percent of all women earning bachelor's degrees in computer science, or employed in computer-related fields, to be African-American or Hispanic.[4]

While gender-related differences in learning and using computers can be documented at all educational levels, their causes and consequences are unclear. Much of the research assumes that women's lower participation rate is either correlated with, or at least shares a common etiology with, women's avoidance of mathematics. Yet this assumption may rest more on prevailing conventions within primary and secondary education that locate computer-based learning within mathematics and science curriculums than upon a carefully contextualized analysis of women's and girls' mathematics and computer-based learning.

RESEARCH ON MATHEMATICS LEARNING

Contemporary research on participation and achievement has relied increasingly on cognitive, affective, and sociocultural factors, rather than biological ones, to explain sex differences.[5] For example, Elizabeth Fennema and Julia Sherman examined differences in mathematics and spatial achievement scores of over twelve hundred ninth-grade students of comparable mathematics background. They found sex differences in mathematics achievement and spatial visualization scores only in those schools where there were also significant sex differences in the students' self-perception of their ability to learn mathematics and the value they placed on mathematics learning.[6] Furthermore, parents' and teachers' expectations for students' learning were not only a significant factor in achievement but also a significant factor in sex differences in learning. (Boys were expected to be better mathematics learners, and it was more important for boys to learn mathematics.) Even in schools where boys and girls performed equally, students perceived mathematics as a male domain. Fennema and Sherman's sample included both urban working-class and suburban middle-class schools, but socioeconomic factors did not predict achievement or attitudinal differences.

In the past decade feminist scholars have built up a richly detailed picture of the ways in which the lives of girls and women differ from those of boys and men and how these differences affect educational and career decisions involving mathematics at critical choice points during the school years. For example, in a follow-up to the 1977 research described above, Julia Sherman compared three matched groups of high school girls who had elected mathematics courses for four, three, or less than three years. Contrary to her expectations, she found that those girls who had taken four years of mathematics were *more* conflicted about sex role expectations and family and career plans than were the other girls.[7] They expressed greater concern about "being smart" in mathematics; they were more likely to admit to "playing dumb" in front of classmates and peers; and they were also more likely to agree that a "mother's place is in the home." Outnumbered by boys in their advanced mathematics courses (13 percent of girls and 57 percent of boys took fourth-year math), these girls did express more positive attitudes abut mathematics and about themselves as potential mathematics learners than other girls did.[8]

Changes not only in perceptions and attitudes, but in contextual factors as well can have a significant impact upon women's learning and career choices in sex-typed domains such as mathematics. Patricia Lynn Casserly, for instance, found that changes in recruitment and teaching strategies for advanced placement (AP) high school courses significantly increased girls' participation in these courses. Female AP students were used as recruitment agents and role models, and bright high school girls were aggressively targeted as potential participants. In addition, AP instructors ensured equal participation in classroom recitation with "turn taking."[9] This significantly reduced girls' silent denigration of their own skills, and it encouraged them to speak out in class even if they thought they might be wrong. Girls enrolled in AP courses also became significantly more likely than other girls to include engineering and science fields in their future career plans.

RESEARCH ON COMPUTER LEARNING

There is a large body of research documenting that sex differences in mathematics performance, where they exist at all, are based on complex interactions of social and attitudinal factors. Yet computer learning research that explains sex differences in performance in terms of males' superior performance in and exposure to high school mathematics may ignore this literature and explain any superior mathematics performance by males in terms of superior, quantitative, reasoning skills.[10]

Here we examine significant exceptions to this approach. However, even where individual studies on girls' and women's performance and participation in computer-based learning do focus upon factors similar to those identified in the earlier research on mathematics learning, no study or group of research studies comprehensively addresses questions and issues dealing with the separate contexts, contents, and values attached to computer learning.[11]

Some studies recognize that social or institutional factors play a role but then fail to question their assumptions about the relevance of mathematics ability to computer aptitude. For example, Faye Dambrot and her associates found lower rates of participation for women in introductory computer programming courses in college, and lower grades for women who did participate, to be significantly correlated with both their relative lack of high school preparation in advanced mathematics and their poorer performance on what is called a "computer aptitude" test.[12] This aptitude test is essentially a measure of mathematics knowledge and experience. Thus, the women's significantly less positive attitudes toward their college computer programming courses were viewed as a side issue unrelated to the other findings: in effect, women are not good at computing, and they do not like it either.[13]

In contrast, other researchers have focused on attitudes as a central factor in women's and girls' computer ability. Jo Sanders and Antonia Stone, for instance, document the implications for attitudes and performance of the ways in which teachers introduce computer-related learning into educational settings. Higher-level computer skills such as programming are usually associated with the male academic domains of math and science and usually are taught by males. Conversely, text processing, simple accounting, and filing programs involve skills that tend to be associated with less prestigious, female-stereotyped vocational tracks. Sanders and Stone find that in this atmosphere, boys sign up for computer-related extracurricular activities in disproportionate numbers. In the few instances where girls are present, they have usually been encouraged to join.[14]

Betty Collis found that a six-week hands-on introductory computer course that was taught only by male teachers had little or no effect on eighth-grade girls' negative attitudes toward computers.[15] The girls in the study were less interested in computers than were boys, less confident about their ability to use computers, and more likely to be negative about the impact of computers on society; and this remained virtually unchanged by the course. In particular, girls in this study who were enrolled in schools with the most extensive computer programs were less positive after taking the course than were other girls. Boys from these schools, however, became significantly more positive about computers after taking the course than other boys were.[16]

To further complicate addressing differences between boys and girls, the girls in Collis's study did not believe their lack of ability and interest was due to the fact that they were female but, rather, saw it as a matter of individual inability or disinterest: "Girls in both grades [8 and 12] strongly agreed with statements about females, in the abstract, being as competent as males with computers. However, as soon as females were asked to assess their own personal competency and self-confidence, they shifted in their attitudes. The typical girl felt that women in general were capable, but that she as an individual was not competent or likely to be a computer user."[17]

A few researchers have documented connections between cultural assumptions, the contexts in which computers are used, and girls' disinterest in computers. For example, Karen Scheingold, Jan Hawkins, and Cynthia Char show how the cultural assumptions that govern the interactions of elementary school children operate to deny young girls credibility, or even visibility, as competent computer users, even when these girls demonstrate the very levels of computer-related knowledge and skills that they supposedly do not have.[18]

Sara Kiesler, Lee Sproull, and Jacquelynne Eccles analyze the ways in which masculine cultural values and stereotypes are incorporated into computer-based learning, work, and play. The high school girls they studied became passive observers ("computer groupies") rather than active participants in many settings; the researchers related this behavior to the pervasive warlike or competitive sports metaphors in much educational and recreational software.[19]

SOME ALTERNATIVE APPROACHES

We have suggested that some important insights may be gained by a more contextualized approach that examines the ways in which preexisting social roles and relationships are replicated within settings for computer learning and how this affects learning outcomes. Indeed, our conversations with women about their encounters with computers resonate with a kind of "knowing more than one can say," as they struggle to express their problems with computer learning from the standpoint of their individual lives and values. For example, this conversation between a woman, her friend, and her husband, suggests a form of resistance to computers that is based on concepts of autonomy and control:

> *Husband:* "I don't know. She just doesn't like to use it. She's bothered by the physical aspects of the thing. The fan. She can't stand the noise the fan makes."
> *Wife:* "No, it's not just the fan."
> *Friend:* "Maybe. . . ."
> *Husband:* "Yes, you are always complaining about the fan."
> *Friend:* "Maybe it's that the computer is so, I don't know, so discontinuous with everything else. With, you know, the ordinary way of getting our work done."
> *Wife:* "That's it. What you just said. I think that is it. It forces you to do things its way, and even though it may be faster, I don't like it."

A community researcher discussed her choices about learning to use a computer in terms of employment politics and policy:

> I love my job, and the issues I get to work on are very important ones, ones that are really interesting to me, too. But eventually, if I want to stay there I am going to have to work on the computer. The statistical simulations they do on the computer are given an enormous amount of weight in developing plans for the community. The trouble is, I have no interest in doing things that way. I don't believe simulations really get at the important issues. And I would have to learn to program the computer. I don't know how to do that. And I don't want to do that all day long.

New technologies are always introduced into a web of existing human settings: physical, organizational, and sociocultural. To understand this technology transfer process, of which computer learning is a part, it is essential to identify the key values that are operative in computer learning settings.

While there are women who express a positive involvement with computers and delight in their capabilities, and men who express doubts or indifferences about computers and "computer jocks," it is women who are expected to avoid computers and who are more often found to do so. We have quoted these two women's voices because the critique implicit in their attempts to frame their ambivalence about computer use suggests themes with which the research literature rarely deals.

Our own observation, based on research, teaching, and consulting experiences, is that few computer learners (including those who learn in work settings) have the breadth of knowledge about computer applications and career options that might allow them to imagine how to use the computer in ways most suited to their individual abilities, interests, and values.[20] Similarly, few children at elementary and secondary levels have access to newer developments in computer technology itself, developments—such as graphics, expert systems, hypermedia, or software designed to support collaborative work—that would allow children to explore their abilities and interests creatively. Yet the computer learning research does not address the implications of these gaps for the ways in which computer knowledge is structured, for example, sex-stereotyped computer tracking.

Moreover, much of the research that documents sex differences in computer aptitude is too simplistic in its treatment of the computer itself. As Jan Hawkins has pointed out, it is individuals who interact with computers, and they will be engaged individually by different skills and applications. Hawkins notes that studies that have reported significant overall differences between boys and girls "tend to describe the computer as a 'unitary topic' rather than attending to the characteristics of the particular situations where differences are found."[21]

RESEARCH ON REENTRY WOMEN

A reentry program for African-American and Hispanic women two-year community college graduates at Polytechnic University, a technological institution primarily known for undergraduate and graduate education in engineering fields, is a particularly good example of the potential benefit to computer learning programs of (1) abandoning assumptions about the correlation between math performance and computer ability and (2) focusing on what skills are being learned, who is teaching these skills, and within what context(s).[22] Fifty-six out of sixty-nine women eventually earned bachelor's degrees in this program (Minority Women in Management and Technical Fields [MIWIM]). To date, eighteen of these women have continued on to earn M.S. degrees in such fields as information management, computer science, and transportation engineering. At the same time as these women were completing their degrees, a second group of nonminority women were reentering at the graduate level as part of a National Science Foundation program in transportation engineering and management. Twenty-six of an initial thirty-three participants completed M.S. degrees in this program.

While the two groups differed in educational background and degree (A.A.S., B.A., B.S.), they proved to be highly comparable in their needs for basic education in mathematics and their attitudes about mathematics. The two-year college graduates had completed an average of 1.9 years of high school mathematics; graduate students in the transportation engineering program had completed an average of 2.1 years. Women in both groups typically were employed in traditionally female occupations: fully half of the National Science Foundation program participants were elementary and middle school teachers; a majority of participants in the MIWIM program were secretaries. They averaged thirty-four years of age and most were married with children living at home. All of the women were required to take trigonometry, calculus, statistics, and computer courses to complete their degrees at both the undergraduate and graduate levels. All exhibited very high levels of mathematics anxiety on the Math Anxiety Rating Scale (MARS) and on other self-report questionnaires, including the Fennema and Sherman scales used to measure attitudes toward mathematics.[23]

All of the women participated in a noncredit review of high school algebra and an introduction to trigonometry before they began their regular college programs. The course, based upon models developed at Harvard University by Deborah Hughes-Hallett and at Wesleyan University by Sheila Tobias, was so effective that all but three participants subsequently passed required college-level precalculus (trigonometry) and calculus or statistics courses.[24]

We examined demographic and attitudinal variables predictive of success in regular college precalculus and calculus courses and success in statistics and computer science courses when such data were available. Data needed to complete this analysis were available for thirty-seven of the fifty-six participants who completed bachelor's degrees in the Minority Women in Management and Technical Fields program and all twenty-six women who earned M.S. degrees in transportation engineering. Because the results for both groups were so similar, we also examined the effect of mathematics-related attitudes on grades in precalculus for a combined sample ($N = 66$).

Previous experience in mathematics did not significantly predict these women's grades in their precalculus and calculus courses. Moreover, it did not predict grades in computer science courses for women who continued in computer-related fields. Age was a predictor for precalculus and calculus courses: women over forty experienced considerably more difficulty in college-level mathematics courses ($R = -.38, P < .001$ [MIWIM]; and $R = -.30, P < .01$). Attitudes toward mathematics, including self-perceived ability, perceived ability in comparison with others, and willingness to take math courses and mathematics anxiety (MARS score), were all strong predictors of the women's grades in their college-level mathematics courses. Combined, these attitudinal variables predicted almost 80 percent of the variability of the women's precalculus course grades.[25] However, while high school math review grades also were significant predictors of both precalculus and calculus grades, and while all mathematics grades reflected overall grade point average to some degree, none of the mathematics grades significantly predicted success in college-level computer courses.[26] The correlational relationships that have been found by other researchers between performance in introductory college-level computer courses and previous mathematics grades or courses may be an artifact of the fact that homework programs assigned in introductory computer courses presume calculus knowledge. We found that when calculus-based problems were eliminated, reentry college women simultaneously taking a first-year programming course and an introductory trigonometry and calculus course were able to complete both. This suggests that previous mathematics experience and measures of aptitude based upon such experience may work more effectively to exclude women than to predict ability in computer courses.

REDEFINING COMPUTER LEARNING

Research on computer learning and ability, if it is to avoid confounding the sex difference findings of mathematics ability research with those of computer learning and participation, must focus its attention on the computer itself and critique the contexts and embedded social contents of computer learning as an essential aspect of research design. While graduate-level and advanced undergraduate-level computer science is in part based on mathematical theory, the design, implementation, and applications of computer technology could be taught in terms resonant with everyday problem solving and logic rather than formal mathematical systems.

Computer technology is highly dynamic. As the use of computers expands in educational and workplace settings, the contexts and applications of their use are rapidly changing so that the presumed closeness of the domains of computing and mathematics knowledge constitutes an increasingly inaccurate portrayal of what experienced and highly skilled computer users describe as being the most advanced types and forms of creative computer-related work.[27] Metaphors for computer technology are moving away from the number-cruncher computer, away from the machine that can replace human action and decision making, and toward an understanding of computing as an interactive process in which the computer becomes an intelligent coparticipant in and facilitator of individual and group communication. This shift reflects the fact that creative computing now relies at least as much upon language, visual design, problem definition, and organizational skills as upon quantitative analysis.

Much of the research on gender differences in computing is based on definitions of computer literacy that fail to take into account the varying contents and context of computing, failing to distinguish clearly between such curricular topics as computer science, software design and programming, the teaching of specific software (such as word processing or spreadsheet packages), and the role of computer technology in our society. Consideration of levels of learning and domains of application of computer-related knowledge and skills should be included in any evaluation of computer aptitude and ability because computer learning, unlike mathematics learning, need not be based on a linear progression in which algebra comes before calculus and calculus before differential equations. Instead, the pieces of computer learning are more like those of a patchwork quilt; they may be joined in a variety of ways, the particular design depending upon the requirements of particular contexts and situations.

The effects of the sociocultural contexts of computing, including the educational and economic structures within which women encounter and work with computers and the attitudes that both shape and are shaped by particular settings, need to be carefully distinguished from effects deriving from the nature of computer-related learning tasks per se.

As in earlier research on women's avoidance of mathematics, we expect that a careful examination of women's computer participation and learning will reveal complex causal patterns of relationships between computer-related attitudes, abilities, and experiences; the nature of the task; and the sociocultural, economic, and educational settings in which women must choose to pursue or avoid computer-related learning and work. Yet because computer and mathematics learning differ in important ways, not all of these patterns of interrelationships will parallel those previously found for mathematics. Although epistemological and pedagogical issues must be evaluated systematically in relation to both mathematics and computer learning, it may be that women's computer learning will prove to be highly dependent upon institutional and economic contexts. (In fact, there is recent solid evidence that the mathematics gender gap is beginning to close.)[28]

An examination of the contexts of computing may reveal that women's choices are governed as much by positive preferences for certain styles of knowing and thinking as by negative stereotypes and discrimination. Although studies that have examined the expression of positive preferences and values in relation to computing are few, the existing literature suggests that an important starting point is the recognition of computing as an activity that incorporates and reflects social relationships and has social and psychological impacts.

Notes

1. R. D. Hess and I. T. Miura, "Gender Differences in Enrollment in Computer Camps and Classes," *Sex Roles* 13, nos. 3/4 (August 1985): 193–203. See also Jo Sanders and Antonia Stone, *The Neuter Computer: Why and How to Encourage Computer Equity for Girls* (New York: Women's Action Alliance, 1987). In an article exploring the impact of a course in computer literacy, Betty Collis found that girls, who were five times less likely to enroll, actually expressed more negative than positive attitudes about computing following the course ("Sex Differences in Secondary School Students' Attitudes toward Computers," *Computing Teacher* 12, no. 7 [April 1985]: 33–36). Others, however, have found that increased opportunities for experience with computers, although less likely for girls, do tend to produce positive attitude change. See Marcia Linn, "Gender Equity in Computer Learning Environments," in *Computers and the Social Sciences* (Providence, R.I.: Paradigm Press, 1985), 19–26; and Marlaine Lockheed and Steven Frakt, "Sex

Equity: Increasing Girls' Use of Computers," *Computing Teacher* 11, no. 8 (April 1984): 16–18.
2. *Women and Minorities in Science and Engineering* (Washington, D.C.: National Science Foundation, 1986): 27–38, 121–33.
3. See S. Dubnoff and P. Kraft, "Gender Stratification in Computer Programming" (University of Massachusetts, Center for Survey Research, Boston, 1980); and John Markoff, "Computing in America: A Masculine Mystique," *New York Times* (February 13, 1989).
4. Computing opportunities for less affluent and minority high school girls, who are less likely to have computers at home, may be available but underutilized due to contextual factors. In a survey of 225 inner-city high school math and science teachers in schools with high minority enrollments, while 95 percent of the teachers reported that computers were available in their schools, the same number also reported that these were used by less than 10 percent of all enrolled students. In addition, over half (54 percent) of the teachers admitted that they did not use the computers. See P. Kramer, *Final Report to the National Science Foundation*, grant no. SER-8160408 (Washington, D.C.: National Science Foundation, 1987).
5. See E. E. Maccoby and C. N. Jacklin, *The Psychology of Sex Differences* (Stanford, Calif.: Stanford University Press, 1974) for documentation of literature that consistently reports significant sex differences in favor of males in mathematics achievement and visual-spatial skills. However, although the authors suggest that these findings support an argument that biological sex differences may be a factor, they do not rule out sociocultural determination as well, since the differences are greater in adults than in children. For a reexamination of much of the data used by Maccoby and Jacklin, see Janet Shibley Hyde, "How Large Are Cognitive Gender Differences? A Meta-Analysis Using ω^2 and d," *American Psychologist* 36, no. 8 (August 1981): 892–901. Hyde demonstrated that gender is a nonsignificant factor in terms of accounting for differences in young people's mathematics achievement. More recently, a similar analysis of visual-spatial abilities not only supports a similar conclusion but raises substantial questions concerning how visual reasoning skills are defined and assessed. See P. J. Caplan. G. MacPherson, and P. Tobin, "Do Sex-related Differences in Spatial Abilities Exist? A Multilevel Critique with New Data," *American Psychologist* 40, no. 7 (1985): 786–99.
6. E. Fennema and J. Sherman, "Sex-related Differences in Mathematics Achievement, Spatial Visualization, and Affective Factors," *American Educational Research Journal* 14, no. 1 (Winter 1977): 51–71. Also see E. Fennema and J. Sherman, "Sex-related Differences in Mathematics Achievement and Related Factors: A Further Study," *Journal for Research in Mathematics Education* 9, no. 3 (1978): 189–203.
7. Julia Sherman, "Mathematics, the Critical Filter: A Look at Some Residues," *Psychology of Women Quarterly* 6, no. 4 (December 1982): 428–44. Greater ambivalence about career opportunities and plans on the part of more talented young women is also described by Matina Horner, "Toward an Understanding of Achievement-related Conflicts in Women," *Journal of Social Issues* 28, no. 2 (1972): 157–75; and by Irene Hanson Frieze, "Internal and External Psychological Barriers for Women in Science," in *Covert Discrimination and Women in the Sciences*, ed. J. Ramalay (Boulder, Colo.: Westview, 1978).
8. Very similar attitudes are found in a survey of 160 high school girls participating in advanced placement courses in mathematics and physics by Patricia Lynn Casserly, "Helping Able Young Women Take Math and Science Seriously in School," in *New*

Voices in Counseling the Gifted, ed. Nicholas Colangelo and Ronald T. Zaffrann (Dubuque, Iowa: Kendall/Hunt, 1979). Girls reported that they often kept quiet in class when they knew the answer because they often did not want to appear to be "too smart." The same girls also said that they often did not speak up because they did not want to appear "too dumb." Forty percent reported playing down their good grades in mathematics in front of classmates and peers, especially male classmates and peers.

9. The role of teaching styles and attitudes and how these may interact with students' own attributions concerning their abilities as mathematics learners, have been explored in a series of research studies by Carol Dweck and her associates. See, e.g., Carol Dweck, "The Role of Expectations and Attributions in the Alleviation of Learned Helplessness," *Journal of Personality and Social Psychology* 31, no. 4 (April 1975): 679–85. Dweck's research indicates that teachers who allow students to use "learned helplessness" attributions about their ability in mathematics ("I'm just not good at math, so why try?") as opposed to persistence attributions ("Mathematics requires that I work hard") are much more likely to produce math-avoidant students. In Dweck's research, junior high school girls outnumbered boys in the "learned helplessness" group in mathematics classrooms by three to one.

10. L. Fox and J. Cohen have also examined how changes in motivational structures and attitudes of mathematically gifted girls, who were identified as part of Project Talent Search, could significantly enhance these girls' mathematics course-taking in high school and their future career plans. See L. H. Fox and J. J. Cohen, "Sex Differences in the Development of Precocious Mathematical Talent," in *Women and the Mathematical Mystique,* ed. L. H. Fox, L. Brody, and D. Tobin (Baltimore: Johns Hopkins University Press, 1980), 164–78; Patricia Lynn Casserly, "Factors Affecting Female Participation in Advanced Placement Programs in Mathematics, Chemistry, and Physics," in Fox et al., eds., 138–63; and L. H. Fox, "Women and Mathematics: The Impact of Early Intervention Programs upon Course-taking and Attitudes in High School," final report to the National Institute of Education for grant no. NIE-G-77-0062 (Johns Hopkins University, Baltimore, 1979). These intervention efforts, although successful, were unable to close completely the gap between boys and girls: the boys were far more likely than equally able girls to participate in advanced or special mathematics programs and to plan on careers in science and engineering fields. It is worth noting that the Project Talent Search junior high school children are the same group whose Scholastic Aptitude Test (SAT) scores were used by Camilla Persson Benbow and Julian Stanley to support their argument for boys' superior mathematical ability. See Camilla Persson Benbow and Julian C. Stanley, "Sex Differences in Mathematics Ability: Fact or Artifact?" *Science* 210, no. 4475 (December 1980): 1262–64, and their responses to comments about this article in "Letters to the Editor," *Science* 212, no. 4491 (April 1981): 118, 121.

11. Studies that report similar correlations between mathematics ability or learning and computer aptitude include C. A. Alspaugh, "Identification of Some Components of Computer Programming Aptitude," *Journal of Research in Mathematics Education* 3 (1972): 89–98; C. Gressard, "An Investigation of the Effects of Math Anxiety and Sex on Computer Attitudes" (paper presented at the American Educational Research Association meeting, New Orleans, 1984); and J. Konvalina, S. A. Wileman, and L. J. Stephens, "Math Proficiency—a Key to Success for Computer Science Students," *Communications of the Association for Computing Machinery* 26 (1983): 377–82.

12. F. Dambrot, M. Watkins-Malek, S. Marc Silling, R. S. Marshall, and J. A. Garver, "Correlates of Sex Differences in Attitudes towards and Involvement with Computers," *Journal of Vocational Behavior* 27, no. 1 (August 1985): 71–86.
13. It is important to remember that correlations between two or more variables do not establish causal connections between these variables; a third (or more) factor(s) may be causing the observed effects. If, as is the case in Dambrot et al. and similar studies, computer aptitude is defined in such a way as to be virtually synonymous with mathematics achievement, then it almost certainly reflects mathematics experience, which we know to be less for girls than for boys after the second year of high school. In such studies the presumed finding of lower computer aptitude for girls is invalid. One measure of computer aptitude that does not depend on previous mathematics knowledge is the Computer Aptitude, Literacy, and Interest Profile (CALIP), created by Mary Poplin and her associates (see Mary Poplin, David Drew, and R. Gable, CALIP manual [University of Texas at Austin, 1984]).
14. Sanders and Stone (n. 1 above). Their Computer Equity Training Project studied junior high school boys and girls in over sixty classrooms in New Jersey, Oregon, and Wisconsin. In addition to school logistics (computers are taught by male mathematics teachers to business, mathematics, and science students), the authors cite voluntary computer use as being an unorganized and solitary activity. Problems with computer software, career awareness, and parental attitudes are also noted as creating significant obstacles for girls.
15. Collis (n. 1 above).
16. However, Lockheed and Frakt (n. 1 above) report that positive experiences with computers were associated with positive attitude changes for girls.
17. Collis, 33–34.
18. See Karen Scheingold, Jan Hawkins, and Cynthia Char, " 'I'm the Thinkist, You're the Typist': The Interaction of Technology and the Social Life of Classrooms," *Journal of Social Issues* 40, no. 3 (1984): 49–61. This article discusses the meaning of computers and the tasks that are presented via the computer for both children and teachers. Interpretations of the computer have powerful implications for how children use computers and structure various tasks. As one example of differential acknowledgment granted to girls' skills, reported by Scheingold, Hawkins, and Char, when children were asked, "Who is the best computer user in the class?" both boys and girls named a boy. However, when the children were asked, "Who would you ask to help you if you got stuck (writing a LOGO program)?" both boys and girls named both girls and boys. While talented girls might be denied public acknowledgment for their skills, the children did not feel girls were less capable as long as the girls were using their skills to help others.
19. The aggressive masculinity of the subculture surrounding the computer is described by Sara Kiesler, Lee Sproull, and Jacquelynne Eccles in their "Poolhalls, Chips, and War Games: Women in the Culture of Computing," *Psychology of Women Quarterly* 9, no. 4 (December 1985): 451–62.
20. See, e.g., A. F. Westin, H. A. Schweder, M. A. Baker, and S. Lehman, *The Changing Workplace: A Guide to Managing the People, Organizational, and Regulatory Aspects of Office Technology* (White Plains, N.Y.: Knowledge Industry Publications, 1985).
21. Jan Hawkins, "Computers and Girls: Rethinking the Issues," *Sex Roles* 13, nos. 3/4 (August 1985): 165–80, esp. 171.

22. The Minority Women in Management and Technical Fields program at Polytechnic University was supported by a grant from the Fund for the Improvement of Postsecondary Education (FIPSE) from 1979 to 1984, Pamela E. Kramer, principal investigator.
23. The Fennema and Sherman mathematics attitude scales (Fennema and Sherman, "Sex-related Differences in Mathematics Achievement, Spatial Visualization, and Affective Factors" [n. 6 above]) consist of eight scales containing twelve Likert-scaled items, each of which includes measures of confidence in one's own ability to learn mathematics, perception of mathematics as a male domain, perception of one's ability to learn mathematics in relation to others, perceived usefulness of mathematics, and willingness to take mathematics (effectance motivation). These are the five scales that we used in addition to a subset of twenty-four items from the Mathematics Anxiety Rating Scale (MARS), which dealt with school-related situations involving mathematics. See R. M. Suinn, C. A. Edie, J. Micotelli, and P. Spinelli, "The MARS: A Measure of Mathematics Anxiety," *Journal of Clinical Psychology* 28, no. 3 (July 1972): 373–75.
24. In brief, this approach combines a solid review of high school algebra with techniques designed to reduce mathematics anxiety and to eliminate "learned helplessness" attributions about one's own abilities. (It is not that you need to have mathematical ability, but it is that mathematics learning requires hard work.) The actual teaching emphasizes word problems and comprehension rather than rote memorization and set problems. It also utilizes group problem solving rather than individual accomplishments (each member of a homework group must understand the solution to a problem and be able to explain it to her peers), peer teaching, and peer tutoring. All of the tutors were minority mathematics and engineering majors at Polytechnic University (most were female). See Deborah Hughes-Hallett, *The Math Workshop: Algebra* (New York: Norton, 1980); and Sheila Tobias, *Overcoming Mathematics Anxiety* (New York: Norton, 1978).
25. The overall regression coefficient for attitudinal factors with mathematics precalculus grades was an astonishing +.93. While this figure reflects the strong individual correlations that were obtained between the various attitudinal measures, which included the Fennema and Sherman mathematics attitude scales and the MARS, it must also be viewed with caution due to the small sample size.
26. Unfortunately, we could not include computer course grades in the regression analysis with mathematics-related attitudes, so we could not determine the extent to which attitudes toward mathematics (as distinct from mathematics performance) may have been related to performance in computer courses.
27. H. Dreyfus and S. Dreyfus, *Mind over Machine* (New York: Free Press, 1987); and T. Winograd and F. Flores, *Understanding Computers and Cognition: A New Foundation for Design* (Reading, Mass.: Addison-Wesley, 1986).
28. Elizabeth Fennema, Thomas Carpenter, and Penelope Peterson, "Teachers' Knowledge of Students' Knowledge of Mathematics Problem-solving: A Correlational and Case Study," *Journal of Educational Psychology* 81, no. 4 (December 1989): 558–69.

Questions for Discussion

1. Pamela Kramer and Sheila Lehman suggest that our assumptions about the differences in men's and women's interest in and proficiency with

computers spring in part from "prevailing conventions within primary and secondary education that locate computer-based learning within mathematics and science curriculums". Does the placing of computer-based learning in math and science programs seem a convention or a logical necessity to you? Imagine for a moment computer-based learning being a part of *all* disciplines. How would such an approach change your attitude toward and interest in computers? Toward the other disciplines?

2. In one study cited by Kramer and Lehman, researchers found that eighth-grade girls were unlikely to respond positively to computer instruction if the teacher was male. In your observation and experience, how important is an instructor's gender to your ability to learn and to appreciate the subject being taught? If the instructor's gender *is* important, in what specific ways should school administrators, teachers, and students work to overcome gender-based barriers?

3. What are your attitudes toward computers? Do you use them for school? For work? For pleasure? If you play computer games, how gender-specific are they?

4. The article ends with the statement that "Women's choices are governed as much by positive preferences for certain styles of knowing and thinking as by negative stereotypes and discrimination." What do you think Kramer and Lehman mean by this statement? Do you believe women and men *do* think and know differently—even when they're thinking about the same things? In your experience, for instance, are men's ways of thinking linear and women's ways more wide-ranging? Do men prefer to work individually and women collaboratively? Are women more comfortable than men with paradox?

Questions for Research and Writing

1. Some people believe that the traditional expectations that boys will pursue careers in math and science and girls will pursue careers in the social sciences, humanities, and arts are no longer valid. Survey men and women from your own and earlier generations. How have perceptions about gender and academic ability changed? To what extent have your respondents been encouraged to conform to, or break from, the academic and career paths traditionally followed by men and women? Ask your respondents to relate particular examples of times when they or others were pushed toward or away from traditional paths. After collecting your information, write an essay arguing for or against changes in our educational system, or analyzing the effect of gender on education. (It may help to interview women and men who have chosen a variety of majors and career paths.)

2. Interview men and women in your own field or in another academic field that interests you. Did the men and women enter the field for

similar reasons? Do they perceive the field—its intellectual challenges, its career possibilities, its ways of looking at the world—similarly? Design interview questions that will help you draw some conclusions about the relationship, if any exists, between gender and academic discipline.

CROSSCURRENTS
Questions for Connecting the Readings in Chapter 4

1. In paragraph 11 of his essay, Neil Postman defines the term *conversation* metaphorically. How is his use of the term similar to or different from the use of that term by other writers in this book? (See, for example, Mike Rose's "Entering the Conversation" in chapter 2.)

2. In choosing Las Vegas as a metaphor for our national character, Postman describes a national character that is bent on "amusement." How would some of the writers in chapter 3 respond to Postman? (See, for example, "Time Squeeze" and "Public Use/Private State.")

3. The authors of "Steal This T.V." are calling for a change in the way we view the relationship between the public and private sectors. Other articles in this book similarly explore this relationship. Find this theme in any two of the other articles in this book and imagine a conversation among the authors. How do Americans view the relationship between the public and the private? Would these authors agree or disagree? Why?

4. Our "descent into triviality" is, Postman tells us, the "residue of an exhausted capitalism." Imagine a conversation among Postman and the writers in chapter 3 who explore the implications of capitalism. Would they agree or disagree with one another?

5. Although they are not writing specifically about education in the United States, many writers in this chapter give us some sense of what they think is right and wrong with our educational system. How might the writers in chapter 2 respond to Postman's implied criticism of the American educational system? What would they think of the definitions of knowledge and cultural literacy advanced on *Jeopardy!* or in E. D. Hirsch's *Cultural Literacy*? How would J. Wade Gilley ("The Distributed University" [chapter 2]) respond to the warnings of Pamela Kramer and Sheila Lehman ("Mismeasuring Women") about the need for schools to attend more to differences in how women and men approach computer learning and use?

6. Compare Deborah Brandt's ideas about literacy (in "Accumulating Literacy") to those in "The Internet's Arrested Development" or in "Steal This T.V." How do they agree and how do they disagree?

7. Brandt suggests that technology has sometimes fostered community and communication. For instance, Sam May wants to sound more like

the voice he hears on the radio. What is the significance of this story? How would other writers in this chapter respond to Brandt's suggestion that technology helps define a larger community?

8. Both Michael Berthold and Susan Neuman talk about ways that television affects ordinary life. In what ways do they seem to agree about this influence—in particular, whether it is positive or negative. In what ways do they disagree?

9. In recent years, a number of researchers have studied the relationship between gender and technology, arguing that technology is very often created by and for men and that women's needs and interests are too often ignored. Imagine a conversation among the authors of "Mismeasuring Women" and "Remote Mothering" (chapter 4), and "Telecommuting" and "Time Squeeze" (chapter 3). What assumptions do these authors share? Where do they agree? Where do they disagree? If the authors of "Introduction to the World of Women's Studies" (chapter 2) were to join the conversation, how do you think they would respond to the arguments about gender and technology?

10. In "Remote Mothering," the authors remind us that cellular telephones have been heralded as devices that can liberate their users from the confines of the home or office and allow them to talk on the telephone while engaged in such other activities as driving, flying, and eating dinner at a restaurant. How do you think the authors of "Time Squeeze" and "Telecommuting" (chapter 3) would respond to advertisers' claims that cellular phones give us more free time?

5

Ethics, Law, and Justice

The United States is, it has been said, a nation of laws, and perhaps because it is, questions about justice abound in our daily lives. But what exactly is the law, and how do we view its relationship to the concept of justice?

Our history as a nation has been strongly influenced by our perceptions of law and justice, of ethical and unethical behavior. Most people feel that beyond or above the laws of our nation, state, and community is a higher law. Thomas Jefferson speaks of this higher law in the Declaration of Independence when he evokes "the laws of nature and nature's God," as a basis for an American right to create a government separate from Great Britain. In "Civil Disobedience" (1848), American essayist Henry David Thoreau argued, "It is not desirable to cultivate a respect for the law, so much as for the right. . . . Law never made men a whit more just; and by means of their respect for it, even the well-disposed are daily made the agents of injustice." As Americans, we see the law as a tool that helps us live peaceful, well-ordered lives, but we place much responsibility for moral decision making on the individual, who, over a lifetime, develops his or her own sense of ethics.

We can begin our conversation about ethics, law, and justice by thinking about what each of us brings to the discussion. Many people have some personal experience with the American judicial system, even if that means simply watching courtroom dramas on television or appearing in traffic court because of a speeding ticket. Today, a variety of legal problems arise in families. Domestic violence, divorce and custody battles, even bankruptcy and other financial problems dominate our cultural landscape. But questions of ethics, law, and justice in our society go far beyond the workings of police stations, courtrooms, and prisons, real or fictional. For example, some of you may know students who have cheated on an exam, plagiarized a paper, or committed some other ethical violation of the university's code of conduct. And your experience with law and ethics will expand as you enter such professions as law, medicine, or science that have established clear and unequivocal rules for the ethical behavior of their members.

In fact, today's legal system and the larger conversations about law, ethics, and justice involve people from many disciplines and professions. For instance, science, medicine, and technology are playing an increasingly important role in the administration of justice and in the workings of the legal system. With the development of forensic science as well as biological and medical advances, many significant legal and ethical questions have been raised that must be addressed in our society. In the academic world, sociologists, psychologists, and even historians are working to explain and explore the issues inherent in preventing crime and punishing criminals. Joining the conversation also are writers and film makers, who, especially in recent years, have both reflected and stimulated our society's enduring fascination with lawyers and the courtroom. Finally, political leaders, too, often raise important legal and ethical issues. In their talk about family values and the American way of life, they often simply assume that we all share the same visions, goals and ethics for our individual lives and our communities. As you think about these concerns, ask yourself: In our diversity, is there a core of ethical values that as Americans we all share? What does it mean to seek justice, to live by the law? What are our rights and responsibilities as citizens? And how do we resolve those conflicts between the social intent of a particular law and the individual's own moral sense?

In the conversations that make up our experience as members of the academic community, questions of law and justice recur frequently. Both written and unwritten laws can be thought of as "texts" that invite a variety of interpretations, some of which result in conflict or strife. As we begin to follow the various threads in this conversation about ethics, law, and justice, think about how we use language to express our beliefs and attitudes, and further, how *legal* language reflects those beliefs and attitudes, whether successfully or unsuccessfully. As you read the selections in this chapter, try to locate your own experience in the context of larger theoretical concerns.

While the readings in this chapter will not even begin to answer—or even identify—all of our questions about ethics, law, and justice, these selections should provide a better sense of the ways in which different disciplines and professions address the concerns of morality and ethics, and of law and justice, in our society. And these readings should help you begin to formulate your own questions about the concerns represented here.

WHAT DOES THE LAW WANT?
Benjamin Sells

> *The following selection is chapter 1 of writer and psychotherapist Benjamin Sells's 1994 book* The Soul of the Law. *This essay helps to lay a foundation for other readings in this chapter by asking us to consider societal attitudes toward the law. Clearly, one premise is that lawyers and nonlawyers see the law through different eyes. Sells uses a literary device known as* personification, *which gives inanimate objects or abstractions human characteristics, to help examine the various ways that we perceive the role and purpose of the law in our contemporary world. Sells also suggests that our attitudes toward the law reflect our attitudes toward relationships with others.*

The most important first step in understanding anything psychologically is to get an image. Images are more complete, more fertile, than concepts because they have a broader range of expression and are therefore more precise. Also, images allow our personal perspectives to coalesce with more enduring psychic patterns. So, in turning a psychological eye to the Law, we first need an *image* of what we are talking about.

I ask the reader to conduct the following experiment:

Imagine you are a psychotherapist. It's mid-afternoon on a Wednesday in October. You're sitting in your office, catching up on some mail. Your next session isn't for a couple of hours, and you're just getting ready to start a letter to a colleague when a knock comes on your door. You quickly double-check your appointment book to make sure you haven't forgotten someone, but no, the blank lines confirm that no one is due until four. You open the door and a person is standing there whom you have never seen before, but who bears a certain distant familiarity.

"Hello," says the person, "I'm the Law. I want to talk with you about some things."

"Come in, come in," you say, not really sure what to make out of this.

"I'm sorry to show up without an appointment," says the Law. "But I just happened to be walking down the street and saw your sign out front. I hadn't really thought about coming to a therapist until about five minutes ago, but then I decided what the hell, I might as well give it a shot. Do you have some time to talk?"

"Sure," you say. "My next appointment isn't for a while yet. Here, let me take your coat. Would you like some coffee? Tea?"

Question One: What does the person who has just walked into your office look like? Be very precise, and try to imagine this person in detail. Is the Law male or female? Old, young, middle-aged? How is the Law dressed? What kind of coat did you take from the Law? Is the Law carrying anything? Does the Law prefer coffee or tea? How does the Law speak, move, sit? Can you see the Law's eyes? What are they like? Try to imagine the Law as clearly as you can, getting as full-fledged an image as possible. Concentrate on the details, and be as accurate as you can.

"So," you say as you both sit down, "what brings you here?"

"Like I said, I was just walking down the street and saw your sign."

"Was there anything in particular you wanted to talk about?'

The Law sits silently for a moment, and appears to be staring at something on the floor halfway between the two of you. Then the Law looks up and says "Yes, I guess there is something bothering me."

Question Two: What does the Law say? What's bothering the Law?

When I have done this experiment with groups, most people, men and women alike, say the Law is an older man, gray-haired and distinguished looking. There is some disagreement about how the Law is dressed, but most people say the coat is an expensive one, maybe camel or leather. Often the Law is carrying a briefcase, sometimes a newspaper or some books. And almost everyone says the Law is a coffee drinker, usually black with no sugar. On rare occasions, lawyers will say the Law is female. On rarer occasions someone will say the Law is both male and female. Other recurring details I've heard about this imaginary person are that the Law is brisk of movement, as if it has somewhere important to go, and that the Law speaks with a measured and careful voice. A few people have commented on the Law's eyes, some saying the Law has steady, piercing eyes while others see them as tired and bedraggled, the eyes of a person who has seen too much.

What did the Law say to you about its troubles? Again, I have found strong similarities in people's responses to this question. Often the Law says it is misunderstood and overworked. But when pressed about deeper concerns, people often imagine the Law saying it is "troubled," sometimes going so far as to use words such as alienated, isolated, anxious, depressed, besieged, and lonely.

Some people, especially lawyers, balk at such questions, finding them offensive or perhaps suspecting they conceal a hidden agenda of some sort. These folks usually maintain that the entire exercise is silly, arguing that you can't personalize an abstraction so it makes no sense to ask whether the Law is male or female, and that this kind of imaginary, fictional exercise is too "touchy-feely" to be of import. This resistance and antagonism to imagination is telling, and we will find it is a recurring theme in our work with the Law.

"What do you mean when you say you're misunderstood?" you ask.

The Law leans back and brushes away an invisible speck of lint. "Well, people don't understand what I'm trying to do for them."

"Do you mean they don't understand intellectually, or they don't appreciate you?"

The Law begins to object to this little hop of interpretation, but then shrugs and says, "Both. They don't understand how I work, or how hard, and they don't appreciate how important I am. Perhaps that sounds arrogant to you, but the fact of the matter is that I don't know what might happen to the world without me."

"Let's come back to that later," you say, sensing that things are moving too fast, that important details are being skimmed over. You refill the Law's coffee and ask, "What is it you *want* exactly? I mean, if you could make things any way you want them to be so you wouldn't feel this way, what would you do?"

Question Three: What does the Law want? How would the Law change things?

"You said a minute ago that people don't realize how important you are. What makes you think that?"

"Are you kidding? My God, everyone bitches about me all the time. I mean I'm O.K. as long as I apply to someone else, but as soon as I prohibit somebody's own pet behavior they go crazy. It's like I'm only supposed to apply to the other guy. And just look at how people talk about my representatives . . ."

"Representatives?" you ask.

"Lawyers," explains the Law. "All of this lawyer-bashing tries to make everything the lawyers' fault. That's just a roundabout way of attacking me, you know."

"But don't lots of people talk about how important the Law is?"

"Yes, almost always as a reaction to violence of some kind—you know, the Law and Order thing. People expect me to crack down on the bad guys but hate me when I try to keep *them* in line. Sometimes I feel like a toxic waste dump—not in my backyard."

"What if people did realize how important you are? How would they act differently from how they act now?"

"I don't want much. If people would just listen to what I tell them and obey me, show a little respect, that would be enough."

"You want to be obeyed?"

"Of course I do. That's what the Law is for isn't it?"

Question Four: Is that what the Law is for?

"You say you want people to obey you, but they don't. Where does that leave you?"

"There's only one thing to do when people get unruly, and that's to force them to comply. Society can't exist without Law; people have to be made to respect and obey me."

"But isn't it impossible to force someone to respect something? I mean, maybe you can make them comply through force, but you can't instill respect that way."

The Law flushes a bit at this remark, and for a second seems on the verge of getting up to leave. You make a mental note that the Law doesn't like being contradicted. But then the Law composes itself, laces its fingers together in its lap and says with studied, almost condescending calm, "People respect strength. I know people don't like to be forced to do something, but it's for their own good. Over time, they'll see I am right."

"What do you think would happen to society without you?"

"Anarchy, pure and simple. Society needs me."

"And why exactly does your absence lead to anarchy?"

"Look at history!" The Law leans forward, hands open now. A point is about to be made. "Human nature has to be restrained. Without an orderly way of organizing society, of resolving disputes, and of ensuring that people do the right thing, we would have people killing each other over the slightest disagreement. Without me, people would shirk their responsibilities. They'd start making up their own ways of dealing with disputes. A lawless society cannot endure."

"But some people say that's pretty much how things are now, even with all the laws already on the book."

"That's just my point. The laws are there but people aren't obeying them. People are ignoring me, they're lawless."

"So what do you want to do about it?"

"There's only one thing you can do when people disobey the Law. You must enforce the Law—make them obey. Lock them up if necessary, fine them, take their rights away, whatever it takes. But the only way to establish and maintain order is through the Law."

We leave our imaginary therapy session now, but I encourage the reader (especially lawyers and law students) to pursue it further. This kind of active imagination is instructive on many levels, revealing not only our personal beliefs about the Law but also deeper, transpersonal themes that give insight into the Law's own personality. Just as novelists talk of their characters taking on a life of their own, so too the Law can be imagined as if it has a life of its own. *The Law that lives in our imagination is far more influential than we might think.* Usually it operates unconsciously, affecting our ideology, our everyday practice, how we think about the Law's role in society, how we relate to concepts like order and obedience, and how we understand larger themes like truth and justice.

The Law that lives in imagination can also offer insight into the Law's unrest. Already, in the short dialogue we have had with the Law, we get a feeling that the Law is bothered by something other than what it actually says, something only hinted at. As in any therapy, what the Law presents as the source of its discontent—people not understanding and not respecting it—is just a starting point for more subtle investigations.

ORDER, OBEDIENCE, OBSESSION

I have noticed an interesting difference in the responses of non-lawyers and lawyers regarding what the Law wants. Most non-lawyers say right off the bat that the Law wants justice. Lawyers, on the other hand, tend to be more diverse in their answers, mentioning things like equality, individual rights, truth, and fairness. It is not uncommon, for example, to hear lawyers say that what is legal doesn't necessarily have anything to do with what is just, or that truth and fairness are only ideals while the Law deals with practical reality. A surprising number of lawyers say none of these high-sounding ideals hit on what the Law wants, and that maintaining social order is the Law's prime concern. But one thing that does emerge when lawyers talk about these fundamental ideas is a kind of tentativeness, as if they aren't used to talking about such things and may even be a bit suspicious of big talk about justice and what have you. In the end, an uneasy consensus often emerges that holds justice up as an unattainable goal while emphasizing social order as an acceptable and achievable substitute.

Once the step is made from idealistic talk about justice to more pragmatic-sounding talk about social order, lawyers seem to be more comfortable. Not that there is agreement on how to achieve order, because there isn't. No, the comfort comes from the very *manner* of the talk, the structures and forms agreed to as the parameters of discussion. It's like scientists who disagree over a theory but nonetheless *do* agree on the efficacy of scientific proof, the use of mathematical forms, and the like. Once lawyers can translate a discussion into a give-and-take over rights and responsibilities they have shifted the discussion to their turf, and with this shift comes the comfort of familiarity. Lawyers, for example, might disagree over how to achieve the Law's desire for order while agreeing on things like the need for objective and dispassionate decision making and the importance of set rules and regulations for ensuring due process, predictability of outcome, and uniformity of result.

I should add that not once, among all of the people I have talked to about the question of what the Law wants, has anyone ever said that the Law wants "peace." This is a significant point, I think, because it suggests that although the Law is interested in maintaining social order, it sees peacemaking as something ultimately beyond its purview. At best, the Law seems to imagine itself as having a peace-keeping mission similar to that of a United Nations force that defines peace only as the absence of conflict. From this perspective, the Law is seen as an outside, occupying force responsible for imposing and maintaining order. As for encouraging a deeper sense of tolerance and understanding that might lead to a lasting peace, that is not the Law's job. The point here is not whether the Law should or should not think this way, but that it *does* tend to think this way and that this self-image has psychological implications.

One of these implications shows up in the Law's stated desire for order and obedience. What is curious here is the tension between the Law's desire to be understood and its more patronizing expectation to be obeyed. It's as if the Law confuses obedience with allegiance, forced acquiescence with willing acceptance. The Law even goes so far as to identify itself with obedience, saying obedience is "what the Law is for."

From a psychological perspective, the Law's identification with obedience and its single-minded emphasis on order have an obsessive ring. Obsession can be defined as a situation in which a single idea or image holds the mind captive, seeking to draw all other perspectives into itself. Usually obsession shows up in symptoms as a peculiar one-sidedness, as when the Law insists that it is misunderstood because others have failed in their obligation to understand it, and that without Law anarchy would necessarily follow. These obsessive ideas repress other possibilities. Perhaps the Law *itself* has failed to find ways to be understood communally, or perhaps the Law's desire for order and obedience is skewing its own self-understanding. Who knows, perhaps it is the Law and not others that needs to deepen its understanding. Perhaps it is the Law that lacks respect for people's natural resistance to its own obsessive desire for obedience and order. Such possibilities fall by the wayside because they are not allowed by the narrow constraints of the obsession.

The Law's obsession with order and obedience also manifests in practicalities: an ever increasing proliferation of legislation, rules, and regulations that suggest there must be a law for every problem; mandatory sentencing statutes decreeing that flexibility means weakness; strict rules of procedure and evidence that attempt to control every phase and detail of the legal process; excessive bureaucracy; courtroom architecture dominated by straight lines and authoritative decor including rows of benches, rectangular tables, elevated benches, fenced-off jury boxes and partitioned witness chairs; the tools of the legal trade with its uniform volumes of carefully indexed and cross-referenced books, and legal pads with their ruled lines; and even the very uniformity of dress and personal mannerism that so readily identifies a person as a lawyer—these things and many others like them suggest a constriction of imagination in favor of the controlling metaphors of order and obedience. "Law" and "Order" are so linked in our common imaginations that they seem to follow as one breath follows another.

Whenever people say they stand for or believe in a particular thing, they also are saying that they don't stand for or believe in a host of other things. That's what definition does. It marks boundaries and seeks to establish the identity of one thing through the exclusion of other things. If I say I'm a Democrat then I imply I'm not a Republican, if a Catholic then not a Protestant, etc. But exclusion by definition doesn't mean these other things necessarily disappear or don't continue to live within a person. I can be a Democrat in name and a Republican by temperament, or I can profess to be a Democrat but consistently vote Republican in the privacy of the voting booth.

The things we exclude through self-definition often reappear in subtle but extraordinarily powerful ways in our lives. Often there is friction between how we perceive ourselves and how others perceive us. Just think about the people you have known who claim to be one way, perhaps are even adamant about it, while their everyday actions reveal otherwise. In fact, one of the great things about being in close relationships is the chance to have running encounters with other people's perceptions of us, people who can be mirrors for our self-conceptions and help us to expand how we see and understand our own identities. But the chance to learn about ourselves from the perceptions of others breaks down if we define ourselves in an unduly narrow and restrictive fashion. Then we start to see symptoms associated with a closed-shop mentality—intolerance, suspicion of others, fear that if I am not the way I think I am then I'm nothing, and a kind of grandiosity masquerading as confidence. The more narrowly people define themselves, the more gets left out. And the more insistent a person is in denying these other possibilities, the more these possibilities live the life of the excluded—constantly trying to find ways to break back into the person's life and gain respect, if not acceptance.

Clues about what is being excluded sometime come in the form of the moralisms we embrace without really thinking about them. The idea here is that we are most unconscious in those places we feel the most normal, mundane, and commonplace—our unconsciousness of them is what makes them feel so normal. So when the Law easily identifies itself with order and obedience it is the very ease of this identification that draws our psychological interest. What exactly is the Law saying? What does it mean by order and obedience? Is it implying that disorder and disobedience are necessarily wrong? What is getting left out? Quite apart from whether such views are right or wrong, moral judgments are not without their psychological implications. Our psychological tradition teaches that the things we repress will eventually return in altered form—repressed sexuality returning as prudishness or in secret perversities, and so on. Furthermore, there seems to be a direct relationship between the force with which we repress things and the power with which they return. If so, then we might expect disorder and disobedience to reappear under various guises in the everyday life of the Law, especially in those places where the Law is most adamant in its demands for order and obedience.

DISORDERLY CONDUCT AND CIVIL DISOBEDIENCE

Despite the Law's concerns that lawlessness is breaking out in society, there is more than ample evidence that lawlessness is breaking out within the Law itself. For example, in the last several years there has been a disturbing rise in incivility among lawyers. Depending on which survey you choose, roughly half of all lawyers think there is a problem with incivility in the legal profession. One survey found that fifty-six percent of lawyers cite "obnoxiousness" as the most prevalent unpleasant quality they encounter in working with other lawyers. Mind you, this is what lawyers are saying about *themselves*.

There are many examples and many degrees of this new incivility: not returning phone calls, saying one thing to opposing counsel in the hall and another thing in front of the court, filing purposefully burdensome and far-reaching discovery requests in an effort to deplete and demoralize the other side, verbally abusing other lawyers and the court, lying, even physical violence. It seems to me that such conduct is a manifestation of precisely the kind of lawlessness that the Law is so concerned about. Why are the Law's own emissaries acting this way?

The usual answers given to this question have a kind of Pavlovian ring to them, positing external factors as stimuli that lawyers respond to with uncivilized conduct. The favorite explanation is that the practice of law is no longer a profession but a business in which concerns for the "bottom line" have supplanted concerns for civility. Stimulus: economic pressure. Response: incivility as lawyers compete for pieces of a smaller pie. Another explanation says incivility results from not having enough judges, arguing that incivility is bound to increase when there aren't enough judges to police legal practice. The first explanation assumes that "business" is inherently uncivilized, while the latter echoes the Law's stated belief that, left untended, people naturally revert to nastiness.

The problem with the stimulus/response analysis is that it tries to explain incivility as merely a result of external pressures. In many ways, the search for external causes of incivility mirrors a broader cultural trend of placing blame elsewhere. Psychology tells us that our personal inadequacies are responses to dysfunctional families (some even apply this meaningless concept to law firms); in politics some people argue for term limitations as the only way to prevent us from re-electing incumbents; in economics we hold foreign nations responsible for domestic shortcomings and assert that if only we had a balanced budget amendment we would be forced to do the right thing; and in society at large we accuse shadowy Drug Lords of being the cause of our national intoxication. Meanwhile, lawyers are blamed as the cause of everything from the litigation explosion to high health care costs. Blame is everywhere but here; with anyone but me.

A different approach to incivility begins to take shape when we remember that narrowly defining oneself in restrictive terms necessarily leads to the return of the repressed. Is it not possible that incivility erupts precisely because of the Law's obsessive desire to identify itself in terms of order and obedience? In other words, what if incivility is not a result of external influences but of an unduly limited self-definition?

"Civility" comes from roots that refer to citizenship and is related to other words referring to members of a household. Under these old meanings, being civilized means being good citizens and householders; to be uncivilized is to betray one's obligations to both society and home.

Being a good citizen might mean being better informed and more broadly involved, caring about what happens to the life of the polis. Viewed through the lens of civic responsibility, community concerns become indistinguishable from so-called individual ones. Perhaps one of the things incivility is pointing to is the need for the Law to be less concerned with imposing order and more involved with engendering a sense of shared community where values are embraced and lived intimately.

It isn't that the Law should be a profession and not a business, which would set up a false and unnecessary opposition between profession and business, but that it needs to be a better neighbor. But this cannot happen as long as the Law retains a defensive posture behind its obsession with order and obedience. When this happens the Law retreats within itself, becomes mean-spirited and short-tempered. You can almost hear the wagons circling. Ironically, when the Law does attempt to respond to incivility, it often does so with calls for more order and obedience, responses likely to guarantee just the opposite.

But there are other things going on here. When the Law says people don't respect it, that it is misunderstood, and that it needs to impose itself more forcefully onto people's lives, I hear talk laced with deep feelings of being cut off, detached, abandoned, disconnected. The very intensity with which the Law attempts to assert its control over society suggests that it currently feels left out, exiled. Note how often the people who make the laws seem to think they are above them; this is an example of how a preoccupation with order and obedience can split a person's perspective into a Me/Them outlook. Similarly, many lawyers complain of an amorphous lack of feeling, a sense of being anesthetized. Things are neither very good nor very bad, but just . . . mediocre. Passion fades, love becomes a parlor game, and inside we don't feel much at all. When this state of affairs reigns over the internal life of a profession or a person, it becomes prone to reaction instead of leadership, violent outbursts occur for no apparent reason, and transient values (order, obedience) replace fundamental ideals (justice, truth). Once the Law is cut off from its passions and forced to be a mere observer and organizer of life, it is just a matter of time before these repressed passions return to demand representation.

Incivility is a love disorder, not a result of working too many hours. We see this even more clearly when we remember some of the societal symptoms clustered nearby: the widespread belief that loyalty is eroding within the legal profession; the growth of an almost pathological individuality insisting that lawyers have to look out for number one because there is no security in relationships; the lingering feeling of emptiness despite material success; the break-up of long-standing partnerships; and the common lament that a life in the Law leaves no room for friends, family, other interests, or even oneself. All of these symptoms suggest that the Law feels divorced from the very society it is intended to serve.

Imposed obedience cannot rekindle the capacity to love. Rather, *incivility itself might be pointing the way by directing the Law to citizenship and householding,* both of which require attention, caring, and interest more than anything else. It is as if the Law is suffering from a lack of oxygen, that it needs air to fuel the combustion hidden in its heart. Moving into the world instead of being applied to it from without can provide this missing component. Everyday concerns, family affairs, matters of the heart—these are places for the Law to turn.

Questions for Discussion

1. How effective is the device that Benjamin Sells uses to personify "the Law" in this essay? How did you respond to it? How does it help draw you into the more complex issues Sells hopes to raise? Does it distract you from the main theme of the essay? Why or why not?
2. Sells suggests that the Law has an "obsession with order and obedience." What causes this obsession, and what are its effects?
3. Sells suggests a tension or conflict between the Law's desire to be understood and its expectation of obedience. In what ways are these two impulses in conflict? Does Sells provide any examples that might help us understand what this means?
4. The reading explores the concept of *incivility*. What does this mean? What are some examples of incivility in your daily life?
5. In what ways do lawyers and nonlawyers view the law differently? What accounts for these differences in attitude? Which view is most compatible with your own ideas?
6. What does Sells mean when he says, "The Law that lives in our imagination is far more influential than we might think." How does our imagination influence our intellectual responses to a problem?
7. What view of human nature do the attitudes reflected by "the Law" suggest? Does the Law, as Sells personifies it, think that people are basically good or basically evil?

Questions for Research and Writing

1. Try Sells's experiment with some of your friends. How do they imagine the Law as a person? In what ways are their responses alike or different from those that Sells mentions in this article?
2. Choose another abstract concept that is very much a part of our contemporary philosophical landscape, for example, democracy, equality, or opportunity. How might a conversation such as the one Sells conducts with the Law play out these ideas? Try to give a "voice" and personality to the concept. What do you learn by doing this?

AM I MY BROTHER'S KEEPER?
Reflections on Compassion and Justice

Leon Kass

> *Leon Kass, a professor at the University of Chicago, originally published the following piece in* The American Enterprise *at the end of 1994. This article raises a number of important questions about the perceived selfishness of today's citizens and about what Kass calls the "bleeding heart" agenda of the traditional liberal. At the heart of his article are issues that have come to the foreground in recent years, as Americans have moved toward a more conservative government and rejected the Democratic social programs of Roosevelt and Johnson. Who, Kass asks, is my brother? And, more important, what does it mean for me to become his "keeper"? When does charity become destructive rather than helpful, and how much should the giver concern himself or herself with the recipient's moral rectitude and self-reliance?*

It has been a year and a half now since the great Mississippi River floodwaters receded, but I am still pondering a jolting appraisal of the disaster that appeared at the time in the *Fourth Estate,* the conservative student newspaper at the University of Chicago. The editorial said (I paraphrase): Don't feel sorry for the people of Davenport, Iowa. These fools deliberately chose not to build levees against possible flooding. Why? Because levees would obstruct their view of the river, and because levees would hamper the growth of riverboat gambling casinos, established to attract tourists and to raise revenues. The city fathers gambled away the city's survival, betting not only on betting but also (and more recklessly) on the cooperation of the river. Thus, the damage in Davenport is not, as it seems, an undeserved and accidental misfortune. It is rather the direct consequence of legislative foolishness. The Davenporters have made their bed, now let them swim in it.

While most of us could only feel compassion at the sight of homes under water and of people desperately trying to defend themselves and their neighbors from the ravages of runaway nature, this complacent young lout seemed to feel nothing but the need to assess responsibility. We wanted to know only when relief would arrive; he wanted only to prove that relief was unjustified. But he started me thinking: Could these people, in some way, have had their troubles coming to them?

Of course they weren't responsible for the flood; that was the work of Poseidon—with a little help from the levee builders upstream. But they had chosen to live in harm's way, or at least not to move out of it. Moreover, their elected community leaders had apparently refused to take prudent measures to reduce the risk of harm. Yet who in our technological age does not tend toward overconfidence regarding Mother Nature, and who in this era of institutionalized humanitarianism is not encouraged to be imprudent by the availability of insurance—here national disaster relief—that compensates us for any loss. People weigh alternative courses of action differently when they think someone else will be paying the bill. Then too, risk taking is not just negative—nothing ventured nothing gained. It is thus hard to calculate what sort of risk taking is unreasonable and what amount too high. And, rational analysis aside, can one really withhold sympathy and assistance once the damage occurs and on a massive scale, once it is seen on television, and once suffering becomes concrete, when names are put with faces of decent now homeless individuals indistinguishable from ourselves, whose complicity, if any, in their misfortune is overwhelmed by the manifest depth of their misery. Are we not our brothers' keepers?

Trying to sort out the rival claims of justice and compassion in this and other natural disasters, I began thinking about the whole range of cases in which we as a society are increasingly being asked, encouraged, and sometimes even compelled to come to the aid of those who refuse to take care of themselves. If we reject indiscriminate compassion for people who bring their troubles on themselves, must we embrace the young editor's hard-nosed view? What, if any, are our moral obligations to those who, in their personal lives, choose to live dangerously, even foolishly?

LIVING DANGEROUSLY

In the most basic sense, simply to be alive and to stay alive means to live dangerously. All life involves danger, all life involves the risk of failure, all life is always losable and eventually always lost. But by living dangerously we usually mean engaging in conduct known to carry more or less obvious and unnecessary extra risks to life and limb, to economic, psychic, or social well-being. Thus defined, living dangerously includes obvious harmful practices such as smoking, heavy drinking, and drug abuse; driving recklessly or without standard safety devices; traveling unnecessarily into dangerous or hostile environments; and engaging in treacherous amusements. It also includes a vast array of unsafe and irresponsible sexual practices as well as excessive gambling, excessive borrowing and spending, and refusing to make good on ordinary obligations in school or on the job. Most of these dangerous activities are legal, only some of them are immoral, but all of them carry risk—sometimes great risk—of self-inflicted harm. In a free society, people will be free by-and-large to run these risks; the question is to what extent everyone else should bear the cost of the resulting harms.

REMEDIES

Even a little reflection shows this to be a massively complicated subject; there are many questions to be disentangled. First, the various risky businesses differ widely, for example, regarding the likelihood, immediacy, and degree of harm. Further, a desire to help does not translate readily into sensible policy proposals. Measures aimed at preventing risky behavior are often difficult to devise; it is notoriously difficult to get people to do what is good for them without tyrannizing them. Measures aimed at remedying the harm afterward may remove disincentives for prudent self-restraint. The availability of an ounce of cure often drives out pounds of prevention. Remedies can even change our view of whether risky behavior is in fact foolish. Not so long ago, a man who had contracted syphilis was, by and large, not an object of pity, and quite apart from the question of his likely immorality. For he had almost certainly consorted with the wrong sort of woman, and carelessly to boot. He also certainly knew that he had brought his troubles on himself. Today, in the age of antibiotics, many sufferers from sexually transmitted diseases overlook their own responsibility; instead they even blame their miseries on society's failure to provide the cure.

Then there is the troubling fact that those who live dangerously also put others at risk. Self-harm harms others—especially one's spouse and children. Reasons to intervene often focus on these innocent sufferers. Yet ironically but not surprisingly, policies designed to fix the works of folly often serve to increase it: for example, we have compassionately spared illegitimate children the opprobrium they once had to bear, but, as a result, many more children are now sired out of wedlock and abandoned with impunity.

Finally, there are the basic moral questions, to which I here give priority. I want to try to get clear what we reasonably ought to expect of one another with regard both to personal responsibility and aid to the suffering. In addition, I want to articulate a principled middle way between the harshness of social Darwinism and the stupidity of no-fault compassion. And, though policy proposals must each be guided as much by what is feasible and effective as by what is right, I suspect that any policies regarding those who live dangerously will be acceptable and welcomed only to the degree that they roughly correspond to our basic moral intuitions.

AM I MY BROTHER'S KEEPER?

Many of our opinions and moral intuitions regarding the rival claims of justice and compassion are rooted in our Judeo-Christian tradition, which, it happens, gives support for all sides of the question. On the one hand, we find many biblical passages that insist on strict justice—giving people just what they deserve—and numerous stories that tie redemption to prudence; for example, Jesus' parables about the talents or about the wise and the foolish virgins. On the other hand, there are many passages that teach charity beyond justice and that praise unqualified love of neighbor in imitation of God's mercy; for example, the parable of the prodigal son. But the primal story about love-of-self and love-of-other, about justice and mercy, and about brotherliness is the story of Cain and Abel.

Cain, you will recall, was ashamed, angry, and jealous because God accepted his younger brother's offering but delayed accepting his own. Not comforted by God's promise that his sacrifice would be lifted "if you do well," Cain murders his brother and rival. When God asks, "Where is Abel thy brother?"—a question designed to make Cain confront himself in his brotherliness—Cain denies knowledge of Abel's whereabouts and adds a lawyerly question of his own: "I know not. Am I my brother's keeper?" God, not deceived, takes Cain's counteroffensive to be a tacit admission of guilt and so forces Cain to confront it fully: "What hast thou done? The voice of thy brother's blood cries out unto me from the ground." This psychologically and morally stunning exchange reveals that Cain's principle "Am I my brother's keeper?" is in fact the maxim of a murderer, an expression of fratricidal intent. To deny responsibility for your brother is, tacitly, to be indifferent to his fate, and in this sense to be tacitly guilty of all harm that befalls him: in short, to say yes even to his death.

Yet we should not judge Cain too harshly; even God treats him mercifully. In Cain's world—the aboriginal human world, prior to law and morals—there seemed to be no cosmic support for morality and no cosmic support for human industry and effort. The fickle powers aloft men attempted to bribe with sacrifices. But in earthly dealings it was every man for himself, and the gods or the devils could look after the hindmost. Seeking to avoid his fate, each man nervously concerned himself with only his own well-being.

We readers of this story, however, learn, implicitly, the following important lessons: the world is ruled not by fickle and arbitrary gods, and the cosmos is not indifferent to our errors. We are responsible for our own conduct, and we will be punished for our misdeeds—but not so much as we deserve: for God is both just and merciful. And, finally, we are—or should be—our brothers' keepers.

MORAL QUESTIONS

But this moral lesson is both far from clear and far from complete. Who exactly is my brother—which is to say, for how many human beings do I bear such fraternal responsibility? If all homicide is really fratricide, and if fratricide is the inner meaning of any and all brotherly neglect, am I therefore really even man's keeper? More importantly, what does it mean to be someone's keeper? The word *keeper, shomer,* means to guard or protect, from a primitive root meaning "to hedge around," as with thorns. Does the duty to guard and protect against outside dangers extend also to dangers one's brother poses to himself? What if he chooses to live dangerously and to court disaster, whether from vice, weakness of will, foolishness, or ignorance?

Am I obliged to help him when he won't help himself? What would it really mean to guard or to help a reckless or a foolish brother? And does the duty to protect from harm imply also a duty to supply positive good, especially after self-inflicted harm has occurred? Does guarding your brother mean picking up after his stupidity?

Consider an example. I have been in an auto accident and damaged my entire liver. My brother is the most suitable donor for a partial liver transplant. Have I a claim on his liver? Not at all. Should my parents—or anyone else—put pressure on him to donate? I believe not. But what does our brotherliness require of him? Should his decision to donate be influenced by the fact that I was responsible for the accident, that I had been speeding on icy roads and not wearing a seat belt? And what if my need of a liver transplant were due not to a onetime auto accident but to a lifetime of alcoholism? Should my brother be obliged to help? Should he be praised for donating? Blamed for not? Does my promise to stop drinking and join AA make a difference? Should some unrelated donor's willingness to donate—or our public policy regarding health insurance—be influenced by whether and how I have brought my troubles on myself?

There can be, of course, no simple or set rules for answering these questions. Much will depend upon the particulars. For example, we are more inclined—and may even be expected—to help alleviate harm caused by foolishness or weakness-of-will than by vice, by a single or occasional episode of folly than by chronic foolhardiness, by dangers undertaken in the course of some serious pursuit than in sheer frivolity, by bad judgment stemming from depression than from insolence, and so forth. Even where one feels a duty to help, any prima facie obligation to do so will surely be limited and perhaps even overturned (1) when one does not know what will be of real help; (2) when assistance will be useless, because refused or squandered; and (3) when there are better or more urgent outlets for one's beneficence, including competing obligations to others.

For these reasons, among others, there are times when it is surely foolish to come to the rescue of foolishness. Moral obligation cannot mean that the remedy for someone else's foolishness is to match or surpass it with our own. The obligation to be even our blood brother's keeper cannot be absolute and unqualified.

Much as we may love our brothers, and much as we should endeavor to care for our neighbor, we are also called to love and care for what is good and right. Indeed, the beginning of morality is the subordination of unqualified self-love and love of your own to the standards of good and bad, justice and injustice. The trick, in moral education, is for parents to exploit the familial attachments and loyalty to one's own to teach habits and principles of proper conduct, principles that we make our own because we recognize them to be good. We are taught to do what's right; we are taught not to make exceptions in our own case; we are taught to accept responsibility for our own lives and conduct—and to expect others to do the same.

AM I MY FOOLISH BROTHER'S KEEPER?

My belief in the importance of accepting and fostering personal responsibility leads me to say for openers that I do not see myself as my foolish brother's keeper. Neither do I regard anyone else as responsible for protecting me from my own follies. Human action is based on human freedom, human freedom is manifested in choice, and human dignity in action resides in making our choices in full cognizance that we are the sources of our deeds and responsible for their effects—including even for their unintended and unanticipated consequences. Self-conscious choice tacitly cheers for justice, for a world in which people get what they deserve. Indeed, a belief in justice is a necessary premise for all human effort. If the world were utterly irrational, if there were no relation between cause and effect, if the cosmos thwarted human attempts to match effort and success, human beings would do little to advance their own cause. And while we all know that the world is far from wholly just, all societies and institutions and most human lives work on the premise that the world makes sense. Moreover, by our responsible practices and by our praise and blame we contrive to have it make even more sense. We read children stories like "The Little Red Hen" to teach them that it is just that those who work for their food should get to eat and those who refuse to work should not. People are pleased when hard work and fair play are rewarded. Our passion for competitive sports is at least partly due to our love of justice: for in this realm of our public life, more than in any other, excellence and playing by the rules are rewarded. At least until recently we did not take kindly to whiners, complainers, and those who blamed others for their own failures. A man who pleaded drunkenness as an excuse for his violence was doubly punished; a woman who went to a man's bedroom and then got drunk could not escape bearing some responsibility for what happened next. America grew strong because people acted in the spirit of the maxim, "By the time a man is 30 he is responsible even for his face."

COMPASSION

But what then about compassion? The claims of compassion might seem to oppose the claims of justice and lead us always to our foolish brother's assistance. Yet if compassion is rightly understood, this turns out to be at most only partly true. In fact, compassion as experienced sentiment—rather than as ideological principle—is actually somewhat allied with justice. The point was already noted by Aristotle in his account of pity: "Pity is a certain pain at manifest or apparent badness, destructive or painful, hitting one who is undeserving, which one might expect oneself or someone of one's own to suffer."

Pity, or what we now call compassion, is not indiscriminate sympathy for suffering. An at least tacit judgment of whether the badness suffered is deserved is implicit in the feeling of compassion.

This is not to say that everyone judges well whether the suffering is deserved; racists think all suffering of the despised race is somehow appropriate, while bleeding hearts are willing to overlook blatant fault—even rape, murder, and terrorism—in those whose suffering they have privileged. But, given half a chance and adequate information, most people pity fittingly, which is to say justly. They feel more pity for crack babies than for their mothers, more pity for the man whose liver failure was caused by a tainted blood transfusion than by chronic alcoholism, more pity for the homeless person who is mentally ill than for the one who has refused for years to seek work. True, we do not always have information enough to judge, and the sight of suffering if sufficiently great can overwhelm all capacity for discernment. But, compassion as sentiment is not, in principle, at war with an interest in justice.

Yet modern life and modern thought have done much to distort the normal operation of compassion, even while elevating it to political principle. Powerful visual images of suffering—horror without context—are television's daily fare, tugging at heartstrings already overstretched far beyond the capacity for normal response. As Aristotle noted, pity is especially aroused by the seeing of evil, by visibly manifest and evident harm or badness; and such evident harms are pre-eminently harms to the body, what he called "destructive or painful" evils. The vivid sight of serious bodily injury, near at hand and suffered by someone like ourselves, fills us with unqualified sympathy, so much so that it can overwhelm other feelings and thoughts.

MEDICAL VIEW

The exploitation of visual images of suffering, especially when shown out of context, corrupts compassion and moves us toward what one might call a merely medical view of the world or, more precisely, the emergency room's view of the world. Ironically, the great success of medicine in alleviating acute illness has encouraged the spread of its nonmoral and no-fault approach to all bodily suffering and its justice-neutral brand of compassion—a point to which I will return. Add to this the political hegemony of compassion as the first proof of public virtue, and we see how we have created a world in which victims gain more sympathy than heroes—indeed they are lionized for their suffering—and, more to the point, despite their own culpability in coming to harm: Do more people think that Magic Johnson is a fool for living dangerously than think he is a hero for going public as a victim? Sympathy and fellow-feeling are of course precious and praiseworthy, but an indiscriminate compassion that is deaf to judgment has little part to play in my being my foolish brother's keeper.

Yet there are other reasons, beyond the inadequate claims of our new breed of compassion, why the principles of strict responsibility and to-each-his-just-deserts, however suitable as a starting point, cannot be the whole story. Given the unpredictabilities of life, it is presumptuous to believe that one can live with perfect forethought and planning, immune to bad results. Besides, there is frequently much virtue in risk taking. Explorers, immigrants, settlers, founders, pioneers, entrepreneurs, investors, scientists, inventors, soldiers, writers, and statesmen all live dangerously and gamble on their ability to make good in the absence of guarantees. Needless to say, not all failure is the result of folly or vice. In recognition of this fact, society prepares partial safety nets to catch those who fall while trying to climb. We abolished debtors' prisons, permit people to declare bankruptcy, and in many other ways embody our sound belief in the rightness of second chances. America is a land internationally famous as the home of the second chance.

We protect risk takers, of course, mainly because we all benefit from the successes of enterprise, not primarily because we applaud dangerous living as such. It does not therefore follow that we are or should be inclined to be softhearted where living dangerously serves no public good. But though difficult to prove, one suspects that there is considerable overlap between those who will face danger for high purpose and those who, for purely private pleasures, are willing to live dangerously. Valetudinarians are not the highest human type; Winston Churchill drank more than his share. Generally speaking, those of us who play safe and sane benefit from the erotic and the adventurous. In addition to their concrete benefactions, the risk-takers remind us all that there is more to life than health, safety, and comfortable preservation. And through their struggles and failures, they also teach us by example the possibilities and limits of our own human cleverness.

LIMITATIONS

Odysseus, the paradigmatically clever and self-reliant man, was made to travel far and to suffer much before he was allowed to win the day of his homecoming. These travels served to teach Odysseus the limitations on human cleverness, primarily through his many encounters with the minions of the earth-shaker Poseidon—god of tempestuous nature—and through his visit to Hades, place of the dead. In Hades Odysseus was given a commission, to be discharged after his homecoming, to carry a sailor's oar inland until he came to a people who knew nothing of the sea and who thus would mistake the oar for a winnowing fan. Here Odysseus was to plant the oar, marking a sailor's grave, in order to teach complacent, clever, and comfortable men about the dangers and irrationalities of the world and to moderate the hubris entailed in rational man's refusal to acknowledge the unavoidability of facing danger, fate, and the permanent possibility of tragedy.

For even more profound reasons, the principle of strict responsibility cannot be the sole standard for assessing the misfortunes of our foolish brethren. For not everyone starts out with a full deck when it comes to living prudently. Differences in rearing and life experience create differences in each person's ability to choose, in the choices we make, and in our capacity to stick by our better choices. The mysterious yet nigh universal phenomenon of moral weakness—that is, knowing the good but not doing it—accounts for much of what we call foolish conduct; and, repeated, it is habit-forming. Aristotle, that great exponent of personal moral responsibility, also taught that "it makes no small difference if we are accustomed this way or that right from childhood, but a very great one, or rather the whole difference." Children are maimed for responsibility both by indulgent parents who shelter them from learning from the consequences of their mistakes and by negligent parents who fail to teach them the importance of avoiding them in the first place. Some people are timid, others bold—often straightway from birth. Inborn influences, no less than environmental ones neither of them of our own making—predispose to success or failure in the battle for self-command. About these things science still knows very little, but enough to suspect that some aspects of intractable and self-harming behavior probably have a genetic foundation—possibly even regarding smoking, alcoholism, and other "compulsive" practices. And, perhaps most important, there are inborn differences in intelligence. One can say to one's child, "Be sensible," but one cannot say, "Be intelligent." Yet if, in this increasingly complex world, it takes more and more intelligence to figure out what "being sensible" requires, lots of people are going to face life with severe but invisible handicaps.

GENERAL INTELLIGENCE

Two years ago I heard social scientist Charles Murray present stunning data that showed that nothing correlated more with success on the job than "g"—general intelligence—a correlation more than double that for the quality or amount of education, letters of reference, success in job interviews, and the like. Everyone in the audience focused immediately on the foolishness of laws that now prevent the use of general intelligence tests in hiring. I wonder how many also felt sadness at discovering that, if Murray's data are right, hard work and the best intentions will never raise many people from the bottom of the heap—all the more so in the hypertechnological age in which a strong back and a willingness to work will not do enough to enable you to prosper.

This does not mean that we stop teaching the young to brush their teeth, do their school work, avoid bad companions, and stay away from drugs, tobacco, and motorcycles. We should still demand and foster personal responsibility and publicly speak as if it were possible for all—at least at some basic level. We should continue to insist on the importance of obeying the law and to hold people accountable for criminal misconduct. But we would do well to remain modest (rather than proud) if we happen to be—at least for now—less foolish than some of our brothers.

On the basis of arguments like these, one might suggest that a decent community will try to care not only for those who are worse off than others through no fault of their own, but even to bear some of the costs of helping those who are partly responsible for their own troubles. This is not so much a matter of justice or of rights: people have no right or claim to receive from life better than they deserve. It is a matter of the common good. We care for our fellow citizens because we are all in this together. The fortunate and less foolish among us have every reason not to be limited by strict proportionality. We can, not least for our own sakes, improve upon justice—in the direction of generosity and care. Acts of beneficence not only contribute to the common good; they are also manifestations of virtue, and as such are central to the flourishing of the benefactors. Rightly understood, philanthropic deeds are not self-sacrificing but self-affirming and self-fulfilling. Thus if our brothers need defense against themselves even more than against outsiders, we should be willing—in principle—to offer it, not least for our own goodness' sake.

"TOUGH LOVE"

The difficulty for us turns out to be not one of intention but of knowledge: What does it really mean to help and to keep? The present hegemony of no-fault compassion is to be blamed not so much for its implicit willingness to care, but for its failure to understand what care really means. For one does not really keep one's brother by helping him in ways likely to increase his foolishness. On the contrary, help aimed at undoing the harms caused by foolishness is insufficient if it is unaccompanied by help aimed at fostering the benefit of assuming moral and personal responsibility. Most deserving of our sympathy and compassion is not our brother's bodily suffering but his inability or unwillingness to stand in the world with freedom and dignity, which is to say, as a responsible source of his own conduct ready and willing to be held accountable for himself and for his actions. Just as the sentiment of compassion-rightly-experienced is natively not immune to judgments of past responsibility, so the exercise of compassion-rightly-practiced is centrally concerned with enabling the recipient to become more willing and able to choose better and to accept responsibility in the future. True compassion, especially toward the remediably foolish, is synonymous in the current lingo with "tough love."

How this is to be accomplished is, of course, a tricky matter, varying case by case, individual by individual, and folly by folly. There are no set rules, no single strategy. Nor is it easy to shift effectively from individualized strategies for the interpersonal and genuinely familial cases to the necessarily statistical approaches of public policy for larger populations, especially since genuine compassion is—quite properly—much harder to mobilize for countless unnamed strangers than for blood brothers. But the sound moral principle of tough-loving prudence is the same in every case, regardless of scale: to foster personal responsibility and a world that approximates justice where people are justly rewarded and punished; at the same time, to foster fellow-feeling and a world in which people are inclined to be generous—and especially generous in helping people morally and spiritually so that they become less in need of and less dependent on such generosity. This means attaching demands and inducements for change of behavior to offers of outright aid in relief of harm; it also means not destroying the public will to generosity with excessive and unreasonable demands upon our compassion.

Frequent and repeated demands exhaust, in most people, the will to give and care. People who are inclined to help a few homeless beggars often find themselves giving to none, owing to the large numbers they now confront on the street. The heart hardens as the groups competing for compassionate assistance multiply—abused spouses and children; racial and ethnic minorities; the urban poor; drug and alcohol abusers; the unemployed and the imprisoned; unwed mothers; flood and earthquake victims; sufferers from AIDS; Bosnians, Somalis, Rwandians, Soviet refuseniks, Iraqi Kurds; Haitian and Cuban refugees, ad infinitum—even as a defense against the pain of impotence and failure to give all that is wanted. Compassion, to be efficacious, must be a sentiment, not a calculation; one cannot keep it flowing on command. As Clifford Orwin remarks in his brilliant essay on compassion, "Compassion resembles love: to demand it is a good way to kill it." And to demand it in pursuit of unreasonable hopes and utopian dreams is to crush it entirely under the weight of cynicism.

THE TRAGEDY OF ENLIGHTENMENT UTOPIANISM

The moral questions—about moral responsibility and fraternity—that we have been considering are not free standing. They rest on and embody deeper intuitions and beliefs about human life in the world and about exactly what kind of a world this is. Embedded in our opinions about what we should morally and politically expect of people and of ourselves are still more fundamental opinions about what we can and should expect from nature, from the cosmos, and from the powers that be that govern the whole. Not surprisingly, our modern moral prejudices are tied to our modern metaphysical ones. The soundness of the former may be no better than the soundness of the latter.

Let us look again at our increasingly medicalized view of life. Illnesses is beyond guilt or innocence; because suffering is suffering, it demands attention. When John Wilkes Booth came to Dr. Mudd on April 15, 1865,

Dr. Mudd attended only to his broken foot, not to where and how he got it. In today's emergency room, botched suicides, ingestions and overdoses, gun shot and knife wounds, broken bones, and overt bleeding cry out for immediate attention: the doctor dare not reason why, his only thought is, "Fix the guy." Even bad behavior that often leads to illness comes itself to be treated either as illness (for example, alcoholism or rage behavior) or sometimes as an inborn hard-wired predisposition that one must not judge in moral terms (such as a penchant for pederasty). The emergency room or medical view of life is the bodily or somatic view of life: it not only focuses on the ills of the body, it finds bodily causes for all seemingly psychic and moral phenomena.

PSYCHOPHYSICS

Drunk on its remarkable successes in the analysis and treatment of acute infectious disease, modern medicine is confident that its materialistic approach to life will unlock all the secrets of mind and heart and will permit for the first time a rational and successful approach to the troubles of the human condition. The fault, dear Brutus, is not in ourselves but in our genes that we are underlings—which is to say, there is no fault or responsibility, only the misalignment of matter. It is stunning how the outlook of the present day pays tribute to the dreams of Descartes, who saw in his newly invented science the possibility of human mastery of nature and through it the relief even of man's psychic and moral troubles: "For even the mind depends so much on the temperament and disposition of the bodily organs that, if it is possible to find a means of rendering men wiser and cleverer than they have hitherto been, I believe that it is in medicine that it must be sought."

Psychophysics, not praise and blame or moral self-command, is as Descartes predicted the wave of the future. It is no longer "God helps those who help themselves," but rather "mankind through a scientific medicine helps everyone regardless."

In fairness to our rationalistic forebears—in whose debt we stand and which debt we gratefully acknowledge—one must note that they were rather unimpressed with how hospitable nature was to human life or with how well the partisans of God were able to enlist His aid on humanity's behalf. They saw, in fact, a cosmos governed by natural necessity basically indifferent to the human world, and a human world itself governed by ignorance, fatalistic superstition, and chance—in short, a terrestrial world seemingly tragic for all human aspiration. They set out to conquer fate and fortune on the basis of the rational understanding of nature—that is, the laws of motion of bodies. Such knowledge would issue in power to predict, and eventually to control, terrestrial and human phenomena—in the limit, to eliminate altogether the role of fortune (and misfortune) through rational mastery. Though they were not themselves political utopians, the founders of modern science, like Bacon and Descartes, set the stage for the vast modern utopian project, in principle, comprehensive and complete: by rational means, to banish Poseidon—and perhaps even Hades—and to remake the world according to human aspirations.

The successes of the modern project have materially improved our lives but they have not made us content. On the contrary, all residual failure and suffering now become increasingly unacceptable. We have come to expect rational medical solutions for all our ailments, and we demand that society provide them. While we wait, we insist on being compensated for harms and losses, regardless of fault. One could, by the way, probably write the history of modernity through the lens of insurance. Insurance was first instituted to compensate seagoing traders for losses to pirates. Thus it originally protected risk takers against deliberate human wrong-doers, and only at sea, that is, where law and government could not protect them from outlaws. Now one can be insured against anything and everything: life is to be both no-fault and no-harm.

POLITICIZATION

But while science forges ahead toward the goal of complete mastery, the continuing presence of personal misery and misfortune becomes primarily the responsibility of the state. Compassion is "elevated" from natural human sentiment to necessary political principle. Society is one big hospital, government one big healer. The technological approach to life—rational mastery through methodical problem solving—finds its political expression in bureaucracy and the welfare state. We go slowly but surely from "Uncle Sam Wants You" to "The Doctor Is In." No longer is the main goal of statesmanship to make secure against interference the natural rights of life, liberty, and the pursuit of happiness, but rather to guarantee universal day care, health care, and hospice care. Driven partly by guilt for its own good fortune, the utopian elite takes up the cudgels for the least fortunate, demanding a politics of compassion on behalf of society's victims—a politics that, ironically, blithely victimizes those hard-working and morally responsible Americans who do not have the margin to be very generous to strangers and who are not yet aboard the train to utopia. The medicalization of politics, the politicization of compassion, and the growing bureaucratization of the rest of life are the logical outgrowths of the modern view of the world.

The not surprising irony of this project for the rational medical-cum-political conquest of fortune is that it leaves most of us less rather than more in control of our own attempt at a prudent life. The project for the human command of nature rests on materialistic ideas about human life that deny human freedom and self-command, and it issues in technologies (and their accompanying bureaucracies) that, in myriad ways, make many of us actually more dependent and helpless in our daily lives.

The bureaucratic enforcement of compassion saps most of the impulse to care for another. For to look on every man as brother, and on every stranger-brother as guiltless victim for whom I am responsible, eventually produces a condition in which I feel myself victimized by the burdens of care, and therefore seek to excuse myself even from my primary duties to those who are nearest and dearest. The utopian project for mastery of fortune through rationalized technique is thus in danger of bringing about the very tragedy it willfully sought to prevent. For to produce a herd of people who don't care for themselves and who then have to rely on unreliable and ineffective powers that are only capriciously responsive to their needs is to recreate the ill-fated and fatalistic world against which Cain rebelled in fratricide—a world that today is returning to our inner cities.

Fortunately there is another world view, between an irresponsible surrender to indifferent fate and an unreasonable belief in human mastery, one still within hailing distance of our collective memory. It was the reigning world view of the West until the coming of the Enlightenment and its newer nihilistic descendants. And it remains the source of our residual moral good sense. It is the sensible, moderate but hope-filled world view of human freedom and dignity under the rule of law, both encouraged and demanded by divine providence. According to received lore, it emerged in the aftermath of a much earlier and more cataclysmic flood than the Mississippi's.

After the Flood, God made a covenant with Noah and with all terrestrial life never again to destroy the earth (see Genesis 9); unruly nature will not utterly crush human aspiration. At the same time, however, human beings undertook to make good on their prospects, to practice moderation and justice, under the rule of law. Though now permitted to eat meat, they moderated their bloodlust by refusing to eat the blood. More important, they held each other accountable for all violence done to one another: "Whosoever sheds man's blood, by man shall his blood be shed; for in the image of God was he created." Recognizing for the first time both his godlikeness and his vulnerability, man lifted himself above the plane of a purely animal existence by freely choosing to become a morally responsible being, whose first rational duty is to be his human brother's keeper and to remove those of his brothers who do not justly honor each man's equal common humanity. A balanced picture of prudent self-command, justice, and fraternity emerges, all under the aegis of a providence that both cares for life and cares for justice. It knows full well the evils and follies that lurk in the hearts of men. But it believes that these troubles of the human condition cannot be eliminated and that they are best addressed by appealing to our better nature, which, even today, is still able to hear the truth in this ancient tale.

Questions for Discussion

1. How much federal assistance would you be willing to grant to the homeowners and businesspeople who knowingly bought property in a flood plain? To those who buy property in earthquake or tornado country?

What assistance—and compassion—do we "owe" to those who cause their own health problems by smoking or drinking? To those who take personal risks when they bungee jump or climb mountains? To those whose head injuries have been caused by failure to wear a bicycle or motorcycle helmet?

2. At one point, Leon Kass asks, "Who exactly is my brother—which is to say, for how many human beings do I bear such fraternal responsibility?" How would *you* answer that question? And how would you answer the next part of his question: "What does it mean to be someone's keeper?"

3. How much is Kass's case influenced by the fact that he is an American citizen writing for an American audience? In other words, what cultural assumptions lie hidden in his essay that people of other cultures might question?

4. What do you make of the maxim "By the time a man is 30 he is responsible even for his face"? Is it an accurate representation of how Americans feel about individual responsibility?

5. Do you agree with Kass that "we have created a world in which victims gain more sympathy than heroes"? What examples besides Magic Johnson substantiate Kass's point?

6. According to Kass, to encourage the success that comes from heroic risk-taking, America has become "a land internationally famous as the home of the second chance." How much evidence have you seen of the willingness of Americans and their institutions to offer a second chance?

7. Kass claims that we all benefit, if only indirectly, from the risk taking of "the erotic and the adventurous." Do you agree?

8. In your experience, what is the connection between intelligence and responsibility? Between success on the job and general intelligence?

9. Look at Kass's use of authority. How effective are his references to the Bible and to early thinkers? What do these references imply about the audience Kass addresses?

Questions for Research and Writing

1. According to Kass, children learn responsibility from their parents and from life experiences, but may also be influenced by genetic predispositions to certain kinds of timid or bold behavior, or even to certain self-destructive behaviors or compulsions. Analyze the complex of factors that have led you to your definition of "responsible behavior" and your ability to act responsibly.

2. Kass argues that we live in a world that is increasingly "no-fault and no-harm," implying that we assume no responsibility for our actions and expect no negative consequences to ensue from them. To what extent do news accounts of the following substantiate his claim: a particular

criminal activity, misconduct by government employees or business officials, or unethical or offensive behavior by sports figures.

3. Survey the citizens of your campus community about the extent to which they feel responsible for being their "brother's keeper." In designing your survey, ask some of the questions Kass himself raises about the extent to which we are more willing to offer charity to those whose actions we condone or to those whom we know best or who are most like us. In analyzing your data, consider how the following characteristics of your respondents have influenced their responses to your questions: age, ethnic and cultural heritage, socioeconomic background, political affiliations, religious training, and so forth.

OUR FALTERING JURY

Albert W. Alschuler

> This essay, published in the opinion journal The Public Interest *in* Winter 1996, explores a number of recent jury verdicts, including the O.J. Simpson verdict in California, in which the jury's response varied greatly from the public's perception of the same evidence and testimony. The author, a University of Chicago law professor, begins by noting that, to an outsider to American society, the current jury system seems "preposterous." Alschuler points out some of the problems inherent in the current system and raises several points for reform. The author suggests that more than just a "flamboyant media event," the O.J. Simpson case may prove to be "the moment when the need for America to reinvent a fair and workable trial procedure became too obvious to deny."

Once I was invited to dinner by an elderly gentleman from China. When my host discovered that I was a law student, he talked about the American legal system. "There, in the courtroom," he said, "are two lawyers. They have been to school for many years. They are wise, able, experienced, and greatly respected in their communities. And above them, at the head of the courtroom, is the judge. He is even older, even wiser, even more experienced, and even more respected than the lawyers. But who decides the case? Twelve people brought in from the street!" The old man laughed.

With youthful enthusiasm, I sprang to the defense of the jury system. Law is too important, I said, to be left to the people who do it for a living. I argued that the jury offers an essential check against overzealous prosecutors and against high-handed judges. To my surprise, the more I talked, the more the old man laughed.

Today's newspaper stories, particularly the ones from California, offer good reason to believe that the old man was right. Our jury system often appears to have grown preposterous. Perhaps one should not criticize a particular verdict without undertaking a review of all the evidence before the jury. When viewed in the aggregate, however, the news accounts of jury verdicts in recent high-profile cases seem troublesome.

STRANGE NEWS FROM THE JURY BOX

The Menendez brothers drove an Alfa Romeo, a gift from their father, to San Diego where they purchased a 12-gauge shotgun. Two days later, they used the gun to kill their father and their mother. Ambushing their parents as the couple watched television, the young men fired the gun 16 times before they were done. Two juries heard their essentially uncorroborated (though tearful) claims of sexual abuse and of a paternal threat to kill them if they made the abuse public. In addition, jurors heard expert testimony concerning scientific research on snails and the "rewiring" of Erik Menendez's brain that occurred as a result of his father's abuse. The jurors were not permitted to hear about a play that Erik Menendez had written 20 months before his crime—a play in which a young man kills his parents with a shotgun for their money. Neither of the juries could agree that the Menendez brothers had committed murder.

When Nicole Brown Simpson and Ronald Goldman were murdered, the manner of their killings suggested a crime of passion. At the crime scene, the police discovered a brown, extra-large Aris Isotoner Light glove, model 70263. This glove's mate was found at the estate of O. J. Simpson, the abusive former husband of Nicole Simpson. Soon after the killings, a limousine driver kept an appointment to pick up Simpson at the estate, but no one appeared to be at home. After the driver repeatedly called the house from his car, he saw a man who looked like Simpson enter the darkened doorway. Simpson then answered the buzzer, saying that he had overslept. DNA testing revealed that stains on the glove found at Simpson's estate matched the blood of Nicole Simpson, Ronald Goldman, and O. J. Simpson. Also on the glove was a hair matching Nicole Simpson's and fibers matching the carpet of O. J. Simpson's Bronco.

Nicole Simpson had purchased two pairs of Aris Isotoner Light gloves, model 70263, just before Christmas in 1990; at most, 240 pairs of these gloves were sold. Photographs and videotapes showed O. J. Simpson wearing similar gloves at football games from shortly after Christmas 1990 through early 1994, the year of the murders. An expert testified that he was "100 percent certain" that the gloves appearing in one photograph were Aris Isotoner Lights, model 70263. The glove found on O. J. Simpson's estate was only one of nearly three dozen blood exhibits connecting Simpson to the murders. Abundant other evidence pointed to his guilt.

Following an eight-month, 23-day trial, a jury deliberated three hours and 40 minutes before finding Simpson not guilty of murder. Mark Fuhrman, the detective who testified that he had found the bloody glove at Simpson's estate, had perjured himself before the jury by denying his use of racial epithets. Moreover, when prosecutors required Simpson to try on the Aris Isotoner gloves at the trial, the gloves did not fit. (A pair of the same model and size that had not been soaked in blood or subjected to forensic testing, however, did fit.) The defense theorized that Fuhrman had discovered a bloody glove at the crime scene, although it had gone unnoticed by others; that Fuhrman had concealed this glove in his sock or elsewhere and carried it to Simpson's estate; and that Fuhrman, without knowing whether Simpson had a provable alibi or whether another person could be shown guilty of the crime, had "planted" the glove.

Many observers were stunned by Simpson's acquittal. Many found the failure to convict the Menendez brothers disturbing. Many also raised their eyebrows when juries acquitted John and Lorena Bobbitt of brutalizing one another; acquitted Damian Williams and Henry Watson of the most serious charges against them following their videotaped attack upon truck driver Reginald Denny during the Los Angeles riots; acquitted Jack Kevorkian of aiding suicide after he had placed a mask over the face of a man with a degenerative muscle and nerve disorder and then pumped carbon monoxide into the man's lungs for 20 minutes; and acquitted Oliver North of all charges of lying to Congress, convicting him only of a single count of obstruction and of two other relatively minor crimes.

TAKING TO THE STREETS

[handwritten annotation: examples of protest due to jury decisions]

Although none of these cases brought protesters to the streets, George Fletcher of the Columbia Law School notes that a number of jury verdicts of the past two decades have. Earlier in our history, Americans marched to protest convictions, such as those of Sacco and Vanzetti; but the recent verdicts sparking outrage and protest have all been full or partial acquittals. These acquittals have come mostly in cases in which the asserted victims of crimes of violence were members of racial or other minority groups and in which the defendants were non-members of these groups.

In 1979, a jury tried Dan White for murdering George Moscone, the mayor of San Francisco, and Harvey Milk, a San Francisco Supervisor and prominent gay activist. The jury accepted White's partial defense of diminished capacity, a defense often called "the Twinkie defense" because a defense expert testified that junk food was one of the influences that had deprived White of the capacity to act with malice. Following the verdict, 5,000 gay men marched on city hall, smashed windows, and overturned and burned eight police cars.

In 1991, a Manhattan jury acquitted El-Sayyid Nosair of killing Meir Kahane, the founder of the Jewish Defense League. The judge who presided at the trial declared that the jury's verdict was "against the overwhelming weight of the evidence and devoid of common sense and logic." Jews in New York and Israel took to the streets in protest. In 1992, a Brooklyn jury acquitted Lemrick Nelson, Jr., of stabbing to death Yankel Rosenbaum during a violent encounter between blacks and Hasidic Jews. Before his death, Rosenbaum had identified Nelson, a black teenager, as his attacker, and the murder weapon had been found in Nelson's possession. Thousands of Hasidic Jews protested the acquittal.

The worst race riot in American history began on April 29, 1992, the day that a California jury failed to convict any of four Los Angeles police officers accused of misconduct, despite the fact that most of these officers had been videotaped kicking and beating Rodney King as he lay on the ground. The jury's action precipitated two days of violence that claimed 58 lives and cost nearly one billion dollars in property damage.

As Fletcher notes, protesters who take to the streets following jury verdicts are unlike other protesters. Whether violent or nonviolent, these protesters do not have an agenda for change; they simply mourn the denial of justice. Their protests may signal an unreflective demand for vengeance against any outsider accused of victimizing a member of their group. In the embrace of "identity politics," these protesters may cheer for blacks over white police officers, or for gays over straights, or for Jews over Muslim fundamentalists.

The new form of protest may, however, indicate the failure of American justice as much as, or more than, it does the Balkanization of American civic life. The indignation of the protesters usually appears justified. Americans take to the streets following criminal trials because our justice system, unlike those of other Western democracies, often acquits people whose guilt of violent crime seems obvious. When a jury reaches a verdict inconsistent with our predilections, we should be able to say that the jurors have heard more of the evidence than we have, yet many of us find it increasingly difficult to say, "We must have been wrong." Perhaps our fellow citizens cannot be trusted, or perhaps lawyers, judges, and television broadcasters have corrupted them.

SKEWED JURIES

Juries represent all of us, but the jurors in publicized cases often seem to have been drawn from the less-informed portions of the community. For example, two-thirds of the prospective jurors in the case of Oliver North were dismissed because they had viewed part of North's Congressional testimony on television or had read about it. Those who remained eligible included one, the jury's eventual foreman, who reported that she never followed the news because "it's depressing," one who said that he read only comics and horoscopes, one who recalled that North was "a head of soldiers or something like that," and still another who declared that he "didn't understand whatever I heard about this case."

The jurors who tried Imelda Marcos included one who had never heard of her and who could not say whether she was a woman or a man—and another who had not heard of Ferdinand Marcos either. A man who said that the media had made him think of the Menendez brothers as wealthy, spoiled kids was struck from the Menendez jury for cause while a woman who said that she read only *Cosmopolitan* and *Water Ski* magazine was accepted. Forty-five percent of the 196 people summoned as jurors for the 1974 trial of John Mitchell and Maurice Stans had attended college, but only one of them served on the jury.

The Simpson jury included only two college graduates. It included no Republicans or independents. Most jurors indicated that they obtained their information primarily from "early evening 'tabloid news' programs." One juror reported that she never read anything "except the horse sheet."

Three-quarters answered yes to the question, "Does the fact that O. J. Simpson excelled at football make it unlikely in your mind that he could commit murder?" When the lead Simpson prosecutor, early in her closing argument, encouraged jurors to take notes, only two did. One juror appeared to doze off repeatedly.

Criticism of the qualifications of jurors is, to be sure, not new, and neither is acquittal of the apparently guilty. American juries have often seemed more tolerant of self-help and of violence than the law on the books says they should be, and "trying the victim" has long been a standard defense strategy.

American juries have been especially tolerant of violence when the victims were black and the defendants white. Skin color sometimes has been, for jurors, a good indicator of who needed killing. In 1955, an all-white Mississippi jury took less than one hour to acquit the defendants accused of killing Emmett Till, a 14-year-old black visitor from Chicago who had accepted a dare and spoken to a white woman. Southern juries in the 1960s repeatedly failed to convict defendants accused on strong evidence of killing civil-rights activists (notably, Medgar Evers, Viola Liuzzo, and Lemuel Penn). At the same time, all-white juries voted not only in the Scottsboro prosecution but also in many others to impose the death penalty on blacks who had been accused, often on doubtful evidence, of raping white women or of homicide. Incidents like the first Rodney King verdict suggest to many that the jury remains an instrument of racial oppression.

In a reversal of historic roles, whites have begun to fear black jurors. The acquittal of O. J. Simpson by a predominantly black jury and the jubilant response to the verdict of many blacks heightened white concern, as did the acquittals of Lemrick Nelson, Jr., in the murder of Yankel Rosenbaum and the partial acquittal of Damian Williams in the beating of Reginald Denny. In Washington, D.C., a black juror forced a hung jury in the case of a black accused of murdering a white aide to Senator Richard Shelby; the jury's foreman had earlier sent a note to the judge accusing this juror of racism and of refusing to discuss the evidence. In Smith County, Texas, black jurors blocked the conviction of a black accused of sexually assaulting a white woman and then cited as a reason the earlier failure of a grand jury to indict a white police officer for killing a bedridden black woman during a botched drug raid.

That enough blacks to block conviction may be playing "payback" or otherwise may be unwilling to convict blacks of crimes of violence against whites is terrifying to many. Whites have begun to experience a glimmer of the fear of our justice system that blacks and other minorities have experienced throughout our history. Of course, most black and white jurors seriously seek justice, and multi-racial juries often reach unanimous verdicts in cases of interracial crime. "Most" and "often" may not inspire confidence, however. In a nation divided by racial sentiment and tolerant of violence, trial by jury increasingly appears to promote lawlessness and self-destruction.

JUSTICE GOES HOLLYWOOD

The perception that racism now cuts both ways is one reason why the mistrust of juries, particularly on the part of whites, may be greater than in the past. More importantly, the American jury now suffers from some of the problems that plague other democratic institutions.

Although in most governmental matters, the framers of the Constitution preferred representative to direct democracy, they trusted citizens, not their elected representatives, to resolve civil and criminal disputes. Lawyers, however, now hire experts to help them maneuver jurors in the same ways that candidates for public office hire experts to tell them how to push voters' hot buttons. When clients have enough money, these lawyers retain consultants to survey community attitudes and to determine which demographic characteristics indicate favorable jurors. They also hire field investigators to interview neighbors or to visit courthouse restrooms in order to discover what prospective jurors are reading. With the help of psychologists, they draft endless lists of complex, multiple-part questions probing attitudes, histories, beliefs, memberships, reading habits, viewing habits, and more. Judges then order prospective jurors to answer these privacy-invading questions upon penalty of perjury. The lawyers conduct lengthy voir dire examinations designed partly to determine jury qualifications but mostly to indoctrinate jurors. They sometimes hire shadow juries to observe trials and debrief the lawyers at the end of each court day.

Television may make it easier for trial lawyers with seemingly hopeless cases to confound fantasy and reality—something that the lawyers for O. J. Simpson apparently realized from the outset. As prosecutors at the preliminary hearing in the Simpson case presented a wealth of incriminating evidence, some of which the defendant's attorneys were seeking to suppress, I wondered why the defendant's lawyers had not sought to have the television cameras removed. Broadcasting the preliminary hearing would ensure widespread knowledge of the damaging evidence even if the judge suppressed it.

My first guess was that the lawyers were just grandstanding—seeking publicity for themselves through a broadcast that could only harm their client. After further reflection, however, I decided that the lawyers were better strategists than I. They realized that the more the Simpson case came to be seen as a television drama, the better their client's chance of escaping punishment. "Cinematization" of the case might make more plausible the scenarios that talk-radio callers, defense attorneys, and jurors would later invent: Simpson's older son, whose DNA is much like his father's, killed Nicole Simpson and Ronald Goldman. Or Colombian drug dealers with very bad eyesight committed the crimes to punish Faye Resnick for not paying her debts. Or racist detectives planted bloody evidence to punish Simpson for marrying a white woman. Or the real murderer is the shoe salesman who testified that Simpson always wears size 12 shoes (no one always wears the same size shoe as he shifts from brand to brand). A basic rule of screenwriting is never to write "on the nose." A scene must not be quite what it seems or what the characters say it is, for the writer must leave room for the imaginative participation of the audience.

HOW TO FIX IT

The American jury trial needs reform. The following measures would help:

1. Eliminate or greatly restrict the ability of lawyers to challenge prospective jurors peremptorily. The frequent exercise of peremptory challenges on the basis of group stereotypes is demeaning to the jurors who are dismissed, and peremptory challenges facilitate lawyers' efforts to stack juries. These challenges also ensure that juries rarely are composed of a defendant's peers and rarely reflect a cross section of the community.
2. Eliminate or greatly restrict the use of lengthy jury questionnaires and voir dire examinations. Both are insulting and invasive of privacy.
3. Eliminate all professional exemptions from jury service. Doctors, firefighters, morticians, and lawyers should be expected to serve.
4. Enforce jury summonses. In some jurisdictions, as many as two-thirds of all jury notices are disregarded, and, despite the warnings printed on the notices, nothing happens.
5. Do not disqualify prospective jurors who have seen news accounts of a case unless they have been exposed to inadmissible evidence or appear unwilling to judge the case on the basis of the evidence admitted in court.
6. Do not sequester juries or order changes of venue simply because a case has been the subject of very intense publicity.
7. Reduce the influence of professional jury consultants—perhaps by making their reports available to both sides. If a lawyer could not gain any partisan advantage by hiring a jury consulting firm, the lawyer probably would not pay the $10,000 to $250,000 per case that these firms charge.
8. Offer jurors instructions on the law at the outset of the trial. As Judge William Schwarzer has observed, the current judicial practice resembles telling jurors to watch a baseball game and to determine who won without telling them the rules until the game is over.
9. Redraft standard jury instructions to enhance their comprehensibility, and permit jurors to take written copies of the court's

instructions with them to the jury room. Allow judges to offer further instructions without fear of reversal for imprecise statements of the law unless these statements seem very likely to prove prejudicial.
10. In a lengthy trial, permit and encourage lawyers to present mini-summations and arguments as the trial proceeds.
11. Permit and encourage jurors to take notes. A minority of courts still forbid note taking, even in cases in which the lawyers must carry personal computers to keep track of the evidence. Other courts, without formally prohibiting note taking, fail to supply paper and pencils or to advise jurors that they are welcome to take notes.
12. Permit and encourage jurors to ask questions of witnesses after submitting these questions in writing for review by the court and counsel.

As helpful as these measures would be, all of them together cannot fix what is fundamentally wrong with the American jury trial. The vices of this institution cannot be corrected simply by improving the care and handling of jurors. Repairing our defective evidentiary rules and trial procedures is much more important.

The opponents of televising trials once argued that viewers would watch only lurid cases such as those in which football heroes were accused of killing their ex-wives. The proponents insisted that broadcasts would educate the public about the workings of the third branch of government. Both were right. Viewers might have watched the Simpson trial for entertainment, but many were appropriately appalled as Judge Lance Ito forced lawyers endlessly to "rephrase the question" for reasons that no one could understand; as he admonished jurors twice a day to perform the astonishing task of forming no opinions while they heard the evidence (they disobeyed); as he excluded obviously significant evidence; as lawyers on both sides forced witnesses to repeat their testimony interminably (How long does it take someone to say that he heard a dog barking at 10:15 P.M.? In an American courtroom, about two hours); as Johnnie Cochran and Marcia Clark played games of legal "gotcha"; as 10 of the initially impaneled jurors and alternates were discharged for their sins (mostly avarice and dishonesty); and as witnesses were never permitted to explain their answers.

LEGAL TURNING POINT

Many lawyers claim that the Simpson case was atypical and that it tells us nothing about the American justice system. Though the Simpson trial was atypical, it tells us a great deal about the legal system. It shows how readily this system can be abused when skillful lawyers have the resources to press it hard. It shows a system in which, in Justice Hugo Black's phrase, the kind of trial a man gets depends upon the amount of money he has.

It also shows a system that can survive only because very few litigants have the resources to invoke the procedures that it offers on paper. Because our legal system cannot deliver on its extravagant promises (Simpson's trial cost the taxpayers more than $8 million), lawyers and judges have effectively repealed the right to jury trial. Ninety-two percent of the defendants convicted of felonies in state courts plead guilty because prosecutors and judges tell them in effect, "You have a right to jury trial, and we have the right to sentence you to 50 years if you exercise it." The criminal justice system's taste for champagne and caviar in the few cases that reach trial seems to be causing its starvation in the many cases that do not, and to judge from the Simpson trial, even the caviar does not taste good. This high-priced trial mortified even lawyers.

During a recent discussion of the Simpson case, someone described what the case meant to her elderly father—that he could no longer believe in something in which he had believed all his life, the American justice system. The Simpson trial will be remembered as a flamboyant media event, but it conceivably could prove to be something more. This trial could mark a turning point in our legal history, the moment when the need for America to reinvent a fair and workable trial procedure became too obvious to deny.

Questions for Discussion

1. If you found yourself in the situation Albert Alschuler describes in the opening paragraph—having to defend the jury system to an outsider—how would you do it?
2. Can you detect any bias or prejudice in Alschuler's apparently objective summary of the evidence in the Menendez and Simpson cases (paragraphs 4–7)? In what ways does this seem like a fair version of the evidence presented to the jury? In what ways does it steer the reader toward a particular conclusion about the verdicts?
3. What does Alschuler identify as the most pressing problems facing the jury system in America today? Which of these problems do you think is most serious?
4. How effectively does the author use a "problem-solution" structure in this essay? Is the essay more effective in describing the problem or in proposing a solution? Why? How might the weaker part of the structure be improved?
5. What role does Alschuler think race or "identity politics" plays in either the controversial jury verdicts or the public's response to them? What does the phrase "Balkanization of American civic life" mean (paragraph 14)?

Questions for Research and Writing

1. Examine more closely one or two of the suggestions for reform that Alschuler mentions at the end of his article. What would be some of the advantages and disadvantages of implementing such reform? What would be the greatest difficulty of effecting such reform?
2. Talk to some people from other countries about their perceptions of the American jury system and about the differences between the American legal system and their own legal system. What do these conversations suggest about the strengths and weaknesses of the American system?
3. Read some newspaper or magazine commentaries about one of the cases listed in paragraph 8. How did observers see the case at the time? What is interesting or important about the media reports of the case?

* better at presenting problem because every problem is backed up with a detailed example whereas the solutions do not give examples of the type of change they would bring about or how they would have affected the mentioned cases.

LAW AND DISORDER
How the Juvenile Justice System Is Letting Kids Get Away with Murder

Craig Horowitz

> *Originally published in* The New Yorker *in early 1994, this article describes a New York Family Court system gone so far awry that it serves neither the young criminals who come through its doors nor the society it is trying to protect. Tracing the path that 15-year-old Jay Perez takes to Family Court and the court's response to his actions, Horowitz makes a compelling case for reform of our treatment of young criminals and in the social system that breeds crime. Writing for a publication that appeals largely to a well-educated, politically liberal audience, Horowitz uses a narrative technique that forces the reader to face the realities of crime for criminal and victim alike; he challenges the reader to discard easy solutions to an increasingly troubling and complex problem.*

By the time 15-year-old Jay Perez slid the gun into the right-hand cargo pocket of his camouflage pants, it was clear that something bad was going to happen. It was a comfortably warm Friday night at the end of August, the kind of night that still brings people outside in a neighborhood like East Harlem. For Perez, the start of the weekend meant little more than another shapeless, forgettable blur of television, fast food, and chillin' with his friends Eddie and Fat John. There were no summer barbecues, no bike rides in the park, no picnics, and no afternoons at the beach. Not for Perez. Maybe he'd get high; maybe he'd go to the movies. Maybe he'd just ride the subway for a while and see what happened. It didn't really matter. There was simply no constructive way to fill the time. And for a troubled teenager from the projects like Perez, a kid with no direction, no aspirations, and no thoughts of the future beyond the end of the day, free time is always dangerous. Perhaps the greatest danger. The last thing he needed was a gun.

Perez got the weapon from a guy he knew in the neighborhood named Frankie Lind. The exchange took place early on Friday evening in the lobby of 20 Paladino Avenue, an unremarkable redbrick building in East Harlem's Robert F. Wagner housing project. Backlit by the soft yellow light of an August sunset, the building looked almost homey. Perez had lived with his mother in a fifth-floor apartment in this building for as long as he could remember. Lind, 19, handed Perez the .25-caliber semi-automatic. It was nickel-plated, with a black handle and a full clip. Though no one knows for sure why Lind gave the gun to Perez, the best guess is he was supposed to sell it on the street. Perez would only say later that he "wanted to hold it for a while."

With the two-five, as he called it, now buried deep inside his pants pocket, Perez and his friends headed for the Village—"a place where a lot of people be at on Friday and Saturday night." But not this Friday night. They walked around aimlessly for a while and then took the subway back uptown. Hungry after their little expedition, Perez and his buddies knocked off some takeout chicken wings. Then Fat John went home and Perez went up to Eddie's apartment. According to Perez, Eddie took the gun and fired one shot from the terrace before the two of them drifted off to sleep.

Saturday started out like a replay of the previous day. After sleeping late and spending most of the afternoon just hanging out, Perez and Eddie rounded up Fat John and watched a bootleg tape of *In the Line of Fire*. When the movie was over, Perez headed home. It was hot again, and it seemed like every resident of the Wagner houses was outside. In a kind of square formed by several buildings, including the one Perez lived in, there was a block party with a D.J. and loud music. On the grass, children ran back and forth under sprinklers turned on to help ease the heat, and in an adjacent playground there was a basketball game in full swing. Perez got the key from his mother, who was visiting someone on the second floor, and went upstairs.

He walked into the apartment and snapped on the television in the living room without even looking at it. It was a few minutes past eight, and the movie *Strapped* had just started on HBO. He went into his room and opened the window. As he stood there for a moment, he listened to the music from the block party. Perez shoved his hand into his pocket and gripped the .25. Slowly he brought it up, pointed it out the window, and fired.

Ana Ruiz never had a chance. The 64-year-old native of Aibonito, Puerto Rico, mother of three and grandmother of six, had just come out of 50 Paladino Avenue. She was perhaps 30 or 40 feet from the entrance to the building when she was hit. The bullet struck her in the back and traveled through her body, puncturing her lung, aorta, and esophagus. Ruiz was coming from the apartment of a grieving friend, where she had gone to pray and offer comfort. In Spanish culture, there are nine days of prayers after a death, and Ruiz was always there for the rosaries when someone in the neighborhood needed to be consoled. On this particular night, she was in a hurry to get home and chose not to stay for coffee and cake because she thought she'd left something on the stove.

As Ruiz lay dying on the ground, with a swirl of hysteria around her, Perez put the .25 back in his pocket, closed the bedroom window, and left the apartment. Though he went to "chill" with Fat John, which means he came out the front door of his building and had a clear view of the frenzy he had caused, he would later claim that at this point he had no idea he'd actually shot anyone. "I didn't know it hit nobody," he would eventually tell detectives at the 25th Precinct. "I didn't know what happened till like Monday or somethin."

Word of the shooting spread so quickly that many of Ruiz's friends were at Metropolitan Hospital as doctors feverishly worked in vain to save her. East Harlem's tight-knit Hispanic community was outraged. A selfless, giving woman, Ruiz was loved and respected by everyone. She was chairwoman of the Ladies of the Holy Rosary Society at the Holy Rosary Church, she bought food for people in the neighborhood, and she worked on behalf of the community with local politicians. Though she had lived in the Wagner houses for only four years, Ruiz had owned a beauty salon at 118th Street and First Avenue for 25 of the 41 years she'd spent in America.

By Sunday, posters asking for information had gone up around the neighborhood, and people talked about little besides the killing. A tips hot line was set up. Cops were all over the case. The housing police alone had eight detectives on it. That evening, there was a candlelight vigil at the spot where Ruiz had been gunned down. Dozens of people placed flowers and candles on a makeshift shrine. They held hands while they prayed and sang songs. Meanwhile, Perez had recklessly begun to brag about his exploits as a shooter.

By Monday, stories about the crime had appeared in the tabloids, and even the *Times* ran something on page three of the Metro section. But given the regularity of grisly crime in the city, the killing of Ana Ruiz didn't merit much coverage. The victim, after all, was a Hispanic grandmother, and no matter how important she was to her family and her community, she simply didn't have the headline appeal of an upscale white person. But on Tuesday, the people of East Harlem showed what she meant to them when they marched from the Wagner houses to the Holy Rosary Church for a memorial service. The crowds were so big that the streets were closed to traffic and the procession was covered by Spanish-language television. In a bitter piece of irony, it is believed that Perez marched to the church with the mourners.

On Thursday, five days after the shooting, Ana Ruiz was buried in Puerto Rico. That evening, Jay Perez was taken to the 25th Precinct by his mother, who had heard that the cops were looking for him. Apparently he mouthed off to the wrong people about the shooting, and word got back to the police. Once Perez was in custody, it was easy work for the detectives. He was cooperative and signed a confession. On Friday morning, the cops called the Ruiz family.

"We were in Puerto Rico for the funeral when we got the call," says Lydia Ruiz, who lived with her mother in the Wagner houses. "It was kind of weird to be happy that they'd made an arrest, because at the same time you're so sad about what's happened. But there was a feeling of . . . thank God, at least we don't have to live with the unanswered questions; that really tears at you."

But the relief would be short-lived. Apprehending the killer was one thing; punishing him was something else entirely. For even though he had admitted to the shooting and even though the cops actually recovered the murder weapon somewhere in the Bronx, there was one element of the case that outweighed all the others: age. Jay Perez was only 15. Which meant—since the district attorney felt the case wasn't strong enough for him to be charged as an adult—that Perez would be tried in Family Court, and the Ruiz family was about to become familiar with an extraordinarily frustrating, ineffective, archaic morass known as the juvenile-justice system. Though they didn't know it at the time, their suffering over this crime was just beginning.

"Where is he? Is everybody else here? Yes? Well, then, please go and find Mr. Jones. Now. If he's not here in twenty seconds . . . ."
"Judge, can I just . . . ."
"I'm counting—nineteen, eighteen . . . . You'd better get moving . . . sixteen . . . ."

With that, the court officer wheeled around and headed quickly for the door. Judge Judith Sheindlin is not someone to be ignored, not in her courtroom. In fact, probably not anywhere. Though it is easy to be fooled by the cream-colored lace collar that softens the look of her black robe, this is a mistake. After twenty years in Family Court—the past seven as the supervising judge in Manhattan—she still brings a ferocious spirit and plenty of attitude to the bench. Tough, impatient, and equipped with a blistering smart mouth, the five-foot-two, 100-pound jurist has no trouble intimidating nearly everyone who comes before her, including the meanest Nike-wearing thugs.

One afternoon, for example, a 15-year-old who had violated his probation was brought in on a warrant. He refused to come in voluntarily. "Your Honor, my client was afraid to come back to your court," said the kid's attorney. "That was very smart of him," snapped the judge, while the boy's mother sat next to him crying. "Listen to me very carefully, sir," Sheindlin told the dazed-looking kid, in a voice that sounded like a wire brush. "You were in detention. You don't want to go back there, do you? I'm gonna put you away if you don't do what you're supposed to. Am I clear, sir?" she screamed from the bench. "Good. Step out." When he'd gone, she turned to the court reporter and said, "Fear is good."

It's a weapon she happily wields all day in her courtroom, through the 30 or 40 cases she typically hears between 9:30 and 5:30. But it is her ability and her willingness to speak out bluntly and passionately that really makes her a fearsome presence in Family Court. Even after two decades in a system that breeds burnout faster than a hospital emergency room, the judge still rails with anger and indignation at anyone not getting the job done or trying to take advantage of the system. "I can't stand stupid and I can't stand slow," she says.

When a kid named Eddie Guzman comes before her, the judge is furious. Guzman is someone she had tried to give a break. Though she had previously revoked his parole on an assault charge when he missed eleven of the first fourteen days of school, she still believed he was worth one more shot. So she tried to scare him by putting him in detention for ten days while attempting to get him into a community-based program. But her judgment—and this is something she hates—had been wrong. Since Guzman was uncooperative and was turned down by the program, he was now back in court.

"What do you do when you're not in school?"

"I be chillin' with my girl."

"You be chillin' with your girl? Am I supposed to understand that?"

"I'm sorry, but that's the way I talk, that's the . . . ."

"It says here you want to go to college and become a lawyer," the judge barks. "You think you get to college by chillin' with your girl? I want you to get something straight, Mr. Guzman. I don't care if you're in jail; you understand that? I still go out to dinner, I still go to the movies, I still see my grandchildren, and I don't ever think about Eddie Guzman. Not ever. So the only one it matters to is you." With that, she sends him away for one year, the maximum allowable sentence.

Everyone is fair game. Inattentive lawyers, poorly prepared social workers, teenagers who don't use birth control, parents who shirk their responsibilities . . . right on up through the "yutzniks" at City Hall. She has been called a racist, a sadist, and a woman who demeans the court with her behavior. Sheindlin, 51, couldn't care less. She is not interested in being politically correct, she's not interested in conforming to make friends, and she's not interested in placidly accepting any old-fashioned rules of decorum when she works in a Family Court system that is bursting at its seams with horrors. "You hear a lot of crap like, 'Well, the system is doing fine and everybody's functioning.' But it's not true. Everybody who looks in the street knows it's not true," Sheindlin says while smoking a cigarette during a short court break one morning. "This is not a popularity contest. You can tell the quality of the work you're doing by the quality of your enemies. And I have made some terrific enemies."

When a woman whose four kids have been in foster care for three years comes to court to have their placement extended, the judge asks simple, commonsense questions. "Why aren't you working? You're an intelligent woman. You should get your own apartment, get a job, and take your kids back."

"I've been, you know, trying, but . . . but it's hard," the woman says, seeming a little embarrassed.

"Either she gets her act together," Sheindlin says to the caseworker, "or we will begin proceedings to terminate her parental rights." The judge now turns to the woman. "You can't sit home all day and do nothing. You have a responsibility for these children. The ball is in your court. I will extend the placement for six months, but don't even think about coming back here for another extension."

There is silence for a moment. The hearing appears to be over, but nobody moves. "Hurry up," the judge suddenly says to the woman. "You don't have much time. You better go out and get a newspaper and start looking for a job."

Finally, the court officer sent searching for Mr. Jones returns with a nervous-looking black man who is the Legal Aid attorney assigned to represent Jay Perez. Like most lawyers working in Family Court and juggling dozens of cases, Willie Jones has an armful of manila folders and a small, black loose-leaf binder with gold letters on the front that read FAMILY COURT ACT. He goes directly to his place at the defense table. "Mr. Jones," the judge says, making no effort to conceal her anger, "why do I have to go scouting for you? You knew I was ready to call this case."

"I'm sorry, Judge, I had to . . . ."

"Never mind. Are you ready now? Can we please proceed?"

It is the third week in October, seven weeks after Jay Perez was brought in by his mother for shooting Ana Ruiz. This is his sixth appearance in court. The earlier court dates were taken up by the usual combination of procedural matters—getting the petition filed that stated the charges, arguments about various pieces of evidence, depositions—and postponements. It was also during this period, however, that the outline of a deal was struck between the prosecution and Willie Jones.

Perez has been charged with first-degree assault and reckless manslaughter. (In one of the many eccentricities of juvenile law, the assault charge comes with the possibility of a longer sentence than the manslaughter charge—three years versus eighteen months.) For his guilty plea, Perez has been offered a reward: The prosecutors will recommend that only the first six months of his sentence, rather than a year, be served in a secure facility (the juvenile equivalent of a maximum-security prison). "When they first told us about the sentence," says Iris Ruiz, "we were like, 'C'mon, he killed our mom; the system has to do more than that.' To me he looks like a career criminal, but maybe that'll be his punishment. He'll spend the rest of his life in and out of jail, and he won't really have a life." Groping to make some sense of the sentencing structure, Maria Curran, one of the prosecutors on the case, says, "Look, three years to a 15-year-old is a lot of time. It's the prime of his life."

Since his confession, Perez has been at Spofford, a juvenile detention center in the Bronx where kids are held until their cases are resolved. The dismal atmosphere at Spofford is best understood through an exchange that took place in Sheindlin's court one afternoon when she sent a 16-year-old probation violator there pending the outcome of a robbery charge against him in criminal (adult) court. Because juvenile records don't automatically show up in criminal court, the judge had no knowledge of the kid's history in the juvenile system, and so released him without bail as a "first time" offender. "Miss, miss, can I get another date? Pleeeese can I get another date?" the kid pleaded, trying to get out of going to Spofford. He was wearing a blue Fila parka, a gray Polo sweatshirt, and black Adidas sneakers. "They're gonna cut me. I got new sneakers. They're gonna cut my face." As the kid was led away by a court officer, one of the lawyers remarked, "I guess he's going to go barefoot tonight." (Rose Washington, commissioner of the New York City Department of Juvenile Justice, which runs Spofford, turned down several requests for an interview.)

Perez, handcuffed and accompanied by a guard, saunters into court wearing the uniform of the street—gray, hooded Champion sweatshirt; big, baggy black jeans that fall below his hips and reveal his underwear; and black suede Nikes. While he sits in court, in a plastic chair that's bolted to the floor, the 15-year-old keeps his head down and bites his nails. His leg bounces nonstop. He never looks up at the judge.

When the case is formally announced, a clearly nervous Willie Jones stands up to begin. In halting, incomplete sentences he seems to be objecting to something and asking for a delay. This is the day Lydia Ruiz is scheduled to testify, and she sits quietly in the back of the court with her sister Iris. Though it's difficult to be sure, Jones appears to have a problem with the murdered woman's daughter's testifying on this particular day. He's not ready, and he seems to be trying to convince Sheindlin that she should grant him a delay. Jones is out of his depth.

"Judge . . . ."

"I know who I am," cracks Sheindlin. "State substantively what your objection is."

"Well, it's really not that specific, Judge; it's just . . . ."

"Then the hearing will commence. The family is in court, Mr. Jones. If you're not ready to question Ms. Ruiz today, she can come back for your cross-examination. But there's no reason not to let her testify."

A wan, nervous Lydia Ruiz takes the witness stand and talks about her mother's work in the community. Though it is obviously difficult for her, Lydia speaks in clear, measured tones. She talks about the Wagner houses and her East Harlem neighborhood. "You'll hear shots in the night, but it's not every night. It's a close-knit community. When I go out now, it takes me twenty minutes to get through everybody asking how I'm doing." But it is when her testimony turns to what happened to her mother that she begins to lose control. "We were all each other had. My parents were orphans when they came to this country," she says, sobbing softly. "My mom helped so many people. My sisters are not the same anymore," she says, sobbing more heavily now. "It's changed everything . . . she didn't deserve to die that way . . . nobody does."

Willie Jones chooses not to cross-examine Lydia Ruiz. The hearing is over, the case is continued for ten days, and everybody files out. Moments later, in the quiet of the small, octagonal courtroom, I can hear Lydia's anguished cries from the hall as she makes her way to the elevator.

The Manhattan Family Court Building on Lafayette Street is an eleven-story black granite fortress with few windows and fewer bright spots. It is a place where the darkest, most disturbing urban nightmares come to life. Opened in 1976 at a cost of $28 million, the building is the perfect metaphor for the system: ugly, oppressively overcrowded, and with a design that no longer meets the demands that are placed on it. Squeezed into this stultifying compound, along with eight courtrooms, are offices and facilities for judges, prosecutors, probation officers, Legal Aid lawyers, child-welfare workers, and mental-health workers, as well as a holding area for kids who are brought in for court appearances.

Everything is covered with a layer of dirt as thick and hard as a protective coating. Crowded public waiting areas are filled with hard orange and blue plastic seats, many of which are broken. Babies cry, anxious adults argue, and there is a thick cloud of acrid smoke that hangs in the air as heavily as the general sense of menace. The first morning I was there, two fights broke out, and each required several court officers to pry the participants apart. One, a scatological screaming match between a man and a woman accusing each other of abusing their baby, ended up in the men's bathroom, which looked as if it had already seen its share of battles. The walls were covered with graffiti, the floor was covered with cigarette butts, doors were ripped off the stalls, toilet-paper holders had been pulled out of the walls, and both urinals were covered with large black trash bags. The other battle took place by the stairs, between two men who were quite clearly not interested in sharing the affections of the same woman.

Rarely seen by the public and rarely talked about, Family Court is a repository for every pathology that afflicts the dysfunctional contemporary family. Battered babies. Babies born drug-addicted, HIV-positive or suffering from fetal alcohol syndrome. Sexual abuse. Abandonment. Hateful custody battles. Termination of parental rights. Foster-care scams. And, of course, it is the place where the fate of kids who vandalize, rob, rape, sell drugs, peddle weapons, and kill is determined. Conceived in simpler, less violent times to protect society's children and change the behavior of delinquents, the court today is rarely capable of doing either. In part, it is a matter of simple arithmetic. Since 1986, cases of juveniles arrested with loaded guns are up 700 percent; robberies, assaults, and group attacks by kids are up 100 percent; sex crimes, 50 percent; custody disputes, 300 percent; parental abuse, 300 percent. And there are now more than 50,000 children in New York City foster care, more than double the number there were just five years ago.

But in dealing with delinquents—the term itself seems quaint, if not ridiculous, when describing today's young predators—the problem is more than just the new math. It is also one of philosophy and outlook. Despite the grim reality in the streets, the juvenile-justice system continues to operate with a basic structure designed when the worst thing kids were doing was shop-lifting or stealing hubcaps. "In terms of the psychology of it," says UCLA professor and nationally known expert on crime James Q. Wilson, whose latest book is *The Moral Sense,* "It's simply an irrational system. There ought to be penalties from the earliest offense, steadily intensifying in severity with the commission of additional offenses, so that juveniles are treated by the state the way we treat our own children. You don't ignore the fact that they're wrecking the house until they finally burn it down. You try to deal with it right away."

The basic job of the juvenile-justice system is to handle anyone under 16 who gets arrested. If the arrested kid is found guilty, the court must then, according to the delinquency statute of the Family Court Act, decide whether the juvenile needs supervision, treatment, or confinement. Ideally, the needs of the child are balanced with the need to protect the community. In Family Court, they like to say they don't punish, they try to change behavior. And indeed, one look at the sentencing structure indicates they're at least half right. Take the charge of group robbery in the second degree. This is not only the most feared crime—the image of being terrorized by several vicious teens has been seared into the contemporary consciousness—it is also the city's most commonly committed juvenile crime. In fact, one of every four robbery arrests nationwide of someone under 16 occurs in New York. The maximum sentence for this is eighteen months. Typically, about half the time is actually served. The maximum sentence for an adult on the same charge is fifteen years.

For all but the most serious offenses, a juvenile never faces more than eighteen months. Second-degree possession of a weapon, for example, which implies intent to use the gun and is one of the most common weapons-related charges, still carries the eighteen-month maximum. An adult arrested on this charge is looking at five to fifteen years. Since 1976, the most serious crimes—armed robbery, rape, kidnapping, arson, sodomy—have been called "designated felonies," and they carry a three-year maximum. This special category was created by the Juvenile Justice Reform Act, a bill enacted the last time juvenile crime caused public outrage. In extraordinary cases—those of habitual offenders, murderers, and the like—five years can be given, but it rarely is. For the most serious crimes, juveniles can be tried in adult court, but while the sentences are tougher than they are in juvenile court, they are still not as severe as they are for adults. "We have all the same problems as the adult system," says prosecutor Elizabeth Brady, "but without the same resolution. At least in the adult system, serious offenders can be put away for 25 years to life."

The system remains more concerned with the criminal than with the crime, and rehabilitation is still paramount. But it is rarely asked whether it is even possible to rehabilitate someone who has grown into his or her teens without moral grounding, without education, and without learning what it means to have real hope for the future. How do you reverse a lifetime of deprivation in six or twelve or eighteen months? "I'm convinced that if you wait until the child's a teenager," says Wilson, "it's too late, and basically all you can really do is take him off the streets. Rehabilitation is rarely realistic at that point." Wilson points out that scholars have looked at many rehabilitation programs across the country and have found that very few produced a drop in the recidivism rate. "The lesson is that by the time they're that age, society can't change them. We simply don't know how to do it, and we better face up to that fact."

A kid who comes into the system is dealt with in a variety of ways. First-time offenders and those who are nonviolent can be put in one of the dozens of privately run, community-based programs around the city. These range in scope and intensity from programs where a kid only has to show up a couple of times a month to what is virtually full-time counseling and supervision. If confinement—it's not called "jail time," it's called "placement"—is the court's determination, then the kid is sent to a state facility run by the Division for Youth. The depth of the problem of trying to rehabilitate these kids is made clear by even a cursory look at the characteristics of the 2,323 kids sent to a DFY facility in 1992. More than 80 percent suffered from at least one serious physical or emotional deficiency—58 percent had a drug problem, more than 27 percent had psychiatric problems, and a quarter were on the special-education rolls at their home schools.

Though he tries to put a good face on things, Jay Silverman, a DFY spokesman, admits that at best it's a struggle. "We are the agency of last resort," he says. "We get the cases nobody else can handle. They may have gone through four or five different kinds of alternatives to incarceration. They may have been warned. They may have been probated. They may have done all sorts of things. When they're finally sent to us by the Family Court, we know we have a difficult task."

As expected, Judge Sheindlin takes a much harsher view. To begin with, she points out that 72 percent of the kids who spend time in a state facility are arrested again. "We're paying for a Rolls-Royce in New York's juvenile-justice system and getting an Edsel," she says, referring to the fact that it can now cost up to $85,000 a year to keep one kid in a state-run facility. "There are places throughout the country that offer far better programs than New York, far more realistic programs that cost the taxpayer a lot less." She mentions Glen Mills in Pennsylvania as one good program that costs less than half of what the DFY spends. "I don't know what the bureaucratic overlay is with the state Division for Youth and how the money really flows. I've asked the question and no one wants to give me an answer."

On the issue of rehabilitation, the judge says that she has had five or six kids over the past year or so who seem to have been turned around. "But so many of the kids have been so deprived throughout their early years that by the time we catch them, you have to be realistic. To give them hope, to help them see a light at the end of the tunnel, to help them see a way other than drugs or mugging or hurting people, you have to teach them a skill. Teach them how to be plumbers or painters. Teach them how to lay carpet or fix cars, so that when they get out there's something they can do. Something that gives them self-esteem, that gives them hope. You can't teach them how to be happy with nothing."

Sheindlin believes that too many of both the community- and state-run programs are unrealistic and waste too much time on things that are useless when a kid's back on the street. She tells a story about someone who works at Covenant House, which has a number of programs for troubled kids. He confidently stated his case that one of these programs is a good one because it successfully pushes kids to get their high-school-equivalency diploma. It's terrific, he said, because it's the only time in their lives that these kids have ever accomplished anything. But Sheindlin is skeptical. "So these kids work their butts off getting a GED, and they give them the piece of paper and they give them a graduation, and everybody has a wonderful day. They have punch and cookies and cake, and then they take their GED and go out to get a job. And then they realize that somebody's been pulling the wool over their eyes," she says in a rising voice. "This GED is gonna get them borscht. Where are they gonna go with a GED? So instead of being a packer at FoodTown they'll be a packer at Food Emporium? Don't fool kids. You have to give them something that's real."

The fact that changes have not been made in the juvenile-justice system can be blamed in large part on the continued allegiance to failed liberal social theories, misguided concern for the kids, and a simple lack of courage and vision in the state Legislature. How else is it possible to explain that a kid picked up with a loaded gun is not fingerprinted if he's under 16? For the past seven years, despite exponential increases in gun-related violence among juveniles, the state Legislature has refused to adopt a proposed change in this law.

The system is now so clogged with serious offenses that there's no longer time or the manpower to handle misdemeanors. "We've doubled our overall case load since 1986," says Peter Reinharz, who heads the Family Court division for the Corporation Counsel. "But the interesting thing is that we've now become almost exclusively a felony practice. Of the 13,000 cases referred to us for prosecution last year, better than 90 percent were felonies. Misdemeanor arrests are rarely even referred to our office anymore for prosecution." Last year, more than 30,000 kids picked up for misdemeanors were issued Youth Division cards and then released. Once called juvenile-delinquent or JD cards, these meant that a police officer would be sent to the kid's house to talk to the parents. They also carried a social stigma. The idea of a kid's being stigmatized is now laughable, and it's no longer considered practical or economically feasible to send a cop to the home when a kid commits a relatively minor infraction. Today, the paperwork is filled out, it's stuck in a file, the kid walks out, and that's the end of it. "The joke when you talk about juvenile crime is that incarceration is now the alternative sentence," says Reinharz.

Despite the crisis, arguments continue to rage over how tough the system should be on kids. "I think there's a small number of very vocal people controlling what the majority would like to see happen," says Sheindlin. "You're no less injured if you're mugged and beaten by a 14-year-old than you are if you're mugged and beaten by a 23-year-old. You're no less victimized; you're no less afraid to leave your house. If we can't rehabilitate these kids, then let's at least isolate them. Is it true that society's responsibility is to protect itself, consistent with the rights of the individual? We're not doing that," the judge says. "We have to change the system to reflect what's out there."

But there are those who argue that the juvenile laws are already severe enough, that getting tougher is not the answer. "The statutes clearly have changed," says Carol Sherman of the Legal Aid Society, referring to the 1976 laws that made it possible to charge 14- and-15-year-olds as adults for some crimes, and also created the designated-felony category. "The crime rate has not gone down. The tougher measures don't seem to have solved the problem or been the answer," Sherman says.

But the lawyers at the Legal Aid Society know they are fighting against growing public horror and outrage over crime and increasing demands that law enforcement get tougher. A *USA Today*/CNN/Gallup Poll found that just about three quarters of those surveyed thought that violent juveniles should be tried and punished as adults. "There are many studies on the failure of punishment as a deterrence," says Lenore Gittis, the head of Legal Aid's Juvenile Rights Division, "especially with young people. It's unreal to them, and in many neighborhoods it's simply a rite of passage. So I really doubt that making sentences two or three or five years longer is going to make any difference. That's not where it's at."

Jay Perez has a history that is more or less typical of today's juvenile offender. Raised in a single-parent home by a mother who has a history of substance abuse, he began his documented troubles when he was suspended from school in the third grade. Within a few years, he was so difficult for school administrators to handle that he was banned altogether for a while and received instruction at home. He has an older brother who, after years of his own problems with the juvenile system, is now in adult prison serving time on weapons and drug convictions. Perez was involved in several incidents of gunplay before the one that killed Ana Ruiz, and when the shooting occurred, he was already on probation for selling drugs.

Or consider the case of Warren White, a six-foot-three, 235-pound 15-year-old with tight cornrows and unlaced Reeboks. White has been a regular in Family Court since he was barely as tall as Judge Sheindlin. But as he got bigger and stronger and older, his crimes got more serious and more frequent. The most recent string includes robbery in the second degree, robbery in the first degree, a robbery in New Jersey in which someone was seriously hurt, and two violent episodes while he was in placement—one in which he used a pen as a weapon, and the other a pencil.

On a recent morning, he was brought before Judge Sheindlin on assault and robbery charges. A psychiatrist testified during questioning by the prosecutor that White suffers from violent fantasies and aggressive tendencies. She recommended restrictive placement (maximum security) for the longest allowable time, and therapy. White, who has an IQ of 77 and is functionally illiterate, has continued to deny any wrongdoing in his arrests.

When White's defense lawyer (called a "law guardian" in the sanitized lexicon of Family Court) began to cross-examine the psychiatrist, the proceedings took on a pathetic, almost absurd quality. Stumbling around, starting and withdrawing questions, the lawyer seemed to be hopelessly groping for something substantial to grab onto. And as slowly as she went, asking the same questions over and over again—despite warnings from the judge—things were made that much slower by the fact that the psychiatrist testifying was hard of hearing. This resulted in the lawyer's having to repeat many of her questions several times.

White, it was revealed, had been sexually abused by an uncle for three years when he was a child and grew up with doubts about his masculinity. He has only recently, according to his lawyer, come to accept that he is homosexual. Isn't it true, his lawyer asked the doctor, that Warren's homosexuality gets him into fights when he's incarcerated because he's taunted and called names like *faggot* by other inmates? Wouldn't he be better off, she continued, in some other kind of setting?

Judge Sheindlin, who had been stringing paper clips together and periodically asking the lawyer if she was almost finished, finally erupted. "Do you have much more for the doctor?" It was as much an order as a question.

"I think what I'm doing is important, Judge."

"No, it's not important," Sheindlin screamed. "Placing him in an environment without violent, straight males is not an option. There is no such facility. If he didn't like restrictive custody last time, if it was that unpleasant, then he shouldn't have committed another robbery."

White remained motionless throughout the hearing, including the moment when the judge gave him five years, the maximum. "He's aggressive, he's predatory, and the community can no longer tolerate that behavior."

Overwhelmed by the severity of contemporary urban problems, the Family Court and the juvenile-justice system are crumbling under the weight of their own cumbersome, outdated framework. It's as if they're fighting a modern, high-tech war with turn-of-the-century weapons. Still, public officials have displayed little interest in addressing the breakdown. Those on the inside don't want to rock the boat or seem to be admitting failure, while elected officials have no interest in getting stuck in the political quicksand of a complex crisis that offers no hope of any kind of short-term dividend. "By all the evidence, the juvenile-justice system is not working," says Professor Wilson, "and something else ought to be put in its place."

The situation has grown far beyond the bounds of an underfunded, overburdened juvenile-justice system. The horrific nature of life in the inner city and the near-total disintegration of the family are now so intractable that it is unrealistic to believe that law enforcement and the courts can do anything other than fail. "What can you expect when you see what goes on here?" says Sheindlin. "What you see here in court is a *fait accompli*. There's a history of failure with these kids, and it's often not their fault. But where do you even begin to attack that?" Governor Cuomo last month announced the creation of a special commission to study New

York's juvenile-justice system. Headed by former City Council president Andrew Stein, the commission is scheduled to begin hearings this month and release its findings by the end of the year. "The report can be written now," says Peter Reinharz. "It's all out there. The people of this city know what they're afraid of. In the year it takes to complete this study, the situation's only going to get worse."

In the meantime, experts have begun to call for a public discussion of root causes at a time when the mere mention of the phrase has become political suicide. "There are resources in this country," says Legal Aid's Lenore Gittis. "How they are directed is a political choice, and political choices depend on pressure. And if the pressure's put on by the public only to build more prisons and not deal with some of the root causes, then we're not going to see much change." Though Gittis says she doesn't believe it's "total political death" to talk about root causes, she can't, when pressed, offer the name of a single elected official who's doing it.

Everyone who works in the system, no matter what his or her political shading, agrees on one thing: The only tool that can break the cycle of violence and suffering on display in Family Court every day is early intervention. Some, like Wilson, have begun to advocate radical measures in this area. He would like to see a system of boarding schools, places where children who are identified as being at risk can be sent as early as possible—perhaps even as infants and toddlers—to be raised out of harm's way. "I am convinced that nothing short of this will work."

Equally controversial are Judge Sheindlin's ideas about birth control and family planning. One morning at around 9:15, before the daily maelstrom began, Sheindlin was in her courtroom having a cigarette and a cup of coffee. It was almost tranquil. Most of the people on the calendar that day were still lined up outside, waiting to come in and pass through the building's lone metal detector. Tom Curtis, a veteran Legal Aid attorney, walked in looking for some folder or other, and he and the judge began to talk. Sadly, he told Sheindlin he'd just finished a case in which he was the law guardian for a newborn baby. His work was done because the infant, born prematurely, had died before getting out of Harlem Hospital. It was the woman's eighth drug-addicted baby.

"I would make it a crime," says Sheindlin.

"What are we talking about here, eugenics? I would think, Judge, that as a member of a minority group you'd be sensitive to what this kind of thinking can be used for and what kinds of difficulties can be visited upon minority groups."

"So what would you do?" the judge asks.

"I don't know."

"If she wants to use drugs, that's her business," says Sheindlin. "If she wants to get pregnant, that's her business. But if she wants to do both, that's my business. If we can't tie her tubes or make her use Norplant, then at least she should be punished. The system has to make people act responsibly. She's inflicting her addictions on another human being."

"It's not born yet," Curtis says, "so you can't really say that. When does it actually become a child?"

It is, of course, an unwinnable argument, and even simply as interesting conversation it is fraught with hazards and controversy. But Sheindlin is nothing if not relentless. When Curtis left the room, the judge turned to me and said, "You have to look at the situation and say, 'This is what's real. This is not what I would like to be real, but this is what's real and what's practical.'" Suddenly her voice filled the courtroom. "Teenagers have to have family planning. I tell them making a baby is easy . . . dogs make babies, fish make babies, birds make babies. But being a parent is hard. If we can't get them to understand this, then we're never going to turn this thing around. It's only going to get worse."

While her words still hang in the warm air, people begin filing into the courtroom. The first scheduled case of the morning is the dispositional hearing for Jay Perez. When everyone is assembled, the case is announced by the court officer. Several items, including a photo of Ana Ruiz with her church group and dozens of letters from friends and neighbors saying how they have been affected by her death and asking that Perez be punished, are entered by the prosecution into evidence.

"Has your client ever seen a picture of the victim, Mr. Jones?" Sheindlin asks.

"I don't know, Judge."

"Why don't you ask him?"

"He says yes, he has."

With that, a television is rolled into the courtroom to play the 31-minute, 16-second videotaped confession given by Jay Perez at two in the morning in the juvenile room of the 25th Precinct. Sitting next to a file cabinet in a metal chair pushed up against a cinder-block wall, Perez calmly and dispassionately answered the questions of assistant district attorney William Greenbaum. Yes, he had the gun. Yes, he pointed it out his window. Yes, he knew there were people down there even though the trees obscured most of his view. Yes, he pulled the trigger. No, he had nothing against his victim. "I seen her around, but I didn't know nothin' 'bout her name or anything." The stark video is remarkable not because Perez showed no sign of remorse but because he didn't show even the slightest glimmer that he comprehended the magnitude of what he had done, that he had taken the life of a woman who meant so much to so many people. The only time during the entire tape when he appeared anything but bored was when he described the operation of the .25 he had used in the shooting.

Perez doesn't watch himself on the television. Iris and Lydia Ruiz, who have seen this tape before, also try not to watch. When it is over, the room is still. Drained, perhaps. Then both sides make perfunctory closing statements. Finally, Sheindlin looks at Perez. "Yo," she screams at him, startling everyone. "Stand up. Do you have anything to say to me or to the family of Mrs. Ruiz?"

"No," he mumbles.

She then gives him three years, with the first six months in secure placement. "Are you sure you have nothing to say, sir?" she asks again. This time he shakes his head no, and the court officer takes him away.

Finally, then, at least one part of the nightmare is over for Lydia and Iris Ruiz. But there is no satisfaction, no real relief. "It's nothing," Lydia says of the sentence. "He gets the same thing if he stole a car. There's no distinction for juveniles; it's all the same, it's so unjust . . ." she says, her voice trailing off. "My mom was always there," says Iris, her eyes moist. "She was the strength for all of us; she held us all together. I miss her faith. I miss her wisdom. You know," she says, crying now and heading down the filthy hallway of 60 Lafayette Street for the last time, "something has to be done. Not for us, of course, but for all the other families."

Questions for Discussion

1. Craig Horowitz's introduction is meant to build suspense that culminates in an inevitable tragedy. How does he create the sense that there was no way to stop the tragedy? How does he use comparison/contrast, word choice, and sentence structure to underscore the sense of inevitability?
2. Horowitz uses a colloquial diction throughout. How effective is his use of an informal language? Why do you suppose he chose an informal diction rather than a more formal, even scholarly one?
3. In describing the events that lead up to the killing, Horowitz paints a word picture so rich in detail that it is easy to picture Jay Perez and his surroundings. Examine two or three of the details and determine why Horowitz included them. Why, for instance, does he tell us what Perez and his buddy ate the night before the killing? Or the names of the movies they watched? Why does he mention that Jay calls the weapon a "two-five" or that some of the children on the street were playing in the sprinklers while others were playing basketball?
4. In paragraph 14, the scene shifts abruptly and dramatically to Judge Sheindlin's courtroom. How effective is this sudden shift? Why do you think Horowitz chose to change his focus so abruptly? Why does he tell the stories of several other defendants in Judge Sheindlin's court before returning to his narrative about Jay Perez?
5. Compare the characterizations of two of the people in this narrative. What do they have in common? How are they different?
6. Have you ever been the victim of a crime? If so, how did you feel about the criminal who victimized you? What sort of punishment did you want that person to face? What did you know about his or her background?

Questions for Research and Writing

1. Judge Sheindlin believes that "there's a small number of very vocal people controlling what the majority would like to see happen. . . . You're no less injured if you're mugged and beaten by a 14-year-old than you are if you're mugged and beaten by a 23-year-old. You're no less victimized; you're no less afraid to leave your house. If we can't rehabilitate these kids, then let's at least isolate them." Design a survey that will test Sheindlin's opinion on your campus or in your community. How do people respond differently to crimes committed by teenagers than to those committed by adults? How would they like the courts to treat first-time juvenile offenders as opposed to first-time adult offenders? Repeat offenders of both age groups? After collecting your survey data, write an essay that either uses your results to argue for reforms in the treatment of juvenile offenders or analyze how the following characteristics of your respondents have influenced their responses to your questions: age, political allegiance, gender, educational background, experiences with crime, and so forth.

2. If you live in an area where you can observe juvenile court hearings, spend a day or two listening to the lawyers' arguments and the judges' responses to them. Compare your observations and conclusions to Horowitz's. How similar are your court's procedures and decisions to those Horowitz describes? How do your observations and Horowitz's lead you to support particular legal reforms?

3. Some of the experts named in Horowitz's article contend that politicians think it is "'total political death' to talk about root causes" of crime. Monitor news magazines, television news programs, newspapers, and other sources of political news for what the politicians in your area have to say about the causes of crime. Write or call local officials and government representatives to get their ideas about the causes of crime. Are these politicians willing to talk about the subject? If they identify particular causes, what ideas do they have to eradicate those causes? Once you've gathered your information, write an essay analyzing how adequately political leaders, and the political system itself, are equipped to deal with the causes of crime.

FINAL JUSTICE
Limiting Death Row Appeals

Mark Hansen

> *A reporter for the* ABA Journal—*the professional magazine for attorneys in which this article first appeared—Mark Hansen examines whether death penalty appeals should be limited. Originally published in 1992, the article notes that both the courts and Congress seem to be moving toward limiting the number and types of appeals that death row convicts can make, the goal of which is to move the process more quickly from conviction to execution. By gathering information from a number of cases across the country, Hansen is able to raise questions not only about the appeals process but about the death penalty in general.*

The death of Warren McCleskey in Georgia's electric chair last fall marked a tuning point in the long and bitter national debate over capital punishment.

During his 13-year odyssey through the legal system, the 46-year-old former factory worker came to epitomize what some say are the failings in the modern administration of capital punishment.

McCleskey, who was executed Sept. 25 for the 1978 murder of an Atlanta police officer, had been the subject of two landmark rulings against death-row inmates by the U.S. Supreme Court.

Death-penalty opponents say that McCleskey's execution makes a strong argument for doing away with capital punishment altogether. To them, the Supreme Court decisions that condemned McCleskey raise the possibility that an innocent man may be put to death in violation of his constitutional rights.

But capital punishment proponents contend that McCleskey's case only shows how a death-row inmate can manipulate the legal process to stave off the execution of a lawful sentence.

To them, McCleskey's repeated appeals are typical of the seemingly endless litigation that makes a death sentence in this country neither swift nor certain.

In a final statement, McCleskey thanked his lawyers and asked the family of his victim for forgiveness. Then he accused Georgia officials of yielding to political expediency and decried the continued use of capital punishment.

"I pray that one day this country, supposedly a civilized society, will abolish this barbaric act," he said.

Civilized or not, the United States, which has about 2,500 prisoners on death row today, is the only Western democracy that still practices capital punishment. In that respect, it remains in the rather strange company of such undemocratic countries as China, Iran, Iraq and Libya. Even South Africa imposed a moratorium on executions last year and many Eastern-bloc nations have since followed suit.

Yet the death penalty, by all indications, is here to stay. Polls show that crime is the number-one concern of most Americans and that most Americans favor the death penalty. President Bush made the war on crime his top domestic priority last year and put death-penalty reform at the top of his crime-fighting agenda. And Congress is considering legislation to increase the number of crimes punishable by death, while curtailing the right of death-row prisoners to appeal their sentences.

Congress, in fact, came close to adopting a law last fall that would have expanded the death penalty to 53 new federal crimes, including, for the first time, offenses other than homicides. Previously, the death penalty had applied to only two federal crimes: airline hijackings that resulted in death and certain drug-related murders.

The proposed legislation, part of a larger anti-crime package that Bush threatened to veto for being too soft on criminals, also would have limited most prisoners to one habeas corpus appeal in the federal courts, provided it was filed within one year of their conviction.

But Bush never got a chance to follow through on his threat. The crime-fighting bill died at the hands of a Republican filibuster in the Senate on Thanksgiving eve after being passed by the House of Representatives earlier in the day.

Besides the president, who wanted tougher restrictions on habeas corpus proceedings, the compromise measure was opposed by most Republicans and Southern Democrats. Also helping to seal its fate were liberal Democrats—who objected to the expanded list of death penalty crimes—and opponents of other provisions of the bill, including one that would have imposed a national five-day waiting period on the purchase of handguns.

While the "reform" effort stalled in Congress, however, an increasingly conservative Supreme Court has continued to rewrite the book on capital punishment. In a series of decisions, beginning with McCleskey's first appeal in 1987, the Court has been doing what the president and the Congress so far have been unable to accomplish.

Led by Chief Justice William H. Rehnquist, who has championed the death-penalty reform movement in Congress, the Court's conservative wing appears to be following its own legislative agenda, according to several legal experts and constitutional scholars. And nowhere was the new majority's intent more clear, they say, than in the Court's handling of death-penalty cases last term.

"This Court seems to have a very aggressive agenda in the death penalty and habeas corpus areas," said Vivian Berger, vice dean of Columbia University's law school and general counsel for the American Civil Liberties Union. "It's almost like they've set out to do what the Congress cannot or will not do."

"There's no question that the decisions of the Court last term not only marked a tilt to the right, but a rewriting of the rules of the game," said Stephen Bright, director of the Southern Center for Human Rights in Atlanta, which handles appeals on behalf of death-row inmates. "If the Court, under this chief justice, doesn't get its way legislatively, it goes ahead and legislates anyway."

Conservatives, on the other hand, welcome the new balance of power on the Court and applaud the current majority's approach to death-penalty legislation. John Scully, a lawyer for the Washington Legal Foundation, which supports capital punishment, said the Court has made the death penalty more effective by closing some of the legal loopholes through which death-row inmates have all too often escaped their fate.

The Court issued three decisions last year with far-reaching consequences for death penalty litigants: *McCleskey v. Zant,* 111 S.Ct. 1454; *Coleman v. Thompson,* 59 U.S.L.W. 4789; and *Payne v. Tennessee,* 111 S.Ct. 2597. And two of those cases were important, experts say, for reasons other than the outcome. In *McCleskey,* the Court settled an issue that Congress had failed to resolve. In *Payne,* it solicited arguments on an issue that hadn't even been raised on appeal.

McCleskey, whose death-row appeals have been compared in influence to the *Roe v. Wade* decision in abortion law, produced two of the Court's most important rulings on capital punishment in the past decade. The first decision eliminated the last broad challenge to the death penalty on constitutional grounds. The second narrowed the avenues of appeal open to all death-row inmates.

On his first go-round, the Court upheld the constitutionality of Georgia's death penalty despite statistics showing that defendants who kill whites are far more likely to receive a death sentence than those who kill blacks. *McCleskey v. Kemp,* 481 U.S. 279.

In a 5-4 decision by Justice Lewis F. Powell Jr., the Court said that although racial bias was "an inevitable part of our criminal justice system," it didn't prove that the death penalty was inherently discriminatory. Unless a defendant could show that bias played a role in his own sentencing, the Court held that a death sentence must be affirmed.

The issue of race in capital sentencing has also been a key point of contention in congressional attempts at death-penalty reform during the last two years. In 1990, the House had included a provision in its anti-crime bill known as the Racial Justice Act, which would have set aside the Court's holding in *McCleskey v. Kemp.*

But the measure died in conference during the closing days of the 1990 session after the Senate refused to go along with it. Reintroduced last year as the Fairness in Death Sentencing Act, it was defeated once again. This time, though, the amendment never made it out of the House.

Under the act, death-row inmates would have been allowed to present statistical evidence to make an initial showing of racial bias in sentencing. If challenged, prosecutors would have had to provide an explanation other than race for the imposition of a death sentence.

Supporters of the act say the evidence of racial disparities in capital sentencing isn't hard to come by. The General Accounting Office, the investigative arm of Congress, analyzed 28 such studies in 1990, and came to the conclusion that there was "a pattern of evidence indicating racial disparities in the charging, sentencing and imposition of the death penalty."

One study by University of Michigan Law School Professor Samuel Gross and Robert Mauro, an associate professor of psychology at the University of Oregon, calculated a "death-odds multiplier" to measure the influence of race on capital cases in seven states. In Georgia, the study showed that killers of whites are nearly 10 times more likely to receive a death sentence than killers of blacks. In Florida, the ratio is about eight to one. In Illinois and Mississippi, it is six to one. And in North Carolina, about four to one.

Another study of one judicial circuit in Georgia showed that while whites represented 35 percent of murder victims, they accounted for 85 percent of the capital cases brought by local prosecutors since 1973.

Prosecutors sought the death penalty in one of three murders involving whites. When the victims were black, they asked for death in only one case out of 17.

"In a very real way, the race of the murder victim determines the outcome in death-penalty cases," said Michael Kroll, executive director of the Death Penalty Information Center, the anti-capital punishment group that conducted the Georgia study. "Although prohibited by the Constitution, a white victim often is a *de facto* aggravating factor in murder trials while a black victim appears to mitigate the crime."

But opponents of the act say the studies purporting to show racial bias in capital sentencing don't prove anything. There are too many factors that enter into a death-penalty decision to eliminate any one variable like race, they say. And there was enough evidence to the contrary to sway Congress and the Court, they point out.

"Nobody can seriously argue that a killer's death sentence was based on the race of his victim," said the Washington Legal Foundation's Scully. "It's a demonstration of their desperation in trying to come up with a plausible argument for doing away with [capital punishment]."

As a practical matter, though, supporters of capital punishment contend that such a law would spell an end to the death penalty.

"If the issue were raised, prosecutors would be placed in the position of having to prove the negative," Scully said. "And that's an impossible job."

McCleskey, however, wasn't content to make legal history once. Last April, he provided a more conservative Court another occasion to cut back on prisoners' rights, this time with a sweeping new rule that effectively eliminates the filing of successive habeas corpus claims. *McCleskey v. Zant*.

Although McCleskey had admitted being one of four men who participated in a furniture store robbery in which a police officer was killed, he maintained all along that he was not the triggerman.

His second appeal was based largely on newly discovered evidence that a fellow inmate was an informant who had been offered a secret deal by prosecutors in exchange for his testimony against McCleskey. The inmate, not surprisingly, testified that McCleskey had confessed to the killing.

A federal judge had ruled in McCleskey's favor, saying that his sentence had been tainted by the prosecution's failure to disclose the deal with his fellow inmate. But the 11th Circuit Court of Appeals in Atlanta overturned that ruling, saying that McCleskey had abused his appellate rights by raising new challenges to his sentence in successive habeas petitions rather than including them all in his first.

In a 6-3 ruling by Justice Anthony Kennedy, the Court agreed, setting out new guidelines that make it all but impossible for a death-row inmate to file multiple federal appeals. The majority said that a prisoner could not raise an issue in a habeas petition if his failure to raise it in a previous petition constituted "inexcusable neglect."

To determine what constitutes a good excuse, the Court adopted a "cause and prejudice" standard, which death-penalty litigators say is virtually insurmountable. While most death-row inmates would have no trouble showing prejudice, they would first have to clear the legal hurdle of showing cause, which the Court has defined as "some objective factor external to the defense [that] impeded counsel's effort to comply with the state's procedural rules." A simple mistake wouldn't do it.

Since McCleskey could have raised the issue in his first habeas petition, the Court said, it was inexcusable for him not to. But critics of the ruling said the Court's new standard places petitioners like McCleskey in a "Catch-22" situation, since much of the evidence to support his second claim was only uncovered after his first petition had been denied. To have raised the issue without the crucial evidence in his first petition, his lawyers would have risked violating their legal obligation not to file frivolous claims, critics said.

"It was basically a kiss-off opinion," Columbia's Berger said. "If McCleskey didn't have cause, who will?"

With McCleskey out of the way, the Court continued to change habeas corpus doctrine. And it put another obstacle in the path of death-row appeals in *Coleman v. Thompson,* this time by closing the courthouse doors to some first-time petitioners.

Roger Keith Coleman's lawyer had missed Virginia's deadline for filing his notice of appeal from the denial of state habeas relief by three days. The Court, by the same 6-3 vote with which it had decided *McCleskey,* held that Coleman's constitutional claims were barred by his lawyer's failure to comply with state procedural rules.

The decision by Justice Sandra Day O'Connor marked the reversal of a long-standing precedent for the Court, overturning a landmark 1963 ruling under which state prisoners were allowed to file federal habeas petitions as long as they did not deliberately try to bypass the state courts. *Fay v. Noia,* 372 U.S. 391. In *Coleman,* the majority replaced that standard with the same cause and prejudice test it had applied to McCleskey.

Coleman had claimed that his lawyer's failure to file a timely appeal constituted ineffective assistance of counsel, which falls within the Court's definition of cause. But since there is no constitutional right to counsel at that stage of a death-row inmate's appeal, the Court said Coleman would have to bear the burden of his lawyer's failure to follow the rules.

"It's the last in a long line of cases in which the Court has held that if a lawyer makes a mistake, the defendant pays for it with his life," Bright said.

Ira Robbins, a professor and habeas scholar at American University's Washington College of Law, said that the *Coleman* and *McCleskey* decisions pretty much sounded the death knell for the federal courts' review of an inmate's constitutional claims.

"I'm thinking of starting my lectures with, 'Once upon a time there was a writ of habeas corpus,'" Robbins said, only partly in jest. "This Court is in the business of elevating form over substance, even if it means that an inmate with a good constitutional claim will be executed. It just happened with McCleskey. And it'll happen again."

Turning their attention from the condemned to the accused, last term the majority also handed death-penalty defendants what could be their worst defeat. They did so by first finding a suitable case, *Payne v. Tennessee,* and then inviting argument on two recent rulings that the Court's conservative wing seemed eager to overturn.

In *Payne,* the Court voted 6-3 to permit victim-impact and character evidence in the sentencing phase of a capital case, overriding two recent precedents, *Booth v. Maryland,* 482 U.S. 496, in 1987, and *Gathers v. South Carolina,* 490 U.S. 805, in 1989, in which the Court had held that such evidence was irrelevant and inflammatory.

Writing for the majority, the chief justice said that because a defendant can present mitigating evidence about his character in the sentencing phase of a capital case, it would be unfair not to allow the same kind of evidence in regard to the victim. He also said the testimony is relevant because it educates jurors about the victim's uniqueness and because the assessment of harm caused by the defendant has long been a factor in determining an appropriate punishment.

The decision is likely to have two practical effects, according to experts and death-penalty litigators. First and foremost, it will probably result in a significant increase in the number of new death sentences. Second, it has the potential to turn the sentencing phase of a murder case into a kind of "moral postmortem" on the relative worth of the deceased, they say.

"Victim-impact evidence will make a big difference in capital cases," Berger said. "It exacerbates everything that is wrong with the way the death penalty operates today."

Berger and others said the use of victim-impact evidence will encourage juries to make life-and-death decisions based on value judgments about the goodness, the popularity and the appeal of the deceased, which they claim will only increase the role that race and class distinctions now play in the sentencing process.

"In reality, only good victims and their families will be vindicated in this fashion," Berger said.

Moreover, if prosecutors are allowed to present positive character evidence about the victim, death-penalty litigators say it may in turn open the door for the defense to present evidence to the contrary.

"What it does is remove the pretense that all people are equal before the law," said David Bruck, director and chief attorney of the South Carolina Office of Appellate Defense. "Of course, it also ignores the fact that all of this evidence about the victim was probably unknown to the murderer at the time he committed the crime."

The majority opinion also is noteworthy for its casual dismissal of precedent, according to experts and the three dissenting justices. "It demonstrates a rather cavalier attitude toward individual rights," Robbins said.

In its opinion, the majority said that adherence to the principle of *stare decisis* is not always wise, particularly in cases involving questions of evidence or procedure that were decided by narrow margins and reached over spirited dissent.

In one stinging dissent, Justice Thurgood Marshall called the majority's view "impoverished," and said the decision was only a "preview of an even broader and more far-reaching assault upon this Court's precedents." Along with a scathing critique of the majority's reasoning, Marshall listed 17 other "endangered precedents" that met the Court's new criteria for ignoring *stare decisis,* including many of its landmark civil rights cases.

"Power, not reason, is the new currency in this Court's decisionmaking," he wrote.

In another dissent, Justice John Paul Stevens accused the majority of pandering to "the current popularity of capital punishment in a crime-ridden society, the political appeal of arguments that assume that increasing the severity of sentences is the best cure for the cancer of crime and the political strength of the 'victims' rights movement.'"

But capital punishment proponents and victims' rights advocates discount the dire predictions of some. Scully, whose organization filed an amicus brief in the case on behalf of the victim's family, said the use of such evidence will bring a new and much-needed perspective to the sentencing process.

"It will show that the victim was a living, breathing person, too," he said. "And it will help show that all victims' lives are valuable and worthwhile."

Scully also rejected the notion that victims could be further victimized by the defense during the sentencing phase of a capital case. "I suspect that a defendant wouldn't have much to gain by attacking the character of the person he killed," he said. "The old cliché that one should not speak ill of the dead might come into play."

While 1991 was a bad year for death-row inmates, it could have been worse. Under the version of habeas reform sought by Bush and passed by the Senate, prisoners who received a "full and fair adjudication" of their constitutional claims on the state level would have been barred from appealing their sentences in the federal courts.

In addition to the usual collection of death-penalty foes, the Senate's crime bill drew strong opposition from an unusual coalition of forces. The Emergency Committee to Save Habeas Corpus, which included three former attorneys general and dozens of state and federal prosecutors, judges, law school professors and members of the organized bar, lobbied hard to kill the measure.

The "full and fair" standard would require only that state courts hold a procedurally correct hearing in order to preclude federal review, critics said, even if the state court decision was dead wrong.

Since more than 40 percent of all death sentences have been overturned on appeal in the federal courts, they argued that passage of the bill would result in the execution of people in violation of the Bill of Rights.

"It essentially means that if you had a trial, you had an appeal, and you weren't taken out and shot at dawn, you've had a full and fair hearing," Berger said.

What's next? The sponsors of the now-defunct crime bill have vowed to resurrect their fight. The chief justice renewed his call for habeas reform in his year-end report on the federal judiciary. And the Court, having bolstered its conservative ranks with the confirmation of Clarence Thomas, already may have signaled its next order of business.

The Court agreed Dec. 18 to hear an appeal by Virginia authorities to a federal court's decision to grant habeas corpus relief to a man in prison on a theft conviction. *Wright v. West,* No. 91-542.

In accepting the case, the Court ordered the parties to address whether federal judges should be required to defer to the findings of state courts in habeas proceedings rather than reweigh the issues themselves.

Experts say the question posed by the Court raises the same concerns presented by the "full and fair" standard in the Senate's ill-fated habeas reform bill. If the Court holds that federal judges must give deference to state court decisions, it effectively will have accomplished the same end, they say.

Some said they don't believe the chief justice will be satisfied until the "full and fair" standard becomes the law of the land. "Once he gets that, the habeas writ, as we know it, will have been completely obliterated," Robbins said.

Questions for Discussion

1. Quoting liberals and conservatives alike, Hansen is careful to provide evidence from both sides of the death penalty argument. Examine his presentation of argument and his use of evidence. How and when does he introduce the words of others? To what extent do his stylistic and rhetorical decisions, for example, word choice and organization, reveal his own attitude about the Supreme Court's decisions on the death penalty?
2. What types of evidence and testimony does Hansen use? Which are most convincing? Why?
3. Hansen cites legal experts on both sides of the issue who acknowledge that death penalty convictions are more common in cases involving white victims than those involving black victims. Some argue that the statistical evidence shows a clear pattern of discrimination and, therefore, the possibility of discrimination must be assumed in a given case; others argue that the burden of proof of discrimination must rest with the individual defendant and his or her legal counsel. Where do you stand on this issue? What leads you to your conclusion?
4. The article mentions that some people are concerned that accused criminals might have to pay for mistakes made by their attorneys. How serious is such a concern? How important should this concern be in any consideration of what the law should be?

Questions for Writing and Research

1. When Hansen wrote his article, the Supreme Court was about to accept a case involving a Virginia court's appeal of "a federal court's decision to grant habeas corpus relief to a man in prison on a theft conviction." Locate and read the court's decision in *Wright v. West*. Does it bear out the fears that "the habeas writ, as we know it, will [be] completely obliterated?"
2. Hansen notes early in the article that the United States, in continuing to use the death penalty, "remains in the strange company of such undemocratic countries as China, Iran, Iraq and Libya." Find a discussion of death penalty laws in these countries. In what ways do they differ in attitude or substance from the laws in the United States? Or find a discussion of why other Western industrial nations, like Great Britain or France, have abolished the death penalty. How might proponents of the death penalty in the United States respond to these arguments for abolishing it?
3. The article suggests that most Americans believe the death penalty is a deterrent to crime. Survey about twenty-five people about their attitudes toward the death penalty. Whatever their stance, on what do they base their conclusions about how criminals and prospective criminals respond to the prospect of capital punishment?

4. For proponents and opponents alike, discussions of the death penalty often become emotional. Monitor news reports and editorials, on television, in the newspapers, and in popular magazines. Do the speakers and writers rely primarily on emotional or logical appeals? Are the foundations of their argumentative appeals legal? Moral? Social? How does the medium in which the argument is presented enable you to predict not only the argument itself but also the rhetorical devices used?

IS THE LAW MALE?
Lynn Hecht Schafran

> *A number of factors, including race, gender, ethnicity, and social class, may well influence our responses to the legal system. This article was published in 1995 in the magazine* Trial, *read mostly by trial attorneys; it is a revised version of ideas that appeared earlier in a symposium in the* Chicago Law Review. *Lynn Hecht Schafran, a project director for the National Organization for Women's Legal Defense and Education Fund, explores how a male bias in thinking about the law may affect both legislation and litigation. Are women's experiences fundamentally different from those of men, and if so, do these differences require us to change the way law is taught and practiced in this country? Schafran's article not only explores basic principles but offers some practical reforms for consideration. Do you think, as the author suggests, that the law and legal practice must recognize the "diversity of human experience"?*

The question "Is the law male?" will be understood by some readers on sight, puzzled over by others as a conundrum, and dismissed by still others as a joke. One way to understand its import is by analogy to how women are treated by the medical profession.

The public has recently become aware of a set of issues that women's health advocates have been discussing for years: the male body as the standard for medical training, research, and treatment. The "maleness" of medicine has been manifested in the use of the male disease model as the norm in medical schools and in the standard definitions of illnesses, in the exclusion of women from clinical drug trials, and in Congress's failure to fund research into women's health problems while putting major money into the illnesses that beset men.

Adherence to the male model in medical schools has meant that physicians are not taught that breast and pelvic exams are part of a complete physical; not taught that illnesses such as ulcers, heart disease, lupus, rheumatoid arthritis, and gallbladder disease affect women and men differently; and not taught to appreciate the psychological impact on women of radical mastectomy and hysterectomy. What medical students have learned is that it is acceptable to tell women to cut off their breasts and cut out their uteri as soon as they are finished having babies.[1]

The use of the male disease model in defining illness has had acute repercussions for female victims of AIDS.[2] Female AIDS victims rarely get Kaposi's sarcoma, an AIDS-related cancer frequently seen in male AIDS victims. But they do get cervical cancer, candidiasis, and pelvic inflammatory disease. Because physicians were locked into the male model of what AIDS looked like, they failed to diagnose and properly treat many female

AIDS victims. Until 1991, the male model of AIDS was also the standard definition used by the Social Security Administration to award disability payments, which locked female victims out of the payments they desperately needed to support themselves and their families.

Women's exclusion from drug trials has made men's response to new drugs the standard, with the result that doctors have little knowledge of how women's physiology and hormones are actually affected by these medicines.[3] For example, the fact that women absorb antidepressants and tranquilizers at a different rate than men has implications for dosages.

In one case, an antidepressant approved without being tested on women caused more seizures in women than in men because of the difference in absorption patterns.

With respect to medical research, a study demonstrating the efficacy of aspirin in reducing heart attacks included 22,071 men and no women. Physicians reading the results of this study had no way of knowing whether women, too, should take aspirin on a preventative basis. One study that determined that heavy caffeine ingestion from coffee drinking did not increase the risk of heart disease and strokes used 45,589 subjects, all male.[4] Women who read this study were not told that caffeine has unique risks for women, such as fibrous cysts of the breast. They were also not told that these risks were not a part of the study and that the findings were gender-specific to men.[5] As to why the overwhelmingly male Congress funded research into heart disease in men while ignoring women's diseases like osteoporosis and breast cancer,[6] Rep. Patricia Schroeder (D-Colo.) observed, "You fund what you fear."[7]

Similarly, the law has treated men's life experience and perspective as the norm. For example, rape laws are a codification of men's fears of false accusations. Fortunately, for more than a decade, a growing number of women in the law and some of our male colleagues have been "asking the woman question," as Duke University law professor Katharine Bartlett puts it, "designed to identify the gender implications of rules and practices which might otherwise appear to be neutral or objective."[8] The "maleness" of law is expressed in many different ways—among them laws and regulations; the cases that lawyers take or refuse; what is taught in law schools; and how judges, juries, and other decision makers interpret, apply, and enforce the laws—and in many, many more areas than is usually realized.

LAWS AND REGULATIONS

Until recently the law was literally man-made, since there were no female legislators, lawyers, or judges, and the consequences for women were not pretty. Women were denied the right to vote, own property, enter into contract, sue in their own names, serve on juries, have custody of their children, or engage in many different types of employment.

During the confirmation hearings for U.S. Supreme Court Justice Ruth Bader Ginsburg, the review of the Supreme Court cases that established her as a pioneer litigator for women's legal rights reminded us that less than 25 years ago Idaho had a law that automatically gave gender preference to men when equally entitled petitioners sought to become estate executors.[9] And the Social Security Act provided less protection to the survivors of working women than to those of working men.[10]

Apart from the rape laws,[11] state and federal laws have been largely purged of their overt anti-woman content. But there are still instances in which "rules and practices which... appear to be neutral"[12] are not. Immigration laws and policies are a paradigm example in their repeated failure to comprehend and allow for the role of domestic violence, rape, and poverty in women's lives.

The Marriage Fraud Amendments of 1986,[13] which were directed at couples married for less than two years, effectively barred battered women who were conditional residents from leaving the abusive relationship. It took four years, but in 1990 feminist lawyers and legislators succeeded in adding a waiver provision to the law that would allow these women to obtain residency status without filing a joint petition with their husbands to remove conditional status.[14]

Then, in 1991, the Immigration and Naturalization Service (INS) issued an interim rule that eviscerated the waiver for victims of "extreme cruelty" such as kidnapping or threats who had not experienced physical violence. The INS required these victims to submit the affidavit of a licensed clinical social worker, psychologist, or psychiatrist attesting to the abuse. Feminist lawyers pointed out that abused immigrant women can rarely locate mental health professionals, much less afford their services.[15]

Feminist legal advocates are still seeking to remedy this inequity and also provide help to abused women in marriages of more than two years' duration who do not have conditional residency. Under the Immigration and Nationality Act,[16] the petition for residency for the alien spouse must be filed by the permanent resident or citizen spouse. The battered alien wife fears that reporting her husband to the police will lead to her deportation, and the husband effectively holds her hostage by refusing to petition for her residency. The federal Violence Against Women Act, which became law in August 1994, allows for self-petitioning by the alien spouse.[17]

Women gang-raped in Haiti and El Salvador because of male family members' political activity have been seeking asylum in the United States.[18] Given how reluctant U.S. women are to report rape to our own authorities,[19] and given the torment experienced by the few immigrant women who have told—or been too ashamed to tell—their stores of rape to U.S. judges,[20] it is painful to learn that the Clinton administration has proposed a plan that would expedite the exclusion of asylum seekers at ports of entry but does not take into account these rape cases. As Hope

Frye, president of the American Immigration Lawyers Association, said, "It's just not possible for a woman to tell a stranger in uniform at a foreign airport the grisly details of how she was gang-raped by people in uniform in her own country."[21]

SHOULD I TAKE HER CASE?

A threshold issue for civil plaintiffs and crime victims is getting into court, which usually requires getting a lawyer to believe in the case. A lawyer who does not realize what he or she[22] does not know about the social and economic realities of women's lives,[23] and who buys into—however unwittingly—the misogynist myths about women's credibility,[24] plays a role in denying women access to justice. A story about a sexual harassment case illustrates this.

A few years ago the Washington, D.C., judicial conference included a presentation on sexism in torts and damages. The judge who organized the panel contacted several lawyers in the hope of finding female plaintiffs as speakers. One lawyer responded with a long letter. I quote extensively from this letter because it provides a singular evocation of what our profession has yet to learn about women's lives, and how that ignorance affects our advocacy and women's access to the courts. The lawyer wrote:

> I had especially hoped to obtain the assistance of one particular former client, whose case was most enlightening to me as an attorney. This lady called several times, nearly hysterical. . . . I tried to avoid talking to her, because she seemed crazy. Finally, our receptionist persuaded me to meet with this lady. Our initial conference started off strangely, as the prospective client asked if I could give her several large manila envelopes. I did, and she placed them strategically on the leather of the chair, before sitting. She explained that she was so upset by the events, that she would sweat profusely whenever she thought about her case.
>
> When she came to my office, she was the chief telephone operator for her private employer. She claimed that the distinguished man who headed the division in which she was employed had harassed her repeatedly, and in most outrageous ways. For instance, as she was photocopying papers, he came up from behind and pressed himself against her buttocks. On one occasion, he called, said it was his birthday, and asked why she had not brought him a card. During lunch, she bought a card and brought it over to his office. He closed the door, grabbed her, kissed her, and brought a hand up under her blouse to touch her breasts. He would call her up, promising "to light such a fire on her tail" that she would never want any other man afterward.
>
> This lady rebuffed and resisted these advances, which occurred in private, without suffering any consequences. But, when on one

occasion he tried to touch her while he was in the company of several of his male assistants, she slapped his hand away. Then, all hell broke loose. Everything she did on the job was wrong, and he devoted himself to breaking her spirit and making her an outcast.

As crazy as all of this sounded, I told this lady I would not represent her until I had spoken with her psychiatrist and psychologist. The client agreed and got up to leave, but first threw away the manila envelopes, which were indeed soaked.

I spoke to her psychiatrist. . . . He told me that there was no evidence of fabrication, and he believed her story. Her psychologist concurred, so we plunged ahead.

The case was assigned to Judge X, and full discovery was held. Still, as of a few days before pre-trial, there was no independent corroboration, and my only strength was the believability of my client. Then, an unrelated woman employed in a different area at the same institution called and asked for an appointment. She came in and told her tale. It turned out that she had been harassed by the same man, in many of the same ways. She was quite willing to be a witness and also directed me to a third person, in yet another department, with similar experiences at this man's hands.

Amazingly, my client and the other two ladies had all brought their complaints to their employer's internal Equal Employment Opportunity Commission office. When a request was made to add these two witnesses at pre-trial, and Judge X discovered that the defendants had known of these other complaints, the case settled rather quickly. . . .

Now the reason I have burdened you with such a long letter is because of my feeling that the objective at this judicial conference is extremely important. I do not think I am any less sensitive than most lawyers, but in this case, I was about to reject a meritorious case because it seemed to be too awful to believe. And I was mistaking the client's desperate cries for justice with hysteria.

I am not saying that I have learned how to do this without making mistakes, but all of us, lawyers and judges, need to remember that unspeakable acts are sometimes committed even by respected people and that the most severely injured of their victims may be the hardest to believe.[25]

This is a moving letter, and I thank the lawyer who wrote it for his willingness to expose his own ignorance in order to further reform. I consider the crucial point of his letter the phrase "[a]s *crazy* as all of this sounded" (emphasis supplied) after the description of the harassment this woman had endured. I believe in verifying clients' allegations, but why did he perceive this woman's story as "crazy"? It certainly does not sound crazy to me.

Georgetown University Law Center professor]Robin West has written about the often strikingly different reactions of women and men to the statistics and specifics about violence and harassment against women. She asks, "Why is my reaction so *different* [than men's]?"

> I attribute it to this: my reality—both internal and external—includes that violence, the pain it causes, and the fear it engenders. Not only have I lived it (and they haven't), but I talk to women (and they don't) and women talk to me (and not them). Like all women I know, I hear narratives of violence which are not heard by any man with the sometimes exception of male therapists. My male colleagues think my neighborhood is safe; they weren't told (I was) the details of a recent rape. I *hear* about the date rapes of students . . . ; my male colleagues do not. . . . I *hear* (men don't) about marital violence. . . . I *hear* women's memories of early sexual abuse. . . . I draw this simple inference: Women and men have wildly different "ignorant" intuitions about the amount of danger, violence, and fear in women's lives because women live it and men don't, and women *tell* other women and not men.[26]

WHAT IS TAUGHT IN LAW SCHOOLS?

Making women's real life experiences visible and understood as they relate to the law means, for example, informing the profession about the actual rates of sexual and domestic assault against women as well as the omnipresent fear of this pervasive violence. This needs to begin in the law schools.

A University of Kentucky law professor[27] begins the rape section of her criminal law course by asking each male student to tell the class what he does on a daily basis to protect himself from sexual assault. The response is a puzzled silence.

Then she asks the female students, each of whom has something to say: I do not go to a certain mall because its parking lot is badly lit. Before I get into my car I look to see if anyone is in the back seat. I do not come to campus at times when there will not be many people around. I sleep with my windows locked no matter what the weather.

The first time the law professor tried this teaching technique one woman said, "I don't worry about anything anymore. I carry a loaded gun," and opened her handbag to take out a pistol. Each year the men in the class are stunned to learn that the fear of rape is a daily reality for their female colleagues and in many ways conditions their lives.[28]

When law professors teach this kind of material without being fully informed themselves, the results can distort reality and mislead students. A few years ago I learned that a lawyer teaching the law and psychiatry course at a New York law school had told his class that it was a good thing if police did not arrest the batterer when they responded in a wife beating case.

When I contacted him, the professor said that he was not teaching that the police should do nothing. He was advocating that they should take the batterer to a hospital for a shot of Thorazine. When I told him that the incidence of domestic violence is not confined to a few men having psychotic episodes, but is in fact an epidemic that crosses all economic, racial, religious, and ethnic lines and is minimally estimated to affect 2 million women every year,[29] he was shocked.

IS THE LAW MALE? LET ME COUNT THE WAYS

In my 1989 book, *Promoting Gender Fairness Through Judicial Education: A Guide to the Issues and Resources,* I listed more than 50 substantive and procedural areas in which gender enters the legal arena. Obviously, the book was written as a tool for developing judicial education programs for judges, lawyers, and law students. But the title can suggest a double meaning.

"Judicial education" is not just what goes on at the National Judicial College or a circuit conference. Lawyers educate judges in the course of every case. Lawyers are the essential complement to the other kind of judicial education, especially because judges have very different notions of what they can take judicial notice of, and they want lawyers to bring this information into the courts.

Promoting Gender Fairness Through Judicial Education covers subjects ranging from abuse and neglect to trial skills, with issues, such as driving while intoxicated, medical negligence, municipal liability, and law and psychiatry in between. The section covering law and psychiatry, for example, addresses a host of gender-related issues, such as battered woman's syndrome and rape-related post-traumatic stress disorder. It also provides research showing how sex-stereotyping can color mental health professionals' evaluations and expert witness testimony in a multitude of legal contexts.

Blaming mothers but not fathers for their children's problems is rampant in the professional literature. Mothers have been indicted for 72 kinds of psychopathology in children, ranging from stuttering to schizophrenia.[30] Although current research demonstrates the fallacy of blaming mothers and points to the genetic origin of many of these problems, not all practitioners have discarded this fallacy.

Stereotyping women as passive and dependent can affect mental health professionals' assessments of competency and fitness in women who are in fact assertive and independent.[31] Research indicates that gender bias among social workers is nearly always against women, and social workers tend to adhere to traditional male and female sex roles, damning the mother or father who does not conform to traditional sex roles in parenting or work.[32]

Lawyers using any psychological testing should be aware of the biases there. For example, in the widely used Minnesota Multiphasic Personality Inventory, responses by female victims of domestic violence may produce results similar to those produced by paranoid personalities.[33] There is an ongoing fight over the *Diagnostic and Statistical Manual of Mental Disorders'* addition of diagnostic categories such as "Self-Defeating Personality Disorder" that can be wrongly used to describe women trapped in abusive situations.[34]

SPREADING THE GOSPEL

The title of this article comes from a series of continuing legal education programs presented by the American Bar Association's Commission on Women in the Profession. In addition to encouraging the audiences at its "Is the Law Male?" programs to learn about feminist legal theory because it enhances advocacy, the commission charges its audiences with bringing this knowledge to their male and female colleagues and encouraging them to use it.

Undoubtedly, many of you reading this have just said to yourselves, "The men I know in this profession are not going to come to a program called 'Is the Law Male?'" And you are right. That is why, when you want to be sure that men as well as women will attend, you should avoid using words such as male, female, gender, and feminist in the program titles. Instead, integrate the material into continuing legal education programs for your local and state bars, your own law office if you conduct in-house training programs, and any teaching you do at law schools.

The 1992 *Report of the Select Committee on Gender Equality of the Maryland Judiciary and the Maryland State Bar Association* provides a model. This report states that by using *Promoting Gender Fairness Through Judicial Education,* the Judicial Institute of Maryland has included gender issues in the following list of programs:

1. Specialty Topics in Addiction
2. The Right to Forego Treatment
3. Marital Property
4. Mental Health Issues Affecting Maryland Courts
5. Contempt
6. Fairness in the Courtroom
7. Demeanor and Efficiency in the Courtroom
8. The Use of Experts in Disputed Custody Cases
9. Expert Testimony in Juvenile and Domestic Court
10. Handling the Chronic Youthful Offender
11. Emergency Ex-Parte Orders
12. Alternative Dispute Resolution
13. Race and the Criminal Process
14. Employment Law[35]

The effectiveness of this integrated approach in attracting an audience is illustrated by a story from Justice Rosalie Wahl of the Minnesota Supreme Court, chair of the Minnesota Task Force for Gender Fairness in the Courts. At a statewide meeting of judges, a session on family law was so popular that judges "were fighting to get into the room."

The session was actually the pilot test of a curriculum on spousal and child support created by the Women Judges' Fund for Justice.[36] Afterward, Wahl overheard two male judges discussing the program and saying, "Well thank goodness we don't have any of this gender stuff—gender education—this time." As Wahl said, "The funny thing is . . . we had a *half day* of it! They didn't even recognize it! It may be that when you label it, some of them don't like it, but they don't recognize it when they see it."[37]

Avoiding program titles with words like "gender" in them is not cowardice. Integrating gender issues throughout legal and judicial training under substantive law headings is the best way to ensure that these issues will not be perceived as something tangential to the real work of the courts.

If these issues are integrated consistently and repeatedly into education programs for law students, lawyers, and the judiciary, then women's perspectives will eventually become integrated into the law and legal practice. Programs titled "Is the Law Male?" will become meaningless once the diversity of human experience is fully recognized.

Notes

1. Isadore Rosenfeld, "Health Care for Women: Taking Affirmative Action," *Vogue,* Feb. 1993, at 134.
2. Philip J. Hilts, "AIDS Definition Excludes Women, Congress Is Told," *N.Y. Times,* June 7, 1991, at A19.
3. Philip J. Hilts, "F.D.A. Ends Ban on Women in Drug Testing," *N.Y. Times,* Mar. 25, 1993, at B8; Reuters, "Heart Research Gaps Are Criticized," *N.Y. Times,* Sept. 16, 1992, at C14.
4. Katrine Ames, "Our Bodies, Their Selves," *Newsweek,* Dec. 17, 1990, at 60, 60.
5. Mary Rose Oakar (D-Ohio), "Caffeine Health Study Excluded Women," *N.Y. Times,* Oct. 11, 1990, at A24 (Letter to the Editor).
6. Heart disease is the biggest killer of women, and men also get breast cancer. The widely held belief that women do not have heart attacks, however, has meant that women have been ignored in the medical research, and that treatment for female victims of heart disease has been too little and too late. Grace Lichtenstein, "Crimes of the Heart," *Mirabella,* Sept. 1992, at 154.
7. Karen Tumulty, "Women in Congress Issue Ultimatum on Abortion," *L.A. Times,* Sept. 15, 1993, at A5, A8.
8. Katharine T. Bartlett, "Feminist Legal Methods," 103 *Harv. L. Rev.* 829, 837 (1990).
9. *Reed v. Reed,* 404 U.S. 71 (1971).
10. *Weinberger v. Weinberger,* 420 U.S. 636 (1975).
11. Dorothy E. Roberts, "Rape, Violence, and Women's Autonomy," 69 *Chi.-Kent L. Rev.* 359 (1993). Rape laws continue to express a supremely male view of the world in their premise, absurd to women but a wishful truth for men, that every

woman is willing to have sex with any man at any time. It is no accident that it was during Indira Gandhi's tenure as prime minister that India switched the burden of proof in rape cases to require men to prove consent. Rafiq Zakaria, *N.Y. Times,* Oct. 20, 1991, at A14 (Letter to the Editor).
12. *See supra* note 8 and accompanying text.
13. Pub. L. No. 99-639, 100 Stat. 3537 (1986).
14. 8 C.F.R. §216.5 (1994).
15. Martha F. Davis & Janet M. Calvo, "INS Interim Rule Diminishes Protection for Abused Spouses and Children," 68 *Interpreter Releases,* June 3, 1991, at 665.
16. 8 U.S.C. §§1101–1525 (1988).
17. H.R. 1133, 103d Cong., 1st Sess. (1993).
18. Deborah Sontag, "Asking for Asylum in U.S., Women Tread New Territory," *N.Y. Times,* Sept. 27, 1993, at A1, A13.
19. Victim studies disclose extremely low rates of rape reporting. Findings range from a high of 16 percent (*National Victim Center & Crime Victims Research and Treatment Center, Rape in America: A Report to the Nation* 6 [1992]) to a low of only 7 percent (*Majority Staff of the Senate Comm. on the Judiciary, 102d Cong., 1st Sess., Violence Against Women: The Increase of Rape in America 1990* 7 [Comm. Print 1991], reprinted in "Violence Against Women: Victims of the System, Hearings on S. 15 Before the Senate Comm. on the Judiciary," 102d Cong., 1st Sess. 180, 194 [1992]).

Rape victims are reluctant to report because they fear retaliation, disbelief, the loss of privacy, and the criminal justice system. Lynn Hecht Schafran, "Writing and Reading About Rape: A Primer," 66 *St. John's L. Rev.* 979, 1013–17 (1993).
20. Sontag, *supra* note 18, at A13.
21. *Id.*
22. Being a woman, even a feminist woman, does not automatically confer knowledge. For example, in her recent *Atlantic* article, "Feminism's Identity Crisis," noted feminist Wendy Kaminer wrote, "[I]n some feminist circles it is heresy to suggest that . . . being raped by your date may not be as traumatic or terrifying as being raped by a stranger who breaks into your bedroom in the middle of the night." *Atlantic Monthly,* Oct. 1993, at 51, 67. Kaminer is apparently unaware that extensive clinical research has shown that a victim's response and recovery are not determined by the relationship between rapist and victim nor the amount of force used to accomplish the rape. Victims of nonstranger rape (the vast majority of victims) often have a more difficult time recovering because the rape was accomplished by gaining the victim's confidence, thus shattering the rape victim's ability to trust anyone again. Schafran, *supra* note 19, at 1018–20 and cites therein.
23. Lynn Hecht Schafran, "Credibility in the Courts: Why Is There a Gender Gap?" 34 *Judges' J.,* Winter 1995, at 5.
24. Lynn Hecht Schafran, "The Less Credible Sex," 24 *Judges' J.,* Winter 1985, at 16.
25. Letter to a judge of the Superior Court of the District of Columbia concerning the 1988 Washington, D.C., Judicial Conference on Racism, Sexism, and Gender Orientation in the Law (Apr. 26, 1988) (for reasons of confidentiality, the names of the lawyer and the judge have been omitted).
26. Robin L. West, "The Difference in Women's Hedonic Lives: A Phenomenological Critique of Feminist Legal Theory," 3 *Wis. Women's L. J.* 81 (1987) (paper prepared for the Feminism and Legal Theory Conference: University of Wisconsin Law School [1986]).
27. Carolyn S. Bratt, Professor of Law, University of Kentucky; B.A. 1965, SUNY at Albany; J.D. 1974, Syracuse University.

28. Margaret T. Gordon & Stephanie Riger, *The Female Fear* (1988).
29. "1986 Bureau of Justice Statistics as Cited in Women, Violence, and the Law: A Fact Sheet: Hearings Before the House Select Comm. on Children, Youth, and Families," 100th Cong., 1st Sess. 3 (1988).
30. Paula J. Caplan & Ian Hall-McCorquodale, "Mother Blaming in Major Clinical Journals," 55 *Am. J. Orthopsychiatry* 345 (1985).
31. *Bias in Psychotherapy* (Joan Murray & Paul R. Abramson eds., 1983).
32. Dennis M. Dailey, "Are Social Workers Sexists? A Replication," 25 *Soc. Work* 46 (1980).
33. Lynne Bravo Rosewater, "The Clinical and Courtroom Application of Battered Women's Personality Assessments," in *Domestic Violence on Trial* 86, 89–90 (Daniel Jay Sonkin ed., 1987).
34. Joan Einwohner, "Controversy Over DSM IIIR Psychiatric Categories Continues to Grow Throughout the Country," 38 *N.Y. St. Psychologist* 19 (1987); *see* Brina Caplan, "Crazy by Definition," *Savvy*, Sept. 1986, at 82.
35. *Report of the Select Committee on Gender Equality of the Maryland Judiciary and the Maryland State Bar Association* 5–6 (1992).
36. The Women Judges' Fund for Justice is the 501(c)(3) education arm of the National Association of Women Judges.
37. As quoted in Jeannette F. Swent, *Gender Bias at the Seat of Justice: An Empirical Study of State Task Forces* 74 (1992).

Questions for Discussion

1. Schafran suggests that men and women will respond differently to the title she's given her article. How did you respond to it? In what ways do you think your background—your gender, your cultural, racial, or ethnic identity, even your political or religious beliefs—has influenced the response you had?
2. How effective is Schafran's analogy of the field of law to the field of medicine? In what ways are the two professions similar in their "maleness"? In what ways are they different? Do you think the origins and consequences of such male-dominated ways of thinking are similar in the two fields?
3. According to Schafran and others, the law is male because its most powerful practitioners—legislators, judges, and attorneys—have, until recently, been almost exclusively male. Similar claims could, perhaps, be made about many professions that have been dominated by one gender or another. Medicine, law, and business have been traditionally "male" professions while nursing and teaching elementary and high school have been traditionally "female" professions. How has gender played a role in our perceptions of the practitioners in these professions and in the way the professions operate? Given the fact that gender barriers have begun to break down, to what extent do you think the professions themselves are changing?
4. Schafran argues that law schools need to change the way law is taught, taking into consideration women's experiences. Do you agree with her?

Should your own teachers approach their disciplines differently to recognize the "diversity of human experience"?

Questions for Research and Writing

1. Schafran asserts that many laws—especially those governing issues of family relations, domestic violence, and sexual relations—are subtly anti-women. Examine laws governing marriage and divorce, child custody, property rights, sexual misconduct, or immigration in your state. Do you detect the anti-women bias Schafran sees? (In doing your research, you might begin with the resources listed in Schafran's own book, *Promoting Gender Fairness through Judicial Education* [1989]).

2. Schafran quotes Professor Robin West's contentions that she and her male colleagues have different reactions to statistics and reports about violence against women because "women live it and men don't, and women *tell* other women [about the danger and violence] and not men" (paragraph 19). Select a recent report about violence against women in your area, and then poll men and women about their reactions to it. To what extent do your findings corroborate Schafran's? (If you prefer, you might do a similar study about violence or bias directed against another group: members of a racial, ethnic, or religious group; homosexuals; people with a particular disability; or men.)

3. Schafran tells us that one law professor at the University of Kentucky polls her students about the precautions they take to protect themselves from sexual assault. Conduct a similar poll among your peers, taking note not only of their words but of their nonverbal responses to your question. Do men and women respond differently to the question? To the idea of the poll itself?

THE RIGHT TO PRIVACY
High-Tech Monitoring in the Workplace

Ellen Alderman and Caroline Kennedy

>   *Advances in communication and technology have clearly changed both our attitudes toward the issue of privacy and our responses to conflict over privacy concerns. Many of us consider privacy one of our most basic and essential rights as Americans, but new electronic databases, communications systems, and surveillance methods may well be encroaching on those rights. In their book* The Right to Privacy *(1995), the authors of the following selection—both attorneys in their thirties—use a number of court decisions to explore the ways in which the legal concept of privacy is being continually defined and redefined in law enforcement, the media, government, and the workplace. In this chapter from the section on privacy and the workplace, the authors present a case that has widespread implications for the use of technology in work environments.*

Alana Shoars is one of those lucky workers who seem to have all the training they will need to succeed in the rapidly changing, technology-driven workplace of the future. Alana breezily offers to demonstrate the three different kinds of e-mail on her desk while describing the virtues and technological challenges of synchronizing worldwide e-mail systems—not to mention the cost advantages! "For instance," Alana volunteers, "I can tell you that to send a one-page electronic message to New York, it costs sixteen cents. To send the same message by fax, it'll be $1.86, by telex $4.35." A true believer, no wonder she has been hired to proselytize for e-mail communication.

Alana says that at her previous job she increased e-mail usage from 48 percent of employees to 94 percent in about nine months—that is, she claims, before she was fired for trying to protect the system.

In March of 1989, Alana was hired as an e-mail administrator for Epson America, Inc., the American subsidiary of the giant Japanese electronics manufacturer. An e-mail system was already in place among the seven hundred employees at the company's Torrance, California, location. During Alana's tenure, the system was connected via MCI to other Epson subsidiaries as well as the 8 million other potential correspondents on the MCI Mail network.

According to Alana, the most important factor in increasing e-mail usage is ensuring confidentiality. She says employees will choose to use the system only if they believe that their communications are private, just like their traditional mail. Thus, ensuring confidentiality was a big part of Alana's job at Epson. In her e-mail training sessions, she instructed employees in the mechanics of selecting a password, the importance of not disclosing that password to anyone, and the procedure for changing the password if it no longer appeared to be secret. According to Alana, under directions from management—and often in the presence of her supervisor, Robert Hillseth—she guaranteed her colleagues that the system was secure and that neither she nor anyone else at Epson had access to their passwords.

In the fall of 1989, Alana began to get a funny feeling about Robert Hillseth. On a couple of occasions, she had walked into his office and noticed that e-mail messages were displayed on his terminal, only to have him, as she describes it, "hit a key real quick to clear it up or blank it out." Alana thought it was "kind of unusual" because, she says, "people don't usually do that unless they're trying to hide something." Also, she recalls that a few colleagues had questioned her about the security of the system, saying that in meetings Hillseth seemed to display "extra knowledge."

Shoars' suspicions peaked on December 20, 1989, when she walked into Hillseth's office to use the phone. She noticed a stack of computer messages on his desk—in fact, all the e-mail messages transmitted to or from the Torrance facility in August and September. Alana was not only horrified, she took it personally. She had no idea how Hillseth could have managed to get hold of what she understood to be confidential messages. She later learned that he had intercepted them as they passed through the electronic gateway between Epson's internal e-mail system and MCI Mail. Worried about what she might be getting into, she picked up a six-inch bundle of pages from the printout and took them with her.

Alana claims she told no one, fearing that e-mail usage among her coworkers would decline, but decided to confront Hillseth in the hope that he would stop. In brief, she says, "he became livid, told me it was none of my damn business what he did, and I'd better keep my mouth shut. He said I would leave the company before he did." Alana adds, "He was right." She also made an appointment with the CEO, who told her he would "take the matter under advisement."

Instead, according to Shoars, on January 25, 1990, Hillseth called her into another office, shoved an envelope at her, and said, "You're terminated immediately." She says he accused her of obtaining her own personal MCI Mail account against company policy, constituting gross insubordination—and he had two intercepted e-mail messages to prove it.

Alana claims that the accusation was a pretext. She explains that she had inquired via e-mail into the possibility of obtaining such an account directly from MCI for her home computer, and Hillseth had misread the message. She also claims that he misread a second message in which a colleague notified Alana that a trial account was in place on the system and she was eligible to test it.

On the other hand, Hillseth asserted that he had printed out and flipped through the electronic messages solely to make sure that the newly installed system was working properly, and to check on problems being reported by users.

Alana also believes that in order to intimidate her, Hillseth falsely told other Epson employees that she "had a gun and had threatened to come back and shoot people." Alana believes he had a phone call placed summoning the local police so that when she left the building she had to cross a phalanx of police officers to get to her car. "I was digging around in my purse for my keys, without my glasses, and the next thing I know these guys have their hands on their guns!"

Alana Shoars' next step was to find a lawyer. Attorney Noel Shipman filed two lawsuits against Epson: a personal suit for wrongful discharge (based on her termination for reporting what she believed to be wrongdoing) and slander (based upon the description of her as a deranged individual with a gun); and a class action suit for invasion of privacy under the California state constitution and California statutes. The privacy suit was filed on March 12, 1991, on behalf of Alana Shoars and seventy-seven other Epson employees at the Torrance facility whose e-mail had been intercepted between August 4 and September 29, 1989. Along with Alana's declaration, Shipman produced over 650 pages of hard copies of e-mail transmissions—the stack Alana had taken with her on December 20.

To Alana, the secret nature of Epson's monitoring was most offensive. What Hillseth had done was wrong, she says, as wrong as reading someone else's mail or listening in on their phone conversations—communications which are protected by law and custom. "I know I'm not supposed to go to somebody else's mailbox and read their mail," says Alana. "I've never seen that in print anywhere, but I know my mother told me that."

Both Alana and her lawyer would soon discover, however, that where e-mail is concerned, such homegrown values are murky at best. And so is the law. Shipman and Shoars were quite surprised to discover that there was no California law specifically covering e-mail. So Alana set out to make some. Quite unexpectedly, she found herself a pioneer in the no-man's-land where rapidly advancing technology has left the law behind.

In order to evaluate Alana's state constitutional claim, the California court had to answer the familiar question: Did Alana and the other Epson employees have an expectation of privacy in their e-mail? From Alana's point of view, the obvious answer was yes. "If there was no expectation of privacy, then we wouldn't have had any passwords," she says. Just like a PIN number on a bank account, the passwords were meant to keep uninvited "visitors" out.

At the heart of Epson's argument, on the other hand, was the idea that what happened to Epson e-mail was up to Epson's management. E-mail belonged to the provider of the service, they claimed, not to the employees who had sent it. Epson's attorney Rick Krantz explains: "Electronic mail is a business device used in a business environment for a business purpose. There is no other purpose for it. It's sitting on a table provided by the employer with the hardware and the software provided by an employer for only one reason, and that reason is to make the employee more efficient." In an increasingly competitive world with razor-thin margins of success, to expect an employer to provide hardware, software, and necessary technical support other than for its own use is simply "not rational," according to Epson's general counsel, Judy Bain.

Epson considered e-mail to be a new tool of business communication which, like the old tools—interoffice memos, business files, and equipment—belongs to the employer. They relied in part on a 1987 Supreme Court case, *O'Connor v. Ortega* which upheld a supervisor's search of an employee's office, desk, and files in a public-sector workplace. The Court held that the employee did have an expectation of privacy in those areas, but that a search of them need only be "reasonable under all circumstances" to outweigh that expectation. No warrant or probable cause is required. Presumably, in a private company where employees do not have Fourth Amendment protection, the standard would be lower and the employer would have even more freedom to search an employee's files or desk. So why not e-mail as well?

Epson attorneys also point out that electronic monitoring is a valuable way for employers to discover wrongdoing by employees—for example, where there is reason to suspect theft or negligence, sexual harassment, or gambling. The most visible case involves a vice president for computer languages at Borland International, a large Silicon Valley software company. In September 1992, he defected to a rival company, Symantec Corporation. When suspicious Borland executives went to close down the man's office, they searched his e-mail box. They found messages he had sent to the Symantec CEO which Borland claims contained top-secret corporate data. They called in the police and filed a civil suit against the man and Symantec. His defense: privacy. Like Alana Shoars, the man claimed his e-mail was confidential and should not be read by his employer.

A further twist on the case shows just how far behind technology has left the law. The Santa Cruz County district attorney acknowledged that he didn't have the expertise to develop the case and allowed Borland to recommend a computer expert and cover $13,000 in prosecution costs. A judge then ordered the entire D.A.'s office removed from the case.

Even in a case of suspected wrongdoing, Noel Shipman remains unconvinced of the need to search employees' electronic files. "You can tell from the bill what they're doing, you can *ask* them what they're doing. I mean, sure, they're on your nickel and they're at the workplace, but there are limits!"

In the absence of any e-mail statute, Shipman argued that e-mail monitoring violated California's laws protecting older forms of communication, specifically telephone calls. California has a strict wiretapping law which provides that in order for anyone to listen in on a telephone conversation, *both* parties to the conversation must consent. The statute provides a $2,500 fine or up to one year in jail for "any unauthorized connection" with any "telegraph or telephone wire, line, or cable, without the consent of all parties, or any unauthorized attempt to learn the contents of any message report or communication while it is in transit over any wire line or cable." Shipman argued that although e-mail is not specifically mentioned, it is a communication captured in transit over a phone line and so the existing statute applied.

From Epson's point of view, technological times had changed. According to Judy Bain, "We have to break out of the paradigm of comparing old to new technology and examine this technology for what it is. It's new and it's different." Epson argued that the existing law applied only to telephone calls. The California legislature had not regulated e-mail; therefore, monitoring it could not be against the law.

The trial court agreed with Epson that e-mail was not covered by the California wiretapping statute. It was not the court's role to extend the law to cover e-mail; rather, the court suggested that the legislature should consider the issue. The court pointed out that the federal government, which began grappling with electronic issues in the Electronic and Communications Privacy Act of 1986, provided an exception for employers. Under ECPA, the provider of the service is not prohibited from examining it, which is just what Epson had argued in its case.

Then, on July 31, 1992, class action certification was denied in the privacy suit. The court found that Shipman failed to provide sufficient proof that Alana and the other Epson workers had an expectation of privacy in their e-mail. The court also found that the submitted e-mail messages were, "with few exceptions," business-related, and that the California state constitutional right of privacy covered only "personal information." The court found "no sufficient legal or factual basis for extending the right to privacy to cover business-oriented communications."

Alana was disappointed, but not surprised, by the judge's opinion. "You can tell he doesn't use electronic mail," she says. "Anybody who doesn't use it doesn't understand the [point of the] passwords." Alana took to signing her correspondence "Alana 'David v. Goliath' Shoars."

Perhaps the most important thing to come out of the case is a new appreciation for the importance of a clear company policy. As Rick Krantz himself says, "Despite the fact that Judy and I are representing corporate America . . . we are concerned like everyone else with our own privacy, our own rights. What we try to do is evolve a policy that makes sense for *us*. We're the ones who have to live with it, and it makes sense to me if I know my limits. . . . No, we don't check our privacy at the corporate door, but at some point we have to draw a line. It is easier in the e-mail context to draw a very bright line than it is to draw a shade."

Noel Shipman accepts the value of the policy approach, but for him it raises a new set of problems. Why should the employer, who already calls the shots, get to draw the line wherever it decides? Shipman is concerned that employees will be asked to give up their privacy rights when they are hired—and that most people will do so, in exchange for a job. "If you sign a waiver saying, 'I agree you can spy on me,' and you exchange that for a salary, you're working for a Nazi, but there you go. You've *sold* your right to privacy," says Shipman. The problem is compounded by the fact that often workers have no real choice and are not compensated for the rights they sign away.

At present, neither companies nor their workers really know what the limits are. The few rulings in the area seem to be going the employers' way, but even that trend is not sure to hold. In the electronic workplace, according to Noel Shipman, "When a worker like Alana Shoars asks, 'Do I have an expectation of privacy in the workplace?' 'Well, maybe' is the answer."

The problem of electronic privacy is growing. The number of e-mail users ballooned from 1 million in 1984 to an estimated 20 million in 1995, according to the Electronic Messaging Association and the consulting firm Arthur D. Little. The evidence suggests that electronic monitoring in general is also on the rise, by computer, by telephone, and even by hidden video cameras. A 1993 survey in *Macworld* magazine reported that 22 percent of companies engaged in searches of employee computer files, voice mail, e-mail, or other networking communications. In companies with one thousand or more employees, the figure rose to 30 percent. Based on survey results, the magazine estimated that 20 million Americans may be subject to computer monitoring on the job. It would appear that while the legality of monitoring is still somewhat unclear, companies are taking advantage of the uncertainty. Only 18 percent have any written policy regarding electronic privacy.

The loudest objections to electronic monitoring come from such workers as airline reservations clerks, customer service personnel, or telephone operators, where automation and a high degree of repetition can result in an increasingly dehumanized environment. Keystroke monitoring (where the computer counts the number of keystrokes per minute), telephone call accounting monitoring (where the number of phone calls per hour and the length of each call are recorded), as well as service observation (where supervisors listen in on calls) and keeping track of unplugged time (measuring time spent away from the computer) are all becoming commonplace.

Women interviewed by 9 to 5, Working Women Education Fund describe the stress caused by excessive monitoring. "The monitoring makes you feel like less than a child, less than a thinking human being.... You have to stop and think from time to time that your ancestors did not cross the ocean in steerage and come through Ellis Island to be treated like this," says Maxine O., a customer service representative for a New Jersey telephone company. Olivia L., the voice on the other end of a Georgia computer manufacturer's technical hot line, describes the monitoring in her office as a combination of phone, computer, and video camera. She says that establishing quotas for phone calls, measuring the time between calls, number of calls, and time on and off the computer system, along with video surveillance in the workroom and lunchroom have all combined to create "the feeling that Big Brother is counting us, listening to us, and filming us all the time."

Office workers are not the only ones who feel they are being shadowed. Already, global positioning systems allow truck drivers to be reached on the road, but can also monitor the length of their rest stops. Cellular phone systems can locate anyone using a phone in their car. And there's more to come. Olivetti and Xerox are developing the "active badge," a device which allows workers to be tracked around the company premises. The badge reveals its wearer's location by emitting an infrared signal every fifteen seconds to a network of wall-mounted sensors around the building. The information provided—including the name and location of the badge-wearer, the number of other badge-wearers in the room, the length of time they have been there, and the nearest telephone extension—are all displayed and updated on a central computer screen. So far, the badge is worn only by a few hundred workers in research centers, but the company plans to introduce it widely in the next couple of years.

In the face of such ominous devices, workplace privacy advocates take some comfort from the hope that eventually employers will discover that excessive monitoring is bad for business. They often cite the example of Federal Express, which pursued a "people first" approach to office automation and downplayed quantitative measurements. Worker productivity and performance increased above what it had been under electronic monitoring.

As far as Alana Shoars is concerned, something good may have come out of her experience. Her personal lawsuit against Epson for slander was settled in 1994 for an undisclosed sum. Although her e-mail class action privacy suit went nowhere and she lost her suit for wrongful discharge, her case raised awareness among both workers and management that electronic monitoring could no longer remain secret.

Questions for Discussion

1. Have you ever used e-mail in school or at work? How does e-mail change the study or work environment? Are these changes positive or negative? Why?
2. Do you agree with Alana Shoars's assumption that employees or students at a university will use e-mail only if they can be assured of its confidentiality? Why or why not? On what did Shoars base her belief that there was an "expectation of privacy" among the users of Epson's system?

3. Do you believe that employers have the right to intercept and monitor e-mail messages? In this case, Robert Hillseth argued that his monitoring of messages was intended to ensure that the system was working properly. Were his actions reasonable? Why or why not?
4. An earlier court decision, *O'Connor v. Ortega,* asserted that an employer may search an employee's office, desk, or files, provided that such a search is "reasonable under all circumstances." What does this phrase mean in practical terms? When would a search of an employee's work area be reasonable? When would it be unreasonable?
5. The authors suggest that employers may change their attitudes toward electronic monitoring in the workplace if they realize that this type of monitoring is "bad for business." How might electronic monitoring actually harm an employer's business? Are employers likely to be swayed by this type of economic argument?
6. Why do you think Shoars lost her lawsuit? Why would the defendant's argument have prevailed here?

Questions for Research and Writing

1. Identify an organization or business where employees use e-mail regularly. Interview several of the employees about their expectation of privacy in their e-mail correspondence. Do your findings confirm the conclusions drawn in this article?
2. In your area do companies that use e-mail frequently have any policies regarding employee use of e-mail or about monitoring? Interview officials in several local businesses or organizations. Is there any consensus on e-mail policies? Do the existing policies seem fair and reasonable?

MORAL OBTUSENESS IN AMERICA
Hadley Arkes

> *Originally published in the conservative opinion journal* The National Review *in 1989, the following article focuses on a subject that has received much attention in recent years: the supposed decline in Americans' sense of moral values. What makes this piece unusual, however, is the attention Hadley Arkes, a professor of jurisprudence at Amherst, devotes to the conflicts among various moral codes. Not content with saying simply that we should all lead more moral lives, Arkes argues that some of what we call "moral" or "professional" codes are simply expedient codes of behavior rather than the immutable laws of a higher morality. The article raises important questions about the origins of that higher morality and about how people recognize the superiority of one code over another in their personal and professional lives.*

This melancholy report was offered, a few weeks ago, by a friend who teaches at the war college attached to one of our military services: His students were all seasoned veterans, in their forties; they had all seen military action; but they were still, twenty years later, the people who had been college students in the 1960s, and they had absorbed much of the secular religion that affected other young people at the time. They were, on the whole, skeptical of the notion of moral truths that held in all times and places. They had served their country in the military, but they were far from clear that there was anything about the American Republic that truly justified the risk of their lives. They could not really say, with Lincoln, that the right of human beings to govern themselves was a right that was "applicable to all men and all times." These soldiers of their country were more disposed to believe, with other people their age, that the understanding of what was right and wrong was always "relative" to a particular "culture" or country. They would not claim, then, that the political regime in America was morally superior to that of the Soviet Union or Vietnam. They would settle for the far more modest claim that our political way of life was at least "ours." And on that basis, we were warranted in hazarding our lives to preserve it.

In this construction, of course, the principles that defined the character of the American Republic would be no different from the rules that marked the character of a club, or defined a regime of play. The rules of the American Constitution, in other words, were hardly distinguishable from the rules of baseball or the rules of chess. In that event, I offered this proposition to my friend at the war college: The willingness of his students to risk their lives for the rules of the American Republic apparently stood on the same moral plane as a willingness to risk one's life to preserve the infield-fly rule or the "institution" of the designated hitter.

My friend agreed that such was indeed their understanding. The only thing he might say in their defense is that it is "our" infield-fly rule, and we are free to change it. And in any system of conventions, in any rules of the game, that is certainly true. We are free to decide that it will require *five* balls outside the strike zone to constitute a "base on balls." But are we really free, in the same way, to alter these axioms of the law: that "people should not be held blameworthy or responsible for acts they were powerless to affect"; that like cases should be treated in like fashion; that people accused of a crime should be presumed innocent until proven guilty; that beings who are capable of understanding reasons deserve to be ruled only with their own consent? We would be far more reserved about "legislating" a change in propositions of this kind. For even the dimmest of us may suspect that these truths are not merely conventional: they are not ours because we have chosen to adopt them; rather, we have adopted them—we have made them "ours"—for the sovereign reason that they are compellingly true.

What we see at work here, in the case of our military officers, is the enduring tension between a morality that is merely conventional, and a morality that is rooted in the laws of reason, in the nature of things, or, as Kant put it, in the nature of "a rational creature as such." It is no small service for any teacher of moral philosophy to make his students alert to that distinction. This much can be said then, at least, for the editors and journalists who shaped the ten-part PBS series *Ethics in America*. It was quite evidently part of their design to bring out vividly to their viewers the tension between a morality merely of convention—a "morality" marked by professionals, cast in "roles"—and a morality that was constantly looking past the system of roles, and appealing to a more exacting moral standard.

From that tension, the designers of this series managed to produce its dramatic action, in the exchanges among the participants. And in that vein, there was probably no moment more dramatic than the moment just after Mr. Mike Wallace had waxed eloquent, by his own lights, in insisting on the integrity of his standards "as a journalist." The journalist in the hypothetical case under discussion had agreed to gauge the "other side" of a war in South Kosan (read: South Vietnam) by traveling with contingents of the North Kosanese. In that position, he might be able to encounter the atrocities committed by the South Kosanese and their American allies. The North Kosanese suddenly come upon a contingent of American troops, and they are about to ambush them. At this point, Mr. Peter Jennings allowed that he would not film the incident. In fact, he thought he might actually try to warn the American troops, even though that might be, altogether, bad manners toward his hosts, who had invited him along for this excursion. For this mild reflex of national loyalty, Mr. Wallace came down upon Mr. Jennings with a severe reproach: as a journalist, his responsibility was to the story. "You're a reporter," said Wallace. "Granted you're an American, but you're a reporter covering combat . . . and I'm at a loss to understand why . . . you would not have covered that story."

The discussion seemed to be settling in with a comfortable sense of the journalist at ease with himself and his professional "responsibilities." Suddenly the lull was broken by the quiet, steely words of George Connell, a colonel in the Marines. Connell spoke with an anger evidently coiled in reserve, and he announced that this display had stirred in him "an utter contempt": there would be an incident, with two reporters wounded in the action, and he would be asked to send some Marines into a contested zone for the sake of extracting those hapless journalists. At that moment, said Connell, he could insist that "They're just journalists, they're not Americans." How can they have it both ways? he asked—as Mike Wallace apparently experienced a mild epiphany, and felt obliged to nod his assent. "But I'll do it," the colonel continued, "and that's what makes me so contemptuous of them. Marines will die going to get a couple of journalists."

With his simple, powerful intervention, Colonel Connell had exposed the moral emptiness of Mr. Wallace's stern lecture on the responsibilities of a journalist: the supposed moral requirements of a journalist had simply reduced to the "interests" of a journalist; and those interests could be served scrupulously in a project that was morally obtuse. But what was it, exactly, that made the course of the journalists morally wrong in this case? Was Colonel Connell simply posing, against the "roles" of journalists, the conventional roles of "Americans"? Was he merely asking them to override their loyalty to the code of journalism by acting on the rule of a wider club: *viz.,* that "Americans should help one another in times of danger"? Did the lesson run any deeper than that? I think it did, but the producers of the series made no provision to ensure that the lesson would be drawn or articulated. And that omission cannot be ascribed to accident. The designers of the series were not shy about imposing structure on these conversations. When it was thought necessary to make a point, they found a way to make it. Apparently, it was part of the purpose of the producers to leave certain questions unaddressed, unarticulated, unresolved, as part of the deeper teaching in the program: namely, that there were, finally, no standards for judging.

If we return for a moment to the case of the journalists and the army, let us imagine that the journalists were trying to report, with detachment, on a war between the forces of syntax and the forces that were seeking to overthrow syntax. The reporters go out to travel with the other side—with the armies that would obliterate syntax in the countries they occupy. And yet, the reporters themselves would have to make use of syntax in offering their reports. One might say, in fact, that they have a deep professional stake in the preservation of syntax. Their own occupations, indeed their way of life, would be rendered unintelligible by its destruction. For them to take a posture of detachment in this conflict would be to deliver themselves into a position of deep incoherence.

But it would hardly be more incoherent than the position of those Western reporters who were willing to travel to North Vietnam in the late war, or travel with the contingents of North Kosanese in the case contrived in the program. For the American reporters understood themselves to be working in the character of a free press. They were not like the "reporters" and photographers who traveled with the Nazi troops to provide photos and stories for propaganda. The American reporters were not agents of the government, but reporters detached, in their independence, to tell an accurate story unshaped by the government. In other words, the "work" of the reporters depended, for its character and integrity, on a free regime, which could sustain a free press. The American reporters could hardly be neutral, then, on the moral differences that separated the American regime from the regime in North Vietnam (or North Kosan). Their way of life was inconceivable if it were detached from the moral premises that defined the character of a free society. It made no more sense for them to pretend that they were indifferent to the moral distinction between a constitutional order and a totalitarian regime than it did for the reporters in our example to claim neutrality in the battle between syntax and its enemies.

Among the professions represented in *Ethics in America,* the journalists were nearly the most witless, and certainly the shallowest, when it came to reflecting, with any seriousness, on the moral grounds of their judgment, or the justification for the way they spent their days. I say "nearly": by far, the prize for glib, or even frightening, vacuity must go to the lawyers. With the notable, sparkling exception of Justice Scalia, the lawyers collected in these programs offered the most dramatic illustration of just how far the profession has drifted from Blackstone's understanding, that the law is an exercise in "commanding what is right and prohibiting what is wrong." The lawyers were all successful men of the world, in private practice, government, or the academy. And yet their varieties of style and intellect were swept away in the logic of a common training, which imparted to these men a common banality. Their uniform tendency was to reduce the law to a system of roles and conventions. They were prepared to acknowledge that those conventions could produce, in many cases, judgments that were patently unjust. But they were content to offer the affable hope that the conventions would work, in the long run, to produce decent results.

These bootless speculations could not disguise, however, the inanities that these worldly men were evidently quite willing to absorb into their characters as part of the ongoing condition of their professional lives. The telling encounter here came in a case of murder that was unfolded, with skill, by Professor Charles Ogletree of the law school at Harvard. The killer claims that he killed reluctantly; he seeks counsel, and every lawyer extends, to this client, the protection and shield of his confidence. As Ogletree kept turning new corners, with new, disturbing facts, the lawyers on the panel preserved their willingness to shelter their client and hold back information from the authorities. Particularly adamant here was Mr. James Neal, from Tennessee. Plainly, Neal had prospered in a field that rewards obduracy, especially when it is allied to a masculine willingness to play rough. The killer finally reveals to Mr. Neal that he was responsible for yet another inadvertent killing; that another man had been convicted for this crime; and that the man who had been wrongfully convicted was about to be executed. With the unpeeling of these facts, one could sense the mood altering in the room. Still, even in the face of these reports, Mr. Neal held his ground: he would not yield up information, even to save the life of an innocent man.

With this move, Professor Ogletree managed to bring forth the conflict between the convention of confidentiality, and the necessary moral imperative to avoid the punishment of the innocent. The conflict made little impression, however, on the mind of Mr. Neal. His obstinacy on this point stirred cries of disbelief on the part of the journalists and academics gathered around him. Faced with this storm of reaction, his combativeness rose to meet it, but his reflex was to hide behind the "Code of Professional Responsibility." He reminded his auditors that his reactions were all quite consistent with the code—as though this piece of intelligence could settle any vexing question and bring ease to any mind overly troubled. Would he really let an innocent man be executed? "Absolutely . . . people die every day. It may sound harsh, but we have values to serve."

As one of the participants pointed out, Neal was citing nothing more than codes legislated by lawyers, and those codes could be counted on not to burden the interests of lawyers with moral duties that were too strenuous altogether. Neal apparently assumed that it was good or desirable for lawyers to be guided by a code. The question he left unaddressed was: Why should we care just what is said in the code for lawyers—unless that code claims to speak about the things that are truly right or wrong? The code summons our respect because it pretends to be something more than another convention: we trust that the jurists are not spinning out rules like the infield-fly rule, which may be convenient or useful, or simply make for an interesting "game." The code becomes something that Mr. Neal tries to invoke in his defense because it pretends to explain what is justified and right. But if the code rests, at its foundation, on real truths, then Mr. Neal need not retreat so lamely to "the code" when he is pressed to give an account of himself. He could explain the justification for his decision by recalling the moral reasons that stand behind the code. And yet, we suspect that he no longer recalls those reasons, if indeed he ever knew them.

If Kant or Aristotle had sought to reach a mass audience, they might have felt compelled to teach their lessons through a format of this kind—*viz.,* by inducing ordinary men and women to speak the moral fallacies of their age. And if the philosophers had sought to dramatize the state of mind sunk in a morality of conventions or codes, they could hardly have produced a character more vivid than Mr. Neal, speaking lines more flinty and banal. But, of course, Kant and Aristotle had compelling reasons for not choosing to teach in this way. No dramatic presentation was likely to take the place of careful, precise, analytic prose, dealing in a systematic way with the most straining and subtle questions of moral judgment. Could we imagine, for example, that Kant's *Critique of Pure Reason* could be distilled into a series on television, or translated for the musical stage? The question answers itself, but that answer, evident to common sense, may produce in turn a facile apology: If Kant had sought to teach through television, might he not have produced a program very much like *Ethics in America*? He, too, would have recognized how hard it is to work through television in laying the groundwork for a philosophical argument: could he really have tried to teach about "synthetic *a priori*" propositions by inducing, say, Ellen Goodman or General Westmoreland to bubble up, on occasion, with the right point? He, too, might have been tempted then to settle for the solution accepted by the producers of this series, i.e., to raise the questions, suggest to the listeners that ethics is a hard business, and encourage them to keep reflecting on these thorny matters.

And yet, it is not really so clear that this was the only alternative, even for people working in television. In one inspired example, Tom Stoppard managed to touch quite deftly on the tension between morality and convention in his play *Professional Foul*. The play was written for television, for a running time that could not have exceeded ninety minutes. And as the phrase goes, it had to include the "production values" of a public entertainment. Still, within the space of ninety minutes, in a production offered mainly for entertainment—with no didactic format, and no pretensions to teach—Stoppard developed the philosophic issues in a manner that would have been far more recognizable to professional philosophers. He also managed to discredit, quite powerfully, the perspective that would reduce morality to a system of etiquette or manners, to the mere conventions of language, or to the rules of a game. Stoppard had his character, Professor Anderson, speak of an understanding of rightness or wrongness that "precedes utterance" and the conventions of language—"an idea of justice which is, for want of a better word, natural." Anderson had delivered himself earlier of these observations:

> If we decline to define rights as fictions, . . . there are only two senses in which humans could be said to have rights. Firstly, humans might be said to have certain rights if they had collectively and mutually agreed to give each other these rights. This would merely mean that humanity is a rather large club with club rules, but it is not what is generally meant by human rights. It is not what Locke meant, and it is not what the American Founding Fathers meant . . . when they held certain rights to be unalienable . . .

Even Stoppard did not quite supply the ground of the argument for natural rights within the compass of his play. But what is remarkable is that he accomplished far more to that end than the producers of this series, even though they could address the subject directly, didactically, in sessions extending over nine hours. And in a program on ethics in America, they did not think it important to point out the connection acknowledged by

Mr. Stoppard, who was not even addressing an American audience: people who hold to the doctrines of cultural relativism, and the morality of conventions, are radically at odds with moral understanding of the men who founded the American Republic. If the producers had cared to go further, they could have offered the modest but telling point that the James Neals in this series were on the side of Stephen Douglas in the famous debate with Abraham Lincoln. But such an observation would have touched one side in these exchanges with the taint of a disreputable argument—a rhetorical move inconsistent with a series that sought so strenuously to avoid the taking of sides.

It was not, then, a want of time, or the limits of television, that accounted for the lessons that were not drawn, or the moral understandings that were not explained, in this series. Stoppard could use his arts of entertainment to support his teaching, and he could do it all far more economically, because he was far clearer that there were indeed lessons to teach. The designers of this series were earnest, thoughtful people, who evidently thought that moral questions deserved the strain of serious reflection. But it became apparent also that, in their understanding of the discipline of moral philosophy, they were very much representative of that modern state of mind that might be called, these days, "ethics in America."

In that state of mind, the understanding of "natural justice"—the understanding of the Founders—is offered as just another one of those moral "points of view" that fill in the current landscape, along with utilitarianism, conventionalism, anti-foundationalism, or nihilism. The Founders spoke about necessary moral truths, but the producers of this series would not presume to suggest that the arguments of Plato and Kant, Aristotle and Lincoln, would refute, decisively, the arguments of relativism or conventionalism, the arguments that are obviously taken so seriously today by men and women successful in their professions: by men and women, that is, like James Neal and Mike Wallace. If the producers had sought to offer a judgment of that kind, they would have been obliged to fill in the groundwork of explanation. But in holding back their judgment and their explanation, they have joined the most common fallacy of their age: they have suggested that our task, in ethics, is to choose between competing points of view, when there are no correct answers. But if there is no way of choosing between these alternative moral arguments, then there is, finally, no rational ground for our moral judgments. If the producers of the program accepted that reasoning, however, they would simply install the premises of relativism and dissolve their problem: after all, if there is no right or wrong answer on moral questions, why is it necessary to strain and reflect and agonize before we decide? Is there a tension between our interests and our duties? But so what? On what ground of reason would the commands of obligation take precedence over the commands of self-interest, or the manifold appeals of the things that simply give us pleasure?

On this point, the telling clues were to be found in the commentaries that bracketed the programs. In one discussion, Dr. Mortimer Rosen (the chairman of the Department of Obstetrics and Gynecology at Columbia) made a moving, unpretentious case for operating on a pregnant, comatose woman for the purpose of saving her child. The mother, in this case, had sought to sustain the child, but then changed her mind as she slipped into her last hours. Predictably, Faye Wattleton of Planned Parenthood found it necessary to reject any suggestion that the unborn child might have a claim to the protection of doctors and judges apart from the will of her mother. Willard Gaylin of the Hastings Center thought it was curious to honor a judgment that departed so suddenly from the matured intentions of the mother to save her child. But the last word went, as it always did, to Fred Friendly, the producer of the series, as he closed the program. Friendly noted that "Dr. Gaylin and Ms. Wattleton disagree in this agonizing conflict. They may both be right."

In that manner, the tension in the argument may be dissolved; but so, too, would the enterprise of moral judgment. Mr. Friendly produced, in this series, some arresting exchanges. But I fear that, through the power of television, he has done for the understanding of ethics what Mr. Bert Lahr managed to do, through *The Wizard of Oz,* to advance our understanding of lions.

Questions for Discussion

1. To what extent is Hadley Arkes right that most of us today believe in a kind of moral or cultural relativism? Is your own ethical code founded on immutable and universal truths or is it relative to your culture and/or country?

2. Arkes makes an analogy between the rules of an individually determined or professional ethic and the rules of any sport or game. How convincing is that analogy? What are the crucial similarities between the two halves of the analogy? The crucial differences?

3. The *National Review* generally appeals to a politically conservative audience. How do Arkes's assumptions and values reflect his own conservative outlook? Which assumptions and values might a politically liberal audience question?

4. How does Arkes's rhetoric—for instance, his word choice, his use of particular images and metaphors, his tone, and his use of previous authorities on the subject—reinforce his stance? Which of his words make particularly strong emotional appeals?

5. What values do you consider "conventions"? Which do you hold to be "moral imperatives"?

6. Arkes begins with an analysis of the ways in which the values of the 1960s have shaped the actions of today's leaders. How will the values of today's generation of college students—your generation—shape the values of the nation's leaders twenty to thirty years from now? How differ-

ent are your generation's values from those of the college students of the 1960s and early 1970s?

Questions for Research and Writing

1. In his opening paragraph, Arkes remarks that military men and women in their forties today were the college students of the 1960s, and he goes on to characterize that generation of college students as "skeptical of the notion of moral truths that held in all times and places." Other commentaries on the 1960s take the opposite perspective: they hold that the opposition to the war in Vietnam and to government policies sprang from a sense of a universal ethical code higher than that of any single country's government and wider than any single country's borders. With these contradictory perspectives in mind, do one or both of the following:

   a. Interview people who are old enough to remember the controversy surrounding the US involvement in Vietnam. Ask how they personally reacted to that involvement and how they see the relationship between their political responses to the war and their moral codes. Then ask them the same questions about their responses to the recent Gulf War and, for older respondents, their responses to World War II or the Korean War. Once you've collected your survey data and quotations, analyze the responses you've received. To what extent is Arkes right that the forty-something generation has seemed to reject the notion of universal moral truths?

   b. Read several commentaries about the Vietnam War that were written during the 1960s and early 1970s by legislators and other politicians, war protestors, and journalists. To what extent do the commentaries reflect their authors' beliefs in a universal and immutable ethical code?

2. If you are very familiar with another culture, compare and contrast one of that culture's moral and legal codes with that of the United States. Because this is a broad topic, you'll probably want to narrow your focus to a single facet of the moral/legal code. For instance, write about the rules that govern one of the following: public behavior or dress, particular types of crimes and punishment, or public speech.

3. Arkes gives the example of journalists torn between codes of journalism and their loyalty to their country. Professionals in many fields face similar tensions: lawyers defend clients whom they know to be guilty of heinous crimes; scientists work on projects that yield knowledge but harm people; engineers design systems that will make transportation easier but damage the environment, and so forth. Write an essay in which you address the question of how professionals in a particular field resolve the conflicts between "professional codes" and a "greater morality." (You might gather data by interviewing or surveying the professionals themselves or by reading the debates between those who come

at an issue from different perspectives, for example, environmentalists and engineers.)

4. Disturbed by the moral ambivalence expressed in the PBS series *Ethics in America,* Arkes contends that television could be a medium for greater moral understanding. Considering the moral values exhibited by a newsmagazine program, opinion show, or documentary, analyze the extent to which Arkes's criticisms of the PBS show could fairly be leveled against those other shows.

FROM JEFFERSON TO THE GULF WAR
How Lawyers Have Lost Their Golden Tongue

Richard Weisberg

> *This essay is an excerpt from Professor Richard Weisberg's book* Poethetics and Other Strategies of Law and Literature, *published by Columbia University Press in 1992. Throughout the book, and in this article in particular, Weisberg is concerned with the connections between language and law, and language and truth. In this essay he explores how legal language and legal writing have changed since the time of this country's founding, beginning his discussion with the work of Thomas Jefferson. Weisberg focuses not only on "language" and "writing" in the abstract, but on representative examples of legal discourse.*

I need not remind this audience[1] of the traditional linkage of law and literature since the early days of the Republic. Perhaps our greatest Revolutionary thinker—Thomas Jefferson—laid claim to the unifying virtues of law and letters. Perennially fascinated by the classics,[2] Jefferson once took the time to produce quite an effective essay on English prosody.[3] As a writer, he achieved greatness by recalling (as he did in every genial act of engineering and inventive brilliance) that form and function, style and substance, always merge in excellent prose. In his sole full-length book, *Notes on the State of Virginia*,[4] Jefferson brought a lawyerlike sense of organization to topics ranging from Virginia's climate and topography to the ambitions of first-decade America. In a sentence aptly emphasized by Robert A. Ferguson, who redeems Jefferson's book from its relative obscurity,[5] the author of the *Notes* perfectly articulates the new land: "Young as we are, and with such a country before us to fill with people and with happiness, we should point in that direction the whole generative force of nature, wasting none of it in efforts of mutual destruction."[6]

This sentence stands as a model for my remarks here. Its force comes from the unity of idealism and practical duty, of nature and reason, of the spiritual and the material—unities that continue to characterize (however great the changes that have occurred) the late twentieth-century practitioner of American law. But beyond this, and in a manner more remote from today's legal climate, the sentence *speaks its meaning*. The words *are* the meaning, nothing less. We find in passages such as this, as Ferguson puts it, "the association of voice with action and control, the assertion of solution within the context of speech, and the glorification of a dialectic or argumentative intellect."[7]

As with those other lawyer-writers of our Republic's founding program—the authors of the Federalist Papers—Jefferson recognized in the 1780s that his prose needed not only to describe but actually to *become* the vision of the new nation. "Young as we are," he begins, in an introductory clause that anticipates the sentence's forcefully personal subject, "we"—*we* must do the work both of the sentence and of the fledgling nation. We find here none of the impersonality of today's legal prose. The writer takes full responsibility for his program, makes it also his reader's, and, in the process, associates "nature" with himself, his reader, and "such a country" as together they will "fill with people and with happiness."

The southern lawyer in particular perhaps proceeded across the next seventy-five years—even while the North began to pursue a more impersonal and gradually alienated voice—to unify his program and his words. Amid such prominent lawyer-writers as John Pendleton Kennedy, Sidney Lanier, George Fitzhugh, A. B. Longstreet, and many others, Edgar Allen [sic] Poe stands almost anomalously as one of the few great southern writers who never studied law.[8]

In the early nineteenth century, of course, one would not contemplate letters without lawyers, or law without the ally of strongly expressive words. Lawyers like Daniel Webster and Richard Henry Dana carried our national vision from one generation to the next, burnishing it with the fire of strong subjects and verbs, of disequilibrating metaphor, of stunning imagery. Yet today, at least until the recent reawakening that takes the name "Law and Literature," the lawyer may think of language as a barrier to thought rather than a carrier of it; he may denigrate rhetoric, style, and narrative to a status of strangeness or even artificiality in legal prose.

On the syntactical level, in sentence after legalistic sentence, the twentieth-century lawyer metamorphoses Jefferson's "we should point" into "it might be said," or "the conclusion may be warranted," or "the effort might be made." Vibrant thoughts and arguments disappear into impersonal constructions and nonresponsible agencies.[9] Jefferson's thought, these days, would be transmogrified as follows: "It is to be hoped that, in view of the youthful qualities of this country, which needs to be filled with people and with happiness, that nature in its various aspects will be permitted to be utilized to those ends, avoiding if and when possible, costly wars." But this unhappy translation of Jefferson leaves us altogether bereft of his original thought.

For Robert Ferguson—as for Oliver Wendell Holmes much earlier in the century[10]—the falling off of legal communication can be directly explained by the increased specialization of modern legal practice. But surely the Jeffersonian lawyer, too, reveled in a sense of high competence and professional expertise. Nor need we assume, even if today's lawyers *are* indeed more specialized, an inevitable gap between expertise and expression. The specialized lawyer needs, as much as the generalist, to write well. Specialized language—"stripped technical discourse" as Karl Llewellyn's esthetics most forcefully puts it[11]—is the law's most beautiful language, and it was not for nothing that the French novelist Stendhal (seeking inspiration) read three pages of the *Code Napoléon* every night.[12]

If increased specialization alone cannot explain the profession's recently degraded use of language, neither can the more cynical view that greedy lawyers deliberately obfuscate so that only they can decipher the law's mysteries. I will return to that heresy shortly. History more than greed explains the bizarre quality of lawtalk, and history also proves that legalese is not always a bar to inclusive communication. Jefferson himself could trace the redundancies "null and void" or "last will and testament" to that day some seven hundred years before his time when the Normans reached England and brought their native tongue's equivalents to the words English lawyers already had carved in stone.[13] Yet there was beauty to those mellifluous phrases, as to their alliterative cousin, "release, relinquish, and remit." As a practitioner, Jefferson surely did not fear the use of such other strange creatures of our legal language, the *fee tail male* and the *estate pur autre vie*; he had protected more than one child *en ventre sa mere*. He seized legal language at its most technical, and he made the language live. Not against the historical grain but fully toward it, he became the powerful protector of "life, liberty, and the pursuit of happiness" for all.

Today, the practitioner's language mystifies and alienates—it does not protect or attract—the laity. But this is due neither to specialization nor to the inevitable obscurity of technical discourse. Rather, the fault lies in the *everyday* use of language. Not in their jargon but in their commonplace syntax do contemporary lawyers lose their audience and surrender their historical place at the center of the nation's discourse. And the costs of this impoverished professional speech have begun to outweigh greatly whatever meager benefits may come from strangeness.

Until law and literature, like Plato's Androgyne, strive to recouple, until the Jeffersonian unities reemerge in legal language, the profession runs at least four considerable risks. Two of these threaten law's relationship with the public; two perhaps more portentously involve the law's sense of itself. These risks are:

1. the risk of ridicule and even rebellion among the laity;
2. the risk of surrendering the law's dominance in American politics and culture;
3. the risk of severe professional dissatisfaction; and
4. the risk of professional ethical relativism.

As a window to the profession's values, the writings of the law have been scrutinized more of late than in the past. People peer at what lawyers write, seeking an index of the profession's goals and beliefs. But if heightened recently, this scrutiny comes from a long and distinguished tradition.

For years, lawyers have been aware of the public's unhappiness with their professional writing. Despite their acute ability to listen carefully and speak well, lawyers found fewer incentives to transcribe such communication skills onto parchment. They came to understand their own prose, and the public suffered through it. But the laity started complaining very early on about legal writing—and, unfortunately for lawyers, the complainants numbered among them our culture's best-known writers.

This criticism, loudest over the past 150 years, finds its modern origins in Shakespeare. It was Dick the Butcher, in the second part of *Henry VI,* who uttered the line that the profession itself seems masochistically to like best: "The first thing we do, let's kill all the lawyers" (IV.ii.73); what we often forget is that the remark refers specifically to the way lawyers write, which the rebel Jack Cade insists can "undo a man" in and of itself. Later, Jonathan Swift would detect in lawyers "a peculiar cant and jargon of their own that no other mortal can understand."

Not coincidentally, however, the upsurge of lay criticism about legal language begins around the time that law was losing its ascendancy over cultural discourse. Thus Charles Dickens, in novel after novel, pillories the legal speech he knew so well. In *Bleak House,* examined earlier in this volume,[14] a host of otherwise dissimilar lawyers manage as a group to startle their lay listeners into reactions of amazement, distaste, even madness and self-destruction. And our own century has (with the exception of the horrific continental worlds of Kafka, Camus, and Solzhenitsyn—where terror and legal language are inexorably linked) produced scathing satire on the writing of lawyers. Notable examples can be found in the very literature of the South that once exalted law and unified it with letters; William Faulkner's lawyers in such novels as *Sanctuary* or *Light in August* distort justice as they speak cleverly but to no ethical purpose.

To one extent or another, these artists share Carl Sandburg's view that [15] "in the heels of higgling lawyers, Bob, / Too many slippery ifs and buts and howevers / Too much hereinbefore provided whereas, Too many doors to go in and out of." Sandburg poetically replicates Keats' pithier remark that "[he] would classify lawyers in the natural history of monsters," and later associates the lawyer's anarchic verbosity, as had Dickens before him, with the lawyer's greed: "When a lawyer is through, what is left? Enough for a mouse to nibble on?"

Such views of lawyers we all know, and they are not lost on the profession either. Lawyers read, often voraciously, and they positively devour satires about themselves. (This self-critical taste in reading comes in part from the lawyer's innate modesty, which I will discuss further on.) Even in popular culture, legal writing is raked over the coals. The sleazy lawyer in the film *Body Heat* (1981) falls not because of his questionable morality; it is ultimately his poorly drafted perpetuities clause that gives him away. A certain knee-jerk formalism and boilerplate mentality defeats the hapless Hamilton Burger time after time as he vies with the more creative and verbally forceful Perry Mason. Formalism and archaism have provided grist for the cartoon writers, too: Motley Crew once portrayed a lawyer hurling Latin phrases at his flabbergasted clients who, upon examining the bill he hands them as they leave, conclude that "Latin lessons must be expensive."

Leave it to that sensitive barometer of cultural pressure, the *New York Times*, to reveal in a 1977 headline that attorneys could no longer even understand one another; as the *Times* put it, "Lawyers Now Confuse Even the Same Aforementioned." By then, change was in the air, for around that time pioneering states were passing the first Plain English statutes,[15] and the federal government was also trying to sweep clean the thick and musty world of regulations, tax advisory opinions, and even briefs to the Supreme Court. The laity was beginning to make itself felt.

If lawyers have, by their words, alienated the individual nonlawyer; if the threat of litigation now must coerce the straightforward discourse that Jefferson always used when addressing a lay audience; if potential clients now think twice before retaining a clumsy wordsmith to verbalize the sensitive moments in their lives—yet the profession faces even a greater risk regarding the outside world. The lawyer's place as the arbiter and the rhetorician of the nation's values may have been permanently surrendered. No longer does a James Madison or a Daniel Webster or an Abraham Lincoln fashion the Republic's aspirations by linking them to simple but elegant speech.

No. For, as a result of a pitched battle across a decade and before television audiences of millions, the verbal struggle has been lost. And who now dominates the discursive center? Not the creative writers; their voices are dispersed and idiosyncratic. Surely not the preachers; they are in disarray or in jail. Not even the journalists, who have sacrificed whatever prose power they once had to the twenty-second sound bite and the pretty face. The winners and at least temporary rhetorical champions are . . . the military.

Think for a moment of the Iran-Contra hearings. Against an army of brilliant lawyers, it was the Army that emerged victorious. Oliver North became a national hero, his interlocutors forgotten (despite the nobility of their purpose), because of the drabness of their speech! North's snappy "Disobey orders? Not this lieutenant colonel! I saluted smartly, turned on my heels, and did my bidding!" easily prevailed over such dreary, verbose lawyers' interrogatories as "At what point in time?" "Did there come a time when . . . ," "At such a time as . . . ," and "On the basis of the above." These preposition sandwiches, which studiously delay the meat of the inquiry, bowed to the strong, active subjects and verbs of the military. This trend continued during the Persian Gulf crisis. A general responded to a question about the usefulness of American airpower with the crisply rendered "Our planes will at least interdict Saddam's tanks." And General Schwartzkopf's direct speech, characterized by pithiness and syntactical force, easily outpaced the puffy self-promotion of Congress as it verbosely debated the wisdom of the military action. Most of those wordy legislators were, of course, trained in the nation's law schools. But whoever (or whatever) is teaching the military to communicate, he, she, or it should be hired by lawyers. Whereas lawyers habitually change nice short verbs into nouns and then make those long abstractions the subjects of their sentences, these colonels and generals reverse the process, making verbs out of nouns, shortening their sentences, and winning the hearts and minds of the American people. Consider the following sentence at the close of a brief: "The ultimate termination of this litigation would be materially advanced by correction at this stage, of the deprivation of due process resulting from denial to X of access to information at issue." No profession so encumbered can long endure. We can learn from the military to avoid lengthening verbs into nouns, such as the *five* abstract nouns ending in "-tion" contained in the sentence. Let us interdict abstractions, wherever possible.

While lawyers risk alienating the lay reader and listener, their poor communication strategies also directly threaten their own inner peace. Poor writing, in my opinion, has produced unhappy lawyers. And here I refer not to the dismal daily task of trying to understand another lawyer's prose; instead, I make the claim that the individual writer's *own* habits produce depression on the job.

Workplace unhappiness pervades all corners of our society, in a way that would have shocked Jefferson and his effusively industrious compatriots. A recent survey reports that 68 percent of American corporate executives dislike their jobs and that 99 percent of that sad group see no possibility of job satisfaction any time in the future! But the American Bar Association has brought this point home to lawyers. Citing a 1990 ABA paper, the *New York Times* revealed that "job dissatisfaction among lawyers is widespread, profound, and growing worse." David Margolick's column continues: "The increased stress of dissatisfaction and billable hours have disturbing and important implications for the profession.... These lie in the area of increasing social dysfunction or destructive behavior by lawyers and the impact of this behavior on themselves, their families, their quality of work and productivity, their firms and their clients."

While draconian, this rhetoric rings true. Given their salaries and their respected place in society, lawyers are not as happy as they should be. Yet in explaining this "dysfunction," the ABA report wrongly substitutes effect for cause. The profession's way of practicing (including the way it communicates) is the cause of the depression, not the reverse. Once the legal profession reclaims its natural birthright and resumes forceful communication both within its own ranks and when it speaks to the laity, I believe that lawyers will regain a Jeffersonian enthusiasm for their craft.

The first step to professional bliss lies, once again, on the path to strong syntax. The lesson is brief and deceptively simple: choose the best subject, grammatically speaking, for the sentence. My experience with hundreds of lawyers has taught me that almost every ill, every sense of powerlessness before the blank page or anger when that page is filled with weak prose, will disappear as soon as this lesson is learned. The lawyer's so-called dysfunction is probably nothing more than a *fear of naming*. When our elementary school teachers taught us not to say, "The cat was eaten by the dog," but rather, "The dog ate the cat," they revealed the key to strong expository writing. By making the subject *dog* (the most active thing present to our thought), we produce a syntactically wonderful sentence. The various faults of the alternative—"The cat was eaten by the dog"—are all eliminated. First, strong verbs follow from strong subjects: *ate* is a good transitive verb, not *was eaten*—a paltry passive that adds flab to the verbiage and nothing to the sense. Five words suffice where seven otherwise afflict us. The reader has a vivid, not just a thorough, reflection of the writer's thought. And the writer has fully expressed his or her own verbal power, without superfluous language, without burning the midnight oil to find the apt phrase. The writer is happier; the reader is ecstatic.

Instead, here are several all-too-typical sentences from the profession:

1. Claimants in this action would be benefited by the Price-Anderson waiver of defenses clause.
2. The Senate-passed version of the bill is not said to be retroactive.
3. Borrowing from the reasoning in the cases, and applying the time worn canons of construction, it may be concluded that the interpretation accorded the predecessor of Section 6511 has been accepted by Congress.
4. The purpose of this memorandum is to determine whether an excise tax may be levied by the Legislature.

In each of these sentences, the writer pushes the true subject off by choosing a false subject, often one that is really the object of the original action. When "claimants," instead of "Price-Anderson waiver," become the first sentence's subject, the awkward and wordy "would be benefited" must be inserted. In the second sentence, the Senate-passed version of the bill "is not said to be retroactive"—here the subject disappears altogether; neither the cat nor the dog shows up. The reader is left to ponder *who* failed to discuss retroactivity, although we have a vague hunch that the Senate itself is the actor. Instead, the writer has chosen an abstraction—"version"—as the subject, creating verbiage and confusion and diminishing the writer's own sense of mastery over the thought that needs expression.

The third sentence exemplifies the legal writer's compulsion to avoid the first person singular. "It may be concluded" trots out four words for the simple "I conclude" that the vertical pronoun allows. How clean! How direct! And how likely to cure that dysfunction conjured by the ABA report. Most lawyers, of course, would almost kill to avoid saying "I." But when, on rare occasions, the writer *is* the subject of his thought, he should be the subject of the written phrase as well.

The fourth example exerts a double-bind passivity: "The purpose of this memorandum" keeps the writer from actually beginning to work; this is called "throat clearing." But while a nervous speaker may be permitted this tick at the outset of a speech, a writer does not enjoy such latitude. Instead, throat clearing becomes fatal, because the writer loses the reader at exactly the moment of fullest attention—the beginning of the sentence, the paragraph, or the document as a whole. And finally, "an excise tax may be levied by the Legislature" parrots the unacceptable "cat was eaten by the dog" paradigm. The final sentence should read simply, "This memorandum determines whether the Legislature may levy an excise tax."

Syntactical weakness does not mean analytical weakness. But lawyers must relearn the essential lesson that thoroughness and effectiveness *need not compete* in the domain of legal communication. Only this will lead to renewed job satisfaction. Why do lawyers habitually push the strong, the real, the active, to the end of their sentences, even sometimes to the end of their paragraphs or entire documents? While two recent experts have asserted fourteen reasons for this phenomenon, thus in part also exemplifying it, I would answer with the "three Ms": modesty, market, and models. Before turning to the last risk of bad professional prose (ethical relativism), I will elaborate briefly on the three Ms.

MODESTY

Unlike their public image, exacerbated by such egocentric television shows as "L.A. Law," or by such glamour-ridden celluloid legal protagonists as Al Pacino, Robert Redford, and Harrison Ford, lawyers are in truth a modest lot. I contend that they take this admirable trait one step too far by transporting it into almost every sentence they write. True, the law itself often eludes facile restatement. But, surely, at the end of a memorandum, the writer has earned the right to say, "I conclude," or even "I believe," instead of the more typical "It might be concluded," or "There is reason to state in closing that . . . " or sundry other depressingly wordy alternatives. Judges need not bury their hard-earned judgments—for which they are, after all, paid—behind passive prose. Lawyers need not deliberately structure first lines of letters or first paragraphs of documents to hide their salient points. The reader cries out for direct information; the lawyer demurs. Such excessive modesty betrays not only the individual practitioner's right to speak up forcefully but also his reader's desire for him to do so.

MARKET

Three related market factors contribute to poor expository prose. First, and most cynically, some say that lawyers deliberately obfuscate to increase their revenues. In this view, hiding the subject and using abstractions are deliberate ploys, designed to extend each matter and justify higher fees. As Dickens opined, "The soul vocation of English law is to make money for itself"—a sentiment echoed by Will Rogers, who once said, "Every time a lawyer writes something, he is not writing for posterity, he is writing so that endless others of his craft can make a living out of trying to figure out what he said." This market explanation for weak writing will not withstand scrutiny. If lawyers knew how to write simply and strongly, they would do so, not only for other lawyers or judges, but also for increasingly demanding clients. Effective writing enhances the lawyer's reputation, the client's satisfaction, and the judge's willingness to see it his or her way.

Next, and almost as cynically, a second market-based assertion posits that the public actually *craves* the mystery and majesty of the law's obscure prose. Without a special language of its own, the law would lose its veneer, its very status. After all, doctors cure real illnesses, architects design real structures, and the military (again!) fights real battles. Lawyers create, or so it is said, a web of words to order and then mask reality, to master it and keep it from the uninitiated, who thenceforth yearn to enter its mysteries. I think there is much to this view, at least historically, but we have already seen this Kafkaesque vision overcome by an activist laity intolerant of legal gobbledygook. The costs of writing obscurely have begun to outweigh the market benefits. Clients have demystified the law; they no longer quake in their boots as they demand from counsel prose they can understand in one reading.

So it is the third market-based explanation, and the least cynical, that strikes me as most accurate. Lawyers spend their professional lives seeking the respect of their colleagues, of those who judge them throughout their careers. These respected insiders base such judgments in large part on the lawyer's written work product. So younger lawyers in particular strive to determine what this most important "market" demands. To the extent that lawyers continue to feel that they *must* provide their colleagues with passive, unassuming, wordy prose, they will in all good faith continue to write poorly. If lawyers believe that they must give judges colorless prose, if they believe that their firm or department demands passive self-effacement, if the whole climate of legal writing reinforces the weakest habits of the profession's prose, lawyers will continue for no economic reason at all to write poorly. But only lawyers truly control the marketplace of legal language, and they are beginning to fortify it. Lawyers are learning that they should not anticipate market rejection when they assert themselves through prose. They have renewed their kinship with Jefferson and his colleagues, who imbibed with their mothers' milk the understanding that thoroughness and forcefulness are allies, not competitors, when lawyers speak and write. They perceive anew that career emoluments follow the salutary turn to strong subject choice. The market demands that the profession redeem its heritage of excellent writing. And this brings us to the third *M* that helps explain our era's disjunction of law and literature.

MODELS

From the moment the novice enters law school, he is pushed toward the flat prose he will use once past the bar. Appellate opinions, the stuff of his first-year training, might inspire—think of this volume's focus upon Cardozo[16]—but few teachers these days stress the link between style and substance that is essential to a knowledge of our system of justice. If the student does well enough to "make law review," he paradoxically will lose whatever good writing skills he might have preserved through that first year. I recall vividly my first staff meeting on an East Coast law journal that shall remain nameless. I received a circular on law review writing; one of its early paragraphs began, "Since the mechanics of writing will vary enormously with the scope and content of the note and with the style and approach of the author." With that sentence fragment proposed as my model, I chose not to read further. Many students today, less passive perhaps than I was, are choosing not to join the law journals. Some start their own. Many of these students retain their native or imbued facility with the written word. So do some who proceed to clerk for judges, thus increasing the chances that the judicial opinion will also serve once again to inspire. But many others regenerate the passive prose that has for so long infected our profession.

When the kind of models proposed in this volume gain ascendancy, when lawyers read at least one novel a month, when senior attorneys again take a personal interest in *how the law means* within their firms, then the third risk of legal communication will be sharply diminished. Lawyers will be happy, exhilarated by the prospects of strong and compelling prose afforded by their profession. And if, too, the stories that lawyers read challenge them to understand their place within the profession and to see that the way lawyers talk affects the potential for justice within every legal situation, then the fourth risk of poor professional communication may also be alleviated. I turn now to that most important of risks.

Poor subject choice, as we have seen, permits the lawyer to hide the true nature of his thought; often it permits the masking of the legal writer himself, as though he were not really responsible for his words. Stories about law reveal the outermost risks of impersonal communication. Such brilliant storytellers as Shakespeare, Melville, Dickens, Twain, and those moderns, William Faulkner, Joyce Carol Oates, John Barth, Toni Morrison, Bernard Malamud, and E. L. Doctorow, link their frequent legal themes to the way lawyers talk and write. When stories talk about law, therefore, a sense of ethics as well as of style emerges (if the two can really be separated).

Storytellers seem to be challenging lawyers to recall the human dimension that remains at the core of their seemingly "technical" discourse. No lawyer who has read *The Bluest Eye* can misperceive the aspirations of those different from himself, those who might not talk or even feel the way a lawyer does; none who has opened himself to *Billy Budd, Sailor* can be insensitive to the pitfalls of deceptive professional speech; none who has read *Bleak House* can ever again blithely mislead a client; all who have read *Intruder in the Dust* will recall that the pursuit of justice in law requires a forged link between words and actions.

So the four risks of our contemporary legal world can be alleviated by a return to the early American fusion of law and letters. The discipline of the 1990s for lawyers will be macronarrative, not microeconomic, in nature. Literature will make the practice of law once again not only enjoyable but fully persuasive, one in which lawyers help—as Jefferson once said—to create a candid world "for the truth of which we pledge a faith yet unsullied by falsehood."

Notes

1. This essay derives from a speech given in Charlottesville in May 1991 as the inaugural lecture of the Friends of the University of Virginia Law Library.
2. See, e.g., Douglas L. Wilson, ed., *Jefferson's Literary Commonplace Book* (Princeton: Princeton University Press, 1989).
3. See "Thoughts on English Prosody," in Merrill D. Peterson, ed., *Thomas Jefferson: Writings* (Washington, D.C.: The Library of America, 1984), pp. 594–622.
4. Ibid., pp. 123–325.
5. See Robert A. Ferguson, *Law and Letters in American Culture*, chapter 2.
6. "Notes on the State of Virginia," in *Thomas Jefferson: Writings*, p. 300.
7. Ferguson, *Law and Letters in American Culture*, p. 242.
8. See Ferguson, ibid., p. 291.
9. See, generally, Richard Weisberg, *When Lawyers Write* (Boston: Little, Brown & Company, 1987).
10. Holmes referred to lawyers as "a little army of specialists." See Ferguson, *Law and Letters in American Culture*, p. 290.
11. See Karl Llewellyn, "On the Good, the True, the Beautiful, in Law," in *University of Chicago Law Review* (1942), 9:224.
12. Stendhal, letter to Balzac, October 28–29, 1840, in H. Martineau, ed., *Balzac, Correspondance* (1968), 3:401, cited in Weisberg, *When Lawyers Write*, p. 4.
13. See David Mellinkoff, *The Language of the Law* (Boston: Little, Brown & Company, 1963), chapter 6.
14. See Weisberg, *Poethetics and Other Strategies of Law and Literature* (New York: Columbia University Press, 1992), chapter 2.
15. For its part, Jefferson's home state proclaimed that "English shall be designated as the official language of the Commonwealth." See Virginia Code Annotated 22.1–212.1.
16. See Weisberg, *Poethetics*, chapter 1.

Questions for Discussion

1. What do you think Richard Weisberg means when he talks about the "degraded use of language"? In what ways does he think language has changed since Jefferson's time?
2. What specific claims about truth and language does this essay make? How does Weisberg support these claims? What sort of evidence or authority does he offer?
3. How effective are the examples Weisberg provides for each of his claims?

4. What does Weisberg mean when he says that contemporary legal writing tends to "threaten law's relationship to the public"? Describe an experience in which you found language (legal or otherwise) threatening or alienating. How did you feel about that experience of language?
5. Does Weisberg offer any remedies or solutions to the problem he identifies in this essay? How reasonable or credible are such proposals?

Questions for Writing and Research

1. Interview a lawyer or judge about his or her experience with professional writing. How did this person learn to write? What kinds of writing are lawyers required to do? Weisberg offers evidence that "workplace unhappiness" is pervasive in the legal profession, partly because of the alienating discourse practitioners use. Does your subject agree?
2. Find examples—in the newspaper, for instance, or in other sources of government or bureaucratic prose—of the tendency that Weisberg describes in contemporary legal writing: "Vibrant thoughts and arguments disappear into impersonal constructions and nonresponsible agencies." Analyze three or four of these examples and speculate on the effects of this prose style in each context.
3. Weisberg asserts that legal writing offers "a window on the profession's values." Is this claim effectively supported in the essay? Why or why not?
4. Do other professions, for example, medicine, engineering, or education, reveal their values through writing? Find several examples of writing from a particular profession and describe and reflect on the values that seem to emerge from the language, style, or structure of the prose.

CROSSCURRENTS
Questions for Connecting the Readings in Chapter 5

1. Leon Kass argues in "Am I My Brother's Keeper" that "The obligation to be even our blood brother's keeper cannot be absolute and unqualified." Would Hadley Arkes agree?
2. Kass and Craig Horowitz address the question of where immoral behavior originates. How fully do these authors (and the authorities they cite) agree with one another? How do their different assumptions and values lead to their differences of opinion? How similar is the evidence they use to support their conclusions?
3. Imagine Arkes and Kass in conversation with one another about the moral standards of today's American citizen. Where would they find themselves in substantial agreement or disagreement? Where would you stand in their conversation?

4. Technology is clearly changing our perceptions of what is legal and what is ethical, as Ellen Alderman and Caroline Kennedy suggest in their essay on high-tech monitoring in the workplace. Compare their legal perspective on technological change with that of authors in chapter 3 (see Merlisa Lawrence Corbett or Juliet Schor) or in chapter 4 (see Charles McGrath or Lana Rakow and Vija Navarro).
5. In his essay "What Does the Law Want?" Benjamin Sells talks about attitudes toward our legal system. What might Sells say specifically about the kinds of problems that Albert Alschuler identifies?
6. Imagine a conversation between Sells and Lynn Hecht Schafran, author of "Is the Law Male?" Would they agree or disagree about fundamental concerns in our legal system? How would Noretta Koertge and Daphne Patai, authors of "Introduction to the World of Women's Studies" (chapter 2), respond to Schafran's claims of bias in the legal system?
7. Both Craig Horowitz's and Mark Hansen's articles suggest that many Americans are concerned that criminals are getting away with crimes. These Americans thus see a need for tougher laws and uncompromising punishments. Does the evidence in these two articles seem to support such concerns? Is this system really letting criminals get away?
8. In their essay on privacy in the workplace, Alderman and Kennedy raise a number of questions about the relationship between one's work life and one's private life. How would the writers in chapter 3, who also explore this boundary between work and play (for example, Stanton Wheeler or Juliet Schor) respond to Alderman and Kennedy's legal perspective? How does this legal perspective differ from the perspective of writers more interested in sociological or psychological trends and consequences?

Appendix A

Voices from Our Past
Conversations in American Cultural History—
An Annotated Bibliography and
Questions for Discussion and Writing

In the preceding chapters, we have focused on *current* conversations: that is, on recently published essays, arguments, and research articles about important issues in contemporary American culture. As the introduction to each chapter suggests, we think that these current conversations arise from enduring questions in American cultural history. In this appendix, we suggest some readings that will provide a better understanding of how today's concerns belong to a longer tradition of American research and writing.

Most of these documents can be found relatively easily in your college or university library, often in literary or historical anthologies. The full texts of some of these readings can even be found on the World Wide Web or in other electronic databases to which you may have access.

Think of the readings listed here as earlier starting points for the conversations introduced in the preceding chapters. These historical sources provide further insight into the topics discussed in the chapters' readings, as well as provide the basis for comparative analysis. We've listed the readings chronologically, rather than topically, because many can be connected to more than one of the chapters of current readings; in earlier times, topics were often defined more broadly than is common today. Thus, many of the readings here belong to more than one "current of inquiry."

In this list we have included works that represent a variety of different perspectives and forms, including fiction, autobiography, political address, and scholarly research, to give you a broad range of authors, viewpoints, and approaches. Among the works listed here are a few of the sources on which the writers represented in chapters 2 through 5 relied for their own contributions to the conversations we present. Historians and other researchers use such source documents—called "primary source" documents—to construct their own interpretations of historical events and movements. The commentaries and interpretations produced are then called a "secondary source." When using primary sources like the ones we list, you need to read them somewhat differently than current articles such as those in this text. That is, you must place yourself in the social and historical contexts that produced such documents, recognizing that earlier texts may have differences in language, style, and allusion. Further, imagine how an author's original audience might have responded to his or her words. Some of these works were spoken before they were published, and many are personal rather than scholarly or objective.

When working with the selections listed in this appendix, think about how the readings in chapters 2 through 5 echo and respond to these historical documents. In what ways are we now engaged in the same conversations as those of the writers represented in this appendix? And in what ways do these voices from the past help you to understand more fully the voices that raise issues in conversation today? At the end of the bibliography, you'll find further, more specific questions called "More Connections: Questions for Linking Past and Present." These are just suggestions for the kinds of connections that can be made. As you think more about the source of today's conversations, you will undoubtedly find yourself making many more such connections between past and present.

SELECTED BIBLIOGRAPHY OF HISTORICAL SOURCES

From Revolution to Civil War

BENJAMIN FRANKLIN, "THE WAY TO WEALTH" (1757). This essay, comprised of some of the best portions of *Poor Richard's Almanac,* conveys the importance of industry and a temperate life. The idea that only those who work hard and diligently and who rein in their passions and natural vices will achieve health, wealth, and wisdom is expounded by "Richard Saunders" in the well-known proverb "Early to bed, and early to rise / Makes a man healthy, wealthy, and wise." It is an aphorism that many Americans, at least those of earlier generations, heard frequently while growing up. It had all the more force, perhaps, coming from Franklin (1706–90), whom we know to be the real man behind the fictitious Richard Saunders, and whom we were taught to respect as one of the country's Founding Fathers.

THOMAS JEFFERSON, "REPORT OF THE COMMISSIONERS APPOINTED TO FIX THE SITE OF THE UNIVERSITY OF VIRGINIA" (1818). Inscribed on the monument above the grave of Thomas Jefferson (1743–1826) are the words "Here was buried Thomas Jefferson, Author of the Declaration of American Independence, Of the Statute of Virginia for Religious Freedom, and Father of the University of Virginia." A man of wide-ranging interests and great intellect, Jefferson saw the University of Virginia as a truly *American* institution, one that would educate the new country's statesmen and thinkers in a manner keeping with the political and moral principles of the new Constitution. For that reason, the university was to be an entirely secular institution, one with no ties to any religious faith; in this way, Jefferson argued, the separation of Church and State would be maintained and, more important, students and faculty would have the freedom to worship as they wished. But Jefferson also saw the university as a place where students would receive firm grounding in the best ideas of his own and earlier ages and where they would also receive the kind of training that would make them welcome in intellectual centers around the world.

RALPH WALDO EMERSON, "THE AMERICAN SCHOLAR" (1837). In "The American Scholar" Emerson (1803–1882) asks his audience—both the listeners of the nineteenth century and the readers who have come after them—to reenvision the American scholar and to create themselves anew. Asking us to discard the old notions that enslave scholars to old books and old ideas, making it impossible for them to create, to act, and to *live,* Emerson hopes to inflame in his audience a new sense of the power of the individual spirit. To rekindle that spirit, the scholar—like all people—must not only acknowledge but also embrace the contraries and uncertainties seen in the world and, in the process, become part of the Universal. The world, for Emerson, is "a shadow of the soul, or *other me,*" and the true scholar makes that connection with the Universal only by refusing to become one of the masses, who simply echo what others have thought and said, living a life of desperate inaction.

HENRY DAVID THOREAU, *CIVIL DISOBEDIENCE* (1848). Henry David Thoreau (1817–1862) is probably more familiar to readers for his sojourn on Walden Pond than for a night spent in a Concord, Massachusetts, jail cell in 1846. Nevertheless, the independence of conscience that inspired Thoreau's act of passive, nonviolent protest against the Mexican War arose from the same independence of spirit that led him to the conclusions he draws in *Walden.* In *Civil Disobedience,* Thoreau explores the relationship between the individual and the state and makes a clear distinction between *law,* the body of rules that govern our society, and *justice,* which involves doing what is right. Thoreau believed that because individual conscience must take precedence over laws enacted by government, the individual must resist laws that conflict with his or her sense of what is right.

HORACE MANN, "THE CASE FOR PUBLIC SCHOOLS" (1848). Public education seems such a part of the fabric of twentieth-century life in the United States that it may be hard to imagine a time when those who wanted to attend school did not have the opportunity to do so. That opportunity is due, in large part, to Horace Mann (1796–1859), who, as the Secretary to the Massachusetts State Board of Education, argued that free public education should be made available to all. Fundamental to his argument is the very idea of social and economic democracy. Mann believed that a society is susceptible to class antagonisms if the members of one class are poor, ignorant laborers and the members of another are wealthy, educated property owners. To dissolve these antagonisms—indeed, to dissolve the class structure—he proposes a system of public education. Such a system will allow for much more than the redistribution of existing wealth; it will enable all people, armed with the intelligence brought by their own education, to create and enjoy their own wealth.

HENRY DAVID THOREAU, *WALDEN, OR LIFE IN THE WOODS* (1854). Along with Emerson and others, Thoreau belonged to a circle of New England intellectuals known as the "Transcendentalists." Reacting against the strict rationalism of the eighteenth century, the Transcendentalists were looking for ways to make sense of the distinctions between self and other, nature and culture, reason and instinct. Theirs was a philosophy of profound idealism, and one that has had a lasting effect on the American character. Thoreau's "Walden Experiment" put Transcendentalist principles into practice. The work chronicles his two-year stay at Walden Pond and records his experiences and reflections, later published as *Walden*. In the sections of the book entitled "Sounds" and "Solitude," Thoreau reflects not just on his relationship to nature—an obvious theme of *Walden*—but on the interplay of nature and technology. In a chapter ostensibly about the way that sound helps to structure his daily experience, Thoreau also reflects on the impact of the railroad, as he observes it from his window.

ELIZABETH CADY STANTON, "ADDRESS TO THE LEGISLATURE OF NEW YORK" (1854). In 1848, in the small town of Seneca Falls, New York, a group of men and women met to discuss the status of women in society. Using Jefferson's "Declaration of Independence" as a model, the convention drafted a "Declaration of Sentiments and Resolutions," offering several proposals to change the legal and social status of women. Here, Elizabeth Cady Stanton (1815–1902) began to find her voice and to define the issues that would engage her energies for the rest of her life. In her efforts to improve the status of women, Stanton directed her attention toward the entire system of American law, which she felt gave men an unfair advantage over women, especially in matters of marriage and childrearing. In 1854, Stanton spoke before the New York State Legislature, comparing the situation of married women—subject to their husband's will and authority—to that of slaves living under their master's tyranny. In this address, she calls for equality of men and women under the law.

REBECCA HARDING DAVIS, "LIFE IN THE IRON-MILLS" (1861). A fictional story, "Life in the Iron-Mills" vividly portrays the working conditions of the mill workers of the time. Trapped in the lifeless world of the iron mill, the protagonist Wolfe displays a genius for sculpture recognized even by those who oversee and profit from his work in the mill. Unable or unwilling to provide the young iron worker with a way out of the mill, they nevertheless help him to believe that he has the *right* to a better life. But because he has no opportunity to secure that right (the right to pursue happiness guaranteed to all Americans in the Constitution), Wolfe is doomed. Although Rebecca Harding Davis (1831–1910) wrote this story without any practical, first-hand knowledge of the poverty or working conditions she describes, a picture so vivid emerges from her work that it is hard to escape its reality. Perhaps today, when some critics are again decrying the mechanization and dehumanization of work, Davis's voice sounds an important warning.

ABRAHAM LINCOLN, "SECOND INAUGURAL ADDRESS" (1865). By March 1865, when Lincoln took the oath of office for the second time, the outcome of the Civil War seemed inevitable, and he undoubtedly realized that American society had been profoundly changed by it. The South had surely lost the war, but the task of reconstructing the Union that he held so dear still lay ahead. Lincoln possessed a simple but elegant rhetorical style, which allowed him to convey his message precisely with a few carefully chosen words. In this Inaugural Address he calls upon this talent to accomplish two clear tasks: to convince the soldiers and citizens of the North that their sacrifices had been justified by the evil of slavery and the intransigence of the South, and to begin the process of healing that would ensure reunification.

The Age of Progress and Reform

SUSAN B. ANTHONY, "WOMEN'S RIGHT TO VOTE" (1873). One of the leaders of the suffragette movement, Susan B. Anthony (1820–1906) gave this speech after her arrest for attempting to vote in a presidential election. At the time, only men could vote, of course, so Anthony's action was as much an attempt to win for women the right to vote as to cast an individual ballot. Although the issue is itself a highly charged one, Anthony's appeals in "Women's Right to Vote" are largely based on reason. She argues that the Constitution does not *bestow* rights upon us but only protects those rights "endowed by [our] Creator." As people, women have the same rights as men and are entitled to the same Constitutional protection of those rights. Anthony refutes those who had argued that the masculine pronouns of the Constitution imply that only men may exercise the rights it contains. If that logic were to be applied consistently, she says, women must then be exempted from criminal law and laws of taxation. Finally, Anthony uses the then recent passage of the Fourteenth Amendment to bolster her case. That amendment states, "The right of citizens of the United States to vote shall not be denied or abridged by the United States, or by any State, on account of race, color, or previous condition of servitude." Noting that, Anthony draws a parallel between the conditions of former slaves and the present "condition of servitude" endured by women whose husbands have the right to discipline them, restrict their freedom of movement, and deprive them of wages. Anthony's speech anticipates many of the arguments made a century later by members of what came to be called the women's movement.

HELEN HUNT JACKSON, *A CENTURY OF DISHONOR* (1881). Helen Hunt Jackson became interested in the treatment of Native Americans after attending a lecture on the subject. Her interest led her to research the subject and, in 1881, she sent the fruits of that research, *A Century of Dishonor,* to the members of Congress. Citing government documents acknowledging broken promises and its own mistreatment of Native Americans, Jackson exposes the ways in which frontiersmen, gold-seekers, and entrepreneurs were allowed simply to exploit Native American tribes. Labeled savage and lazy by those who would deprive them of their land and their way of life, Native Americans had none of the rights of American citizens. In *Century of Dishonor,* Jackson calls both Congress and the American public to action: Only by granting Native Americans the rights of citizenship and by recognizing their claims to their own lands, can the US government prevent further cruelty and redress the injustices it has committed.

ANDREW CARNEGIE, *THE GOSPEL OF WEALTH* (1889). In this book Carnegie proposes not to change the methods by which wealth is accumulated in America, but rather to emphasize the duties and responsibilities of those whose efforts have brought them such wealth. A self-made multimillionaire in the steel industry, Andrew Carnegie (1835–1919) believed in a special brand of philanthropy, by which those whose energy and talent had resulted in great wealth distributed their excess to those in need. Somewhat prophetically, Carnegie recognizes that as the disparity between rich and poor grows wider, society as a whole will suffer. Carnegie urges the wealthy to lead a modest, not lavish life, and to spend their money on creating institutions that will work toward improving society. He also points to the dangers of passing on wealth to the next generation, who may become lazy and useless as a result of their inherited riches. Carnegie focused much attention on education and literacy, in particular, by endowing public libraries across the nation.

SAMUEL GOMPERS, "WHAT DOES THE WORKING MAN WANT?" (1890). Hoping to gain for themselves the fruits of their own work and a share of the nation's prosperity, many factory and mill workers joined the union movement to demand shorter hours, higher wages, and better working conditions. Among the leaders of the labor movement was Samuel Gompers (1850–1924), the founder of the American Federation of Labor (now combined with the Congress of Industrial Organizations to become the AFL-CIO). Gompers delivered the speech "What Does the Working Man Want?" on May 1, 1890, as part of his campaign for the eight-hour workday. This campaign was bitterly opposed by the managers and entrepreneurs of the time, who argued that a reduction in the workday would inevitably lead to reduced production and, consequently, a reduction in the national prosperity. Although Gompers is here addressing an audience of union members and workers who would naturally be inclined to support his position, he also attempts to address the concerns of managers and entrepreneurs who would oppose him. To their argument that productivity would decline, he responds with an assertion that "the history of the country . . . shows the reverse." To their fears that the working man would waste any extra leisure time or drink it away, he responds that a man with more time would find himself able to *think* more.

CHARLOTTE PERKINS GILMAN, *WOMEN AND ECONOMICS* (1898). In many of her writings, Charlotte Perkins Gilman (1860–1935), focuses on the economic dependence of women on their husbands, fathers, and sons and asserts that the arguments justifying this situation are both unacceptable and illogical. Anticipating arguments made by working women of later decades, Gilman says that, in doing the hard physical labor of the household, women have proven false the contention that they are incapable of fulfilling the obligations of the workplace. In that case, she asks, why are women denied the chance to work for pay? The immediate reply is that women must devote their time and energies to their maternal duties. Here, too, Gilman finds the argument flawed, noting that so much of women's time goes to nonmaternal duties—the care of the household—that it is clear they have ample time to devote to a paid job. Gilman's approach is especially interesting in that she avoids appeals to emotion and morality and builds an argument on the principles of logic.

THORSTEIN VEBLEN, *THE THEORY OF THE LEISURE CLASS* (1899). Thorstein Veblen (1857–1929) introduces economic concepts that are still widely held today. Among them is the concept of "conspicuous consumption," a term still used to describe some Americans' habit of buying goods they don't need simply to establish publicly their social class. This habit is only one of those Veblen ascribes to the leisure class, but throughout his book he makes clear that this class is defined largely by its distance from true industry. It sustains itself by subjugating those who do the necessary work—often women and those with less physical prowess. Veblen argues that a leisure class can develop only in a predatory culture, in which the necessities are obtained easily enough as to enable the existence of such an unproductive class.

HENRY ADAMS, "THE VIRGIN AND THE DYNAMO" (1900). "The Virgin and the Dynamo" is the most famous chapter of Henry Adams' experimental, never-quite-finished autobiography, *The Education of Henry Adams*. Here he explores late nineteenth-century ambivalence toward science and technology, reflecting on symbols of force and power. The occasion for these reflections is the World's Fair in Paris (April through November 1900), for which Samuel P. Langley, an American scientist and inventor, acted as his guide. Adams is impressed with how much science and technology have advanced in just seven years since he attended the world exposition in Chicago. As the two men contemplate the great machines, Langley himself is at a loss to explain just how electricity works, and this idea of forces beyond our control and comprehension follows Adams throughout the chapter. He uses symbols to explain the difference between present and past—between a world governed by an "anarchical" symbol like the dynamo and a world governed by a unifying symbol like the Virgin.

W. E. B. DU BOIS, THE NEGRO PROBLEM (1903). In the early years of the twentieth century, a great deal of debate centered on the proper education for what was then called the Negro population. At the time, many, including some influential African American leaders, believed that for many of the emancipated slaves the road to economic independence began with an *industrial* education that would ensure that every man learned a trade. Others, among them W. E. B. Du Bois (1868–1963), argued otherwise. In this book, Du Bois, who helped found the National Association for the Advancement of Colored People (NAACP) several years later, proposes that a tenth of the African American population be given the opportunity and encouragement to attend college. That tenth will, he argues, not only benefit themselves but in turn influence others of their race to develop their minds and pursue educations.

UPTON SINCLAIR, THE JUNGLE (1906). People today sometimes talk of novels as "only fiction," but many such works have had a tremendous impact on the social, political, or moral beliefs of their time. One such influential work is Upton Sinclair's (1878–1968) *The Jungle*. A fictional account of work and factory conditions in Chicago's meat-packing industry, this book tells the story of an immigrant factory worker subjected to the harsh working conditions in the Chicago stockyards and exploited by the upper-class owners, policemen, and political bosses who take advantage of his inability to speak English and his ignorance of American ways of life. Although the socialist Sinclair meant for his readers to respond to his horrifying descriptions of poverty, starvation, and exploitation, the public responded instead to the almost incidental descriptions of the unsanitary conditions that surrounded the processing of meat in the stockyards and to the claims that processed meat was often falsely labeled. In direct response to Sinclair's fiction, President Theodore Roosevelt convened a commission to investigate the conditions in the Chicago stockyards. When that commission substantiated Sinclair's story, first Roosevelt, and then the general public, pressured Congress to ignore the intense lobbying and bitter denials of the meat-packing industry. Only six months after *The Jungle*'s appearance as a book (it first appeared in serial form), Congress passed the Pure Food and Drug Act and the Beef Inspection Act. Sinclair's novel has rightly earned him a place as one of the country's most successful "muckrakers."

ANZIA YEZIERSKA, THE BREAD GIVERS: A STRUGGLE BETWEEN A FATHER OF THE OLD WORLD AND A DAUGHTER OF THE NEW (1925). Anzia Yezierska (1885?–1970) wrote her novel *The Bread Givers* in 1925, twenty-four years after she and her Russian-Polish parents immigrated to the United States. Although fiction, the book reveals much about the educational experience of immigrants in early twentieth century America. Like many immigrants of the time, the heroine, Sara Smolinksy, enters college with little experience of the world in which most of her classmates live. While they have lives of privilege and relative wealth, she has worked hard all her life and remained in poverty. While they have lived in an open, airy landscape filled with greenery and sunshine, she has lived in the tenements of New York. And, finally, while many of them see college life as "being out for a good time," Sara sees it as a serious business that will help her escape her past and allow her independence from her father.

MERIDEL LE SUEUR, "WOMEN ON THE BREADLINES" (1932). A reporter and writer of fiction, Meridel Le Sueur (1900–1996) belongs to a school of political realism intent upon bringing into focus some of the grim realities of life in the United States. "Women on the Breadlines" paints a picture of Depression-era hunger, poverty, and hopelessness so vivid and wrenching that an early editor called it too "defeatist in attitude." What makes Le Sueur's work both unusual and powerful is that it tells the stories of particular women trapped by the poverty and despair of urban life during the 1930s. Le Sueur describes the horror of women forced to sell their clothes and bodies because no one will buy their labor and women so emaciated that not only their bones but their hidden tumors become almost visible. What for many of us seems a long-ago decade of economic deprivation becomes, in Le Sueur's descriptions, a portrait of real women desperate to escape the traps of hunger, poverty, and unemployment in a world that gives them little opportunity to do so.

JOHN DEWEY, *EXPERIENCE AND EDUCATION* (1938). One of the most influential educational theorists of the twentieth century, John Dewey (1859–1952) helped engender wide-reaching changes in teaching methods and goals of education. Dewey argues that each child's experience of the world is different, not only because personal environments and histories differ but also because each individual reacts to and interacts with his world in a unique way. For that reason, no single curriculum can meet the needs of every student. By acknowledging the personal needs and environmental realities of each student's life, a teacher can, however, create an environment that will encourage students to interact positively with their worlds. A founder of the "progressive" movement in education, Dewey encourages us to shift our attention away from a standard curriculum designed for all students and focus more attention on making education valuable to students with different backgrounds, needs, talents, and desires.

The Post-Industrial Age

UNITED STATES SUPREME COURT, *BROWN V. BOARD OF EDUCATION OF TOPEKA, KANSAS* (1954). In Louisiana in 1896, a man of mixed racial heritage named Homer Plessy argued that a state law "providing for separate railway carriages for the white and colored races" was unconstitutional. The

Supreme Court disagreed. In *Plessy v. Ferguson* it established the standard of "separate but equal" in race relations—a standard that stood as law for nearly half a century. In 1954 a case came before the Supreme Court which would effectively make the "separate but equal" standard obsolete in public education. With it's decision in *Brown* the Court effectively ended segregation in public schools throughout the nation. As the Court notes in its opinion, segregation has a detrimental effect on children; segregated schools simply can never be made equal. The principles articulated in the *Brown* decision have had an enormous impact on American life. Not only was racial desegregation in public school mandated as a result, but other groups, such as the handicapped, have argued for equal access to public facilities. Recent cases involving the admission of women to all-male military academies are based on the principles articulated in *Brown*. While individual opinions differ greatly, as a society we generally accept that "separate" facilities are by definition "unequal."

DWIGHT D. EISENHOWER, "FAREWELL ADDRESS: THE MILITARY-INDUSTRIAL COMPLEX" (1961). president Dwight D. Eisenhower (1890–1969), whose eight-year term as president ended with the election of John F. Kennedy in 1960, used his farewell address to warn Americans about the changes in American politics resulting from the expanded influence of the military and the defense industry. Eisenhower, himself a career military man and World War II hero, argued that the existence of a permanent armaments industry was unprecedented in American history, and he expressed concern that these changes may have grave implications for "the very structure of our society." Though we generally think of the 1950s as an era of social and political complacency and economic prosperity, this speech makes us recognize that this complacency was only a thin veneer covering deeply troubling tensions, and that economic prosperity came in large part from massive defense spending.

STUDENTS FOR A DEMOCRATIC SOCIETY, "THE PORT HURON STATEMENT" (1962). By the end of the 1960s, three major political figures had been assassinated, an unpopular war had shattered the political future of President Lyndon Johnson, and the American university had lost its reputation for ivory tower seclusion. In the forefront of the decade's battles were a number of student groups, among them the Students for a Democratic Society. Although in later years the SDS came to be associated with a violent militancy, its early proclamations, including this one, are characterized by an intense idealism and a tone of reason. These largely white, middle-class students aimed to use their own positions of relative privilege as a platform for action against the wrongs they saw. They argue in "The Port Huron Statement" that the United States needs to turn away from its obsession with Cold War politics and militarism and rededicate itself to the needs of its own citizens, particularly those afflicted with the diseases of poverty and racism.

MICHAEL HARRINGTON, *THE OTHER AMERICA* (1962). In the early 1960s, when Michael Harrington (1928–) wrote *The Other America,* many Americans believed this country was a land of unparalleled opportunity. Many were shocked by Harrington's assertions that there were over 50 *million* people living in poverty in the United States. Most Americans had, after all, never seen large numbers of the poor, never seen the dilapidated houses in which they lived, never faced the illness and hopelessness that shortened their lives. Harrington's book, which influenced the social programs advanced by both Presidents Kennedy and Johnson, forced Americans to rethink their complacent notions about their country's economic realities. In it, Harrington argues that poverty had not been eradicated but merely hidden. With the growth of the suburbs and interstate freeways, middle- and upper-class Americans no longer saw the poor and could more easily forget their existence. As he puts it, the poor "made the mistake of being born to the wrong parents, in the wrong section of the country, in the wrong industry, or in the wrong racial or ethnic group. Once that mistake has been made . . . most of them would never have a chance to get out of the other America." An appeal to Americans' moral and social conscience, Harrington's book provides a sobering antidote to our notion of the 1950s and early 1960s as an era of affluence and moral ease.

MARTIN LUTHER KING, JR., "LETTER FROM BIRMINGHAM JAIL" (1963). It is hard to imagine a figure who more fully dominates the landscape of the 1960s than Martin Luther King, Jr. (1929–1968). King, a young Baptist minister, emerged as a leader in the civil rights movement during the bus boycott in Montgomery, Alabama, in 1954. In April 1964, King was jailed in Birmingham when he participated in nonviolent demonstrations there. King wrote his famous "Letter" in response to a published statement by eight Birmingham clergymen who opposed King's activities in their city. This letter is important because it reveals King's political and social philosophy more fully than does the oratorical eloquence of "I Have a Dream." A number of key definitions emerge from "Letter from Birmingham Jail." First, King asserts the interrelatedness of all communities and seeks to clarify the goals and purposes of what he calls "direct nonviolent action." But beyond the specifics of his own nonviolent campaign, King's letter seeks to define injustice and to explore the ways and means of achieving justice.

MARSHALL MCLUHAN, *UNDERSTANDING MEDIA: THE EXTENSIONS OF MAN* (1964). By the 1960s, the television set, which had been a mere curiosity a decade before, had become ubiquitous in American homes. Not only did most homes have one, but this new technology transformed the way that people viewed their world. Born in Canada and educated in England at Cambridge University, Marshall McLuhan (1911–1980) was a university professor in both the United States and Canada. One of the first writers to take a critical look at the impact of technology on media, he explains in this book—in which he coined the phrase "the medium is the message"—"any technology gradually creates a totally new human environment." McLuhan examines how new electronic technologies affect the community and relationships within that community. Whereas the mechanical age (beginning with the invention of print) was characterized by fragmentation and isolation, the electronic age brings people together, abolishing time and space. As a result, McLuhan argues, detachment from the world is no longer possible in the technological age.

LYNDON B. JOHNSON, HOWARD UNIVERSITY ADDRESS (1965). When Lyndon Johnson (1903–1973) became president after the assassination of John F. Kennedy in November 1963, the country was faced with two major issues: its increasing involvement in the Vietnam War and the growing passion of the civil rights movement. Although Johnson's presidency was defined for many by his inability to extricate the country from its military involvement in Vietnam, Johnson himself wanted to focus more attention on the building of a Great Society that would benefit all Americans. In his address at Howard University, Johnson affirms his commitment to the principles of the civil rights movement. The history of slavery and discrimination has, he tells his audience, threatened the family structure of African Americans and too often made poverty endemic to their lives. For that reason, no amount of legislation alone will solve the problems that beset the African American population; America's white people must be willing to provide African Americans with opportunities for education, training, and work. Johnson's address is a call to end the centuries of hatred and oppression that have made equal opportunity so elusive.

JAMES MEREDITH, *THREE YEARS IN MISSISSIPPI* (1966). In October 1962, James Meredith made history simply by attending his first class at the University of Mississippi. An African American, Meredith had sought to defeat white supremacy by winning admission to the formerly all-white university, a goal he achieved only after a long struggle in the courts. In his book, Meredith describes the court battles that preceded his entrance into the university and the personal struggles he faced as he attended class each day. Until he graduated from the University in August 1963, federal marshals stood outside each of Meredith's classes and accompanied him as he walked about the campus. And, until he graduated, Meredith was subjected to racial epithets and even death threats. His book reminds us of the personal as well as political and social harm that racism causes.

CLARK KERR, "THE URBAN-GRANT UNIVERSITY" (1967). In a speech to the Phi Beta Kappa Gamma Chapter of the City College of New York, former University of California President Clark Kerr (1911–) asks us to envision a new kind of university—one modeled on the land-grant universities that were created with the Morrill Act of 1862. Land-grant universities were established as places where students and professors might devote themselves to the study of agriculture and industry. Here Kerr proposes "an urban-grant university" located in the towering skyscrapers of urban centers, which would draw students and professors interested in finding solutions to problems confronting many of today's urban centers. Thirty years after Kerr's address, there are no urban-grant universities and no prospects for them. However, Kerr raises some important questions about the role of the university—should it be primarily a peaceful haven for its scholars and students, a research institution serving government and industry, or a center for the study of the sociological problems that beset the modern city?

MORE CONNECTIONS
Questions for Linking Past and Present

1. In the *Breadgivers,* Anzia Yezierska's heroine, Sara Smolinky, enters college excited by its promise and fearful of her inability to fit in. In his autobiography, James Meredith also describes his status as an "outsider" entering college for the first time. Among the writers whose work appears in this text, Mike Rose (chapter 2) writes most specifically about the experiences of first-year college students. Imagine a conversation among Smolinky, Meredith, and Rose. What would they say their experiences have in common? What would they say makes their experiences different from the others'? Finally, if these three were to give advice to the outsiders that have come after them, what would each say?

2. Americans often pride themselves on their individuality and personal independence. Both in our literature and in our lives, we have often made heroes of the "lone ranger," the man or woman who succeeds with little help from the larger community. Throughout this text, the double-edged theme of independence and isolation/alienation has appeared again and again. Certainly we see it in Rose's autobiographical description of his first days in college (chapter 2). Among the works in our annotated bibliography in Meredith's autobiographical piece; in Yezierska's fictional story about a young immigrant's college experiences; in Henry David Thoreau's "Civil Disobedience"; and Martin Luther King's "Letter from Birmingham Jail." But issues of individuality, independence, and alienation also surface at least occasionally in works like Ralph Waldo Emerson's "The American Scholar," Rebecca Harding Davis's "Life in the Iron-Mills," Horace Mann's "The Case for Public Schools," and John Dewey's *Experience and Education* (all mentioned in the annotated bibliography) and in Leon Kass's "Am I My Brother's Keeper?" (chapter 5). Examine the concept of the individual in (or against) society in at least three or four of the readings presented in chapters 2–5 or listed in this appendix. To what extent do the authors agree about the appropriate relationship between the individual and the society? The most common relationship? Where would *you* stand in their conversation about independence and isolation/alienation?

3. For generations, Americans have grown up with the notion that they can get anywhere if they just work hard and "pull themselves up by their bootstraps." This work ethic is, many have said, at the heart of American culture. Others—not just in our time but in previous times as well—have argued otherwise, bemoaning the loss of the work ethic, especially, it seems, in the younger generation. Perhaps the debate results more from tensions and competition among generations than from any real change in the work ethic. Or perhaps our willingness to work really has declined or our ideas about the nature and purpose of work really have changed. Among the writers in our annotated bibliography, look at the works by Benjamin Franklin, Andrew Carnegie, Samuel Gompers, and Thorstein Veblen. How would Franklin (or Richard Sanders, the speaker in "The Way to Wealth") respond to the ideas of Gompers, Carnegie, or Veblen? How might any of these earlier writers have influenced the definitions of work presented by the various writers in chapter 3 (especially Reg Theriault, Herbert Applebaum, Juliet Schor, and Stanton Wheeler)?

4. During the nineteenth and twentieth centuries, higher education in the United States blossomed, and most Americans now live fairly near a two- or four-year college or university. Despite the apparent success and popularity of the American educational system, however, educators, politicians, parents, and students continue to debate some very fundamental questions about the nature and purpose of higher education. Many of the earlier writers presented in the annotated bibliography define what they see as the essential function of the college or university, and these definitions vary considerably. Read the works by Thomas Jefferson, Ralph Waldo Emerson, and Clark Kerr. Then imagine yourself in a conversation with these writers and thinkers. Each of them has a firm idea of what education should be and what it should do, but their visions may have been formed by political, social, and economic conditions that no longer exist. In this conversation, explain which of their ideas still have merit at the end of the twentieth century and which would need modification to suit modern conditions, assumptions, and values. In the end, your goal is to convince them that you have a definition of "higher education" that will strengthen American colleges and universities. To help you form your own ideas about the ideal college or university education, look at some of the writers in chapter 2 who are responding to the problems and promises of higher education in the 1990s and consider the new definitions of literacy advanced by Deborah Brandt ("Accumulating Literacy") in chapter 4.

5. Americans have long had a love-hate relationship with science and technology. We are often intrigued and impressed by the advances that science and technology have helped us make in such areas as medicine, space exploration, transportation, and communication; at the same time we are fearful of the science that could unleash unknown horrors, or the technology that could slowly undermine human relationships. Use the readings in this text to trace our attitudes toward science and technology. How do attitudes formed in earlier decades and centuries influence current attitudes? Some readings to con-

sider are J. Wade Gilley's "The Distributed University" (chapter 2), Juliet Schor's "Time Squeeze," and Merlisa Lawrence Corbett's "Telecommuting" (chapter 3), all of the readings in chapter 4, and the following readings listed in this appendix: Thoreau's *Walden,* Davis's "Life in the Iron-Mills," Henry Adams's "The Virgin and the Dynamo," and Eisenhower's "The Military-Industrial Complex."

6. In "What Does the Law Want?" (chapter 5), Benjamin Sells paints a scenario in which the Law, troubled by poor health, seeks psychiatric counseling. Imagine that this figure of the Law is being examined by a panel of "psychiatrists" from among the writers represented in this appendix. Among those you might include in your panel, for instance, are Thoreau, Abraham Lincoln, Susan B. Anthony, Helen Hunt Jackson, Upton Sinclair, Michael Harrington, Martin Luther King, Jr., Lyndon Johnson, and James Meredith. How would these people advise the Law to heal itself? (To determine what ails the Law, look also at other essays in chapter 5.)

7. In the nineteenth and early twentieth centuries, Elizabeth Cady Stanton, Charlotte Perkins Gilman, Susan B. Anthony, and Meridel Le Sueur addressed issues about the status and equality of women that are still being debated today. If these earlier writers were suddenly to appear before them, how would the following writers respond to their questions about the status of women in today's American society: Daphne Patai and Noretta Koertge ("Introduction to the World of Women's Studies" [chapter 2]), Joan Ryan ("Little Girls in Pretty Boxes" [chapter 3]), Lotte Bailyn ("Two Women at Work" [chapter 3]), Pamela E. Kramer and Sheila Lehman ("Mismeasuring Women" [chapter 4]), and Lana F. Rakow and Vija Navarro ("Remote Mothering" [chapter 4])?

8. At the heart of several selections in the annotated bibliography is a sense of what it means to live in a democracy. Use some of the works listed here to come to your own understanding of what "democracy" means. In addition to the works that most explicitly raise the question—the works of Thomas Jefferson and Henry David Thoreau, for instance—you might also look at the writings of Horace Mann, Lyndon Johnson, Helen Hunt Jackson, Michael Harrington, Susan B. Anthony, and Meridel Le Sueur. What other writers in this text might you invite to join the conversation? Why?

Appendix B

Research and Knowledge
A Short Guide to Gathering and Using Outside Sources

Many of the questions following the readings in this book ask you to do some kind of research—in other words, to use a source outside the reading to aid you in forming your own opinion of the validity of the author's message. When you hear the words "academic research" or think about writing a research paper, you may think about going to the library and finding books on a particular topic. If you are a freshman, you may have little experience using your college or university library—which, especially at large research universities, will be dramatically different from the high school or public library you have used in the past. You will find that college and university libraries not only have more volumes, but also have a wide array of other sources, such as special collections, microfilm and microfiche resources, electronic databases, and specialized indexes to journals and periodicals. Though finding sources in the library can be an important part of the research process, you should also begin to broaden your notion of what sources are and what research really is. The purpose of this appendix is to introduce you to a variety of strategies for finding outside sources to explore the issues and questions raised by this book and to support your own arguments and ideas about these and other topics.

For most people, academic research is somewhat like detective work. Above all, you must be creative and have good problem-solving skills. Whether you are searching a library database, formulating a survey, or conducting a research interview, you need to be willing to try several different angles or approaches when first attempts fail to produce useful information. While writers may dream about finding a perfect source, what they usually find instead are small pieces of the puzzle, as they build their opinions piece by piece, idea by idea. In addition, it is quite common to miscalculate how valuable a source will be until you have carefully analyzed it. In the end, a source that you considered unimportant may give you the most useful and interesting insight on your topic. As you become comfortable with a variety of strategies and approaches, research will prove to be both rewarding and exciting. Because there is no single right way to do research, though you will want to build a repertoire of research strategies that work best for you.

IDENTIFY A RESEARCH QUESTION THAT WILL LEAD YOU TO A THESIS QUESTION

A topic for a research project usually evolves from other reading you have been doing, sometimes in textbooks or other required course materials and sometimes from personal, general interest reading. Some instructors may ask you to keep a reading journal, in which you can reflect on your reading assignments, or a "clipping file," where you can collect newspaper or magazine articles and notes about things you see and hear that are related to ideas you are exploring in a course. Once you have some general knowledge of a topic, you will be ready to start your research project.

A research project will usually be more productive if, early in the process, you are able to formulate a *research question* about the general topic you want to explore. For instance, if you are writing about technology in higher education, frame your interest in the topic as a question. Something like "In what ways has technology changed college classrooms?" will help you to focus your research and evaluate your sources more carefully. Your research question may not be the same question as your thesis question, but it is a necessary starting point that will give your research a sharper focus and a more purposeful direction than if you just begin with a general topic. In large libraries, especially, you may find that beginning your research with just a topic, rather than a question, will prove overwhelming. So, by taking the time early in the process to formulate a research question, you will save time and frustration as you begin to work with the myriad of sources available to you.

The discovery process, using your research question, should help identify a narrower, more particular issue or problem that interests you. However, many writers get into trouble early in a paper because they decide on a thesis before they've thought about how they might approach their topic and what evidence and examples they might use in their discussion. It's as if they've decided on the design and structure of their building without determining whether any of the building materials are available.

Deciding on a definite thesis statement too early can lead to a writer's feeling paralyzed, because that statement may seem permanent and inflexible. Thus, it helps to think first about a *thesis question*—a narrowed, sharply focused question that offers points of analysis and opens itself up to further questions. If you are assigned a topic, you can often simply move words around to form a question. For example, a topic like "analyze the ways that technology has changed college classrooms" becomes the research question "In what ways has technology changed the college classroom?" That question will guide your research well, but it will not help you shape your paper.

To find a thesis question that will give the paper an analytical point, you need to narrow and sharpen your research question. You might ask, for instance, "How does 'distance learning' benefit and harm college students?" Such a thesis question promises an analytical paper in which you examine a complex system and report on its advantages and disadvantages. If, on the other hand, you feel that your goal is to argue a point, such a thesis question could be transformed even further: "Given its benefits and drawbacks, when and how should colleges use 'distance learning' methods?" or even "Do the advantages of 'distance learning' methods outweigh any disadvantages?" In other words, the kind of thesis question you ask will be determined in part by the kind of paper you have been asked to write. Whatever your goal, though, a strong thesis question provides a strong foundation for the research and writing that follow.

Thus, as you begin your research, take a broad approach, asking general questions to avoid overlooking any important sources and to maintain as many options as possible for narrowing and refining your topic. As you move closer to the problem or issue you want to examine in your paper, make your questions more precise and specific and sharpen the edge of controversy in them. It is very important to cast each step in the process as a question; once you stop asking questions and begin stating topics, the attitude of inquiry so essential to research writing is lost.

DEVELOP GOOD NOTE-TAKING SKILLS

As you learn to work with research sources, you will need to develop effective strategies for keeping track of the information and ideas you gather. You must keep accurate information about all your sources in order to prepare a bibliography or list of works cited, in addition to carefully recording the ideas and quotations you take from a source. It is equally important to find a way to distinguish in your notes between your own ideas (those that evolve in your own mind as you are reading) and the ideas that originated with the author of the source you are using. If your notes are not clear, you may not remember later exactly how much your own insight depended on what you read in the source. Borrowing another writer's ideas without giving him or her credit constitutes plagiarism.

Many academic writers use a notecard system: one set of notecards for bibliographic information, and one set of notecards for each idea gleaned from those sources. As you take notes from your sources, you might record direct quotations, paraphrase facts or opinions you find, or even summarize a long section of a source. Knowing whether you need a direct quotation or merely a summary, or whether you have one idea or several, may be difficult, especially in the early stages of your research. For this reason, notecards may work best for research projects that already have a clear structure and focus, as well as for large projects that use many sources. Other ways of organizing your notes may work just as well, especially if you are only using a few sources in your research.

Other writers find it easier in the beginning stages of a project to simply take detailed notes on the computer or on lined paper, sorting and reorganizing the information according to subtopics or major sections of the paper at a later stage of the project. Many writers develop a file folder system to sort their notes, or make photocopies of possibly relevant portions of their sources rather than taking notes. You might consider making photocopies of shorter sources, such as journal articles or book chapters. Keeping your own copies allows you to review a source more than once and to underline and comment on the most important information. For many people, it is becoming easier to keep "notecards" in a computer, making use of special computer programs designed for note taking or adapting general database programs. Many of these programs will generate your bibliography in whatever documentation form required by your instructor. Verify the form you are using before you begin your research, so that you can record complete and accurate bibliographic information for each source you locate.

FIND OUT WHAT SOURCES YOUR LIBRARY HAS, AND LEARN HOW TO LOCATE THEM

Most college or university libraries offer classes, tours, and printed reference materials to inform users of the library's sources and the best way to find them. While some libraries still rely primarily on a paper card catalogue retrieval system, most libraries (even some in small towns) now have electronic card catalogues. Although the electronic card catalogues at different institutions will be similar, the specific search tools may be quite different, so it is important to learn all you can about searching in the system that your library uses. Most electronic systems enable you to search by author, title words, other key words (such as words appearing in a specially prepared abstract of the source), and subject headings (often specific Library of Congress headings), and to narrow your search to a particular time frame. Each approach may provide different results. Different sources—such as books, audiovisual materials, magazines, scholarly journals, newspapers, specific articles from books and periodicals, and reports of conferences and meetings of scholarly societies—may need to be searched for, identified, and located in different ways.

Books are obviously the easiest thing to locate in a library, but books often do not provide the most recent information on a topic. Therefore, learn how to find periodicals in your library. Periodicals not only offer the most up-to-date research in a field, but they often include review articles that summarize and evaluate the most recent books. Most likely, periodicals will provide you with sources more narrowly focused than, say, a book on your topic will be.

Many research libraries contain electronic references to periodicals as part of the on-line card catalogue or as separate CD-ROM databases that contain abstracts or full-text versions of articles, which can make the research process move much more quickly. In libraries without electronic search capabilities, you will need to use special indexes to periodicals. The most common is *The Readers' Guide to Periodical Literature,* which will help you locate articles in most mainstream, general interest periodicals. Other indexes exist for specific disciplines; check with your reference librarian about which periodical indexes are available and how they are used.

Above all, do not be intimidated by the size or unfamiliarity of your college or university library. The more you know about your library, the more certain you will be of finding the most valuable and reliable information available.

CONSIDER USING NONPRINT SOURCES OF INFORMATION

Much valuable information, especially on very current topics or issues, may be found in such sources as video and audio tapes, films, photographic collections, or CD-ROM. While your library catalogue (especially the electronic catalogue) may help you find such materials, you may want to look outside the library for other useful and relevant sources. For example:

- Local or regional museums may have exhibitions that could prove useful.
- Inexpensive commercial CD-ROM reference materials are available for a variety of fields and topics.
- Documentaries or news programs broadcast on television may relate to your topic of research. Local television stations often make videocassettes of newscasts and other programming available free or for a nominal charge. In addition, most television and radio networks such as PBS (Public Broadcasting System) or NPR (National Public Radio) have sites on the World Wide Web as well as toll-free numbers for ordering copies of television or radio programs. (Your instructor may be able to obtain funding for a source that several students would use.)
- Video sale and rental stores often have vast collections of documentaries.
- Your college or university library may have a separate repository for audiovisual materials, to which your instructor may have access.

START A CLIPPING FILE OF CURRENT MAGAZINE AND NEWSPAPER ARTICLES

Some students have been able to use a technique employed by professional writers. As you read newspapers or magazines each day, clip or photocopy articles that may be of interest to you later on and file them under broad topics. After you've collected a number of articles, review them to further categorize them and file them into smaller subtopics. (You may also want to review them periodically to eliminate articles that no longer seem interesting or useful.) Since your development as a writer depends on reading widely and actively, consider spending twenty minutes or so each week in your library's current periodical room, browsing the shelves for articles that have not yet been indexed, reading newspapers from other cities, and finding out what is being written and published on particular topics. Many students are surprised to find that major metropolitan newspapers like the *New York Times* or *Washington Post* cover most topics in greater depth than smaller city newspapers can.

Not only will a clipping file provide you with potentially valuable sources for formal research assignments, but it may offer you some issues, questions, or problems for informal writing, such as journal entries or reader responses. Recurring themes in clipping files often lead to topics for papers or to questions for more extensive research projects.

BROWSE THE WORLD WIDE WEB

You have probably heard of the Information Superhighway, but you may wonder how it can help you locate information for an academic research paper. First, the term Internet refers to a worldwide computer network that links other computer networks together, allowing users to access remote databases and files that they can read or retrieve, to send electronic mail, and even to participate in "real-time" conversations with other users on-line. The World Wide Web (WWW) allows users to access "sites" on the Internet and to create on-line documents that incorporate text, graphics, and even sound and video. To use the WWW, you need an Internet connection and special "Web browsing" software, such as Mosaic or Netscape. You can probably access the WWW from your college or university library or computer center, and you may be able to get software that will allow you to access the WWW from your home or dorm. Many commercial computer services provide Internet access (much like phone service) for a fee; and commercial on-line computer services like America On-Line, CompuServe, and Prodigy provide their subscribers with "gateways" to the Internet and the World Wide Web. Individual Web pages will often provide you with "links" to other related or relevant sites. Literally hundreds of millions of documents have now been stored on the WWW, allowing individuals almost instantaneous access to enormous amounts of information on almost any topic imaginable. Browsing the Web may help you to identify "experts" on your topic. Web pages often provide you with e-mail addresses, which you can use to contact the author of a Web document or one of his or her informants. The information you find on a Web page may allow you to make further inquiries about your topic.

Although you must always be a cautious consumer of information retrieved from the WWW, if you learn to use this resource wisely, you may find invaluable insights that will make your research project both exciting and creative. As with almost any research tool, you will get better at both retrieving and evaluating such information with practice. If you want to use the Web to locate information, you will need to learn how to sift through all this information to find what you really want and need.

Using a Search Engine

Your Web browsing software will provide you with at least one and often several *search engines*. A search engine works in some ways like an electronic card catalogue, allowing you to retrieve Web documents on a particular topic. But these search engines are far more flexible and powerful than most database search tools. For instance, you may want to research whether or not family leave policies are good business for US corporations. You might begin by typing the phrase "family leave policies." A search query like this may identify 10,000 documents or more. Thus you may want to add additional qualifiers such as "large corporations." You will still identify many documents, but the search engine will sort the documents in order of importance; that is, presenting you first with the documents that seem to most completely match your search query.

But what kinds of documents will you find on the WWW? Given the example above, you might find a statement from a major political party, an opinion article from an on-line magazine, a college professor's lecture notes, an entry in a news archive, a noted researcher's annotated bibliography, or the home page of a Fortune 500 corporation. Each one of these documents might give you a slightly different piece of the puzzle you are trying to put together. In short, you may find many useful documents that you would not be able to locate (at least without much effort, knowledge, and energy) in any other way.

Apply Critical Reading Skills to WWW Documents

Documents on the WWW will challenge you to use your most highly developed critical reading skills. Remember that almost anyone with a computer and a little technical knowledge can "publish" on the WWW. The author of a document you recover may be a 12-year-old or a respected scholar, and it may not be obvious at first whether the information is reliable. If the author or organization has many documents linked to a home page, you might have to click on several links before learning what you need to know about the author's identity. Once you know the source or author of a document, you will need to assess the author's reliability and credibility as well as the document's timeliness.

At the end of this appendix are some guidelines for evaluating all kinds of sources, including WWW documents. Remember, however, that Web sources have not undergone the rigorous process of review, evaluation, and revision expected of most published sources; thus we need to judge them even more critically than other published sources. Some Web documents may, in fact, be copies of articles published elsewhere, in which case you should use the earlier, and possibly more accurate, version of the document. With Web documents, it is especially important to consider the authors' bias or prejudice about a topic, the extent of their research (including how well such research is documented and supported), and the reasons they have published a Web page. For example, does an author have any commercial or political purposes that might affect how he or she interprets or presents the information in the document? Is the piece intended to serve as propaganda for a social or political organization? If so, does that make the source more or less useful to you? Even propaganda that comes from a political or social organization with its own strong agenda may provide you with valuable insights into other points of view. Your task is to evaluate each source critically and carefully.

Keep Accurate Bibliographic Data

You can usually either print a WWW document or save it as a file to your computer disk, but make sure to note the author, title, and date of the document. Also, record the date that you found or accessed the page, since information on it may change over time. Further, pay close attention to the document's URL (universal resource locator). This WWW address (for example, the URL for the Michigan State University home page is <http://www.msu.edu>) allows another user to find the site quickly and should be part of any bibliographic citation if you use this source. The URL may not appear on the document page you print or save, so you may need to make a separate note of it, perhaps cutting and pasting it and other URLs to a computer file on your own disk. Many Web browsers, such as Netscape, also allow users to "bookmark" Web sites; a user can then go to the list of bookmarks and return quickly to a site marked earlier.

USE OBSERVATIONS AND SITE VISITS TO FIND OUT MORE ABOUT YOUR TOPIC

Much of what we learn about a topic may come from observing for ourselves what happens in particular situations. By visiting a particular place—such as a shopping mall, an amusement park, a daycare center, or an electronics factory—we can learn much about the atmosphere and culture of that place. The insights gained from careful, objective observation may help us to understand more fully our own relationship to the world around us.

In some places and situations, you will be able to observe unobtrusively, without asking permission. Whether you want to study the behavior of animals in the zoo or of teenagers at the shopping mall, you can probably do so without even making your presence known. If, on the other hand, you wanted to observe an elementary school classroom or your college board of trustees meeting, you might need to obtain permission ahead of time. Consider carefully how you will conduct yourself during the observation. Most observers are by definition not participants in the events or situations they are consciously observing. But if you have made an appointment to visit a school or factory, there may be opportunities to ask questions or elicit explanations from someone in charge. In planning your observation, decide if you can learn what you need silently—by merely watching, listening, or taking notes—or if you need to discuss your observations with someone familiar with the place or situation. Sometimes a short preliminary observation session will help you not only to decide not only the answers to these questions but to determine exactly what behavior you want to observe in the setting.

As you observe, use your senses—seeing, hearing, touching, tasting, smelling—as a checklist, to determine if you are gathering all the details you can about the place or situation. You might also construct a list of questions ahead of time to consider as you observe. Make your questions as objective as possible, calling for description rather than evaluation. Let's take the example of visiting a daycare center to learn more about the effects of daycare arrangements on both parents and children. The preliminary list of questions might include such questions as

- "How are spaces in the center arranged?"
- "Are there both indoor and outdoor play areas?"
- "How do children respond when their parents leave them?"
- "How does the center handle meals and snacks?"
- "In what ways do the children interact with each other?"
- "How do teachers handle problems with discipline or misbehavior?"
- "What emotions do the children exhibit?"

GATHER INFORMATION FROM RESEARCH INTERVIEWS

Interviews give you the chance to learn firsthand from experts on a topic or issue. Your interview subject may be an expert because of his or her profession, scholarly or teaching activities, or personal experience. Interviews are often a good first step in the research process, because they may help you identify key issues or problems related to your topic, thus allowing you to narrow your research question. Talking with an expert may also help you make better sense of the print sources you uncover. An interview might also provide a good final source of information, filling in gaps or explaining concepts that you encountered in your other research.

Interviews are most successful when you prepare carefully and plan how to process the information you receive from your informant. Before the interview:

- *Choose your subject carefully.* Select an expert—someone who can provide you with the best information regarding your topic. Try to determine whether your subject will really be able to discuss the topic clearly and specifically. Choose someone who is willing to participate in your project and can enjoy the process. Don't select someone who seems reluctant or hesitant about sharing knowledge or experiences.
- *Plan your questions ahead of time.* Consider the wording of the questions you want to ask. Will your questions elicit facts when you need facts, and opinions when you need opinions? Don't ask questions that might lead your subject to think you've already made up your mind about the topic or have already decided what you think he or she should or would say. Usually yes-or-no questions are not effective;

include open-ended questions in your repertoire. Because you never know exactly how an informant will respond to your questions, design more questions than you think necessary. While many interviewers find a "script" or sequence of questions useful, you should be able to revise the script in your mind as the interview unfolds. Include some questions designed primarily to put your informant at ease; however, be certain that such questions can lead to a discussion of the information and opinions essential to your research.

- *Consider your own attitudes about the process.* Your informant's attitude toward the interview will depend largely on you. If an interviewer is careless, haphazard, or apathetic about conducting the interview, the informant will probably respond in kind. But if an interviewer takes the process seriously and prepares carefully, the informant will probably be more forthcoming and provide more useful information. Whenever you interview someone, keep in mind that the subject is doing you a favor, and be thoughtful and courteous about the kinds of questions you ask and the manner in which you ask them.

During the interview:

- *Don't begin asking questions right away.* Even if you know your informant well, don't begin firing questions. Take some time to talk to your informant about the purpose of your project and about your own hopes and goals for the interview. Try to reassure him or her that you are genuinely interested in learning. Perhaps most important, try to make the subject comfortable with the process.
- *Listen carefully to what your subject says.* Often, interviewers are so busy thinking up or choosing the next question that they don't listen carefully to the answer to the question they have just asked. (This is especially true when interviewers use tape recordings.) Your informant's response may indicate to you a new line of questioning or the need for a follow-up question. Furthermore, if you show your informant that you are using good listening skills, he or she is more likely to open up to you and even volunteer information that goes beyond the questions you ask. So, although you certainly should consult your script of questions and take notes, you should also remain flexible and open throughout the interview.
- *Pay attention to more than just words.* As in many situations, it isn't just *what* the informant says but *how* he or she says it that will reveal information to you. Your subject's body language or gestures may reveal certain emotions or attitudes that are not conveyed in the words he or she uses. Include the nonverbal information in your notes.
- *Make sure you have heard correctly.* Echo back in your own words what you thought the subject said ("So, you are saying that . . . ?"). Ask

your informant to confirm especially important ideas ("Do you mean that . . . ?"). Again, this helps let your subject know that you are really listening.
- *Take notes; tape if possible.* The answer to this question depends on many things, not the least of which is your access to a reliable recording device and your willingness to replay the tape of the interview and take notes later. But if your informant would be uncomfortable with note taking, or if you have particularly poor note-taking skills or memory, then tape recording the interview may be necessary. If you don't tape the interview, write down some direct quotations to use in your paper. (You may polish your informant's phrasing to make it more clear.) Even if you tape the interview, take some notes to remember things such as gestures or facial expressions, that won't be picked up on the tape. The tape recorder may make the informant anxious or nervous. Reassure him or her that you are more likely to get accurate information if you record the conversation. However, if your informant objects to the tape recorder, don't insist. You will get the best possible information only if your informant feels comfortable about the process. If you don't use a tape recorder, take careful, precise notes, and verify all facts and quotations with your informant.
- *Give the interview closure.* Since your informant has provided you with valuable information, be sure that you thank him or her appropriately. Before you leave, you should also ask the informant to sign a release form, if necessary.

After the interview:

- *Review your notes as soon as possible.* Make sure that you got all the information you wanted and that your notes are complete and clear. Take some time immediately to record your impressions about what was most important. Consider writing a quick, informal response right after the interview to begin organizing the information you received while it is fresh in your mind.
- *Consider arranging a follow-up interview.* You may think of some additional questions you wish you had asked, especially after you begin planning your paper. Make sure that you can contact your informant again to verify information or solicit additional facts and opinions. In any event, you may want to ask your informant to verify any direct quotations or specific facts that you attribute to him or her.

CONDUCT RESEARCH SURVEYS

Throughout this book we have suggested that you conduct surveys to help you determine other people's opinions and formulate your own arguments. One of the advantages of doing surveys is that, in the process of asking other people to respond to your questions, you will probably see some arguments that you might not otherwise have encountered. Survey respondents can help make you a more "honest" writer, reminding you of the need to acknowledge and address opposing points of view, providing you with supporting arguments that you may not otherwise have considered, and giving you a sense of how people's backgrounds and experiences have led them to their opinions.

Identifying Informants for a Survey

In conducting a survey, first decide whom you will survey. For an essay on how mothers' working outside the home affects family life, for instance, you would probably devise a questionnaire for working mothers, their husbands, and their children. A survey of only one of these groups (say, the college-aged children of working mothers) would undoubtedly yield biased results. If, on the other hand, you were writing an essay specifically focused on the ways in which the children of working mothers respond to their mothers' working, you might want to survey only children. Even then, though, you need to identify a diverse sample. If the essay is to address all children, you wouldn't, for instance, want to survey only college-aged people about their attitudes or only students in elementary school. Nor would you want to survey only men, only women, only first-year students, or—and this is sometimes hard—only your own friends.

Getting a Representative Sample of Opinions

This point is perhaps the most important. In collecting survey results, make sure to get as representative a sample of responses as possible. No one expects you to get a scientifically valid sample; you simply don't have the time, resources, or training to do that. Nevertheless, readers will expect you to be as fair as possible about whom you survey and how you phrase the questions. If you survey only your friends, you're likely to get opinions from people who are too much like you, and that may prevent you from considering other, equally valid points of view.

So how do you go about collecting survey data? You might begin by asking your friends or classmates or people at your workplace, at your church, or on your sports team. But don't stop there. Ask each of those respondents to give you the names of two or three other people whom you might contact. That way, you'll move away from your small circle of friends and acquaintances and, as the circumference of the circle widens, gain a larger and more representative sample. Achieving such a sample will help you see the full complexity of the issue you're studying.

Asking Survey Questions

Of course, before you can distribute the survey, you have to compose it. First include a series of questions about a respondent's background. In our example about attitudes toward working mothers, for instance, it might be helpful to know a respondent's age, gender, and parental status. With such information you can analyze the ways in which fathers, mothers, and children, or men and women, answer the questions differently. Surveys work best when they comprise a mix of both questions with easily tabulated answers and open-ended questions. Yes/no or multiple choice questions, for instance, allow for easy tabulation. You can quickly determine the percentage of responses for each group of respondents (men/women; children/young people/middle-aged people/senior citizens; science majors/humanities majors; people of varying incomes or political philosophies; and so forth). That way, you'll be able to analyze the extent to which answers seem to be determined in part by factors like age, gender, educational background, ethnicity, religion, or culture. Easily tabulated results can also be obtained from questionnaires that ask respondents to select from a list those opinions with which they agree, to rank items in their order of importance, or to rate their degree of agreement or disagreement on a scale from "strongly disagree" to "strongly agree."

Open-ended survey questions are useful as well. Although many respondents will not want to take the time to write out long answers, many others will also welcome the chance to give you some sense of the reasons for their beliefs. What they say will help you expand upon your own arguments, giving you more support or alerting you to places where you need to reconsider your ideas or find opposing arguments. Sometimes you can even ask respondents to tell you a short anecdote in support of their opinions; in the process you will begin to better understand what lies behind their opinions, and you'll find some examples that may prove useful as you write your essay.

Whatever kinds of questions you decide to include (and, again, use a mix), phrase questions as objectively and clearly as possible. A question like "How much do working mothers harm family life?"—even when it includes a choice like "not at all"—seems to presuppose a particular response. A question like "Do you think working wives and mothers spend too little time with their children and their husbands?" not only presupposes an answer (the writer seems to think mothers shouldn't work) but it also could confuse a respondent. What happens if the respondent thinks that working wives and mothers need to spend more time with their children but that they don't need to spend more time with their husbands? In fact, what is "too little time"? Make certain that all the concepts in your survey questions are clear and that you avoid compound questions that may lead to confusing responses. And make sure that your questions allow for diverse views on the subject.

Analyzing Survey Responses

You may decide to analyze and use your surveys as what we call *anecdotal evidence*—that is, their value comes from the "stories" that the responses tell about the topic. Depending on how you constructed the survey, you may be able to use them as *statistical evidence*—that is, for the quantitative conclusions you can draw from a relatively large sample. Each approach to analyzing surveys is appropriate in different situations. However you end up using survey results, you should include a copy of the survey as an appendix to your paper.

Surveys are, then, yet another kind of research tool to help you write more thoughtful and thorough arguments and analyses. Used well, they can help you refine your own ideas and construct an argument that will convince readers of your expertise, your fairness and honesty, and the thoughtfulness and validity of your ideas.

EVALUATE YOUR SOURCES

Students are often afraid that they will be unable to find anything on a particular research question, but if you are both creative and meticulous in your search strategies, you will almost certainly find more information and ideas about your topic than you really need for the assignment. Several of your sources may provide essentially the same information; you need to decide which is the best source, offering the most complete and reliable information. Also, your initial search will probably identify many more possible or likely sources than you will use. Because the number of sources you can use is limited by your time and by the assignment, how can you select the most useful and appropriate sources for your paper from among those you located in your initial research? The choices you make at this point may well determine the success of your final paper. Please consider the following criteria as you select the sources for any formal research paper you write:

- *Do you have the most recent sources available?* While having the most current sources is certainly more important in some fields than in others, make sure that your sources are not obsolete or outdated. Not only will the most recent sources reflect the most recent developments, but they will usually incorporate the thinking of earlier writers, much as your own discussion of the topic will incorporate the thoughts of writers who have tackled this subject before you.

- *Do you have the most reliable sources?* Consider how an article was researched, what the author's goals were, and where the article was published. What is the author's expertise, perspective, or experience with the issue? What is the author's bias? Why do you think that the information in the source is reliable? You may not agree with all that a source says (in fact, you should locate sources with which you disagree), but you should understand the author's purpose, motives, and methods. It is important to consider where and under what circumstances a source was published. In short, do you think that the author is qualified to write about this topic? Why?

- *Do you have reasonably well-written sources?* Has the author presented his or her ideas with clarity and careful development? (You may find logical errors, factual inconsistencies, or weak evidence in a source;

however, a reliable and well-written source is likely to present a coherent and reasonable opinion on the topic.) Use the "rules of argument" described in chapter 1 of this text to help you judge the strengths and weaknesses of each source. Choose your strongest, best-written sources because they will make your paper more authoritative.

- *Do you have a diversity of opinions?* If several sources provide virtually the same information, simply choose the best one (based, at least in part, on the criteria indicated above) and find other sources that provide you with different information or opinions. Don't choose all your sources from authors with the same or similar political, social, or educational perspectives or from authors who provide the same interpretations of phenomena. You should know what those on both sides of a controversy have to say. By relying on sources that reflect views different from yours, you demonstrate to your reader that you know and understand what your opposition says. Acknowledging an opposing argument clearly makes your rebuttal much more effective.

INTEGRATE SOURCES AND INCORPORATE QUOTATIONS

In academic writing, we lend authority to our own words and ideas by connecting what we have to say with what others have said about the same subject. We are always building on knowledge created and disseminated by others. When we use sources, we are illustrating the ways in which our reading has influenced our writing. Synthesizing the ideas of others with our own generates new ideas or new ways of looking at old ideas. By recognizing and synthesizing the views of others, you can become a more authoritative participant in the conversations you encounter in your academic career. As suggested elsewhere in this book, academic writing builds on the knowledge of other writers you encounter as a reader.

You *must* make it clear to your reader that certain words or ideas originated not with you, but with another writer or speaker. As we noted earlier, a failure to make sources clear usually constitutes plagiarism, which most colleges and universities take seriously, whether such unattributed "borrowing" was intentional or accidental. Thus, you must take careful, documented notes when you read, so that you will be easily able to trace the source of an idea or the unique expression of an idea. And remember, sources are not only printed or published documents. If you borrow ideas from a speaker or lecturer, if you download information from a World Wide Web site, or if a friend lets you read a paper she had written on a similar topic, each of these is considered a source, which you must acknowledge and document in your paper. If you are ever uncertain about whether a source should be acknowledged or how it should be documented, speak with your instructor.

Once again, developing your experience as both a reader and writer will help you learn when to indicate the source of a fact or idea, and when such citation is unnecessary. The kinds of decisions that you have to make when you use sources will certainly be more difficult if you know little about a field of study or topic. A few basic rules may make it easier to decide how to use the information you glean from your sources. Obviously, you must indicate the source for any direct quotation or paraphrase you take from another source, as well as for a thesis or theory that you borrow from another writer in the process of building your own thesis. But if an idea or theory seems widely accepted by authors of a number of sources—and if you express this idea in your own words—a citation is probably not necessary. Similarly, if a fact seems widely accepted as true and correct, you probably need not include a citation, especially if the fact appears in a number of different sources. In contrast, the facts gathered as the result of specific studies or experiments and those that appear in a relatively obscure source must be documented. When you are uncertain about documenting an idea or fact, it is, as a rule, better to acknowledge a source than not to do so.

Developing your own ideas with information gleaned from other sources is a process that usually involves three clear steps. First, you make an assertion. Second, you offer a fact or opinion from a source that helps to support that assertion. Finally—and this is the step that many writers fail to take—you must explain very clearly how the source supports the assertion with which you began. Never assume that your reader sees in a passage from a source exactly what you see, or interprets facts as you have. Your goal here is not simply to rephrase or repeat the cited source. You must make explicit the connection between your ideas and the insight your source provides.

You may use and acknowledge your sources in a number of different ways. You must often choose between using a *direct quotation* from a source or using a paraphrase or summary of the other writer's ideas. It is not an arbitrary or haphazard choice, but one based on what you want to accomplish in your paper. A direct quotation is most important when the language or style of the source is particularly valuable to you or cannot easily be put in your own words. A direct quotation should never be simply "patched into" your own analysis. Rather it should be integrated as smoothly as possible into your own writing. Rather than leave a quotation alone, in a sentence by itself, provide an introduction to the quotation, easing the transition from your own writing to the source. Whenever possible, integrate key phrases from the quotation, surrounded by quotation marks, into your own sentence. Try to make the shift from your own words to those of your source as smooth as possible. Doing so will make your writing more coherent.

In shorter papers, avoid using long block-style quotations. The reason is simple: The more you allow your sources to say, the less you will be able to say yourself, so choose the words you want to quote carefully. Whenever you do quote more than four or five lines from a source, you will need to indent this long quotation (often called a "block quote"), and omit the quotation marks. Rarely, if ever, should a block quote appear at the end of a paragraph. Always analyze and explain long quotations, and give yourself the last word in the paragraph.

Often it will be sufficient to simply *paraphrase* what another writer says. Paraphrasing is putting another writer's words into our own words, that is, explaining someone else's ideas in words that come more naturally to us. Writers will often paraphrase theories and concepts that they borrow from a source. A paraphrase is also useful when the language and style of the source is not particularly important to you, or when the style of the source is so different from your own style that it would be difficult to integrate a quote into your own analysis.

Sometimes you will want not to paraphrase something from another writer but to condense it into fewer words, leaving out much of the detail. This is called a *summary* of the source. A summary is useful when your source includes much more detail than is relevant to your own subject or purpose; when you use a general theory or idea, but do not need to include the examples and details that another writer uses to develop it; or when you want to orient your reader to the larger context of a particular section of the source on which you want to focus.

You can use a variety of appropriate formal conventions to identify your sources. These "documentation systems" vary among academic disciplines. For example, a literary scholar will rely on the citation system developed by the Modern Language Association (MLA), while a social scientist may rely on the *Chicago Manual of Style* or the citation system of the American Psychological Association (APA). Sometimes a special documentation style will be used. Always ask your teaching assistant, instructor, or professor which documentation style is appropriate for the formal work you do in a particular course. A formal documentation system will probably be required for most papers involving research in more than one source. Examples of various documentation styles should be available in the reference section of your college or university library.

Credits

DON ADAMS and ARLENE GOLDBARD, "Steal This TV: How Media Literacy Can Change the World." Reprinted from *The Independent Film and Video Monthly,* a publication of the Foundation for Independent Video and Film. Used with permission of the authors. Don Adams and Arlene Goldbard (icd@wwcd.org) are writers and consultants who have worked together since 1978.

ELLEN ALDERMAN and CAROLINE KENNEDY, "The Right to Privacy: High-Tech Monitoring in the Workplace" from *The Right to Privacy.* Copyright © 1995 Ellen Alderman and Caroline Kennedy. Reprinted by permission of Alfred A. Knopf, Inc.

ALBERT W. ALSCHULER, "Our Faltering Jury." Reprinted with permission of the author and *The Public Interest,* Number 122, Winter 1996, pp. 28–38. Copyright © 1996 by National Affairs, Inc.

HERBERT APPLEBAUM, "Work—Past, Present, and Future." Reprinted from *The Concept of Work: Ancient, Medieval, and Modern* by Herbert Applebaum by permission of the State University of New York Press. Copyright © 1992 Herbert Applebaum.

HADLEY ARKES, "Moral Obtuseness in America" from *The National Review,* June 16, 1989, vol. 41, no. 11. Copyright © 1989 by National Review, Inc., 150 East 35th Street, New York, NY 10016. Reprinted by permission.

LOTTE BAILYN, "Two Women at Work: Balancing Work and Family" from "Interlude II: Nancy Wright: Success?" and "Interlude III: Elizabeth Gray: Failure?" reprinted with the permission of *The Free Press,* a division of Simon & Schuster from *Breaking the Mold: Women, Men, and Time in a New Corporate World* by Lotte Bailyn. Copyright © 1993 by Lotte Bailyn.

MICHAEL C. BERTHOLD, "*Jeopardy!,* Cultural Literacy, and the Discourse of Trivia" from *Journal of American Culture* 13.1, Spring 1990. Used with permission of the publisher.

DEBORAH BRANDT, "Accumulating Literacy: Writing and Learning to Write in the Twentieth Century" from *College English* 57.6, October 1995. Copyright © 1995 by the National Council of Teachers of English. Reprinted with permission.

MERLISA LAWRENCE CORBETT, "Telecommuting: The New Workplace Trend" from *Black Enterprise,* June 1996. Copyright © 1996 Black Enterprise Magazine, New York, NY. Reprinted with permission. All rights reserved.

CHESTER E. FINN, JR., and BRUNO V. MANNO, "Behind the Curtain" from *Wilson Quarterly,* Winter 1996. Reprinted with permission.

J. WADE GILLEY, "The Distributed University" from *Thinking about American Higher Education: The 1990s and Beyond.* Copyright © 1991 American Council on Education. Reprinted with permission.

MARK HANSEN, "Final Justice: Limiting Death Row Appeals" from *ABA Journal,* March 1992. Reprinted by permission of the ABA Journal.

CRAIG HOROWITZ, "Law and Disorder: How the Juvenile Justice System Is Letting Kids Get Away with Murder" from *New York,* January 10, 1994. Reprinted with permission.

DAVID M. HUMMON, "College Slang Revisited: Language, Culture, and Undergraduate Life" from *Journal of Higher Education,* vol. 65, no. 1, January/February 1994. Reprinted by permission. Copyright © 1994 by the Ohio State University Press. All rights reserved.

PHILLIP E. JOHNSON, "The Creationist and the Sociobiologist: Two Stories about Illiberal Education." Reprinted from *California Law Review,* vol. 80, no. 4, July 1992, pp. 1071-1090 by permission. Copyright © 1992 by The California Law Review, Inc.

LEON KASS, "Am I My Brother's Keeper? Reflections on Compassion and Justice" from *The American Enterprise,* November/December 1994. Reprinted by permission of *The American Enterprise,* a Washington-based magazine of politics, business, and culture.

PAMELA E. KRAMER and SHIELA LEHMAN, "Mismeasuring Women: A Critique of Research on Computer Ability and Avoidance" from *Signs: Journal of Women in Culture and Society,* 16:1, 1990. Reprinted with permission of the authors and The University of Chicago Press.

GEORGE D. KUH, JOHN H. SCHUH, and ELIZABETH J. WHITT, "Some Good News About Campus Life" from *Change,* September/October, 1991. Reprinted with permission of the Helen Dwight Reid Educational Foundation. Published by Heldref Publications, 1319 Eighteenth Street, N.W., Washington, D.C. 20036–1802.

CHARLES MCGRATH, "The Internet's Arrested Development" in *The New York Times,* December 8, 1996. Copyright © 1996 by The New York Times Co. Reprinted by permission.

SUSAN B. NEUMAN, "Television and Reading in the Lives of Young Children" from *Literacy in the Television Age: The Myth of the TV Effect,* Ablex Publishing Company, 1991. Reprinted with permission from Ablex Publishing Corporation.

DAPHNE PATAI and NORETTA KOERTGE, "Introduction to the World of Women's Studies" from *Professing Feminism.* Copyright © 1994 by Daphne Patai and Noretta Koertge. Reprinted by permission of BasicBooks, a division of HarperCollins Publishers, Inc.

NEIL POSTMAN, "The Medium Is the Metaphor" from Amusing Ourselves to Death. Copyright © 1985 by Neil Postman. Used by permission of Viking Penguin, a division of Penguin Books USA Inc.

LANA F. RAKOW and VIJA NAVARRO, "Remote Mothering and the Parallel Shift: Women Meet the Cellular Telephone" from *Critical Studies in Mass Communications.* Copyright © 1993 Speech Communication Association. Used by permission of the Speech Communication Association.

MIKE ROSE, "Entering the Conversation." Reprinted with the permission of The Free Press, a division of Simon & Schuster from *Lives on the Boundary: The Struggles and Achievements of America's Underprepared.* Copyright © 1989 by Mike Rose.

JOAN RYAN, from *Little Girls in Pretty Boxes.* Copyright © 1995 by Joan Ryan. Used by permission of Doubleday, a division of Bantam Doubleday Dell Publishing Group, Inc.

LYNN HECHT SCHAFRAN, "Is the Law Male?" from *Trial,* August 1995. Copyright © 1995 Lynn Hecht Schafran. Used with permission of the author. Lynn Hecht Schafran, Esq., Director, National Judicial Education Program (a project of the NOW Legal Defense and Education Fund in cooperation with the National Association of Women Judges).

JULIET B. SCHOR, "Time Squeeze: The Extra Month of Work" from *The Overworked American: The Unexpected Decline of Leisure.* Copyright © 1991 by BasicBooks, a division of

HarperCollins Publishers, Inc. Reprinted by permission of BasicBooks, a division of HarperCollins Publishers, Inc.

BENJAMIN SELLS, "What Does the Law Want?" from *The Soul of the Law*, Element Books, Inc., 1994. Reprinted with permission of the publishers.

REG THERIAULT, "Old Blue Collars, Young Blue Collars, and That Little Place You're Going to Get in the Country" from *How to Tell When You're Tired: A Brief Examination of Work*. Copyright © 1995 by Reg Theriault. Reprinted by permission of W.W. Norton & Company, Inc.

RICHARD WEISBERG, "From Jefferson to the Gulf War: How Lawyers Have Lost Their Golden Tongue" in *Poethetics and Other Strategies of Law and Literature*. Copyright © 1992 by Columbia University Press. Reprinted with permission of the publisher.

STANTON WHEELER, "Double Lives" from *The Nature of Work*, Erickson, ed., Yale University Press, 1990. Reprinted by permission of Yale University Press.

SUSAN WILLIS for the Project on Disney, "Public Use/Private State" from *Inside the Mouse: Work and Play at Disney World*, pp. 184–198. Copyright © 1995 Duke University Press. Reprinted with permission.

Index of Authors and Titles

Accumulating Literacy: Writing and Learning to Write in the Twentieth Century, DEBORAH BRANDT, 263–273, 346, 470
ADAMS, DON, and GOLDBARD, ARLENE, Steal This TV: How Media Literacy Can Change the World, 240, 286–291
ADAMS, HENRY, The Education of Henry Adams, 463; The Virgin and the Dynamo, 463–464, 471
Address to the Legislature of New York, ELIZABETH CADY STANTON, 460
ALDERMAN, ELLEN, and KENNEDY, CAROLINE, The Right to Privacy: High-Tech Monitoring in the Workplace, 425–432, 455
ALSCHULER, ALBERT W., Our Faltering Jury, 376–385, 455
Am I My Brother's Keeper?: Reflections on Compassion and Justice, LEON KASS, 360–375, 454, 469
The American Scholar, RALPH WALDO EMERSON, 459, 469
ANTHONY, SUSAN B., Women's Right to Vote, 461, 471
APPLEBAUM, HERBERT, Work—Past, Present, and Future, 224–237, 237, 472
ARKES, HADLEY, Moral Obtuseness in America, 433–442, 454

BAILYN, LOTTE, Breaking the Mold: Women, Men, and Time in the New Corporate World, 163, 175
———, Two Women at Work: Balancing Work and Family, 163–175, 238, 473
The Beef Inspection Act, U.S. CONGRESS, 466
Behind the Curtain, CHESTER E. FINN, JR., and BRUNO V. MANNO, 44–56
BERTHOLD, MICHAEL C., Jeopardy!, Cultural Literacy, and the Discourse of Trivia, 274–285, 347
The Bill of Rights, 264
BRANDT, DEBORAH, Accumulating Literacy: Writing and Learning to Write in the Twentieth Century, 263–273, 346, 347, 470
The Bread Givers: A Struggle between a Father of the Old World and a Daughter of the New, ANZIA YEZIERSKA, 464–465, 469

Brown v. Board of Education of Topeka, Kansas, U.S. SUPREME COURT, 465–466
CARNEGIE, ANDREW, The Gospel of Wealth, 462, 470
The Case for Public Schools, HORACE MANN, 459–460, 469
A Century of Dishonor, HELEN HUNT JACKSON, 461–462
Civil Disobedience, HENRY DAVID THOREAU, 459, 469
College Slang Revisited: Language, Culture, and Undergraduate Life, DAVID M. HUMMON, 106–128, 129
The Concept of Work: Ancient, Medieval, and Modern, HERBERT APPLEBAUM, 224
The Constitution, 460, 462, 463
CORBETT, MERLISA LAWRENCE, Telecommuting: The New Workplace Trend, 176–181, 238, 457, 473
The Creationist and the Sociobiologist: Two Stories about Illiberal Education, PHILLIP E. JOHNSON, 57–78

DAVIS, REBECCA HARDING, Life in the Iron Mills, 460–461, 469, 471
Declaration of Independence, THOMAS JEFFERSON, 462
DEWEY, JOHN, Experience and Education, 465, 469
The Distibuted University, J. WADE GILLEY, 87–93, 238, 348, 473
Double Lives, STANTON WHEELER, 143–151, 238
DUBOIS, W.E.B., The Negro Problem, 464

The Education of Henry Adams, HENRY ADAMS, 465
EISENHOWER, DWIGHT D., Farewell Address: The Military-Industrial Complex, 466, 471
EMERSON, RALPH WALDO, The American Scholar, 459, 469, 470
Entering the Conversation, MIKE ROSE, 2, 22–23, 131, 348
Experience and Education, JOHN DEWEY, 465, 469

Final Justice: Limiting Death Row Appeals, MARK HANSEN, 403–412
FINN, CHESTER E., JR., and MANNO, BRUNO V., Behind the Curtain, 44–56, 129

FRANKLIN, BENJAMIN, *Poor Richard's Almanac*, 458; The Way to Wealth, 458, 470
From Jefferson to the Gulf War: How Lawyers Have Lost Their Golden Tongue, RICHARD WEISBERG, 443–454

GILLEY, J. WADE, The Distributed University, 87–93, 129, 238, 348, 473
GILMAN, CHARLOTTE PERKINS, *Women and Economics*, 463, 471
GOLDBARD, ARLENE, and ADAMS, DON, Steal This TV: How Media Literacy Can Change the World, 240, 286–291
GOMPERS, SAMUEL, What Does the Working Man Want?, 462–463, 470
The Gospel of Wealth, ANDREW CARNEGIE, 462

HANSEN, MARK, Final Justice: Limiting Death Row Apeals, 403–412, 455
HARRINGTON, MICHAEL, *The Other America*, 467
HOROWITZ, CRAIG, Law and Disorder: How the Juvenile Justice System Is Letting Kids Get Away with Murder, 386–402, 454, 455
Howard University Address, LYNDON B. JOHNSON, 468
HUMMON, DAVID M., College Slang Revisited: Language, Culture, and Undergraduate Life, 106–128, 129

The Internet's Arrested Development, CHARLES MCGRATH, 252–262, 346
Introduction to the World of Women's Studies, DAPHNE PATAI and NORETTA KOERTGE, 79–86, 238, 349, 457, 473
Is the Law Male?, LYNN HECHT SCHAFRAN, 413–424, 455

JACKSON, HELEN HUNT, *A Century of Dishonor*, 461–462, 471
JEFFERSON, THOMAS, *Declaration of Independence*, 350, 460, 462
———, Report of the Commissioners Appointed to Fix the Site of the University of Virginia, 460–461, 473
Jeopardy!, Cultural Literacy, and the Discourse of Trivia, MICHAEL C. BERTHOLD, 274–285
JOHNSON, LYNDON B., Howard University Address, 468, 471
JOHNSON, PHILLIP E., The Creationist and the Sociobiologist: Two Stories about Illiberal Education, 57–78, 129
The Jungle, UPTON SINCLAIR, 464

KASS, LEON, Am I My Brother's Keeper?: Reflections on Compassion and Justice, 360–375, 454, 469
KENNEDY, CAROLINE, and ALDERMAN, ELLEN, The Right to Privacy: High-Tech Monitoring in the Workplace, 425–432, 455
KERR, CLARK, The Urban-Grant University, 468–469, 470
KING, MARTIN LUTHER, JR., I Have a Dream, 467; Letter from Birmingham Jail, 467, 469, 471
KOERTGE, NORETTA, and PATAI, DAPHNE, Introduction to the World of Women's Studies, 79–86, 129, 238, 457, 473
KRAMER, PAMELA E., and LEHMAN, SHEILA, Mismeasuring Women: A Critique of Research on Computer Ability and Avoidance, 332–346, 471
KUH, GEROGE D., SCHUH, JOHN H., and WHITT, ELIZABETH, J., Some Good News about Campus Life: How "Involving Colleges" Promote Learning outside the Classroom, 94–105, 129

Law and Disorder: How the Juvenile Justice System Is Letting Kids Get Away with Murder, CRAIG HOROWITZ, 386–402
LE SUEUR, MERIDEL, Women on the Breadlines, 465, 471
LEHMAN, SHEILA, and KRAMER, PAMELA E., Mismeasuring Women: A Critique of Research on Computer Ability and Avoidance, 332–346, 471
Letter from Birmingham Jail, MARTIN LUTHER KING, JR., 467, 469
Life in the Iron Mills, REBECCA HARDING DAVIS, 460–461, 469, 471
LINCOLN, ABRAHAM, Second Inaugural Address, 461, 471
Little Girls in Pretty Boxes, JOAN RYAN, 152–162, 473

MANN, HORACE, The Case for Public Schools, 459–460, 469, 471
MANNO, BRUNO V., and FINN, CHESTER E., JR., Behind the Curtain, 44–56, 129
MCGRATH, CHARLES, The Internet's Arrested Development, 252–262, 346, 455
MCLUHAN, MARSHALL, *Understanding Media: The Extensions of Man*, 467–469
The Medium Is the Metaphor, NEIL POSTMAN, 242–251
MEREDITH, JAMES, *Three Years in Mississippi*, 468, 469, 471
The Military-Industrial Complex (Farewell Address), DWIGHT D. EISENHOWER, 466, 471
Mismeasuring Women: A Critique of Research on Computer Ability and Avoidance, SHEILA LEHMAN and PAMELA E. KRAMER, 332–346, 347, 471

Moral Obtuseness in America, HADLEY ARKES, 433–442
Morill Act, U.S. CONGRESS, 470

The Nature of Work: Sociological Perspectives, KAI ERIKSON and STEVEN PETER VALLAS, 143
NAVARRO, VIJA, and RAKOW, LANA F., Remote Mothering and the Parallel Shift: Women Meet the Cellular Telephone, 316–331, 455, 471
The Negro Problem, W.E.B. DUBOIS, 464
NEUMAN, SUSAN B., Television and Reading in the Lives of Young Children, 292–315, 347

Old Blue Collars, Young Blue Collars, and That Little Place You're Going to Get in the Country, REG THERIAULT, 133–142, 237
The Other America, MICHAEL HARRINGTON, 467
Our Faltering Jury, ALBERT W. ALSCHULER, 376–385

PATAI, DAPHNE, and KOERTGE, NORETTA, Introduction to the World of Women's Studies, 79–86, 129, 238, 457, 473
Plessy v. Ferguson, U.S. SUPREME COURT, 468
Poor Richard's Almanac, BENJAMIN FRANKLIN, 458
The Port Huron Statement, STUDENTS FOR A DEMOCRATIC SOCIETY, 466
POSTMAN, NEIL, The Medium Is the Metaphor, 242–251, 346
PROJECT ON DISNEY and WILLIS, SUSAN, Public Use/Private State, 210–223
Public Use/Private State, SUSAN WILLIS and PROJECT ON DISNEY, 210–223, 238, 348
The Pure Food and Drug Act, U.S. CONGRESS, 466

RAKOW, LANA F., and NAVARRO, VIJA, Remote Mothering and the Parallel Shift: Women Meet the Cellular Telephone, 316–331, 455, 472
Remote Mothering and the Parallel Shift: Women Meet the Cellular Telephone, LANA F. RAKOW and VIJA NAVARRO, 316–331, 347, 471
Report of the Commissioners Appointed to Fix the Site of the University of Virginia, THOMAS JEFFERSON, 460–461
The Right to Privacy: High-Tech Monitoring in the Workplace, ELLEN ALDERMAN and CAROLINE KENNEDY, 425–432
ROSE, MIKE, Entering the Conversation, 2, 22–23, 128, 129, 131, 348, 471
RYAN, JOAN, Little Girls in Pretty Boxes, 152–162, 473

SCHAFRAN, LYNN HECHT, Is the Law Male?, 413–425, 455

SCHOR, JULIET B., Time Squeeze: The Extra Month of Work, 132, 182–209, 238, 457, 472, 473
SCHUH, JOHN H., KUH, GEORGE D., and WHITT, ELIZABETH J., Some Good News about Campus Life: How "Involving Colleges" Promote Learning outside the Classroom, 94–105, 129
Second Inaugural Address, ABRAHAM LINCOLN, 461
SELLS, BENJAMIN, What Does the Law Want?, 350–359, 455, 471
SINCLAIR, UPTON, *The Jungle,* 464, 471
Some Good News about Campus Life: How "Involving Colleges" Promote Learning outside the Classroom, GEORGE D. KUH, JOHN H. SCHUH, and ELIZABETH J. WHITT, 94–105
STANTON, ELIZABETH CADY, Address to the Legislature of New York, 460, 471
Steal This TV: How Media Literacy Can Change the World, DON ADAMS and ARLENE GOLDBARD, 286–291, 346
STUDENTS FOR A DEMOCRATIC SOCIETY, The Port Huron Statement, 466

Telecommuting: The New Workplace Trend, MERLISA LAWRENCE CORBETT, 176–181, 349, 473
Television and Reading in the Lives of Young Children, SUSAN B. NEUMAN, 292–315
The Theory of the Leisure Class, THORSTEIN VEBLEN, 463
THERIAULT, REG, Old Blue Collars, Young Blue Collars, and That Little Place You're Going to Get in the Country, 133–142, 237, 472
THOREAU, HENRY DAVID, Civil Disobedience, 459, 469, 471; *Walden,* 459, 460, 473
Three Years in Mississippi, JAMES MEREDITH, 468
Time Squeeze: The Extra Month of Work, JULIET B. SCHOR, 132, 182–209, 238, 348, 349, 473
Two Women at Work: Balancing Work and Family, LOTTE BAILYN, 163–175, 238, 473

U.S. CONGRESS, The Beef Inspection Act, 466
U.S. CONGRESS, Morill Act, 19, 470
U.S. CONGRESS, The Pure Food and Drug Act, 466
U.S. SUPREME COURT, *Brown v. Board of Education of Topeka, Kansas,* 465–466
U.S. SUPREME COURT, *Plessy v. Ferguson,* 468
Understanding Media: The Extensions of Man, MARSHALL MCLUHAN, 467–469
The Urban-Grant University, CLARK KERR, 468–469

VEBLEN, THORSTEIN, *The Theory of the Leisure Class*, 463, 470
The Virgin and the Dynamo, HENRY ADAMS, 463–464, 473

Walden, HENRY DAVID THOREAU, 461, 462, 473
The Way to Wealth, BENJAMIN FRANKLIN, 458, 470
WEISBERG, RICHARD, From Jefferson to the Gulf War: How Lawyers Have Lost Their Golden Tongue, 443–454
What Does the Law Want?, BENJAMIN SELLS, 350–359, 455, 471
What Does the Working Man Want?, SAMUEL GOMPERS, 462–463
WHEELER, STANTON, Double Lives, 132, 143–151, 237, 238, 457, 472

WHITT, ELIZABETH J., KUH, GEORGE D., and SCHUH, JOHN H., Some Good News about Campus Life: How "Involving Colleges" Promote Learning outside the Classroom, 94–105, 129
WILLIS, SUSAN, and PROJECT ON DISNEY, Public Use/Private State, 210–223, 238
Women and Economics, CHARLOTTE PERKINS GILMAN, 463
Women on the Breadlines, MERIDEL LESUEUR, 465
Women's Right to Vote, SUSAN B. ANTHONY, 463
Work—Past, Present, and Future, HERBERT APPLEBAUM, 224–237

YEZIERSKA, ANZIA, *The Bread Givers: A Struggle between a Father of the Old World and a Daughter of the New*, 464–465, 469